# THE WORLD OF
# ROMAN COSTUME

WISCONSIN STUDIES IN CLASSICS

*General Editors*

Barbara Hughes Fowler and Warren G. Moon *(1945–1992)*

# The World of
# Roman Costume

Edited by

Judith Lynn Sebesta and Larissa Bonfante

THE UNIVERSITY OF WISCONSIN PRESS

The University of Wisconsin Press
114 North Murray Street
Madison, Wisconsin 53715

3 Henrietta Street
London WC2E 8LU, England

Library of Congress Cataloging-in-Publication Data
The world of Roman costume / edited by Judith Sebesta and Larissa Bonfante.
    292 p.        cm.—(Wisconsin studies in classics)
    Includes bibliographical references and index.
    ISBN 0-299-13850-X
    1. Costume—Rome—History.   2. Dress accessories—Rome—History.
3. Costume—Rome—Symbolic aspects.   I. Sebesta, Judith.
II. Bonfante, Larissa.   III. Series.
GT555.W67        1994
391'.00937'6—dc20        93-12709

# CONTENTS

# ILLUSTRATIONS

# ABBREVIATIONS

| | |
|---|---|
| *AA* | *Archäologischer Anzeiger* |
| *AAAH* | *Acta ad archeologiam et artium historiam pertinentia*, Institutum Romanum Norvegiae et Roma |
| *ABull* | *The Art Bulletin* |
| AIA | Archaeological Institute of America |
| *AJA* | *American Journal of Archaeology* |
| *ALFPer* | *Annali della Facoltà di Lettere e Filosofia, Perugia* |
| *ANRW* | *Aufstieg und Niedergang der römischen Welt* |
| *AntPl* | *Antike Plastik* |
| *BA* | *Bollettino d'Arte*, Rome |
| *BABesch* | *Bulletin Antieke Beschaving* |
| BAR | British Archaeological Reports, International Series |
| *BCAR* | *Bullettino della Commissione Archeologica Comunale di Roma* |
| *BIBR* | *Bulletin de l'Institut historique belge de Rome* |
| *BJ* | *Bonner Jahrbücher* |
| *CIL* | *Corpus Inscriptionum Latinarum* |
| *CISem* | *Corpus Inscriptionum Semiticarum* |
| *CP* | *Classical Philology* |
| *CQ* | *The Classical Quarterly* |
| DAI | Deutsches Archäologisches Institut, Rome |
| DarSag | C. Daremberg and E. Saglio. *Dictionnaire des antiquités grecques et romaines*. 5 vols. in 10. Paris, 1877–1919. |
| *GMusJ* | *The J. Paul Getty Museum Journal* |
| Helbig | W. Helbig. *Führer durch die öffentlichen sammlungen klassischer Altertümer in Rom*. Vol. 1. 4th ed. Ed. H. Speier. Tübingen, 1963. |
| *IGR* | *Inscriptiones graecae ad res romanas pertinentes* |
| *JDAI* | *Jahrbuch des Deutschen Archäologischen Instituts* |
| *JHS* | *Journal of Hellenic Studies* |
| *JIES* | *Journal of Indo-European Studies* |
| *JRS* | *Journal of Roman Studies* |
| *JWAG* | *Journal of the Walters Art Gallery* |
| LCL | Loeb Classical Library |
| *MAAR* | *Memoirs of the American Academy in Rome* |
| *MDAFA* | *Mémoires de la délégation archéologique française en Afghanistan* |

| MEFRA | *Mélanges d'Archéologie et d'Histoire de l'Ecole Française de Rome, Antiquité* |
| NSc | *Notizie degli Scavi dell'Antichità* |
| PAPhS | *Proceedings of the American Philosophical Society* |
| PdP | *Parola del Passato* |
| RE | A. F. von Pauly and G. Wissowa. *Real-Encyclopädie der klassischen Altertums-Wissenschaft*. Stuttgart, 1894–. |
| REL | *Revue des Etudes Latines* |
| RhM | *Rheinisches Museum* |
| RM | *Römische Mitteilungen* |
| RM-EH | Römische Mitteilungen Ergänzungsheft |
| RVV | *Religionsgeschichtliche Versuche und Vorarbeiten* |
| SBAW | *Sitzungsberichte der Bayerischen Akademie der Wissenschaften Philos.-Hist. Klasse*, Munich |
| SHA | Scriptores Historiae Augustae |
| TAPA | *Transactions and Proceedings of the American Philological Association* |
| YCS | *Yale Classical Studies* |
| ZPE | *Zeitschrift für Papyrologie und Epigraphik* |

# CONTRIBUTORS

HENRY BENDER   is Adjunct Associate Professor of Classics at Villanova University and Teacher of Latin and Greek at St. Joseph's Preparatory School in Philadelphia. He is currently preparing a new, expanded edition of his book, *Roman Civilization: An Archaeological Perspective* (1985).

LARISSA BONFANTE,   Professor of Classics at New York University, is the author of *Etruscan Dress* (1975), *The Etruscan Language* (with Giuliano Bonfante, 1988), and articles on early Rome, ancient dress, and nudity in ancient art.

DOUGLAS R. EDWARDS,   Associate Professor of Religion at the University of Puget Sound, is the author of articles on Josephus, the ancient romances, and the New Testament. In 1992 he co-directed excavations at Jotapata, a Greco-Roman site in Israel. His book, *Religion and Power: Jews, Christians, and Pagans in the Roman East,* will be published by Oxford University Press.

RICHARD A. GERGEL,   Professor of Art History in the Department of Art at Central Michigan University, studies Roman imperial and Byzantine art. His principal field of research deals with the analysis and interpretation of Roman imperial cuirassed statue breastplate and lappet iconography.

BERNARD GOLDMAN,   Professor Emeritus of Ancient Art, is the author of *Reading and Writing in the Arts* (1978), *The Sacred Portal* (1986), and *The Ancient Arts of Western and Central Asia* (1991). He coedits the *Bulletin of the Asia Institute.*

NORMA GOLDMAN,   Adjunct Professor in the College of Lifelong Learning at Wayne State University, is coauthor of *Latin via Ovid* (now in its seventh printing), *English Grammar for Students of Latin,* and *The Lamps of Cosa.*

JULIA HESKEL,   Assistant Professor of Classics and History at Yale University, works primarily in the field of fourth-century Greek history. She is currently preparing a book on Philip II of Macedon.

LAETITIA LA FOLLETTE,   Assistant Professor of Art History at the University of Massachusetts at Amherst, is working on a book on imperial building in Rome between A.D. 217 and 312.

LUCILLE A. ROUSSIN   is on the staff of the University of South Florida excavations at Sepphoris, Israel. She has taught at Yeshiva University, Sarah Lawrence College, and the Cooper Union. She has published several articles on late Roman Palestine.

JUDITH LYNN SEBESTA,   Professor of Classics at the University of South Dakota, is the author of *Carl Orff, Carmina Burana: Cantiones Profanae* (1985). She is currently studying the Roman stola.

SHELLEY STONE,   Associate Professor of Art History at the University of California at Bakersfield, has published on Roman sculpture and pottery.

ANN M. STOUT,   Lecturer in Art History at Macalester College, has published on jewelry in the later Roman and early Byzantine periods.

# Preface

JUDITH LYNN SEBESTA

When Jane Goodall watched the Gombe chimpanzees fashioning tools out of twigs and using blades of grass to "fish" ants out of nests for food, her observation made obsolete the old definition of *Homo sapiens* as the "tool-using primate." More recently, chimpanzees and gorillas have learned to use symbol boards which resemble large typewriters with symbols imprinted on the key squares rather than letters. By tapping the key squares, the apes construct their own original sentences and even create new expressions to communicate with behavioral scientists. If, as such experiments indicate, apes possess true linguistic ability, then the definition of *Homo sapiens* as the "language-using primate" is also obsolete. Yet, while chimpanzees in zoos have been seen to drape yarn, ribbon, or cloth around their heads and bodies, their activity cannot be termed "clothing themselves." Perhaps the best current definition of *Homo sapiens* is "the clothing-using primate."

If clothing is defined as any covering or adornment of the body, then clothing first appeared in the mid-Paleolithic period, when Neanderthals stained the bones of their dead with red ochre during burial. While Neanderthals may have clothed themselves by fastening fur skins together with bone or thorn pins, any such garments have long since disintegrated. The earliest definite indication of clothing are the bone needles with carefully cut eyes that survive from the upper Paleolithic, Aurignacian period. The earliest surviving textile remnants come later, from the Neolithic period.

Our knowledge of prehistoric clothing has been much increased by the discovery in September 1991 of a partially freeze-dried Bronze Age corpse in the Italian Tyrol. The man, who died from causes yet to be ascertained, was dressed in carefully constructed leather garments and boots insulated with straw. Tattoos, in the form of short, parallel dark lines, adorned his lower back and skin behind his knees.

While his clothing was well suited to an Alpine environment, he may have been tattooed for personal, psychoreligious, or sociocultural reasons. Earlier attempts by anthropologists to trace the invention of clothing (including adornment such as jewelry and tattoos) to a single reason, whether for environmental protection, concealment of the genitalia, attraction of a mate, or advertisement of social status and/or social function, have now given way to an understanding of clothing as arising out of a complex of motivations. The 1988 National Endowment for the Humanities seminar titled "The Religious, Social, and Political Significance of Roman Dress," directed by Professor Larissa Bonfante, presented the opportunity to extend the still-young field of the anthropology of clothing into the classical world.

What conclusions we seminar participants drew about this fascinating topic are presented in this book. These chapters, however, also reflect certain questions we were unable to resolve: for instance, why prostitutes and adulteresses were required to wear the toga. Such questions resulted in lively seminar discussions and produced a camaraderie which is demonstrated by the illustrations in this volume from Norma Goldman's fashion show (now famous in classical circles) held toward the end of the seminar. This camaraderie has not dissipated in the subsequent years, as the production of this book shows.

As the Roman world was the most cosmopolitan of ancient societies, the seminar was appropriately held in one of the most modern cosmopolitan cities, Rome. In the evenings, after the day's research in the American Academy, the main site of the seminar, we participants walked around the city, observing the modern manifestations of the religious, social, and political significance of dress. Nationalities of tourists and foreign students studying in Rome were easily identified by the distinctive costumes of the visitors. The fashionable elite of the Via Veneto paraded in their elegant designer clothes down to the antique restoration shops near the Tiber to place orders with the artisans, who, dressed in plain, serviceable, work-worn clothing, proudly wore the craftsman's hats they daily folded out of newspaper—a contrast of social rank and function, revealed through apparel, as great as that once seen in ancient Rome. Martial would have been amused to find that the popular color of the Roman youth that year was the yellowish green *(galbinus)* so popular among the vulgar rich of his day.

We seminar participants thank the director, Joseph Connors, and the staff of the American Academy at Rome for their gracious hosting of the seminar. We owe a particular debt of gratitude to the librarian, Lucilla Marino, the assistant librarian, Antonella Bucci, and the staff of the Academy's library, who efficiently and tirelessly assisted us in locating materials and references, whether in the Academy library itself or in the other research libraries of the city. The scope of our individual research was broadened by several colloquia with scholars visiting the Academy: Nancy de Grummond, Nicholas Horsfall, Gerhard Koeppel, Thomas McGinn, and Brian Rose. We wish also to acknowledge the assistance offered to us by the Deutsches Archäologisches Institut of Rome.

# THE WORLD OF
# ROMAN COSTUME

# Introduction

LARISSA BONFANTE

In the view of the Greeks and Romans, language and dress identified a nation.[1] The ancient languages of Italy have been studied systematically since the mid–nineteenth century, and the discipline of historical linguistics has made important contributions to our knowledge of these ancient civilizations.[2] Dress, in contrast, has often been considered a frivolous and superficial aspect of culture, though its representation in Greek and Latin art and literature is currently attracting the attention of classicists—art historians, philologists, historians, archaeologists—interested in identifying divine images, social classes, mythological figures, symbols, and allegories.

In the academic area the study of costume history is coming into its own. Several centers have been established. A new institute in Italy, the Polimoda of the University of Florence, is affiliated with New York's Fashion Institute of Technology. Museums have been taking the subject seriously and have organized important historical exhibits, such as the Metropolitan Museum's "Dress in the Time of Napoleon." The psychological aspects of dress, and of nudity as a costume, have been the subjects of books and articles.[3]

There is less need now than in the past to argue for the usefulness of a study of ancient dress for an understanding of social institutions, status symbols, family life, daily life, iconography, and much else. Greeks, Etruscans, and Romans were concerned about what they wore and how they appeared in life and after death. Descriptions of garments, jewelry, hairstyles, and accessories can inform us about social structure and religious ritual, and since clothing was the outward, visible sign of differences in cultures, its representation can illuminate the interrelationships among Greeks, Etruscans, Romans, and the peoples of Asia Minor and the Near East.

The study of ancient dress has been accumulating a respectable bibliography, after a break following the basic works in the 1920s and 1930s of Margarete Bieber for Greek dress and Lillian Wilson for the Roman toga and other Roman garments. Specialists in Greek and Roman sculpture in particular have focused recent research on questions of dress, probably because three-dimensional art offers better opportunities than painting for one to study the actual model behind the more or less stylized representations of specific fashions. The date of a monument can often be deduced much more reliably by the form and type of dress than by stylistic analysis alone. Recent studies contribute important material on the dress of the Roman provinces.[4]

The history of the study of ancient dress has yet to be written. The formal study of costume began in 1589 or 1590, when Cesare Vecellio (ca. 1530–1600) published in Venice a book illustrated with figures representing peoples of different lands. Travelers' diaries and journals also recorded examples of exotic dress.[5] As Nancy de Grummond's article "The Study of Classical Costume by Philip, Albert, and Peter Paul Rubens" points out, the study of "antique costume" was popular in the sixteenth and seventeenth centuries. Rubens' son Albert, an archaeologist and historian who knew how to use ancient texts and interpret ancient monuments, contributed important information on Roman symbolic garments. Apparently the first to realize that the Roman tunic was adorned with stripes of different width (the *angustus clavus* or the *latus clavus*) which suited the status or role of the wearer, he wrote *De re vestiaria veterum,* a monograph on ancient clothing, which was

Seated female figure wearing a toga. Courtesy of the Tullie House Museum, Carlisle, Cumbria, England.

devoted to ancient dress, was also republished by Dover in 1963.[9] To the dress of the Near East and Egypt have been dedicated books, published in this century, based on the evidence of pictorial representations on ancient monuments.[10]

The articles in Daremberg and Saglio's *Dictionnaire* (1877–1919) are still invaluable for the information they give us: they were written in a period when *realien* was an important subject, taught in universities by professors who held prestigious chairs of Greek and Roman Antiquities. The works by Bieber and Wilson belong in this tradition, which is finding in our own days a renewed vigor. Scholars have once more been paying serious attention to Greek and Roman fashions and garments. In the field of Roman art and history, in particular, they have been able to reach important conclusions by focusing on details of dress and their ancient connotations.

Both the Roman toga and the paenula are now subjects of longer studies and monographs.[11] An exhibit of Roman art in the time of Augustus and Paul Zanker's studies have featured interesting discussions on the stola and the toga, their use and significance.[12] I have written both on Etruscan influence on Roman ritual dress and the triumph and on the visual sense of fourth-century art and literary descriptions, that is, on Roman dress in its early and final phases. A controversy connected with the celebration of the Roman triumph at Rome concerns the dress worn by the victorious general. It was described as being the same as the dress of the statue of Jupiter Optimus Maximus in his temple on the Capitoline Hill. Did this similarity imply that the general's extraordinary privileges were in fact divine honors? Eventually—originally it meant that historically both costumes dated to Etruscan times, in the sixth century B.C.

In the fourth century the emperor Julian, as Pontifex Maximus and head of the pagan religion, was very much concerned with the question of the holy images, warning a priest of the dangers connected with the use of sacred images, but he accepted them in deference to the traditions of the Roman forefathers. He also spoke of priestly dress and its proper use. He instructed priests to be magnificently dressed when they performed their functions, but not to exhibit the sacred vestments as objects of curiosity for the crowds: "We priests ought to show moderation in our dress, in order that we may win the goodwill of the gods, since it is no slight offence that we commit against them when we wear in public the sacred dress and make it a public property, and in a word give all men an opportunity to stare at it as though it were something marvellous. For whenever this happens, many who are not purified come near us, and by this means the symbols of the gods are polluted. Moreover, what lawlessness it is, what arrogance towards the

published in Antwerp in 1665, eight years after his death.[6] Lorenzo Guazzesi of Arezzo wrote a monograph on Etruscan dress in the eighteenth century.[7] In the nineteenth century, interest in ancient dress resulted in a number of publications which are still used today. *Costume of the Ancients*, by Thomas Hope, a collection of engravings of figures from Greek and Roman monuments, "a work intended solely for the easy reference and ready application of actual practitioners in art," which appeared in 1812, was republished as a paperback by Dover as late as 1962.[8] *A History of Costume*, by the German Painter Carl Köhler (1825–76), a scholarly work based on evidence from art, archaeology, and the remains of actual garments, a third of which was gods for us ourselves when we are not living the priestly life to wear the priestly dress!"[13] It is clear that some attributed a magical power to the sacred garments of the priests. From the time of Josephus, in a different religion and geographic area, we hear echoes of other heated discussions of the power and significance of the dress of priests: as Douglas Edwards states in chapter 9, "These objects . . . recall and represent the universe." It is this visual aspect of Roman history in various periods which scholars have often ignored.

Dress for a Roman often, if not primarily, signified rank, status, office, or authority. An artistic monument was just as often a document to be "read" with a particular meaning in mind. The dress worn by the participants in an official scene had legal connotations. In a society that had no regular newspapers, radio, or television, the official means of communication were mostly visual: coins, statues, paintings, relief sculpture. The visual language used consisted of gestures, clothing, attributes. Because Roman dress was more loaded with meaning than was Greek dress, questions of its form and symbolism arise more often than with Greek dress in historical studies of social problems, status, gender, religion (priestly dress,[14] the triumph[15]), as well as in art historical studies.

In antiquity these visual distinctions in dress were the subject of study and of anecdotes. That the rounded toga of the Romans was immediately distinguished from rectangular Greek himation or pallium, for example, is shown by the fact that the toga-wearing Italian inhabitants of Asia were picked out of the crowd by Mithridates' assassins in 78 B.C. (Athenaeus, *Deipnosophistai* 5.213). Augustus, on a visit to Capri, ordered an exchange of dress and language between Greeks and Romans, in a spirit of vacation fun: "For the several remaining days of his stay, among little presents of various kinds, he distributed togas and cloaks as well, stipulating that the Romans should use the Greek dress and language and the Greeks the Roman."[16]

Roman authors also wrote about costume and ways of dressing as elements of style, manners, custom, and culture: they obviously considered this an important subject. Modern scholars have, on the whole, tended to undervalue this production. In his account of the rise of culture and progress in crafts, art, music, and letters, Lucretius (*De rerum natura* 5.1350–60) briefly notes the development of wool-working, following the primitive use of skins for clothing.[17] Varro, and Suetonius, in his (lost) *De genere vestium*, recorded much interesting material on dress and its traditions, used and cited by fourth-century commentators such as Servius. A lover of antiquities, Hadrian helped Suetonius collect the information he needed, from which the latter drew anecdotal evidence from the lives of the Roman emperors and their entourages. In a famous passage, for example, Suetonius illustrates Augustus' old-fashioned tastes and even his character by his choice of language and dress.[18] Probably on a more personal, "ethical" level, was Maecenas' *De cultu suo* (On his way of life, or perhaps simply, His style), a work which we know from its title and a few short fragments.[19] Maecenas' consciously informal, unconventional way of dressing and ornate style of poetry were criticized in Seneca's *Epistles*.

A few passages from Seneca will serve to show how the Romans held that the style of a man's language and dress reflected his character and how closely connected language and dress were in Roman minds.[20] Writing to Lucilius, Seneca explains that a man's speech is just like his life.

Exactly as each individual man's actions seem to speak, so people's style of speaking often reproduces the general character of the time, if the morale of the public has relaxed and has given itself over to effeminacy. . . . How Maecenas lived is too well-known for present comment. . . . Does not the looseness of his speech match his ungirt attire? . . . his eloquence was that of an intoxicated man—twisting, turning, unlimited in its slackness. . . . Can you not at once imagine, on reading through these words [there follow some examples of Maecenas' "baroque" literary style] that this was the man who always paraded through the city with a flowing tunic? For even if he was discharging the absent emperor's duties, he was always in undress when they asked him for the countersign. Or that this was the man who, as judge on the bench, or as an orator, appeared with his cloak wrapped about his head, leaving only the ears exposed, like the millionaire's runaway slaves in the farce? . . . These words of his, put together so faultily, thrown off carelessly, and arranged in such marked contrast to the usual practice, declare that the character of their writer was especially unusual, unsound and eccentric.

Seneca goes on to criticize those who "pluck out, or thin out, their beards, or who closely shear and shave the upper lip while reserving the rest of the hair and allowing it to grow, or . . . those who wear cloaks of outlandish colors, who wear transparent togas, . . . they endeavor to excite and attract men's attention, and they put up with even censure, provided that they can advertise themselves. That is the style of Maecenas and all the others who stray from the path, not by hazard, but consciously and voluntarily." Elsewhere in the same epistle, the connection between dress and personal morality is made explicit: "When the soul is sound and strong, the style too is vigorous, energetic, manly; but if the soul lose its balance, down comes all the rest in ruins."

The relation of an overly "rich," recherché, even outrageous style in dress and language to the luxurious condition of the Roman state is also addressed. "This fault is due sometimes to the man, and sometimes to his epoch. When prosperity [*felicitas*] has spread luxury far and wide, men begin by paying closer attention to their personal appearance [*cultus*]. . . . When the mind has acquired the habit of scorning the usual things of life, and regarding as mean that which once was customary, it begins to hunt for novelties in speech also; now it summons and displays obsolete and old-fashioned words; now it coins even unknown words or misshapes them; and now a bold and frequent metaphorical usage is made a special feature of style [*cultus*], according to the fashion which has just become prevalent."[21]

In Latin literature the word *cultus* is often used to signify personal adornment, style of dress. Deriving from the root meaning of "dwelling in," "training the person," "tilling the ground," "observing obligations toward the gods" *cultus corporis,* "personal style of dress or ornament," "getup," is not too far in meaning from *cultus vitae,* "mode or standard of living." The appearance and the dress of the triumphator, and of the emperor, are matters of great importance.[22] Cicero's and Quintilian's practical advice to orators on the proper way to drape and wear the toga is less philosophical, though it brings up the question of propriety.[23] We seem to hear the voice of an English gentleman reproving someone for the moral lapse of wearing the wrong regimental tie.

Seneca's moral criticism of Maecenas sets the tone for a work of the second century A.D. usually held to be enigmatic: Tertullian's *De pallio.* Maecenas' *De cultu suo* also in some ways precedes Tertullian's *De pallio* in its psychological and ethical concerns.[24] Tertullian's writings devoted to dress (he dealt with this subject in four different works) have puzzled generations of critics. In *De pallio* Tertullian distinguishes garments according to their propriety: certain garments are appropriate to men or women, to specific situations, times, and places. But he has a far more spiritual view of what is involved in the change from the rounded toga of the Roman citizen to the simpler square pallium, which still characterized the Greek philosopher. He speaks of cosmic changes, comparing the microcosm of costume, dress, and human habits to the macrocosm of nature, and he contrasts the unchanging nature of God to the changing phases of human history. In *De pallio,* Tertullian attributes the change of fashion to custom, as distinct from nature. "Changing one's type of clothing is not blameworthy if it touches only custom, rather than nature. There is a great difference between the respect due to one's own time and religion. Custom should be faithful to the times, nature to God."[25] Here too we are aware of the philosophical, moral Stoic background. The subject of Tertullian's work, now generally agreed to be one of the last ones he wrote, has left scholars perplexed, for they felt the subject matter was slight, frivolous, and superficial. But Tertullian composed three other works on costume, none of them frivolous or superficial: *De cultu feminarum, De virginibus velandis,* and *De Aaron vestibus.* (The latter is lost; it is thought to have referred to the dress of the high priest.) Involved are important questions: the place of Christian men and women in this world, their appearance, their involvement, and their loyalty.[26]

Much later, Julian's *Misopogon* (The beard-hater) also dealt with dress, in a bitterly polemic justification of the emperor's decision to wear the beard of a philosopher, thus consciously breaking with Constantine's creation, the image of a smooth-shaven, statuelike icon of the emperor, and returning to the image of the philosopher-emperor—a man, not a god.[27] In this period of late antiquity the questions of classical attire gain even more importance; we get much more of our information on early Roman and Etruscan traditions of dress from fourth-century commentators like Servius on Vergil, who preserved passages from such earlier works as Suetonius' *De genere vestium,* because it was important to retain a tradition that was dying out on the one hand, and was in danger of being destroyed by the barbarians on the other.

In the sixth century Johannes Lydus, in his *De magistratibus,* a handbook on contemporary bureaucracy, described in detail the official dress for the Fathers or Patricians, including the mantle, white leggings, black sandals, and leather thongs that are represented in art in this period.[28] He did not realize it, but the barbarians had won: people now wore long sleeves and long pants, traditionally the sign of a barbarian, contrasting with the draped garments of the classical period.

The present volume is the outcome of a seminar held in Rome in the summer of 1988, and it derives its unity from its subject, the social, religious, and historical significance of Roman dress. The subject is particularly appropriate for the Romans, for the hierarchic, symbolic use of dress as a uniform or costume is part of Rome's legacy to Western civilization. Connected to this tradition were the conservative tendencies of Roman religion, a religion or ritual that was constantly relevant in every area of public life. There was no real difference in kind, for example, between the dress of a priest or a magistrate. In each case the individual's authority was recognized visually, by means of his or her uniform, costume, or "habit," which did not change according to the vagaries of fashion but remained official and immutable. New forms of costume might be adopted, but old forms were continued too.[29]

The unity of this volume rests not only on the identity of the subject and the body of material consulted but also on the contributors' awareness of different approaches. All of us had in mind, just as the Romans did, the artistic representations of the garments and costumes to which we refer. These, along with references in the writings of Greek and Roman authors that have come down to us, constitute our main body of evidence. Remnants of actual garments are rare, but examples of ancient shoes, jewelry, and textiles are examined in contributions by Norma Goldman, Ann Stout, Judith Sebesta, and Lucille Roussin. The following chapters illustrate how a variety of approaches can be used to deal with this rich store of material available to us, bringing us closer to an understanding of Roman art and society as well as the reality of daily life.

We are dealing with a time span of well over a thousand years and with a wide variety of peoples, customs, beliefs, and individuals. Yet there was some unity and much continuity in all this diversity. Roman conservatism makes it possible to trace the form, significance, and transformation of much Roman dress through long periods of Rome's history. We can find Etruscan influence in Roman ritual costume and Roman influence in some of the ecclesiastical dress of later periods.[30] We are not dealing with such problems in this book, however. What we attempt to do is to explain, in a basic way, what Roman dress consisted of, what we can find out about it, and what this in turn can tell us of the world of the Romans who wore and represented these garments, costumes, and accessories.

Various approaches illustrated in the present volume include the archaeological or antiquarian, which attempts to reconstruct the ancient reality; the philological, which analyzes literary descriptions or references that give us a clue to the author's purpose; cultural or anthropological, which tries to re-create the beliefs, rituals, and mental habits of a people; and the historical, which attempts to re-create a particular geographic, political, religious, social, or economic situation by means of visual as well as literary, epigraphic, or other more conventionally historical evidence.

How did Roman citizens, ladies, or slaves dress when they got up in the morning? How were these clothes made? What fabrics were used, and when? What colors did you see when you walked down to the Forum on a fine day in Rome?[31] What were Roman shoes like? And what did one wear on different occasions? These are questions answered in Judith Sebesta's and Norma Goldman's chapters. Jewelry, less perishable but more valuable than other items of dress, can be studied from actual pieces that have survived. A comparison of such jewels to those represented on the sixth-century Byzantine emperor and empress and their entourage as pictured on contemporary portraits on coins or on the mosaics at Ravenna, for example, yields fascinating results, as Ann Stout shows.

Another question that needs to be addressed is the message communicated to the viewer by the person's or the artist's choice of clothing. Two essays focus on the ritual element of dress, important in every culture, pre-eminent for the Romans. Laetitia La Follette describes the wedding dress of the bride, along with related rituals and symbols. In his contribution on the toga, Shelley Stone traces the form and fortune of this garment, providing a much-needed account of historical changes in toga styles from the first century B.C. to the fourth century A.D. (Art historians, who often date a monument from the shape, size, and manner of draping togas represented on it, will be particularly grateful to have this up-to-date study in English.) There are some telling parallels in these two chapters, which between them deal with the ritual dress of men and women, characterizing men as citizens and women as brides and future *matres familiae*. Toga and bridal dress are involved in the initiation rites or *rites de passage* of boys and girls in Rome as they move from childhood to adolescence and start to take their places in the adult world of their parents. As early as age twelve or thirteen years a boy put aside his little boys' toga, with a dark red border, and the good-luck charm, or bulla, he had worn at his neck from the time he was a baby. He now started to wear the plain white woolen toga of the Roman citizen. At about the same age, or when she was only a little older, a girl put away her doll, her ball, and other toys and and prepared for marriage. She wore a veil and a special dress and fixed her hair in a prescribed style, in a special ritual so old that its original meaning had long since been lost. Such traditional elements must have been embraced by her much as the throwing of the rice and the wearing of "something borrowed, something blue" are accepted by the modern bride, who takes them as appropriate for the sanctity and importance of a ceremony that will mark a deep change in her life.

The garments of women were not generally as officially significant as those of magistrates. The dress of the Vestal Virgins was an exception. The toga was used by girls and prostitutes, as several of the contributors remind us. A unique example of a second-century monumental statue of a seated *togata* from Britain representing a female divinity shows a typically provincial misinterpretation of the powerful Roman symbol of the toga (fig. Intro.1). Roman women also used dress and jewelry to show off their status. This is shown nowhere better than in the words of the Roman tribune L. Valerius, who in 195 B.C. championed women's right to display marks of honor. His speech strikingly confirms the importance of dress in such a context: "No offices, no priesthoods, no triumphs, no honorary insignia, no gifts or spoils from war can come to [women]; elegance and adornment and apparel—these are the insignia of women."[32]

The interesting results obtained from a study of references to dress in literature illustrate the usefulness of such an approach and should encourage others to pay more attention to such material. Julia Heskel's and Henry Bender's analyses of the types and contexts of garments and costumes mentioned in selected works of Cicero and Vergil bring out the way these ancient authors made use of religious, social, and historical connotations, as well as their audiences' expectations of proper attire, in the late republic and early empire. A similar reading of Josephus, by Douglas Edwards, reveals much about the attitudes and assumptions of both Romans and Jews in the world of first-century A.D. Palestine and makes an intriguing complement to Lucille Roussin's account of dress in the Mishnah. Social distinctions, religious traditions and rituals, and political and national issues were all at stake in this world of the first and second centuries A.D.

History and the geographic range of the empire provide the focus for another group of contributions. Dress serves to distinguish friend and foe in war and in peace; divine and imperial figures; wife, prostitute, and defeated barbarian mother with child; soldier and private citizen. Richard Gergel has discovered a rich treasure trove of historical reliefs in an unsuspected place: the decorated breastplates of Roman imperial statues in armor, like the much-studied statue of Augustus of Prima Porta. He has, furthermore, identified a great many standard symbolic, mythological, and allegorical figures, distinguishing, on the basis of their dress, the national origin of barbarian captives and geographic personifications. Sometimes the figures on these breastplates provide us with information with which we can even determine protagonists, place, and outcome of a specific military confrontation.

The contribution of Bernard Goldman on Graeco-Roman dress in Syro-Mesopotamia deals with Roman influence in western Asia from the first century B.C. through the fourth century A.D. as illustrated by the adoption and adaptation of the draped Graeco-Roman dress, in contrast to the native or Iranian Parthian fitted costumes. This influence varies with geographic area: the closer an Asian city is to the Mediterranean or to a major commercial highway, the more prominent are Graeco-Roman features. It also varies with status, occasion, and gender: women for some reason tend to wear more Western dress.

Changes in outlook in the Roman world are marked by a change in dress. So the pallium, the traditional rectangular Greek garment which to the mind of Tertullian and others signified ancient philosophy, is promoted as a distinctively Christian costume. By the fourth century the pallium ceases to be used for ordinary dress, but it continues to be used in art. The emperor Honorius, at the turn of the fifth century, passed a series of laws forbidding the wearing of barbarian dress within the city of Rome—leather garments, pants, and other un-Roman dress. In spite of the severe penalties—permanent exile and loss of civil rights—the tide could no longer be turned.[33]

The arrangement of the contributions is not chronological, though Laetitia La Follette's account of the dress of Roman brides, part of an ancient ritual, contains elements that can be traced to the early days of Rome, taking us back—or so the later Romans believed—to the time of the legendary Romulus. At the other end, Ann Stout's brief survey of the jewelry of the late Roman and Byzantine period illustrates the change in taste from simple adornment to lavish displays as a reflection of change in the imperial court, while the contribution of Bernard Goldman on the garments worn by the more or less westernized inhabitants in Roman Asia Minor allows us to glimpse the complex situation that existed by the fourth century on the eastern boundaries of the Roman Empire.

Within Rome, the transformation of classical dress marks the end of the classical world. Peter Brown, in *The World of Late Antiquity* (1971), indicates the growing recognition of costume as important for the re-creation of ancient ideas, as well as daily life: "Small things betray changes more faithfully, because unconsciously. Near Rome, a sculptor's yard of the fourth century still turned out statues, impeccably dressed in the old Roman toga (with a socket for detachable portrait-heads!); but the aristocrats who commissioned such works would, in fact, wear a costume which betrayed prolonged exposure to the 'barbarians' of the non-Mediterranean world—a woolen shirt from the Danube, a cloak from northern Gaul, fastened at the shoulders by a filigree brooch from Germany, even guarding their health by 'Saxon' trousers."[34] H. I. Marrou, in his *Décadence romaine ou antiquité tardive?* (1977), begins with a chapter, "The Revolution of Dress," on the change from draped classical dress to modern fitted, sewn garments.[35] It is at this point that our research naturally and logically terminates. We leave to others the study of this fascinating revolution as well as other topics related to the study of Roman dress, only hoping that what is covered in this volume illustrates a methodology and enhances a body of information that may serve as guides to future research.

NOTES
1. Vergil, *Aeneid* 8.722–23: "gentes quam variae linguis, habitu tam vestis et armis." Cf. Polybius, *Historiae* 2.17. A. S. F. Gow, "Notes on the *Persae* of Aeschylus," *JHS* 48 (1928): 142–52; L. Bonfante, *Etruscan Dress* (Baltimore, 1975), 1.

2. See the useful survey in A. Morandi, *Epigrafia Italica* (Rome, 1982), 17–18. For Latin words for clothing, weaving, and dress belonging to an Indo-European group, see G. Devoto, *Storia della lingua di Roma,* vol. 1 (1939; Bologna, 1983), 8–9; G. Devoto, *Origini Indoeuropee* (Florence, 1962), 203–4 (colors), 239, 243–45, 272, 332–33 (dress), 102, 107, 385 (weaving). E. J. W. Barber, *Prehistoric Textiles* (Princeton, 1992), 260–83.

3. Scuola del Costume e della Moda, Università degli Studi di Firenze. Metropolitan Museum of Art, "Dress in the Time of Napoleon," 1989. See also the Holman symposium on ancient Egypt, "Costumes and Hairstyles in the New Kingdom: Reality, Image and Status," Fordham University, March 9, 1991. On psychology and nudity, see J. C. Flügel, *The Psychology of Clothes* (London, 1966); L. Bonfante, "Nudity as a Costume in Classical Art," *AJA* 93 (1989): 543–70; E. J. W. Barber, "The PIE Notion of Cloth and Clothing," *JIES* 3.4 (1975): 294–320; A. Hollander, *Seeing through Clothes* (New York, 1978).

4. Greek and Roman sculpture: B. S. Ridgway, "The Peplos Kore, Akropolis 679," *JWAG* 36 (1977): 49–61; eadem, "The Fashion of the Elgin Kore," *GMusJ* 12 (1984): 29–58; E. B. Harrison, "Notes on Daedalic Dress," *JWAG* 36 (1977): 37–48; eadem, "The Shoulder-Cord of Themis," in *Festschrift Brommer,* ed. U. Höckmann and A. Krug (Mainz, 1977), 155–61; S. C. Stone, "The Imperial Sculptural Group in the Metroon at Olympia," *AA* 100 (1985) 378–91; K. D. Morrow, *Greek Footwear and the Dating of Sculpture* (Madison, Wis., 1985); A. Stewart, *Greek Sculpture* (New Haven, Conn., 1990); K. Fittschen, *Die Bildnistypen der Faustina Minor und die Fecunditas Augustae* (Göttingen, 1982).

Provincial dress: R. Birley, *Vindolanda: A Roman Frontier Post on Hadrian's Wall* (London, 1977); J. Garbsch, "Die norisch-pannonische Tracht," *ANRW* 2.12.3 (1985): 546–77; M. Gebühr, *Der Trachtschmuck der älteren römischen Kaiserzeit im Gebiet zwischen unterer Elbe und Oder und auf den westlichen dänischen Inseln,* Göttinger Schriften zur Vor- und Frühgeschichte, Band 18 (Neumunster, 1976); J. P. Wild, "The Clothing of Britannia, Gallia Belgica and Germania Inferior," *ANRW* 2.12.3 (1985): 362–422; Ch. Peyre, "L'ornement . . . Gaulois," *Studi Romagnoli* 14 (1963): 255–57; A. Böhme, "Tracht und Bestattungssitten in den germanischen Provinzen und der Belgica," *ANRW* 2.12.3 (1985): 423–55; R. Koch, "Die Kleidung der Alemannen in der Spätantike," *ANRW* 2.12.3 (1985): 456–545.

5. See J. L. Druesedow, "In Style: Celebrating Fifty Years of the Costume Institute," *The Metropolitan Museum of Art Bulletin* (Fall 1987).

6. N. de Grummond, "The Study of Classical Costume by Philip, Albert and Peter Paul Rubens," *Ringling Museum of Art Journal, International Rubens Symposium* (1983): 78–93, esp. 81–82.

7. N. de Grummond, "Rediscovery," in *Etruscan Life and Afterlife,* ed. L. Bonfante (Detroit, 1986), 40.

8. T. Hope, *Costumes of the Greeks and Romans* (1812; New York, 1962).

9. C. Köhler, *A History of Costume,* ed. and augmented by E. Sichart (1928; New York, 1963).

10. M. Tilke, *Entwicklungsgeschichte des orientalischen Kostüms* (Berlin, 1923); J. Vercoutter, *L'Egypte et le monde égéen préhellénique* (Cairo, 1956).

11. On the toga, see H. R. Goette, *Studien zu römischen Togadarstellungen* (Mainz, 1990); F. W. Goethert, "Studien zur Kopienforschung, 1: Die stil- und trachtgeschichtliche Entwicklung der Togastatue in den beiden ersten Jahrhunderten der römischen Kaiserzeit," *RM* 54 (1939): 176–219; H. Gabelmann, "Römische Kinder in *Toga Praetexta,*" *JDAI* 100 (1985): 497–541. On the paenula, see F. Kolb, "Römische Mäntel: Paenula, Lacerna, Mandye," *RM* 80 (1973): 69–167, pls. 22–46.

12. P. Zanker, *The Power of Images in the Age of Augustus,* trans. A. Shapiro (Ann Arbor, Mich., 1988), 162–66, 319, 327; catalog of the Berlin show, *Kaiser Augustus und die verlorene Republik* (Berlin, 1988), Cat. 158–59, 171.

13. Julian, *Letter to a Priest,* trans. W. C. Wright, in *The Works of the Emperor Julian,* 3 vols. LCL (Cambridge, Mass., 1913–23), 1:332–35; L. Bonfante-Warren, "Emperor, God and Man in the IV Century: Julian the Apostate and Ammianus Marcellinus," *PdP* 99 (1964): 405. On the Jewish high priest's clothing, see D. Edwards, chap. 9 in this volume.

14. The identification of social classes depicted on funerary reliefs, for example, or of the relationship of the children on the Ara Pacis to the family of Augustus has been established chiefly by an examination of the garments worn by these figures, and their connotations. See D. E. E. Kleiner, *Roman Group Portraiture: The Funerary Reliefs of the Late Republic and Early Empire* (New York, 1977); B. Rose, "Princes and Barbarians on the Ara Pacis," *AJA* 94 (1990): 453–67, with bibliography. For the clothing of women, see J. Sebesta, chap. 2 in this volume. For the controversial question of slaves' dress, see, most recently, K. R. Bradley, "Roman Slavery and Roman Law," *Historical Reflections / Réflexions Historiques* 15 (1988): 477–95: "When recently installed as Rome's new emperor, the young Nero was informed by his mentor Seneca that 'a proposal was once made in the senate to distinguish slaves from free men in their dress'; but, Seneca continued, 'it then became apparent how great would be the impending danger if our slaves should begin to count our number,' and presumably . . . the proposal in the senate was dropped" (477). This lack of distinction in dress between slave and master is mentioned elsewhere in ancient literature: see T. Wiedemann, *Greek and Roman Slavery* (Baltimore, 1981), 68–69, 223, cf. 176. A "Spartan gibe claimed that in the streets of Athens [one] could not distinguish between a slave and a citizen"; H. D. F. Kitto, *The Greeks* (Baltimore, 1957), 132. Posidonius in turn remarked that Etruscan house slaves dressed more luxuriously than was appropriate to their slave status; see Diodorus Siculus, *Bibliotheca* 5.40; J. Heurgon, *La vie quotidienne chez les étrusques* (Paris, 1961), 50, 71. On Vestal Virgins, see M. Beard, "The Sexual Status of the Vestal Virgins," *JRS* 70 (1980): 12–27.

15. For the triumph, see L. Bonfante-Warren, "Roman Triumphs and Etruscan Kings: The Changing Face of the Triumph," *JRS* 60 (1970): 49–66; H. S. Versnel, *Triumphus* (Leiden, 1970), 59–93. For the dress of the emperor, see R. Delbrueck, *Spätantike Kaiserporträts von Constantinus Magnus bis zum Ende des Westreichs* (Berlin, 1933); A. Al-

földi, "Insignien und Tracht der römischen Kaiser," *RM 50* (1935): 1–171.

16. "Sed et ceteros continuos dies inter varia munuscula togas insuper ac pallia distribuit, lege proposita ut Romani Graeco, Graeci Romano habitu et sermone uterentur"; Suetonius, *Augustus* 98.4.

17. C. Bailey, ed. and trans. *Titi Lucreti Cari de rerum natura libri sex,* 3 vols. (Oxford, 1947–63), 5.1350–60, and 1423–29.

18. Suetonius, *Augustus* 86–87. Suetonius' *De genere vestium* is cited in Servius, *In Aeneadem* 7.612.

19. H. Bardon, *La littérature latine inconnue* (Paris, 1956), 15–16. For Maecenas as an author, see F. Harder, "Über die Fragmente des Maecenas," *Wissenschaftliche Programm, Berlin* 63 (1889): 1–23. On Maecenas' dress and morals in Roman eyes, see Heurgon, *La vie quotidienne,* 318–28.

20. Seneca, *Epistles* 114.4–8, 21–22; translations by R. M. Gummere, in *Seneca: Ad Lucilium, Epistulae Morales,* LCL (London, 1925), 3: 303–5.

21. Cf. *Epistle* 122.7: "Do you not believe that men live contrary to Nature who exchange the fashion of their attire with women?"

22. C. Lewis and C. Short, *Oxford Latin Dictionary,* s.v. "cultus."

23. On Cicero, see E. H. Richardson and L. Richardson, Jr., "*Ad Cohibendum Bracchium Toga:* An Archaeological Examination of Cicero, 'Pro Caelio' 5.11," *YCS* 19 (1966): 251–68. See also J. Heskel, chap. 7 in this volume. For Quintilian, see S. Stone, chap. 1 in this volume.

24. J. C. Frédouille, *Tertullien et la conversion de la culture antique* (Paris, 1972), 443–78, with bibliography. See also A. Nazzaro, *Il 'de pallio' di Tertulliano* (Naples, 1972).

25. Tertullian, *De pallio* 4.2: "Habitum transferre ita demum culpae prope est si non consuetudo sed natura mutetur. Sat refert inter honorem temporis et religionem. Det con-

suetudo fidem tempori, natura deo." See Frédouille, *Tertullien,* 462–63, on commentators who have found the work to be "frivole et légère." Yet even Frédouille speaks of the "disproportion entre l'importance du thème invoqué et l'insignificance du motif" (465). Hugh Witzmann's contribution to the seminar on the *De pallio* of Tertullian and the iconography of the Junius Bassus sarcophagus unfortunately could not be included in this volume.

26. L. Raditsa, "The Appearance of Women and Contact: Tertullian's *de habitu feminarum,*" *Athenaeum* 73 (1985): 297–326.

27. J. Bidez, ed. and trans., *L'Empereur Julien: Oeuvres complètes,* 2 vols. (Paris, 1932, 1942); English translation, Wright, *Works of the Emperor Julian,* vol. 2. Bonfante-Warren, "Emperor, God and Man," 401–27, esp. 418.

28. John the Lydian, *De magistratibus* 1.16.3. P. Brown, *The World of Late Antiquity* A.D. *150–750* (London, 1971), 28–29.

29. L. Bonfante-Warren, "Roman Costume: A Glossary and Some Etruscan Derivations," *ANRW* 1.4 (1973): 584–614.

30. For Etruscan influence, see Bonfante-Warren, "Roman Costume," 584–614. For Christian transformation, see Kolb, "Römische Mäntel," 69–167, pls. 22–46.

31. On colors, see Barber, "PIE Notion," 294–320; G. Bonfante, "I nomi dei colori in indoeuropeo," *Archivio Glottologico Italiano* 73 (1988): 153–54.

32. Livy 34.8–9; translation by N. de Grummond, in *Guide to Etruscan Mirrors,* ed. N. de Grummond (Tallahassee, Fla., 1982), 180.

33. J. L. Murga, "Tres leyes de Honorio sobre el modo de vestir los romanos," *Studia et Documenta Historiae et Iuris* 39 (1973): 129–86.

34. Brown, *World of Late Antiquity,* 21.

35. H. I. Marrou, *Décadence romaine ou antiquité tardive?* (Paris, 1977).

# PART I
# ROMAN GARMENTS, HAIRSTYLES, ACCESSORIES

# The Toga: From National to Ceremonial Costume

## 1

SHELLEY STONE

Of the garments worn by the ancient Romans, the toga was that which was most characteristically Latin. Vergil (*Aeneid* 1.282) called the Romans the *gens togata*, and the nationalistic associations implied by that phrase are echoed in other ancient sources.[1] According to Dionysius of Halicarnassus (*Roman Antiquities* 3.61), the toga was originally worn by both Romans and Etruscans, although the latter called the garment the *tebenna*.[2]

Because of the sparse survival of early Roman art, the nature of the early toga is known primarily through literary references, although a number of Etruscan works of art depict the tebenna.[3] Unlike the rectangular Greek himation (Latin pallium), the toga was always at least half elliptical with rounded ends.[4] It was originally worn by both men and women (by men without an undergarment save a loincloth, the subligaculum), and hence it was the national garment of the early Romans.[5] It was even worn into battle after having been tied securely around the waist, a mode of draping called *cinctus Gabinus* which survived into later ritual associated with war.[6]

By the second century B.C. the toga was worn over a tunic (*tunica*) and was reserved for adult males; by the time of Augustus, an adult female wearing the garment was considered a prostitute.[7] Nevertheless, signs of the universal character of the toga as a garment survived into the empire, since it was worn by young girls until the age of twelve (i.e., until puberty).[8] The toga was generally woven from wool and, hence, was well suited to a people whose early economy was heavily based on the herding of sheep. It may be assumed that the garment early served also as a blanket at night, although it likely was woven into a fairly thin cloth.[9] Despite evidence

that it was declining in popularity by the time of Augustus, the toga survived as a ceremonial garment throughout the empire and was always considered the garment to be worn by the Roman man conducting public business.[10]

In keeping with the Romans' emphasis on depicting status through costume, the toga early evolved different forms of decoration which distinguished the rank within Roman society of its wearers. According to Dionysius of Halicarnassus (*Roman Antiquities* 3.61) and Pliny the Elder (*H.N.* 8.4), the Etruscan kings of Rome wore elaborately decorated togas. The toga picta continued to be used during the republic by triumphing generals and, later, by the emperors.[11] The toga purpurea was also worn by kings; eventually the emperor alone could wear the purple toga.[12]

The decorative treatment of the toga evolved during the Etruscan period. What had the most importance for the later history of the garment was a purple stripe of approximately two to three inches in width along the border of the robe. A toga so decorated was called a *toga praetexta*, and its use was reserved for magistrates and high priests.[13] According to Pliny the Elder (*H.N.* 9.63.136), this first appeared in Rome during the reign of Tullus Hostilius in the seventh century B.C. He also states (*H.N.* 8.74.197) that the toga praetexta of Servius Tullius survived at Rome until the death of Sejanus (A.D. 31). The garment was also worn by young boys of the upper classes until the age of fourteen to sixteen, when they adopted the toga virilis.[14] A relatively early example of the toga praetexta can be seen in the bronze statue (fig. 1.1) of the early first century B.C. known as the Arringatore, where the stripe runs along the lower border of the garment.[15] The imperial toga praetexta can be

Fig. 1.1. The Arringatore, bronze statue of an Etruscan municipal magistrate named Aule Meteli, ca. 100–75 B.C. He wears the bordered toga praetexta over a tunic with stripes. Museo Nazionale Archeologico, Florence. Photo from DAI, Rome, neg. 63.599.

Fig. 1.2. Painting depicting a togate *genius familiaris* between two Lares, from the Lararium in the House of the Vettii, Pompeii. Photo: Alinari (Anderson) 24875.

seen in the central *genius familiaris* of the Lararium of the House of the Vettii at Pompeii (fig. 1.2).[16] There the purple stripe runs around the border of the sinus or overfold on the right side of the figure as well as along the lower border of the robe. The magisterial character of the *genius* is also indicated by the vertical purple stripes on his tunic, since these appear to be the broad stripes *(latus clavus)* reserved for the senatorial class. The members of the equestrian class were allowed to wear narrow stripes on their tunics *(angustus clavus)*.[17]

Besides the toga praetexta, the Romans created other forms of the toga to indicate precisely the status or the nature of the wearer. The normal toga of the average male citizen was called *pura* to describe its natural color (likely an off-white or grayish hue).[18] Another specific type of toga was the toga pulla (or dark toga), which was worn only in times of mourning. Wearing it at another time was not only inappropriate but also inauspicious (Cicero, *In Vatinium* 12.30, 13.31).[19] The toga candida, an artificially whitened toga, was worn by candidates seeking office.[20]

We have seen that the earliest form of the toga is little known due to the rarity of artistic renditions. The first significant surviving togate statue depicts an Etruscan magistrate named Aule Meteli (Aulus Metellus) (fig. 1.1), but since it dates to the period of the Social War (the first quarter of the first century B.C.), it undoubtedly shows the mode in which a Roman of that date would have worn the toga.[21] This is confirmed by the fact that similar *togati* appear on the Census relief of the so-

Fig. 1.3. Grave relief of a married couple from the Via Statilia, Rome, ca. 75–60 B.C. Conservatori Museum, Rome. Photo from DAI, Rome, neg. 29.172.

called Altar of Domitius Ahenobarbus from Rome of ca. 100 B.C.[22] The bronze statue is often called the Arringatore (the Orator) since it shows Meteli in the act of addressing an audience. He wears a toga over a tunic with sleeves to the elbow. The toga is considerably less full than is the later imperial toga (compare fig. 1.2), but its draping conforms to the basic method of wearing the toga throughout its history. First an entire side of the garment was loosely rolled into folds. One end of the side with these folds was placed against the lower left leg of the wearer, then passed up the left side and over the shoulder. The rest of the toga was then wrapped loosely

around the back and placed beneath the right arm in order to facilitate the use of the arm. Then the remainder of the garment was brought around the chest and thrown back over the left shoulder, concealing the end of the toga from which the drapery started (see fig. 1.4d). As shown by the statue, the bottom hem of the garment extended to the lower shins. The rolled folds running up the left side, around the back, beneath the right arm, and diagonally across the chest could be easily adjusted in order to achieve this length. The basic unwieldiness of the garment is clearly apparent; the left arm must be held against the side to hold the cloth in place on the left shoulder, since it is nowhere pinned and the weight of the cloth alone maintains the draping. The doubling of the woolen cloth over the left side made the toga quite warm in the hot Mediterranean summers of Italy, and the garment's impracticality increased as it became larger in its imperial form.

The toga of the Arringatore conforms well to what little is known of the early form of the garment from surviving literary references. It is often called the *toga exigua* from a remark by Horace (*Epistles* 1.19.12–14) which refers to Cato's "skimpy" toga.[23] This term, however, while it is often used by modern scholars to designate the republican toga, is merely a witticism and probably does not represent a common ancient usage.

During the first century B.C. Rome (and Italy) underwent an intense period of Hellenization. The draping of the toga proved subject to Greek influence also, as can be seen in a funerary relief of a couple from Rome in the Conservatori Museum (fig. 1.3) of the second quarter of the first century B.C.[24] The couple may belong to the newly important freedman class, since the funerary reliefs of freedmen illustrate their newly acquired *romanitas* and male figures consequently wear the toga.[25] The woman on the tombstone is depicted in the *pudicitia* (modesty) pose commonly used in late republican and early imperial funerary sculpture to portray feminine virtue.[26] The man wears a toga much like that of Aule Metli, but the folds which on the Arringatore run under the right arm now have been loosened, and the cloth has been pulled up over the crooked arm and held in place beneath the neck in what has been called an arm-sling.[27] As has been noted, this method of wearing the toga is similar to a common draping of the himation and likely represents Greek influence, although it appears on Etruscan statues wearing the tebenna as early as the fourth century B.C.[28]

This style of the toga further restricts the use of the arms and is mentioned by Quintilian (*Institutio oratoria* 11.3.138), who notes that this method of covering the arms precluded expansive gesturing while speaking. He also states (11.3.143) that Plotius Gallus and Nigidius Figulus, two rhetoricians of the mid–first century B.C., recommend that the lower edge of the toga hang to the ankles "like the Greek pallium."[29] The longer toga necessitated by this latter recommendation can be seen on statues slightly later in date than the grave relief, and the longer toga with the "arm-sling" continued to be depicted until the turn of the era.[30] The increase in the amount of cloth required by lowering the bottom hem represents a trend which continued into the early imperial age.

The greatest number of the surviving monuments depicting *togati* belong to the early empire of the late first century B.C. and first century A.D. The longest surviving discussion of the garment, in the *Institutio oratoria* of Quintilian, also belongs to this period, since it was written at the end of the first century A.D. In his Book 11 (3.137–44), Quintilian clearly indicates the significance of the garment during the early empire, since his avowed purpose in writing this section of his manual is to ensure that an orator be well received in his speech through proper attire. He makes it clear that the toga must be worn while orating (since no other garment is mentioned as possible oratorical garb) and that improper draping of the garment could seriously impair a budding political career.

Despite this evidence of the toga's authority in governmental circles, it is equally clear from other sources that by the imperial period the toga was becoming largely a ceremonial garment. Augustus was forced to require that citizens wear it in the Forum (Suetonius, *Augustus* 40), while Juvenal comments that in his day (the first quarter of the second century) "there is a great part of Italy where no one wears the toga until they die" (*Satires* 3.171–72).[31] Apparently even the Roman upper classes eschewed the toga by the later first century. Martial refers to the pleasures of country life, where there is "never a lawsuit, the toga is scarce, the mind at ease" (10.47.5), and he and other authors of the same period use the term *toga* as synonymous with client status (clients were forced to wear the toga in order to accompany their patrons to the Forum).[32] At the same time, legislation was passed during the early empire that enshrined the toga as the definitive garment of the Roman male; by the middle of the first century foreigners and exiles were apparently denied its use lest they be mistaken for citizens.[33]

One of the likely reasons for the decline in popularity of the toga was its increasing unwieldiness. The most familiar form of the garment is that which developed during the late first century B.C. and which remained the dominant style into the second century A.D. During this period the toga became extremely large. The width of a developed imperial toga of the first century A.D. was fifteen to eighteen feet (4.8–5.0 m, as opposed to slightly over twelve feet or 3.7 m in that of the Arringatore), and it was consequently impossible to don the garment without aid (figs. 1.4a–d and 1.5a, b). Its tendency to slip from its draping made it unsuitable for any physical endeavor. It is therefore not surprising that the imperial toga was avoided by all other than those who devoted their lives to public service. It should also be noted that as the garment's size increased, it became heavier and, consequently, warmer.

Visually, the imperial toga is distinguished from its republican predecessors by two new features, the sinus (the overfold) and the umbo (literally, "knob"). The sinus represents the loosening of the loosely rolled folds running diagonally across the chest (often referred to as the balteus, or sword belt) in order to form a decorative emphasis over the torso (see figs. 1.2–3). Its evolution is unknown, although it may represent observation of a similar use of an overfold over the torso on the himatia of some Greek statues.[34] To form the sinus, the toga was folded nearly in half, and the doubled cloth was rolled into the loose folds which ran around the upper body. The institution of this feature thus determined the increased dimensions of the imperial toga. The actual sinus first appears where the bunched folds emerge from underneath the right arm. At that point, some of the folds were loosened to allow the cloth to fall like an apron across the torso (see figs. 1.4b–c, 6–12, 14, 16). The umbo was a largely decorative clump of drapery pulled up from the folds of the toga which ran up the left side of its wearer (figs. 1.4a, b). Its purpose was apparently to help to hold the draping together (much as a towel knotted around the body would, but less efficiently), but it swiftly became a characteristic decorative aspect of the imperial toga and rapidly increased in size at the beginning of the first century A.D.

These new features of the toga evolved during the reign of Augustus, since they appear in early form on the processional friezes of the Ara Pacis (fig 1.6) and by the first decade of the first century A.D. reached the form which they maintained with few changes for the next century (see figs. 1.7–10). Figure 1.5a shows the change in size of the toga from the time of the Ara Pacis to the first century A.D. The surviving members of the imperial family (save Augustus) on the south frieze of the Ara Pacis (commissioned in 13 B.C. and dedicated January 30, 9 B.C.) include five *togati* who illustrate the new style of draping the garment and who demonstrate the garment's use and significance in Roman society.[35]

The *togati* begin with the tall figure of Marcus Agrippa, who has covered his head with part of the garment. This suggests that he is about to enter sanctified ground and witness the sacrifices associated with the dedication of the altar; such a figure *capite velato* (with

Fig. 1.4a

Fig. 1.4b

Fig. 1.4a–d. Reconstruction of the imperial toga pura, showing the mode of
draping popular during the first century A.D.
a. First stage of draping.
b. Creation of the sinus and the umbo.
c. View of the front with draping completed.
d. View of the back with draping completed.

Fig. 1.4c

Fig. 1.4d

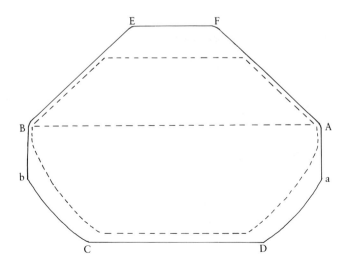

Fig. 1.5a. The outline of the imperial toga as it was woven during the first and second centuries A.D. The dotted lines indicate the dimensions of the toga as seen on the Ara Pacis. After Wilson, *Roman Toga*, fig. 27a.

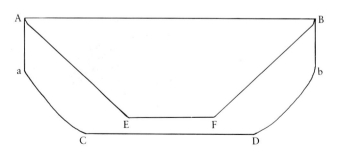

Fig. 1.5b. The outline of the imperial toga after it was folded to create the sinus. After Wilson, *Roman Toga*, fig. 27b.

19

Fig. 1.6. South frieze of the Ara Pacis, Rome, showing a procession of members of the imperial family in 13 B.C. Courtesy of the Fototeca Unione at the American Academy in Rome, neg. F.U. 3247 F.

head covered) demonstrates the virtue of piety toward the gods, since priests covered their heads while sacrificing. An examination of Agrippa's garments shows how this was achieved at the time of the Ara Pacis. The umbo was first pushed back down to become again a part of the vertical portion of the toga resting against the left side. The bunched fabric on the left shoulder and across the back was then drawn up to cover the head. When the ceremony was over and the participant in a rite had left sacred ground, the portion of the toga covering the head could easily be replaced on the shoulder and rolled back into its original position and the umbo restored. Directly behind Agrippa in the foreground is a small child dressed in a tunic, followed by Augustus' wife, Livia, who has her head covered in the same way as Agrippa.[36] Behind her moves her son Tiberius, who may be loosening his umbo with his right hand in order to cover his head.

Following Tiberius is a woman (Antonia Minor) who looks back toward a man in military garb who has been identified as her husband and Tiberius' brother, Drusus the Elder. Between these figures stands a small togate child, likely their son Germanicus. He wears around his neck the bulla, the protective amulet traditionally worn by Roman boys prior to their official assumption of manhood.[37] Some of the adult male *togati* on the Ara Pacis were magistrates and priests and would thus have worn the toga praetexta, as would the small boys, but

the purple stripes on these and their tunics were rendered in paint which does not survive today.[38] Behind Drusus and grasping his cloak stands another togate boy who is several years older than Germanicus. He looks back at a slightly older girl clad in a voluminous palla or mantle (hence she is over twelve years of age).[39] Her palla is draped like a toga which combines the "arm-sling" of the late republic with the sinus, but its squared lower border indicates that it is a palla. A similar conflation of two styles of draping can be seen on several togate figures on the north frieze of the Ara Pacis, while some of the *Quirites* there depicted show the older style of draping without the sinus popular during the period of the Triumvirates.[40] The coexistence of two styles of draping the toga suggests that the period of the Ara Pacis (ca. 10 B.C.) was one of transition from the late republican style of toga to the new and fuller fashion characteristic of the empire, an observation supported by other monuments of the same period.[41]

Behind the little girl in figure 1.6 stands yet another adult *togatus* (presumably her father) in the same pose as Germanicus.[42] It is interesting to observe the positioning of the left arms of these *togati*. The arm is held crooked in order to hold the heavy fabric on the left shoulder. The last figure also depicts a gesture likely necessary when walking in an imperial toga; he grasps the umbo with his left hand in order to keep it from slipping down and disappearing. It is clear from these figures that the toga of the imperial age was neither suited to much movement nor easy to maintain in its fashionable draping, factors which no doubt contributed to its gradual decline in popularity. Nevertheless, the imperial toga was a stately and impressive garment, and this, together with its traditional associations, ensured its survival as ceremonial clothing.

On the Ara Pacis the sinus reaches to the middle of the right thigh of each figure (see Quintilian, *Institutio oratoria* 11.3.167). The length of this new feature of the toga swiftly increased. By the first century A.D. it reached to just above the knee, as can be seen in a statue of M. Nonius Balbus (fig. 1.7), a distinguished inhabitant of Herculaneum who was much honored there late in the reign of Augustus.[43] His toga has a long and elegant sinus but does not show the umbo, again demonstrating the transitional character of the reign of Augustus for togate style; thereafter virtually all *togati* wear some form of the umbo.[44] The "balteus" of Balbus' toga is unrolled and loose and suggests that he has just released an "arm-sling" in order to free his right arm. But save for this and the absence of the umbo, Balbus' toga is essentially a clumsier version of that worn by Augustus in the elegant sacrificing image of late Augustan date from the Via Labicana in Rome (fig. 1.8).[45] The increased size of the toga on this statue is attested by the fact that the cloth falls over the left foot, rather than above the ankle, as on the Ara Pacis (fig. 1.6). This must have made walking in the toga even more difficult than previously; Caligula is recorded to have tripped on the end of his toga while leaving the amphitheater (Suetonius, *Caligula* 35.3), likely a not uncommon accident. Augustus has covered his head without loosening his large umbo, another sign of the increased size of the toga of the first century A.D. (compare Agrippa on the Ara Pacis, fig. 1.6, and the *genius familiaris* of the House of the Vettii, fig. 1.2). The extreme linearity of the multiple folds visible on this statue as well as on that of Balbus probably indicate that the classicistic style popular in this era has led the sculptors to take some liberties with the character of the cloth, rather than reflecting any change in the weight of the fabric used for the toga.

The close correspondence of the two images also demonstrates that fashions of draping the toga popular in the capital (where most innovations may be presumed to have developed) swiftly spread throughout Italy.[46] Nevertheless, it is important to emphasize that exact fashions in draping the toga were not enforced during the first century and that some individuals at any given time may have eschewed the most current trend in favor of the familiar authority of earlier style. Thus, just as the individuals of the north frieze of the Ara Pacis show two styles of draping the toga, one late republican and the other the fuller fashion favored by the imperial family on the south frieze (fig. 1.6), so the magistrates at the left end of the Tiberian *Vicomagistri* relief wear togas close to the style favored by the imperial family on the Ara Pacis, while the younger *togati* at the right end of the same relief are draped in the mode of figure 1.8 of the first decade of the first century A.D.[47] Such variations must have existed at all times; they warn the modern scholar that changes in fashion must be used cautiously as chronological indicators.

By Augustus' death the early imperial toga had achieved the basic style of draping that it would retain for a century, with only minor variation. By the middle of the first century the cloth on sculpted images had regained the flowing folds characteristic of wool, but the basic draping of the garment had changed only in that the sinus now dipped below the knee. This can be seen in a fine *togatus* (fig. 1.9) which was once part of a Claudian group of the Julio-Claudian family at Caere.[48] As shown by the toga of the Neronian *genius familiae* of the House of the Vettii at Pompeii (fig. 1.2), the sinus soon crept back above the knee; as noted earlier, the figure also shows the imperial method of draping the toga praetexta.[49] The same basic style of draping seen in the man from Caere persisted throughout the second half of the first century. Despite a more baroque treatment of the folds to create sculptural contrasts of light and shadow, the same draping is seen on the well-known togate statue of Titus in the Vatican (fig. 1.10).[50] On both statues the toga falls over the feet and to the ground, and both show a full sinus stretching to the region of the knee and a large umbo. Titus' sinus can serve as an illustration of his contemporary Quintilian's instructions on achieving the most elegant draping of this feature: "The overfold is most becoming if it falls a bit above the lowest point of the tunic [which should] fall a little below the knee."[51]

It is somewhat ironic that Quintilian's account, the longest surviving tract on the toga, was written in the late first century, when the garment was becoming increasingly unpopular. In the same years Martial (4.66) suggests that it was worn by the lower classes only on holidays (that is, at religious festivities), and in the next generation Juvenal, as we saw, states that many Italians wore it only when buried (*Satires* 3.171–72). In the early third century the Christian apologist Tertullian inveighed against the discomforts of the toga while praising the pallium *(De pallio)*. It thus seems clear that by the second century the toga was worn by most Romans only on formal or festive occasions. The artistic record is misleading because of the public and status-oriented nature of Roman art; although togate statues declined in number after the first century, they remained common into

Fig. 1.7. M. Nonius Balbus of Herculaneum, early first century A.D. Museo Nazionale Archeologico, Naples. Photo: Alinari, P.I.N. 11110.

Fig. 1.8. Augustus, *capite velato*, from the Via Labicana, Rome, early first century A.D. Museo Nazionale delle Terme, Rome. Photo: Alinari 30157.

the fourth century owing to the toga's authority as the garment worn to conduct public and religious matters and as the definitive Roman male costume.[52]

Roman sculpture depicting the emperors suggests that the imperial toga as developed during the first century continued to be the favored costume of the ruler through the third century, but the same monuments indicate that new styles of draping developed between the second and the fourth centuries. On the Arch at Beneventum dedicated in 114 (fig. 1.11), Trajan wears his toga in essentially the same way as Titus did forty years earlier (fig. 1.10). The only differences in the two garments are that Trajan's ends more sensibly slightly above the ankles and that his sinus has become wider and deeper, dipping well below the knee and spreading broadly across his lower body.

The reliefs illustrated in figure 1.11 depict Trajan entering Rome and greeting businessmen and/or officials in Rome or Ostia while gods look on in the background. This refers to his efforts to improve commercial access to the capital through improving the harbor at Ostia.[53] All of the foreground figures in the panel above are togate save the lictors surrounding the emperor, but only Trajan wears his garment with the traditional umbo. The three businessmen or officials show a new treatment of the roll of folds which, as Quintilian noted (*Institutio oratoria* 11.3.140), extends diagonally across the chest like a sword belt (balteus). These are now twisted together more tightly and pulled up higher on the chest than previously. A part of the underlying cloth resting on the left side has been pulled out over the diagonal roll of folds, but the cloth for this is no longer drawn from the region of the waist (as on the traditional umbo) but has now been pulled out of the roll of folds which rests on the left shoulder and chest and folded over the "balteus" into a rough triangle.[54]

This new style of draping the toga seems clearly to represent an effort to better secure the garment at the point (the left shoulder) where it was most often subject to slippage. A clearer depiction of the new style of draping the toga can be seen on the figure directly preceding Trajan (likely the *praefectus urbi*) on the *Adventus* relief below the harbor panel, and Trajan appears in this style of toga on his column in Rome.[55] The limited literary evidence on the later history of the toga suggests that the cloth pulled out over the shoulder was still called the umbo, although it no longer resembled a knot or a boss.[56]

The same modes of draping continued throughout the second century, as can be seen on a panel relief from a triumphal Arch of Marcus Aurelius which depicts the emperor sacrificing at the Capitolium (fig. 1.12).[57] There the emperor wears his toga in the early imperial mode, while the toga of the *genius senatus* standing immediately behind him shows the triangular shoulder umbo. It

is significant that in the other surviving panel reliefs on which the emperor appears togate he again is draped in the early imperial style, while on the *Liberalitas (Largitio)* panel now on the Arch of Constantine the five other *togati* show the shoulder umbo.[58] This suggests that the shoulder umbo was the most popular style during the second century and that the toga of the early empire was worn by the emperor on formal occasions due to its traditional associations.

One of the figures on the *Liberalitas* panel (the figure at the extreme left seen from behind) wears a short toga which ends above his knees; the same style can be seen on the diminutive flautist to the right of the altar on the Sacrifice panel (fig. 1.12). It has been suggested that this is the toga worn by the common people who were seldom depicted in Roman art, and whose costume is thus little known.[59]

An interesting togate statue of Hadrian sacrificing with his head veiled (fig. 1.13) from the 130s illustrates yet another mode of draping the toga.[60] It has neither sinus nor umbo, and the "balteus" is quite loose. The effect is to make the toga look very similar to a himation, yet the rounded lower edge, together with what seems to be the praetextate stripe appropriate to a high priest, indicates conclusively that Hadrian wears the toga. The peculiar draping of the garment, which appears on only one other statue known to me, probably represents a fleeting Hellenization popular during the reign of the most philhellenic of emperors.[61] On two panel reliefs in the Capitoline Museum, Hadrian appears in the toga with the shoulder umbo.[62]

The "himation" toga seen in figure 1.13 appears to disappear with Hadrian, but both other styles of draping the toga in the second century continued to be used throughout the third century. Septimius Severus appears draped in the early imperial mode on the Arch of the Argentarii of 204 (fig. 1.14), and the only surviving figure in its pendant relief on the other pier, Caracalla, is draped in the same way.[63] On the Palazzo Sacchetti relief of around 205, all of the figures, including Septimius, are draped with the shoulder umbo.[64]

On the Attic frieze of the Arch of Septimius Severus at Leptis Magna of 206–9, however, while Septimius appears in the Sacrifice scene wearing the early imperial toga, most of the other *togati* on the frieze (including two representations of the emperor) wear a new style of toga featuring broad, smooth bands of stacked folds.[65] If we consider a detail of the central section of the *Concordia Augustorum* relief (fig. 1.15), this style can be understood. There Caracalla, at the left, wears the early imperial toga, but both Geta, at the center of the imperial trio, and Septimius wear the new style with bands. Three bands of stacked folds adorn their togas. The first would have been made by folding the cloth which was placed over the left side to commence the draping back and forth several times to create a stacked series of folds of the same width (about four to five inches or ten to fifteen centimeters). This band runs up between the legs and over the left shoulder. A second folded band begins at the middle of the chest and is pulled out over the "balteus" cloth on the chest and the left shoulder just as in the toga with the shoulder umbo. A final band of stacked folds runs around the lower edge of the sinus, which reaches to the upper shin.

This style, which is generally called the banded toga (it is sometimes also referred to as the *toga contabulata*, a modern Latinization), became in various forms the final mode of draping the garment. This fashion first appears in nascent form on busts of the later second century and clearly represents a development from the toga with the shoulder umbo.[66] The band across the chest served the same function as the shoulder umbo, since it was drawn out over the left shoulder to hold in place the gathered sinus, which had been thrown over the shoulder.[67]

The formality and discomfort of the banded toga were criticized by Tertullian in the early third century (*De pallio* 5). He condemns the difficulty of creating the folded band: "There was [earlier] no need of a skilled person who should the day before from the beginning make folds and smooth them down more elegantly and place in *forceps* the whole mass of the contracted umbo."[68] From this passage it seems likely that the band running across the chest was called the umbo and that the bands were created by a valet, who pressed the toga overnight in a *forceps* (presumably some sort of press). In order to maintain this arrangement for any length of time it must also have been necessary to fasten the folds together, likely by concealed stitching.[69]

The banded toga became the most popular mode of draping the garment in the third and fourth centuries, although it is clear that earlier styles of draping survived. A fragmentary biographical sarcophagus in Naples (fig. 1.16) dates to ca. 260 and shows four different ways of draping the toga.[70] It is generally called the Brother Sarcophagus because the same bearded individual (presumably the man buried there), who appears four times overall, is paired at its center as if he were identical twins. The man appears in the early imperial toga at the right end, where he marries his wife. In the center he appears twice, at the right clad in the toga with the shoulder umbo as a senator and to the left in the philosopher's pallium (himation). At the left end he appears as a consul wearing a banded toga flanked by senators in banded togas.[71]

In this final scene the consul's sinus still hangs loosely across his legs, but from other representations it is clear that this was done only when the figure was at rest. It seems to have become fashionable by the middle of the third century to carry the lower end of sinus in the left hand or across the left arm while walking, as seen in both of the figures flanking the consul on the Brother Sarcophagus. This was no doubt necessitated because the cloth thrown over the left shoulder easily slipped from beneath the band pulled over it and because the enormous length of the third-century sinus made walking difficult.[72] It should be remembered that the sinus on the banded toga of the consul not only extends below the knee but also includes four stacked bands of pressed folds of cloth. Since, when the sinus was carried over the left arm, the lower legs below the knee would have remained exposed in the tunic popular in Quintilian's day, the third-century tunic was lengthened to cover the lower legs to the middle of the shin.[73] The coexistence of three styles of draping the toga in the third and the early fourth centuries seems confirmed by their simultaneous appearance on the Brother Sarcophagus and other sarcophagi of the period, as well as on the *Decennalia* base of 303 in the Forum.[74]

At the same time it is clear that the most popular fashion of wearing the toga in its last period was with folded bands. By the middle of the third century, two styles of banded toga existed, as evidenced by the Brother Sarcophagus. At its left end the two flanking attendants of the togate consul wear banded togas in the style of the Arch of Septimius Severus at Leptis Magna (fig. 1.15); that is, the band across the chest starts at the breastbone. The consul, however, wears a new style in which the band begins beneath the left arm and runs across the chest over the right shoulder. This style of draping the toga can be seen also on a statue of a Roman in the Villa Doria-Pamphili (fig. 1.17a) of about the same date as the Brother Sarcophagus.[75] It first appears on busts of the 220s.[76]

The mode of achieving this arrangement is not totally clear. The problem is how the folded bands can hang directly between the legs and, without distortion, extend across the chest to the right armpit (where the bands must have been fastened in some way). Lillian Wilson reconstructed this type of toga by cutting out a portion of the corner of the cloth (fig. 1.17b), which allows the portion with the bands to zig over from the middle of the body to the armpit without pulling on the stacked folds between the legs.[77] The band across the chest is formed by folding back and forth the section of the sinus labeled *E–C* on the diagram. This alteration in the shape of the toga seems likely, since figures wearing the banded toga in the fourth century show a style of draping in which the shape of the toga was further altered and which is a clear development from the toga of the statue

Fig. 1.9. *Togatus* from a group of the imperial family, A.D. 40s, found at Caere. Museo Gregorio Profano, Vatican Museums. Photo: Musei Vaticani, Archivio Fotografico L.14.106.

Fig. 1.10. Statue of Titus, A.D. 71–81, found on the Esquiline Hill, Rome. Braccio Nuovo, Vatican Museums. Photo: Musei Vaticani, Archivio Fotografico IX.14.19.

Fig. 1.11. Panels from the city side of Trajan's Arch at Beneventum, A.D. 114–18. *Below*, Trajan enters Rome; *above*, Trajan is thanked by businessmen and/or officials for fostering commerce by building the harbor of Ostia. Photo: Alinari, P.I.N. 11501.

Fig. 1.12. Panel relief from an arch of Marcus Aurelius, ca. A.D. 175–85. Marcus Aurelius sacrifices before the Temple of Capitoline Jupiter. Conservatori Museum, Rome. Photo: Alinari (Anderson) 1732.

Fig. 1.13. Hadrian, *capite velato*, A.D. 130–38. Conservatori Museum, Rome. Photo from DAI, Rome, neg. 55.212.

Fig. 1.14. Septimius Severus and Julia Domna sacrifice. Passageway relief on the Arch of the Argentarii, Rome, A.D. 204. Photo: Alinari 28856.

Fig. 1.15. *Concordia Augustorum* relief of Septimius Severus and his coregent, Caracalla. From the Arch of Septimius Severus at Leptis Magna, A.D. 206–9. Photo from DAI, Rome, neg. 61.1701.

Fig. 1.16. The Brother Sarcophagus, ca. A.D. 260. Museo Nazionale Archeologico, Naples. Photo from DAI, Rome, neg. 70.1505.

Fig. 1.17a. Togate man, ca. A.D. 260. Villa Doria-Pamphili, Rome.
Photo from DAI, Rome, neg. 8158.

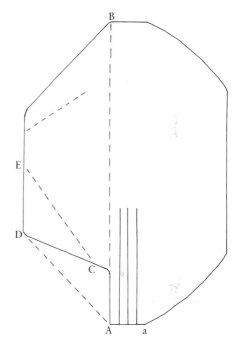

Fig. 1.17b. Lillian Wilson's reconstruction of
the shape of the toga in fig. 1.17a. Dotted lines
indicate the dimensions of the imperial toga.
After Wilson, *Roman Toga*, fig. 53.

in the Villa Doria-Pamphili. It is clear, however, that the alteration must have followed the introduction of this style of toga, since it responds to the needs of the draping.

This style can in fact be created without altering the basic shape of the garment, if the portion of the sinus which is placed against the left side to commence the draping is folded beneath the stacked folds between the legs. If the folds running up between the legs are then attached to the tunic at the waist, where it was belted, a portion of the sinus cloth can be unfolded above the waist to the right armpit. This style of draping was likely created in this manner, although an earlier school of students believed that a separate piece of cloth was needed to produce the band across the chest on the banded toga.[78] This is not necessary and seems alien to the traditional character of the toga in Roman society. It seems best to me to see the toga throughout its history as a single piece of cloth whose cut was modified very slowly to achieve various styles of draping.

The *togatus* in the Villa Doria-Pamphili presents the best surviving evidence for concealed stitching binding the stacked folds together. Faint pairs of parallel lines can be observed on each of the bands; these do not appear on earlier representations of the toga and are best explained as depicting concealed stitching.[79]

During the fourth century the most popular form of the toga was clearly that with folded bands. The *Decennalia* base of 303 shows the latest surviving appearance of the toga with the shoulder umbo, but several *togati* show that the early imperial fashion of draping the garment survived, at least in artistic renditions, until the end of the fourth century.[80] Some of the *togati* from this period use earlier bodies mated with new portrait heads, and it is consequently unclear whether this style of toga was worn or whether it represents a conscious anachronism designed to recall the earlier empire.[81] It seems reasonable, however, to assume that the early imperial toga continued to be worn in the fourth century during traditional religious ceremonies (such as the *Suovetaurilia* depicted on the *Decennalia* base).

Otherwise the banded toga predominates. It is worn by all of the *togati* on the Constantinian friezes of the Arch of Constantine of 312–15.[82] Figure 1.18 shows the central section of the *Liberalitas* relief on the north face of that monument. The figures now wear their tunics to the ankles; the two at the extreme right of the detail wear two tunics each, an undertunic with long sleeves and a shorter overtunic with sleeves to the elbows. This became common practice in the fourth century.[83] The togas are quite short, extending to just below the knee. The entire sinus, including the "balteus" folds, which once extended diagonally across the chest, is carried across the left arm, but a band extends across the breast

of each *togatus* just as in the statue in the Villa Doria-Pamphili. This indicates that a section of cloth must have been extended to the right armpit from the portion of the toga which was placed as a band of folds between the legs. The band was then laid across the chest; it runs over the left shoulder and across the back (as can be seen in the *togatus* second from the left in fig. 1.18). This portion of the toga then reemerges in the front of the body as the sinus. As noted earlier, it would have been necessary to attach the band across the chest by some concealed means beneath the arm. A close examination of the *togati* in figure 1.18 reveals that now only two bands of folds adorn their togas. One runs up between the legs and over the left shoulder, where it has been placed beneath the second band across the chest. This first band then runs down the left side of the back. The proportions of this toga thus have been reversed from those of the early imperial toga, since the sinus portion now has become larger than the portion which once constituted the main body of the garment.

In addition, two anomalous *togati* are depicted in figure 1.18. The man receiving coins in his up-stretched sinus from the enthroned Constantine does not show the folded band across his back, and it must be assumed that, in his eagerness to receive the money, he has disturbed the stacked folds which made up the band. A similarly draped figure can be seen at the left. It is, however, perhaps not worth quibbling about the lack of naturalistic details in the togas given the rigidly hieratic and nonnaturalistic style used for the Constantinian sculpture of the Arch of Constantine.[84]

This style of draping the toga seen on the Arch of Constantine seems to have remained in fashion in Rome throughout the fourth century. Numerous Christian sarcophagi of the second quarter of the fourth century have portrait busts of men who wear this style of toga.[85] The ivory diptych honoring Probianus, the *vicarius* (commander of the military detachment) of Rome around 400 (fig. 1.19a) shows on its left wing Probianus enthroned, wearing a military cloak (Latin paludamentum, Greek chlamys) over a tunic, and surrounded by similarly clad secretaries to either side and below.[86] On the right wing (fig. 1.19b) he appears enthroned wearing the toga. On this wing, his flanking secretaries wear the paenula (a kind of mantle) over their tunics. On this wing Probianus is hailed from below by togate senators; one is shown from the front, and the other from the rear, making it possible to evaluate the draping of the garment. Both senators wear two tunics beneath togas, which are draped in the same manner as those in the *Liberalitas* scene on the Arch of Constantine. The long sinus is carried over the left arm of each figure. A sign of the decreasing naturalism in the sculptural style of this

Fig. 1.18. Detail of central section of the *Liberalitas (Largitio)* relief on the Arch of Constantine, Rome, A.D. 312–15. Photo: Alinari, P.I.N. 17325.

period can be seen in the jog which the folds take from between the legs to the left side of the senator to the right. The rear view of the left-hand figure is interesting, since the folds across the back do not take the form of a band but rather are loosely twisted as in a traditional toga (compare the figure seen from the rear in fig. 1.18).

The final form of the toga is an extremely complex garment which seems to have been popular mainly in the eastern Mediterranean, while the more traditional banded toga seen on the diptych of Probianus remained the favorite in Rome and the Western Empire. The eastern form of the toga appears on eastern works such as the base of Theodosius' obelisk, erected in 390 in Constantinople, but it also appears, exceptionally, in Rome in the later fourth century in two virtually identical togate statues of consuls, probably father and son, each of whom waves in his right hand the *mappa,* or handkerchief used to start the chariot races in the Circus.[87]

The finer of these two statues, depicting an older man, is shown in figure 1.20. He wears a long-sleeved tunic

under another tunic with sleeves to the biceps. His toga is at first barely recognizable as such, since the section which was placed between the legs and over the left leg has been subsumed by the sculptor into the folds of the upper tunic and must be located through knowledge of the toga. One must therefore assume that this section of the garment was arranged so that its lower border coincided with the lower border of the upper tunic. The sinus is enormous and would drag on the ground if the magistrate did not carry its lower portion over his left arm.

As Lillian Wilson long ago noted, because the right arm is raised it can clearly be seen that the band of drapery which runs across the chest continues around the man's back, unlike the band of the other late togas which have been considered.[88] This band, which is not made of pressed and stacked folds as in the Western banded toga, corresponds to the "balteus" folds which run across the back and chest in a traditional toga. It thus seems, at first glance, that the Eastern style of banded toga corresponds more closely to the traditional

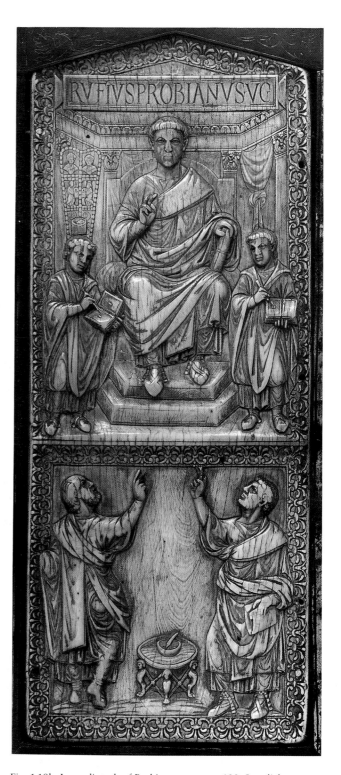

Fig. 1.19a. Ivory diptych of Probianus, ca. A.D. 400. Staatliche Museen, Berlin. Photo: Bildarchiv Foto Marburg 250.936.

Fig. 1.19b. Ivory diptych of Probianus, ca. A.D. 400. Staatliche Museen, Berlin. Photo: Bildarchiv Foto Marburg 250.937.

Fig. 1.20. Togate magistrate holding the *mappa*, ca. A.D. 400. Capitoline Museum, Rome. Photo from DAI, Rome, neg. 38.1322.

style of draping the garment than the banded toga popular in the West during the fourth century. Although the back of the statue is cursorily worked and it is accordingly difficult to evaluate the exact cut of this late version of the toga, it is clear that the end of the sinus was thrown back over the left shoulder to hang down the back.[89] It is held in place by cloth from the "balteus" which was pulled out over all of the cloth on the shoulder. But no point of transition between two sections of cloth is visible on the back; rather the band of drapery continues uninterrupted around the upper body.

As Wilson has shown, one way to create this feature is to have a long strip of drapery of about twelve inches (31 cm) in width attached to a main body of cloth of severely reduced length (height when draping) but of width close to that of the traditional imperial toga. The long strip was attached to the main body of the toga at the center of what corresponds in draping to the height of its wearer. The toga is then little more than a band and a sinus. In this reconstruction, the strip of cloth was first laid between the legs and over the left leg. It was then drawn over the left shoulder and completely around the body. At this point the main portion of the toga would be behind its wearer. The main body of cloth was then wrapped around the back and across the front, with its end, as in the toga with the shoulder umbo, thrown over the left shoulder, where it was tucked beneath the band of drapery. The result is a purely ceremonial costume unsuitable for any physical movement, which has little of the functional qualities associated with clothing.

At this point we have reached the end of the history of the toga. The fourth century was the last century when the toga remained popular as garb for ceremonial occasions. By the fifth century it was replaced in depictions of those in power by military costume and elaborate court robes which herald the development of medieval Byzantine court costume. In the later fourth and fifth centuries its traditional associations with priestly functions also caused the toga to mutate into the stola of the Catholic priest.[90] The history of the toga thus parallels that of the *gens togata* which it clothed, beginning as the multipurpose wrap for small Latin communities of herdsmen and subsistence farmers and mutating into a stately garment for the ruling elite. The final versions of the toga are part of the elaborate costume of court ritual associated with the late Roman Empire and, like the government of that age, look forward to the magnificence of the Byzantine Empire and medieval Catholicism as much as they reiterate the glory of earlier Roman government.

## NOTES

1. For other ancient authors who refer to the *romanitas* of the toga, see Athenaeus, *Deipnosophistai* 5.213; Suetonius, *Augustus* 40; Horace, *Odes* 3.5.10. Macrobius (*Saturnalia* 6.5) says that Vergil borrowed the designation *gens togata* from Laberius (d. 43 B.C.). *Togatus* was often used to designate an Italian. See Cicero, *Philippics* 5.5.14, *Pro Sulla* 30.85, *De Oratore* 1.24.111; and H. Bender, chap. 8 in this volume. See also Bonfante-Warren, "Roman Costume," 613, for *toga* and *togatus* as legal terms to designate Italians or Roman citizens. During the empire legislation was introduced to compel Romans to wear the toga in the Forum; see Suetonius, *Augustus* 40. Later, noncitizens were forbidden to wear it; see Suetonius, *Claudius* 15.2; Pliny the Younger, *Epistles* 4.11.3. Citizens in the provinces wore the toga to show their status as Roman citizens; see Seneca, *Apocolocyntosis* 3; Tacitus, *Agricola* 21. Italians were dressed in the toga for their funerals; see Juvenal, *Satires* 3.171–73. The standard work on the toga is now that of H. R. Goette, who presents a listing of the ancient sources (in Latin and Greek) which mention the toga (*Togadarstellungen*, 10–19). This chapter was completed before the appearance of Goette's monograph, and references to it are incorporated into the notes insofar as has proven possible.

2. See also Servius, *In Aeneadem* 2.781, and Tertullian, *De pallio* 1.1 Two late sources state that the toga evolved under Peloponnesian Greek influence. See Suidas, s.v. "tebennos"; and Pollux 7.61. This seems to me to be dubious, but see Goette, *Togadarstellungen*, 2–3, for acceptance of this idea.

3. On the tebenna, see Bonfante, *Etruscan Dress*, 15, 39, 45, 48–55, 102; and Bonfante-Warren, "Roman Costume," 590–92. For statuettes and statues wearing the tebenna, see E. H. Richardson, *Etruscan Votive Bronzes* (Mainz, 1983), 220, 231–42, types 2 and 4; idem, "The Etruscan Origin of Early Roman Sculpture," *MAAR* 21 (1953): 110–16; G. Hafner, "Etruskische Togati," *AntPl* 9 (1969): 25–44; D. Strong, *Roman Art*, 2d ed. (Harmondsworth, Eng., 1988), 34. For examples on Etruscan sarcophagi and urns of the third through the first centuries B.C., see W. Weber, *Die Darstellungen einer Wagenfahrt auf römischen Sarkophagdeckeln und Loculusplatten des 3. und 4. Jahrhunderts n. Chr.* (Rome, 1978), 95–106; P. J. Holliday, "Processional Imagery in Late Etruscan Funerary Art," *AJA* 94 (1990): 73–93.

4. Dionysius of Halicarnassus, *Roman Antiquities* 3.61; Quintilian, *Institutio oratoria* 11.3.139; Scholiast on Persius 5.14; Isidore, *Origines* 19.24.3; Athenaeus, *Deip.* 5.213. See also L. Wilson, *The Roman Toga* (Baltimore, 1924), 27–29; L. Bonfante and E. Jaunzems, "Clothing and Ornament," in *Civilization of the Ancient Mediterranean: Greece and Rome*, vol. 3, ed. M. Grant and R. Kitzinger (New York, 1988), 1404. I follow Wilson's reconstruction of the form of the garment. Goette (*Togadarstellungen*, 3–4) reconstructs the garment as a half-circle in its republican form, and as an elliptical oval in its imperial form.

5. For its early use by both men and women, see Varro, in Nonius 14.867 L, and Servius, *In Aeneadem* 1.282. According to Arnobius, *Adversus nationes* 2.67, the *togula puellae* (i.e., that worn before age twelve) was dedicated to Fortuna Virginalis, presumably after a ceremony akin to a boy's donning of the toga virilis at the Liberalia (see below, n. 14). For its early wear without an undergarment, see Aulus Gellius, *Noctes Atticae* 6.12; Livy 8.13; Pliny the Elder, *Historia naturalis*

34.23; E. H. Richardson, *The Etruscans: Their Art and Civilization* (Chicago, 1964), 134. Cato the Younger self-consciously asserted his "old Roman virtue" by wearing his toga without a tunic; see Plutarch, *Cato minor* 6.3; Asconius, on *Cicero pro Scauro* 30. Aeneas is depicted on the Ara Pacis togate, but without a tunic; see Strong, *Roman Art*, pl. 38, and B. Andreae, *The Art of Rome* (New York, 1977), fig. 270.

6. On the *cinctus Gabinus*, see DarSag 5:352, s.v. "toga" (Courby); Wilson, *Roman Toga*, 86–88; Bonfante-Warren, "Roman Costume," 596–97; Goette, *Togadarstellungen*, 7. See Valerius Maximus 3.1.1 for the only ancient reference which seems to associate it directly with battle. The other ancient references comment on the cultic use of this draping, but these all seem to be related to war: the consul so girt when he unbarred the gates of war (Vergil, *Aeneid* 7.601–15); the consul so girt when he sacrificed for the army (Livy 10.7.3). The reasons for Fabius sacrificing *cinctus Gabinus* in Livy 5.46.2 are unclear. Servius' comments on the draping indicate that it was originally a Sabine garment (*In Aeneadem* 7.712) and that it was pulled up over the head (at least while sacrificing) and tied around the waist (*In Aeneadem* 5.755). Isidore (*Origines* 19.24.7) preserves the longest description, but this seems somewhat confused. Either the *cinctus Gabinus* had some obscure cultic origin, or it survived from the time when the toga was the only garment worn and this girding was a way of securing the toga to prevent its slipping off at an inconvenient time in battle. When it was actually used in battle, the toga was probably not pulled up over the head as described by the ancient references, since they describe a magistrate or a priest sacrificing. Rather, the cloth must have rested on the left shoulder or been rolled around the waist. Since the left arm held a warrior's shield, less mobility was needed there, and the cloth on the shoulder and arm would afford some additional protection to the side presented to an opponent in battle. The right arm was free to wield a spear or sword, while the girding around the waist secured the garment for active wear so that the warrior need not fear tripping over his garment while moving rapidly.

7. On the tunic, see L. Wilson, *The Clothing of the Ancient Romans* (Baltimore, 1938), 55–71; Goette, *Togadarstellungen*, 8–9. On togate prostitutes, see Cicero, *Philippics* 2.44; Horace, *Satires* 1.2.63; Martial 2.39, 6.64.4, 10.52; Juvenal, *Satires* 2.68–70; Sulpicia in Tibullus 4.10.3 (3.17.16 LCL); and J. Sebesta, chap. 2, and J. Heskel, chap. 7, in this volume. For other sources, see Goette, *Togadarstellungen*, 6 n. 42.

8. See Goette, *Togadarstellungen*, 5; Gabelmann, "Römische Kinder," 517–38; Wilson, *Roman Toga*, 27, 51; F. W. Goethert, "Toga," *RE*, 2. ser., vol. 12 (1937): 1653. Several depictions of young girls in the toga survive on the Ara Pacis and elsewhere; see Goette, *Togadarstellungen*, 80–82.

9. See Varro, in Nonius 867–68 L, on the use of the toga as a blanket, and also Arnobius, *Adv. nat.* 2.67. On the material and the weaving of the toga, see Wilson, *Roman Toga*, 34, 70–72; Wilson, *Clothing*, 16–27, 38; Bonfante and Jaunzems, "Clothing and Ornament," 1387–89. Pliny the Elder (*H.N.* 8.74.195) notes that from early times togas were sometimes woven from a cloth of poppy-stem fiber mixed with flax. The toga may have been woven in different weights of cloth for summer and winter wear; see Goette, *Togadarstellungen*, 4, 6–7.

10. On the significance of the wearing of the toga while conducting public affairs, see Livy 3.26.7–10; Nonius 653 L; Quintilian, *Institutio oratoria* 11.3.137; SHA *Hadrianus* 22.2; Tertullian, *De pallio* 5; Cassius Dio frag. 39.7; *Codex Theodosianus* 14.10.1. Clients met and accompanied their patrons in the toga; see Tacitus, *Dialogus de oratoribus* 6; Martial 10.18.4, 10.74.3, 11.24.11; Juvenal, *Satires* 7.142; Seneca, *Epistles* 4.2. Cicero (*De oratore* 3.42) states that the toga was used metaphorically by the Romans to refer to peace; this is echoed in his *In Pisonem* 29.72 and 30.73; Velleius Paterculus 1.12.3; SHA *Marcus Aurelius* 27.3; Dio Cassius 41.17.

11. On the toga picta, see Goette, *Togadarstellungen*, 6; Wilson, *Roman Toga*, 84–85. Florus (1.5.6) states that Tarquin wore the toga picta. As Bonfante-Warren ("Roman Triumphs," 61–62, 64–65) notes, however, it was not developed until the third century B.C. (see Festus 209 M). Before that date the toga purpurea had been worn by kings; see also Plutarch, *Romulus* 25. For triumphing generals in the toga picta, see Livy 10.7.9 and 30.15.11–12. Until the time of the emperor Gordian (late 230s A.D.), emperors wore a state toga picta on ceremonial occasions; see SHA *Tres Gordiani* 4.4.

12. On purple-clad kings, see Livy 28.4.11, 30.15.11, and 31.11.12; Bonfante-Warren, "Roman Triumphs," 57–59, 61, 63. Dio Cassius (49.16) says that Julius Caesar authorized the wearing of purple by magistrates in the last years of the republic; see also Goethert, "Toga," 1660, and n. 11 above. No literary reference survives which states that the Roman emperor wore a purple toga (see, however, SHA *Severus Alexander* 40.6), but several togate statues in purple porphyry survive which presumably represented emperors in their robes of state; see R. Delbrueck, *Antike Porphyrwerke* (Leipzig, 1932), 49, 54–58, 96–100. Goette (*Togadarstellungen*, 45–49) has recently divided these between the early second century A.D. and the Tetrarchic period.

13. See Isidore 19.24.16; Pliny the Elder, *H.N.* 8.74.195; Goette, *Togadarstellungen*, 4–5; Gabelmann, "Römische Kinder," 499–500; Wilson, *Roman Toga*, 51–52; R. Delbrueck, *Die Consulardiptychen und verwandte Denkmäler* (Berlin, 1929), 51–52. Goette and Gabelmann both point out that it changed in the early imperial period. On the toga praetexta, see Livy 34.7.2; Goette, 4–5; Wilson, 18–19, 51–56; Bonfante-Warren, "Roman Costume," 591. On the protective symbolism of the praetexta, see J. Sebesta, chap. 2, and J. Heskel, chap. 7, in this volume.

14. On the toga virilis, which was first donned at the Liberalia on March 17, see Ovid, *Fasti* 3.713; Cicero, *Philippics* 2.18.44, *De amicitia* 1.1, *Pro Sestio* 69.144, *Epistulae ad Atticum* 5.20.9 and 6.1; Livy 26.19.5, 42.34.4; Suetonius, *Claudius* 2.2; Seneca, *Epistulae* 4.2. It is also referred to as the *toga libera*, a reference to the freeing of the youth from paternal control; see Ovid, *Fasti* 3.771; Propertius 4(5).1.132.

15. On the Arringatore, see T. Dohrn, *Der Arringatore*, Monumenta Artis Romanae 8 (Berlin, 1968); Goette, *Togadarstellungen*, 21, 106 A a 2; L. Bonfante, *Etruscan Dress*, 190, illus. 109; G. M. A. Hanfmann, *Roman Art* (Greenwich, Conn., 1964), 81–82, no. 48; N. Hannestad, *Roman Art and Imperial Policy* (Aarhus, 1988), 34; Wilson, *Roman Toga*, 25–34 (dated to the third century B.C.).

16. See Goette, *Togadarstellungen*, 100, 174 K IV 7 (with a list of other paintings of togate figures in Lararia), and color pl. 1; T. Fröhlich, *Lararien- und Fassadenbilder in den Vesuv- städten*, RM-EH 32 (Mainz, 1991), 279 L70, and color pl. 7; H. Kunckel, *Der römische Genius*, RM-EH 20 (Heidelberg, 1974), 17–18.

17. On stripes on the tunic, see Goette, *Togadarstellungen*, 8–9; Wilson, *Clothing*, 59–64; Bonfante-Warren, "Roman Tri- umphs," 59, 63–64. Although the stripes were generally desig- nated in Latin by the singular form, it is clear that there were two stripes, one on each side of the body.

18. E.g., Cicero, *Epistulae ad Atticum* 5.20.9, 9.17.1, 9.19.1. See also Catullus 68.15; Pliny the Elder, *H.N.* 8.74.194.

19. On the toga pulla and its color, see Wilson, *Roman Toga*, 50. Festus (236 M) states that it was only proper attire at a funeral. Sidonius (*Epistles* 5.7) preserves a witticism about people who do everything incorrectly: "They wear white togas to funerals, and dark togas to weddings" *(albati ad exsequias, pullati ad nuptias)*. See also J. Heskel, chap. 7 in this volume.

20. The toga candida was worn by men seeking office; see Isidore 19.24.6. They were hence called *candidati*. For other terms used by ancient authors in describing the toga, see Goette, *Togadarstellungen*, 1660.

21. For the Arringatore, see n. 15 above. Dohrn, *Der Arringatore*, pl. 4, illustrates the back of the statue.

22. On the Census relief, see M. Torelli, *Typology and Struc- ture of Roman Historical Reliefs* (Ann Arbor, Mich., 1982), 5–16; Zanker, *Power of Images*, 12–14; Goette, *Togadar- stellungen*, 20–21, 106 A a 4; R. Bianchi Bandinelli, *Rome: The Center of Power* (New York, 1970), 56, fig. 53; Hanf- mann, *Roman Art*, 103–4, no. 99.

23. "Quid? si quis vultu torvo ferus et pede nudo / exiguaeque togae simulet textore Catonem / virtutemne rep- raesentet moresque Catonis?" For other references to Cato the Younger's toga, see n. 5 above.

24. The garment worn by the man has been correctly identi- fied as the toga in Kleiner, *Roman Group Portraiture* 145–46; Goette, *Togadarstellungen*, 108 A b 16; and H. G. Frenz, "Untersuchungen zu den frühen römischen Grabreliefs," Ph.D. diss., University of Frankfurt, 1977, pp. 63–65. It has often been suggested that he wears the pallium, but it seems highly unlikely that a Roman would have been depicted on his tombstone in Greek dress (see Juvenal, *Satires* 3.171–73, and n. 31 below). The lack of curvature on the lower edges of the garment is likely assignable to the sculptor's clumsiness; com- pare Goette, *Togadarstellungen*, pls. 1 A a 4 (the censor on the Altar of Domitius Ahenobarbus) and 2 A b 3. For identifica- tions of the garment as a pallium, see M. Bieber, *Ancient Copies: Contributions to the History of Greek and Roman Art* (New York, 1977), fig. 605; Helbig 2.427, no. 1631. The most complete examinations of the late republican toga are Goette, *Togadarstellungen*, 20–28, and D. E. E. Kleiner and F. S. Kleiner, "Early Roman Togate Statuary," *BCAR* 87 (1980–81): 125–33. See also Richardson and Richardson, "*Ad Cohiben- dum Bracchium*," 251–68, where, however, the conclusions about the existence of concurrent styles of draping seem too broad.

25. On freedman grave reliefs, see Kleiner, *Roman Group Portraiture*, 144; Zanker, *Power of Images*, 163; Goette, *Togadarstellungen*, 24–25. As Bianchi Bandinelli (*Center*, 94) points out, the couple depicted in fig. 1.3 are probably mem- bers of the middle class rather than freedmen.

26. See M. Bieber, *The Sculpture of the Hellenistic Age*, 2d ed. (New York, 1961), 131–33, 176, and Bieber, *Ancient Copies*, 132–33.

27. See Kleiner, *Roman Group Portraiture*, 78, 81, 146, 150; Kleiner and Kleiner, "Togate Statuary," 127; Goette, *Togadarstellungen*, 24–26. Hafner, "Etruskische Togati," 40– 41, notes that this style of wearing the toga dates back to the fourth century B.C.

28. Kleiner, *Roman Group Portraiture*, 159–60. As she notes, the fashion is based ultimately on Greek statues of the later fourth century B.C. such as the Lateran Sophokles and the Naples Aischines. See Bieber, *Ancient Copies*, 129–30, figs. 581–82. Closest to the Roman fashion is a Hellenistic variant of the style best seen in the portrait of Dioskourides on Delos; see Bieber, *Ancient Copies*, 130, fig. 584; J. J. Pollitt, *Art in the Hellenistic Age* (Cambridge, Eng., 1986), 286, no. 15, fig. 289. It should be pointed out that both modes of draping the toga (those seen on figs. 1.1 and 1.3) can be found on Etruscan stat- ues of the fourth through second centuries B.C.; see Hafner, "Etruskische Togati," 40–42.

29. "Togam veteres ad calceos usque demittebant ut Graeci pallium." See Richardson and Richardson, "*Ad Cohibendum Bracchium*" for illustrations of this style of wearing the toga.

30. See Goette, *Togadarstellungen*, 24–27, 107–12 A b *(Die toga im pallium-typus)*; Wilson, *Roman Toga*, 39–42, figs. 9–11; Kleiner, *Roman Group Portraiture*, 147–49, fig. 37 (early Augustan, ie., 30–13 B.C.), fig. 66, fig. 12 (dated 13 B.C.–A.D. 5), which is identical to Bianchi Bandinelli, *Center*, 95, fig. 103. See also D. E. E. Kleiner, "Private Portraiture in the Age of Augustus," in *The Age of Augustus*, ed. R. Winkes (Louvain, 1985), 109–11, 125; Kleiner and Kleiner, "Togate Statuary," 126, 133. Goette (27, 112 A c) notes a variant of this type which combines the "arm-sling" with the sinus of the imperial toga and which he dates as Augustan-Tiberian.

31. "Pars magna Italiae est, si verum admittimus in qua / nemo togam sumit nisi mortuus." In the succeeding lines (173–77) Juvenal states that even the aediles wore only tunicas during summer festivals. Suetonius (*Augustus* 44.2) suggests that Augustus had enacted legislation forbidding individuals wearing Greek dress to sit below the *summa cavea* of the theater.

32. Martial 10.47.5: "Lis numquam, toga rara, mens quieta." For togate clients, see references in n. 10 above.

33. Suetonius, *Claudius* 15. Pliny the Younger, *Epistles* 4.113.

34. E.g., Bieber, *Sculpture*, figs. 132–35, 138–39, 163–66, 176, 249, 779–81. The style probably appears as early as the second half of the fifth century B.C., when the original of the Dresden Zeus has generally been placed; see J. Boardman, *Greek Sculpture: The Classical Period* (London, 1985), fig. 228.

35. On the Ara Pacis, see E. Simon, *Ara Pacis Augustae* (Greenwich, Conn., 1967); Strong, *Roman Art*, 80–84; D. E. E. Kleiner, "The Great Friezes of the *Ara Pacis Augustae*," *MEFRA* 90 (1978): 757–85; Hannestad, *Roman Art*, 62–74;

S. Settis, "Die Ara Pacis," in *Kaiser Augustus und die verlorene Republik* (Berlin, 1988), 400–425. For a convenient summary of the identifications of the figures on the north and south friezes, see H. V. Bender, "Portraits on the Ara Pacis: A Comparison of Current Theories," *The Augustan Age* 4 (1985): 1–16. On the toga of the Ara Pacis, see Wilson, *Roman Toga*, 43–49.

36. The small child wears only a tunic and has a torque around his neck. Hence he is not dressed in Roman costume and has been plausibly identified as a barbarian client protected by the imperial family; see Simon, *Ara Pacis Augustae*, 19; J. Pollini, *The Portraits of Gaius and Lucius Caesar* (New York, 1987), 27; B. Rose, "Princes and Barbarians," 453–67. Others see him as Augustus' grandson Gaius, explaining his odd attire as "Trojan" and depicting him as the leader of the cavalry at the *Lusus Troiae* of 13 B.C.; see Torelli, *Typology*, 48; P. J. Holliday, "Time, History and Ritual on the *Ara Pacis Augustae*," *ABull* 72 (1990): 548 n. 37. See also Settis, "Die Ara Pacis," 416; Bender, "Portraits," 3–4, 6–7; Gabelmann, "Römische Kinder," 523.

37. On the bulla and its significance to the Romans, see Cicero, *In Verrem* 2.1.58.151–52, where Verres is alleged to have impoverished a boy who was then forced to sell his bulla, an act which apparently was to be regarded as a sacrilege. Following the assumption of the toga virilis, the bulla was dedicated to the Lares; see Persius 5.30–31. The bulla derived from venerable Etruscan tradition but virtually disappears after the first century A.D.: see R. Higgins, *Greek and Roman Jewelry* (Berkeley, 1980), 141–42, 173–75, 180; M. Amorelli, "Bulla," in *Enciclopedia dell' Arte Antica Classica e Orientale*, vol. 2 (Rome, 1959); Gabelmann, "Römische Kinder," 510–24, 537; Goette, *Togadarstellungen*, 104. The latter also mentions a group of Severan reliefs in North Africa which depict bullas (52–53, 139 B b 177–79). See also A. Stout, chap. 5 in this volume.

38. See Wilson, *Roman Toga*, 52–58.

39. The traditional identification of these children as Gnaeus Domitius Ahenobarbus (consul A.D. 32 and Nero's father) and his sister Domitia has been questioned by R. Syme, "Neglected Children on the *Ara Pacis*," *AJA* 88 (1984): 583–89, and reaffirmed by J. Pollini, "Ahenobarbi, Appuleii and Some Others on the *Ara Pacis*," *AJA* 90 (1986): 453–56. Gabelmann ("Römische Kinder," 523) thinks that Domitia wears a toga.

40. See Andreae, *Art of Rome*, figs. 272–73; Settis, "Die Ara Pacis," figs. 186–87; Kleiner, *Roman Group Portraiture*, 151.

41. See n. 30 above.

42. He is generally identified as Lucius Domitius Ahenobarbus, husband of Augustus' niece Antonia Maior; see Pollini, "Ahenobarbi," 453; Bender, "Portraits," 11; Torelli, *Typology*, 50; Settis, "Die Ara Pacis," 416.

43. On the date of Balbus, see L. Schumacher, "Das Ehrendekret für M. Nonius Balbus aus Herculaneum (AE 1947, 53)," *Chiron* 6 (1976): 165–84; S. Muscettola, "Nuove letture borboniche: I Nonii Balbi ed il Foro di Ercolano," *Prospettiva* 28 (1982): 2–16. For further bibliography, see Goette, *Togadarstellungen*, 113 A d 4.

44. For other togate statues with the same style of draping, see Goette, *Togadarstellungen*, 113 A d 1–3, 5–8.

45. This figure of Augustus is generally dated ca. A.D. 10; see Goette, *Togadarstellungen*, 31, 115 B a 32; H.-G. Niemeyer, *Studien zur statuarischen Darstellung der römischen Kaiser*, Monumenta Artis Romanae 7 (Berlin, 1968), 82, no. 4; Zanker, *Power of Images*, 127–28; A. Giuliano, ed., *Museo Nazionale Romano: Le Sculture* 1.1 (Rome, 1979), 274–77, no. 170 (inv. 56230). Goethert regarded the statue as early Tiberian ("Studien zur Kopienforschung," 186–87). Helbig 3, no. 2300, dates this statue to the reign of Claudius, which is unlikely given the linear treatment of the drapery. Even less likely is the assertion of M. Hofter ("Porträt", in *Kaiser Augustus*, 323–24, no. 168) that the statue may possibly date to the 20s B.C. The toga on the statue clearly postdates the Ara Pacis. Also on this statue, see M. R. Di Mino and M. Bertinetti, *Archeologia a Roma: La materia e la tecnica nell'arte antica* (Rome, 1990), 136. For similar *togati*, see Goette, *Togadarstellungen*, 115–24 B a 32–244; Goethert, "Studien zur Kopienforschung," 1887–88; Zanker, *Power of Images*, figs. 108–9, 130. The style of draping the toga changed little during the first half of the first century, and certainty in dating individual statues is difficult. Goette (*Togadarstellungen*, 29–37) presents a closely argued series that presumes that nuances of changes in styles of draping were closely observed by Italian sculptors during this period, a theory which is based on relatively few works which are securely dated. Even in the case of imperial portraits, the date at which an image was made is often disputed. As an example of the problems in evaluating portrait statues in this period, see the bibliography on the group of the imperial family found at Velleia. This group has been fully published in C. Saletti, *Il ciclo statuario della basilica di Velleia* (Milan, 1968). Saletti distinguished Tiberian, Caligulan, and Claudian phases. Other authors, notably H. Jucker, "Die Prinzen des Statuenzyklus aus Velleia," *JDAI* 94 (1979): 204–40, and Goette, *Togadarstellungen*, 32–33 (with further bibliography), have offered other dates for the *togati*, all within the same twenty-year period of A.D. 30–50. See also Goette (120 B a 144) for a statue of Tiberius found at Herculaneum, which he places in his Claudian series, noting, however, that the statue has been associated with an inscribed base dated A.D. 36/37 (*CIL* 10.1414). On the problems in closely dating *togati* during the first century A.D., see D. Kent Hill, "An Unknown Roman Togatus," *Antike Kunst* 15 (1972): 27.

46. See Goethert, "Studien zur Kopienforschung," 187, and K. Fittschen, review of H.-G. Niemeyer, *Studien zur statuarischen Darstellung der römischen Kaiser*, *BJ* 170 (1970): 542–43.

47. For the *Vicomagistri* relief, see D. Strong, *Roman Imperial Sculpture* (London, 1961), 93, no. 51; T. Hölscher, "Historische Reliefs," in *Kaiser Augustus*, 396–97, no. 224; Goette, *Togadarstellungen*, 117 B a 77.

48. Goethert, "Studien zur Kopienforschung," 202–4; A. Giuliano, *Catalogo dei ritratti romani del Museo Profano Lateranense* (Vatican City, 1957), 22–38, esp. 27, no. 30; Goette, *Togadarstellungen*, 122–23 B a 186. The head attached to this statue may not belong with it. For similar *togati*, see Goette, 121–26 B a 164–266; Goethert, 203–6; and Hanfmann, *Roman Art*, 84, no. 53.

49. See n. 13 above on the imperial toga praetexta.

50. Hanfmann, *Roman Art*, 84–85, no. 54; M. Wegner in Helbig 1, no. 417; Niemeyer, *Studien*, 84, no. 12; G. Daltrop, U. Hausmann, and M. Wegner, *Die Flavier: Römische Herrscherbild* 2.1 (Berlin, 1966), 23, 39, 93. Goette (*Togadarstellungen*, 40, 127 B a 290) maintains that the portrait of Titus was not the original head attached to the body and suggests that the figure originally depicted Nero. He cites similarities in the drapery to the well-known togate youthful Nero from Gabii (124–25 B a 245, pl. 10.4) which is datable to 50/51. Titus' toga, however, also shows some similarities to the drapery on the togate Trajans on the Arch at Beneventum of A.D. 114 (see fig. 1.11, especially the upper relief). Similar *togati* appear on the Cancellaria reliefs of ca. 90–96, although the reliefs are more classicizing in style than the Titus and show flatter, less dramatic folds; see Goette, 41, 128 B a 316, pl. 12.5; Andreae, *Art of Rome*, figs. 389–90; Hanfmann, *Roman Art*, 109–10, nos. 110–11; Hannestad, *Roman Art*, 132–39; Strong, *Roman Art*, 94, no. 61. Goette here poses a problem that seems to me insoluble. Virtually all *togati* have their portrait heads inserted into separately worked bodies, and there are many examples of the reuse of the bodies with new portraits. If one accepts that the head of Titus replaced an earlier head, then given the statue's quality and its senatorial calcei patricii, it should have depicted an emperor. Stylistically, the statue represents a step beyond that seen in the statue from Caere (fig. 1.9) and other works assigned to the reign of Claudius, so it should date after ca. 50. It cannot date after the death of Titus in 81. If the head of Titus is a secondary addition, then his portrait must have replaced one of Nero, and the original statue must, in view of the mature body, date between 60 and 68 (Nero was born in 37). The Titus portrait seems likely to have been made between 71 and 79, when Titus was the designated successor of his father, Vespasian. The sculptors active in this period no doubt worked under both Nero and Vespasian. There is clearly a stylistic direction to Roman sculpture in the first century A.D., but can we truly distinguish stylistic differences between decades? Can we be sure that the Roman sculptor was aware of his duty to pursue the new stylistic course of each successive decade in his career? It is a salutary warning concerning the dangers of a too rigid stylistic classification to reflect that the same sculptor could have made the togate body and the head of Titus (fig. 1.10) whether or not the head replaced an earlier portrait of Nero.

51. Quintilian, *Institutio oratoria* 11.3.140: "Sinus decentissimus, si aliquanto supra imam tunicam fuerit"; 11.3.138: "ita cingatur, ut tunicae prioris oris infra genua paulum."

52. The continuing significance of the toga in public affairs is clear from two references in SHA. Hadrian (SHA *Hadrianus* 22.2) ordered senators and knights to wear the toga in public and is said to have always worn it in public himself when he was in Italy. Severus Alexander (SHA *Severus Alexander* 40.7) is said to have done the same.

53. See Andreae, *Art of Rome*, figs. 419 and 421; Goette, *Togadarstellungen*, 42–43, 130 B b 9; F. J. Hassel, *Der Trajansbogen in Benevent: Ein Bauwerk des römischen Senates* (Mainz, 1966), 13, 16; Hannestad, *Roman Art*, 182.

54. On this style, see Wilson, *Roman Toga*, 74–75; Goette, *Togadarstellungen*, 54–59; Goethert, "Studien zur Kopienforschung," 1558. The earliest appearance of this style of draping is on the Arch of Titus in Rome (ca. 80–82); see Goette, 55, 141–42 C a 17, 128 B a 315, pl. 32.1–2.

55. For the identification of the figure as the *praefectus urbi*, see Hassel, *Trajansbogen*, 13; Hannestad, *Roman Art*, 182. Trajan and other figures on his column wear the shoulder umbo in several scenes; see I. S. Ryberg, "Rites of the State Religion in Roman Art," *MAAR* 22 (1955), figs. 55 and 57; Goette, *Togadarstellungen*, 142 C a 18, pls. 32.3–4, 33.1–2. For Trajan's appearances in the traditional toga of the first century on the column, see Goette, 43, 130 B b 8, pl. 14.4–5. *Togati* with the new style of draping also appear on the so-called *Anaglypha Traiani* (of either Trajanic or early Hadrianic date); see M. T. Boatwright, *Hadrian and the City of Rome* (Princeton, 1987), 182–90; Goette, 55, 142 C a 20, pl. 33.3; Hannestad, 193–94; Bianchi Bandinelli, *Center*, 255, figs. 282–83; Strong, *Roman Art*, 96–97, no. 80. All of the *togati* on the Monument of Philopappos in Athens of 114–16 are draped in the traditional mode of the first century; see D. E. E. Kleiner, *The Monument of Philopappos in Athens* (Rome, 1983), 81–83, 90–91; Goette, 44–45, 131 B b 17, pl. 17.4–5.

56. Tertullian, in *De pallio 5*, calls the folded band which runs across the chest in the banded toga of the third century the *umbo*. This suggests that the term was also used for the folds drawn out on the shoulder in the second-century style of draping the garment. For this text, see n. 68 below and L. Bonfante's introduction to this volume. See also Goette, *Togadarstellungen*, 4.

57. See I. S. Ryberg, *Panel Reliefs of Marcus Aurelius*, AIA Monographs 14 (New York, 1967), 21–27. E. Angelocoussis, "The Panel Reliefs of Marcus Aurelius," *RM* 91 (1984): 141–205, presents a more plausible reconstruction of the arch. See also Hannestad, *Roman Art*, and Goette, *Togadarstellungen*, 137 B b 124.

58. Ryberg, *Panel Reliefs*, 71–76; Andreae, *Art of Rome*, fig. 531. Ryberg (22–23) suggests that the style of the first century had by the late second "become a feature of ceremonial dress." The meaning of this is unclear, since the toga was, by the imperial age, a ceremonial garment in whatever form it took. It seems clear that the traditional toga remained authoritative in the second century, especially in scenes of sacrifice; see Goette, *Togadarstellungen*, 42. Besides the examples mentioned in the text, it is worn by Aurelius on the *lustratio* and Triumph panels, and by the *genius senatus* of the *profectio* relief. For these, see Ryberg, *Panel Reliefs*, 15–20, fig. 9a, and 28–43, figs. 19 and 20; Andreae, figs. 524, 529, 533; Goette, 137 B b 125–27. Marcus Aurelius also appears in the traditional toga in scene 30 on his column (180–93); see Goette, 137 B b 128, pl. 24.4; Ryberg, "Rites," fig. 58. The *togati* on the Great Antonine Altar at Ephesus all show the traditional style of draping. See Andreae, figs. 505 and 508; Hannestad, *Roman Art*, 201–4 and fig. 126; Goette, 136–37 B b 123, pl. 23.2. A tombstone of an aedile found at Ostia (?) dating to the first half of the century shows him clad in a traditional toga; see Bianchi Bandinelli, *Center*, 263, fig. 294; E. Kitzinger, *Byzantine Art in the*

*Making* (Cambridge, Mass., 1977), 11, pl. 10; Goette, 131 B b 26 (with further bibliography). The Antonine or Severan pulpit reliefs of the theater *skene* at Sabratha depict both the traditional toga and the toga with the shoulder *umbo;* see G. Caputo, *Il teatro di Sabratha,* Monografie di Archeologia Libica 6 (Rome, 1959), 19–20; T. Kraus, *Das römische Weltreich,* Propylaen Kunstgeschichte 2 (Berlin, 1967), fig. 232; Goette, 138 B b 154. Antonine "biographical" sarcophagi generally show their principal figures in the traditional imperial toga; see N. Kampen, "Biographical Narration and Roman Funerary Art," *AJA* 85 (1981): pl. 7, fig. 1; pl. 8, fig. 8; pl. 9, fig. 10 and fig. 12; pl. 12, fig. 24. See also G. Koch and H. Sichtermann, *Römische Sarkophage,* Handbuch der Archäologie 3 (Munich, 1982), 97–101; L. Reekmans, "La *dextrarum iunctio* dans l'iconographie romaine et paléochrétienne," *BIBR* 31 (1958): 40–42. Goette (83–98 and 159–69, list S) presents a discussion and a catalog of sarcophagi on which togate figures are represented.

59. Wilson, *Roman Toga,* 83. The short toga worn by the flautist was noted also by Ryberg, "Rites," 22. For the citizen seen from behind at the extreme left of the *Liberalitas* relief, see Ryberg, *Panel Reliefs,* 73, fig. 49; Andreae, *Art of Rome,* fig. 531; Hannestad, *Roman Art,* fig. 143; Strong, *Roman Art,* 98, no. 94; Goette, *Togadarstellungen,* 142 C a 30, pl. 34.4. If a short toga was indeed worn by the common citizen, perhaps it is significant that Martial twice refers to a client as a person wearing a small toga (*togulatus,* 10.74.3 and 11.24.11) and refers to a poor man's *togula* (4.66).

60. K. Fittschen and P. Zanker, *Katalog der römischen Porträts in den Capitolinischen Museen und den andern kommunalen Sammlungen der Stadt Rom,* vol. 1, *Kaiser- und Prinzenbildnisse* (Mainz, 1985), 53–54, no. 51; Helbig 2, no. 1174. Goette (*Togadarstellungen,* 29, 133 B b 56) sees this statue as reiterating a republican style of draping the toga. He notes (48–49) that Hadrian's love of things Greek seems to have affected depictions of the toga during his reign.

61. Rome, Museo Nazionale del Terme, inv. 1010: Giuliano, *Le Sculture* 1.2, 251–252, no. 46. See Goette, *Togadarstellungen,* 51, for mention of an unpublished *togatus* at Ostia.

62. These depict an *Adlocutio* and an *Adventus;* see Boatwright, *Hadrian,* 231–34, illus. 55–56; Goette, *Togadarstellungen,* 142 C a 24–25, pls. 34.1–2. The head of the emperor is restored on both, and the exact identity of the ruler as well as the date (Hadrianic or early Antonine) hence remain open.

63. Andreae, *Art of Rome,* fig. 554; Goette, *Togadarstellungen,* 138 B a 152. On the arch, see E. Nash, *Pictorial Dictionary of Ancient Rome,* vol. 1 (London, 1968), 88–91; Hannestad, *Roman Art,* 277–83; Strong, *Roman Art,* 101, no. 112; R. Bianchi Bandinelli, *Rome: The Late Empire* (New York, 1971), 70.

64. Andreae, *Art of Rome,* fig. 556; Hannestad, *Roman Art,* 268–70; Strong, *Roman Art,* 100–101, no. 111; Goette, *Togadarstellungen,* 55, 142 C a 31, pls. 35.1–2.

65. On the arch at Leptis, see Andreae, *Art of Rome,* 580, figs. 557–60; Hannestad, *Roman Art,* 270–77; Strong, *Roman Art,* 225–28; Goette, *Togadarstellungen,* 138 B b 153, pls. 25.6, 38.1–2.

66. See Goette, *Togadarstellungen,* 57–59, 71–74. The banded toga can first be seen in bust form on a grave relief of early Antonine date from Ostia, now in the Vatican. See R. Calza, *Scavi di Ostia,* vol. 5, *I Ritratti,* part 1 (Rome, 1964), 85, no. 132 (dated to the reign of Hadrian); H. Jucker, *Das Bildnis im Blätterkelch* (Lausanne, 1961), 174 (dated early Antonine); Goette, 149 L27, pl. 51.4. The first absolutely dated appearance of the banded toga is on togate busts on the Arch of Marcus Aurelius and Lucius Verus at Tripoli; see S. Aurigemma, *L'arco quadrifronte di Marco Aurelio e di Lucio Vero in Tripoli,* suppl. 3, *Libya Antiqua* (Rome, [1970]), 36. A bust of Lucius Verus in Berlin wears an early form of the banded toga, but it is not clear if the bust belongs to the head; see C. Blümel, *Katalog der Sammlung antiker Skulpturen, suppl. vol., Römische Bildnisse* (Berlin, 1933), 32 R76, pl. 49.

67. This arrangement can be clearly seen on fig. 1.18, the *Liberalitas* panel from the Arch of Constantine, in the figure viewed from behind to the left of the emperor in the center.

68. "Adeo nec artificem necesse est qui pridie rugas ab exordio formet et inde deducat nitidius, totum contracti umbonis figmentum custodibus forcipibus assignet"; translation from Wilson, *Roman Toga,* 78. See also Goette, *Togadarstellungen,* 57. On Tertullian, see T. D. Barnes, *Tertullian: A Historical and Literary Study* (Oxford, 1971), esp. 229–31 on the *De pallio.*

69. Wilson, *Roman Toga,* 79.

70. Andreae, *Art of Rome,* pl. 142; Goette, *Togadarstellungen,* 86–87, 161 S 32; Koch and Sichtermann, *Römische Sarkophage,* 103; N. Himmelmann-Wildschutz, "Sarkophag eines gallienischen Konsuls," in *Festschrift für Friedrich Matz* (Mainz, 1962), 110–24.

71. On the interpretation of this sarcophagus, see Himmelmann-Wildschutz, "Sarkophag," 114–18, and Goette, *Togardarstellungen,* 86–87.

72. See Goette, *Togadarstellungen,* 55, 61; Wilson, *Roman Toga,* 98–103. The earliest clear example of this fashion in on the Arch at Beneventum (Goette, pl. 15.1), although the headless *genius senatus* (?) on the Triumph panel of the Arch of Titus seems also to show the gesture (Goette, pl. 32.1–2). See also Delbrueck, *Consulardiptychen,* 45. For other examples of this fashion on sarcophagi, see Goette, pls. 76.3, 77, 80.3, 82.4, 84.2, 85.2; Andreae, *Art of Rome,* figs. 597–98; Bianchi Bandinelli, *Empire,* fig. 56. It is interesting that the processional side of the *Decennalia* base (Andreae, fig. 607; Goette, 145 D 12, pl. 42.1) of A.D. 303 shows four headless figures in banded togas, all of whom carry the sinus over the left arm. The figure at the left of these is seen from behind but seems to wear the traditional toga (see Wilson, *Roman Toga,* 103). On the main side of the base, where a sacrifice is depicted (Andreae, fig. 608; Goette, 140 B b 187, pl. 28.3), the *togatus* to the left of the altar wears the shoulder umbo but carries his sinus over his arm. The same attitude can be seen on the *Liberalitas* (fig. 1.18) and *Oratio* panels of the Arch of Constantine. For the *Oratio* panel, see Andreae, fig. 629; Bianchi Bandinelli, fig. 69; Goette, 145 D 13.

73. For Quintilian's instructions on the length of the tunic, see n. 51 above. On the lengthening of the tunic in the later empire, see Wilson, *Clothing,* 67–68.

74. See, for example, the sarcophagus from Acilia in the Terme Museum: Goette, *Togadarstellungen*, 94–95, 164 S 59, pls. 79.1–2 and 86; Andreae, *Art of Rome*, pl. 143; Hanfmann, *Roman Art*, 121–22, no. 137; Strong, *Roman Art,* 102, no. 124; Giuliano, *Le sculture* 1.1, 298–304, no. 182. See also Andreae, pl. 147. On the *Decennalia* base, see Hannestad, *Roman Art*, 309–11; H. Kähler, *Das Fünfsaulendenkmal für die Tetrarchen auf dem Forum Romanum*, Monumenta Artis Romanae 3 (Cologne, 1964). See also Andreae, fig. 607–10; and Goette, 145 D 12, pl. 42.1, and 140 B b 187, pl. 28.3.

75. H. von Heintze, "Drei spätantike Porträtstatuen," *AntPl* 1 (1962): 7–9, 17–24; Goette, *Togadarstellungen*, 60–61, 145 D 1; R. Calza, ed., *Antichità di Villa Doria Pamphili* (Rome, 1977), 299–300, no. 372.

76. The earliest representation of this style of draping is a bust in the Capitoline Museum of the youthful Severus Alexander; see Fittschen and Zanker, *Katalog*, 17–21, no. 99 (dated A.D. 222–24); Goette, *Togadarstellungen*, 67, 151, L50 pl. 54.1. This portrait has, however, been identified as Philip, Jr., of the later 240s; see H. B. Wiggers and M. Wegner, *Caracalla, Geta, Plautilla, Macrinus bis Balbinus* (Berlin, 1975), 191–92. A toga in which the band stretches across the chest is worn by a bust of Severus Alexander (dated to the later 220s) in the Uffizi. See Wiggers and Wegner, 186–87; G. Mansuelli, *Galleria degli Uffizi: Le sculture parte 2* (Rome, 1961), 116–17, no. 147; Goette, 150–51, L48 pl. 54.2. It may also be seen on well-known busts of Pupienus (A.D. 238) and Philip the Arab (r. A.D. 247–49) in the Vatican; see Goette, 151, L58 pl. 55.1 (Pupienus), and 151–52, L62 pl. 55.3 (Philip). For a similar bust of Philip in the Uffizi, see B. M. Felletti Maj, *Iconografia Romana Imperiale da Severo Alessandro a M. Aurelio Carino*, A.D. 222–285 (Rome, 1958), 93, no. 18, pl. II.10.

77. On the toga worn by this statue, see Wilson, *Roman Toga*, 94–97; Goette, *Togadarstellungen*, 59–60.

78. See E. Hula, "Die Toga der späteren Kaiserzeit," *XXIV. Jahresbericht des k.k. zweiten Obergymnasiums in Brunn* (1895): 7–13; C. F. Ross, "The Reconstruction of the Later Toga," *AJA* 15 (1911): 24–31.

79. See Goette, *Togadarstellungen*, 61, 68. Similar lines may be seen on the bands of the togas of the diptych of Probianus of ca. 400 (fig. 1.19).

80. For the shoulder umbo on the *Decennalia* base, see Goette, *Togadarstellungen*, 55, pl. 35.3; Andreae, *Art of Rome*, pl. 608; Hannestad, *Roman Art*, fig. 190. A sarcophagus in Rome of the late third century shows the same style; see Kunckel, *Der römische Genius*, 82, S15, pl. 27.2. On the *Decennalia* base, the sacrificing Caesar wears the traditional toga, as does the figure at the left end of the *Processus* panel (n. 72 above). Another sacrificing figure in a traditional toga is in the Ostia Museum and has been dated ca. 300; Andreae, pl. 149. Goette (49, 133 B b 58, pl. 19.5) dates this statue to the reign of Hadrian. A further example of the same period is in the Villa Doria-Pamphili; see Calza, *Villa Doria Pamphili*, 304–5, no. 377. Four porphyry statues wearing traditional togas have been dated around 300; see Delbrueck, *Antike Porphyrwerke*, 96–100; R. Calza, *Iconografia Romana Imperiale da Carausio a Giuliano, 287–363 d.C.* (Rome, 1972), 108–12, nos. 14–17. Goette (45–59) would place a number of these in

the second century, probably correctly. For another traditional *togatus* of Diocletianic date, see Calza, *Iconografia*, 92–93, no. 2. A fine gilded bronze, likely the image of an emperor, wearing the traditional toga was found at Emona in Yugoslavia and is often dated to the mid–fourth century; see B. Brenk, *Spätantikes und frühes Christentum: Propyläen Kunstgeschichte*, suppl. vol. 1 (Berlin, 1977), no. 380. Goette (42–43, 130 B b 5, pl. 14.2) believes that this statue was made in the early second century A.D. A statue of Virius Audentius Aemilianus found at Pozzuoli stood on an inscribed base which can be securely dated around 370; see M. Napoli, "Statua ritratto di Virio Audenzio Emiliano consolare della Campagna," *BA* 44 (1959): 107–13; Kraus, *Weltreich*, 264, no. 334a. Goette (52, 139 B b 166, pl. 26.2) believes this statue was made in the Severan period and was reused in the second half of the fourth century, but I do not find his stylistic parallels compelling. One of the latest statues wearing this style of toga was found at Ostia and dates to the later fourth century; Goette, 53–54, 140 B b 182, pl. 27.5–6; Hanfmann, *Roman Art*, 87, no. 59; Bianchi Bandinelli, *Empire*, fig. 343 (discussed 437); Kraus, 264–65, fig. 334b.

81. For reused togate bodies, see H. Blanck, "Wiederverwendung alter Statuen als Ehrendenkmäler bei Griechen und Römern," Ph.D. diss., University Cologne, 1963, pp. 33–47; Giuliano, *Le Sculture*, 35–36, no. 26; Goette, *Togadarstellungen*, 134 B b 65. The problems of evaluating this type of statue can be seen in the lack of agreement over the date of the togate body, which bears a portrait of Dogmatius dated to A.D. 326–33 by its inscribed base. The body has been considered *spolia* taken from a portrait of the second half of the third century (Helbig 1, nos. 1133–34). F. W. Goethert ("Studien zur Kopienforschung," 216, pl. 50.2) dates the body to the Trajanic period, and Blanck (31–32) dates it to the reign of Hadrian. Goette (134 B b 83) places it in his Hadrianic–early Antonine group. A. Giuliano (*Catalogo*, 81–82, no. 99) considers the body's date to be the same as that of the head.

82. On the Constantinian frieze of the Arch of Constantine, see Kitzinger, *Byzantine Art*, 7–9; Bianchi Bandinelli, *Empire*, 73–80; Strong, *Roman Art*, 276–78; Hannestad, *Roman Art*, 323–25; R. Brilliant, "Scenic Representations," in *The Age of Spirituality: Late Antique and Early Christian Art, Third to Seventh Centuries*, ed. K. Weitzmann (New York, 1979), 67–69, no. 58; Goette, *Togadarstellungen*, 145 D 13. For similar *togati* on works of the period ca. 300–330, see Bianchi Bandinelli, fig. 56; Wilson, *Roman Toga*, fig. 54; G. Wilpert, "Zum Sarkophag eines christlichen Konsuls," *RM* 65 (1958): 100–120; Reekmans, "La *dextrarum iunctio*," 60–77.

83. Wilson, *Roman Toga*, 98, 104; idem., *Clothing*, 67–68.

84. See Kitzinger, *Byzantine Art*, 7–9; Bianchi Bandinelli, *Empire*, 73–80; Strong, *Roman Art*, 276–78.

85. For the "Dogmatic" sarcophagus, see Kitzinger, *Byzantine Art*, 24, pl. 41. For the portraits on the sarcophagus of Adelphia, see W. Volbach and M. Hirmer, *Early Christian Art* (New York, 1961), pl. 39. See also Strong, *Roman Art*, 288, fig. 220; and E. Dinkler, "Abbreviated Representations," in *Age of Spirituality*, ed. Weitzmann, 399, fig. 53; 400, fig. 56 (from southern France). Other sarcophagi with this type of toga include Vatican 31427, 31456, 31532, 31535, and 31551.

86. On the diptych of Probianus, see J. C. Anderson, "Diptych of Probianus," in *Age of Spirituality*, ed. Weitzmann, 55–56, no. 53; W. Volbach, *Elfenbeinarbeiten der Spätantike und des frühen Mittelalters* (Mainz, 1976), 54–55, no. 62; Delbrueck, *Consulardiptychen*, 45, 250–56, no. 65; Goette, *Togadarstellungen*, 170 K II 1.

87. For these statues, see Goette, *Togardarstellungen*, 62, 146–47 E 8–9, pls. 46.1–2; Helbig 1, no. 1491; Volbach and Hirmer, *Early Christian Art*, 324, no. 64. For Theodosius' base, see Goette, 62, 147 E 17, pls. 46.3, 47.1–3; Bianchi Bandinelli, *Empire*, 352–57, figs. 335–36; Hannestad, *Roman Art*, 332–38; Volbach and Hirmer, 322–23, pls. 54–55; Strong, *Roman Art*, 317–19, figs. 254–55; Brilliant, "Scenic Representations," 107–8, no. 99; Kitzinger, *Byzantine Art*, 33–34, figs. 60–61. For similar *togati* in the East, see Goette, 146–47 E 1–7, 10–16, and 18; J. Kollwitz, *Oströmische Plastik der theodosianischen Zeit* (Berlin, 1941), 81–88, 92, 94–113; Bianchi Bandinelli, 356, fig. 337; Delbrueck, *Consulardiptychen*, 13–15, figs. 6–8 (Column of Arcadius).

88. See Wilson, *Roman Toga*, 104–10, on this statue.

89. See Wilson, *Roman Toga*, 106, fig. 66, for a drawing of the back.

90. See Goette, *Togadarstellungen*, 99–100, and Delbrueck, *Consulardiptychen*, 43–54, on male ceremonial costume in the fourth through the sixth centuries. Goette (170–72 K 1–29) lists the diptychs which depict *togati*, with bibliography. The exact names of the items of clothing worn are disputed by scholars; compare, for example, Volbach and Hirmer, *Early Christian Art*, 329, no. 96, and Delbrueck, 93–95, no. 3, on the costume of the consul Felix (A.D. 428). See also Bonfante-Warren, "Roman Costume," 594–95, 600. L. Wilson (*Roman Toga*, 110–15) considers the garments worn on the diptychs of the fifth and sixth centuries togas but admits that they have mutated far from the Roman imperial toga. See also L. Heuzey, *Histoire du costume antique* (Paris, 1922), 274; P. E. Schramm, "Von der Trabea triumphalis des römischen Kaisers über das byzantinische Lorum zur Stola des abendländischen Herrscher," in *Herrschaftzeichen und Staatssymbol* 1 (Stuttgart, 1954), 26–30.

# Symbolism in the Costume of the Roman Woman

# 2

JUDITH LYNN SEBESTA

When a Roman man dressed himself, he put on his *habitus*, a garment imbued with symbolism. The various forms of his toga indicated his status and function in Roman society. The toga pura, of natural, undyed wool, denoted citizenship. The toga praetexta, adorned with a purple band along one edge, marked a magistrate. The dark wool of the toga pulla signified mourning, while the specially whitened wool of the toga candida drew attention to the office seeker. The toga, in its various forms, was so distinctive a dress among Mediterranean cultures that Vergil called the Romans the "toga-clad people."[1]

In a manner similar to their husbands, patrician women varied their costume according to their position and function in Roman society. Widows were easily distinguished from wives, and the "mothers of the family" *(matres familiae)* from other matrons. Yet comparatively speaking, the costume of the Roman woman has received little attention. Discussions of her mode of dress in textbooks on Roman culture, in general, limit themselves to pointing out that the stola was the distinctive dress of the Roman wife or describing the ritual costume of the Roman bride. Recently, however, scholars have begun to pay more attention to aspects of feminine costume. For example, Kampen has used the costume of Ostian working women in her investigation into their lives and status, and MacMullen has discussed how widespread among various classes and in various provinces was the custom of veiling. Gabelmann has reconstructed the costume of the patrician girl from statues and reliefs. Sensi has examined the costume of the head—hairstyles, veils, and mantle coverings—as an indicator of the status and social function of women.[2]

Not only veils but also the other garments of women served as indicators of their status and social function.

In addition, garments had a numinous dimension and function, imparted by a prescribed color or fiber. What was the religious and social symbolism that underlay the costume of the aristocratic woman?

### PUELLA INGENUA (Freeborn girl)

Costume: *toga praetexta,*
braided hair tied with a *vitta, lunula*

Freeborn boys *(liberi ingenui)* wore the toga praetexta. This toga was like that of the adult male's but had a narrow, reddish purple *(purpura)* woven border along one long edge. Under this the boy wore a tunic which was further distinguished by two purple woven stripes, or clavi, which extended from his shoulders to the hemline. Around his neck hung a locket made of gold, silver, bronze, or leather (bulla), enclosing an amulet, which was often phallic in nature.

While this formal costume for freeborn boys is well known and illustrated on a number of monuments and statues, there is comparatively little documentation, visual or literary, on the formal costume of the freeborn girl *(puella ingenua)*. What evidence we have suggests that in certain respects it was similar to her brother's.

In investigating the costume of the freeborn girl, Gabelmann found four examples of girls dressed in a toga praetexta. His earliest representation is a statue dating to the mid–first century B.C. The girl, accompanied by her mother, wears her toga with her right arm wrapped in the toga and held against her breast.[3] Consequently it is difficult to see what garment she wears underneath the enveloping toga. Other examples are the young girl on the north side of the Ara Pacis, whose undergarment is also hidden; the daughter of a freed-man depicted on a mid–first century A.D. grave relief at Ince Blundell Hall; and the Cologne statue of Poblicia, which dates to the fourth decade of the first century A.D.[4] The latter two wear tunics. As the girl in a toga on the south side of the Ara Pacis clearly wears a chiton under her toga, however, it would seem that a tunic with clavi was apparently not a necessary part of her formal dress, and we may hypothesize that any tunic worn by a girl did not have clavi.

To Romans of the late republic and empire, the toga praetexta was a sign of rank, as their explanations of its origin show.[5] It and the bulla were called the "sign of free birth" (signum libertatis) for boys because at first only patrician boys wore them.[6] The right to wear both of these items was extended to sons of freedmen during the Second Punic War, provided that the boys' mothers were matres familias.[7]

Gabelmann suggests that the use of the toga praetexta by girls was an adoption of the boy's costume.[8] It is possible, however, that girls "originally" wore the toga praetexta, for the toga was according to Roman tradition the earliest form of dress for both men and women: "Varro says . . . that once the toga was the common garment for both night and day, for both women and men" (Nonius 541 M).[9] If both men and women wore the toga, then we might reasonably suppose that children of both sexes also wore the toga. Second, the ancient, original marriage rite of confarreatio required children dressed in togae praetextae to lead the bride to her husband's house following the marriage. Such children had to have mothers and fathers who were still living; they had to be patrimi et matrimi. The antiquity of such a rite suggests that girls as well as boys originally wore the toga praetexta.[10]

The conjunction of the toga praetexta with the bulla indicates that the praetexta band was in origin apotropaic, a protective border worn during sexual immaturity, when the child was most defenseless against evil. When the male child had sexually matured, the toga praetexta was put off along with the protective amulet of the bulla. Persius' description of this rite clearly indicates that the child's toga praetexta was a garment of protection: "As soon as the purple ceased to be a protection to me, a timid child, and the bulla dedicated to the Lares hung on their altar . . ." (5.30). Quintilian also points out that the protective power lay in the purple color of the praetexta band: "I swear to you upon that sacred praetexta—by which we make sacred and venerable the weakness of childhood" (Institutio oratoria 340). Festus adds that obscene or impure words were not to be uttered in the presence of a child clad in a toga praetexta. Such impure spech would injure the child and

make him or her ritually impure for assisting in sacrifices as camillus or camilla.[11]

A praetexta border had to be made of wool, whether it served as a border for a toga or some other ritual garment. Though wool was the most common fabric for Roman clothes, it was endowed with an apotropaic and ritual significance. For example, the praetexta garments of priests and of magistrates (who performed such religious rites as the taking of auspices) had to be made of wool, and wool was used in purification rites such as that of the Luperci.[12]

The purple color was associated with blood; the Romans and Greeks spoke of purple blood as we do blue blood. As blood symbolically represents life, the wide range of red hues, which for the Romans included the hue purpura, has been used in cultures throughout the world to protect those who are seen as particularly helpless and defenseless against evil forces, such as babies, children, pregnant women, and women lying in. For the Romans, the hues of red protected nascent life, which is why Quintilian says that purpura and coccum (purple and scarlet) were hues not suitable for the elderly.[13]

While her brother wore the golden bulla containing a protective amulet, the freeborn girl apparently did not. Four of the five examples of a girl wearing a toga praetexta mentioned above wear no amulets of any kind; the absence of this object is particularly noticeable in the Ince Blundell Hall relief, which also depicts the girl's brother wearing a large, prominent bulla. A girl might wear a necklace of some sort, however, perhaps with an amuletic crescent moon (lunula), such as is worn by the girl on the north frieze of the Ara Pacis.[14]

The boy ceased to wear the toga praetexta when he reached puberty; his mature sexual status was then signified by his all-white toga virilis. Menarche signified for the girl that she had safely survived the weakness of childhood and was now sexually mature. Like her brother, she put off the toga praetexta: "Soon when her toga praetexta yielded to the marriage torches . . ." (Propertius 4.11.33). In an act analogous to her brother's dedication of his toga praetexta to the household Lar, the girl dedicated hers to Fortuna Virginalis.[15] She did not assume her final adult garments, however, until she passed through one additional stage, that of the bride, for she, unlike her brother, changed families upon marriage and so put herself under the protection of her husband's Lar. This rite of passage required the special protective ritual garments of the bride.

Her passage from the authority of her father to that of her husband was also signified by a change in how she dressed her head. As a child, she had worn her hair carefully combed, braided, and tied with a single woolen band (vitta).[16] The Romans used woolen bands to indicate that an object was ritually pure and dedicated to or connected in some way with the gods. Woolen bands were also worn, for example, by Vestals and, when attached to animals and altars, indicated that the objects were consecrated and under divine protection. While no author specifies the color of the young girl's woolen band, white would seem to be the most likely, as white woolen bands were used by Romans in rites concerning the gods, while vittae purpurae were used in funeral rites and in rites concerning the infernal gods.[17] Lastly, the young girl had left her hair uncovered when she went outdoors. During the subsequent stages of her life she would veil her head in public, an action which had ritual significance.

### NUPTA (Bride)

Costume: *tunica recta, reticulum luteum,*
*seni crines, vittae, flammeum, cingulum*
with *nodus Herculaneus*

On the night before her wedding, the bride donned the tunica recta. Ritual required that the bride weave this and her yellow hairnet (reticulum luteum) on the oldest kind of loom, the upright loom.[18] The white, woolen tunica recta was doubly protective, as wool was the fabric ritually used for religious garments. As a fabric wool was additionally hallowed for the Romans by its antiquity of use, and the bride's use of it signified that she was capable of weaving for her husband.[19] White was the color associated with the gods, consecration, and purity. The reddish orange color of her hairnet was likewise protective, analogous to the hue purpura.[20]

On the day of the wedding, the bride's head was additionally protected by the ritual hair dressing of the seni crines, with its white woolen bands.[21] This most ancient form of hair dressing signified her chastity, *pudor.*[22]

Binding her tunica recta and "locking up" her chastity was her belt (cingulum), which ritual required to be made from the fleece of a ewe. The wool was intertwined into the form of a cord to represent the tying and binding of herself and her husband. The cord was knotted in the knot called *Herculaneus,* which her husband untied only when the couple reclined in the marriage bed. This knot was made by doubling one end of the cord into a loop; the other end was threaded through the loop, around the doubled cord, and then out of the loop. Considered a difficult knot to untie, it portended for her husband the procreative power of Hercules, who had begotten seventy children.[23]

Totally covering her hair and face, and indeed much of her body, was the flammeum, the bridal veil. Its ritual hue of yellow-red (luteum) protected the bride as she passed from the protection of her family's Lar to that of

her husband's.[24] The scholiast on Juvenal calls the reddish yellow hue "bloodlike" and explains that it "guarded" the blushing modesty of the bride, just as the toga praetexta had protected her from any obscene words or sights.[25] As the color of this veil was also that of the Flaminica Dialis who presided in the marriage ceremony, it thus had a sanctifying, protective aura.[26]

The veiling of the bride was, per se, a protective act since it hid her from the sight of evil spirits and made her unable to see anything which could be construed as an evil omen as she passed from the protection of the Lar of her father's house to that of her husband's. Her veiling is analogous to her husband's veiling his head with his toga during sacrifice, which signified his participation in a religious act and also protected him from seeing an evil omen. After the bride received from her husband's hands fire and water, an action which welcomed her into her new family, she placed a coin on the altar of her husband's Lar and another coin on the altar of the Lar of her new district. Her dangerous transition was now complete.[27] The act of veiling her hair thus took on a new symbolism for the rest of her life.

### MATRONA (Matron)

Costume: *stola, vittae, palla*

The costume of the matron signified her modesty and chastity, her *pudicitia.* It consisted of her distinctive dress, the woolen stola, which was worn over a tunic; the protective woolen bands which dressed her hair; and the woolen palla or mantle, which was used to veil her head when she went out in public.

While to modern women of Western countries, the Middle Eastern custom of veiling women seems to signify social inequality and even inferiority, to modern women of the East it is a symbol of their honor and of the sanctity and privacy of their family life. In Islamic society today, respectable women veil to protect their honor and to signify their respectability. If a man does not show them respect, their kinship group will feel shamed and will likely take serious steps to avenge the collective family honor. Veiling in Islamic society also is a way of protecting against the evil eye. In fact, the Arabic word for veiling is related to the word for the amulet worn to counteract the evil eye.[28]

There are some indications that the Romans viewed veiling in a general way like modern Islamic society. In discussing the veil, Isidore comments that the head "is the sign of marital rank and power. For man is the head of woman, and the veil is over the head of the woman" (19.25.4).[29] As the veil symbolized the husband's authority over his wife, the omission of the veil by a married woman was a sign of her "withdrawing" herself from marriage, as an anecdote about Sulpicius Gallus, a consul in 166 B.C., shows. Gallus divorced his wife because she had left the house unveiled, thus allowing all to see, as he said, what only he should see.[30] When his wife omitted her veil, she in effect excluded herself from the rank of matron, and Gallus' divorce was a ratification of the exclusion her bare head had expressed.[31] As in the case of the bride, the veil also protected the married woman from religiously impure things, limiting the likelihood of her seeing some omen, object, or act that would diminish her purity.

The protection provided by the veil in public was paralleled by the protection provided to the woman's head by the woolen bands with which she bound her hair. Just as the sacrificial woolen bands indicated that an animal was dedicated to the gods and was pure, so the matron's bands both protected her from impurity and indicated her modesty.[32] Hair bound with vittae was so distinctive a style that by itself it signified the married woman. Ovid speaks of the "honor of the vittae."[33] When Plautus' Palaestrio requires a prostitute to disguise herself as a matron, he specifically directs: "Lead her here dressed just in the matrons' way with hair combed and tied with woolen bands so that she can pretend to be your wife" (*Miles Gloriosus* 790–93).

Just as integral to the matron's costume was the stola, the dress reserved for the chaste married woman. Commenting that the vitta covers modest hair, Ovid acknowledges that his amatory verse is not suitable for the matron: "Be far from here, you signs of purity, thin vittae and long stola which covers the feet" (*Ars amatoria* 1.31–32).[34] Though Bieber correctly described the stola in 1920, the erroneous description of the garment as a long gown adorned with a distinctive flounce, or instita, persists in many descriptions of the clothing of the Romans. Bieber argued that Horace's words *veste subsuta instita* should be understood as meaning "a dress suspended from the sewed-on straps."[35] The institae thus were straps on each shoulder to which the cloth forming the dress was attached (fig. 2.1). The stola resembled a modern slip, though made of fuller material which hung in distinctive folds, or rugae, and by its length covered and protected the body down to the midstep from pollution from religiously impure things.

Like the child's toga praetexta, the stola also denoted social rank. Matrons were defined as those who had the right to wear the stola.[36] Originally, as in the case of the toga praetexta of the child, such women were of patrician rank, but sometime before the Second Punic War freedwomen married to Roman citizens gained the right to wear the stola.[37]

Stola and vittae remained the basic costume of the chaste married woman throughout her life. Subsequent

Fig. 2.1. Woman dressed in a stola from Isola Tiberina, Rome, early first century A.D. Museo Nazionale Archeologico, Naples, inv. 121216. Photo from DAI, Rome, neg. 56.232.

changes in her family status were signified by changes in hairstyle or head covering.

MATER FAMILIAS (Mother of the family)

Costume: *stola, vittae, tutulus, palla*
The rank of the "mother of the family" depended upon that of the "father of the family," according to Paulus, who states: "The *mater familias* is not called such before her husband is called *pater familias;* nor is more than one woman in the family able to be called by this title" (Festus 112.27 L).[38]

The mother of the family was distinguished from the matron by her distinctive hairstyle, called the *tutulus.* This hairstyle was commonly worn by Etruscan women in the late sixth and early fifth centuries B.C. As this was the time of the Etruscan domination of Rome, the aristocratic mothers of the family presumably adopted this hairstyle at this time.[39] The tutulus is thought to have been created by dividing the hair into sections, drawing these tresses up and piling them high on the crown of the head and fastening them by wrapping them with vittae. The somewhat conical shape of the tutulus was likened to a boundary stone *(meta)*. This resemblance for the Romans may not have been accidental, for, like such stones, the tutulus had a sacred, protective quality. According to Varro, the tutulus and its woolen bands served as a protection for the head and were similar in function to the headdress of priests conducting the rites of the *Argei:* "These priests are called *tutulati,* 'protected by the tutulus,' as they customarily wear on their heads something which resembles a conical marker. The tutulus is so called from the way *matres familias* wear their twisted locks of hair on the tops of their heads enveloped in a vitta. This was called a tutulus either because it protected [*tuendi*] the hair or because the highest place in the city, the citadel, was called the safest [*tutissimum*]" (*De lingua Latina* 7.44).[40] The fact that the tutulus was also worn by the Flaminica Dialis underscores its apotropaic symbolism.[41]

### VIDUA (Widow)

#### Costume: *ricinium, stola? vittae?*

The last change in married status of the woman was widowhood. If she held the title of mother of the family, she lost this title unless she had sons still living: "Nor can a widow be called by this title [*mater familias*] who has no sons" (Festus 112.29 L).[42] A woman signified her widowhood by covering her head with the ricinium, in place of the palla. The ricinium seems originally to have been a garment of general use, a woman's garment analogous to the man's toga. According to Festus, "the ricinium is any kind of square garment; the Twelve Tables interpret the ricinium as a man's toga (?) used by women, and made praetexta with a purple stripe" (Festus 342.20 L).[43] Varro emphasizes the antiquity of the ricinium when he says that it was the most ancient garment for women, just as the laena was for men, and his comments give us some idea of its appearance. He derives the word from *reicere,* "to throw back," and explains: "It is so called from the fact that women use it double-folded, that is, they throw backward half of it, and it is called ricinium from *reiciendo*" (*De lingua Latina* 5.132).[44]

By the end of the sixth century, as a passage in the Twelve Tables indicates, the ricinium had become a garment worn by women as a sign of grief, whether in mourning for a family member or in times of public trouble: "In adverse times and in mourning, when women lay aside all fine and costly clothing, they put on the ricinia" (Nonius 542 M).[45] The ricinium is likely to have been dark colored, like the man's mourning toga pulla, which was made from naturally dark wool. The

"red" hue of the praetexta also symbolized mourning, for red was associated with death, according to Varro, through the blood shed by victims sacrificed to the dead and through the blood which flowed as women scratched their faces in grief at funerals.[46]

The ricinium was worn by the widow during the year prescribed for mourning.[47] Traditional Roman morality, however, praised the widow who remained *univira,* "the wife of one man only," until her death. Was the ricinium then worn by the widow for the rest of her life as a sign of her perpetual mourning for her husband? Would she also have worn vittae and stola to signify her continued chaste loyalty to her deceased husband? Our sources, unfortunately, are silent about other items of the widow's costume.

### INNUPTA (Adult unmarried woman)

#### Costume unknown

How common the situation of the never-married adult daughter in a patrician family was is hard to say, but doubtless there were some. Such a woman was also called a widow: "A widow is not only she who once had been a bride but also that woman who has not had a husband . . . she is similarly called a widow because she is unpaired" (*Digest of Justinian* 16.242.3, 33.1.22).[48] Was her dress then similar to that of a woman who had lost her husband? Though it is hard to imagine an adult unmarried woman wearing the child's toga praetexta, we cannot impose our own sense of congruity on the Romans. If the unmarried adult woman did adopt a different costume, at what age would she have done so?

Likewise, we know nothing about the costume of the woman divorced for reasons other than adultery. Would she have worn vittae and stola to signify her chastity?

### ADULTERA (Adulteress)

#### Costume: *toga*

We do know the costume of the adulteress. Loss of chastity was grounds for divorcing a wife. No longer a matron, the woman was not permitted to wear the stola and vittae. Instead, according to custom, the woman divorced for promiscuity wore a plain toga.[49] The symbolism behind the assumption of the toga would seem not to be that the woman had assumed the sexual freedom allowed males, but that she had lost her status and role as a sexually mature woman in Roman society. If you were a married woman, you wore a stola; if you were not, you wore a toga, praetexta if you were still a child, plain if you were an adulteress.[50]

We know most about the costume of the Roman woman for those stages in which she exercised her most important role in Roman society, the role of the mother. Distinctive costume marked the various aspects of this role, whether it be as potential mother (girl, bride), actual mother (matron, mother of the family), or past mother (widow), or as one excluded from this role (e.g., as adulteress). The quality inherent to each of the stages of the role of mother was the quality of purity, whether it be the innocence of the young girl, the virginity of the bride, the modesty of the wife, or the marital loyalty of the widow, for upon this quality depended the biological continuance of the family and its clan. In each stage of the Roman woman's life, costume served as a visual and tactile reminder of the virtue she should maintain and for which she should be respected.

## NOTES

1. Vergil, *Aeneid* 1.281. On the toga, see Bonfante-Warren, "Roman Costume," 390–92, 612–13. All translations in this chapter are the author's.

2. N. Kampen, *Image and Status: Roman Working Women at Ostia* (Berlin, 1981); R. MacMullen, "Women in Public in the Roman Empire," *Historia* 29 (1980): 208–18; Gabelmann, "Römische Kinder," 497–541; L. Sensi, "Ornatus e status sociale delle donne romane," *ALFPer*, n.s., 4 (1980–81): 55–102.

3. Statue of mother and daughter in toga praetexta: Conservatori Museum, Rome. See Gabelmann, "Römische Kinder," 565 Abb. 4.

4. Ince Blundell Hall relief: B. Ashmole, *A Catalogue of the Ancient Marbles at Ince Blundell Hall* (Oxford, 1929), 87, nr. 222, pl. 34. Poblicius-Monument, Roman-German Museum, Cologne: H. Gabelmann, "Die Frauenstatue aus Aachen-Burtscheid," *BJ* 179 (1979): 239, Abb. 21.

5. Macrobius (1.6.7–13, 15–16) offers four theories which explain the toga praetexta as a symbol of rank and honor:

1. The first toga praetexta was worn by Tullus Hostilius because it was the costume of Etruscan magistrates. It continued to be regal costume. When the fourteen-year-old son of Tarquinius Priscus distinguished himself in battle against the Sabines, Tarquin praised the boy in a public assembly and awarded him honorific insignia consisting of the golden bulla and toga praetexta as marks of his courage.

2. Tarquinius Priscus wished to emphasize the respect due to freeborn boys and ordered that such should wear the golden bulla and toga praetexta, provided that their fathers had held a curule magistracy or merited the stipend for a horse.

3. The toga praetexta was an honor awarded a boy who helped rid Rome of a plague.

4. The first boy born of one of the Sabine women was given the right to wear the toga praetexta.

6. Scholiast on Juvenal 5.164.

7. Macrobius 1.6.13–14.

8. Gabelmann, "Römische Kinder," 520–21.

9. Servius, *In Aeneadem* 1.282, considers the *ricinium* and *cyclas* a form of the toga, that is, a garment wrapped around the body. Both Servius and Varro agree that in the early period of Roman history, both men and women wore a wrapped rather than a fitted garment, that is, a tunic.

10. Festus 282 L, s.v. "patrimi et matrimi." DarSag 4.1, 349–50.

11. Festus 283 L: "Praetextatis nefas erat obsceno verbo uti, ideoque praetextum appellabant sermonem, qui nihil obscenitatis haberet." Macrobius (1.6.17) also connects the "red" of the praetexta with the purity of the sexually immature child.

12. J. Pley, "De lanae in antiquorum ritibus usu," *RVV* 11.2 (1911): 13, 46–47. See also E. Samter, *Familienfeste der Griechen und Römer* (Berlin, 1901), 54. Those magistrates who conducted blood sacrifices wore togae praetextae. W. W. Fowler, in *Religious Experience of the Roman People* (London 1922), 176, argues that the toga praetexta was worn by primary or secondary agents in sacrificial acts, that is, by priests, magistrates, and children who served as *camilli* or *camillae*. Children in general, however, were not secondary agents in blood sacrifices, and only a few would serve as assistants. In regard to children, Fowler's comment that the red hue of the praetexta symbolized life and strength probably identifies the underlying symbolism.

13. E. Wünderlich, "Die Bedeutung der röten Farbe in Kultus der Griechen und Römer," *RVV* 20.1 (1925): 90; Quintilian, *Institutio oratoria* 11.1.31.

14. Plautus (*Rudens* 1194) has Palaestra say that her father gave her a golden bulla on the day of her birth. Mau, however, thinks that Plautus here is translating the word *perideraia* in the original Greek play and that this line cannot be taken as evidence for girls' wearing the bulla. See A. Mau, "Bulla," *RE*, vol. 3.1 (1897): 1048, and J. Marquardt, *Das Privatleben der Römer* (Leipzig, 1886), 85. Gabelmann has found no representations of girls wearing bullas and states that instead girls might wear other amuletic necklaces such as the lunula; see Gabelmann, "Römische Kinder," 520–21, 523.

15. Arnobius, *Adversus nationes* (2.67) asks if the Romans still dedicate the small togas of their daughters to "Virginal Fortune": "Puellarum togulas Fortunam defertis ad Virginalem?" The temple of Fortuna Virginalis was in the Forum Boarium next to that of Mater Matuta.

16. Nonius (236 M) comments that "underage girls went bare-headed, with hair combed and bound with vittae"; "minoris natu capite aperto erant, capillo pexo, vittis innexis crinibus." See Sensi, "Ornatus," 56.

17. DarSag 5: 949–57.

18. Festus 342.30 L says that "the men's garments are called 'straight,' and fathers see to it that they are made for their sons for the sake of good omen; the term has been taken over for the bride's garment because the bride weaves it on an upright loom while standing"; "rectae appellantur vestimenta virilia, quae patres liberis suis conficienda curant ominis causa; ita usurpata quod a stantibus et in altitudinem texuntur." On the various head coverings of the bride, see Sensi, "Ornatus," 57–59.

19. Festus 102.1 L states that "the new bride customarily sits on a woolen fleece, either because it is an old custom and people in the past were clothed with fleece, or because the task of wool-working gave proof that she was ready to be a helpmeet"; "in pelle lanata nova nupta consedere solet, vel propter morem vetustum, quia antiquitus pellibus homines erant induti, vel quod testetur lanificii officium se praestaturam viro."

Sebesta / *The Costume of the Roman Woman*   51

20. Wünderlich, "Die Bedeutung," 38.

21. On the vitta of the bride, see Propertius 4.3.15 and 4.11.33.

22. Festus 454.23 L explains that "brides have their hair dressed in the senes crines because this is the most antique hairstyle. Indeed the Vestal Virgins dress their hair this way whose chastity \*\*\*\*"; "senes crinibus nubentes ornantur, quod [h]is ornatus vetustissima fuit. Quidam quod eo Vestales virgines ornentur quarum castitatem viris suis + sponoe \*\*\* a ceteris." See also Bonfante-Warren, "Roman Costume," 596, 612.

23. Festus 55.63 L observes that "the new bride is girded with a belt which her husband unties in the marriage bed; it is made from wool, so that, just as wool, wrapped in skeins, is coiled up in itself, thus her husband is girded and bound along with her. Her husband loosened this binding, which was tied in a Herculanean knot for the sake of good omen, so that he himself should be as fortunate in begetting children as was Hercules, who begot seventy sons"; "cingillo nova nupta praecingebatur, quod vir in lecto solvebat, factum ex lana ovis, ut, sicut illa in glomos sublata coniuncta inter se sit, sic vir suus secum cinctus vinctusque esset. Hunc Herculaneo nodo vinctum vir solvit ominis gratia, ut sic ipse felix in suscipiendis liberis, ut fuit Hercules, qui septuaginta liberos reliquit." See also DarSag 4.1, 87–88.

24. On the hue of the flammeum, see Pliny the Elder, H.N. 21.46, 10.128. On red as a bridal color, see Wünderlich, "Die Bedeutung," 36–37.

25. The scholiast on Juvenal 6.224–26 says that "the flammeum is the kind of cloak with which women cover themselves on their wedding day; it is blood-colored for the purpose of guarding their blushing"; "flammea genus amicti quo se co-operiunt mulieres die nuptiarum; est enim sanguineum propter ruborem custodiendum."

26. The feet of the Flamen's marriage bed were smeared with luteum. On the symbolism of the hue of the flammeum, see Samter, Familienfeste, 47. Also Sensi, "Ornatus," 73–74.

27. On the ritual of the two Lares, see G. Dumézil, Archaic Roman Religion vol. 1 (Chicago, 1970), 341–42.

28. E. W. Fernea and R. A. Fernea, "Symbolizing Rules: Behind the Veil," in Conformity and Conflict: Readings in Cultural Anthropology, ed. J. P. Spradley and D. W. McCurdy (Boston, 1987), 104–12.

29. "Signum enim maritalis dignitatis et potestatis in eo est. Caput enim mulieris vir est, inde et super caput mulieris est."

30. Valerius Maximus 6.3.10.

31. MacMullen, "Women in Public," 208–18, argues that veiling came to be less common among women of higher classes in the Western Empire during the early empire than in the East because of the influence of the imperial court. Nonetheless, a number of statues exist showing an empress veiling her head with a palla.

32. MacMullen, "Women in Public," 208. In other cultures the head is imbued with a particular sanctity. To the Cambodians, for example, it is extremely sacred and not to be touched by anyone save the person to whom it belongs. On the vittae of the matron, see Sensi, "Ornatus," 60.

33. Ovid, Ars amatoria 3.483: vittae honore.

34. Ovid, Epistulae ex Ponto 3.351–52. Ovid, Ars amatoria 1.31–32: "Este procul, vittae tenues, insigne pudoris / quaeque tegis medios, instita longa, pedes."

35. M. Bieber, "Stola," RE, 2d ser., vol. 7 (1931), 56–62. See also Bieber, Ancient Copies, 23. L. Sensi ("Ornatus," 59–60) identifies the stola as a mantle, but Isidore, whom Sensi cites as his source, uses the word stola only in its Greek sense meaning "covering."

36. Festus 112.26 L.

37. Macrobius 1.6.13–14. The longa veste in this account is understood to denote the stola, which is frequently described by this phrase.

38. "Mater familiae non ante dicebatur quam vir eius paterfamiliae dictus esset; nec possunt hoc nomine plus in una familia praeter unam appellari."

39. Bonfante-Warren, "Roman Costume," 596, 614. See also Sensi, "Ornatus," 61–64.

40. "Tutulati dicti hi, qui in sacris habere solent ut metam; id tutulus appellatus ab eo quod matres familias crines convolutos ad verticem capitis quod habent vitta velatos dicebantur tutuli sive ab eo quod id tuendi causa capilli fiebat sive ab eo quod altissimum in urbe quod est, Arcs, tutissimum vocatur." See also Festus 485.12 L. The color of the vittae in the tutulus of the mater familias is nowhere specified, though the Flaminica bound her hair with vittae purpurae; see Festus 484.32 L.

41. DarSag 2.2, 1169–70. The Romans also called the head covering of the flamines a tutulus; see Bonfante-Warren, "Roman Costume," 611–14. A. Ernout and A. Meillet, Dictionnaire étymologique de la langue latine, 4th ed. (Paris, 1959), 1024, suggests that tutulus may be an Etruscan word related in some way to the name of the priapic deity Tutunus. E. Baldwin Smith suggests that the tutulus of the Flamen may have been a form of the "celestial helmet"; see Smith, The Dome: A Study in Architectural Symbolism (Princeton, 1950), 5, 77–79. If so, the tutulus of the Flaminica would seem also to have this latent symbolism. Sensi ("Ornatus," 62) traces the Etruscan tutulus to the Greek kekruphalis but this is a style in which a cloth covers the hair like a snood. The hair is caught up in the cloth at the back, not the top of, the head, and as vase paintings, statues, and reliefs show, this head covering was worn by women of all ages and conditions. On the kekruphalis, see DarSag 3: 812–16. Helbig's suggestion that the hairstyle of the tutulus was derived from a bonnet called a tutulus might explain why flamines, whose headdress was properly called the pileus, were called tutulati; see W. Helbig, "Über den Pileus der alter Italiker," SBAW (1880): 515. On woolen priestly garments, especially that of the Flaminica, see Pley, "De lanae," 3–39.

42. "Sed nec vidua, hoc nomine [sc. mater familias], quae sine filiis vocari potest."

43. "Ricinium omne vestimentum quadratum hi qui XII interpretati sunt esse dixerunt + vir toga + mulieres utebantur, praetextam clavo purpureo." Servius (In Aeneadem 1.282) also states that the toga was the original garment for women: "togas autem feminas habuisse, cycladum et recini usus ostendit." See also Sensi, "Ornatus," 65, who describes the ricinium

as a short shawl. It would seem that by the time of Nonius the ricinium had been replaced by the *mafurtium*, which he defines as a short mantle (542 M): "ricinium, quod nunc mafurtium dicitur, palliolum femineum breve."

44. "[Ricinium] quod eo utebantur duplici, ab eo quod dimidiam partem retrorsum iaciebant, ab reiciendo recinium dictum. Laena quod de lana multa, duarum etiam togarum instar . . . ut antiquissimum mulierum ricinium, sic hoc duplex [laena] virorum." L. Bonfante-Warren ("Roman Costume," 608–9) points out that the laena was called *duplex* because it was draped over both shoulders, front to back. *Duplex* in reference to the ricinium, however, seems to mean "folded in half." The unfolded pallium was called the *pallium simplex;* see Nonius 869 L.

45. Nonius 542 M quotes Varro as saying in his *De vita populi Romani:* "ec quo mulieres in adversis rebus ac luctibus, cum omnem vestitum delicatiorem ac luxoriosum postea institutum ponunt, ricinia sumunt." Cicero, *De legibus* 2.23.59, quotes a passage from the Twelve Tables which limits expenses for mourning and funerals, allowing only "three ricinia and a small [?] purple tunic and ten flute players"; "tribus riciniis et tunicla purpurea et decem tibicinibus."

46. Wünderlich, "Die Bedeutung," 46–48. Varro as quoted by Servius, *In Aeneadem* 3.67.

47. Seneca, *Epistles* 63.13, states that "our ancestors gave women one year for mourning, not that they should mourn that long, but that they should mourn no longer than one year"; "annum feminis ad lugendum constituere maiores non ut tam diu lugerent, sed ne diutius." H. Stadler, "Ricinium," *RE,* 2d ser., vol. 1 (1914), 799–802.

48. Livy (1.46.7) uses *vidua,* "unmarried woman," as an expression parallel to *caelebs,* "bachelor."

49. See Juvenal 2.68; Martial 2.39, 10.52; Cicero, *Philippics* 1.18.44; and Marquardt, *Privatleben,* 44 n. 1.

50. Isidore (*Origines* 19.25.5) says that in the past a matron taken in adultery wore an *amiculum,* which he describes as the prostitute's linen pallium. He adds that in his day, in Spain, the amiculum was a garment signifying feminine honor. But two outer garments, toga and amiculum, would be unnecessary, and Isidore seems to be conflating the adulteress' toga with the prostitute's amiculum. L. Sensi, following Isidore, states that the unchaste woman wore the amiculum only; Sensi, "Ornatus," 65–66. See J. Sebesta, "Togate Prostitutes and Adulteresses" (forthcoming).

# The Costume of the Roman Bride                     3

LAETITIA LA FOLLETTE

In many cultures even today, the bride wears special clothing on her wedding day, ranging from the white dress and lacy veil common in the West to more elaborate ceremonial costume in other parts of the world. The Roman bride was similarly marked by special costume, for the wedding, the most important rite of passage for a Roman girl, symbolized her initiation into womanhood and her new status as wife. In contrast to the initiation of the Roman boy, which involved the adoption of a new body garment, the toga virilis (manly toga), the most distinctive elements of the bride's special costume concerned her head and hair.[1] These elements included a special way of dressing the hair, the seni crines (six tresses), and a special veil, the flammeum (flame-colored). Both the appearance and the ritual connotations of coiffure and veil can be reconstructed, since certain Roman priestesses shared these bridal accoutrements. The hairstyle was part of the costume of the Vestal Virgins, and the Flaminica Dialis wore the flame-colored veil. Although this chapter surveys all the elements of the Roman bridal costume, detailed discussion will focus on this distinctive bridal apparel and its ritual significance.

Most of the evidence for bridal costume comes from literary accounts, in particular from the late second-century A.D. epitome by Sextus Pompeius Festus, who has preserved for us the Augustan scholar Verrius Flaccus' lost treatise on the meaning of words, the *Libri de significatu verborum*.[2] Occasionally articles of bridal costume can also be identified in Roman wall painting and sculpture. Although it is not possible to trace the development of Roman bridal costume over time, it may be argued that the general conservatism of Roman society in matters of ritual as well as status allows us to assume that much of the basic nuptial scheme outlined here

would have been recognized by aristocratic Romans from the late republic through the third century A.D. In any case, this compilation of the literary and artistic evidence for the costume of the Roman bride should prove a helpful first step to further research on the topic.[3] In the following sections, the most important literary descriptions of Roman bridal dress are followed by a brief discussion of any relevant artistic representations.

### THE "STRAIGHT" DRESS (TUNICA RECTA)

In both clothing and custom, Roman male and female initiations share a number of similarities. Just as the boy laid aside his child's bulla and toga praetexta to assume the toga virilis, so the girl put aside her toga along with her toys prior to the wedding.[4] Both the girl and the boy then put on the same new garment, the tunica recta, or straight tunic, so called because it was woven on a special type of loom. Our chief sources for the tunica recta are Festus and Pliny the Elder, who trace the origins of the garment back to the period of the Etruscan kings. Pliny writes: "Marcus Varro informs us on his own authority that the wool on the distaff and spindle of Tanaquil (also called Gaia Caecilia) was still preserved in the Temple of Sancus and also that in the shrine of Fortuna [was] a pleated royal toga made by her, which had been worn by Servius Tullius. Hence arose the practice that maidens on their marriage were accompanied by a decorated distaff and spindle with thread. Tanaquil first wove the straight tunic of the kind worn by novices and by newly married brides" (H.N. 8.124). Festus says that on "the eve of their wedding day, for good luck, maidens go to bed dressed in royal white tunics and yellow hairnets, both woven (by them) standing in front of the upright loom, just as is the custom also in the giving of the toga virilis (to boys)" (364.21 L). In both passages the straight tunic is considered a "royal" garment, which subsequently became the Roman ceremonial dress for both sexes. According to Pliny, the first such tunic was woven by Tanaquil, the wife of Tarquinius Priscus, the first Etruscan king of Rome (traditionally 616–578 B.C.). The bridal garment, of wool or linen, was woven by the young bride-to-be on the old-fashioned upright loom as part of the bridal preparations. The upright or warp-weighted loom produced a much wider piece of cloth (over two meters wide) and thus a fuller garment, which probably only needed one side seam.[5] The weaving of tunic and hairnet by the bride was also a symbolic act, since after the wedding she would be responsible for the weaving of her family's clothes, as indicated by the distaff and spindle mentioned as bridal accoutrements by Pliny.

After this unisex garment, the bride's special costume diverged from the young man's. The toga he put on was off-limits to any woman of repute after childhood.[6] Instead of the toga, the bride wore a special flame-colored veil and placed a wreath atop her hair, which was dressed in a special way. The religious significance of covering one's head is known from other Roman rituals, such as the *capite velato*, in which the man covered his head with the toga during sacrifices.[7] Both bridal customs and literary sources, however, document the particular importance the Romans attached in early times to the covering of the head of the sexually mature woman. Valerius Maximus (first century A.D.) reports that Sulpicius Gallus (third to second century B.C.?) divorced his wife for uncovering her head in public, an anecdote which clearly indicates that a chaste woman was one who kept her hair covered.[8] Women depicted on tombstones are most typically in the pose called *pudicitia* (modesty), in which they have drawn the mantle (palla) up over their heads, holding part of it in front of their faces. The anecdote, and this gesture, suggest that the Roman practice may go back to the age-old notion, still prevalent in the Middle East, that a woman's sexual powers are concentrated in her hair.

The hairnet (reticulum), also woven on the upright loom according to Festus, is the first of several head or hair ornaments associated with the Roman bride. This preliminary hair restraint, along with the tunic, was worn to bed on the night before the wedding but was dedicated to the Lares before the wedding itself.[9] Its color is significant since yellow is also the color of the most important bridal garment, the bridal veil.

### THE BRIDAL VEIL (FLAMMEUM)

According to both ancient texts and artistic representations, the veil was the most prominent feature of the Roman marriage costume. The Romans apparently thought of the bride as one who was "clouded over with a veil." Festus explicitly links the Latin verb *nubere*, "to be married," "to take a husband," with the Latin word for "cloud," *nubes*: "Nuptials are so called because the head of the bride is wrapped around with the bridal veil, which the ancients called 'to cloud over' or 'veil'" (174.20 L).[10] Visual illustration of this "clouding over" of the bride can be found as early as the sixth century B.C. An Etruscan relief from Chiusi shows a fringed cloth garment, hanging cloudlike over the muffled and partially visible figures of the bridegroom, bride, and priest or attendant. In her discussion of this relief, Margherita Guarducci relates the cloth cloud to the bridal veil and sees it developing from a covering originally shared by both bride and groom into the later veil exclusively worn by the bride.[11]

If the veil was the most characteristic element of Roman bridal costume, it has also been the most misunderstood. One recent discussion describes it quite misleadingly as a red handkerchief.[12] While the Latin word for the veil, *flammeum*, is cognate with the adjective *fiery* or *flamelike*, the literary sources make clear that the veil was not red, but a deep yellow, the color of the flame of a candle. The mistaken notion of a red flammeum appears to stem from an anonymous scholiast of the latter part of the fourth century, who in commenting on one of Juvenal's *Satires*, glossed the flammeum as "a kind of cloak with which women cover themselves on their wedding day; it must be kept bloody red in color, on account of the blushing of the bride."[13] This statement flatly contradicts the other more reliable ancient testimony on the flammeum. The most important descriptions again come from Pliny the Elder and Festus. Pliny writes: "I understand that yellow was the earliest color to be highly esteemed and was granted as an exclusive privilege to women for their bridal veils" (H.N. 21.46). Festus says that "the garment known as the flammeum is worn by the Flaminica Dialis, that is the wife of the [Flamen] Dialis and priest of Jupiter, the cloth of which is the same color as lightning" (82.6 L). He also writes: "The bride is wrapped in the flammeum as a good omen, because the Flaminica, the wife of the Flamen [Dialis], to whom divorce was not permitted, used to wear it constantly" (79.23 L). Pliny describes the color of the flammeum as *luteum*, a shade of yellow he tells us was used exclusively for bridal veils. Pliny uses the same word for an egg yolk, which suggests a deep yellow, bordering on orange.[14] This color is not inconsistent with the description in Festus, since a bolt of lightning would appear as a bright flash of yellow.

The clue to the significance of the color and by extension of the bridal veil itself comes from the second Festus passage. Here Festus tells us explicitly that the bride wore the same veil as the Flaminica Dialis, the Roman priestess who could not divorce her husband, the Flamen Dialis and priest of Jupiter. In other words, the bride wore the flammeum as a good omen for a lasting marriage and lifelong fidelity to one man. By association with the Flaminica Dialis, the faithful wife par excellence, the yellow bridal veil symbolized constancy. The etymology of *flammeum*, from "flame," Latin *flamma*, further suggests that the veil may have been a symbol of the life-giving flame of the hearth, which would be tended by the bride in her new home.[15]

Further confirmation of the yellow color of the bridal veil may be found in representations of brides in Roman wall painting. An example of the first half of the first century A.D. from the Villa Imperiale at Pompeii shows a bride with a diaphanous yellow veil seated on a bridal bed.[16] Scholars have also recognized Roman bridal elements in the painted frieze of the mid–first century B.C. in the Villa of the Mysteries at Pompeii. The scene immediately to the right of the entrance to the room has been identified as one of bridal toilette, in which a standing attendant dresses the hair of a seated bride, while two cupids look on, one holding up a mirror so that the bride can admire herself. The older woman or Domina shown seated on an ivory couch to the left of the entrance features further bridal accoutrements: the betrothal ring and the marriage contract lying beside her on what must be the bridal bed.[17] Given the presence of so many elements of Roman bridal custom, the deep yellow mantles worn by the brides should be identified as flammea, even though they are bordered with a purple stripe.[18] Although the purple stripe is nowhere mentioned as part of the bride's flammeum, such borders symbolize special status and as such are often a feature of Roman priestesses' clothing.[19] The presence of the purple stripe may perhaps be explained by the Dionysiac context of the rest of the frieze, indicating that these brides are being initiated into a Dionysiac cult.

The painting termed *The Aldobrandini Wedding* from an Augustan house in Rome also includes a flammeum, although it is not shown on the bride herself, but rather resting next to her on the bridal bed.[20] Here the goddess of love seated next to the bride must be trying to persuade the young girl to put on the marriage veil. The reluctance of the bride-to-be is reinforced by the enveloping cloak underneath which she hides. The outcome, however, is not in doubt: not only have the bridal preparations begun on either side of the central group, but the bride has already donned the Roman bridal shoe, the *luteum soccum* or yellow bridal slipper mentioned in the nearly contemporary poem of Catullus.[21]

Thus, on the basis of both the literary and artistic

sources, we can assume that the Roman bridal veil was deep yellow in color, the color of an egg yolk and a bolt of lightning. It was a substantial mantle and in several artistic representations covers much of the upper body. This veil, also worn by the Flaminica Dialis, was apparently a symbol of constancy and lifelong fidelity because of its ritual association with the faithful wife of the priest of Jupiter.

### BRIDAL COIFFURE
### (COROLLA, SENI CRINES, HASTA CAELIBARIS)

"The young bride used to wear a small crown under her bridal veil, of flowers, *verbenae,* and herbs she picked herself" (Festus 56.1 L). In the painting from the Villa Imperiale, the bride wears what appears to be a diadem under her veil. This is the bridal corolla or crown, a wreath of flowers and herbs the bride was supposed to pick herself. According to Festus, the wreath contained *verbenae,* leafy twigs from aromatic shrubs used in religious ceremonies, but Catullus also mentions marjoram *(amaracum),* one of the flowers associated with Venus.[22] The wreath is thus clearly a symbol of fertility. On a third-century A.D. sarcophagus in Naples, a bride is shown placing just such a wreath on her head with the assistance of Juno Pronuba, attendant of brides.[23]

The bridal hairstyle, however, is rarely visible in artistic representations, even though a special coiffure for the bride is attested as early as Plautus, in the second century B.C.: "The thing to do is to humor him, and fix up your hair for the wedding" (*Mostellaria* 226). Also, "You are to take her home to your house at once, then bring her back here all got up like a married woman, the usual headdress, hair done high in ribbons, and she's to pretend she's your wife" (*Miles Gloriosus* 790–93). The second passage in particular suggests that the hair was piled high on the head like the tutulus, or high bun, of the Flaminica.[24] The difference between the hairstyle of the matron described here and the bridal coiffure in the first passage in unclear. The former used ribbons (vittae), while more explicit descriptions of the bridal hairdo stress the arrangement of the hair tresses.[25] Both, however, involve the putting up and binding of the hair. For more detail on the bridal coiffure, we must again turn to Festus: "Brides are adorned with the seni crines [six-tressed coiffure] because it is the most ancient style for them. This is also why the Vestals are so adorned, [since this hairstyle guarantees?] the chastity of brides to their husbands" (Festus 454.23 L).

Despite some textual difficulties in the passage, Festus clearly states that Roman brides and Vestal Virgins shared the seni crines coiffure, which was a sign of chastity. The precise meaning of the phrase *seni crines* has been debated, since it appears only here.[26] The most commonly accepted interpretation is that *seni* is the equivalent of *sex* and that the description is that of a six-tressed hairstyle, although this still does not clarify precisely how the hair was arranged. Both an arrangement with vertical spiral locks falling on either side of a central part and a high bun made up of horizontal sections of hair have been proposed. Recently two new alternative and apparently mutually exclusive interpretations for *seni* have been suggested, meaning either "twisted and bound" or "cut".[27] Although either of these alternatives might make it easier to reconstruct the bridal coiffure, the numerical interpretation (*seni* as six) is supported by a previously unnoticed passage in Martial: "I saw them, Vacerra, I saw those bags they would not hold as payment for two years' worth of rent: your red-headed wife, the one with the seven-tressed hair, walked off with them" (12.32.2–4).

Although some scholars have taken the expression *septem crinibus* here to mean bald, this does not convince me, since the wife is also described as a redhead.[28] It seems more likely that *septem crinibus* is a play on the seni crines, the canonical bridal coiffure. Thus Martial would be sketching the portrait of an unfaithful wife by referring to her (irregular) bridal attributes. Like the worn-out flammeum in Juvenal's sixth *Satire*, the modified bridal hairdo (seven-tressed instead of six) marks the unfaithful spouse. Understood in this way, the passage makes it clear that by the first century A.D., *seni crines* was understood by the Romans to refer to a six-tressed hairstyle, not to cut or bound hair. While the significance of the number six remains obscure, it should perhaps be related to the number of the Vestals, who share this bridal attribute.[29]

The shared coiffure highlights the common features of Vestal and bride. Both had to be virginal, yet both were associated with fertility and the life-giving hearth, the bride with that of her household, the Vestal with that of the state.[30] Vestals were also considered the brides of Rome through the intermediary of the Pontifex Maximus, who greeted the new Vestal with the words "Thus, beloved, I seize you" *(ita te amata capio),* in a version of the old-fashioned form of the Roman wedding, the *manu captio,* or the seizing of the bride by force.[31] Since the hairstyle of the Roman bride is obscured by her veil in most artistic representations, the study of depictions of Vestals would seem to afford the best opportunity to reconstruct the bridal hairdo.[32]

### THE HEADDRESS OF THE VESTAL
### (SUFFIBULUM, INFULA, VITTAE)

Most statues of the Vestals, such as the series of statues from the Atrium Vestae in Rome or a recently published head from the British Museum (figs. 3.1–2),[33] show the priestesses veiled with the suffibulum, a short veil described by Festus as white, bordered with purple, and fastened with a fibula, hence the name which means "pinned below."[34] In the sculptural examples, this veil is generally worn further back on the head than the bridal flammeum, so that the Vestals' hairstyle can be observed. As is clearly visible in figure 3.2, under her veil the Vestal wears an infula, a white fillet of wool which has been coiled around her head at least five times. The ends of this fillet normally fall to the shoulders in long loops (as seen in the Vestal now in the Terme Museum) or strands (as seen in figs. 3.4–5). This fillet and its pendant strands, or vittae, are described by Servius: "The infula is a band similar to a diadem, from which ribbons hang down on either side; most are broad and twisted [and in color they are] red and white" (*In Aeneadem* 10.538). The significance of these headbands is made clear by those who wore them. These included sacrificial victims, priests, and suppliants seeking asylum.[35] Seneca describes the infula as a protecting emblem, one which sets a person or object apart as inviolate.[36] As a symbol of inviolacy and ritual purity, the fillet is also found in the Roman wedding, though not worn by the bride. Rather the doorjambs of the bride's new home are decorated with these fillets, rubbed down with oil or grease.[37]

H. Jordan has suggested that the turbanlike arrangement of the infula seen in several of the portrait statues of Vestals from the Roman Forum and in figure 3.1 is a cloth substitute for the seni crines hairstyle of the bride. Despite the fact that only some representations of Vestals depict a sexpartite infula (all dated to the second century A.D.), Jordan's proposal has been widely accepted.[38] Several earlier monuments, in fact, both of relief and portrait sculpture, feature the fillet as a scarflike piece of cloth which was wrapped around the head, then was tied at the nape of the neck, and finally fell to the shoulders in ropelike strands. This arrangement is seen in figures 3.3–4, a late Flavian or early Trajanic head from the Atrium Vestae, and figure 3.5, a somewhat later Trajanic portrait now in the Uffizi. Both heads are thought to represent the same Vestal.[39]

Especially worthy of note in these two heads is the presence of short hair locks both in front and in back of the ear (these are most easily seen in the profile view of the Atrium Vestae portrait, fig. 3.4, and in fig. 3.5, the three-quarters view of the Uffizi piece). These locks are not wisps of hair that have escaped the hairdo but are clearly rendered as cut locks.[40] That the Vestals' hair was cut short is attested by Pliny the Elder: "Still older, though its age is uncertain, is the one called the hair tree, because the Vestals' hair is brought to it" (*H.N.* 16.235).[41] The depiction of the Vestal on frieze B of the

Fig. 3.2. Detail of the fillet of the Vestal in the British Museum. Courtesy of the Dept. of Greek and Roman Antiquities, British Museum, neg. 88636.

Fig. 3.1. Portrait head of a life-sized statue of a Vestal Virgin of the Trajanic period. British Museum, London, inv. 1979.11–8.1. Courtesy of the Dept. of Greek and Roman Antiquities, British Museum, neg. 88632.

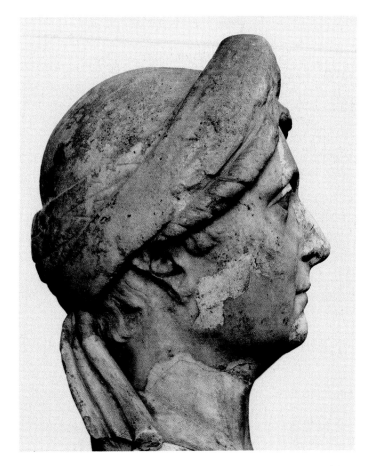

Fig. 3.4. Profile of the Vestal head from the Atrium Vestae. Courtesy of the Soprintendenza Archeologica di Roma, neg. 921.

Fig. 3.3. Portrait head of a life-sized statue of a Vestal Virgin (late Flavian-early Trajanic from the Atrium Vestae, Rome, now in the Forum Antiquarium, inv. 634. Courtesy of the Soprintendenza Archeologica di Roma, neg. 921.

Fig. 3.5. Late Trajanic portrait bust of a Vestal Virgin, now in the Uffizi, Florence, inv. 1914/150. Photo: Alinari/Art Resource, New York neg. 1292.

Fig. 3.6. Detail of the head of a Vestal Virgin from frieze B of the Cancelleria reliefs (late Flavian), now in the Lateran Museum, Vatican. Photo by author.

Cancelleria reliefs (late first century A.D.) shown in figure 3.6 is further corroboration that adult Vestals continued to wear their hair short.[42] How can we reconcile the representation of this Vestal, shown with short hair cinched by the infula, with all the others in which the Vestals appear to have long hair? The solution to this apparent contradiction must lie in the criterion used to date Vestal portraits, namely the similarity of their coiffure to that of women of the imperial family.[43] Van Deman has pointed out that the dress shown on statues of the Vestals is not their own but is rather borrowed from late classical sculpture. It would appear that the treatment of their hair is similarly modeled on that of contemporary imperial women and thus does not accurately reflect the way the Vestals wore their hair.

The contrast between the Trajanic coiffure of long braids and "Schildfrisur" and the short locks visible on the Atrium Vestae and Uffizi heads (figs. 3.4–5) can thus be explained. The short locks reflect the Vestals' actual

hairstyle, a short "bowl" cut similar to that represented on the nearly contemporary Vestal in the Cancelleria relief (fig. 3.6), while the Trajanic coiffure assimilates the Vestal with other important women of the day.

The disparity between the representations of Vestals in portrait statues and their ritually prescribed dress was not complete, since the infula is faithfully represented, and sometimes the suffibulum as well. The short hairstyle of the Vestals argued for here in fact provides support for Jordan's identification of the arrangement of the fillet with the seni crines: clearly the reason a cloth substitute for the six-tressed hairstyle was needed was because the Vestals' hair was cropped short. It does not follow, however, that the bride's hair was cut short: the literary passages cited above make it clear that the bridal hairstyle involved putting the hair up in a six-tressed style worn on top of the head.[44]

The seni crines coiffure, worn by brides and imitated by the arrangement of the infula of the Vestals, is therefore reconstructed here as a style in which the hair is parted into six tresses, or braids, probably three on either side of a central part, with the tresses or braids then twisted or braided and wound around the head in a turbanlike arrangement. The style probably resembled the matronly tutulus with vittae described by Plautus and others.[45]

The final element of the bridal coiffure to be discussed is the hasta caelibaris, literally, the "celibate spear," used to dress the bride's hair in the seni crines style. Ovid, Plutarch, and Arnobius all refer to the custom of stroking or parting the bride's hair with this implement:

Nor will the curving spear dress your virgin hair. (Ovid, *Fasti* 2.435–36)

Why do they part the hair of brides with the point of a spear? (Plutarch, *Roman Questions* 87)

Some also say that the custom of parting the bride's hair with the point of a spear is a reminder that the first marriage was attended with war and fighting. (Plutarch, *Romulus* 15.5)

When you come together in marriage, do you spread out the toga on the marriage bed and invoke the genius of the husband? Do you caress the hair of the bride with the celibate spear? Do you dedicate the little girls' togas at the shrine of Virgin Fortune? (Arnobius, *Adv. nat.* 2.67)

Festus offers four explanations for the custom of caressing the bride's hair with a spear:

The head of the bride used to be dressed with the celibate spear which had been planted in the body of a gladiator thrown aside and killed, so that
A) in the same way the spear had been joined with the gladiator's body, the bride would be joined with her husband, OR
B) because matrons are under the tutelage of Juno Curitis, who is so called from the spear carried [by her image], which is called in the language of the Sabines *curis*, OR
C) because the spear predicts that the brides will bring forth brave men, OR
D) because by nuptial law, the bride is subjected to the command of her husband and the spear is chosen because it is the most important of weapons and [is a symbol] of power. (Festus 55.3 L)

Although modern scholars have explained the hasta caelibaris as a hairpin or, even more ingeniously, as a hair hook used to thread ornaments into the hair as it was braided, the passages from Plutarch and Festus cited above strongly suggest that a real weapon was used.[46] Surely the simplest interpretation is to be preferred, namely that the hair was parted and perhaps also separated into six tresses with this spear, then twisted or braided on the top of the head, where it would have been held fast by wreath and veil.[47]

The symbolic meaning of the act is far more interesting than the actual gesture. Of the myriad explanations, I find N. Boels' thesis that the spear conjured up powers

in the bride's hair the most attractive.[48] The hair of the sexually mature woman was, as we have seen, a potent reservoir of the powers of fertility.[49] Boels has pointed out the close connection between marriage and the combing of the hair of the Flaminica Dialis in Roman religion and has suggested that the combing of the Flaminica's (and by extension, any woman's) hair was symbolic of conjugal union. Thus the touching of the spear to the bride's hair, according to Boels, meant the conjuring up of the woman's fertility. Others, such as M. Cary and A. D. Nock, however, have seen the magic contained in a woman's hair as more malevolent and thus interpret drawing the spear through the hair as an exorcism of evil spirits.[50]

The spear itself was an emblem of magical and ritual power to the Romans, as Alföldi has demonstrated and, indeed, as Festus in the passage cited explicitly states.[51] But surely we miss the point if we see the act of the hasta caelibaris as merely the exercise of legal sovereignty over the bride by her husband.[52] After all, the spear became the emblem of legal authority primarily as a result of its use as the killing weapon par excellence.[53] At the heart of the practice of the hasta caelibaris lies the deliberate juxtaposition of the (male) realm of war and the (female) sphere of the family. Female magic in the hair meets male magic in the spear, a spear we are told has already killed. According to Pliny the Elder, a spear that had killed became a talisman for new life and specifically guarded against difficult labor.[54] It thus seems plausible to suggest that in the rite of the hasta caelibaris, the spear also served as a talisman, as a *porte bonheur*, guarding against a difficult or sterile marriage.

A similar juxtaposition of the military with the domestic sphere is also found in Roman art, specifically in sarcophagi of the third century A.D., which frequently illustrate domestic concord, with the *dextrarum iunctio* or handshake of the bridal pair, alongside the successful military exploits of the deceased.[55] Like the act of the hasta caelibaris, these scenes balance opposing principles: war and peace, the foreign and the domestic, public triumph and private bliss.

I suggest that the hasta caelibaris makes much more sense as a real spear, which was touched to the head of the bride in a gesture not of menace but of empowerment. Just as the bridal hairstyle, used with modifications by the Vestals, symbolized the girl's chastity, and her bridal veil, modeled after that of the Flaminica Dialis, symbolized constancy and fidelity, so too the celibate spear performed a symbolic and ritual function, that of talisman for a peaceful, happy, and fertile union.

The costume of the Roman bride thus illustrates the newly empowered status of the girl, as she is initiated into womanhood on her wedding day. The dress and customs associated with it are consistent with the stress laid in Roman marriage on the idea of the consent of the principals, epitomized by the handshake, and their mutual affection symbolized by the ring, concepts which have shaped our own marriage customs.[56] The tunica recta, the very first article of clothing the Roman bride put on, was associated with the Etruscan nobility of early Rome. Her veil, the flammeum, and the six-tressed seni crines hairstyle were also archaic elements, which she shared with the most powerful priestesses of Rome, the Flaminica Dialis, and the Vestal Virgins. Thus through her costume and hairstyle, the bride became noble, sacred, chaste, and fertile, with all the power of each attribute. And like the girl herself, the spear, symbol of war and death, was transformed to play a life-giving and empowering role in her initiation: it became a good-luck charm launching the bride on her own *champ de bataille*.

## NOTES

I am grateful to Larissa Bonfante, Katherine Geffcken, Julia Heskel, Judith Sebesta, Michelle Salzman, and Rex Wallace for their comments and suggestions on this chapter. Translations of the ancient sources are taken from the Loeb Classical Library editions, save for those translations of Festus and the scholiast on Juvenal, which are my own.

1. The toga virilis became standard public attire for the youth thereafter. In contrast, most of the bridal garments appear to have been worn for a much shorter period of time, perhaps only the day of the wedding. For a discussion of the toga, see S. Stone, chap. 1 in this volume.

2. Verrius Flaccus, one of the most erudite scholars of the Augustan Age (his work was one of Pliny the Elder's sources), preserves much earlier republican material. All passages in the epitome of Verrius Flaccus by Festus (later further epitomized by Paul) refer to the Teubner text of W. M. Lindsay, *Sexti Pompei Festi: De verborum significatu cum Pauli epitome* (Leipzig, 1913).

3. Greek bridal practices have recently seen a revival of scholarly interest; see J. Redfield, "Notes on the Greek Wedding," *Arethusa* 15 (1982): 181–201; J. Oakley, "The Anakalypteria," *AA* 97 (1982): 113–18; R. Hague and J. Oakley, *The Wedding in Ancient Athens* (Madison, 1993). The extensive ancient testimonia on Roman bridal costume, however, have not been reviewed systematically since H. Blümner, *Die Römischen Privataltertümer*, Handbuch der klassichen Altertumswissenschaft 4.2.2. (Munich, 1911), 349–53. Some discussion of Roman bridal garments has appeared in surveys of Roman dress, such as Wilson, *Clothing*, 138–45, and Bonfante-Warren, "Roman Costume," 584–614, esp. 596. Specific aspects of Roman bridal apparel and headgear have been the focus of two Italian scholars recently, although neither is solely interested in the costume of the bride: Sensi, "Ornatus," 60–64, and M. Torelli, *Lavinio e Roma: Riti iniziatici e matrimonio tra archeologia e storia* (Rome, 1984), esp. 31–50. Roman marriage rites are briefly treated in

I. Jenkins, *Greek and Roman Life* (Cambridge, Mass., 1986), 40; for a full treatment, see DarSag, s.v. "Matrimonium", and S. Treggiari, "Roman Marriage," in *Civilizations of the Ancient Mediterranean,* vol. 3, ed. M. Grant and R. Kitzinger (New York, 1988), 1343–54.

4. Propertius 4.11.33; Arnobius, *Adversus nationes* 2.67 (toga dedicated to Fortuna Virginalis). Earlier the toga, like the hairnet, may have been dedicated to the Lares of the household; see n. 9 below.

5. On the upright or warp-weighted loom and (linen?) tunic, see J. P. Wild, *Textile Manufacture in the Northern Roman Provinces* (Cambridge, Eng., 1970), 68–69; Bonfante and Jaunzems, "Clothing and Ornament," 1388, 1403–4; and E. J. W. Barber, *Prehistoric Textiles* (Princeton, 1991). Wilson (*Clothing,* 138) believes the tunic was woolen; see also her discussion of the tunica recta, 57–58. The girl's tunic was tied with a Hercules knot, to be loosened by her husband on their wedding night (Festus 55.20 L)

6. On togate prostitutes and adulteresses, see S. Stone, chap. 1, and J. Sebesta, chap. 2, in this volume.

7. See Bonfante-Warren, "Roman Costume," 606.

8. Valerius Maximus 6.3.10. Funerals, according to Plutarch (*Roman Questions* 14), constituted the exception. For the symbolic importance of head and hair and the different treatment of girls and women, see Sensi, "Ornatus," 55–56.

9. Dedication of the hairnet to Lares: Nonius Marcellus (early fourth century A.D.), *De compendiosa doctrina,* ed. W. M. Lindsay (Leipzig, 1903), 869, 7–9 (Varro frag., 463). See also P. E. Mottadeh, "The Princeton Bronze Portrait of a Woman with Reticulum," in *Festchrift Leo Mildenberg,* ed. A. Houghton et al. (Wetteren, Belgium, 1984), 203–8, for complete discussion of Roman hairnets with reference to artistic representations. On dedication of dolls, see *Creperia Tryphaena: Le scoperte archeologiche nell' area del Palazzo di Giustizia* (Rome, 1983).

10. Although the ancient association of *nubes* and *nubo* has often been accepted by scholars (e.g., Ernout and Meillet, *Dictionnaire étymologique,* 448–49), my colleague Rex Wallace has pointed out to me that recent linguistic work indicates the roots are probably not the same: see C. Watkins, *The American Heritage Dictionary of Indo-European Roots* (Boston, 1985), 62, s.v. *sneubh-*, "to marry," Latin *nubere* and *sneudh-*, "mist," "cloud," Latin *nubes* also J. Pokorny, *Indo-germanisches etymologisches Wörterbuch* (Bern, 1959), 977–78.

11. M. Guarducci, "Il *conubium* nei riti del matrimonio etrusco e di quello romano," *BCAR* 55 (1929): 205–24.

12. Torelli, *Lavinio,* 33: "*flammeum,* un fazzoletto rosso.*" This is a common mistake; cf., e.g., Blümner, *Privataltertümer,* 350; Sensi, "Ornatus," 73; Beard, "Sexual Status," 15 and n. 24.

13. Scholiast on Juvenal, *Satires* 6.224–26. For the date, see E. Courtney, *A Commentary on the Satires of Juvenal* (London, 1980), 56. Courtney implicitly rejects the testimony of the scholiast in his explanation of the flammeum as orange at *Sat.* 2.124, p. 143.

14. Pliny the Elder, *H.N.* 10.148: "The chick itself is formed out of the white of the egg, but its food is in the yolk." On

*luteum* as the color yellow, and the flammeum, see J. André, *Etudes sur les termes du couleur dans la langue latine* (Paris, 1949), 151–53, 115–16.

15. Probably also relevant here is the ritual of fire and water, part of the Roman wedding ceremony, but unfortunately it is only alluded to in the sources: Varro, *De Lingua Latina* 5.61; Festus 87.21 L; Plutarch, *Roman Questions* 1. N. Boels, "Le statut religieux de la Flaminica Dialis," *REL* 51 (1973): 81, also sees the flame-colored veil as a symbol of fertility.

16. All the paintings in this house must date before the earthquake of A.D. 62: see W. Archer, "The Paintings in the Alae of the Casa dei Vettii and a Definition of the Fourth Pompeian Style," *AJA* 94 (1990): 110 n. 37; against, e.g., U. Pappalardo, "Die Villa Imperiale in Pompeij," *Antike Welt* 16.4 (1985): 3–15. For a color illustration, see A. Maiuri, *Roman Painting* (Skira, N.Y., 1953), 106. Pappalardo identifies the bride in Room A as a poet (12) but acknowledges her similarity to the bride in the Aldobrandini wedding, discussed below. The figure's costume is clearly bridal, even if adopted here for a female Greek lyric poet.

17. Bridal toilette: M. Bieber, "Der Mysteriensaal der Villa Item," *JDAI* 43 (1928): 313; O. Brendel, "The Great Frieze of the Villa of the Mysteries," in *The Visible Idea* (Washington, D.C., 1980), 115, 119. Betrothal ring described by Aulus Gellius 10.10: Bieber, 312 n. 5; Brendel, 119. Wedding contract: Bieber, 329; Brendel, 119 and n. 65. The bridal elements are also stressed in J. M. C. Toynbee, "The Villa Item and a Bride's Ordeal," *JRS* 19 (1929): 67–87. I am not convinced by F. L. Bastet, "Fabularum dispositas explicationes," *BABesch* 49 (1974): 206–40, that these figures must be goddesses (Aphrodite and Hera), not mortals, given the absence of the bridegroom in the toilette scene (218–20) and the presence of a footstool for the Domina (238).

18. For color illustrations of the entire frieze and details of the two brides, see Andreae, *Art of Rome*, figs. 27–31. Brendel, "Great Frieze," 136 n. 65, sees the yellow veil as characteristic of the Roman bride, although he mistakenly believes it to feature a purple seam. E. Simon, in contrast, identifies the color as the saffron yellow of Dionysus, and thus a Greek rather than a Roman element; Simon, "Zur Fries der Mysterienvilla bei Pompeji," *JDAI* 76 (1961): 119. It is also possible that the color represents both. In that case, we would have a tidy combination of the Greek and Roman elements here in the conflation of flammeum yellow with Dionysiac saffron, just as Dionysiac and Roman purple (as in the praetexta stripe) are fused.

19. Purple border as symbol of special status *(praetextum)*: Bonfante-Warren, "Roman Costume," 591, 614; Bonfante and Jaunzems, "Clothing and Ornament," 1402–3. The Vestals too wore a veil with a purple border: Festus 475.4 L. The figure of Ariadne on the east wall of the frieze of the Villa of the Mysteries also has a purple stripe on her mantle, though here the mantle is white, not yellow. A number of other figures in the painted frieze also have purple-bordered kerchiefs or mantles; see the illustrations in Andreae, *Art of Rome*, figs. 27–31.

20. For a color illustration of this painting, see Maiuri, *Roman Painting*, 30. Flammeum on the bed next to the bride: K. Quinn, *Catullus' Poems* (New York, 1973), 266 (on Catullus 61.8). Like the frieze in the Villa of the Mysteries, this

painting combines Greek and Roman bridal elements. On the Greek or Hellenistic elements in the painting, see L. Curtius, "Zur Aldobrandinischen Hochzeit," in *Vermächtnis der antiken Kunst*, ed. R. Herbig (Heidelberg, 1950), 119–40; P. H. von Blanckenhagen and B. Green, "The Aldobrandini Wedding Reconsidered," *RM* 82 (1985): 83–98. Roman elements, in particular the fire and water ritual mentioned above: B. Andreae, "Igni et aqua accipi," *Römische Quartalschrift* 57 (1962): 1–16.

21. Yellow shoe *(luteum soccum):* Catullus 61.8–10, "Seize the joyful bridal veil, come now come, cast the yellow shoe on the snowy white foot"; "flammeum cape, laetus huc / huc veni niveo gerens / luteum pede soccum."

22. *Verbenae:* Servius, *In Aeneadem* 12.120, "We call *verbenae* all sacred branches, like laurel, olive, or myrtle." *Amaracum:* Catullus 61.6–7, "Bind your brows with flowers of fragrant marjoram, put on the wedding veil"; "cinge tempora floribus / suave olentis amaraci." On marjoram as a flower of love, see R. D. Williams, *The Aeneid of Virgil, Books 1–6* (London, 1972), 210 (on *Aeneid* 1.693–94). See also A. C. Andrews, "Marjoram as a Spice in the Classical Era," *CP* 56 (1961): 73–82, a reference I owe to Laura Voight.

23. On the Gallienic sarcophagus in Naples, see Andreae, *Art of Rome*, fig. 142.

24. Plautus, *Mostellaria* 226: "soli gerundum censeo morem et capiundas crines." Plautus, *Miles Gloriosus* 790–93: "ut ad te eam iam deducas domum / itaque eam huc ornatam adducas, ex matronarum modo, / capite compto, crines vittasque habeat, adsimuletque se / tuam esse uxorem." On the tutulus worn by the Flamenica Dialis, see Bonfante-Warren, "Roman Costume," 596; Bonfante, *Etruscan Dress*, 75–76; and J. Sebesta, chap. 2 in this volume. On the tutulus and vittae as matronly prerogatives, see Sensi, "Ornatus," 60–64.

25. It should be noted that Propertius (4.3.15–16, "nec recta capillis / vitta data est"; and 4.11.34, "et acceptas altera vitta comas") uses vittae as a symbol of the wedding, but this is perhaps to be explained as part of the conflation of bridal and matronly attributes so frequent in Latin poetry. See, e.g., Juvenal 6.224–26 and Martial 12.32.4, discussed below, for examples of unfaithful wives described in bridal terms. In Propertius, the reverse would hold; the bride is characterized through matronly attributes.

26. The precise phrase is *seni crines*, not *sex crines* as it is often cited, in, e.g., Beard, "Sexual Status," 16; E. B. Van Deman, "The Value of the Vestal Statues as Originals," *AJA* 12 (1908): 324–42; S. Walker, *A Portrait Head of a Life-size Statue of a Vestal*, British Museum Occasional Paper 22, Department of Greek and Roman Antiquities, New Acquisitions 1, 1976–79 (London, 1981), 17. I thank Susan Walker for a copy of the latter publication.

27. Vertical spiral locks: Torelli, *Lavinio*, 33–34. Torelli appears to identify all the female terracotta heads from Lavinium as brides, despite the fact that they wear quite different hairstyles. Of his figs. 15–32, only the piece illustrated on 36–37, figs. 16–17, has three ringlets on either side of the head. His figs. 20–21 have only two ringlets on either side of the head, and the other examples simply feature short, combed hair. In two instances (38, figs. 18–19), the hair is clasped in

barrettes and is covered with a kerchief. Thus the vertical spiral locks arrangement fits only some of Torelli's examples from Lavinium. This arrangement does not account for the passage in Plautus, nor does it match the coiffure of the Vestals. High bun: Bonfante-Warren, "Roman Costume," 396, and Bonfante, *Etruscan Dress,* 75–76. Bound or cut hair: G. Giannecchini, in Sensi, "Ornatus," 91–92.

28. Martial, *Epigrammata ad codices parisinos accurate recensita,* vol. 3 (Paris, 1825), 30 n. 4: "crinibus septem. id est uxor tua calva." I have been unable to find any other commentary which discusses the meaning of the phrase. I am indebted to Rex Wallace for bringing the Martial passage to my attention and for running a scan of *crines* on the Ibycus program, which revealed only two instances of *crines* with a numerical adjective: this passage in Martial and that of Festus 454.23 L cited earlier.

29. Although G. Giannecchini in Sensi, "Ornatus," 91, sees no religious significance in the number six, Festus 475.12 L seems to retain (albeit garbled) elements of an explanation for the number, which he associated with the three Roman tribes: "Sex Vestae sacerdotes constitutae erant, ut populus pro sua quisque parte haberet ministram sacrorum, quia civitas Romana in sex erat distributa partes: in primos secundosque Titienses, Ramnes, Luceres." Perhaps each tribe needed two Vestals (one senior and a junior apprentice?). For more on the significance of *seni* and the proper interpretation of the seni crines, see R. Wallace and L. La Follette, "Latin *seni crines* and the Hair Style of Roman Brides" *Syllecta Classica* 4 (1992): 1–6.

30. Venus Mater: H. Jordan, *Der Tempel der Vesta und das Haus der Vestalinnen* (Berlin, 1886), 52–53. Agricultural rites performed by the Vestals: L. A. Holland, *Janus and the Bridge* (Rome, 1961), 316–22. Vestals and life-giving fire: Plutarch, *Camillus* 20.139. Sexual ambiguity of the Vestals: Beard, "Sexual Status," 12–27.

31. Seizing of the Vestal: Aulus Gellius 1.12.9–14. *Manu captio:* DarSag, s.v. "Matrimonium"; also F. Guizzi, *Aspetti giuridici del sacerdozio romano: Il sacerdozio di Vesta,* Pubblicazioni della facoltà giuridica dell'università di Napoli 62 (Naples, 1968), 31–66, 124–39.

32. For a list of monuments depicting the Vestals, see F. Magi, *I rilievi del palazzo della Cancelleria* (Rome, 1945), 90–93. Only the Vestals' heads and hair dress are of concern here, not the rest of their clothing. The garments are generally difficult to distinguish in most of the reliefs; see I. S. Ryberg, "Rites," figs. 22a (Ara Pacis), 26 (Sorrento base), 27 (Palermo relief) and 36f (Ara Pietatis). The portrait statues of the Vestals from the Roman Forum are equally untrustworthy: as E. B. Van Deman has indicated ("Vestal Statues as Originals," 324–42), the drapery and poses of the figures reflect fifth- and fourth-century Greek statuary.

33. Vestal in the British Museum (figs. 3.1–2): Walker, *Portrait Head,* 17–19, 50, figs. 31a–c. I thank Susan Walker for her assistance in procuring the photographs of the head reproduced here and Maxwell L. Anderson for bringing this head to my attention. The veil and hairstyle of the piece are virtually identical to those of several Vestals from the Roman Forum: Jordan, *Der Tempel der Vesta,* 43–56, pls. 8–10; see

also Van Deman, "Vestal Statues as Originals." The best-preserved example from the Forum, Jordan's no. 10 and Van Deman's fig. 15, is now in the Terme Museum (inv. 639, dated to the Antonine period): see E. Talamo, in Giuliano, *Le sculture,* cat. no. 165, 269–70.

34. Suffibulum: Festus 475.4 L; cf. Varro, *De lingua Latina* 6.21.

35. Sacrificial victims and priests: Festus 100.7 L, s.v. "infulae"; L. Bonfante, "Human Sacrifice on an Etruscan Urn," *AJA* 88 (1984): 537–39. Vestals: Prudentius, *Contra Symmachum* 2.1086, 1094–95. Priests of Ceres: Cicero, *In Verrem* 6.50.110. Priests of Apollo and Diana: Vergil, *Aeneid* 2.430, 10.538. Arvals: Aulus Gellius 6.7. Suppliants seeking asylum: Caesar, *Bellum civile* 2.12; Tacitus, *Historiae* 1.66. On the infula and vittae, see also Bonfante-Warren, "Roman Costume," 608, 614; and DarSag, s.v. "infula," for illustrations of the fillet on sacrificial animals.

36. Seneca, *Epistles* 14.11: "One must therefore take refuge in philosophy, as this pursuit not only in the eyes of the good, but also in the eyes of the moderately bad, is a sort of infula (a protecting emblem)." Both in appearance and in function, the infula resembles the Greek *agrenon,* a string of wool that has been carded but not yet spun, the strands of which are held together with knots at regular intervals. It is this type of fillet that was wrapped around the omphalos at Delphi and is still used to ward off evil in parts of Cyprus today; see E. Gullberg and P. Åström, *The Thread of Ariadne,* Studies in Mediterranean Archaeology 21 (Göteborg, 1979), 44–45.

37. Lucan, *Pharsalia* 2.355: "No white fillet ran this way and that to the posts of the door"; "[nulla] infulaque in geminos discurrit candida postes." See also Pliny the Elder, *H.N.* 29.30: "The old Romans assigned to wool supernatural powers, for they bade brides touch with it the doorposts of their new homes"; "lanis auctoritatem veteres Romani etiam religiosam habuere postes a nubentibus attingi iubentes."

38. Jordan, *Der Tempel der Vesta,* 47–48, esp. pl. 8, figs. 1–3. Other second-century examples with the sexpartite turban: Antonine Vestal in the Terme Museum (E. Talamo, 269–70, in Giuliano, *Le sculture);* Hadrianic-Antonine heads from the Palatine (Magi, *I rilievi,* 41). Jordan's hypothesis has been accepted by Walker, *Portrait Head,* 17; and H. Jucker, "Bildnis einer Vestalin," *RM* 68 (1961): 96. It had been rejected by H. Dragendorff, "Die Amtstracht der Vestalinnen," *RhM* 51 (1896): 286–87.

39. These heads have been most fully published in Jucker, "Bildnis," 93–102, esp. pls. 28–30. Inv. 634 appears to be the same head, though much restored, as that published by Jordan, in *Der Tempel der Vesta,* as pl. 9, fig. 11. I am grateful to the Soprintendenza Archeologica di Roma for the two photographs of this portrait published here as figures 3.3–4, and to Shelley Stone for his assistance in procuring them. I also thank Julia Hairston for her help with the Alinari photo of Uffizi, inv. 1914/150, published as figure 3.5.

40. Compare Jucker, "Bildnis," pls. 28–29. The hair is thick and bluntly cut, not fine and of different lengths, as one would expect of wisps escaping the hairdo.

41. "Lotos . . . incerta eius aetas, quae capillata dicitur, quoniam Vestalium virginum capillus ad eam defertur." Compare

Festus 50.12 L: "They used to call the hairy tree the one on which they used to hang cut hair."

42. Cancelleria Vestal (fig. 3.6): Magi, *I rilievi*, 28, fig. 31; 92 (discussion), and pl. 19. On the short haircut of the Vestals, see R. Lanciani, "L'atrio di Vesta," *Notizie degli scavi di Antichità* (1883): 461, with references to earlier authorities. Lanciani's observation is cited with bemusement by Jordan (*Der Tempel der Vesta*, 48) and is categorically rejected by Jucker ("Bildnis," 96). More recently, both Sensi ("Ornatus," 68) and Giuzzi (*Aspetti giuridici*, 110–11) discuss the cutting of the Vestals' hair.

43. Jucker, "Bildnis," 100, for inv. 634, dated to late Flavian–early Trajanic period on the basis of hairstyle; pp. 96–97, for the dating of the Uffizi head to the reign of Trajan on the basis of the same criterion. See also Walker, *Portrait Head*, 18; E. Talamo, in Giuliano, *Le sculture*, 270, for the similar use of hairstyle for the dating of the Vestal portraits in the British Museum and the Terme Museum.

44. E.g., Plautus, *Mostellaria* 226; Martial 12.32.2–4. Compare the representation of brides on third-century sarcophagi, such as Ryberg, "Rites," pl. 59, fig. 95, or the sarcophagus cited above in n. 23, where it is clear that the bride's hair is long and done up under the veil. I cannot follow Sensi, "Ornatus," 68–69, who associates the seni crines of the bride with a ritual haircut, designed to instill a sense of chastity (i.e., shame) in the bride.

45. The clearest representation of the preparation of the hair is that found in the bridal toilette scene from the Villa of the Mysteries at Pompeii: see n. 17 above. On the tutulus and vittae, see nn. 24–25 above; cf. also Ovid, *Ars amatoria* 1.31, and Servius, *In Aeneadem* 7.403, on vittae as sign of matronly *pudor*, or sexual continence.

46. Sensi, "Ornatus," 59: *ago crinale*. Torelli, *Lavinio*, 36–37: "qualcosa di molto simile ad un attuale uncinetto per lavorare a maglia . . . piccoli ferri uncinati [per] fermare le treccioline a qualsivoglia ornamento perforato." Torelli in particular seems to have confused the spear Festus refers to with the *uncus*, the hook used to drag, not the dead gladiators from the ring, but the bodies of condemned criminals to the Tiber; on the distinction, see G. Ville, *La gladiature en occident des origines à la mort de Domitien*, Bibliothèque des Ecoles Françaises d'Athènes et de Rome 54 (Rome, 1981), 36–37, 425 n. 146. See also H. Le Bonniec, "Le témoignage d'Arnobe sur deux rites archaïques du mariage romain," *REL* 54 (1976):

117, on the long tradition of the misidentification of the hasta as a hairpin. As Le Bonniec points out, such hairpins did exist but were never referred to as hastae.

47. As suggested by Jenkins, *Greek and Roman Life*, 40.

48. Boels, "Le statut religieux," esp. 93–94.

49. The bride, in principle if not in fact, was considered sexually mature. On the age at marriage, see B. Shaw, "The Age of Roman Girls at Marriage: Some Reconsiderations," *JRS* 77 (1987): 30–46.

50. M. Cary and A. D. Nock, "Magic Spears," *CQ* 21 (1927): 127.

51. A. Alföldi, "Hasta-Summa Imperii," *AJA* 63 (1959): 1–27; Alföldi's title comes from Festus 55.3 L, cited above.

52. Le Bonniec, "Le témoignage d'Arnobe," 128–29.

53. Alföldi, "Hasta," 2, 8, 18–19.

54. Pliny the Elder, *H.N.* 28.33–34: "It is said that difficult labour ends in delivery at once, if over the house where is the lying-in woman there be thrown a stone or missile that has killed with one stroke each three living creatures—a human being, a boar and a bear. A successful result is more likely if a light-cavalry spear is used, pulled out from a human body without the ground being touched"; "ferunt difficiles partus statim solvi, cum quis tectum in quo sit gravida transmiserit lapide vel missili ex his qui tria animalia singulis ictibus interfecerint, hominem, aprum, ursum. probabilius id facit hasta velitaris evulsa corpori hominis, si terram non attigerit."

55. Ryberg, "Rites," figs. 90 (from Mantua), 91 (in the Uffizi), and 92 (in Los Angeles). Each shows a military scene or parade on the left, with the marriage scene on the right of the sarcophagus front.

56. See F. Gies and J. Gies, *Marriage and the Family in the Middle Ages* (New York, 1987), 20–23, on the legal formula "consent, not intercourse, makes the marriage" *(nuptias consensus non concubitus facit)* and the tradition of the betrothal ring, placed on the fourth finger of the left hand (Aulus Gellius, *Noctes Atticae* 10.10) because a vein there led directly to the heart. For illustrations of the *dextrarum iunctio* (clasping of right hands) so frequently shown on marriage sarcophagi of the third century A.D., see Jenkins, *Greek and Roman Life*, 40, figs. 47–48 (a ring and a relief, both in the British Museum); Ryberg, "Rites," figs. 90–92 (sarcophagi); and A. M. McCann, *Roman Sarcophagi in the Metropolitan Museum of Art* (New York, 1978), 124–29, figs. 157–65.

# *Tunica Ralla, Tunica Spissa:* The Colors and Textiles of Roman Costume

## 4

JUDITH LYNN SEBESTA

Roman husbands must have listened wryly to one speech of the slave Epidicus in the eponymous Plautine comedy. In the course of describing to his master his son's new love, Epidicus lists the colors and textiles currently in hot demand by Roman women of fashion: "the close-knit tunic, the gauzy, the little sky blue linen caplet, the wrapped, the golden-banded, the marigold yellow, or the red-orange . . . the sea blue, the downy, the walnut brown, or the waxy yellow" (229–35). Two hundred years later, when advising women to wear colors most complimentary to their complexions, Ovid lists the colors currently available in Roman markets:

You need no woolen dress blushing with Tyrian dye. When there are so many cheaper colors, why madly spend all your income on your dress? There are dresses the color of the cloudless sky, when the south wind brings no showers, and the color similar to you, ram, who once, it is said, bore Phrixus and Helle away from Ino's plots. This dress imitates the waves and is named after them; I could willingly believe it covers the nymphs. This one imitates saffron . . . this one the myrtles of Paphnos, this purple amethyst, this white roses, that the Thracian pale gray crane; Amaryllis, you may walk in a dress of chestnut or almond, and wax has given its name to yellow fleece. (*Ars amatoria* 3.169–72)

Nor was the interest in new fabrics and colors entirely limited to women. P. Lentulus Spinther was the first to use the very expensive double-dyed purple *(purpura dibapha Tyria)* for the praetexta of his toga when curule aedile in 63 B.C.[1]

Though the style of Roman dress remained basically the same during the republic and early empire, clearly the Romans, men and women, were interested in varying the colors and textures of their clothing through dyes and different fabrics.[2] Such interest in dyes and fabrics reflected the basically hierarchial Roman society and the struggle to distinguish or to change social rank by the members of the higher and lower social orders. This interest also had socio-economic dimensions such as the establishment of various *collegia* of dyers, weavers, even patchworkers, and ultimately had an impact on the economic development and prosperity of provincial cities.

Tracing the social importance of dyes and fabrics and the trade in such materials draws upon archaeological and literary sources, which are unfortunately scanty for the earlier centuries. Consequently, this examination has been divided into four periods: regal, early and middle republic, late republic and Augustan, and early empire (to A.D. 200).

### REGAL PERIOD

During the regal period, the eighth to sixth centuries B.C., and indeed in all periods, the major fabric was wool. Doubtless many of the fleeces went undyed, and clothing color was varied only by the natural hues of the sheep such as *albus* (white), *niger* (very dark brown or black), and *coracinus* (deep black). A sheep from Canusium was *fuscus* in color; its brown wool had a reddish tinge. Cicero noted that this wool served in his time as the poor man's "purple," and it may in this period have served as purple for the poor and perhaps the rich as well. Wool from Pollentia, Tarentum, and Liguria was *pullus* in color, evidently a dark brown or brownish black that by the middle of the republic had become a color ritually associated with mourning and self-abasement. Wool of such colors, if not produced by the sheep around Rome and Latium, would be available through trade.[3]

Wool was made into felt long before it was spun and woven. Felt is made by beating, rolling, and pressing wool, or other animal hairs, into a compact material. The hair or wool fibers may be further securely matted by application of an alkaline liquid "glue." Warm and waterproof, felt made excellent hats and shoes.

While wool can be dyed—and the Romans preferred to dye the fleece rather than the cloth—linen was very difficult to color with the dyes available to the Romans. Instead, linen was worn mostly in its natural color, a grayish brown, or was bleached by long exposure to the sun to produce a whiter color.[4] Flax was cultivated in Italy during the prehistoric period, certainly by Etruscans, from whom the Romans purchased linen if they did not grow flax and produce linen themselves. Nevertheless, the use of other fibers from prehistory continued, such as nettle fiber, whose preparation is very similar to that of linen. Felt and fabric made from goat hair, too, were doubtless used in clothing where durable, coarse cloth was suitable, such as for cloaks, shoes, and slippers.[5]

According to tradition, the Romans knew of lamé cloth, at least during the late regal period. Tarquinius Priscus is said to have celebrated a triumph wearing a gold tunic. This tradition is not implausible, for in the Regolini-Galassi tomb (first half of the seventh century B.C.) there were found the remains of a woman's robe which had been heavily embroidered in gold. Likewise, a funerary urn found at Chianciano and dated to the seventh century B.C. or earlier contained fragments of a purple linen fabric mixed with bits of gold, the remains of a purple and gold chiton or shroud.[6]

More difficult is the determination of what dyes were used by the Romans during the regal period. The kings and rich citizens could probably afford Etruscan cloth and garments and any dyed cloth or dyes sold by the Etruscans or by other foreign merchants.[7] Purple dye and purple-dyed garments, according to Roman tradition, were used by Romulus, Tullus Hostilius, and other kings.[8] While the purple dye could have been brought from the eastern Mediterranean by Greek traders, another, somewhat closer source in the late regal period may have been Massilia and its environs, where the Greeks had established a trading center with the Celts in the sixth century B.C.[9]

Knowledge of other textile colors available to the Romans is limited. Etruscan tomb paintings show clothing in red, yellow, green, and blue, a range of colors limited more perhaps by the paints available to the artist than the dyer's dyes. It is reasonable to conjecture, however, that the Romans in this period used the dyes that were in use in prehistoric Europe. Blue hues were obtainable from woad, a plant introduced to northern Europe from the south, or from several species of berries and plants, indigenous to Italy and areas along the amber trade routes. The dwarf elder (Sambucus ebulus) produced a blue dye, and Pliny the Elder mentions the heliotrope (Heliotropium tricoccum), bilberry or whortleberry (Vaccinium myrtillus), and hyacinth (Hyacinthus orientalis) as other sources of blue dye. Yellow hues were obtained from the madder plant, which also yielded red by a different dye process, as its name, Rubia tinctorium, reveals. Red hues were also yielded by the weed called lamb's quarters (Chenopodium album) and dye bedstrow (Gallium palustre), and again through variations in the dyeing process, these plants yielded hues of yellow as well. Other sources of yellow were the centaury (Serratula tinctoria) and weld plant (Reseda luteola); the latter yielded the yellow-red hue luteus which became the ritual color of the bride's veil by the late republic. Purple dye sources included the bilberry, Vaccinium myrtillus; one wonders if cloth dyed with this vegetable dye, rather than imported purple dyed cloth, was employed by the Roman kings in imitation of Etruscan nobles. Black could be obtained from a dye of iron salts, with tannic acid from oak galls serving as the mordant, though this process reduced the strength of the textile fibers.[10] Doubtless other dyes were used, and more hues may have been made by double-dyeing wool in vats of different colors, such as green from wool dyed with madder and bilberry.[11]

Roman tradition ascribed to Numa the organization of the first college of dyers.[12] If indeed such an organization can be credited to the regal period, it reflects a growing demand for dyed clothes and for the dyes themselves. Such a demand would be handled more efficiently by a collegium than by an individual household, as dyeing on a large scale requires not only a supply of dye sources but also space and an ample supply of water and fuel. Doubtless, also, households were glad to get rid of the obnoxious smells coming from the dyeing process.

### EARLY AND MIDDLE REPUBLIC

The list of women's clothing fashions rattled off by Epidicus shows that, in a sense, a fashion industry had developed around the Roman woman by the middle republic. She could choose a linen or woolen loose-woven, gauzy tunic (ralla) or one closely woven (spissa).[13] She could further vary her wardrobe through a range of colors: caltulus (marigold yellow), crocotulus (reddish orange), carinus (walnut brown), cerinus (brownish yellow), cumatilis (sea blue), caesicius (sky blue). The other terms Epidicus lists seem to refer more to style than to color: indusiatus (undertunic), subparum (linen shift), subnimium (slip?), basilicum (royal), *exoticum* (foreign). The tunica patagiata had its neckline adorned by a gold band (patagium).[14] The *plumatilis* tunic may have had a soft pilelike down (plumeus), created by teasing the woolen fibers, or it may have been a forerunner of the tapestry cloth called *plumata* of late antiquity.[15] Nor does Epidicus' list exhaust the possible colors and styles. Elsewhere Plautus mentions the *flammarii* and the *molocinarii,* dyers of reddish orange and mauve, respectively.[16]

The *violarii,* also mentioned by Plautus, were dyers of a violet hue of purple, receiving their dyestuffs from the East, especially Tyre. Such a hue was required for the clavi of the Roman male tunics, the borders of the children's togae praetextae, and the borders for magistrates as well. Presumably it was the hue of the limbus, the purple band sewn on the hem of a woman's tunic. In addition, the increase in wealth among the senators and equites and their exposure to the use of purple in Greece and the East led to a greater demand for this hue, especially in the second century.[17] At least one noble family, the Furii Purpureones, had a cognomen indicating that a good percentage of its wealth was derived from the purple trade. And one wonders if Juba smiled cynically to see the Roman nobles he castigated as venal buying purple manufactured at the purple dye works he established at Mogador off the coast of Africa.[18]

Another luxury dye color was that called *puniceus, phoenicius,* or *poenicius.* A brilliant scarlet, it was derived from the whelk (*Buccinum undatum*) which lived in the sea around Tyre and along the Phoenician coast.[19] A cheaper equivalent of this hue was *ferrugineus,* the purplish color of the hyacinth. Plautus' Palaestrio disguises his master, Pleusicles, as a shipmaster wearing a hat and short cloak of this color.[20]

Plautus' list of colors in *Epidicus* indicates that the dyers of Rome were able to produce varied hues through different preparations and mordants or—though the two are not mutually exclusive—that the Romans carried on a dye and fabric trade with countries whose dyers were so adept. The shops of the fora displayed bolts of dyed fabric, and ready-made clothing was sold there by the *vestiarii,* dealers in ready-made clothing. Used clothing was sold to a special group of clothing dealers, the *centonarii,* or patchworkers, who pieced together cloaks and quilts for slaves from cast-off tunics and togas. By the late republic the *centonarii* had formed a college; probably every town had at least one "patcher," and it is likely that much of the slaves' clothing was increasingly bought at the market, in addition to that made "in spare moments" at home.[21]

The growth of the *latifundia* after the Second Punic War facilitated the breeding of sheep for improved wool, for only such estates had flocks large enough for selective breeding and the capital assets for supporting the long-term returns inherent in breeding ventures. By the first century B.C., strains of sheep naturally lacking pigmented fleece had been bred to produce pure white fleece, the most suitable for dyeing.[22] To protect this highly prized wool, whether white or colored, the Romans practiced "jacketing" their sheep. Jacketed sheep (*oves tectae*) wore woven wraps over their bodies to protect the long fibers of their wool from brambles they primarily fed upon, as well as from weather, seeds, and dirt. These impurities, along with the sweat of the sheep's own bodies, could constitute as much as half of the weight of the sheared fleece. Pliny recommended Arabian wool for the best jackets.[23]

Italian centers of fine wool production lay primarily in the south, including Luceria in Apulia and Brundisium and Tarentum in Calabria. Wool from the latter was so fine that it could be spun into diaphanous material, and Tarentine rams were used in breeding programs around the growing empire. Dark-colored wool (*pullus* and *fuscus*) was produced at Pollentia, tawny wool at Canusium.[24]

Through their involvement during the second century B.C. in the politics of Asian cities and monarchies, the Romans came upon the breed of Asian sheep with reddish (*erythraeus*) wool mentioned by Columella. Such contacts, and the Romans' increasing wealth, also enabled them to purchase linen from Egypt in increasing quantity. Egyptian linen was a luxury good; when Rabirius was appointed financial supervisor of Ptolemy Auletes, he exported to Puteoli ships filled with Egyptian linen as well as Egyptian glassware.[25] Egyptian linen, well known for its quality in the Mediterranean, was far better than that made from Italian flax. Various regions of Italy, however, continued to grow flax and produce linen for sale well into imperial times. Such linen was in sufficient demand by Romans that its production had grown beyond home production to the large-scale manufacturing level, for Plautus mentions the *lintones* as an established group of tradesmen. By the end of the fourth century B.C. these *lintones* had learned how to whiten linen to a dazzling brightness by sulphuric fumes; Livy mentions the brilliant white tunics worn by the Samnites in 301 B.C. The Roman acquisition of Punic Spain and Sicily—the latter particularly had a well-developed fabric industry—provided additional sources of linen and other clothing; these two countries, along with Sardinia, supplied Roman troops with clothing in 203 B.C.[26]

A totally new fiber for Romans in this period was cotton, apparently first introduced to the eastern Mediterranean through the conquests of Alexander the Great. Though Herodotus was aware that cotton was produced in India (he thought it came from trees!), there is no indication of its use in Greece, at any rate not until the Macedonian conquests. As cotton was called *carbasus,* a word coming from Hebrew, it is reasonable to suppose that it was in use in the Persian Empire, which then encompassed Judaea. Since Macedonian soldiers first came across cotton, Strabo's comment that cotton was first used for pillows and saddle padding is not surprising.[27]

Though Caecilius Statius is the first to mention cotton, in his *Pausimachus* (ca. 190 B.C.), the Romans doubtless had begun its use earlier. Carbasus made a durable fabric, and as it dried quickly when wet, unlike wool, the Romans used it for theater awnings and curtains. Unlike linen, it was easy to dye, and the bright colors of the awnings and curtains must have delighted the crowds.[28] The Romans often wove cotton with linen to produce a material called *carbasus lina.* This mixture of fibers resulted in a material more pliant than pure linen, yet one which, when pressed, had a smooth, semilustrous surface. Cotton was also interwoven with wool to produce a lightweight, warm fabric.[29]

Eastern foreign policy also introduced the Romans to a new luxury fabric made in Pergamum. Though Pliny credits Attalus I with the invention of gold embroidery, it is more likely that Attalus I began the production of this embroidery on a large scale by setting up government-owned workshops. Because of his promotion of this exotic and costly material, it was called Attalic and appeared in Rome sometime after 189 B.C. The vogue for this material and for other items embroidered in gold really began, however, as a result of Attalus II's bequeathal of his kingdom to Rome in 132 B.C., which sent to Rome not only his personal gold-embroidered clothing but also tapestries embroidered in golden thread.[30]

LATE REPUBLIC AND AUGUSTAN ROME

The last century of the republic saw an even greater sophistication in the use of clothing, dyes, and luxury fabrics for social display. The traditional toga was changed under Augustus from a rough-textured garment into one with a smooth, even finish, the toga rasa, by alternately teasing the woolen nap with hedgehog bristles or thistles and then clipping it closely with shears.[31] During this time, the first century B.C., the continuing expansion of the empire brought Romans into contact with new sources of dye and gave them the means to obtain them. New dye hues transformed any fabric into a luxury item.

Ovid advised Roman women to develop sophisticated taste in selecting those colors most complimentary to their complexions rather than vulgarly emphasizing

their wealth by wearing without discrimination only dresses dyed with expensive *purpura dibapha Tyria.* Those of dark complexion should wear white *(albus),* those of light complexion dark gray *(pullus).*[32] In addition to these, he proposes for women's consideration several other hues: two blues, three yellows, one each of green and purple, two browns, one light gray, and (perhaps) one light pink.[33]

The two blues are described as being like the air *(aer)* and the waves *(undae).* Ovid defines the first as the blue of a cloudless sky, presumably a light blue color.[34] The color similar to the waves may be identical to Plautus' *cumatilis,* a sea blue.[35]

The three yellows include a color similar to the Golden Fleece, *aureus.*[36] The second, *croceus,* obtained from saffron *(Croceus sativus),* was a red-orange or yellow with orange overtones. Ovid calls it the color of Eos' garments.[37] The third yellow, *cereus,* was the color of unrefined wax, a strong brownish yellow. Perhaps it is to be identified with *cerinus,* mentioned by Plautus.[38]

The color like Paphian myrtle trees *(Paphiae myrti)* that Ovid mentions was most likely a dark green. Ovid elsewhere calls the myrtle *nigra,* though *paphias* may indicate a particular shade of myrtle green, rather than being solely a poetic "love" reference.[39] Ovid's color like purple amethysts *(purpureae amethysti)* was later called *amethystina* or *amethystina purpurea* by Pliny and, like the precious stone, was a violet color.[40]

It is more difficult to identify Ovid's *albentes rosae. Albens* denotes a very light gray; it frequently modifies things not a pure white, such as bones and poplars. While Ovid possibly has in mind here a rose of a grayish white color, he may also mean a rose color that is particularly pale.[41] Ovid contrasts this color to one like the Thracian crane *(Threicia grus).* Presumably Ovid is referring to the common European crane, which is gray in color.

Ovid names two brown hues. One is the color of *glandes* (chestnuts), a dark brown with red undertones. The second is the color of *amygdala* (almonds), a very light tan color. By no means has Ovid exhausted the color possibilities open to women; he notes that there are as many hues available to his readers as there are colors of spring's flowers—and more.[42]

While some of Ovid's colors may have been used as far back as Plautus, the blues produced by indigo were apparently new in the late republic. Indigo *(indicum)* was known to Vitruvius, and its import is likely to have begun under Augustus, for Pliny says that indigo had begun to be imported "not long ago" at a cost of seven denarii a pound. That it was made from a plant was apparently unknown to him, for at first he believed it was made from foam on reeds or a black scum which stuck to copper dye pans. Later, having acquired more definite knowledge, he describes it as a white powder; it now cost twenty denarii a pound.[43] Indigo was extracted as a colorless soluble from the leaves of the indigo plant *Indigofera tinctoria*, which, when fermented, becomes an insoluble indigo. Vitruvius, however, regarded indigo as a mineral, probably because it was exported from India in dried chunk or brick form. When mixed with water, Pliny notes, indigo produced a marvelous mixture of purple and blue.[44]

Despite its association with Eastern kings and despots, purple as a status color remained in great demand, resulting in the introduction of several new hues.[45] According to Vitruvius, the color purple had four basic hues: dark, pale, blue, and red *(ater, lividus, violaceus, ruber)*.[46] All of these were made from a dye liquid produced by crushing the marine gastropod *Murex conchylium* with iron rods and further pulverizing the shards in a mortar. The liquid, *ostrum*, was exported mixed with honey as a preservative.[47] The basic reddish hue of this liquid was frequently called *ostrinum, ostrum rubens, ostrum sanguineum,* or *ostrum puniceum.* It was used as a dye for clothes and coverlets.[48]

Cornelius Nepos relates that *violaceus*, a violet hue of purple, came into use during his youth when it sold at one hundred denarii a pound. After this, he says, the hue *ruber Tarentinus* came into vogue, followed later by the *purpura dibapha Tyria*, which then cost more than a thousand denarii a pound. As P. Lentulus Spinther first used this double-dyed Tyrian purple in his toga praetexta when curule aedile, its introduction can be dated to 63 B.C. *Purpura dibapha Tyria* (twice-dyed Tyrian purple) was made by dipping wool first into a bath of the *ostrum* produced by the *Murex pelagium;* this dyed the wool a green color *(viridis)*. Then the wool was immersed in a vat of *ostrum* from another species of gastropod, the *Murex bucinum.* The overlay of purple on green produced a color Pliny likens to that of congealed blood, black but gleaming, the *purpureus sanguis* of Homer, he adds. During the last years of the republic and the early years of the principate, *purpura dibapha Tyria* was extremely costly, a *magnificum impendium,* according to Pliny.[49]

*Conchyliatus* is first mentioned by Cicero, Catullus, and Lucretius, suggesting that it too was introduced at this time. To make this hue dyers diluted the juice of the *Murex pelagium* with water and human urine in equal quantities, using a lesser amount of the juice than in producing the hue *purpura dibapha Tyria.* Pliny adds that the pale lavender of *conchyliatus* was much admired.[50]

A possible hue of purple, *thalassinus,* seems to have been introduced at this time, but its hue is disputed,

some authorities leaning toward a clear blue, others toward a sea green. This hue is mentioned only by Lucretius in a passage which implies that it is particularly costly, however, and so it is most likely a hue of purple.[51]

Another variant hue of purple was *hysginum;* this word also denoted the dye producing this hue. This unusual purple dye was made from the female of a parasitic scale insect *(Kermococcus vermilio)* infesting a small oak bush, *Quercus coccifera,* native to the Near East. The female insect retained her eggs in her body; these developing young actually yielded the coloring agent. Just before they hatched, the female insects were collected; by now reduced to egg sacks, they resembled berries *(cocci)* clinging to the bushes and were thought to be such fruit by Pliny. The egg sacks were killed by exposure to vinegar, left to dry, and exported in the form of cakes or granules.

*Coccinus* or *coccineus* was the unadulterated brilliant scarlet hue produced by this insect. It is first mentioned by Horace and the author of the *Ciris;* by Pliny's time it was a hue particularly reserved for the paludamenta of generals. The production of *hysginum* is vaguely described by Pliny; he says only that the fabric was first dyed with the crushed, liquified egg sacks and then dyed a second time with a mixture of mineral mordants and Tyrian dye. The resulting *hysginum* was a red-purple hue.[52] As only the female scale insect produced these dyes and thousands of them were necessary to yield an ounce, *coccinus* and *hysginum* were expensive hues.

Roman interest in conspicuous expenditure as a sign of rank and wealth was expressed not only by the use of new dyes and combinations of dyes but also by the use of new fibers, such as silk. A wild silkworm supplied the material of the infamous *vestes Coae,* produced in the third century B.C., but only in the late republic do we find Propertius, Horace, Tibullus, and Ovid referring to *bombycina, serica,* and *metaxa,* all terms for silk.[53] At this time the Romans obtained silk from Cos and Assyria and from China through the Hellenistic East. Use of silk was not limited to women. Men also wore it at dinner parties and in the summer, notwithstanding Tiberius' law condemning it as effeminate apparel.[54]

Egypt also supplied luxury textiles for the Roman market. These were sold during the reign of Augustus at the Horrea Agrippiana just south of the Forum between the Vicus Tuscus and the Clivus Victoriae. In addition to the fine Egyptian linens from the different nomes, each with its distinctive weave, the stalls displayed the prized *lodex,* a Laodicean weave copied from that produced at Arsinoe, and Alexandrian *polymita,* a damask woven out of a great number of threads.[55]

Not too far away from these *horrea,* alongside the

Tiber docks, were dealers in slaves' and workmen's clothing. In addition to the patchwork produced by the *centonarii,* brown wool from Canusium in Apulia could be bought there for slaves' garments, while workmen or their wives bargained over the triple twill fabric imported from Gaul. This particularly thickly woven cloth was so tough that it could be cut only with a saw, according to Martial.[56] There, too, could be bought warm and waterproof cloaks, made of felt, which began to appear toward the end of the first century B.C. These garments, called *gausapae,* were particularly useful in the harsher climes as the Romans advanced northward into Europe.[57]

Nonetheless, wool remained the main source for fabrics, and the *latifundia* owners in Italy and the provinces continued to direct their efforts into breeding sheep with finer, or whiter, or unusually colored wool. While viewing the games at Gades in Spain, the elder Columella was struck by the unusual colors of wild rams imported from Africa for one of the beast hunts. By breeding them and their progeny with domesticated ewes, including those of Tarentum, particularly prized for their fine wool, he was able to produce a strain of exotically colored sheep.[58]

Breeding practices improved the sheep of northern Italy to such an extent that their wool came to be preferred to that of sheep from southern Italy. White wool produced in the Po Valley, around Padua, Parma, Mutina, Altinum, and in the Timavus River valley, was so fine that these areas grew to be the main centers of Italian wool production. Slaves working in factories provided a steady flow of woven cloth. Comments of Columella and other authors comparing weaves and durabilities of the cloth suggest that these factories established standards of production.[59]

These factories and the imported fabrics mentioned earlier contributed to the decline, so lamented by Augustus, of the time-honored custom of the wife and daughters of a household weaving its clothing. Shops in Rome and other towns sold ready-made clothing for both master and slave. Though Columella assumes that the sheep of the *latifundia* would provide wool for the female slaves to spin and weave in their spare time, he comments that, though homespun is just right for stewards and the higher class of slaves to wear, it is too good for slaves and not good enough for their masters.[60]

The second most important fabric, linen, was increasingly imported from various provinces. The linen of Syracuse was particularly fine, and Verres derived much of his wealth from the weaving and dyeing industry of Syracuse and the rest of Sicily.[61] Even the Gallic tribes of the Cadurci had produced linen for export long before Caesar's conquest.[62]

The Romans did not limit the use of linen to clothing. Interwoven with cotton, it inspired conspicuous consumption in the form of brightly dyed sails and awnings. Such "backdrops" can be considered analogous to clothing in presenting a public persona. Q. Catulus first used such awnings to create a dramatic backdrop when he dedicated the new Capitolium in 69 B.C. Caesar stretched awnings—made with Gallic linen, perhaps?—from his mansion over the Forum and Via Sacra right up to the Capitol.[63] Other uses of linen for "show" included the production of napkins for that important Roman custom of the banquet. Catullus received a gift of napkins made from Spanish Saetaban linen, reputed the best linen in Europe. So prized were these napkins that they were stolen from him by an ungrateful dinner guest![64]

### EARLY EMPIRE

The fuller documentation for the first to third centuries A.D. clearly reveals the use of color and fabric for social status symbols and covert social weapons by the aristocracy and social climbers. More luxury colors were introduced, and the range of shades of earlier luxury hues increased, reflecting the unending contest of social one-upmanship. Literary evidence also identifies some hues as definitely vulgar, proving indeed that clothes made the man.

An interesting variation of the social contest in clothing is shown by the restriction of hues of purple to the emperor and his family by Caligula and Nero, though breaches of this interdiction occurred.[65] The emperor also emphasized his status through fabric. The imperial wardrobe included garments of silk interwoven with gold thread, cloth-of-gold, and bejeweled cloth, fabric out of the purse range of even the very rich.[66] This imperial interest in using clothing as a display of status is a precursor of the use of jewelry as imperial insignia during the later empire.

The vulgar rich favored hues of startling color such as the newly introduced *cerasinus, prasinus* or *prasinatus,* and *galbinus,* not only because they were expensive dyes but also because they were new. *Galbinus* was a hue of yellow, apparently a rather sickly hue, as Pliny likened it to the oriole called *galgulus,* whose pale yellow plumage had a green tinge. Deriving its name from the Greek word for pea, *prasinus* was a very strong green with blue overtones, which became the uniform color of the Greens, a circus faction.[67] Cherry trees *(cerasia)* were first imported in 74 B.C. from the area of the Pontus by Lucullus, whose interest in cuisine led him to appreciate this delightful fruit. *Cerasinus* doubtless denoted a bright red and appears to have been a favorite color of Fortunata in the *Satyricon.*

Two other, less expensive color favorites were *russus* (*russeus, russatus*) and *venetus*. *Russus, russeus*, and *russatus* denote a fairly bright red. First used for *vela* in the theater during the late republic, this bright red became a favorite color, along with the more costly *cerasinus*, for those of vulgar taste such as Trimalchio and Fotis. *Russeus* and the dark blue *venetus* were also the colors of circus factions.[68]

As political offices lost their traditional prestige during the early empire, becoming imperial patronage appointments, the aristocracy sought new ways of showing their status through clothing, either by conspicuously disdaining "status dressing" like the Stoics or by demanding, as Pliny notes, that dyes challenge the flowers.

The shades of purple were increased during the first century A.D. Purple, in order to remain a status color, had to evolve new hues, for as its older hues became more common, they lost some status. Pliny comments that *purpura dibapha Tyria* was then being used to cover dining couches! He lists *purpura Tyria, purpura dibapha*, and *purpura laconica*, increasingly darker shades of rose purple. In the violet range he names *amethystinus* and *ianthinus*, the latter named from the Greek word for the violet. Other new purple shades made from murex dyes included that of the heliotrope (*heliotropium*), presumably a reddish blue-red, sometimes light, more often deeper in tint; that of the mallow (*malva*), a bluish blue-red; that of the late-blooming violet (*viola serotina*), which Pliny describes as the strongest of these hues; and the reddish violet hue *hyacinthinus*, first mentioned by Persius. Lastly, *Tyrianthina* is the color of Martial's *urbica* (*vestis*). André identifies this hue with the purple color produced by dyeing cloth first in *ianthinus* and then in *purpura Tyria* to produce a violet purple.[69]

*Coccinus*, the brilliant scarlet made from the kermes or scale insect, was in such demand as a luxury dye that, in addition to the Asian production, a large kermes dye industry developed in Spain. The dye produced from the kermes living on the holm oaks around Emerita in Lusitania was particularly prized for its color and served as a cash crop for the poor; Pliny estimates that the average Spaniard was able to pay at least one out of every two tribute installments by collecting the insects. In addition to the kermes industry in Galatia, Cilicia, Pisidia, and Spain, kermes production centers also existed in Gaul, Africa, and Sardinia, the latter producing the poorest quality dye.[70]

The demand for these luxury hues was so great that it led to the creation of counterfeit dyes. Gallic *tinctoria*, for example, were able to replicate through vegetable dyes the hues *purpura Tyria* and *conchyliatus* as well as all other colors, Pliny notes. One of these counterfeit methods is actually illustrated by dyed, unspun wool found in the Bar Kokhba caves, on which indigo and kermes were used to replicate *purpura Tyria*. Another counterfeiting process used madder and indigo, and papyri give many more dyers' formulas for counterfeit dyes.[71]

One last status hue was *callainus*, whose name was formed from the Greek word for turquoise. Pliny's comments on the turquoise gem suggest that this hue shaded toward the green rather than toward the blue. *Callainus* was an esteemed luxury hue; a silk dress dyed *purpurea et callaina* was given to Isis at her shrine in Nemi.[72]

Despite Tiberius' condemnation of silk as effeminate, this lustrous material continued to be in great demand during the early empire. Most of it was imported from China through northern India, in addition to cotton and other kinds of cloth, though India produced its own wild silk which was dark brown. The demand for silk and other exotic items such as spices led to the discovery under Claudius of the direct trade route around Arabia by the trader Hippolis. To facilitate the Indian trade, Trajan cleaned out the Nile–Red Sea canal, and Hadrian built a new road around the Red Sea. The frontier policy of Rome from Augustus to Trajan was directed, in large part, by the desire to circumvent Parthia and gain direct control of raw silk, silk yarn, and garments from China.[73]

Nonetheless, silk remained so expensive that the silk merchants of Rome and other towns primarily sold it in the form of thread which was interwoven with other kinds of thread. These *serica* or *subserica* (silk mixture) garments still were costly enough; Marcus Aurelius included his *serica* garments, along with those made with gold thread (*aurata*) when he auctioned off his imperial wardrobe at Trajan's market to pay for his Marcomannic wars. According to tradition Heliogabalus was the first to wear a pure silk (*holoserica*) garment. Even for an emperor, such a garment was horrendously expensive: a similar garment owned by Aurelian was valued at its own weight in gold.[74] Though the Romans wove much of this imported silk themselves, some weaving was also done in Persia, and then the product was sold to Roman merchants. Egypt, with its interest in producing luxury materials, produced a considerable quantity of silk-linen cloth, often further adorning it with woven bands, squares, or panels depicting Bacchus, fauns, maenads, and other mythological figures, to decorate tunics and mantles.[75]

Silk did not become the sole fabric of social display; the donation recorded at Nemi included a purple linen tunic with gold clavi.[76] Gold-embroidered Attalic cloth remained part of the luxury wardrobe as well. Agrippina the Younger, empress of Claudius, once wore a military cloak made entirely of gold while watching a mock naval battle. Hadrian received a gold-embroidered chlamys as a gift. Herod Agrippa owned an only slightly less flashy mantle made of silver. Less wealthy people contented themselves with a mixture of gold and other thread. A graffito in the *officina coactiliaria* of the felter M. Vecilius Verecundus of Pompeii mentions a *tunica lintea aurata*. Jewels were also sewn on garments. Caligula wore a paenula heavily embroidered and accented by jewels, and Nero bestowed a dress covered with jewels on his mother.[77]

For the only moderately rich, somewhat less costly fabrics of social display available at Roman shops throughout the empire included embroideries and cotton textiles woven in a checked pattern from Babylon; fine muslin cloth made of mallow fiber from India for Roman banquet dress, which was perhaps belted by a damask girdle, one cubit wide, also from India; and painted muslins and painted cloth from Egypt.[78] Egypt also produced cloth varied by resist dyeing. Gaul also produced checkered cloth, though Pliny does not say whether it was made of wool or linen.[79]

The Gallic woolen industry benefited from the Roman conquest. Prior to Caesar the Gauls wove the rough, long hair of their sheep in its natural colors, but under Roman rule demand for fine products improved the quality of the wool and facilitated the growth of extensive dye and weaving industries. The sheep of the Belgae, in particular, had a fine reputation for their wool. From the lands of the Cadurci, Caleti, Ruteni, Bituriges, Morini, and Treveri came woven goods of such quality that they were sold around the empire, making such inroads on trade that, in an attempt to regain some of the market they had lost to the northern Gauls, the weavers of Asia Minor began to make imitation Nervian cloaks![80]

The effect of the demand for woolens under Roman occupation proved a mixed blessing for Britain. In Silchester, and probably other cities as well, the dyeing industry came to be a dominant economic factor. The hill country of Britain proved to be excellent pasturage for sheep, as it did many centuries later, and the imperial house established weaving mills to encourage the expansion of wool production, resulting in the growth of *latifundia* and depopulation in the "sheep country."[81]

Two new woolen garments were the cilicium and the amphimallium. Augustus' weak constitution led him to wear in winter, in addition to his woolen toga, a woolen "undershirt," four tunics, and leggings. Perhaps it was he who personally began the curious new fiber import in the form of the cilicium, an especially warm cloak made of the hair of the goats which abounded in the hills of Cilicia. In addition, their hair was made into socks and leggings—doubtless appreciated by the emperor![82] He

would have liked the new felt cloak, the gausapa, which appeared in the mid–first century A.D. Pliny comments that "cloaks that are shaggy on both sides (amphimallia) have recently come into use, along with villous stomach belts, and a *tunica lati clavi* is now for the first time being woven in the style of a gausapa." This fashion interest in rough texture is an aspect of the increasing influence the clothing of conquered nations and tribes of Europe had on Roman dress. Other garments borrowed from the Gauls at this time, or earlier, include the cucullus and bardocucullus, cloaks for cold, windy days. The latter, a shaggy garment, was waterproofed by the natural oil of the wool.[83]

The growth in the use of linen, begun in the late republic, continued. Linen materials of various qualities were now imported from a number of areas around the Mediterranean, in addition to the linen supplied from Italian districts. Pliny rates the flax of Spanish Saetabis as prime in all Europe, followed by that produced by the Italian town of Retovium near the Alia and Faenza. Though the former was not bleached, it was fine in texture and had no nap, which pleased some customers, but, Pliny comments, not all. The thread of the flax produced by Retovium was of uniform quality and tough; if you tested it with your teeth, it would produce a twang, Pliny says. For this reason it cost twice as much as other linen. Linens of Faenza were preferred for their whiteness. Other linens produced in the area around the Alia were used unbleached and rated third best in Europe. The linen workers in this area processed much of the flax in caves, where, it was thought, the humidity improved the quality of the fabric. Other areas of Italy producing flax included Latium, Falerii, and Paelignium. The linen produced in these areas was used only after being fulled to a brilliant whiteness, and in texture it closely resembled wool.[84]

Next in quality was the linen of *Hispania citerior*. That produced by Tarragon was the best, due to the quality of the water used for retting the flax. Local towns were very keen to maintain the quality of their linen manufactures and held contests for the women in weaving and cloth-making.[85]

Gaul also produced linen, and from there its manufacture had spread across the Rhine by the mid–first century A.D. Centers of linen production were in the areas of the Cadurci, Caleti, Ruteni, Bituriges, and Morini, and Pliny adds that the Gallic women now preferred linen dresses to wool.[86]

Other areas from which Rome imported linen included the Phasis Valley and Elis; the latter's flax was as fine as Judaean but not as yellow in color. It was woven at Sparta and Patrae into linen.[87] Egyptian linen, however, continued to enjoy its good reputation, though

Pliny comments that it was not very durable. The Egyptians exported four kinds, named for the four districts in which they were produced: Tanitic, Pelusiac, Butic, and Tentyritic. These linens were exported not only westward but also to Arabia and India in exchange for their materials.[88] Yet gradually the linen of Cilicia and Syria supplanted Egyptian linen. The sandy plain around Damascus was especially suited for flax growing, and the flax plantations in the area of Berytus were famous throughout the East. Linen weaving was a major industry in Galilee, Laodicea, Sidon, Byblos, Tyre, and in Scythopolis, where in the late empire an imperial weaving house was established.[89]

The development of the Roman fabric, dye, and clothing industries shows that the use of clothing and adornment for status display, so well known in late antiquity, was already present in early Rome. The paucity of information for the early periods limits our understanding of the economic impact these industries had on the social development of early republican Rome, but the extent of their economic importance in the late republic and early empire is easier to assess. What is most interesting, perhaps, is the development of the dye and fabric trade, a trade greatly fostered by the imposition of a unified government, into an important source of income for several provinces. The local importance the dye and fabric industry could have is illustrated by Babylon, where the commercial importance of linen was so great that whenever the price of linen fell 40 percent or more, the shofar (ram's horn) was blown, and citizens uttered prayers![90]

Other benefits besides provincial income included the improvement of breeds of sheep, as in Spain and Italy, and the creation of new industries, such as large-scale weaving in northern Gaul. Yet the empire-fostered trade could have negative effects, too, on a long-established industry which relaxed its standards or used inferior raw material, as, for example, in the displacement of the weaves of Asia Minor by the cloaks made by the Nervii of Gaul.

## ROMAN DYES AND MORDANTS

Attempts to reproduce the colors of Roman dyes can yield only approximate results for several reasons. First, we have scanty knowledge about how the dyes were prepared, for both the techniques and the dyes used were trade secrets, handed down from father to son. The increased demand for dyed stuffs in Hellenistic times, however, resulted in experiments to produce good colors with less costly dyes; in these experiments lie the beginnings of chemistry. The Egyptian dyers in particular conducted such experiments, and their new processes were recorded by Bolos of Mendes in his treatise on dyeing,

the *Baphika*, in the second century B.C. His work was a major source for Pliny the Elder.

Second, even dyers who followed such recipes exactly would obtain different results each time due to inexactness of measurements, whether of dyestuffs used, of time, or of temperature of the dye solutions. Additional variations of color resulted from the natural impurities in the dyestuffs or in the fabric fibers. Indeed, textile fibers themselves react differently to the same dye because of their chemical compositions. Vegetal fibers contain only carbon, hydrogen, and oxygen, while animal fibers also contain nitrogen and sulphur, which can cause problems in dyeing. Because wool is hydroscopic, it takes up dye very readily; yet impurities such as dirt and oil in the wool affect its ability to absorb water, resulting in uneven dyeing of fibers. The strength of a dyestuff obtained from vegetable matter may vary according to the season in which it is harvested or to its physical state; fresh madder may be twice as potent as madder in dried root form. Geographic distribution can affect the potency of a dyestuff; Indian indigo gives better color results than does indigo from Central America.[91]

Color fastness varied, too. *Fastness* means that the coloring matter and fibers are permanently united. This union should not be disturbed (and the color changed) by washing, perspiration, rubbing, fulling, or exposure to light. It is possible, however, for a color to be fast for washing but not when exposed to light. Four ways of dyeing fibers were used in antiquity: direct dyeing, dyeing with reduced color solutions, mordanting, and resist dyeing.

Direct dyeing was used most often with animal fibers. When mixed with water, a basic dyestuff would combine with the wool to form a lake (colored salt) on the fiber. In dyeing wool with true purple, the dyer would pretreat the wool with an extract of soapwort (*Saponaria officinalis*) to ground the color and to give the wool a brighter hue.

Fibers could also be dyed with reduced color solutions through vat dyeing. For example, fibers would be dyed with indigo that had fermented in vats. Deeper shades were obtained by repeatedly soaking the fibers in the vat, vegetable fibers for a few minutes at a time, wool fibers for an hour or more each time. Depending upon the dyestuff used and the fiber to be dyed, the vats would have to be heated to various temperatures.

Mordants in antiquity were usually employed before actual dyeing; rarely were mordant and dye combined to form a lake. The mordant adheres to the fibers and fixes the dye color on the fiber while it soaks in the dye vat. Various mordants were used, including urine, natron, and potash. Pliny distinguishes between white alum, which was used for bright colors, and black alum, which was used for more somber colors. The former presumably was a potash alum, the latter an alum with other metal ions.[92] Alum was used in preparing wool for dyeing it *hysginum;* other dyestuffs used with mordants included madder, kermes, saffron, archil, weld, and indigo.

In resist dyeing, the dyers applied different mordants or mordants of different strengths to the cloth, making a pattern, and then dipped the cloth into a vat of a single color. The chemical action of the mordants resulted in the dye's producing different tints or even hues on the cloth.

Despite the care taken by dyers, dyeing remained a process which produced colored goods of unpredictable fastness. Direct-dyed goods were particularly subject to fading when washed, but the bright Mediterranean sun or the harsh cleaning of woolen fabrics with urine affected the dyed garment. It was not uncommon for a customer to request a fulling establishment *(fullonica)* to recolor a cleaned garment, though there were those who specialized in redyeing faded clothing *(offectores).*[93]

## NOTES

1. Pliny the Elder, *H.N.* 9.137.
2. For an example of a stola made from a very crinkly material, see the Flavian statue of a woman in the Museo Nazionale Archeologio, Naples, inv. 4320.
3. Pliny the Elder, *H.N.* 31.14; Columella 7.2.4; Cicero, *Pro Sestio* 8.19. I was unable to include information from Barber's *Prehistoric Textiles* in this chapter.
4. J. R. Forbes, *Studies in Ancient Technology,* 6 vols. (Leiden, 1955–60): 4: 94.
5. Barber, "PIE Notion," 295; Forbes, *Ancient Technology* 4: 62. Examples of textiles found in Mesopotamia dating from the third century B.C. to the third century A.D. demonstrate the combinations of fibers employed by weavers which were also possible for Roman weavers, viz. flax or hemp and wool, and rush and wool; see H. Fujii, "Some Roman Textiles from At-Tar Caves in Mesopotamia," *Mesopotamia* 27 (1987): 219.
6. Pliny the Elder, *H.N.* 33.62–63. On the Regolini-Galassi tomb and lamé in antiquity, see G. P. Shams, *Some Minor Textiles in Antiquity* (Göteborg, 1987), 12, 14. On the Chianciano urn, see Bonfante, *Etruscan Dress,* 11.
7. Important dyeing centers during the Etruscan period were Populonia and Vetulonia; see F. Brunello, *The Art of Dyeing in the History of Mankind* (Vicenza, 1973), 104.
8. Pliny the Elder, *H.N.* 9.136.
9. The Celts exported, in the sixth century B.C., textiles, leather, and furs; see P. S. Wells, *Culture Contact and Culture Change: Early Iron Age Europe and the Mediterranean World* (Cambridge, Eng., 1980), 64. According to F. Benoît, "Recherches sur l'hellénisation du Midi de la Gaule," *Annales de la Faculté des Lettres, Aix-en-Provence,* n.s., 43 (1965): 195–211, purple dye was manufactured at Massilia.

10. Black was also obtained by successively dyeing fibers the primary colors. When this process was discovered in antiquity is unknown, but it is illustrated by the Bar Kokhba textiles; see Y. Yadin, *The Finds from the Bar Kokhba Period in the Cave of Letters* (Jerusalem, 1963), 278–79.
11. Forbes, *Ancient Technology* 4: 112, 99, 124. A secondary color such as green could be produced by weaving yellow and blue fibers together. This process is not mentioned in any ancient source, however, nor is it illustrated by the Bar Kokhba textiles; see Yadin, *Finds from the Bar Kokhba Period,* 271–72.
12. Plutarch, *Numa* 17.
13. On the different weaves illustrated by the Bar Kokhba textiles, see Yadin, *Finds from the Bar Kokhba Period,* 188–94. These garments illustrate the tapestry weave, the main weave employed in making woolen textiles; the rep or ribbed tabby, mainly used for linens; and the American tabby, also used primarily for linens. Variations on the way the weft is shot through the warp threads affect the texture and durability of the material.
14. Festus M221; Nonius 540.6.
15. On *vestes plumatae* known in late antiquity, see Marquardt, *Privatleben,* 538–39, who identifies them with the *polymita* damask of Alexandria. The term is applied to intricate tapestry work because it is as multicolored as the plumage of birds; cf. Prudentius, *Hamartigenia* 294, and Adhelmus 15. The term *plumatus,* however, may have changed its designation between ca. 200 B.C. and A.D. 300. Wilson, *Clothing,* 154, suggests decoration with feathers.
16. On *flammarii,* see Plautus, *Aulularia* 510; André, *Termes de Couleur,* 115–16. On *molocinarii,* see Plautus, *Aulularia* 514; André, 198.
17. On purple as a status color in the republic, see M. Reinhold, "History of Purple as a Status Symbol in Antiquity," *Latomus* 116 (1970): 37–47.
18. Pliny the Elder, *H.N.* 6.201.
19. Plautus, *Mostellaria* 310; Pliny the Elder, *H.N.* 9.134; André, *Termes de Couleur,* 88–90.
20. Plautus, *Miles Gloriosus* 1178–79; André, *Termes de Couleur,* 105–11.
21. On *vestiarii,* see Plautus, *Aulularia* 508–16; Forbes, *Ancient Technology* 4: 233. On homespun slaves' clothes, see Columella 12 *praef.* 9–10, 12.3.6. Cato, 57, recommends that a tunic and a sagum be given to a slave every other year; the old clothing was to be made into patchwork. He further suggests that each slave be given a pair of wooden shoes every other year.
22. Varro, *De re rustica* 2.2.4; Columella 7.2.5. See also J. M. Frayn, *Sheep-Rearing and the Wool Trade in Italy during the Roman Period,* ARCA 15 (Liverpool, 1984).
23. Pliny the Elder, *H.N.* 8.190. Varro *De re rustica* 2.2.18. The practice of jacketing sheep has recently been reintroduced, but with jackets made of polyethylene rather than of natural fibers; see N. Hyde, "Wool: The Fabric of History," *National Geographic* 173 (May 1988): 578–79.
24. T. Frank et al., *An Economic Survey of Ancient Rome* 5 vols. (Baltimore, 1933–40), 5: 165; Columella 7.2.3–5. Pliny

the Elder (*H.N.* 8.7.3) describes wool from Canusium as *fulvus;* Martial (14.127) describes it as very similar on color to honey-sweetened wine.

25. Columella 7.2.4; Cicero, *Pro Rabirio Postumo* 40.

26. Plautus, *Aulularia* 512; Livy 9.40.3, 30.3.2. Pliny the Elder (*H.N.* 19.21), however, states that the fiber from the stems of one kind of poppy were interwoven with flax to give a gloss *(candorem)*. Elsewhere he mentions that the use of closely woven poppy fiber for togas goes back as far as the Second Punic War (8.195).

27. Herodotus 3.106; Strabo 15.693.

28. Nonius M548; Lucretius 4.75–76.

29. Propertius 4.64; Fujii, "Roman Textiles," 219.

30. Pliny the Elder, *H.N.* 33.149. Gold thread is known to have been produced as early as Exodus 39.3 and was used in Babylon and Assyria for royal tunics; see Shams, *Minor Textiles,* 13; and Frank et al., *Economic Survey* 1: 240, 354, and 4: 818.

31. Pliny the Elder, *H.N.* 8.195. Pliny also mentions that under Augustus the toga of Phryxian wool came into use, but he does not further describe it. See also Forbes, *Ancient Technology* 4: 93–94, and J. P. Wild, "Textiles," in *Roman Crafts,* ed. D. Strong and D. Brown (New York, 1976), 176. This teasing and clipping process also produced the tunica rasa; see *Ephemeris epigraphica* 8: 154, no. 624.

32. André, *Termes de Couleur,* 71–72. This natural dark hue of wool, between black and brown, was produced by the sheep of Pollentia and of Baetic Corduba. Ovid's suggestion indicates that *pullus* was an acceptable nonmourning color, for women at least. A synonym for *pullus* as a mourning color is *anthracinus,* used by Varro according to Nonius (M550), a word derived from the Greek for "coal." This black color Nonius defines as the color of mourning clothes.

33. Ovid, *Ars amatoria* 3.170–92.

34. André, *Termes de Couleur,* 182.

35. Ibid., 194, 268.

36. Ibid., 155–56; Columella 7.2.3–4.

37. André, *Termes de Couleur,* 153–54.

38. Plautus, *Aulularia* 510; André, *Termes de Couleur,* 157–58.

39. André, *Termes de Couleur,* 196–97.

40. Pliny the Elder, *H.N.* 9.139; André, *Termes de Couleur,* 196–97.

41. André, *Termes de Couleur,* 29, 30, 111–12.

42. Ovid, *Ars amatoria* 3.185–87.

43. Pliny the Elder, *H.N.* 33.163, 35.43 and 46, 37.84. Forbes, *Ancient Technology* 4: 111, suggests that the scum may be the indigo scum collected from the bamboo stirring rods (Pliny's reeds) used in the process, or even the scum of Tyrian purple.

44. Vitruvius 7.9.8; Forbes, *Ancient Technology* 4: 110–12. Pliny the Elder, *H.N.* 35.46: "mixturam purpurae caeruleique mirabilem."

45. Pliny the Elder, *H.N.* 9.63, 137; Reinhold, "History of Purple," 42–44.

46. Vitruvius 7.13.1. He gives the geographic distribution of these variant hues as *ater,* Pontus and Gaul (i.e., the north); *lividus,* the north and west; *violaceus,* the east and west; *ruber,* the south.

47. T. F. Butler, *Roman Galley beneath the Sea* (Leicester, 1964), 65. The galley discussed in this book sank during Nero's reign off Ibiza, Spain.

48. Nonius M549: "ostrinum ab ostri colore qui est subrubeus"; "*ostrinum* is named from the shellfish color which is reddish." On synonyms for *ostrinum,* see Lucretius 2.35; *Aetna* 331; Seneca, *Medea* 99; Vergil, *Aeneid* 2.67; Valerius Flaccus 2.342; Statius, *Thebais* 4.265; Propertius 2.29.26; Nonius M549; André, *Termes de Couleur,* 102–3. On its use for clothes, see Varro, *De re rustica* 133.9; for coverlets, Propertius 1.14.20.

49. Pliny the Elder, *H.N.* 9.137. Nepos was born in 100 B.C.

50. Pliny the Elder, *H.N.* 9.138.

51. André, *Termes de Couleur,* 104.

52. Pliny the Elder, *H.N.* 9.140–41. He says that the parasitic kermes insect of Emerita Lusitania in Spain and the kermes insect of Galatia were particularly valued for their superior hue. As the kermes is a scale insect living on plant stems, Romans misidentified it as the seed *(coccus)* of the plant; hence the name of the pure color of the dye is *coccinus.* The Romans quite possibly used this dye earlier in the republic, obtaining it either through trade or through their acquisition of Punic Spain or North Africa, but its use is documented only in the last century of the republic. On this insect and other species of *cocci* insects related to it and used for dyes, see Forbes, *Ancient Technology* 4: 101–4. On the use of this dye for paludamenta, see Pliny the Elder, *H.N.* 22.3.

53. Propertius 1.22; Horace, *Satires* 1.2.101; Tibullus 2.3.53, 4.29; Ovid, *Ars amatoria* 2.298.

54. Tacitus, *Annals* 2.53.1. On the silkworm and silk apparel, see Pliny the Elder, *H.N.* 11.76–78. On Coan "silk," see Aristotle, *Historia animalium* 5.19. Silk is mentioned by poets under Augustus and the Julio-Claudian emperors, but not afterward; see Frank et al., *Economic Survey* 4: 823.

55. Forbes, *Ancient Technology* 2: 31; 4: 234, 235, 237. Pliny the Elder, *H.N.* 8.196; Frank et al., *Economic Survey* 2: 388.

56. Forbes, *Ancient Technology* 2: 31; 4: 232, 233. Martial 9.22.9; 14.127, 129, 143.

57. Pliny the Elder, *H.N.* 8.192; Forbes, *Ancient Technology* 4: 91. Caesar, *Bellum civile* 3.44. Pliny says the *gausapa* first appeared in his father's lifetime. The Romans also believed that felt treated with vinegar would withstand even iron weapons. Caesar's soldiers padded their armor with felt when facing Pompey's archers.

58. Columella 7.2.5. Pliny the Elder (*H.N.* 8.190) calls Tarentine sheep "the most praised" for their fleeces.

59. Frank et al., *Economic Survey* 5: 166, 204; Columella 7.2.3–5; Forbes, *Ancient Technology* 4: 22–24.

60. Frank et al., *Economic Survey* 5: 166; Columella 12 *praef.* 9–10, 12.3.6; Suetonius, *Augustus* 73. Though wives and daughters of the rich families did not follow the example of Augustus' women, many of their household slaves were engaged in weaving cloth which would be sent to independent tailors for fashioning into garments. This cloth also could be

sold commercially. Atticus made clothing for Cicero; even so the orator had on occasion hired weavers. See H. J. Loane, *Industry and Commerce of the City of Rome, 50 B.C.–200 A.D.* (Baltimore, 1938), 69–70.

61. Frank et al., *Economic Survey* 3: 289.

62. Wells, *Culture Contact*, 62, 64, 71, 90; Forbes, *Ancient Technology* 4: 33–35.

63. Pliny the Elder, *H.N.* 19.22–24. He regards attempts to dye linen as a sign of mad extravagance *(insania)*.

64. Catullus 12, 25; Pliny the Elder, *H.N.* 19.9.

65. Reinhold, "History of Purple," 49–50.

66. K. D. Matthews, "The Imperial Wardrobe of Ancient Rome," *Expedition* 12.3 (1970): 2–13.

67. On *prasinus*, see André, *Termes de Couleur*, 192. On *galbinus*, see Pliny the Elder, *H.N.* 30.96, and André, 148–50. On *cerasinus*, see André, 118.

68. On *russeus*, see André, *Termes de Couleur*, 77, 83–84. On its vulgarity, see Petronius 27.1. On *venetus*, see Cassiodorus, *Var.* 5.34.2, where he distinguishes it from a clear blue. Vegetius 15.7, mentions its later use as a naval camouflage color; see also André, 181–82.

69. Pliny the Elder, *II.N.* 9.137, 21.27, 21.45–46; André, *Termes de Couleur*, 195–98; Persius 1.32; Martial 1.53.5.

70. Pliny the Elder, *H.N.* 9.141, 16.32, 22.3.

71. Pliny the Elder, *H.N.* 22.3. By varying the amount of alum and iron mordants, dyers were able to produce various shades of purple; see Wild, *Textile Manufacture*, 81. See also Yadin, *Finds from the Bar Kokhba Period*, 279.

72. Pliny the Elder, *H.N.* 37.110; Solinus 21; Isidore, *Origines* 16.7.10; André, *Termes de Couleur*, 192–93; *CIL* 14.2215.

73. Forbes, *Ancient Technology* 4: 239. Inscriptions of silk merchants have been found at Gabii, Naples, Rome, and Tibur; see M. P. Charlesworth, *Trade-Routes and Commerce of the Roman Empire* (Cambridge, Eng., 1924), 62, 68, 105, 110. The silk trade was highly regulated by the Chinese. Some surviving government documents record the origin, dimensions, weight, and price of each silk consignment; see C. G. Seligman, "The Roman Orient and the Far East," *Smithsonian Report* (1930): 550. For fabrics exported from Rome to India, see J. I. Miller, *The Spice Trade of the Roman Empire, 29 B.C. to A.D. 641* (Oxford, 1969), 204, 206, 207. See also L. Casson, *The Periplus Maris Erythraei* (Princeton, 1989).

74. K. D. Matthews, "The Imperial Wardrobe," *Expedition* 12 (1970): 2–3; Miller, *Spice Trade*, 205.

75. Seligman, "Roman Orient," 555; S. Liebman, "Contact between Rome and China," Ph.D. diss., Columbia University, 1953, 234; Forbes, *Ancient Technology* 4: 243.

76. *CIL* 14.2215: "et lentea purpura cum clavis aurea."

77. Pliny the Elder, *H.N.* 33.63; Josephus, *AJ* 19.8.2; Matthews, "Imperial Wardrobe," 3, 6, 18.

78. Frank et al., *Economic Survey* 5: 294; Miller, *Spice Trade*, 195, 208; Martial 5.79; Forbes, *Ancient Technology* 4:243. Samples of fabric with alternating checks of reddish orange and dull reddish yellow have been found; see Fujii, "Roman Textiles," 225.

79. Pliny the Elder, *H.N.* 35.150; Forbes, *Ancient Technology* 4: 132; Fujii, "Roman Textiles," 101–3.

80. Frank et al., *Economic Survey* 3: 445, 587, 682; Charlesworth, *Trade-Routes*, 94, 195.

81. Frank et al., *Economic Survey* 3: 86, 106, 107.

82. Charlesworth, *Trade-Routes*, 93.

83. Pliny the Elder, *H.N.* 8.193. Though the etymology of *gausapa* is unknown, it would seem likely to be the name of a Celtic or Germanic garment. Columella 1.8.9; Martial 1.53.5 (he complains that the grease of the bardocucullus smears off on others' garments), 10.76.8, 14.128.1; Juvenal, *Satires* 3.170.

84. Pliny the Elder, *H.N.* 19.9, 13; Frank et al., *Economic Survey* 5: 156.

85. Pliny the Elder, *H.N.* 19.13; Charlesworth, *Trade-Routes*, 164.

86. Pliny the Elder, *H.N.* 19.7–8, 13; Frank et al., *Economic Survey* 5: 156.

87. Charlesworth, *Trade-Routes*, 104, 120, 125.

88. Pliny the Elder, *H.N.* 19.13–14. Such linen the Romans traded to India in return for silk; see Charlesworth, *Trade-Routes*, 68.

89. Frank et al., *Economic Survey* 5: 294; Charlesworth, *Trade-Routes*, 48, 50. In the archives of L. Caecilius Iucundus of Pompeii was found a document noting a quantity of linen imported from one Tolomaeus of Alexandria; see E. La Rocca et al., *Guida archeologica di Pompei* (Rome, 1976), 205.

90. Frank et al., *Economic Survey* 4: 191. I am thankful to Lucille Roussin for this reference.

91. J. Adrosko, *Natural Dyes in the United States*, U.S. National Museum Bulletin 281 (Washington, D.C., 1968), 17, 21.

92. So suggests K. C. Bailey, in H. Rackham, ed., *Pliny: Natural History* (Cambridge, Mass., 1961), 9: 396 n. a.

93. Forbes, *Ancient Technology* 4: 142.

# Jewelry as a Symbol of Status in the Roman Empire

## 5

ANN M. STOUT

Throughout Rome's history a tension existed between the desire for showy gold, gem-encrusted jewelry and the restraint appropriate to republican values of simplicity and modesty. The ancient authors tell story after story of the excesses of adornment by certain individuals and rulers contrasted with the rejection of such behavior by others. The revered Roman matron Cornelia, mother of Tiberius and Gaius Gracchus, when asked to show her jewels, presented her sons, saying, "These are my jewels." This virtuous example is countered by Pliny the Elder's story of Lollia Paulina (one of the wives of Caligula) who paraded herself at an ordinary wedding entertainment "covered with emeralds and pearls which shone in alternate layers upon her head, in her hair, in her wreaths, in her ears, upon her neck, in her bracelets, and on her fingers."[1]

The elder Pliny blamed Pompey the Great's victory over Mithridates and his subsequent triumph in 61 B.C. for the Roman taste for pearls and gemstones. Gold vessels inlaid with gems, thirty-three pearl crowns, and even Pompey's portrait rendered in pearls were some of the opulent objects paraded before the Roman populace.[2]

While the East is often seen as the key to a shift in Roman taste, there were lavish ornaments closer to hand in the rich heritage of Etruscan jewelry. Pieces from the late Etruscan period (fourth century B.C.) featured large convex surfaces of embossed sheet gold sometimes worked in repoussé. Typically such pieces were fashioned into hollow pendants (bullae) which served as amulets, a series of pendants suspended from gold wire necklaces, or into beads clustered together in earrings.[3]

Not only the ancient literature but also surviving artistic monuments and archaeological finds show that jewelry distinguished people in many ways in Roman society. In time, special imperial jewelry evolved which became part of the insignia of the emperor. This chapter will first present an overview of the various ways jewelry indicated status among ordinary citizens. Then the development of the special jewelry which set the emperor (and, in time, the empress) apart and signified imperial power and authority will be investigated.

Off and on throughout Rome's earlier history the use of jewelry was regulated by law. The law of the Twelve Tables of 450 B.C. limited the amount of jewelry that could be buried with the dead. More important, concerning what people could wear while still alive, the Lex Oppia, passed in 215 B.C., limited the amount of gold a Roman lady could wear to one-half ounce. Even though the sumptuary laws were not rigorously enforced, the idea remained that modesty in adornment was a valuable republican virtue. At the same time, the wearing of jewels and jewelry by men was considered effeminate. The elder Pliny rails against the emperor Caligula for wearing "effeminate slippers sewn with pearls."[4]

According to the ancient authors, the two most visible forms of jewelry which distinguished Roman citizens by their rank in the republic were the bulla and the gold ring. Pliny the Elder relates that Tarquinius Priscus was the first to present his son with a golden amulet after he had killed an enemy in battle, and from that time on the amulet continued to be worn by the sons of those who served in the cavalry. This bulla had been a favorite ornament of the Etruscans and continued to be favored by the Roman nobles as an amulet for children. The bulla could not be worn by slaves; therefore its presence is also an indication of the child's free status. One bulla from a site near Ferrara, Italy, was found to contain remains of resin. The resin was used to hold and fix delicate perfumes.[5]

In the republic, the gold ring was reserved for particular classes of people or for special occasions. Nobles who had held curule office and their descendants in the male line had this privilege from 321 B.C., while the equites acquired the right by 216 B.C. By the Third Punic War military tribunes possessed the right.[6] Pliny the Elder goes on to say that senators did not usually wear the gold ring but that those "going on an embassy" wore the gold ring in public and an iron ring in private. All of this changed in the reign of Tiberius, when the right to wear the ring depended on whether one was freeborn (as well as one's father and grandfather) and owned four hundred thousand sesterces. Along with the right to wear the ring went the privilege of sitting in the first fourteen rows of the theater. By A.D. 197 Septimius Severus granted permission to all soldiers to wear the gold ring.[7]

It had also become customary for married women to wear a gold ring before the second century A.D. Tertullian mentions this custom, and the monuments verify it. Witness the Domina in the Villa of the Mysteries frieze (buried by the eruption of Mt. Vesuvius in A.D. 79) who attends the ceremony wearing a gold ring. This ring set a woman apart, showing her betrothed state. The elder Pliny tells us that the usual betrothal gift to a woman was an iron ring without a stone.[8]

Sometimes under special circumstances the earlier restrictions were lifted. Dio Cassius relates how Augustus was so grateful to a certain freedman, Antonius Musa, who had restored him to health that he granted him the right to wear the gold ring as well as a gift of money.[9]

Moreover, wealthy Romans collected antique rings and especially the engraved gems which were originally fitted into them and served as signets. Pliny the Elder tells about several collectors of ring cabinets (Sulla's stepson Scaurus, Pompey the Great, and Julius Caesar). Some of these valuable collections were presented to Roman temples.[10]

The signet ring of the emperor Augustus took on special status as imperial insignia, or a sign of authority. Two of Augustus' earlier signet rings, featuring sphinxes, were used by personal advisers when Augustus was absent and letters or proclamations needed to be signed in his name. Later he signed his documents with a signet depicting Alexander the Great, as well as a signet with his own likeness, carved by the famous artist Dioscurides. When Augustus was very ill in 23 B.C. "he arranged everything as if he were about to die . . . and handed his ring to Agrippa." Possibly this was Augustus' way of showing whom he favored for the suc-

cession. Another instance in which a reigning emperor gave jewelry to a presumed successor occurred later when Nerva presented Trajan with a precious diamond after appointing him Caesar. Still later Trajan presented the same diamond to Hadrian so that he was encouraged to hope for the succession.[11]

Another kind of gold ring featured the likeness of the emperor and was given only to those individuals who had free access to his person. The elder Pliny tells us how this custom was instituted by Claudius but then revoked by Vespasian, who wanted all to have equal access to him. The custom of depicting members of the imperial family was revived in the late empire. One gold ring in the Rheinisches Landesmuseum, Trier, seems to depict Fausta, the wife of Constantine, or Helena, his mother. A number of other rings have survived with inscriptions of various kinds. Some of them are indications of imperial favor: one in Trier, for example, has the words *Fidem Constantino* engraved on the band and top.[12]

Other Roman jewelry from the first four centuries A.D. can be seen in surviving artistic monuments, such as frescoes at Pompeii and Herculaneum, mummy portraits, and sculptured tombs at Palmyra, and in numerous hoards discovered throughout the empire.[13] Barbel Pfeiler has distinguished two major trends in Roman jewelry of the first and second centuries: Italo-Roman and Hellenistic-Roman. To the first she attributes geometric shapes, linear decoration, and an interest in color. In the other she sees a stylized naturalism of Hellenistic animal and human motifs. In the third century she notes the new decorative technique of *opus interrasile* (openwork), a stronger polychromy, and the piling up of colored stones in more massive pieces.[14] Pfeiler's conclusions seem confirmed by mummy portraits, which show a progression in the size and amount of jewelry from the first century to the fourth. Mummy portraits from the first century often feature a woman wearing one simple gold chain with a golden pendant (often a crescent) or one jeweled necklace. Earrings are also simple, being made up of a single pearl or simple gold shapes: hoops, disks, or balls. Such arrangements are further verified in surviving frescoes and mosaics from Pompeii and Herculaneum.[15] In the second century, two or three necklaces were favored with one of them containing colored semiprecious stones; earrings typically had three or four sets of pendants hanging from a horizontal bar. These trends are visible in the mummy portrait now in the Getty Museum (fig. 5.1). Later portraits from the fourth century often feature coins or medallions incorporated into more massive neck rings. Snake bracelets, a holdover from the Hellenistic period, were popular throughout the first four centuries A.D.[16] Visual evidence of the mummy portraits is reenforced by

Fig. 5.1. Fayum mummy portrait. From the collection of the J. Paul Getty Museum, Malibu, California, inv. 81.AP.42, attributed to the Isadora Master, ca. A.D. 100–125, encaustic and gilt on a wooden panel wrapped in linen, height 13 1/4 inches, width 6 3/4 inches.

Fig. 5.2. Fragment of belt or breast ornament with large medallion of Constantius II and small medallion. Roman, mid–fourth century. Walters Art Gallery, Baltimore, inv. 57.527 AB.

the publication of more and more hoards from the Roman period, giving us a clearer picture of what people actually wore.[17] Major treasures, including women's jewelry from Lyon and Naix (dated to about A.D. 200), show pieces remarkably like those earrings with pendants hanging from a bar which are depicted in second-century mummy portraits. Several necklaces have gold links interspersed with semiprecious and precious stones, but others feature much larger, faceted stones. Fourth-century treasure hoards found in Czechoslovakia, Hungary, and Romania have produced solid gold neck rings and bracelets, openwork bracelets and pendants with mounted medallions or coins, and brooches of semi-precious stones.[18]

Taking the artistic monuments and the surviving jewelry together, one notes an appreciation of Greek gold work in bands and chains in the early empire. Semiprecious and precious stones such as onyx, lapis lazuli, cornelian, emeralds, sapphires, rubies, and especially pearls were worked into gold settings, often alternating with the gold work in rings, necklaces, earrings, and bracelets. Stones also served as pendants and amulets. Amber was also prized for amulets because of its supposed medicinal value.[19]

Medallions and coins were increasingly incorporated into jewelry in the third and fourth centuries as single pendants hung from chains or in bracelets or in groups suspended from necklaces. Many of these have come to light in elaborate openwork *(interrasile)* settings. Presumably they were gifts from the reigning emperor and would designate the wearer as one enjoying imperial favor. A particularly interesting example is in the Walters Art Gallery (fig. 5.2). The gold medallion of Constantius II (A.D. 337–61) in an openwork frame appears to have been part of a belt because of the gold strap in five links adjacent to it. Hanging from the frame are three gold chains ending with a central teardrop stone and a smaller stone on one side. The other stone seems to be missing.[20] In later centuries gold medallions and coins were massed in impressive gold settings attached to plain hollow neck rings. The coins in these arrangements range from the fourth to the seventh centuries. Procopius of Caesarea reports that Justinian's general Belisarius presented his soldiers with bracelets, necklaces, and monetary gifts. In the Byzantine period such coin ensembles were remounted to include Christian medallions as a focal point.[21]

Perhaps the greatest profusion of jewelry worn at one time can be seen in the surviving sculpted tombs from Palmyra (laid waste in the third century A.D.), where the deceased is commonly portrayed atop her sarcophagus arrayed with multiple necklaces, bracelets, rings, earrings, brooches, and hairpieces. Several of these pieces

Fig. 5.3. Palmyrene relief. Ny Carlsberg Glyptotek, Copenhagen.

Fig. 5.4. Ceiling fresco from beneath the cathedral, Trier. Photo courtesy of Bischöfliches Dom-und Diözesanmuseum, Trier, inv. 85.89.7.

have hanging pendants and jewels, as a surviving example in Copenhagen shows (fig. 5.3). A hairpiece exceedingly similar to that seen in the Copenhagen relief, with three stone settings surrounded by pearls and three hanging pendants terminating in two outer pearls and a central sapphire, is in the possession of the British Museum. It was found at Tunis and is dated to the third century.[22]

A clear trend in the later empire is toward a greater massiveness in jewelry. Women's bracelets are wide and heavy-looking; often a stone is mounted in the center. Necklaces feature larger stones. An excellent monument showing these trends is the fourth-century ceiling beneath the cathedral in Trier featuring frescoed portraits of women wearing large jewels in necklaces, in bracelets, and in their hair (fig. 5.4). These women have been identified as members of Constantine's family.[23]

Even though later Roman jewelry tends to be showier, it is important to point out that this trend was also true of Hellenistic Greek jewelry. A case in point is the Olbia Treasure at the Walters Art Gallery dated to the first century B.C. Among the most magnificent pieces are two

articulated gold bracelets featuring many rows of colored semiprecious and precious stones, granulation, and beading.[24]

In the later empire it was common for men to wear large, prominent crossbow fibulae. Pliny the Elder complained about the beginnings of this trend with gold brooches worn by the tribunes. Many are inscribed with the names of reigning Augusti and again indicate imperial favor. Good examples of large, gold crossbow fibulae can be seen in German collections such as in Trier, where one fibula is inscribed on the bow with the names of Constantine and Licinius Augustus, and with that of Servandus (presumably the recipient) on the underside.[25] Interestingly, another place to see late Roman jewelry is on Christian sarcophagi, where husband and wife frequently appear in a *clipeus* showing off their massive bracelets, necklaces, and crossbow brooches amid Christian iconography, despite the admonitions of Tertullian.[26]

Another category of jewelry was awarded on special occasions. Some of this special jewelry was awarded to soldiers who had distinguished themselves in battle, and

Fig. 5.5. Cornucopia Cameo. Kunsthistorisches Museum, Vienna, inv. IX A 63.

Fig. 5.6. Painted roundel of Septimius Severus and family from Egypt. Antikenmuseum Berlin, Staatliche Museen Preussischer Kulturbesitz, inv. 31329. Photo by Ingrid Geske-Heiden.

Fig. 5.7. Medallion of Tacitus, A.D. 276. Staatliche Museen zu Berlin, Münzkabinett.

other pieces could be worn only by the emperor. The elder Pliny relates how gold necklaces were given to foreign soldiers while Romans got silver ones. These were large necklaces called torques, worn by the Etruscans and the Gauls as well as the Persians.[27] Gold crowns, however, were given to Roman soldiers. Crowns play a prominent part in honors awarded to the Roman ruler by the Senate or given to him by conquered potentates and kings. One could contrast Pompey's lavish triumph mentioned above with that of Augustus in 29 B.C. Augustus would not accept the gold required for making the crowns voted to him, so the Romans viewed his triumph with pleasure, since they did not have to make sacrifices for his glory. Suetonius mentions several types of crowns awarded by the Senate for distinction in the field: the civic crown with oak leaves for saving lives of Roman citizens; the laurel crown, a sign of victory for the general in his triumph; the mural crown for the one who scaled an enemy wall; and the naval crown, featuring the beaks of ships. Claudius was awarded the naval and the civic crowns after his victories in Britain. Aside from gold crowns made to look like oak or laurel wreaths, victorious generals were also given laurel wreaths and garlands of flowers by the people themselves. Tiberius was supposed to have had such faith in the laurel wreath that he would put one on when the sky wore an ugly look to make him lightning-proof. One of the honors voted to Julius Caesar by the Senate was the privilege of wearing a laurel wreath on all occasions. Dio Cassius tells us that Augustus was granted the right to wear the triumphal crown (corona triumphalis) at all festivals in 29 B.C. Later, in 25 B.C., he was voted the privilege of always being able to wear it on New Year's Day. Caligula wore the oak leaf crown at public spectacles.[28]

Cameos of the first-century emperors give more detailed information about the type of wreaths or crowns worn than do coins, which are often generalized or damaged. Three different types are visible in the Cornucopia Cameo, housed in the Kunsthistorisches Museum in Vienna: the mural crown worn by Agrippina the Younger, the laurel wreath over a helmet worn by Livia, and the oak wreath worn by Claudius and Tiberius (fig. 5.5).[29]

Another type is the rampart crown, said to have been awarded to Aurelian for victories over the Goths, in addition to the other types of crowns mentioned above. In some cases the mural crown is conflated with a rostra crown. A good example of this type is seen in the coinage issued jointly by Augustus and Agrippa in 12 B.C.[30]

There is also abundant evidence that laurel and oak crowns were jeweled. A head of Marcus Aurelius (A.D. 161–80) wearing a laurel wreath with a large central jewel is in the Archaeological Museum in Istanbul.

Septimius Severus (A.D. 193–211), along with the rest of his family, wears the laurel crown embellished with several jewels in a painted roundel from Egypt (fig. 5.6). A portrait of Diocletian (A.D. 284–305), also in the Istanbul museum, shows him wearing an oak crown with a large central jewel.[31]

Another category of crowns is priestly. Elagabalus (A.D 218–22) was accustomed to wearing a jeweled crown in carrying out his priestly duties to the sun god. Earlier references to priestly crowns, without jewels, can be found in Suetonius. Domitian, when presiding over a festival dedicated to Capitoline Jupiter, wore a gold crown engraved with the images of Jupiter, Juno, and Minerva in the company of priests who wore similar crowns carrying the emperor's likeness. Actual crowns have survived in England and Naukratis and are thought to have been used by priests in cult ceremonies. The British finds are of bronze, originally fitted with ornaments and plaques. They are dated roughly from the late second to the fourth centuries A.D. The Egyptian gold example, dated to the first century A.D., is embossed with inscriptions and busts of Helios, Horus, and Demeter. No mention is made of attached ornaments. Many sculptures of priests and priestesses from the second through the fourth centuries wear crowns, incorporating rolled diadems, fillets, and/or laurel wreaths, atop damaged and thus unidentifiable busts.[32]

The radiate crown was used sparingly by the Romans until the third century. Strong associations with the sun god and the Hellenistic monarchies which also favored the radiate crown may have led most rulers to choose other emblems in the early empire. Occasionally it was used as a mark of honor, as on a coin showing the deified Augustus radiate after his death. Nero is depicted as the radiate sun on the reverse of an aureus, but most coinage shows the emperor laureate.[33] The third-century emperors depicted themselves radiate much more frequently in their coinage. Severus, Caracalla, Posthumus, Aurelian, Tacitus, and several others wear the radiate crown on their coinage.[34] Historians recount that Gallienus appeared in public wearing a radiate crown, and the surviving coinage depicts him so crowned.[35]

Still another type of imperial jewelry is the diadem. A plain band or fillet tied in the back, this headgear is associated with Alexander the Great and symbolizes absolute monarchy.[36] Because of the strong republican spirit which dominated much of Rome's early history, in theory if not in practice, the diadem was not adopted as the official Roman imperial insignia until the time of Constantine the Great. Before him, various emperors wore it, but their doing so was always criticized in the ancient literature. One senses the shock of Suetonius when he reports that Caligula "nearly assumed a royal diadem" at a dinner with foreign kings and that Titus had worn a diadem at the consecration of the Apis bull at Memphis, lending credence to rumors that he planned to revolt against his father and make himself king in the East. Antoninus Elagabalus was supposed to have worn a jeweled diadem at home in order to increase his beauty and make his face look more like a woman's.[37] Alföldi has noted that Gallienus wore the band-diadem in a festival issue of the newly opened mint in Milan which strongly imitated issues of Alexander the Great.[38] When Zenobia, the female ruler of Palmyra, assumed the diadem to show her independence from Roman power, Aurelian could not ignore her challenge. He ultimately conquered her and led her captive in his triumph. By the end of the third century, however, Diocletian and Maximian were not only not accountable to any legislative body, but they also wore the imperial diadem and robes trimmed with jewels and had an elaborate ceremonial for any who would approach them.[39]

It is very difficult to find evidence in the ancient literature for imperial brooches. A brooch, or fibula, would have been needed to clasp the civic (as well as the military) cloak of the emperor. Alföldi has suggested that when military tribunes were given jeweled, golden brooches in the third century as official presents, it was necessary to make the emperor's brooch stand out as being even more magnificent.[40] According to the Scriptores Historiae Augustae, Gallienus (A.D. 253–68) appeared in Rome, where emperors had always worn simply the toga, in a purple cloak with jeweled and golden clasps, a jeweled sword belt, and jewels on his boot laces. Carinus (A.D. 282–185) was also supposed to have worn a jeweled clasp and belt. Examples of a jeweled brooch in surviving coins of Gallienus and Carinus are not found, but Tacitus (A.D. 275–176) wears a rosette brooch which appears to be jeweled (fig. 5.7).[41] This love of luxury was clearly rejected by earlier emperors; Hadrian had no gold ornaments on his sword belt or jewels on his clasps, and Alexander Severus removed from the imperial footwear and garments all the jewels that Elagabalus had used.[42]

Jewelry thus played a prominent role in Roman society in distinguishing one's rank and state. Among Roman citizens it indicated whether you were an aristocrat, whether or not you had imperial favor, or whether you were married or betrothed. In all periods it spoke of one's wealth. Depending on the inscriptions, it could denote political or religious affiliation. Of course, as time went on some jewelry displayed specifically Christian inscriptions, signs, and iconography: rings, pendants, and belt buckles featured the cross, phrases such as "Holy, Holy, Holy, Lord God of Hosts," and images of Christ holding a cross or of saints being crowned by

Christ.[43] The use of jewelry by Roman emperors varied. Some reveled in the wearing of gems and bracelets; Caligula even had gems on his shoes.[44] Others seemed to emulate Augustus' example by choosing not to display unnecessary pomp.

In the late empire two new forms of jewelry evolved which became associated with the imperial insignia of the emperor and empress and were visible signs of their power and authority. One of these is the jeweled brooch with three pendants which holds together the chlamys (civic cloak) on the right shoulder. It is not discussed by the ancient authors, to my knowledge, until the time of Procopius in the sixth century and does not appear in the surviving monuments until the time of Constantine's struggle for power with Licinius in the early fourth century. From the time of Constantine the Great to the time of Justinian, one can follow the evolution of this new brooch form as well as that of another new form: a jeweled diadem which evolves into a jeweled crown with hanging jewels on the sides called *pendilia*. I propose to trace the development of these two imperial insignia through imperial coinage, silver plate, sculpture, ivories, and other mosaics, beginning in the time of Constantine. These special jewels reach a climax in the dedication mosaics of Justinian and Theodora in San Vitale, Ravenna. The wearing of the imperial insignia in the form of jewelry is not limited to the San Vitale mosaics but continues to play a part in Byzantine imperial costume for several centuries.[45] The San Vitale mosaics demonstrate the culmination of this development, which then becomes codified for succeeding emperors and empresses. Moreover, it is apparent that the Justinianic jewelry is accurately portrayed, since several pieces of late Roman and early Byzantine jewelry recovered from treasure hoards strongly resemble pieces visible in the mosaic.

San Vitale was founded in A.D. 526 by Bishop Ecclesius, who died in 532. His successor, Maximian, was appointed in 546. San Vitale was dedicated in 548, so the mosaics were probably completed between 546 and 548.[46] The imperial couple, Justinian and Theodora, appear with their respective retinues, located in the apse on opposite lateral walls (figs. 5.8 and 5.9).

On the left wall, the emperor stands in the center of the composition dressed in his civil costume, not his military or consular costume. The civil costume is marked by the chlamys, a long cloak reaching the ankles and decorated with a tablion, an elaborately patterned rectangular cloth, featuring green birds in red circles on a gold background. The chlamys is worn over a white tunic with long fitted sleeves trimmed in gold. Justinian's shoes are red and jeweled.[47] Standing to Justinian's left is a man identified either as Julianus Argentarius, asso-

Fig. 5.8. Justinian and entourage, apse mosaic, San Vitale, Ravenna. Photo from DAI, Rome, neg. 57.1744.

Fig. 5.9. Theodora and entourage, apse mosaic, San Vitale, Ravenna. Photo from DAI, Rome, neg. 57.1760.

Fig. 5.10. Detail of Justinian. Photo from DAI, Rome, neg. 57.1751.

Fig. 5.11. Detail of Theodora. Photo from DAI, Rome, neg. 57.1764.

ciated with the building of several important churches, or, alternatively, as the governor of Italy.[48] Next comes Bishop Maximian. To Maximian's left are two members of the clergy. To Justinian's right stands a man identified as Belisarius, conqueror of Ravenna, followed by an unidentified member of the court and several guards. It will be noted that none of the other members of the group wear jewelry similar to Justinian's. Members of the military wear torques, and members of the court wear crossbow brooches.

Across the apse, Theodora stands surrounded by ladies-in-waiting to her left and unidentified dignitaries or members of the court on her right. Male members of the court wear crossbow brooches, while women attendants wear jeweled necklaces and earrings. None, however, are as finely arrayed as is the empress. Theodora wears a purple chlamys bordered with gold, which depicts on the hem the three magi bringing gifts to the Christ child. Under the chlamys she wears a white tunic bordered with gold and colored designs, and gold shoes.

The attention given to jewelry in the mosaics represents the culmination of the gradual development of pomp and ceremony at the imperial court over at least

two centuries. Both Justinian and Theodora wear enormous jeweled crowns which evolved from the imperial diadem. Justinian's is adorned with short pendilia. Theodora's crown, with long pendilia extending past her shoulders, developed from the snood covered by a diadem. In addition, she wears hoop earrings with three successive jewel pendants, a choker necklace probably of emeralds, and an enormous, lunate jeweled necklace with pendant jewels covering her shoulders.

One of the most important pieces of jewelry making up the imperial regalia that Justinian and Theodora wear is the large brooch with three pendant jewels. Justinian's is easier to see, as it is not covered by a necklace (fig. 5.10). The top part of the brooch is a rosette consisting of a large central stone surrounded by pearls. The brooch has an upturned foot worn at the shoulder and three jewels suspended on gold chains or wires, the imperial insignia. Part of Theodora's brooch is visible on her right shoulder above her necklaces, while the three pendant jewels are visible below (fig. 5.11).

Three kinds of evidence exist today which help us better to understand the significance of this imperial jewelry. Remains of actual jewelry from archaeological

Fig. 5.12. Onyx brooch from Osztropataka. Kunsthistorisches Museum, Antikensammlung, Vienna, inv. VII B 306.

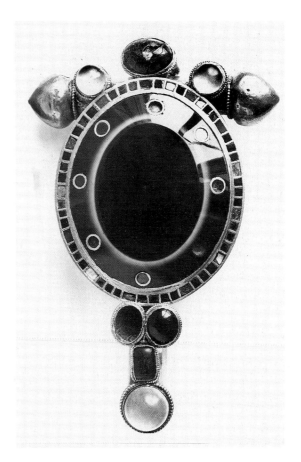

Fig. 5.13. Sardonyx brooch from Szilágy-Somlyó. Magyar Nemzeti Múzeum, Budapest, inv. 122/1895.1.N70.

excavations and treasures parallel pieces depicted in the mosaic, suggesting that Justinian's and Theodora's jewelry is accurately represented. Representations of jewelry on imperial coinage, silver plate, portrait sculpture, consular diptychs, and nonimperial mosaics from the late Roman and early Byzantine periods enable us to follow the development of the special jewelry which came to signify imperial authority. Finally, we have the literary evidence of Procopius, who describes the brooch with three pendant jewels as part of the imperial insignia.

Brooches have been recovered from third- and fourth-century treasures. Predecessors of Justinian's brooch, they illustrate an increasing taste for large, colored semi-precious stones used in showy jewelry. From the first half of the third century comes an oval brooch from Osztropataka (in present-day Czechoslovakia) which incorporates a single onyx stone in an openwork frame. From it hang two double gold chains with small gold leaf motifs at the ends (fig. 5.12). A similarly shaped piece in the British Museum, imitating sardonyx with

two club-shaped pendants hanging from it, is fitted to a gold link necklace. This piece dates to the third century.[49] The later fourth-century site of Szilágy-Somlyó in present-day Romania has produced a sardonyx brooch in a cruciform shape with a large encased sardonyx below the crossbar and with smaller, rounded stones adorning the crossbar and the foot (fig. 5.13). The Szilágy-Somlyó piece is also interesting because it has two loops on the underside of the head, suggesting the original presence of two hanging elements. A profile view shows the upturned foot similar to the one on Justinian's brooch. A gold brooch from the later fourth-century site of Nagy Mihály in present-day Czecho-slovakia has onyx, almandine, amethyst, and glass paste stones worked into a triangular shape, from which hang three gold chains ending in teardrop stones (fig. 5.14). Still another interesting piece is a chalcedony cameo with busts of Diocletian and Maximian, who was appointed co-Augustus with Diocletian in 286. The cameo has been set in gold; from it hang three tear-

Fig. 5.15. Chalcedony cameo with busts of Diocletian and Maximian. D.O. 47.14, Byzantine Visual Resources, © 1991, Dumbarton Oaks, Washington, D.C.

Fig. 5.14. Gold brooch from Nagy Mihály. Kunsthistorisches Museum, Antikensammlung, Vienna, inv. VII B 307.

Fig. 5.16. Earrings from Piazza della Consolazione treasure. D.O. 28.12, Byzantine Visual Resources, © 1991, Dumbarton Oaks, Washington, D.C.

Fig. 5.17. Necklace from Lambousa, Cyprus. Published by permission of the Director of the Department of Antiquities of the Republic of Cyprus, the Cyprus Museum, inv. J.429.

87

shaped jewels of beryl, emerald, and green glass (fig. 5.15).[50] This is the first example we have of three pendant jewels decorating an imperial cameo that have taken on visual importance as the imperial insignia.

Good examples of Byzantine jewelry have come to light from the Piazza della Consolazione treasure found near Rome in 1910 and now in the Dumbarton Oaks collection. Like Theodora's earrings, earrings from this collection have a gold hoop, from which is suspended a pearl encased in a gold ring, an emerald in a plain setting, and finally a pear-shaped sapphire (fig. 5.16).[51] A necklace from Lambousa, Cyprus, is also close to that worn by Theodora, with its amethyst stones alternating with pearls threaded on small pieces of gold wire (fig. 5.17).[52] Very close to the elaborately jeweled necklace of Theodora's lady-in-waiting (only slightly less sumptuous than Theodora's) is a necklace of gold openwork plaques mounted with three rows of stones from which hang seventeen pendant jewels on gold wires. Originally over one hundred pearls, emeralds, and sapphires (or aquamarines) decorated this lunate-shaped necklace, which resembles a large collar when worn. Now in Berlin, it comes from a treasure of uncertain provenance in Egypt (possibly from Antinoe). Dated to the sixth century, it represents a long tradition of excellent gold and jewel workmanship in Constantinople, its supposed place of manufacture (fig. 5.18).[53]

Aside from the few pieces of surviving jewelry, evidence for the development of imperial regalia can be sought in official imperial portraits in many media, especially in the coinage. I will trace the insignia for the emperor first. As we have already seen in figure 5.7, an early ancestor to the imperial brooch is visible on a coin issued during the reign of Marcus Claudius Tacitus (A.D. 275–76). The brooch, small and without pendant jewels, is in the form of a rosette. There may have been a break of several decades in the production of such brooches, for the rosette brooch does not show up again until the coinage of Constantine, during the period A.D. 310–15 (fig. 5.19).[54]

Constantine's headgear revived some Hellenistic favorites. The radiate crown (see fig. 5.19) was favored by him until his supposed conversion. It would appear that Constantine hedged his bets; Zosimus in *Historia nova* 2.31 describes the pagan shrines the emperor set up in Constantinople after founding his new capital in 330. In 324 Constantine defeated Licinius, his last rival to sole power as Augustus. According to Josef Deer, Constantine first wore the diadem at the celebration of his *Vicennalia* in 325. At that time, the jeweled diadem appears in his coinage, and it continues to be a regular feature of the imperial portrait.[55] A good example of a Constantinian portrait showing both the diadem and the jeweled brooch is a coin from 336–37 (fig. 5.20).[56] The diadem has laurel leaves alternating with jeweled rosettes and short ties on the back of the diadem where it is tied onto the head. The ties appear to have been made of chains with teardrop jewels on the ends. No pendants appear on the brooch; it features a large central jewel surrounded by eight smaller ones in a square design. An upturned foot tops the piece, while another jewel can be seen at the bottom.

It is important to note that while the Tetrarchic system established by Diocletian was still functioning, three pendant jewels on the brooch fastening the cloak were reserved for Roman officials with the rank of Caesar or Augustus; for example, three pendants decorate the cameo of Diocletian and Maximian as co-Augusti from the end of the third century (fig. 5.15). Therefore it is not too surprising to see three pendants on brooches worn by Licinius I and Licinius II in their coins issued in 321 (figs. 5.21 and 5.22). In 317 Licinius II was named Caesar in the East, and his father, Licinius I, had been named junior Augustus in 308 along with Diocletian, Galerius, and Maximian. By 313 Licinius and Constantine shared the rule of the empire, East and West, as Augusti.[57] Although Licinius I and Licinius II wear small brooches with three pendant jewels, neither wears a diadem. Constantine, on his later coinage (fig. 5.20) after he had defeated Licinius in 324 and was the sole Augustus, wears both a larger jeweled brooch (but without the three pendants) and a large jeweled diadem.

After Constantine died in 337, his sons shared the rule of the empire. In a coin from 342, Constans, who ruled the West from 340 to 350, wears a jeweled diadem with a large central rosette and a rosette brooch with three hanging pendants.[58] Constantius II, who was sole emperor in 355, is shown wearing a rosette brooch with three jewels barely projecting and a large jeweled diadem in a gold medallion from 355.[59] Much earlier, however, when he was celebrating his *Vicennalia* in 343, he wears a diadem and a brooch with three hanging pendants on a silver bowl found at Kerch (fig. 5.23). Thus, from the 330s to the 350s the imperial jeweled brooch took many forms.

The jeweled diadem also took different forms. From the time of Constantine through the fourth century, the jewels either alternated with leaf elements (as in fig. 5.20) or assumed two rows. In both cases, the focal points were a large central jewel above the forehead and jeweled ties fluttering behind. Ammianus Marcellinus comments that Julian "wore a magnificent diadem set with gleaming gems" when he celebrated quinquennial games as an Augustus, one which was so much nicer than the "cheap crown" he had worn at the beginning of his principate. By examining the surviving coinage, one

Fig. 5.18. Lunate necklace from Egypt. Antikenmuseum Berlin, Staatliche Museen Preussischer Kulturbesitz, inv. 30219.505. Photo by Jutta Tietz-Glagow.

can see that by the time of Valens and Valentinian I (A.D. 364–65), the jeweled diadem with a large central jewel with ties and attached jewels as well as the jeweled brooch with three pendant jewels are reserved for imperial rank and make up the imperial insignia. From now on the jeweled brooch and the diadem become larger and larger, as evidenced on the Missorium of Theodosius I (A.D. 388).[60]

A contrast exists, however, in a monument depicting the jewelry that someone in authority but of nonimperial rank was allowed to wear. A two-pendant brooch is worn by Aphrodisius, governor of Hermopolis, on the triumphal arch mosaic in Santa Maria Maggiore, Rome (A.D. 432), suggesting that his rank allows him to wear two pendants but not three.[61]

The next major change in the appearance of the diadem involves the jewels hanging from the sides, referred to as pendilia. The earliest pendilia on the sides of the diadem have been assigned to Honorius by Josef Deer and are visible in the consular diptych of Probus from A.D 405 (fig. 5.24, left).[62] Pendilia can also be seen hanging from the sides of the diadem of the colossal bronze statue at Barletta, dated to the 450s (fig. 5.24, right).

From now on, changes are more a matter of degree than kind. The pendilia on the sides of the diadem and the jeweled rosette brooch with the three pendants continue in use, with slight variations, down to the time of Justinian. They are visible in other media besides his dedication mosaic. The ensemble was present in one of Justinian's medallions, now unfortunately lost but known from casts.[63] Moreover, headless porphyry statues wearing three-pendant rosette brooches can be seen in the Archbishop Museum in Ravenna and in the Kunsthistorisches Museum in Vienna.[64]

Fig. 5.19. Double gold solidus of Constantine, A.D. 310–15. Staatliche Museen zu Berlin, Münzkabinett.

Fig. 5.20. Solidus of Constantine, A.D. 336–37. Reproduced by courtesy of the Trustees of the British Museum, inv. 121672.

Fig. 5.21. Aureus of Licinius I, A.D. 321. Reproduced by courtesy of the Trustees of the British Museum, inv. 121675.

Fig. 5.22. Aureus of Licinius II, A.D. 321. Civiche Raccolte Numismatiche-Milano, inv. 3165.

Fig. 5.23. Silver bowl of Constantius II from Kerch, A.D. 343. Photo courtesy of the Hermitage State Museum, St. Petersburg, inv. 14744.

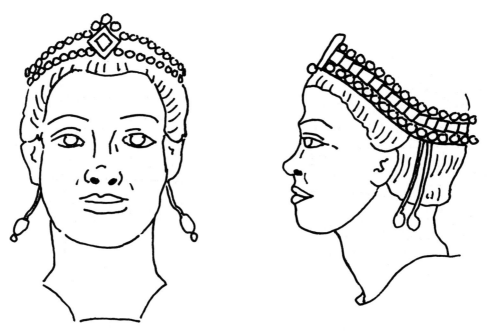

Fig. 5.24. *Left,* drawing of detail of ivory diptych of Probus, ca. A.D. 400, after Volbach, *Elfenbeinarbeiten,* pl. 1; *right,* drawing of detail of the colossal statue at Barletta, A.D. 450s, after Delbrueck, *Spätantike Kaiserporträts,* pl. 120.

Fig. 5.25. Solidus of Flaccilla, A.D. 383. Reproduced by courtesy of the Trustees of the British Museum, inv. 132897.

Fig. 5.26. Dupondius of Livia, A.D. 22–23. From Kent, *Roman Coins*, pl. 41, no. 159.

Fig. 5.27. Medallion of Helena, A.D. 325. From Kent, *Roman Coins*, pl. 161, no. 639.

Fig. 5.28. Solidus of Licinia Eudoxia, A.D. 455. Reproduced by courtesy of the Trustees of the British Museum, inv. 209098.

The brooch with three pendant jewels is not worn by an empress with the rank of Augusta until late in the fourth century. Flaccilla, wife of Theodosius I, wears one in A.D. 383 (fig. 5.25). From then on, all empresses with the rank of Augusta wear the triple-pendant brooch in their coinage.[65]

Surviving imperial coinage suggests that the headgear worn by the Augusta changed form during the imperial period. Numerous examples of women elevated to the rank of Augusta can be seen in their coin portraits. Livia, the first empress to be given the title Augusta by Augustus, is thought by Giacosa to be shown in the guise of the personified virtues of Pietas, Iustitia, and Salus Augusta (Justice, Piety, and Health or Safety) on coinage minted under Tiberius in honor of his mother.[66] On a dupondius issued by Tiberius in A.D. 22–23, a young, idealized woman faces right, wearing a triangular hairpiece of Greek Hellenistic type (fig. 5.26). Holum has pointed out that this type of headgear is associated with the stephane worn by goddesses and is not a true diadem, as it does not tie in the back.[67] Several other empresses with the title Augusta appear in official coinage with the same type of solid triangular headgear worn atop various hairstyles. Examples include Plotina, Marciana, Matidia (wife, sister, and mother-in-law of Trajan), Sabina (wife of Hadrian), Julia Domna (wife of Severus), and other more obscure empresses from the late third and early fourth centuries.[68] Still other empresses, such as Faustina, wife of Antoninus Pius (ca. A.D. 150), and Fausta, wife of Constantine the Great, were awarded the rank of Augusta but do not wear headgear in their coin portraits. Helena, mother of Constantine the Great, who was elevated to Augusta with Fausta in 324, wears a jeweled band. Helena's band is restrained compared with later examples and has no ties (fig. 5.27). Kenneth Holum and Maria Alföldi have expressed the opinion that Helena's simple band is more like a hair ornament and is not meant to denote the diadem or the imperial insignia because it lacks the large forehead jewel and ties at the back.[69] By contrast, the emperor Constantine's diadem has a large forehead jewel and ties at the back (fig. 5.20). Helena does wear considerably more jewelry than we have seen on other coin portraits of Augustae: a necklace with two strands of jewels and earrings with two jewels. This is a trend that accelerated during the next two centuries.

According to Holum, the first female empress to have the diadem denoting the imperial insignia is Flaccilla, wife of Theodosius I. Her diadem is large and jeweled like her husband's, with a large forehead jewel, rosette jewels, and jeweled ties in the back (fig. 5.25).[70] One can clearly see that her hair is brought forward at the top of the arrangement and is also visible at the bottom of the

Fig. 5.29. Procession of the Virgins mosaic, Sant'Apollinare Nuovo, Ravenna. Photo from DAI, Rome, neg. 58.603.

diadem. The Augustae from then on wear the diadem with large forehead jewel and jeweled ties fluttering in back, in addition to the imperial three-pendant brooch. Another trend is the increasing amount and size of jewelry worn by the Augusta. Flaccilla's necklace has large stones, her earring has two pendant stones, and she wears elaborate jeweled pins in her hair surmounting the diadem.

A noteworthy change in style comes with the empress Licinia Eudoxia (wife of Valentinian III, A.D. 425–55), whose headdress now has pendilia on the sides which are much longer than the emperor's (fig. 5.28).[71] Two strands of pearls hang down on each side of her head to her shoulders. Three radiating spokes project from the top of her head on either side of a double cross form. She also wears a triple-strand necklace in addition to pearl earrings and the three-pendant brooch.

It is interesting to note the use of jewelry in nonimperial mosaics at about the same time. On the triumphal arch of Santa Maria Maggiore in Rome, a woman interpreted as the Virgin sits as a regal figure in her newly elevated role of Theotokos. She is dressed in a gold overgarment adorned with a large rosette brooch under her breasts which is held in place by a double strand of pearls. She also wears jewels in her hair. Three jewels appear above a gold band, with one jewel below.[72] This jewelry, however, does not correspond to the imperial insignia. The brooch is in the wrong position, not being on the right shoulder, and it lacks the three pendant jewels. The hair ornament does not have the ties or the pendilia. Rather, the woman is adorned as are the virgins in the procession mosaic in Sant'Apollinare Nuovo in Ravenna, dating to the time of Justinian. The virgins wear double-stranded jeweled bands with rosettes in their hair and rosette brooches under the breasts attached by double strands of pearls. None of these virgins wear the imperial three-pendant brooch or the diadem with ties or pendilia (fig. 5.29).

A sculptured head in Castello Sforzesco, Milan (thought to represent Theodora, Galla Placidia, or possibly Pulcheria, thus dating between A.D. 450 and 540), wears a snood or cloth covering the hair with triangular projections on each side of the head (fig. 5.30). The thin cloth is covered with a diadem adorned by a large central jewel. Unexpected are the three jewels hanging from the diadem which encircles the snood. Furthermore, as revealed in an overhead photograph published by Siri Sande in 1975, a double strand of jewels flanked by a single strand of jewels passes over the top of the head perpendicular to the horizontal diadem.[73] Furthermore, the diadem (with top-of-the-head additions) is tied in a knot at the back, showing its long heritage of ties (fig. 5.31). Finally, a side view shows short pendilia on the diadem, which only reach to the hairline at the ears (fig. 5.32), possibly indicating an intermediate stage as well as suggesting an identification of an empress earlier than Licinia, who was represented with long pendilia. The three pendants visible on the Milan head must stand for the imperial insignia which we have seen on brooches and one cameo from the late third and early fourth centuries. Perhaps the empress wore the three-pendant headpiece when her costume did not require a brooch to fasten a cloak. Another incomplete head in the Side Museum, judged Theodosian in date, shows a headdress with three pendants resting on bangs in a similar manner.[74] In the Milan example, the bangs and hair show underneath the snood or crownlike cap, and the rest of the hair is concealed by the cloth of the snood.

In similar examples in the Louvre, the Palazzo dei Conservatori, and St. John's Lateran, the diademed snood conceals all of the hair except a little at the nape of the neck. None of these examples have visible pendilia. A possible identification of these heads is based on facial

Fig. 5.30. Head from Castello Sforzesco, Milan. Photo from DAI, Rome, neg. 4732.

Fig. 5.31. Detail of knotted tie on the back of Milan head. Photo from DAI, Rome, neg. 4273.

Fig. 5.32. Side view of Milan head, showing short pendilia. Photo from DAI, Rome, neg. 43.335.

similarities to an ivory diptych leaf in the Kunsthistorisches Museum in Vienna identified as Ariadne (fig. 5.33), as well as a similar one in the Bargello in Florence. The ivories, dated to about 500, show an empress wearing a snood, diadem, long pendilia, lunate necklace and earrings. Minor differences include a brooch with two pendant jewels visible in the Vienna diptych leaf and a projecting group of three jewels at the top of the headpiece in the Florence diptych leaf.[75]

Theodora's headpiece in the dedication mosaic in San vitale (fig. 5.11) appears to sum up the elements seen in the examples above. No hair is visible from the front. Two jeweled, triangular projections protrude from the top of her headpiece. The diadem, consisting of two strands of pearls on either side of almond-shaped and rectangular jewels, is still visible and also has the top-of-the-head addition as in the Milan head. At the top of her

head the additional diadem element supports two teardrop jewels flanking a larger one, as in the Florence diptych. Below the diadem, jewels adorn the rolled cloth snood, as in the Lateran head and Ariadne diptychs. The headpiece appears too stiff to be a snood and should probably be called a crown. As Sande has pointed out, Theodora's attendants have cloth-type coverings over their hair, but these differ from the empress' in their lack of jewels and apparent softness.[76]

There is no such progression for the crown surviving in the male imperial portraits. Justinian's portrait in the dedication mosaic shows three strands of jewels separated by solid bands of red and black, making the headpiece appear to have much more substance than a diadem through which one can see the hair (fig. 5.10). Justinian's hair is visible only at the bottom, implying that the crown of his head is covered. Moreover, the jeweled strands extend further out toward the top instead of coming inward and conforming to the natural rounded shape of the head. This headpiece must be the equivalent of Theodora's crown and would appear to be the first occurrence of a male crown with no other intermediary types surviving after the codification of the jeweled diadem in the fourth century. Justinian wears a similar massive crown, with hair visible only at the bottom, in a mosaic in Sant'Apollinare in Classe (fig. 5.34).

Our last evidence for the significance of jewelry as imperial insignia is literary. Procopius of Caesarea describes the Roman insignia given to Armenian satraps at the time of Justinian.[77] These included a purple cloak with a gold insert (tablion) fastened with a golden brooch, in the middle of which was a precious stone; three sapphires hung from the brooch by loose golden chains. Procopius goes on to describe the tunic of silk adorned with decorations of gold and red boots reaching to the knee "of the sort which only the Roman emperor and the Persian king are permitted to wear."

This last remark suggests that Persia was one source for the increased love of pomp and splendor seen in the late Roman and early Byzantine courts. Persian rulers from Darius to Shapur I are shown with sumptuous jewelry in representations ranging from mosaics to carved rock reliefs. Torques, earrings, jeweled necklaces, bracelets, diadems, and crowns decorate Eastern rulers in the Alexander Mosaic now in the Museo Nazionale Archeologico in Naples as well as in the Bishapur reliefs of Shapur I.[78] The love of jewelry is especially noticeable in Palmyrene grave stelae of A.D. 200–250 (fig. 5.3). The rosette brooch, as well as brooches and hair ornaments with two, three, and four pendant jewels, occur in Palmyrene reliefs. The three-pendant brooch appeared first on coins and plate issued by Licinius I and Licinius II, who ruled the Eastern Empire. The cameo with the three pendants depicting Diocletian and Maximian, however, was found in Rennes, France. Moreover, Maximian's assignment was the province of Gaul.[79] Other jewelry with suspended pendants has been found in the West in present-day Czechoslovakia and Romania.

Although certain motifs could have been borrowed from the East, the impetus for showy jewelry was present in Rome already, as is shown by the portrait from about A.D. 200 of Septimius Severus and his family wearing jeweled wreath crowns (fig. 5.6). Moreover, the treasure unearthed from Lyons with its gold and jeweled pieces shows that a taste for large, showy jewelry was already in the West by A.D. 200. It continued unabated, as witnessed by the Trier frescoes of the jeweled Constantinian ladies, Christian sarcophagi of the fourth century, and surviving jewelry hoards.

It was always fashionable to adorn oneself richly with

Fig. 5.33. Ivory diptych of Ariadne, ca. A.D. 500. Kunsthistorisches Museum, Antikensammlung Vienna, inv. X 39.

Fig. 5.34. Mosaic of Justinian in Sant'Apollinare in Classe. Photo from DAI, Rome, neg. 58.1155.

jewelry in the Roman and Byzantine periods, the showier the better as time went on. Andreas Alföldi has pointed out that the Romans were forced into the use of regalia because of Rome's status as a world power: they had to be taken seriously by their adversaries. Moreover, as more and more jewelry gifts were given to members of the military and the court, the imperial jewelry had to be even more grand and visible.[80] Jewelry was also used to enhance religious images of the Virgin Mary and of anonymous saints in the mosaics at Santa Maria Maggiore in Rome and in Sant'Apollinare Nuovo in Ravenna. It was only fitting that the emperor, who was now Christian and served as God's representative on earth, should inspire awe by means of his regalia.

The precedent for the use of crowns is clear from surviving priestly crowns and sculptures of crowned priests. In time, the regalia of the emperor was extended to the empress. What is important to note in the San Vitale mosaics is the fact that Justinian's and Theodora's jewelry is imperial and is worn by no one else. They alone have the prerogative of wearing the jeweled crown with pendilia and the large rosette brooch with three pendant jewels. By the mid–sixth century, this special jewelry was firmly established as a symbol of imperial power and authority.

### NOTES

I would like to give special thanks to Larissa Bonfante for her assistance in researching this chapter and to the staff of the library at the American Academy in Rome. I wish also to express my gratitude to the following individuals and institutions for their assistance in procuring the photographs for this chapter: Dr. Winfried Weber, museum director, Bischöfliches Dom und Diözesanmuseum Trier, Trier; Flemming Johansen, director, Ny Carlsberg Glyptotek, Copenhagen; the Walters Art Gallery; the J. Paul Getty Museum; Vera Zalesskaya, curator of the Byzantine Collections, Hermitage Museum, Leningrad; the British Museum; Dr. Kurt Gschwantler, Kunsthistorisches Museum, Antikensammlung, Vienna; Dr. Gertrud Platz, Antikenmuseum, Staatliche Museen, Preussischer Kulturbesitz, Berlin; H.-D. Schultz, Kustos, Staatliche Museen zu Berlin, Münzkabinett, Berlin; Dr. Kelmut Jung, Photographic Section, Deutsches Archäologisches Institut, Rome; Dr. Attila Kiss, Magyar Nemzeti Múzeum, Budapest; Dumbarton Oaks, Washington, D.C.; Cyprus Museum, Nicosia, Cyprus; and Rodolfo Martini, Raccolte Archeologiche e Numismatiche, Milan.

1. B. Radice, *Who's Who in the Ancient World* (New York, 1980), 93; Pliny the Elder, *H.N.* 9.58.

2. Pliny the Elder, *H.N.* 37.6.

3. M. Cristofani and M. Martelli, *L'oro degli Etruschi* (Novara, 1983). I am grateful to Larissa Bonfante for this reference.

4. On the Lex Oppia, see M. Cary and H. H. Scullard, *A History of Rome* (New York, 1978), 67, 191. On Caligula's slippers, see Pliny the Elder, *H.N.* 37.6.

5. Pliny the Elder, *H.N.* 33.4; Juvenal, *Satires* 14.4; Macrobius, *Saturnalia* 1.6, 9; Propertius, *Elegies* 5.131, 132. For the perfumed bulla, see G. M. A. Hanfmann, "Daedalos in Etruria," *AJA* 39 (1935): 189. Pliny the Elder (*H.N.* 13.7) says that resin was applied to prevent the evaporation of perfume.

6. F. H. Marshall, *Catalogue of the Finger Rings: Greek, Etruscan, and Roman* (Oxford, 1968), xviii–xx; Pliny the Elder, *H.N.* 33.18; Appian 8.104.

7. Pliny the Elder, *H.N.* 33.4.10; 33.8; Herodian, *History* 3.8.4.

8. Tertullian, *Apologeticus* 6. See R. Seaford, *Pompeii* (New York, 1978), 75, for a color plate of the matron who wears a prominent gold ring with a large red stone. On the betrothal gift of a ring, see Pliny the Elder, *H.N.* 33.4.12.

9. Dio Cassius *Romaika* 53.30.3.

10. Pliny the Elder, *H.N.* 37.1–5.

11. Ibid., 37.1–4; Dio Cassius, *Romaika* 51.3.5–7; Suetonius, *Augustus* 2.50; SHA *Hadrianus* 3.8. Quotation from Dio Cassius 53.30.2.

12. Pliny the Elder, *H.N.* 33.12. Rheinisches Landesmuseum Trier, *Trier Kaiserresidenz und Bischopssitz* (Mainz, 1984), 115–16, pl. 33a and b.

13. B. Pfeiler, *Römischer Goldschmuck des ersten und zweiten Jahrhunderts n. Chr. nach datierten Funden* (Mainz, 1970), 105–6. See also Higgins, *Greek and Roman Jewelry;* F. H. Marshall, *Catalogue of the Jewellery: Greek, Etruscan and Roman* (Oxford, 1969); M. Henig, "Continuity and Change in the Design of Roman Jewellery," in *The Roman West in the Third Century*, BAR 109 (Oxford, 1981), 127–43; C. Barini, *Ornatus Muliebris* (Turin, 1956).

14. Pfeiler, *Römischer Goldschmuck.*

15. A. de Franciscis, *The National Archeological Museum of Naples* (Naples, n.d.), figs. 5, 16, 17. See also M. Grant, *The Art and Life of Pompeii and Herculaneum* (New York, 1979), 4, 66.

16. A. F. Shore, *Portrait Painting from Roman Egypt* (London, 1962), 12–16, pls. 2, 3, 11–14, 18. See also H. Zaloscer, *Porträts aus dem Wüstensand* (Vienna, 1961); and D. L. Thompson, *Mummy Portraits in the J. Paul Getty Museum* (Malibu, 1982), pls. 1 and 3, figs. 11, 17, 34.

17. D. Charlesworth, "Roman Jewellery Found in Northumberland and Durham," *Archaeologia Aeliana*, 4th ser., 39 (1961): 1–36 and plates; idem., "The Aesica Hoard," *Archaeologia Aeliana*, 5th ser, 1 (1973): 225–34. A. Maiuri, *La casa del Menandro e il suo tesoro di argenteria* (Rome, 1932); A. Comarmond, *Description de l'écrin d'une dame romaine trouvé à Lyon en 1841* (Lyon, 1844).

18. A. Böhme, "Frauenschmuck der römischen Kaiserzeit," *Antike Welt* 9 (1978): 3–16. For treasure hoards from Petrijanec, Osztropataka, Starcevo, and Szilágy Somlyó, see R. Noll, *Vom Altertum zum Mittelalter: Kunsthistorisches Museum* (Vienna, 1958), pls. 14, 31, 32, 35–40.

19. Pliny the Elder, *H.N.* 37.30, 44. See also D. Strong, *Catalogue of the Carved Amber in the Department of Greek and Roman Antiquities* (London, 1966).

20. A. Garside, ed., *Jewelry: Ancient to Modern* (New York, 1979), 119–20, nos. 328, 330; C. C. Vermeule, "Numismatics in Antiquity," *Swiss Numismatic Review* 54 (1975): 5–32. See also Marshall, *Catalogue of the Jewellery,* for earlier exam-

ples, e.g., no. 2727, a third-century gold necklace with an aureus of Severus worked into a pendant.

21. Procopius, *The Gothic War* 7.1.8. For a sixth-century pectoral, composed of fifteen coins depicting emperors in military dress, which has been identified as a collection of military trophies belonging to a distinguished military commander or an emperor, see K. R. Brown, "Pectoral," in *Age of Spirituality*, ed. Weitzmann, 318–19, no. 295. Another, Christian example is a medallion depending from a coin arrangement very similar to no. 295. The medallion shows on the obverse the Annunciation and, on the reverse, the miracle of Cana; see Brown, "Pectoral," 319–21, no. 296, and color pl. 8.

22. For other examples from Palmyra, see D. Mackay, "The Jewellery of Palmyra and Its Significance," *Iraq* 11 (1949): 160–87, pl. 58:2. For an example from Tunis, see Marshall, *Catalogue of the Jewellery*, 339, pl. 66, no. 2866.

23. W. Weber, *Constantinische Deckengemälde aus dem römischen Palast unter dem Trierer Dom* (Trier, 1984), fig. 15, possibly depicts Constantia with her jewelry box.

24. Garside, *Jewelry*, 94–103, no. 283.

25. Pliny the Elder, *H.N.* 33.12; Rheinisches Landesmuseum Trier, *Trier Kaiserresidenz*, 111–14, no. 31.

26. F. Deichmann, G. Bovini, H. Brandenburg, *Repertorium der christlich-antiken Sarcophäge Rom und Ostia* (Wiesbaden, 1967), pl. 40; Tertullian, *De pallio* 1.8.

27. Bonfante, *Etruscan Dress*, 143–44 and esp. nn. 95 and 98 for ancient references.

28. Pliny the Elder, *H.N.* 33.10, 11. Dio Cassius, *Romaika* 42.19, 49, 51.21.4. Suetonius, *Claudius* 5.17. Herodian 2.11.6, 2.13.12. Suetonius, *Tiberius* 3.17, 3.69; *Julius Caesar* 1.45. Dio Cassius, *Romaika*, 51.20.2–3, 53.26.5. Suetonius, *Caligula* 4.19.

29. F. Klauner et al., *Das Kunsthistorisches Museum in Wien* (Vienna, 1978), 325, pl. 40. See also Alföldi, "Insignien," pl. 22.

30. SHA *Aurelianus* 13. For coins of Augustus and Agrippa, see J. P. C. Kent, *Roman Coins* (New York, 1978), 278, pl. 39, no. 137.

31. For portrait heads of Marcus Aurelius and Diocletian, see J. Inan and E. Rosenbaum, *Roman and Early Byzantine Portrait Sculpture in Asia Minor* (London, 1966), 76, pl. 27.2–3, no. 44, and 85, pl. 39.3–4, no. 61. For the roundel, which is in the Antikenmuseum, Berlin, see Thompson, *Mummy Portraits*, 26, fig. 46; Strong, *Roman Art*, fig. 184.

32. Herodian 5.3.6 (Elagabalus) and 12.4 (Domitian). For examples of bronze crowns, see J. M. C. Toynbee, *Art in Roman Britain* (London, 1962), 177–78, pls. 139–41. For the Naukratis crown, see Marshall, *Catalogue of the Jewellery*, xlv, no. 3045; 364, pl 70. For the sculptures, see Inan and Rosenbaum, *Portrait Sculpture*, 109, pl. 65, no. 111; 124; pl. 85.1–2, no. 143; 128, pl. 87.1–2, no. 151; 139, pl. 103.1–2, no. 174; 141–42, pl. 104.1–2, no. 178; 148–49, pl. 111.3–4, no. 190.

33. Alföldi, "Insignien," 139f. See also Kent, *Roman Coins*, pl. 49, no. 171; pl. 54, no. 191.

34. Kent, *Roman Coins*, 303, pl. 110, no. 379; 306, pl. 115, no. 404; 315, pl. 133, nos. 503 and 504; 318, pl. 139, no. 534; 319, pl. 141, nos. 538 and 539.

35. SHA *Duo Gallieni* 16; Kent, *Roman Coins*, 314, pl. 131, no. 488.

36. Alföldi, "Insignien," 145. W. Smith et al., *A Dictionary of Greek and Roman Antiquities* (London, 1901), 619–20, notes that Alexander adopted the diadem after his conquest of Darius.

37. Suetonius, *Caligula* 4.52; *Titus* 11.5. SHA *Antoninus Elagabalus* 13.

38. Alföldi, "Insignien," 148 n. 2.

39. SHA *Tyranni Triginta: Zenobia* 30. On Diocletian and Maximian, see J. C. Rolfe, ed., *Ammianus Marcellinus* LCL (Cambridge, Mass., 1935). E. Gibbon, *Decline and Fall of the Roman Empire* (New York, 1981), 204–5, mentions that the diadem (in the form of a broad white fillet set with pearls) which Diocletian ventured to use was an ornament detested by the Romans as the "odious ensign of royalty." There is, however, some disagreement about whether Diocletian did wear a diadem; see Alföldi, "Insignien," 149–50.

40. Alföldi, "Insignien," 65 and n. 4.

41. SHA *Duo Gallieni* 16; *Carus, Carinus, et Numerianus* 17. See also Kent, *Roman Coins*, 319, pl. 141, no. 537.

42. SHA *Hadrianus* 10; *Severus Alexander* 4.

43. Garside, *Jewelry*, 153–54, nos. 427, 428, 433, 435.

44. Pliny the Elder, *H.N.* 33.6.

45. I am grateful to Bernard Goldman for information on the three-pendant brooch, which continues after the San Vitale mosaics and which played a part in Sasanian imagery. See his "The Imperial Jewel at Taq-I Bustan," in *Archaeologia Iranica et Orientalis*, ed. L. De Meyer and E. Haeriuck (Ghent, 1989), 831–46. See also O. G. von Simson, *Sacred Fortress: Byzantine Art and Statecraft in Ravenna* (Chicago, 1988), pl. 27, "The Granting of the *Autokephalia*," Sant'Apollinare in Classe, Ravenna.

46. Simson, *Sacred Fortress*, 23; Delbrueck, *Consular-diptychen*, 36–40.

47. P. Grierson, *Byzantine Coins* (London, 1982), 30–32.

48. Simson, *Sacred Fortress*, 24–27; W. Bendazzi and R. Ricci, *Ravenna: Mosaics, Art History, Archaeology, Monuments, Museums* (Ravenna, 1987), 30.

49. For the Osztropataka brooch, see A. Riegl, *Late Roman Art Industry*, trans. R. Winkes (Rome, 1985), 195, pl. 2. For the imitation sardonyx pendant, see Marshall, *Catalogue of the Jewellery*, 319–20, pl. 61, no. 2745. Another brooch, in the Capitoline Museum, Rome, is in the form of an engraved oval amethyst with two hanging gold chains with gold leaf pendants; see Barini, *Ornatus Muliebris*, 102–3. I am grateful to Larissa Bonfante for this reference.

50. Riegl, *Late Roman Art Industry*, 3. See also N. Fettich, *Der zweite Schatz von Szilágy Somlyó* (Budapest, 1932), 21–23. Recently A. Kiss has dated the brooches found at Szilágy Somlyó to the fifth century; see his "Der Zeitpunkt der Verbergung der Schatzfunde I und II von Szilágysomlyó," *Acta Antiqua Academiae Scientiarum Hungaricae* 30 (1988): 401–16.

For the Nagy Mihály piece, see Riegl, *Late Roman Art Industry*, 195, pl. 4; Klauner et al., *Kunsthistorisches Museum in Wien*, 53; Noll, *Vom Altertum zum Mittelalter*, pl. 26. For the cameo, see G. M. A. Richter, *Catalogue of Greek and*

*Roman Antiquities in the Dumbarton Oaks Collection* (Cambridge, Mass., 1956), 15–19, pl. 6, no. 11. The three-pendant motif has a Greek predecessor. In the British Museum, a Greek gold pendant, dated to the fourth to third centuries B.C., has three suspended chains ending in pomegranate beads; see Marshall, *Catalogue of the Jewellery*, 231, pl. 40, no. 2064.

51. M. C. Ross, *Byzantine and Early Mediaeval Antiquities in the Dumbarton Oaks Collection*, vol. 2, *Jewelry, Enamels, and Art of the Migration Period* (Washington, D.C., 1965), 1, pl. 1.

52. Cyprus Museum, *Jewellery in the Cyprus Museum* (Nicosia, 1971), 53, pl. 36. A similar necklace is in the collection of the Walters Art Gallery in Baltimore; see M. Mitchell, ed., *Objects of Adornment: Five Thousand Years of Jewelry from the Walters Art Gallery* (Baltimore, 1984), 110, no. 106.

53. See also K. R. Brown, "Necklace," in *Age of Spirituality*, ed. Weitzmann, 310–11, fig. 284.

54. For a double gold solidus showing the rosette brooch, see Kent, *Roman Coins*, pl. 163, no. 647.

55. J. Deer, *Der Kaiserornat Friedrichs II* (Bern, 1952), 47. See Alföldi ("Insignien," 145–49) for a discussion of the diadem; he relates that Diocletian did not accept the diadem even though he had the title of Dominus.

56. See Kent, *Roman Coins*, 331–32, pl. 165, no. 653, for a solidus from Constantinople.

57. See also Kent, *Roman Coins*, 158, no. 623; 328, pl. 159, no. 622. See Rheinisches Landesmuseum Trier, *Trier Kaiserresidenz*, 156, cat. no. 50: 1 and 2; 135–37, for examples of silver plates which show Licinius and his son wearing pendant brooches. See also J. P. C. Kent and K. S. Painter, *Wealth of the Roman World, A.D. 300–700* (London, 1977), 20–21, cat. no. 1, for the "Munich Treasure," a bowl of Licinius I (A.D. 321–22); also 73, 164, cat. no. 373, which shows a multiple aureus of Licinius I and Licinius II (A.D. 320) in which both are nimbed and wear brooches with two double pendant jewels.

58. Kent, *Roman Coins*, 347–48, pl. 167, no. 664.

59. Ibid., 335, pl. 173, no. 683.

60. Ammianus Marcellinus 21.1.4. Kent, *Roman Coins*, 337, pl. 177, no. 698, an aureus of Valentinian I. For the Missorium of Theodosius, see Delbrueck, *Spätantike Kaiserporträts*, pl. 96; K. J. Shelton, "Missorium of Theodosius," in *Age of Spirituality*, ed. Weitzmann, 74–76, no. 64. For an example of a portrait of Constantine wearing a double row of jewels on his head, see the bronze head of Constantine in the National Museum of Belgrade and J. D. Breckenridge, "Head of Constantine I," in *Age of Spirituality*, ed. Weitzmann, 16–18, no. 10.

61. H. Kantorowicz, "Gods in Uniform," *PAPhS* 105 (1961): 387; S. Spain, "The Promised Blessing: The Iconography of the Mosaics of S. Maria Maggiore," *ABull* 61 (1979): 519–40, figs. 3 and 5.

62. Deer, *Der Kaiserornat*, 43–44; Volbach, *Elfenbeinarbeiten*, 20–30, pl. 1, no. 1.

63. J. D. Breckenridge, "Medallion of Justinian I," in *Age of Spirituality*, ed. Weitzmann, 45, no. 44.

64. For the Ravenna statue, identified as Theodosius or Justinian, see Bendazzi and Ricci, *Ravenna*, 163–64. The Vienna statue is dated to the second quarter of the fourth century, the period of Constantine, Licinius, and their descendants.

65. See Kent, *Roman Coins*, 339, pl. 182, no. 718; G. Giacosa, *Women of the Caesars: Their Lives and Portraits in Coins*, trans. R. Holloway (Milan, 1977), pl. 64; and esp. K. G. Holum, *Theodosian Empresses: Women and Imperial Dominion in Late Antiquity* (Berkeley, 1982), 32, 34.

66. Giacosa, *Women of the Caesars*, 108 and 23–24, pl. 5. Kent (*Roman Coins*, 281, pl. 45, no. 159) does not agree that it is Livia who is shown in these personified virtues but terms the representations "female bust[s]."

67. Holum, *Theodosian Empresses*, 33. See also M. Alföldi, *Die constantinische Goldprägung* (Mainz, 1963), 93f. The dupondius is in the British Museum. A triangular stephane, dated to the late fourth to third centuries B.C., was found at Madytus in the Troad; see Higgins, *Greek and Roman Jewelry*, 158, pl. 45C.

68. Kent, *Roman Coins*, 293, pl. 78, nos. 272, 273, 274; 295, pl. 84, no. 291; 304, pl. 111, no. 639.

69. Giacosa, *Women of the Caesars*, pl. 60; Kent, *Roman Coins*, pl. 161, no. 639. The coin depicting Helena is in the Louvre. Holum, *Theodosian Empresses*, 33; Alföldi, *Die constantinische Goldprägung*, 93f.

70. Holum, *Theodosian Empresses*, 34.

71. Giacosa, *Women of the Caesars*, 127, pl. 70. See also Kent, *Roman Coins*, pl. 192.

72. See Spain, "Promised Blessing," fig. 27. Spain presents the interesting interpretation that the woman in gold may represent Sarah, who also experienced a supernatural birth (530–31).

73. S. Sande, "Zur Porträtplastik des sechsten nachchristlichen Jahrhunderts," *AAAH* 61 (1975): figs. 46–48. See also R. Delbrueck, "Porträts byzantinischer Kaiserinnen," *RM* 28 (1913): 310–57, pls. 8–18.

74. For the incomplete head, see Inan and Rosenbaum, *Portrait Sculpture*, 90, pl. 42.3–4, no. 67.

75. The Lateran head appears in Sande, "Zur Porträtplastik," figs. 9–11. For the Louvre head and the Vienna diptych, see J. D. Breckenridge, "Head of Ariadne," in *Age of Spirituality*, ed. Weitzmann, 30–31, no. 24, and "Diptych Leaf with Ariadne," 31–32, no. 25. See also Klauner et al., *Kunsthistorisches Museum in Wien*, pl. 58, AS Inv. X 39. Both diptychs are shown in Volbach, *Elfenbeinarbeiten*, 49–50, pl. 27, no. 51.

76. Sande, "Zur Porträtplastik," 72.

77. Procopius, *De aedificiis* 3.21–27.

78. Franciscis, *Museum of Naples*, 38–39; Brown, *World of Late Antiquity*, pl. 11. See also Kent and Painter, *Wealth of the Roman World*, for Sasanian jewelry adorning kings of the third through fifth centuries (144, 146–47, nos. 305, 307, 308).

79. Richter, *Catalogue of Greek and Roman Antiquities*, 17–18.

80. Alföldi, "Insignien," 59, 65, 147.

# Roman Footwear

6

NORMA GOLDMAN

One can practically walk in the footsteps of the ancient Romans by investigating their footwear at home and abroad. It is possible to identify the many ways they devised for covering, protecting, elevating, and decorating their feet, which provide an interesting display of variety and ingenuity from Etruscan through imperial Roman times. These varieties always reflected Roman ideas of class, rank, trade, and profession. Senators, knights, priests, actors onstage, soldiers, citizens, and noncitizens all wore distinctive dress and footwear, appropriate to their roles in life. Footwear cannot be ignored in a consideration of the whole picture of costume (along with clothing, hairstyle, and jewelry), and the shoe styles give evidence for both indigenous costume and for changing fashion in Rome and in the provinces.[1]

Our knowledge about footwear comes from a variety of sources—visual, archaeological, and literary. Visual materials include paintings, sculpture, and mosaics, all representations by artists showing real or imaginary footwear on humans, gods, or heroes (fig. 6.1). Archaeological finds include leather, wood, cork, or metal fragments from which shoes in antiquity were actually made. On the *limes* in the northern provinces—Germany, the Netherlands, and England—many of these finds of leather sandals, shoes, and boots have been preserved in continuously wet contexts. Carbonized sandal soles have been remarkably preserved in Etruria (fig. 6.2).[2] Fiber and leather sandals have been preserved in Egypt, and sandals have been excavated in the Near East, where the climate has been continuously dry (fig. 6.3a).[3] Perishable felt, straw, cork, or plant fibers have not survived in Italy or France, although some remains of gold repoussé decoration on leather or fabric footwear have

been found in a recently excavated Celtic tomb (fig. 6.3b).[4]

Literary sources about Roman footwear include many references by ancient authors in poetry and in prose, culminating in the *Edict of Diocletian* (A.D. 301), which lists many varieties of sandals, shoes, and boots from the late third century A.D.[5] Isidore of Seville (A.D. 602–36) in his *Origines* included a section on footwear. This was a seventh-century reworking of Varro's original work on shoes, no longer extant.[6] In using literary sources, however, one must always take into account the nature of the work (poetry, essay, narrative, lexicon, price list), since extraneous factors of meter, artistic license, and change of meaning may have affected the choice and interpretation of various words for footwear. Carol van Driel-Murray adds the following caution in her discussion of footwear from an archaeological site on the northern *limes:* "It is the lack of awareness of the changes taking place in Roman footwear through time which renders the link between text and illustration . . . tenuous in the extreme. A similar caution applies to the use of both terminology and prices in Diocletian's Price Edict, since observed changes in technology by the end of the 3rd century mean that even where terms are familiar from earlier references, the articles themselves had changed beyond all recognition."[7]

As with other aspects of Roman life and culture, there are Greek forms antecedent to, or contemporary with, Etruscan and Roman styles in footwear that first influenced Roman fashion and later in turn were influenced by the Romans as the empire spread in the Mediterranean world. Tracing these styles has been made an easier task by Katherine Dohan Morrow's recent study, *Greek Footwear and the Dating of Sculpture,* in which

101

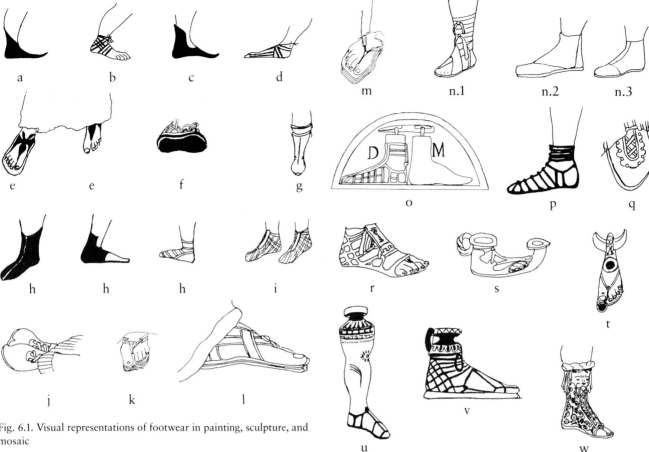

Fig. 6.1. Visual representations of footwear in painting, sculpture, and mosaic

**Footwear in Painting**

a. Tomb of the Baron, Tarquinia: Flute player wearing calcei repandi

b. Tomb of the Augurs, Tarquinia: Phersu wearing crepidae

c. Tomb of the Augurs, Tarquinia: Augur wearing calcei repandi

d. Tomb of the Leopards, Tarquinia: Flute player wearing crepidae

e. Villa of the Mysteries, Pompeii: Terrified initiate wearing sandals

f. Villa of the Mysteries, Pompeii: Ariadne, central panel, with sole of crepida facing viewer

g. Villa of the Mysteries, Pompeii: Flagellante wearing a boot or buskin

h. Museo Nazionale Archeologico, Naples: Bakery shop customers, father and son. Male to left of father wearing calcei and son wearing crepidae

i. Museo Nazionale Archeologico, Naples: Aeneas being treated for a wound on the thigh, wearing crepidae

**Footwear in Sculpture**

j. Villa Giulia Museum, Rome: from Caere, terracotta sarcophagus depicting a couple on a couch, with the wife wearing calcei repandi

k. Capitoline Museum, Rome: Juno wearing sandal with thick platform sole, indented between large and second toes

l. Museo Nazionale Archeologico, Naples: Apollo wearing sandal (solea) with platform sole, indented between large and second toes

m. Hadrian's Villa, Tivoli: Karyatid wearing sandal with thick platform sole (no toe indentations)

n. Ara Pacis, Rome: 1. Flamen wearing calceus patricius
2. Rex Sacrorum wearing pero or calceus
3. Agrippa wearing pero or calceus

o. Capitoline Museum, Rome: Tombstone of C. Julius Aelius, a shoemaker, showing the right and left lasts (formae), with a caliga on the left one

p. Trajan's Column, Rome: Soldier wearing caliga

q. Norwegian Institute, Rome: Statue of an empress wearing calceus decorated with pearls

r. Metropolitan Museum of Art, New York: Ivory foot wearing trochas (gallica?)

s. Offenbach Shoe Museum: Marble foot lamp wearing trochas

t. British Museum, London: Terracotta lamp in the form of a foot, wearing a sandal with yoke-thong arrangement

u. Villa Giulia Museum, Rome: Leg vase wearing sandal of simplified crepida style

v. British Museum, London: Foot vase wearing crepida

w. Museo Nazionale Archeologico, Naples: Spirit of Rome, wearing dress parade boot

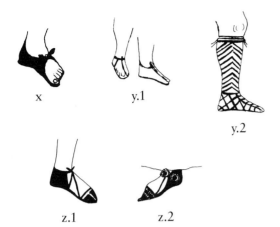

x

y.1

y.2

z.1        z.2

Fig. 6.1. Visual representations of footwear in painting, sculpture, and mosaic *(continued)*

Footwear in Mosaics

x. Museo Nazionale Archeologico, Naples: House of Cicero street musicians wearing soft sandals (soleae)

y. Piazza Armerina, Sicily: 1. Young courtier attendant wearing sandals
2. Courtier sacrificing, wearing buskins

z. San Vitale, Ravenna: 1. Courtier wearing latchet shoe tied at ankle
2. Justinian wearing flowered, jeweled latchet shoe tied at ankle

Fig. 6.2. Etruscan wooden sandals outlined in bronze. Original leather hinges are missing. End of sixth century B.C. Note the imprints of the toes in the right sandal. Bisenzio, tomb 80, Villa Giulia Museum, Rome, inv. 57156. Photo courtesy of the Villa Giulia Photo Archive.

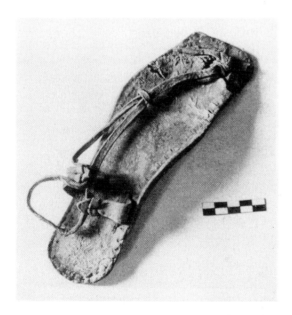

Fig. 6.3a. Woman's sandal from the terrace of the North Palace, ca. A.D. 130. Y. Yadin, *The Excavation of Masada, 1963/64, Preliminary Report* (Jerusalem, 1965), pl. 22B. Photo courtesy of Israel Exploration Society.

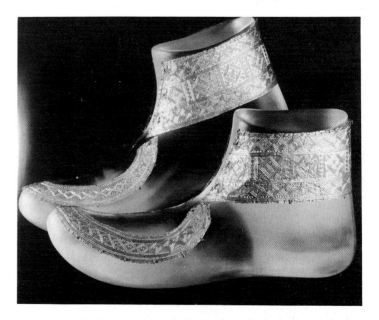

Fig. 6.3b. Gold repoussé decoration from felt or leather shoes excavated in a Celtic tomb. The curve of the decoration indicates that the shoes probably had turned-up toes. From A. Hartmann, "Die Bronze- und Goldfunde aus dem Fürstengrab von Hochdorf," in *Der Keltenfürst von Hochdorf,* p. 145, fig. 165.

Morrow catalogs typical examples of sandals, shoes, and boots on sculpture during five period styles: archaic, severe, classical fifth century, classical fourth century, and Hellenistic.[8] One of the problems in the Roman world is that similar styles appear, disappear, and reappear many times in the course of a thousand years of Roman history, making dating difficult. Compare, for example, how often shoes with pointed toes have been popular in American footwear, have disappeared, and then have reappeared, even in one's own lifetime. The same phenomenon in fashion must have occurred to some extent in the Roman world, although there does seem to be a ritual consistency in the representations of sandals, shoes, and boots for certain kinds of occasions and for certain classes and occupations. On monuments of assured date, such as the Ara Pacis and Trajan's Column, we have visual guidelines for several basic types of footwear that are firm and reassuring, even though the representations carry no labels identifying them as one type or another.[9] One common feature, however, is that most of the monuments represent footwear made of leather.

LEATHER

Leather goods from the waterlogged deposits in the northern provinces appear among archaeological finds, showing the use of leather in the ancient world for tents, more rarely for clothing (jerkins and breeches), for military gear (belts, shield coverings, horse trappings), but most commonly for footwear, both soles and uppers. Especially in military contexts, such as in the army camp at Vindonissa near Basel, Switzerland, there must have been constant need for hides to supply the army with boots (caligae). Hides for the caligae were of fine quality and sometimes, like pottery, were stamped with the maker's name. There is a reference to an army boot maker (caligarius) from Aquilea in the Po Valley, and we know that there was in Rome a Vicus Sandalarius, indicating an area for the sale of sandals, which in Rome were mostly made of leather.[10]

The civilian population depended on leather for footwear, and trade in hides was an important part of ancient commerce. Animal skins of goat, sheep, cow, bull, or ox were scraped and tanned by being impregnated or infused with a liquid made from tree bark, galls, mineral salts, or some form of "tannin." Commonly used were oak, spruce, or fir bark; sometimes a colorant was added in the tanning process. The process seems to have been an obnoxiously smelly one, and tanneries were not popular as neighboring shops. Tanning vats were found beneath the present Church of Santa Cecilia in Trastevere, and the tanning industry was probably kept "across the river," out of the central city, because of the smell.[11]

On the hair side, each animal skin has a distinctive grain, enabling experts to tell of what animal the leather was made. Most people generally wore shoes of natural color, but those who could afford the more expensive dyed leather wore shoes of black, red, or other colors. Black was produced by using melanteria, a copper vitriol containing iron; sometimes the leather or shoes were blackened with tar or pitch, and thus arose the Greek name pissyrgos (pitch worker) for a shoemaker. But other colors—white, gold, and purple—appear in Diocletian's Edict of prices in the beginning of the fourth century. A fourth-century reference mentions a guild of tanners, a guild of three hundred slipper makers, and makers of heavy nailed boots (caligarii), as well as makers of crepides, crepidarii. At Ostia there was a guild of dealers in hides.[12] At Pompeii, the organization of a leather craft industry and shoe industry is apparent; a wealthy magistrate may have supplied the leather for individual shoemakers. The tanning establishment was near the Stabian Gate in Regio 1.52, and the shops appear in Regio 7.1.41–42. In this shop were found tools for working leather, which included knives, chisels, awls, and a moon-shaped rocking cutter.[13] No leather finds from Pompeii have appeared, however. The leather either disintegrated or was thrown out in excavation.

Where leather finds have been excavated in the northern provinces, researchers have studied the kinds of leather used in footwear construction, the types of footwear, sizes (with population projections based on the sizes), and stitching patterns. A new body of comparative information is beginning to appear as the actual leather finds are being published. Restoring the crumpled leather finds from waterlogged wells, ditches, and riverbeds in the northern provinces has become a new branch of archaeological research, with the attendant problems of storing wet leather and cleaning and stabilizing it. After the leather has been safely dried, various techniques are used to rehydrate and restore the oils necessary to preserve and display the footwear. Drawing of footwear patterns is an important part of the process before and after restoration, both to record the shape and size prior to drying in order to determine shrinkage and to define the technology used in construction. This is best done while the recovered finds are still wet. Experts in photography, radiology, and retreating the finds then work on the leather to document, analyze, and restore suppleness. New drawings are made of the restored products.[14] At Saalburg, a modern shoemaker has reproduced some of the more interesting of the civilian shoes, and the modern reproductions, along with the

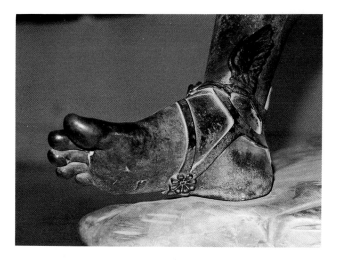

Fig. 6.4. Statue of Mercury resting, attributed to Lysippus, detail. Museo Nazionale Archeologico, Naples.

patterns, are displayed next to the restored originals in the Saalburg Museum.

### BARE FEET

The unshod foot is not unusual in real life, and probably many Romans went barefoot, particularly in rural areas. In art, however, the unshod foot offers many interpretations. In real life one goes barefoot for various reasons: for comfort when a foot is sore; for the aesthetic pleasure and freedom associated with touching the earth; for the safety of sailors walking on the wet deck of a ship; for religious reasons, while standing on holy ground or performing a sacred ritual; and for the simple economic reason of poverty. Doubtless many ancient Romans, the city poor, slaves, and those in rural areas, walked barefoot. We have no record of whether they wrapped their feet in straw or other fibers to protect them from the cold or from harsh terrain. Artists usually depicted the upper classes in sculpture. Many times these images show the foot bare to indicate divinity, heroization, religious sanctity, or piety. Augustus, for example, in the Prima Porta sculpture is unshod, obviously an allusion to divinity (see fig. 12.1). The bronze sculpture of seated Mercury from the Naples Museum shows the god shod in elaborate winged sandals which have no soles. Obviously the god would need none, for he had no need to walk on earth (fig. 6.4).

### PERONES

Slave owners on the great *latifundia* must have provided some simple foot covering to keep farm workers shod, thereby keeping farms in efficient operation. Peasants and farmers had a simple boot or shoe of natural-col-

ored leather, which seems originally to have been called the *pero*. Literary evidence for the term makes it a matter of conjecture of just how the shoe looked, and few identifiable artistic representations of the lower classes exist. Literary testimony says that those who had attained magistrate status wore the enclosed Roman shoe or calceus, and all others wore the pero.[15] Vergil refers to the pero as the rustic shoeboot of the hardy men from Praeneste who came to fight with Aeneas with one foot bare and the other shod in rawhide (*Aeneid* 7.722). Juvenal says that mountain peasants tell their sons that a real man does not disdain to wear "knee-boots" *(perone alto)* when it is icy-cold outside (*Satires* 14.185). If the adjective *alto* has to be added to *perone*, then the shoeboot may have been low or ankle-high by implication. What it looked like is difficult to judge, since there seems to be many forms of the pero, carved by sculptors and pictured by painters. John Pollini, in his study of Augustan sculpture on the Ara Pacis, refers to the low shoeboot worn by some of the men as the pero, in contrast to the calcei patricii or senatorii worn by the priests and Augustus, although these lower shoeboots could be just as logically called calcei.[16]

The problem of assigning terms for the various kinds of footwear in Rome and in the provinces is complicated by the use of accepted "archaeological" terms for sandals *(soleae)*, closed shoes *(calcei)*, military boots *(caligae)*, sewn slippers *(socci)*, and one-piece shoes *(carbatinae)*, retained for convenience in cataloging. We shall never know for sure whether the Romans themselves consistently referred to the various shoe styles by these terms, despite, or perhaps because of, the literary evidence, which varies from author to author and changes over years of Roman history. The best that can be done is to piece together the hints we get from the writers with the visual evidence from the artists and from the finds. Van Driel-Murray, in her text preceding the catalog of the footwear from the Legio I Minervia am Bonner Berg, has cautioned against the definitive use of these terms, especially when only soles have been preserved and the uppers are missing.[17] Sandal soles, however, are easily identifiable by the hole for the thong, that slender strap which sometimes is preserved but more often is missing.

### SOLEAE, SANDALIA

The idea of separating or protecting the foot from the ground *(solum)* by sandals (soleae or sandalia) may be a Greek or Etruscan importation into Rome, but it could also easily be an idea independently developed to meet a practical situation, since many people all over the world seem to have developed a sandal of some sort. Roman sandals, however, display an interesting variety of strap

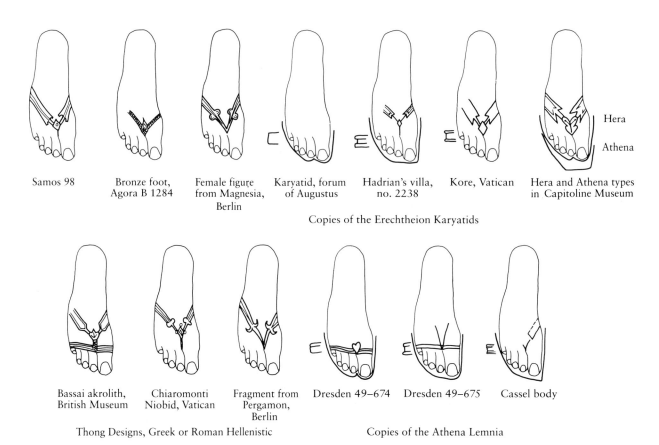

Samos 98

Bronze foot,
Agora B 1284

Female figure
from Magnesia,
Berlin

Karyatid, forum
of Augustus

Hadrian's villa,
no. 2238

Kore, Vatican

Hera and Athena types
in Capitoline Museum

Hera

Athena

Copies of the Erechtheion Karyatids

Bassai akrolith,
British Museum

Chiaromonti
Niobid, Vatican

Fragment from
Pergamon,
Berlin

Dresden 49–674

Dresden 49–675

Cassel body

Thong Designs, Greek or Roman Hellenistic

Copies of the Athena Lemnia

Fig. 6.5a. Greek and Roman sandal strap styles of the Hellenistic period. From Morrow, *Greek Footwear,* pp. 169–70.

Fig. 6.5b. Sandals worn by Juno. Capitoline Museum, Rome. Photo courtesy of the Capitoline Museum Photo Archive, inv. 5.

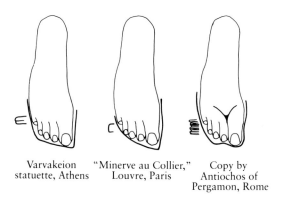

Varvakeion statuette, Athens    "Minerve au Collier," Louvre, Paris    Copy by Antiochos of Pergamon, Rome

Fig. 6.6. Copies of Athena Parthenos' multilayered platform sandal. From Morrow, *Greek Footwear*, p. 170.

and thong arrangements that seem to have Etruscan or Greek antecedents, although even these may belong to common Mediterranean styles. A popular kind of sandals in antiquity in the Mediterranean world is similar to one commonly sold today: a sandal sole is held to the foot by a thong inserted into the sole separating the large and second toe and attached to a yoke of upper straps which are also attached to the sole on the sides. The ancient strap decorations varied as much as do those displayed today in shop windows, with leather thongs, cords, or patterned straps attached to soles composed of layers of leather or, less often, made of wood. Morrow has drawn the varied styles of Greek and Hellenistic sandal straps, many of which appear also on Roman statues and paintings during all periods of Roman art (figs. 6.5a–b).[18] Sandals from Egypt and the Near East display many of the same types of strap arrangements, although the forty-one Egyptian ones from Karanis (first century B.C. to first century A.D.) in the collection at the Kelsey Museum in Ann Arbor, Michigan, are not made of leather but of wrapped, plaited, or sewn palm fiber, both for the basketry sole and the straps. Every civilization around the Mediterranean basin made sandals from whatever materials were locally available.

In the seventh century B.C. the sophisticated Etruscans even hinged the two-part wooden sole with leather, as evident in the carbonized sole outlined with metal from a tomb at Bisenzio, now in the Villa Giulia Museum in Rome. Leather hinges (no longer extant) connected the two parts, and a bronze frame held the contoured sole together (fig. 6.2). Even the impression of the toes still marks the sole, an eloquent "footnote."[19] These thick-soled sandals seem to have been popular throughout Etruscan times, since actual fragments of them have been found in early tombs, and they are represented on later monuments. A pair stands on the floor beside the bed of the woman in the third-century B.C. Tomb of the Reliefs at Cerveteri (Caere). The style was even exported or imi-

tated in Athens, the "fashion capital of the world. When elegant Athenian ladies in Aristophanes' time flocked to their shoe merchants or shoemakers to buy a pair of Etruscan sandals, they were perhaps buying these sandals with high hinged soles, rendered even more exotic by their golden laces."[20] If indeed the idea of the sandal did come originally from Greece, it soon returned with embellishments, for one Greek variety was called *tyrrhenica*, referring to the sandal with a thick wooden multilayered sole with gilded straps possibly worn by Athena Parthenos, according to contemporary literary evidence, a style copied in later Roman platform sandals (fig. 6.6).[21]

Paintings, mosaic, and sculpture depict the many varieties of sandals common in Italy throughout all periods of the Roman Republic and the Roman Empire. The artwork from the Bay of Naples gives examples of every type of footwear, including sandals. In the room of the initiation in the Villa of the Mysteries at Pompeii, wall paintings show female votary attendants wearing a simple kind of soft sandal with covered heel and a thin sole, similar to the ones worn by the street musicians in the mosaic from the House of Cicero (fig. 6.7). The female in scene 7 wears the sandal tied at the ankle in a soft leather knot with an extra strap over the vamp, which narrows as it extends to the toe thong (fig. 6.8).

One of the most elegant of the soled sandals is the one worn by Apollo in the red porphyry seated figure in the central hall in the Naples Museum (fig. 6.9). The feet and sandals are carved in white marble and show clearly inch-wide straps tooled with a plain raised border in a fine design of a buttoned yoke holding the sole to the foot with the thong between the large and second toe, and with extra crossing straps to complete the pattern over the instep. The sandal is classic in style and could be sold today in any fashionable shoe store.

How much the Romans along the Bay of Naples were indebted to the Greeks for such a sophisticated style in footwear is impossible to say. As in so many other aspects of fashion for house, home, and daily life, Greek artisans may have done the work, or Romans may have imitated Greek styles. If the footwear is found on a work of art excavated on Italian soil, however, then it can be classed as "Italian" or "Roman," even if the hand that executed the work of art (or made the shoe) was Greek, or if a Roman copyist deliberately repeated a Greek image.[22] Morrow has discussed footwear on Roman copies of original Greek sculpture, and she concludes that although some copyists faithfully reproduced all the features of the original statue, including the footwear, some fused later fashions with earlier styles. A clear example of the latter occurs in the Roman representations of the Karyatids from the Erechtheum in Athens as copied in the upper register of the porticos of the Forum

Fig. 6.7. Soft sandals worn by street musicians, mosaic, House of Cicero. Museo Nazionale Archeologico, Naples.

Fig. 6.8. Soft sandals worn by the terrified initiate in scene 7 of the paintings in the room of the Dionysiac initiation in the Villa of the Mysteries at Pompeii. Photo from Maiuri, *La villa dei misteri*, pl. 7.

Fig. 6.9. Apollo Citaredo wearing sandal with buttoned thong. Museo Nazionale Archeologico, Naples, no. 6281.

Fig. 6.10. Karyatid wearing the unindented platform sandal, detail. From Hadrian's Villa at Tivoli. Photo by Kim Hartswick.

of Augustus and along the pool of the Canopus at Hadrian's Villa. On the Erechtheum Kore C from the British Museum, the only one with extant footwear, the sandal is of an Attic type with unindented sole, but on the later Roman copies in the upper register of the Forum of Augustus, a Hellenistic sole with indentation between the large and second toe is used. At Hadrian's Villa, the Karyatids along the Canopus Pool again wear sandals with the Attic unindented sole (fig. 6.10).[23]

Indoors, various kinds of sandals were worn by all, nobles and slaves alike. Obviously they varied in quality and style, and people of the lower classes probably wore sandals outdoors as well. Literary evidence implies that only citizens of high status were entitled to wear the special kind of enclosed Roman shoe called *calcei patricii* or *senatorii.* Such restrictions would probably not have extended to the simple calcei in the northern provinces, where climate would have affected what was appropriate wear and the archaeological evidence shows footwear of the enclosed type for citizens and noncitizens alike.

An artistic representation of a substantial sandal with wide straps crisscrossing the vamp seems to have been both practical and popular in the Roman world (fig. 6.11). The style has Greek antecedents in sandals that Morrow classifies as *trochades* on the foot of a philosopher from Delphi, on the bronze foot fragment from the Antikythera wreck, and on a marble foot fragment from Delos. The style even echoes that of the famous Hermes of Praxiteles from Olympia.[24] The Roman version, clearly the same kind of sandal, has low, solid uppers along the sides, tapering to the toe section, which is bare. The solid sides, however, have horizontal slots along the top through which the wide laces are threaded to crisscross three times before going through large ankle loops. They are then tied in a neat bow at the top. The Roman example has a leaflike triangular tongue extending from the bottom of the laces down over the otherwise bare toes. The sober young magistrate Marcellus, sitting in the center of the upper gallery of the Capitoline Museum in Rome, wears these elegant sandals. They are more substantial than open-thong or strap sandals, and Morrow claims that, according to literary sources, they are similar to Greek trochades but that they are also similar to carbatinae in being pulled together by lacing through loops.[25] Aulus Gellius says that *gallicae* was a new word coming into use about the time of Cicero, who uses it in his *Philippics,* complaining that Anthony ran around outdoors improperly clad in "Gallic sandals and a cloak" (Aulus Gellius 13.22).

At the time of Diocletian, the Greek word *trochadia* appears as the equivalent for the Latin word *gallicae* in the *Edict* (9.12–14): *De Soleis et Gallicis,* men's rustic

Gallic sandals (perhaps for farm workers?), listed at eighty denarii a pair for double-soled and at fifty denarii a pair for single-soled. *Gallicae cursuriae* (for runners) were priced at sixty denarii a pair. Both of these seem to have been substantial sandals, and their use for farm workers and runners would imply sturdy construction. Morrow indicates in her glossary that the name *trochades* (diminutive, *trochadia*) is derived from the Greek verb *trecho,* "to run," suggesting the use of the sandal for runners. After a span of many years, however, the name by the time of the *Edict* may have referred to quite a different kind of shoe or sandal.

A second type of footwear listed along with the Gallic sandal in the *Edict* is called the *taurina,* meaning only that it was made of ox or bull hide. The varieties in the *Edict* are, for women, double-soled at fifty denarii a pair, single-soled at thirty denarii a pair (9.15–16). Sandals appear in the section "De Soleis Babylonicis et Purpureis et Foeniceis et Alvis" as *inauratae* (gilded) costing seventy-five denarii, and *lanatae* (possibly lined with wool or felt?) costing fifty denarii (9.24–25). One does not usually imagine a sandal being lined with wool, although some types of cork slippers in London from St. Magnus House had felt insoles. Perhaps the taurina was a more substantial, built-up shoe. The luxury of being decorated with gold, however, obviously made the gilded footwear, whatever its form, more valuable than the kind providing the comfort and warmth of fleecy sheepskin or warm felt.

What do the actual leather sandal finds add to literary references and artistic representations? From sites in the Netherlands, Germany (Saalburg, the Bonner Berg, Mainz, and Cologne), and England (along the Thames embankment in London and at Vindolanda, the Roman fort on the Stangate Road just south of the Roman Wall), there are hundreds of sandal soles, as well as some complete sandals, showing the remains of layered leather soles, three to seven layers thick, some with thongs still intact, some only with the holes for thong attachments, and many with hobnails on the soles in a variety of patterns (figs. 6.12a–b).[26] These have been preserved in continuously damp contexts—in wells, ditches, and marshy bogs, and beneath a clay layer that sealed out air. That there have been no such consistent climatic conditions in Italy and Gaul probably explains the lack of such archaeological remains in these two important areas.

The sandals display a great variety of shapes and sizes: there are foot-shaped ones, which would fit a normal foot; narrow, pointed-toed sandals for women and children; and even unusual ones with an exaggerated, wide foresection for men and boys, measuring almost three to four inches across the toe (fig. 6.13).[27] Carol van Driel-Murray in her classification of sandals notes this

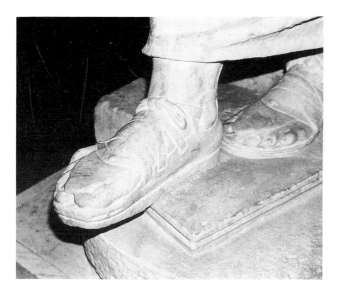

Fig. 6.12b. Sandal sole showing hobnail "follow me" pattern, possibly worn by a prostitute. Römisch-Germanisches Zentrals Museum, Mainz. All of the photos by the author in the RGZM are thanks to the kindness of the RGZM Director Ernst Künzl.

Fig. 6.11. Statue of Marcellus, wearing gallicae or trochades, detail. Capitoline Museum, Rome. Photo courtesy of Capitoline Museum Photo Archive, inv. 603.

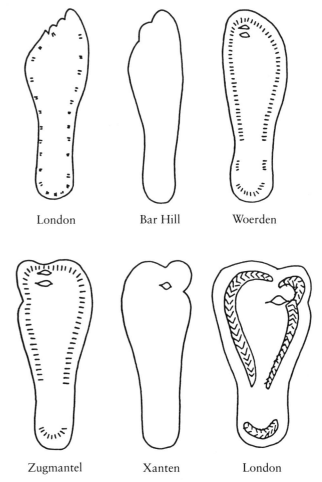

London          Bar Hill          Woerden

Zugmantel          Xanten          London

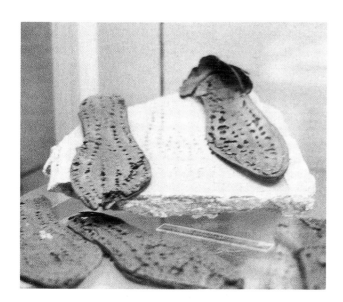

Fig. 6.12a. Sandal soles from Saalburg showing holes from the hobnails. Saalburg Museum.

Fig. 6.13. Sandal development, first to third centuries. From Van Driel-Murray, "Roman Footwear," fig. 5.

110

curious and fascinating change in style for the first through the third centuries A.D., when there was first a naturally-shaped sandal sole for all—men, women, and children. Then in the first quarter of the second century divergent male and female styles appeared, with the woman's sandal becoming more narrow and the toe more pointed, while the man's sandal became blunter and more broad. In the third century appeared the strange exaggeration of the toe section for men's sandals; smaller-sized soles also had wide toe sections, indicating that children, probably boys, also wore this unusual style. The position of the toes, shown by wear on the sole, indicates that the foot remained in a normal position, and the style did not last into the fourth century. Van Driel-Murray suggests that this style probably shows the power of a militaristic society and the favored position of soldiers influencing civilian garb in the provinces.[28]

Although the straps on most of the sandals have disappeared, the holes for the thongs are still quite evident, as is a variety of sophisticated stitching patterns on the soles, made before hobnailing. Some soles are stamped with the maker's mark or the leather tanner's mark; some are merely decorated on the inner sole. Many are hobnailed, since the practical Romans found that what was good for the army in preserving the shoe against wear was good for the civilian population as well. The patterns for the hobnails are also apparent in sandals from all of the sites, with first an edging of hobnails all around the outer edge of the sole and then a variety of designs on the interior, such as S-shapes, leaves, circles, roundels, and triangles.

One complete sandal from the Roman fort at Saalburg shows a stone centered in the wide strap that covers the instep.[29] A similar complete sandal appears at Vindolanda with an undecorated wide strap; it is stamped with the name of the tanner or maker, Lucius Aebutius, son of Titus. It was recovered from the praetorium of the third fort, dated about A.D. 102. Similar in having a wide vamp strap is a soccus or sewn slipper from New Fresh Wharf in London. This one has an elaborate tooled design in the center of a wide strap over the vamp, and examination by X-ray fluorescence has detected gold with a trace of copper in the patterned area. The delicate tooling of the decorated area is extraordinary, with a variety of circles in rows and scale patterns, edged with an intricate, tooled border design (fig. 6.14).[30] The three examples are similar only in having a wide strap across the vamp rather than the slender thong or narrow strap, and they testify to wearers with discriminating taste.

Excavations in England at Billingsgate Buildings in 1974 and at New Fresh Wharf (St. Magnus House) in 1985 in London reveal the same interesting progression of fashion in sandals as that documented by van Driel-Murray on the Continent. Of the nearly 150 leather shoes from New Fresh Wharf, which date from early to mid–third century, there are thirty-three sandals, and these are more numerous in larger sizes than those found at Billingsgate, which date from the late first to the mid–second century.[31] Such evidence suggests that sandals had become more popular with the adult population in the third century. The sandals are of two kinds: the traditional narrow standard version, with and without hobnails, with ten examples, and the broad version, with twenty-three examples. Only the soles of the sandals remain; the upper straps have disappeared. The broad-toed variety seems to be an unusual extreme in fashion in contrast to earlier Roman slender sandals. It is certainly related to the same wide version found at Saalburg, although the dating of the continental version is not so secure.[32] On the Continent, these strange wide-toed versions appear in both adult and children's sizes, the latter miniature versions of the adult sandal. One example from New Fresh Wharf in London even shows the human touch of a mend, with an extra piece of leather attached at the toe held by the thong.

Sandals often appear serving for functions other than as footwear. An interesting depiction of a sandal as a musical instrument appears in the illustration of a marble statue of a faun playing a foot organ (scabillum), which is made of wood or metal attached to a sandal, and clashing cymbals attached to each hand at the same time.[33] Roman marble, bronze, or terracotta lamps were sometimes fashioned in the form of feet shod in sandals (fig. 6.15).[34] Sandals in the form of a pair of glass bottles are a prize exhibit in the Roman-German Museum at Cologne. They are clear glass with colored thongs; when filled, they would have taken on the color of the contents (fig. 6.16).[35]

Sandals were removed when one reclined on the dining couch and were requested at the end of the banquet evening. To ask for one's sandals (poscere soleas) was to announce to the host the intention of departing. Clearly sandals were aesthetically pleasing, a source of delight as well as a practical foot covering.

## SCULPONEAE

Also classed as sandals are simple slip-on clogs with a thick wooden sole and a broad strap across the vamp, almost identical to Dr. Scholl's popular clog of today without the buckle.[36] The name sculponeae, applied to these clogs, evidently refers to the carving (sculpere) done to shape the wooden soles, sometimes with heels carved into the bottoms and sometimes hobnailed (fig. 6.17). Sculponeae appear in finds of footwear in Ger-

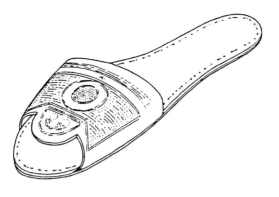

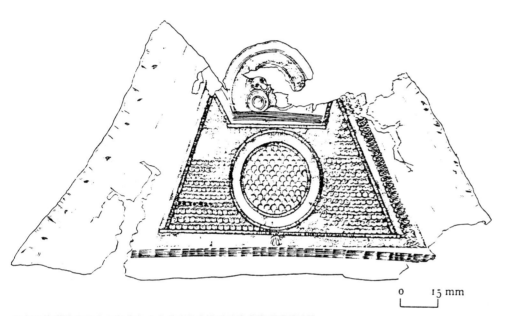

Fig. 6.14. Sewn slipper from New Fresh Wharf in London, third century A.D. The wide strap across the vamp has a central decoration. P. Mac-Connoran in "Footwear," *The Roman Quay at St. Magnus House,* fig. 8.28. Copyright © The Museum of London and the London and Middlesex Archaeology Society.

0    15 mm

Fig. 6.15. Terracotta footlamp showing network straps of sandal with hobnails. Photo courtesy of the Römisch-Germanisches Museum Rheinisches Bildarchiv, Cologne, published by A. Möhring, *Kölner Jahrbuch.*

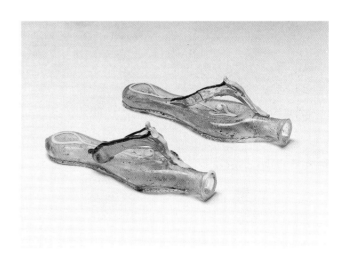

Fig. 6.16. Glass sandals from Cologne, 24 cm long. Second half of third century A.D. Photograph courtesy of the Römisch-Germanisches Museum Rheinisches Bildarchiv, Cologne, neg. 136277.

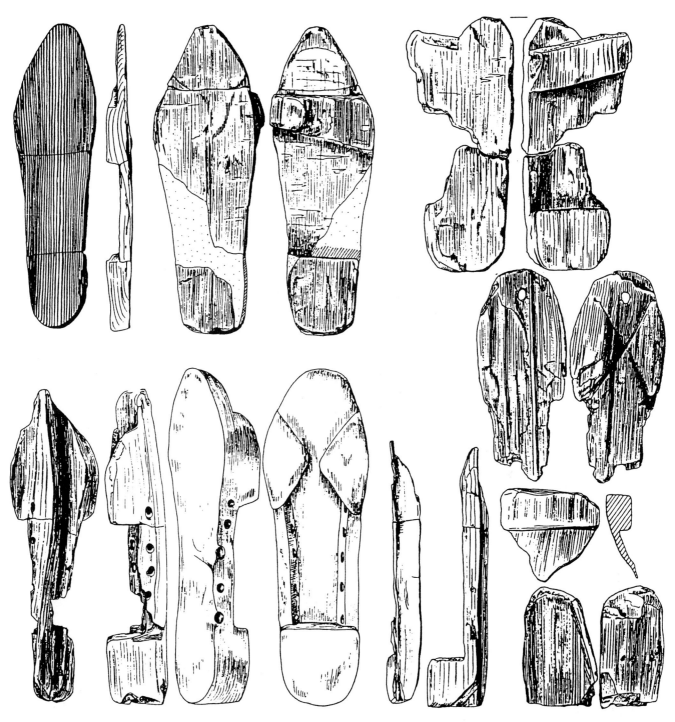

Fig. 6.17. Wooden soles of carved sculponeae. From *Saalburg Jahrbuch* 22 (1965): pl. 30.

many from Saalburg, from Mainz, and from Cologne, and in England from Vindolanda on the Roman Wall.[37] These date from the first through the third century A.D., and they show various degrees of preservation of both the wooden sole and the wide band across the vamp, which was often carelessly cut from a scrap of leather. Many have the metal nails still attached at the sides, and one at Vindolanda even has cork insets in the sole. Obviously such a practical, slip-on style lasted for centuries in various parts of the Roman Empire. The high wooden sole protected the foot from damp conditions, and it did not wear out as quickly as did a leather sole, even with hobnails on the bottom. The endurance of the style is evidenced in many parts of the world where "pattens," "sabots," and clogs of various kinds have continued in use to the present time for outdoor wear, and the style is found in bath complexes everywhere.

### CREPIDAE

In both Greece and Italy, sandals with a complicated network of upper straps, sometimes covering the toes and sometimes leaving the toes exposed, were known by a special name: *crepidae*, a Latin form of the Greek name *krepides* t̶ ̶ ̶ ̶ ̶ ̶ ̶ ̶ ̶ ̶ ̶ ̶ ̶ ̶ ̶ ̶ ̶.[38] The
network (̶ ̶ ̶ ̶ ̶ ̶ ̶ ̶ ̶ ̶ ̶ ̶ ̶ ̶ ̶ ̶ ̶ t̶
interwove ̶ ̶ ̶ ̶ ̶ ̶ ̶ ̶ ̶ ̶ ̶ ̶ ̶ ̶ ̶ :
lozenges, ̶ ̶ ̶ ̶ ̶ ̶ ̶ ̶ ̶ ̶ ̶ ̶ ̶ e
Greek an ̶ ̶ ̶ ̶ ̶ ̶ ̶ ̶ ̶ ̶ ̶ ̶ l
leather cu̶ ̶ ̶ ̶ ̶ ̶ ̶ ̶ ̶ ̶ ̶ ̶ e
military ̶̶ ̶ ̶ ̶ ̶ ̶ ̶ ̶ ̶ ̶ )f
the non-̶ ̶ ̶ ̶ ̶ ̶ ̶ ̶ ̶ ̶ ̶ e
network ̶ ̶ ̶ ̶ ̶ ̶ ̶ ̶ ̶ ̶ ̶ ̶ ls
of vario ̶ ̶ ̶ ̶ ̶ ̶ ̶ ̶ ̶ ̶ ̶ )r
thong. C ̶ ̶ ̶ ̶ ̶ ̶ ̶ ̶ ̶ ̶ ̶ d-
ing the a̶ ̶ ̶ ̶ ̶ ̶ ̶ ̶ ̶ ̶ ̶ )t
a regula ̶ ̶ ̶ ̶ ̶ ̶ ̶ ̶ ̶ ̶ ̶ )f
crepidae̶ ̶ ̶ ̶ ̶ ̶ ̶ ̶ ̶ ̶ ̶ ̶ is
depicted̶ ̶ ̶ ̶ ̶ ̶ ̶ ̶ ̶ ̶ ̶ ̶ ne
Mysteri̶ ̶ ̶ ̶ ̶ ̶ ̶ ̶ ̶ ̶ ̶ al
figure of the new bride of Dionysos, ̶ ̶ ̶ ̶ ̶ ̶ rs only one sandal; the other, sole out, faces the viewer with its many straps in disarray (fig. 6.1f). Ariadne's one bare foot perhaps indicates her partial apotheosis, perhaps merely her state of relaxation. Crepidae are also evident in paintings across time, from the Tarquinia tomb paintings (figs. 6.1b, d) of the fifth century B.C. to paintings in the Naples Museum from the first century A.D. They seem to be worn by both males and females. Morrow differentiates between *krepides* and *trochades*: the latter, she says, have solid leather uppers covering the heel and sides of the foot but only laces and straps over the toes, although a mixture of the two styles often occurs.[39]

An ivory foot encased in a crepida-style sandal, displayed in the Metropolitan Museum in New York, is loosely dated by the museum to the imperial period (fig. 6.18). The sandal is similar to the kind that Morrow has described in her catalog of Greek sandals from Pergamon, blending looping features of the *trochades* over the instep with those of the network-heeled crepides, but it lacks a sole, making it more like a carbatina. In addition, a lingula, or overlapping decorated wide tongue, covers the bow of the lacing at the ankle and extends over the crossed laces at the instep. According to Morrow, this overfolding tongue does not appear on sculpture in Greece until the second century B.C. and attests to rising Roman power in Greece and Asia Minor. Because the material is ivory and the carved designs are of a most elegant nature, the sculpture probably represented someone of great importance or wealth.

### CARBATINAE

Included with Roman crepidae is the single-piece moccasin-type shoe referred to in all the catalogs as a carbatina. There is some question about the word itself, since it appears neither in the *Oxford Latin Dictionary* nor in the *Thesaurus Linguae Latinae*, although a version of it, *carpatina* or *carbasina*, does exist (the former, of Greek origin, in a single lewd Catullus reference, 98.4). For archaeological cataloging, however, the word *carbatina* has been accepted, referring to single-piece footwear. This shoe was known in the Greek world: it consisted of a single piece of leather with holes along the edges. A cord laced through the holes drew the edges together. Sophisticated versions of it appear on the *limes,* where the entire shoe, both the sole and the sides, is similarly cut from one piece of leather. The sides end in patterns of loops, usually of graduated sizes, smaller at the toe and larger at the ankle. A lace or thong is threaded through the loops to pull the entire shoe together. On the Roman *limes* in Germany and England the carbatina seems to have been a popular kind of shoe, allowing for a variety of loopwork decoration (fig. 6.19a). It was usually sewn up the heel. Its distinctive feature is the network of loops, with a central lacing which raises the sides over the vamp and instep and even around the ankle. Usually there is no undersole or inner sole, but it would be possible to add an undersole attached beneath the bottom to reinforce the central section, which would become the midsole. An inner sole could be added to protect the foot from the turned points of the hobnails, if they were added. Thus the caliga might be considered a form of carbatina, although it is no longer so classified by van Driel-Murray, since the carbatina usually has no inner or outer sole.[40]

Van Driel-Murray suggests that carbatinae of Britain

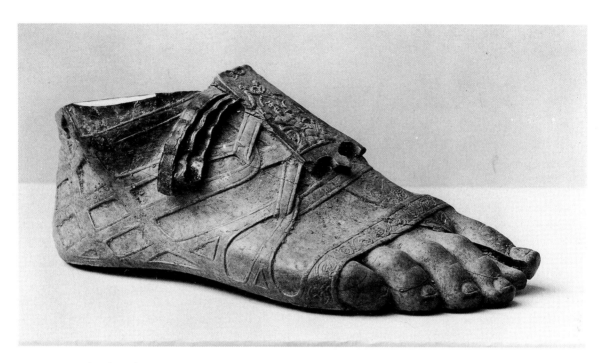

Fig. 6.18. Ivory foot from the imperial period, unknown provenance. This form of sandal combines that of the crepida and other forms, with a lingula or tongue covering the wide lacing. Metropolitan Museum of Art, New York, inv. 25.78.43, gift of John Marshall. Photo courtesy of the Metropolitan Photograph and Slide Library.

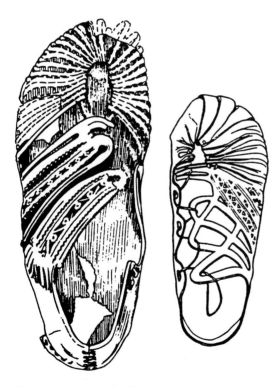

Fig. 6.19a. Drawing of carbatina design showing the cutting pattern for the ornate cutwork. From Busch, "Die römerzeitlichen Schuh- und Lederfunde," pl. 1, no. 3.

Fig. 6.19b. Carbatina from an excavation, with modern reconstruction, above. Saalburg Museum.

and Germany are different from pre-Roman Iron Age styles, though alike in principle. Under Roman rule, native populations of Celts, Germans, and Britons may have accepted Roman elements in footwear design, perhaps blending indigenous and Roman elements. When styles of the Iron Age disappeared locally in Britain and Germany, they were replaced by a carbatina similar in design and comfort, but rather different in appearance. Carbatinae seem to have been very popular, to judge from the finds at the various sites; there are 116 examples from Saalburg alone. The exhibition cases at the Saalburg Museum in which the carbatinae are displayed contain on the back wall the cutting patterns for some of the shoes, and a local shoemaker has made modern reconstructions based on the clever cutting design, so that the modern reconstruction is shown alongside the ancient preserved shoe (fig. 6.19b).

Etymologically the word *carbatina* is very interesting, for *carbasina* refers to the heavy linen cloth used in sails of ships, and certainly the use of heavy, durable sailcloth for a soft, moccasin-type shoe is logical for shoe construction. When leather was then substituted for cloth, the name may have remained as a vestigial reminder of the original construction. Though carbatinae appear in all of the sites on the *limes*, they are absent from the artistic depictions in Italy, unless some of the crepidae are carbatinae (if cut from single pieces of leather).

During the first century A.D. the carbatina seems to have been symmetrical, with loops of equal length on each side of the shoe. During the second and third centuries, however, a fashion of lengthening the loops over the instep on the outside of the shoe caused the carbatina to be made with shorter loops on the inner side, forming an asymmetically shaped shoe (figs. 6.20a–b). Some of the cutting patterns are most ingenious, and all kinds of variety in the loop design and in delicate cutting and tooling for the loops were devised. This footwear seems to have been a most popular style for the civilian population, both male and female, and it was especially ideal for children, whose feet were constantly increasing in size.

CALCEI

For Roman citizens, sandals were appropriate footgear for indoors with the tunic and stola but were not appropriate for outdoor wear with the toga and palla. Aulus Gellius quotes T. Castricius, an arbiter of taste, as reprimanding young noblemen for wearing sandals outdoors with tunic and cloak, instead of wearing calcei with toga (13.22). These calcei, shoes entirely encasing the foot, were a Roman contribution to ancient footwear in the Mediterranean world.

Calcei first appear in Italy as the Etruscan calcei repandi with pointed toes, reputedly owing to Ionian or Near Eastern influence.[41] These pointed-toed shoes are apparent in Etruscan tomb paintings (figs. 6.1a, c) and most clearly in the neat, tiny shoeboot of the Caere woman on the couch with her husband, now in the Villa Giulia Museum (figs. 6.21a–b). Her shoeboots are laced carefully up the front and bound at the top with a wide strap above the ankle. The style with pointed toes, evident also in the painting of the three central figures in the Tomb of the Baron at Tarquinia, seems to have been a general shoe style for men and women for a short time in Etruria, only from about 550 to 475 B.C.[42] Cicero says that the pointed-toe calcei repandi are reserved for images of Juno Sospita in later times, and visual representation of the many styles of blunt-toed calcei seem to bear out his observation.[43]

The pointed, upturned toe went out of style, but the calceus itself continued for centuries, and all enclosed Roman shoes and shoeboots may be classed as calcei, enclosed footwear for all levels of society. Calcei appear at archaeological sites for civilians of all levels everywhere in the Roman world. Many versions of these calcei continue throughout Roman history, the most impressive perhaps being the calcei patricii and calcei senatorii. These may have been distinguished from the calcei equestres by both quality and color, since the patrician and senatorial versions, called the *mulleus*, may have been a distinctive red color associated with the color of the expensive red mullet fish so prized in Roman cuisine.[44] Caesar is supposed to have worn high red shoeboots in his triumphal victory parade (Dio Cassius, *Roman History* 43.43.2). Perhaps he thus continued the emphasis on red as a way to distinguish the classes, since the black equestrian boot seems identical in general shape to the red one of the senators and patricians, but its color is more sober and less expensive. One can guess, however, that quality of the leather and careful workmanship were also factors distinguishing even the shoeboots of the patricians from those of the senators, since by the time of the *Edict of Diocletian* the calcei patricii were selling for 150 denarii, while the calcei senatorii cost 100. There is no literary or artistic evidence to indicate exactly how the equestrian shoeboots differed from those of the senator, but the *Edict* (9.7–9) lists them at a considerably lower price, 70 denarii a pair. Made centuries earlier, the bronze Arringatore, whose tunic with narrow stripes (clavi) indicates equestrian rank, wears elegant shoeboots that seem otherwise identical to the ones worn by later nobles and patricians (see fig. 1.1). Probably materials and workmanship separated the shoes produced for the highest nobility, just as such factors today make the difference between a shoe produced in the workshops of Gucci or Florsheim from those sold

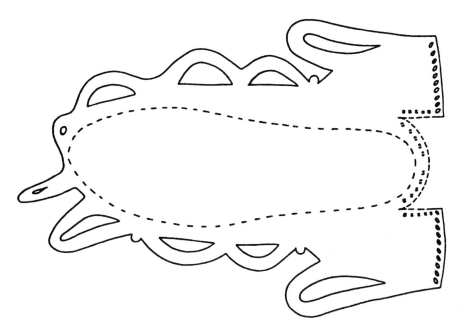

Fig. 6.20a. Cutting pattern for carbatina from Saalburg. From Busch, "Die römerzeitlichen Schuh- und Lederfunde," pl. 1, no. 6.

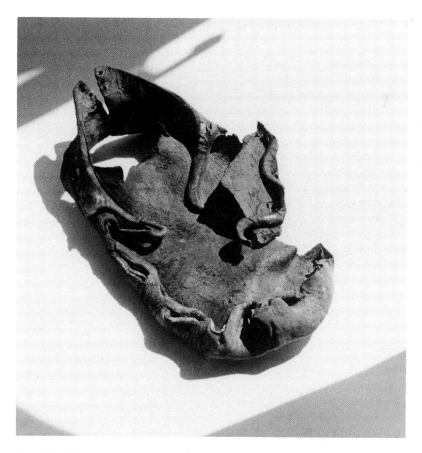

Fig. 6.20b. Vindolanda carbatina, made from pattern similar to the one from Saalburg. Photo taken in the Vindolanda Museum storeroom, thanks to the kindness of Director Robin Birley.

Fig. 6.21a. Etruscan couple reclining on the couch. Terracotta sculpture from Caere, ca. 525 B.C., now in the Villa Giulia Museum, Rome.

Fig. 6.21b. Calcei repandi, neatly laced, worn by the woman reclining beside her husband. Photo courtesy of the Villa Giulia Museum Photo Archive.

from the racks at K-Mart, without much variation in the basic style of the product. The confusion over red as the color for the patrician or senatorial boot may have resulted from the fact that most senators were originally patricians entitled to wear red boots. When many men of former equestrian rank began to be enrolled as senators, the color distinction of the more outstanding red for patricians would have provided an excellent way to distinguish the landed gentry from the nouveau riche, just as the wide clavi (about three inches wide) on the tunic of the patrician senator distinguished the nobleman from the equestrian, who was allowed to wear only narrow clavi (about one inch wide) on his tunic. Such class distinctions were clear and obvious to all, and the shoeboot in style and color was consistent with the status of the wearer. The luna, a crescent-shaped decoration that was inserted in one of the ties of the calceus, also as an indication of status, is not represented in painting or sculpture. It does appear in several literary references, and the use of the luna would have been another method by which the class-conscious Romans could have tagged themselves as belonging to one social group or another.[45]

Calcei patricii, senatorii, and equestres appear on many statues of noble Romans, from the Arringatore (the Orator) of late republican time to sculpture of the midempire. The style remained constant, with minor variations. This calceus for knight and senator was a shoeboot entirely encasing the foot and ankle, distinguished by its four straps tied in two knots in front. It was put on by inserting the foot into the front through a vertical cut on the inside of the uppers, which allowed the shoe to open wide. Four leather straps called corrigiae, two on each side of the front and back, narrowing as they extended upward, were wrapped around the ankle several times, sometimes over a tongue, and were tied high around the leg, anywhere above the ankle to midcalf. The long strips left over from the knot of the first tie were allowed to hang down or were sometimes tied to the foot by the two narrower back straps attached between the sole and the heel. These were wound further down around the ankle and lower leg and sometimes held the upper leftover straps in place to prevent the wearer from tripping. The two knots tied in front provided the decoration, the extra ends often hanging loose. These shoeboots appear on statues of the flamines from the Ara Pacis (fig. 6.22).[46] Excellent versions are carved on the two equestrian statues of Balbus and of his son in the Naples Museum. A fine rendering of the calcei patricii appears on the newly exhibited equestrian bronze statue of Domitian or Nerva in the same museum. On this imperial figure, the leather covering the toes on the front of the calceus is so thin as to appear

almost transparent, with the toes clearly delineated. The soft leather seems almost socklike.[47] The same elegant, double-knot shoeboot appears on the equestrian statue of Marcus Aurelius, recently restored and returned to a protected courtyard of the Capitoline Museum. An examination of the underpart of the boot suggests that the straps might have consisted of one long continuous strip of leather attached under the shoeboot to the upper by the undersole. The same soft, socklike covering is represented in bronze over the toes (figs. 6.23a–b). Such consistency in style indicates a continuation of ritual footwear. Obviously pride was associated with wearing the calceus patricius, since it, like the traditional tunic and toga, survived centuries of use.

If the identification and dating of the just under life-size statue in Rome's Norwegian Institute by L'Orange is correct, the elegant figure of an empress is made even more impressive by the fancy calcei she wears (fig. 6.24). L'Orange interprets the small, round raised decoration at the inner border of each of the lacing holes as pearls, and he calls the figure a third- or fourth-century empress on the basis of both the ornate shoes and the cloak, which only an empress is entitled to wear. The laced shoes are a classic style of the ankle-high calceus for women.[48]

What evidence is there for calcei from excavated sites? Oddly, there are so far no actual calcei patricii from the leather finds from the northern provinces. Most of the finds have been excavated in refuse or dump sites—wells and ditches—and probably no nobleman ever discarded such expensive leather footwear.

Van Driel-Murray dates the various styles of excavated calcei at Vindolanda from A.D. 90 to 400, divided into eight phases of occupation. The importance of this type, which appears in sizes for both adults and children, is that it has been found all over the Roman world from Britain to Dura-Europos, suggesting a style that was practical for many parts of the empire.[49] In her preliminary review of the Vindolanda finds, van Driel-Murry has dated the most basic of the standard Vindolanda calcei to about A.D. 90–120. This calceus has solid sides sewn up the toe and laced through oval holes over the instep and ankle. Even when decorated lacing loops or cutout patterns were added, as in the more elaborate, cutout style (fig. 6.25), the basic pattern for the boot remained the same.

Another version of the calceus is an eyelet boot (which van Driel-Murray dates to about A.D. 180–230), whose uppers are cut from a single piece of leather in an ingenious fashion that includes a long lace for each side cut in a tapering curve that arcs over the top of the cutting pattern, making conservative use of the leather (fig. 6.26). The ankle-high shoeboot was sewn together up

Fig. 6.22. Ara Pacis, detail showing the Flamen Dialis priests wearing calcei patricii and the Rex Sacrorum *(on right)* wearing a simple calceus without straps. Photo courtesy of Gerhard Koeppel.

Fig. 6.23a. Statue of Marcus Aurelius. Capitoline Museum, Rome. Photo courtesy of the Capitoline Museum Photo Archive.

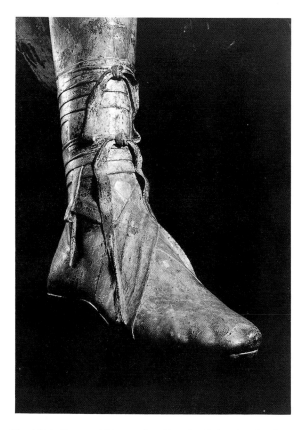

Fig. 6.23b. Statue of Marcus Aurelius, detail showing the elegant calceus patricius. Capitoline Museum, Rome. Photo courtesy of the Capitoline Museum Photo Archive.

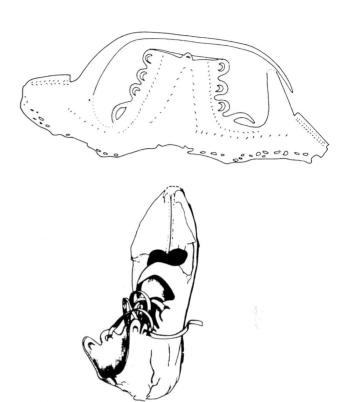

Fig. 6.24. Statue of empress, detail showing calceus neatly laced, with pearls decorating the edges of the lacing holes. Norwegian Institute in Rome.

Fig. 6.26. Eyelet shoeboot calceus sewn up the toe, with arcing laces extending from the sides, cut from a single piece of leather. Found at both Vindolanda and Saalburg. From Busch, "Die römerzeitlichen Schuh- und Lederfunde," pl. 10, no. 199.

Fig. 6.25. Enclosed shoeboot calcei from Vindolanda with uppers pierced by careful cutwork to form lace-like sides. The owners may have worn colored "socks" or linings inside to show off the pattern of the cutwork. Vindolanda Museum.

the toe section, with a triangular tip added at the toe for reinforcement. A sole was then hobnailed to the undersection.[50] This same style of boot has been found at Saalburg dated to about the mid–third century A.D.; both the restored leather find and the modern reconstruction are displayed in the Saalburg Museum, with the cutting pattern shown on the wall.

In the northern provinces, calcei are found in numerous styles, sometimes with solid sides, but sometimes with uppers pierced with an awl or cut with a knife into decorative patterns of diamonds, circles, squares, and rectangles in various designs over the heels and sides. They are usually shoes that today seem more appropriate for women or children, but at Vindolanda they are found mostly in large, male sizes. Many have such fine decorative punchwork as to appear almost lacelike. They date from about A.D. 100–20. Most were sewn up the toe with reinforcements along loopholes at the edges, through which lacing would have pulled the sides together. They would have been shown off most effectively with colored socks or linings underneath, and one, according to van Driel-Murray, has the remnants of such a lining. At Vindolanda there are even several pairs of matching calcei, one (which van Driel-Murray dates after A.D. 200) with a cutwork design over the pointed toe section. Most were soled, and some were also hobnailed, requiring an inner sole to cover the tips of the nails. They have been recovered near camp sites and from towns that grew up outside the camps, giving evidence of a civilian population that included women and children in towns adjacent to the camps, despite official injunctions against soldiers marrying or "fraternizing."[51]

## CALIGAE

The soldier's military boot, the caliga, also seems consistent throughout years of use in many campaigns in various parts of the Roman world during the early empire. This was the regulation foot covering for all soldiers up to the rank of centurion. It was cut from a single piece of leather, like a carbatina, but with a tough, thick, hobnailed sole, made from excellent-quality tanned cow or ox hide.[52] An inner sole protected the foot from the turned hobnails. The uppers consisted of a network of cutout leather or interlaced narrow leather straps, covering the instep and ankle but leaving the toes bare; the boot was double-strapped or laced above or around the ankle. Perhaps on the long march the bare toes kept the feet cool, as would the network of straps. Drusus in military garb was assigned the caliga on the Ara Pacis procession by a later restorer, although this is clearly a reworking of his left foot, not matching the original sketchy shoeboot of the right foot.

Naturally Trajan's Column displays hundreds of soldiers wearing caligae, both foot soldiers and cavalrymen. Isidore of Seville says that the name caliga may have evolved from the word callus, meaning "hard leather," or from the idea that the boot was tied on. He adds that caligae were nailed all around the sole with small hobnails (Origines 9.34), and the finds from sites on the limes bear this out. These hobnails are graphically shown on the Trajanic frieze on the inner panel of the Arch of Constantine, where the caliga is shown from the side. Hobnailing became common on civilian footwear as well, since it saved the expensive leather soles from wearing out.

Hobnailing on Roman footwear is referred to in the Mishnah (Shabbat 6.2) as the difference between Roman and local footwear. The hobnails caused one Roman soldier to slip on the marble flooring of the Temple during the attack by Roman soldiers, as described by Josephus.[53] The thunderous sound of an attack by a hobnailed army (the caligati) must have been terrifying.

The military boot does not seem to change from one area of the empire to another during the first century, but by the second and third centuries it seems to have gone out of style in the northern areas. Van Driel-Murray says that no strap-style caligae have so far been excavated at Vindolanda, suggesting that they had gone out of style by A.D. 90, at least in Roman Britain. They may have been replaced by the plain or cutwork calcei, by the calceus with solid sides, or by the campagus militaris as the official army boot. The meaning of the word caliga seems to have undergone a radical change by the fourth century, as evidenced by the references in the Edict of Diocletian. A version of it without hobnails for farmers and mule drivers sold for 120 denarii, and another, for soldiers and without hobnails, sold for 100 denarii (9.5, 5a, 6). There must have been more substantial, enclosed military boots for northern climates, but if there were, they are unrecorded. The Edict of Diocletian lists a shoe called campagi militares selling for 75 denarii (9.11). Since the Edict modifies campagi with militares, it seems safe to assume that this might be the shoeboot for the soldier covering the entire foot, as distinguished from the caliga with its network of straps. As evidence of the problems of changes in meanings, Saglio defines campagus as a Byzantine shoe, the kind worn by emperors such as Justinian in the sixth-century Ravenna mosaic, a significant change from the earlier meaning.[54] The Edict lists the cost of the lasts (formae) preceding the section on caligae: for the largest size, one hundred denarii; for the second size, eighty; for women's shoes, sixty; and for children's shoes, thirty (9.1–4). The inclusion of the last two items indicates that caligae had undergone considerable change by A.D. 301 and now were shoeboots for anyone. If the caliga even appeared without hobnails, then its most characteristic feature as military footwear had disappeared.

Actual leather caligae in the style duplicated on monuments have been recovered from excavations on the *limes,* at first-century sites, and they are exhibited in the museums and in the storerooms in Germany and England. In the Roman-German museums at Mainz and Cologne, in the Mainz Landesmuseum, in the Offenbach Shoe Museum, and in the Shoe Museum at Northampton and the Museum of the City of London, there are finds of caligae complete with their hobnailed soles that have been excavated from sites where continuously damp conditions have preserved both the leather and the metal (figs. 6.27a–b).

Robin Birley has represented his Roman soldier in the Roman Army Museum near Vindolanda wearing the traditional caligae, which he has had stuffed with raw wool to protect the feet from the cold. This practical device would have been needed in the northern provinces, and it was repeated at the Corbridge Museum on the Stangate. Either raw wool or socks, of which there is a woven example at Vindolanda along with a reference in a letter, would have been necessary in the cold climate on the *limes.* Soldiers may also have wrapped their legs in sheepskins, as demonstrated in the Housesteads Museum replica of a soldier. Van Driel-Murray says that the caliga went out of style by the end of the first quarter of the second century A.D. and that depictions of it on monuments are more a recording of a memory than an actual representation. She adds that by the second century soldiers' footwear had become indistinguishable from that of the rest of the population.[55] At Dura-Europos in the Near East, an enclosed calceus is listed as a "soldier's boot." There are many such "boots" from the northern frontier as well, where they would have been more practical as military footwear than caligae made of thin strips of leather.[56]

In general, however, van Driel-Murray lauds the caliga as an ideal marching boot, providing support for foot and ankle, cut out in sensitive places to avoid chafing and to allow ventilation, adjustable with the straps to allow for swelling during hot weather, and with an uncovered toe to allow for variation in length. Even the nailing pattern on the undersole is not random: the characteristic D-shaped pattern distributed the support where needed. The pattern identified footprints of soldiers, even on drying clay tiles.[57] This pattern is echoed almost two thousand years later on the bottoms of modern sport shoes.

## BOOTS

In art works, high boots were reserved for horsemen, deities, warriors, heroes, personifications of the city, generals, and emperors. Images of gods wear boots, as do both the lad reading to the initiate in the first scene and the flagellante in the painting of the Dionysiac initiation in the Villa of the Mysteries at Pompeii. There are no archaeological finds documenting that such boots ever existed, although they appear on many sculptures and in paintings.

The most elaborate of all boots are the ones decorated with a feline head. These are almost knee-high and are here termed "dress parade" boots. Morrow does not give them a name separate from her heading of boots as *endromides* or *embades,* footwear that could be "put on."[58] The Hellenistic Greek high boots worn by hunters and deities, which are decorated with ornate scrolls and vegetal patterns and lined with *piloi* and *pellytra,* liners mde of thin leather, which sometimes had overhanging flaps on their top edges, appear on the Pergamon Altar Gigantomachy figures. Morrow speculates on whether they actually existed as boots or whether they are the result of artistic license. She concludes that they are authentic because they are lined with soft leather to prevent rubbing, a convincingly human touch.

These fancy dress parade boots continue into the Roman world, appearing on statues of heroes, gods and goddesses, and emperors, and on a symbolic statue of the spirit of Rome in the Naples Museum (fig. 6.28). Around the tops are liners, somewhat like flaps, sometimes with a feline head attached in front, details which appear as early as mid–fifth-century B.C. Greece and continue through the Hellenistic period into Roman times.[59] This kind of footwear seems to have been preserved as an honored style throughout the Greek and Roman worlds. The Greeks refer to such protective layers and overhanging flaps around the top of the boots as *piloi.* There does not seem to be an equivalent Latin word. The uneven edges of the animal skin are bound by a decorative cord around the top of the boot, and these uneven edges hang down all around the top, explaining the curious tops of the edges of the Lares' boots on the images from the shrines in Pompeii; the tops are shown flying out as if the figure were dancing or in motion (see fig. 1.2). Sometimes the paws of the animal (or flaps of similar shape) are also preserved in sculpture or painting.

This style is a dramatic extravagance in boot construction, obviously reserved for the most wealthy, most honored, most powerful, and most revered. Depicted in relief and free-standing sculpture, the style is shown on statues of Diana, and it appears on representations, original and restored, of emperors, heroes, and important deities, such as Mars from the Capitoline Museum (fig. 6.29). Perhaps that is why a version of it appears in the painting of the Priapic figure in the entrance hall of the House of the Vettii in Pompeii.

Fig. 6.27a. Reconstruction of the Mainz caliga (accurate except for missing hobnails) on the statue of a soldier. Römisch-Germanisches Zentral Museum, Mainz.

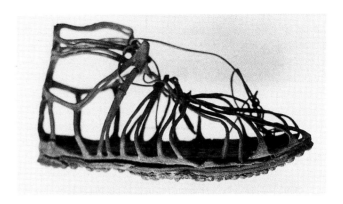

Fig. 6.27b. Actual preserved caliga with hobnailing intact. Römisch-Germanisches Zentral Museum, Mainz.

Fig. 6.28. Spirit of Rome, wearing "dress parade" boot. Farnese Collection, Museo Nazionale Archeologico, Naples.

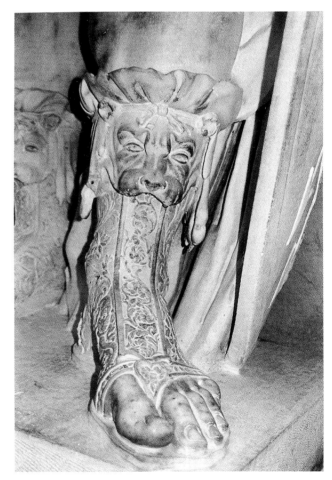

Fig. 6.29. Statue of Mars, detail showing dress parade boot. Restored legs. Capitoline Museum, Rome. Photo courtesy of the Capitoline Museum Photo Archive.

124

There is no archaeological evidence that these dress parade boots ever existed. Perhaps boots of such status, like the calcei patricii, were never thrown away and thus do not appear in dump sites, down wells, or in ditches, the places where archaeologists have discovered leather finds.

Not all aristocrats are depicted wearing such decorative shoeboots. On the Ara Pacis, neither Augustus nor Agrippa, who by this time, according to Meyer Reinhold, would have attained patrician status, wears the dress parade boot. Augustus wears calcei patricii, but both the Rex Sacrorum and Agrippa wear the undecorated soft shoeboot that encases the ankle with a double fold of leather, as do most of the other nobles and magistrates. No one wears the fancy dress parade boot. Perhaps Augustus is maintaining the myth of his being simply *princeps*. The word *pero*, assigned for all footgear below magistrate level, is used by Pollini for all of the boots on the Ara Pacis relief that are not the calcei patricii worn by Augustus and by the priests. By the word *pero* he is referring to the shoeboot with soles about one-half-inch thick and soft, leather-enclosed uppers, sometimes with an additional fold, like an Ace bandage, encasing the ankle or hanging over the ankle in a loose extra layer.[60] Perhaps this type of footwear might be referred to simply as the calceus, the comfortable shoeboot for outdoor wear when the patrician was not attending a formal meeting. Versions of it appear on Trajan's Column, worn by Trajan himself, and on the Arch of Constantine, worn by Trajan, Marcus Aurelius, Hadrian, and others. The magistrates in the entrance hall of the Naples Museum also wear a more highly decorated form of this dignified and elegant shoeboot (fig. 6.30). It seems to be the general foot covering for nobles, magistrates, and official attendants.

COTHURNI AND SOCCI

Footwear for the stage included the cothurnus, suitable for tragedy, and the soccus, suitable for comedy. The cothurnus was another version of the boot, a three-to-five-inch thick-soled high boot or buskin, associated with Dionysus and worn by tragic actors. These boots were worn in tragedies by the actors to increase their height, and the boots then came to symbolize tragic drama.[61] Pliny the Elder exaggerates the weight of the boot as excessive *quingentum pondo* (five hundred [?] in weight). Frontinus speaks of an aged man elevated by *altissimis cothurnis* (very high stage boots). Juvenal refers to one of the women as shorter, since she is described with *nullis cothurnis* (no stage boots). Pliny the Younger, in a letter describing his two neighboring villas, one on a rock overlooking the lake and the other at the seaside, refers to one as his "Tragedy," supported as it were by a lofty buskin, and the other as his "Comedy," as if resting on a humble sock.[62]

The soccus, suitable for comedy, was a soft, low-heeled or loose-fitting slipper originally worn by Greeks and comic actors. Like the cothurnus, which became symbolic for tragedy, the soccus came to symbolize comedy.[63] Offstage it seems to have been worn first mostly by women. In the *Edict of Diocletian*, six different varieties are listed in a section devoted to foreign or luxury footwear: *socci purpurei* or *Foenicei* (purple or Phoenician), selling for sixty denarii a pair; white, no price listed; *biriles* (for men), indicating that by the time of Diocletian men were also wearing socci, at sixty denarii a pair but for women at fifty; *inauratae* (golden or gilded), at eighty denarii a pair; and at the same price *socci Babylonici purpurei sive albi* (Babylonian purple or white) (9.18–23). Obviously what had begun as a style for the stage had become a style popular with the audience as well. By the end of the third century the soft indoor slipper had become quite popular. The addition of another sturdier shoe or boot covering the soccus might result in the present etymology of *sock*.

SHOE OR BOOT LININGS (SOCKS)

Robin Birley has displayed in one of the Vindolanda exhibition cases a single, almost intact, woven child-size sock shaped like a foot and sewn across the toe (fig. 6.31). This unique find was excavated from this site on the Stangate just south of the Roman Wall. That the entire sock is extant is a miracle, since most other textiles are preserved in fragments. Yet in Greek and Roman times, there must have been foot coverings in cloth, felt, or soft, suedelike leather worn inside sandals, shoes, or boots. The Japanese use such socks today, with the thong for the sandal pushing the sock into the groove between the toes. Some socks are even designed with the built-in indented groove. Greek and Roman linings may have been shaped like the Vindolanda example or may have been simply "puttee"-like strips of cloth wound around the feet, ankles, and legs to protect them from cold and chafing. In her preliminary review of the Vindolanda footwear finds, Carol van Driel-Murray has referred to a sewn-in lining of colored cloth inside two of the fancy cutwork design shoes. She suggests that women may have shortened their skirts a bit to show off such lined shoes and that officers may also have worn colored socks to display their shoeboots with cutwork designs.[64]

According to Morrow, the Greeks had as liners *hoi piloi* (flaps from inside hanging over the tops of boots, perhaps even attached to the boots) and *ta podeia* (liners which she equates with Roman *impilia*, from *empilion*, a felt slipper, related to the *podeia*, felt shoes to be worn under boots or sandals). Morrow's bronze foot fragment (no. 269 from Olympia) clearly shows the stipled sock inside the sandal covering the foot except for the ends of

Fig. 6.30. Statue of magistrate, detail showing calceus, before A.D. 79. Museo Nazionale Archeologico, Naples.

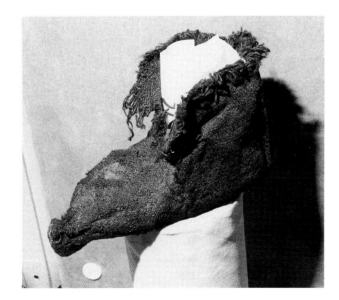

Fig. 6.31. Well-preserved child's sock, Vindolanda Museum. Photo: B. Goldman.

the first two toes.[65] The Etruscan calcei repandi with pointed toes could have been made of felt as well as of leather (figs. 6.1a, c). Boots worn over such felted styles would have been practical in cold climates. Certainly for protection against chafing as well as the cold, such felt slippers or soft, thin leather "socks" must have been worn. When the sculpture depicts the outline of the toes on the equestrian statues of Domitian-Nerva or of Marcus Aurelius, one wonders whether this effect reflects the use of thin, suedelike leather (Greek, *pellytra*) for uppers on such elegant footwear. There does not seem to be a word for this thin leather in the Roman world, though the soft skins of small animals used in the dress parade boots tied around the tops would belong to this group. There are, however, many words for skins of animals; for example, the word *pellicula* appears on an inscription describing a man who earned his living from making wool-lined army boots: "Qui caliculis lana pelliculis vitam toleravit suam" (He earned his livelihood from army boots lined with wool). Could *lana* have referred to felt or woolen lining for army boots? The evidence for socks from Vindolanda is explicit in a letter recording a shipment of socks, sandals, and underpants. Martial uses the word *udones* to refer to woolen socks made from African goat hair.[66] Thus we know that the concept of socks existed. Whether they were shaped or simply strips of cloth is not clear.

### SEWN LOW STRAP SHOES OR LATCHET SHOES

As the Roman world moved into Byzantine times, another enclosed shoe, cataloged as a calceus by modern historians because it consisted of a separately cut sole and upper, began to appear on the *limes*, both in Germany and England, and in the Eastern world as well. The shoe was no longer nailed; sewing (which had frequently appeared in combination with nailing) now began to replace nailing as the means for attaching the uppers to the edge of the sole. The uppers might be solid or perforated leather, and a few covered the ankles, but most were low. In the sixth-century mosaics at San Vitale in Ravenna, Theodora's shoes (only the toes are showing) seem to be decorated with pearls down each side (see fig. 5.9). Justinian seems to be wearing latchet shoes decorated with jeweled flowers (see fig. 5.8), although Saglio calls this shoe a *campagus*. The courtiers flanking Justinian all wear latchet shoes.

The Romans clearly had fashioned footgear suitable for all occasions, for all ranks of society, and for different professions. Although classical authors are not as specific on every type of footwear, the visual monuments, reliefs, sculptures-in-the round, and paintings help to identify and clarify the variety and appropriate footwear for priests, magistrates, nobles and their attendants, and the military.

What was worn by the common folk, who are not represented in paintings or sculpture, is more difficult to determine. But now that excavations on the northern *limes* are revealing the actual leather finds as evidence to complement the representations in art, we are beginning to have a clearer idea of what the Romans wore. Where dating is possible, a pattern of style changes has already begun to emerge. For example, the soldiers on the northern frontier were no longer wearing the thin-strip caligae after the first decades of the second century A.D. but were wearing a more practical enclosed shoeboot, not different from civilian styles. What is frustrating, because of the lack of Italian and Gallic evidence, is the discrepancy between the actual leather finds and the representations in art. Until there are actual leather finds from Italy itself, we do not know whether the styles on the sculpture and in the paintings depict real footwear. When artists have been so meticulous, however, in representing the figures in such realistic detail, it would seem strange or unnatural if they invented or improvised the footwear, except of course for the gods and heroes.

## NOTES

1. C. van Driel-Murray, "Roman Footwear: A Mirror of Fashion and Society," in *Recent Research in Archaeological Footwear,* Association of Archaeological Illustrators and Surveyors, Technical Paper 8 (n.p., 1987), 32–33.

2. This pair of well-preserved sandals has carbonized high wooden soles, hinged in the center at the instep with leather (no longer extant) and outlined in bronze.

3. Sandals from Masada have been preserved; see Y. Yadin, *Masada: Herod's Fortress and the Zealots' Last Stand* (London, 1966), 57, 196. Nails and the sole from a caliga have been recovered from a cave at Ketef Jericho; see J. Patrick, "Hideouts in the Judean Wilderness," *Biblical Archaeology Review* 5 (1989): 50–51. For a soldier's boot, a child's sandal, and a child's pair of shoes from Dura-Europos, see P. V. C. Baur and M. I. Rostovtzeff, eds., *The Excavations at Dura-Europos: Preliminary Report of Second Season of Work* (New Haven, 1931), 69, pl. 10. An intact pair of child's sandals has been recovered from Egypt and is now exhibited in the Northampton Leather Museum, England. The Kelsey Museum basketry finds of twenty-four fiber soles from Karanis can be accessed from the new computerized database, nos. 8450–57; 1.0832–47. Contact Robin Meador-Woodruff at the Kelsey Museum, University of Michigan, Ann Arbor, Mich. 48109.

4. See A. Hartmann, "Die Bronzeund Goldfunde aus dem Fürstengrab von Hochdorf," in *Der Keltenfürst von Hochdorf* (Stuttgart, 1985), 145, fig. 165, for Celtic shoes of felt or leather (no longer extant) elaborately decorated on the sides

with curved, wide strips of gold *repoussé,* which would have been sewn to the shoe. Isidore (*Origines* 19.34) says that Roman shoes were originally made of willow (osiers).

5. *Edict of Diocletian 9.5–25.*

| 1 | DE FORMIS CALICARIBUS. | |
|---|---|---|
| 1a | Formae calicares maximae | centum. |
| 2 | Formae secundae mensurae | octaginta. |
| 3 | Formae muliebres | sexaginta. |
| 4 | Formae infantiles | triginta. |
| 5 | DE CALIGIS. | |
| 5a | Caligae primae formae mulionicae sibe rusticae, par sine clavis | CXX. |
| 6 | Caligae militares sine clabo | centum. |
| 7 | Calcei patricii | centum quinquaginta. |
| 8 | Calicae senatorum | centum. |
| 9 | Calicae equestres | septuaginta. |
| 10 | Calicae muliebres, par | sexaginta. |
| 11 | Ca(m)pagi militares | septuaginta quinque. |
| 12 | DE SOLEIS ET GALLICIS. | |
| 12a | (Gall)icae biriles rusticanae bisoles, par | octaginta. |
| 13 | (Gall)icae biriles monosoles, par | quinquaginta. |
| 14 | (Gal)licae cursuriae, par | sexaginta. |
| 15 | (Tau)rinae muliebres bisoles, par | quinquaginta. |
| 16 | (Taurin)ae muliebres monosoles, par | triginta. |
| 17 | (DE SOL)EIS BABVLONICIS ET PVRPVREIS ET FOENICEIS ET ALVIS. | |
| 17a | (Soleae) Vavulonicae, par | centum viginti. |
| 18 | (Socci) purpurei sive foenicei, par | sexaginta. |
| 19 | (Socci albi, par) | . . . . . . . . . . . |
| 20 | (Soc)ci bi(riles, par) | LX. |
| 21 | (So)cci muliebres, pa(r) | L. |
| 22 | (I)nauratae | LXXX. |
| 23 | Socci Babulonici purp(urei sive albi) | LXXX. |
| 24 | Taurinae inauratae | LXXV. |
| 25 | Taurinae lanatae | (qui)nq(uaginta). |

6. Isidore, *Origines* 19.34.

7. C. van Driel-Murray, "Roman Footwear from a Well in the Ostkastell Welzheim" (forthcoming).

8. Morrow, *Greek Footwear.*

9. The Ara Pacis reliefs can be dated to January 30, 9 B.C., when the altar was dedicated. Trajan's Column, dedicated in A.D. 113, documented the two campaigns against the Dacians in A.D. 102–3 and 105–6.

10. *CIL* 6.9796.

11. Pliny the Elder, *H.N.* 17.51; Martial 6.93.1–4; Juvenal, *Satires* 14.203.

12. *CIL* 6.1682, 9494, 9225, 9284; 10.4549.2.

13. An excellent discussion of leather appears in J. Waterer, "Leatherwork," in *Roman Crafts,* ed. D. Strong and D. Brown (London, 1976), 179–93. Forbes's discussion of leather in *Ancient Technology* 5: 48–63; on the industry at Pompeii, see p. 55.

14. For restoration techniques, see J. A. Spriggs, "Aspects of Leather Conservation at York," in *Recent Research in Archaeological Footwear,* Association of Archaeological Illustrators and Surveyors Technical Paper 8 (N.p., 1987), 43–46, with valuable bibliography. Spriggs describes the various products used to clean and restore the leather: Vulpex soap in white

spirit, methylated spirits, and glycerol. One restoration even required deep freezing and freeze drying; F. Pertegato, "Tecniche di lavorazione delle calzature rinascimentali," in *Il costume nell'età del Rinascimento* (Florence, 1988), 347–49.

15. For a general discussion of all types of Roman footwear, see DarSag: *calceus, caliga, campagus, cothurnus, crepida, embas, endromis, pero, soccus, solea.*

16. J. Pollini ("Studies in Augustan Historical Reliefs," Ph.D. diss., University of California, Berkeley, 1978, appendix 1, pp. 133–36, 170–72) refers to the shoes worn by all but the priests and Augustus himself on the Ara Pacis as perones. Pollini is presently revising and expanding his material into a new work, *The Image of Augustus: Art and Ideology,* in which he will be reviewing his work on the footwear problem on the Ara Pacis.

17. C. van Driel-Murray, "The Leatherwork," in "Funde aus der Fabrica der Legio I Minervia am Bonner Berg," by C. van Driel-Murray and M. Gechter, *Beiträge zur Archäologie des Römischen Rheinlandes* 4, *Rheinische Ausgrabungen* 23 (1984): 16. In this reference Carol van Driel-Murray cautions about the use of Latin terms for Roman footwear: "The generally accepted archaeological division into military boots *(caligae),* closed shoes with a nailed sole *(calcei),* sandals *(soleae),* sewn slippers *(socci)* and one-piece shoes *(carbatinae),* is retained for convenience, despite the very considerable differences in treatment of the upper. It is unlikely that the varied footwear here [the 1 Minervia legion at the Bonner Berg] (and elsewhere) regarded as *calcei* or *soleae* would all have been termed as such by the Romans themselves, but the terms are commonly accepted, and, in view of the nature of the literary evidence, it is unlikely that an accurate and acceptable ancient terminology could be devised to suit the needs of archaeologial description. Of necessity, archaeological description is technological, while ancient nomenclature—even if used consistently by the various authors—is liable to refer to visual characteristics such as color, material used or imitated, general appearance or even the status of the wearer, quite apart from the shifts in meaning throughout time to which articles of fashion are particularly prone." The archaeological terms above are used in the present chapter.

18. Morrow, *Greek Footwear,* 164–69; DarSag 4.2: 1387–90, s.v. "solea."

19. The Bisenzio sandals are of carbonized wood, but the height of the sole, the metal outline, and the attachments for the leather hinges are all clearly apparent; L. Bonfante includes a description of the sandals and their appearance in Etruria and in Athens in *Etruscan Dress,* 60.

20. Bonfante, *Etruscan Dress,* 60; cf. Morrow, *Greek Footwear,* 62, 183, no. 77.

21. See Morrow, *Greek Footwear,* 200–201, nos. 29–31, for the discussion of the *tyrrhenica* and its possible appearance on the Athena Parthenos; in her glossary (183), Morrow suggests that "Phidias carved his Athena Parthenos wearing them," although she says that Evi Touloupa of the Acropolis Museum does not agree and says that the sandals were really Attic *krepides.* Morrow based her identification on the fact that a fifth-century comic poet, Kratinus, refers to them as *tyrrhenica,* "Etruscan [sandals]."

22. M. Wheeler has helped to clarify the Greek and Roman

contributions to art in *Roman Art and Architecture* (London, 1964), 23–24.

23. Morrow, *Greek Footwear,* 171–73.

24. Ibid., 126, fig. 97; 126–27, figs. 98–102; 128, fig. 103; 79, figs. 59a–c.

25. Ibid., 63–64, 84–86, 114–17, 146. Both C. van Driel-Murray and M. Rhodes of the London Museum consider gallicae as carbatinae (personal correspondence from van Driel-Murray, August 20, 1991).

26. The Saalburg leather finds have been published in A. L. Busch, "Die römerzeitlichen Schuh- und Lederfunde der Kastelle Saalburg," *Saalburg Jahrbuch* 22 (1965): 158–210, pls. 1–40. J. Göpfrich has published "Römische Lederfunde aus Mainz," *Saalburg Jahrbuch* 42 (1986): 5–26, figs. 35–47. M. Schleiermacher has published the finds from Cologne: "Römische Leder- und Textilfunde aus Köln," *Archäologisches Korrespondenzblatt* 12 (1982): 205–12, pls. 12–20. C. van Driel-Murray published the finds from the *limes* ("The Leatherwork," 5–56). Van Driel-Murray, who also published the finds from the Netherlands, is currently cataloging the leather footwear finds from Vindolanda, prior to publication. There are over three thousand pieces of footwear to catalog, according to Robin Birley, director of the Vindolanda excavations and museum. Cf. Birley, *Vindolanda,* 123ff., figs. 63–66. P. MacConnoran has cataloged the finds from the Thames embankment in London in "Footwear," in *The Roman Quay at St. Magnus House,* ed. L. Miller, J. Schofield, and M. Rhodes (London, 1986), 218–25.

27. Mainz sandals with wide toes are cataloged by Göpfrich ("Römische Lederfunde"). She indicates that of the thirty-one sandal soles (p. 16), ten belong to the broad-toe variety (nos. 33–50, figs. 38–39). Schleiermacher ("Römische Leder- und Textilfunde," 210–11, figs. 17–20) has included only the normal-shaped soles, although in the leather find drawers in the Roman-German Museum in Cologne, to which museum director Hansgard Hellenkemper and Professor M. Schleiermacher generously gave me access, several wide-toed varieties have been cataloged. Busch in the catalog from Saalburg lists only one wide-toed variety ("Schuh- und Lederfunde," pl. 7, no. 144). P. MacConnoran in the finds from New Fresh Wharf, however, has cataloged twenty-three of the thirty-three sandals as belonging to the "broad sandal" variety ("Footwear," 222–23, nos. 8.17–24). The Vindolanda finds await final publication by van Driel-Murray.

28. Van Driel-Murray, "Roman Footwear: A Mirror," 34–35.

29. On the Saalburg sandal, see Busch, "Schuh- und Lederfunde," pl. 6, no. 122; p. 165, no. 4. The thong makes it a sandal, but the flat, sewn sole is like that of the soccus from London.

30. The Vindolanda sandal awaits publication by van Driel-Murray. See MacConnoran, "Footwear," 224–25, for the London version of a soccus.

31. MacConnoran, "Footwear," 221; Miller, Schofield, and Rhodes, *Quay,* 117–21. MacConnoran divides her catalog into nailed shoes (calcei or caligae), one-piece shoes (carbatinae), sandals (soleae), and stitched shoes (socci). She refers to all sewn footwear as socci.

32. MacConnoran, "Footwear," 222, 223; van Driel-Murray, "Roman Footwear: A Mirror," 34–35. See Busch, "Schuh- und Lederfunde," 165, no. 3; pl. 7, no. 144. See also Göpfrich, "Römische Lederfunde," 20–22.

33. A. Rubenus, *De re vestiaria,* vol. 2 (Antwerp, 1655), 187–88. The statue is now in the Uffizi in Florence.

34. F. L'Hoir, "Three Sandalled Footlamps," *AA* 98 (1983): 225–37.

35. D. B. Harden, *Glass of the Caesars,* Catalogue of Glass from the Corning Museum Exhibition of Ancient Roman Glass (Corning, N.Y., 1987), no. 66, pp. 136–38; U. Kaltwasser, *Die Kölner in der Römerzeit* (Cologne, 1977), 35–36; J. Bracker, "Das Frauengrab Köln, Severinstrasse 129," *Gymnasium* 79.5 (1972): 389–95, pl. 6.

36. DarSag, s.v. "Sculponeae."

37. Busch, "Schuh- und Lederfunde," 173–74, pl. 30; Van Driel-Murray, "The Leatherwork," 10, no. 1. E. Vigeon, "Clogs or Wooden Soled Shoes," *Journal of Costume Society* (1977), offprint, discusses wooden-soled shoes in England from the Renaissance up to modern times.

38. *Krepides:* Morrow, *Greek Footwear,* 46–48, 63–64, 73–75, 83–84, 145–46, 180 (no. 46); DarSag 1.2: 1557–60.

39. Morrow, *Greek Footwear,* 64.

40. See D. Baatz, "Carbatina—ein lateinischer Schuhname?" *Saalburg Jahrbuch* 42 (1986): 65–67, on the word *carbatina* and the use of the word in cataloging. See also DarSag 1.2: 915–16, fig. 1182, s.v. "carbatina"; Busch, "Schuh- und Lederfunde," pls. 1–5, nos. 1–116; Göpfrich, "Römische Lederfunde," 18–20, nos. 28–32; Van Driel-Murray, "Roman Footwear: A Mirror," 34–36. Van Driel-Murray classes sewn shoes, single-piece shoes, and military boots together in her discussion of the Bonner Berg site ("The Leatherwork," 16–19). See Schleiermacher, "Römische Leder- und Textilfunde," 211, figs. 15–16.

41. According to Bonfante (*Etruscan Dress,* 60–61), the early calcei are a version of Greek *endromides.* See DarSag 2.1: 615–16, s.v. "endromis."

42. Bonfante, *Etruscan Dress,* 60–61. The earliest known examples, however, are of ca. 575 B.C. (Murlo sculptures).

43. Ibid., 61–62; 131, nn. 8–11, 25, 38.

44. DarSag 1.2: 815–20, s.v. "calceus."

45. There are, to my knowledge, no representations of the luna in art. Literary references include Juvenal, *Satires* 7.192, "adpositam nigrae lunam subtexit alutae"; and Isidore, *Origines* 19.34.4, "patricos calceos Romulus reperit IV corrigiarum assutaque luna."

46. See Pollini, "Augustan Historical Reliefs," appendix 1, pp. 133–36; 170–72, nn. 190–211, for the evidence on the discussions of the colors of the calcei patricii and senatorii and the description of what Pollini terms the *pero.* These shoe-boots could also be termed *calcei.*

47. G. Macchiaroli, *Domiziano-Nerva, la statua equestre: Una proposta di ricomposizione* (Naples, 1987), 31–33, figs. 28a–b and 29a–b.

48. H. P. L'Orange, "Statua di un'imperatrice," *AAAH* 4 (1969): 93–99, pls. 1–9. See p. 97 on the shoes with pearls and n. 1 on shoes decorated with jewels as an imperial style.

49. Van Driel-Murray, "Roman Footwear from a Well." See also C. van Driel-Murray, "Shoes in Perspective," *Studien zu den Militärgrenzen* 3 (1986): 141.

50. C. van Driel-Murray has kindly supplied this information in the manuscript for her forthcoming publication of the Vindolanda finds.

51. Calcei from van Driel-Murray, "Roman Footwear: A Mirror," 37, fig. 6; "Römische Leder- und Textilfunde," 209, figs. 12–14; Göpfrich, "Römische Lederfunde," 41–43, figs. 67, 67a, 68, 68a, 82, 83, 91; pp. 22–24 (only six calcei are cataloged). Busch, "Schuh- und Lederfunde," 165, nos. 9–11, pl. 10, no. 199; pl. 11, nos. 210–11, pl. 12, nos. 212–13; pl. 13, nos. 215–16; pl. 15, nos. 221–24; pl. 17, nos. 262–63. L. Allason-Jones, *Women in Roman Britain* (London, 1989), 61, 118–22. British Museum, Department of British and Medieval Antiquities, *Guide to the Antiquities of Roman Britain* (London, 1951), 10–11.

52. DarSag 1.2: 849–50, s.v. "caliga." Markus Junkelmann, in *Die Legionen des Augustus: Der römische Soldat im archäologischen Experiment* (Mainz, 1986), has reconstructed the caligae, copied from ancient monuments, and they appear in graphic form on the dust jacket. Even more accurate reconstructions were made for Carol van Driel-Murray ("Roman Footwear from a Well") by the Ermine Street Guard, but even these do not include the strips that are apparent in the Mainz caliga over the front toes (figs. 6.27a–b).

53. Josephus, *BJ* 6.1.8. Josephus uses a Homeric Greek phrase, *ta hupodemata peparmena puknois . . . helois,* "shoes thickly studded with nails" (*Iliad* 1.246, 11.633), indicating that hobnailing the bottoms of army boots was known in Homeric warfare, at least when Homer described it.

54. DarSag 1.2: 862–63, s.v. "campagus."

55. Van Driel-Murray, "Roman Footwear: A Mirror," 33.

56. C. van Driel-Murray, "Leatherwork in the Roman Army," in *Exercitus Institute for Pre- and Protohistory* 2.2, 23–27 (Gloucester, n.d.), 8–9.

57. Ibid., 9.

58. Morrow, *Greek Footwear,* 178. Other discussions of boots appear on 64–68, 87–88, 123–25, 136–39.

59. Ibid., 132–35, figs. 112–22.

60. Pollini, "Augustan Historical Reliefs," 133–36.

61. DarSag 1.2: 1544–48, s.v. "cothurnus." Morrow, *Greek Footwear,* 180, no. 42; 122–23; 147–48.

62. Pliny the Elder, *H.N.* 7.83; Frontinus, *Stratagems* 1.2.10; Juvenal, *Satires* 6.506; Pliny the Younger, *Epistles* 9.7.3.

63. DarSag 4.2: 1365–66, s.v. "soccus."

64. C. van Driel-Murray has kindly supplied this information in the manuscript for her forthcoming publication of the Vindolanda finds.

65. Morrow, *Greek Footwear,* 64–67, 69, 87–89, 110, 137, 148–49. For examples, see 132–35, figs. 112a and b through 122a and b; 124–25, figs. 119–22a and b; 150, fig. 124; 182, no. 60, for a definition of *hoi piloi,* and no. 62 for *ta podeia.* The Greek dictionary defines *ta podeia* as the ragged edges formed by the feet and tail of the skin of animals, that is, like the linings for the tops for the dress parade boot.

66. *CIL* 9.3193; P. G. Bahn, "Letters from a Roman Garrison," *Archaeology* 45.1 (1992): 60–65; Martial 140.1–3.

# PART II
# ROMAN COSTUME AND
# LITERARY EVIDENCE

# Cicero as Evidence for Attitudes to Dress in the Late Republic

7

JULIA HESKEL

Clothing has played an important role as a distinguisher of profession and social rank in all societies. All sorts of uniforms perform these functions. We have only to think of the blue shirt, pants, badge, and cap which reflect the authority of the policeman, on the one hand, and the tuxedo, which reflects the status of the aristocrat, on the other. Conversely, the departure from uniforms or accepted forms of dress signifies a departure from social conventions. The example of blue jeans in the 1960s immediately comes to mind.[1]

Rome was no exception to this rule. The Romans had various "uniforms" for both men and women in different situations. In civil life, the toga was considered the official garb of the Roman citizen. In military contexts, soldiers were distinguished by the sagum and their commanders by the paludamentum.[2] As in other cultures, individual Romans occasionally broke from these conventions. The evidence for such exceptions during the late republic is limited, however, because the archaeological evidence for clothing in this period, which is scanty at best, concerns only "uniforms," such as the toga of the Roman citizen.[3] We need to turn to the literary evidence and, in particular, to Cicero, the most important contemporary source for late republican attitudes to dress. This chapter will deal with only his speeches, which contain by far the greatest number of references to clothing in the Ciceronian corpus. Cicero most often refers to the dress of Roman magistrates and especially to dress that was inappropriate for the specific occasion under discussion. He criticizes the clothing of a few particular individuals, the most important being C. Verres, M. Antonius, P. Clodius Pulcher, and P. Vatinius. The majority of these references focus on four types of

clothing: Greek dress, dress and undress, transvestism, and the clothing of mourning rituals.

The forensic bias of any given speech makes it difficult for us to know if the individual actually wore the clothing Cicero accuses him of wearing. This poses no problem for our purposes, as it is not important to determine whether he was telling the truth. It is important, rather, that Cicero used this material to attack his opponent, with the knowledge that his contemporaries considered the particular outfit inappropriate for the occasion at hand. Thus, his charges reveal the dress code of late republican society. It is clear that the conservative Romans took this code quite seriously.

## ROMAN OFFICIALS IN GREEK DRESS: THE CASE OF C. VERRES

The first time we find Cicero using the charge of wearing inappropriate clothing, he directs it at a Roman official who dressed like a Greek. His principal target is C. Verres, the former governor of Sicily whom he prosecuted for extortion in 70.[4] Cicero refers to Verres' clothing five times in the *Verrines*, and in each case, he weaves the charge into an elaborate attack on Verres' propraetorship.

In the *Fourth Verrine*, Cicero recounts how Verres set up a workshop to expropriate valuable treasures that he had taken from his Sicilian subjects: "The ornamental work that he had torn from dishes and censers he now proceeded to attach so ingeniously to the outside of the golden cups, and so cleverly to the inside of golden basins, that anyone would have supposed them designed for the purpose; while our governor himself, who tells us that it was his own watchful attention that kept Sicily at peace, used to sit in this workshop for most of the day, wearing a *tunica pulla* and a *pallium* . . . For who has not heard of this workshop, of the golden vessels, and of that man's *pallium?*" (*Verr.* 4.54–55).[5] The orator contrasts Verres' claim to have protected Sicily with the facts that prove the very opposite: he spent his days in the workshop, and he wore a tunica pulla and a pallium, that is, decidedly Greek clothes, rather than the proper Roman tunic, which was white and had the *latus clavus*, and the paludamentum normally worn by a governor.[6] Cicero uses rhetorical means to show that Greek dress was an important component of Verres' scandalous behavior: he ends the passage with a tricolon stating where Verres was, what he was doing, and what he was wearing.[7]

In the *Fifth Verrine*, as in the *Fourth*, Cicero contrasts the governor's illicit activities with the way he was supposed to behave. He repeatedly emphasizes the fact that Verres completely neglected his duties as praetor because he spent so much time on the beach with women.[8] In section 40 of this speech, Cicero cites several crises that Verres failed to deal with, including a meeting with an embassy from Valentia:

When the Valentini came to you and a distinguished and noble man, Marcus Marius, spoke on their behalf and asked you, since you had the authority and title of praetor, to deal with this situation and put yourself in charge to destroy that small band of men, you not only shirked this duty, but at that very time there you were on the beach with that woman of yours, Tertia, whom you had brought along with you, in full view of everyone; and when you gave your answer to the people of a town so famous and important as Valentia, you were wearing a *tunica pulla* and a *pallium*.

According to Cicero, Verres neglected his duties by spending time with his mistress when he should have been meeting with the Valentian ambassadors. Moreover, when he finally did meet with them, he was again dressed in a tunica pulla and a pallium. This behavior constituted more than a disregard for the social conventions that went with his office: it was an insult to the people of Valentia. Surely they believed that, when meeting with ambassadors from an important town, the governor should wear official Roman dress to show his respect for the prestige of that town. This is a clear reference to a Roman "uniform," and modern parallels spring to mind: the dark suit a lawyer wears to court, for example, reflects respect for the judge and the judicial process.

Another reference that Cicero makes to clothing in this speech appears in his discussion of Verres' neglect of his juridical duties:

But that very Hannibal, who thought that in his camp promotion should be by merit and not by birth, became so much

attached to this woman Tertia that he took her off with him when he left his province. And also during those days, when he spent his time in banquets with women, dressed in a purple *pallium* and an ankle-length *tunica*, people were not irritated or troubled about the fact that the chief magistrate was absent from the forum, no legal decisions were pronounced, and no judgments were made. People were not annoyed that that entire coast resounded with women's voices and band music, while in the forum there was complete silence of lawsuits and the law, for it was not the law or the courts that seemed absent from the forum, but violence and savagery and the cruel and undeserved plundering of property. (*Verr.* 5.31)

Cicero contrasts what the governor was doing with what he should have been doing: he spent his time in banquets with women instead of in the forum, and he wore an ankle-length tunic and a purple pallium instead of the knee-length Roman tunic and the paludamentum, which was probably scarlet and extended to about mid-calf.[9] This account is more elaborate than the one in the *Fourth Verrine*. No doubt Cicero had literary motives for adding the details of color and length: the alliteration of *pallio purpureo talarique tunica* would not have escaped his audience. But these details also prove that these clothes were Greek. There is evidence from other speeches of Cicero and from Gellius that the ankle-length tunic was considered effeminate.[10] Cicero did not wish to make an issue of this in the *Verrines*, however; rather, he wanted to stress the immorality of Verres' liaison with Tertia.

In sections 86 and 87, Cicero again speaks of Verres' Greek clothes, this time when he discusses how Verres' neglect of his duties had harmed the fleet:

That diligent governor viewed the fleet in his command only as long as it sailed past his most disgraceful banquet; he himself, moreover, who had not been seen in many days, at that time showed himself for a little while to his soldiers. That Roman governor stood there on the shore in *soleae*, wearing a purple *pallium* and an ankle-length *tunica*, and leaning on his little woman; and often enough before that any number of Sicilians and Roman citizens had seen him in this costume. . . . Cleomenes . . . imitated him by spending whole days drinking in a tent pitched on the shore.

The one time in days Verres is actually present to discharge his duties as governor, he has just come from a banquet, drunk, and he is dressed in a purple pallium, ankle-length tunic, and soleae. Cicero has added shoes to complete the picture: soleae are, notably, sandals that are meant to be worn only indoors.[11] Verres is said to be wearing them because, in his state of intoxication, he neglected to put on proper shoes when he left the banquet in his tent.[12] In his drunken stupor and his apparel, he is even more debauched than he was earlier. It can be no accident that in this same passage Cicero mentions Cleomenes, the commander of the fleet, who followed Verres' degenerate example. The governor was so far gone that he set an example of immorality even for Greeks.

In the last of this series of attacks on Verres' Greek dress, Cicero poses a hypothetical situation in which Verres' father, acting as one of the jurors at his trial, says to his son:

You, here in this illustrious province, among our loyal allies and honorable countrymen, amid the dangers by which the province was menaced spent day after day idly carousing on the beach. You, all that time, were never to be found at home, never to be seen in the forum. Your guests at those banquets were married women, the wives of our Sicilian allies and friends. You introduced to the society of such women your son wearing a *toga praetexta*—my grandson—so that, at the most unstable and dangerous period of his life, his own father's lifestyle might set him an example of vicious living. You, while a governor in command of your province, showed yourself wearing a *tunica* and purple *pallium,* you because of your passion and lust robbed the *legatus,* appointed by the Roman People of the command of the fleet and handed it over to a Syracusan, your soldiers in Sicily lacked produce and grain, and because of your wantonness and greed, a fleet of the Roman people was captured and set on fire by pirates. (*Verr.* 5.137)

This passage reiterates the claim that Verres' immoral activities brought great harm to Sicily and the Roman people. Cicero adds to this an equally serious charge: in behaving this way, the governor set a bad example for his son, who was *praetextatus,* that is, dressed in the toga praetexta, the correct attire for Roman boys.[13] Whereas in section 87 Verres is said to have been the model of illicit behavior for Greeks to emulate, in this passage he is said to have corrupted his own son. Surely the irony of the improperly dressed father acting as a model for the properly dressed son, who was of an impressionable age, would not have been lost on the audience.

All of Cicero's references to Verres' dress have certain elements in common. First, they describe him as wearing a pallium and tunic. Despite some variation in details, the orator makes the same point every time: Verres was not wearing what he should have been wearing. He wore Greek, not Roman, clothing. The dark tunic and purple pallium are meant to be contrasted with the paludamentum he should have been wearing, and likewise the ankle-length tunic is meant to be contrasted with the proper shorter one. Second, Cicero stresses repeatedly that it is a Roman governor who was wearing Greek clothes. In all five passages he uses the word *praetor* or alludes to the office.[14] This governor did not perform his proper duties regarding embassies, legal decisions, and the fleet. Verres is said to be in a workshop or at banquets on the beach instead of where he belonged. Third, each passage emphasizes the immorality of Verres' behavior, whether it was the greed he displayed in stealing precious objects from his subjects or the intemperance

and lust he displayed in carousing with women. He acted immorally, like a Greek, and he dressed the part. By repeating variations on this theme a number of times, Cicero unremittingly leads his audience to this conclusion.

The castigation of Romans for having Greek morals was nothing new. During the late third and second centuries, orators inveighed against individuals for being corrupted by Greek vices.[15] There is even evidence that suggests Romans frowned upon those who wore Greek dress.[16] Cicero relied on this attitude to convince his audience of the immorality of Verres' behavior: by wearing a tunic and a pallium in official situations, the governor had disgraced his Roman office and shown his true character.

If we had only these examples, we might conclude that Cicero himself was personally outraged by Roman magistrates who wore Greek dress. His speech *Pro C. Rabirio Postumo* of 54, however, provides quite a different picture. Rabirius was a knight who was prosecuted for his financial involvement with Ptolemy Auletes, the king of Egypt. In the following passage, Cicero defends Rabirius' wearing of Greek apparel:

Reproach him therefore as much as you will, with his constant wearing of the *pallium,* and with his use of some other ornaments not belonging to a Roman; on every occasion of your making any such allegation, you do but repeat the self-same statement—that he rashly lent money to the king, and that he trusted his fortunes and his reputation to the royal caprice. He had acted rashly, I admit; but what was done could not be undone; and either he had to don the *pallium* at Alexandria, in order to wear the *toga* at Rome, or he had to retain the *toga* and fling away all his fortunes. I have often seen not only Roman citizens but high-born youths, and even some senators of eminent family, wearing a *tunica pulla* not in their country seats or their suburban villas, but in the populous town of Naples, as a form of foppish self-gratification. In the same place many saw the great general, Lucius Sulla, wearing a *pallium;* and you can all see on the Capitol the statue of Lucius Scipio, who conducted the war in Asia and defeated Antiochus, wearing not only a *chlamys* but also *crepidae.* And these men were unassailed even by popular talk, let alone by judicial proceedings. Still more easily beyond question will the plea of necessity afford a defence to Publius Rutilius Rufus; he, having fallen into the hands of Mithridates at Mytilene, escaped the cruelty which the king showed to all wearers of the *toga* by changing his apparel. That Rutilius, then, who was to our fellow-countrymen an example of courage, of old-time honor, and of wisdom, and who was moreover an ex-consul, donned *socci* and a *pallium,* and none at that time imputed the blame to the man, but all to the necessity in which he found himself; and shall Postumus be arraigned for wearing a garment in which lay his sole hope of one day recovering his fortunes? (*Rab. Post.* 25–27)

This passage indicates that people of Cicero's day generally believed it wrong for upper-class Romans to wear Greek clothing abroad, although it could be excused by special circumstances. It implies, moreover, that this charge was often made in legal proceedings because inappropriate clothing was believed to mirror inappropriate behavior. Postumus' opponents accused him of acting like a Ptolemaic official instead of looking after Roman concerns, and they criticized his shedding of the toga because they saw this act as a symbolic renunciation of Roman citizenship.[17]

Cicero's defense of Postumus rests on proving the paradoxical statement that wearing non-Roman clothing was necessary for him to save his position as a Roman citizen. It is evident from this argument that Cicero himself did not object to Greek dress in certain circumstances; nor did some of his peers. Apparently it was sanctioned in private and in Greek cities. And yet, the examples Cicero cites show how difficult it must have been to find material to support his case. Naples, the one city he chooses to mention, is, notably, a Greek one. Furthermore, the individuals he cites, L. Sulla, L. Scipio, and P. Rutilius Rufus, are all exceptional in that they had served Rome with distinction in the East. The depiction of Sulla in a pallium surely applies to the period after his return from his Eastern campaigns, most likely after his dictatorship: not only did he retire to Campania, which had a large Greek population, but also by this time he would not have been concerned with propriety.[18] The example of Scipio is also suspect, because Cicero cites only the clothes on his statue, not knowledge of his actual habits.

Cicero reserves the discussion of P. Rutilius Rufus for last because, of the three men, his situation was most similar to Postumus': his dealings with an Eastern king forced him to wear the pallium instead of the toga. This certainly is not the whole story. Rufus had left Rome in exile after his conviction in 92 and returned to the East.[19] He may have become a citizen of Mytilene and shed the toga at this time. But in view of a Posidonius fragment, it is also possible that, like many other Romans, he took up Greek dress to escape execution by Mithridates.[20] Clearly, Cicero is suppressing part of the truth in order to liken Rufus' situation to Postumus' and to claim that each man's ability to survive depended on his choice of apparel. The orator thus uses the subject of clothing to imply that Postumus, like Rufus, had all the important Roman virtues and was a model "of courage, of old-time honor, and of wisdom."

Cicero's apparently contradictory statements on Romans who wore Greek dress enable us to make certain inferences about this practice. It is likely that some officials were happy to wear Roman clothing because they wished to maximize the distance between themselves and the Greeks under their jurisdiction. They wanted their subjects to know they were different. Presumably they insisted on speaking Latin as well.[21] But this evidence shows even more compellingly that magistrates wore Roman clothing abroad because Romans at home generally thought they should. Anything less was considered an affront to the *dignitas* of Rome. These two reasons bring to mind the British viceroys who wore official white uniforms in India, although they were no doubt quite uncomfortable in so warm a climate. The viceroys wanted their subjects to know who they were, and at the same time, this dress was mandated by the local English community. Wearing this uniform was thus a way of obtaining respect from both elements of the population.

And yet, as Cicero recognizes, not all Romans wore Roman clothing in his day or even long before. Some men, both officers and civilians, wore Greek clothing in southern Italy and in the East because it was comfortable and appropriate leisure wear. But since Romans typically must have associated Greek clothing with immoral behavior, Cicero uses this attitude to his advantage when attacking Verres. Conversely, in his defense of Postumus, he stresses how mistaken this attitude is and makes a point of attributing to Rufus all important Roman virtues. It is likely, therefore, that Cicero and his contemporaries did not make Greek dress an item for criticism unless the appropriateness of the individual's behavior was in question.

DRESS AND UNDRESS:
THE CASE OF M. ANTONIUS

In the *Philippics,* the series of speeches directed against M. Antonius in 44 and 43, Cicero again uses the subject of clothing as a means of criticizing his opponent's actions as a magistrate. It is not surprising that the *Second Philippic,* the most rhetorically elaborate of the series and essentially a personal and political attack on Antonius (and the only one of the series that was not delivered), contains the greatest number of references to clothing; there are four different passages here, while there is one in the *Third Philippic* and one in the *Thirteenth.*[22] All but one of these allusions concern clothing Antonius wore as a magistrate in specific situations.

When narrating the circumstances of Antonius' return to Rome after campaigning in Gaul for the consulship of 44, Cicero says:

And now, the manner of his return from Narbo—and he was asking why *I* turned back so suddenly, abandoning my journey! . . . As for your question, *how* did I return, to begin with, it was by daylight, not darkness; secondly, it was in *calcei* and a *toga*, not in *gallici* and a *lacerna.* . . . No infamy I have ever seen or heard of was more outrageous. You looked upon yourself as a former master of horse, you were standing for the consulship, or rather asking for it, the following year: and you rushed through the townships and colonies of Gaul, the region where we used to canvass for the consulship when that office was stood for and not asked for, in *gallici* and a *lacerna*! (*Phil.* 2.76)

According to Gellius, the term *gallicus* for a shoe first came into use shortly before Cicero's day.[23] This is a rather curious statement, for it implies that Gallic shoes were virtually unknown to Romans of the republic. We are not told what type of shoe this was, but like the *lacerna*, it must have been worn in the north. There are two ways to interpret Antonius' behavior. It is possible that he had not stopped to change to the proper dress of the candidate, the white toga and *calcei*, which Cicero himself had worn during his own campaign.[24] Alternatively, he may have been trying to fit in with the natives in order to win their votes. If that is true, Antonius resembles the politicians of our own day who campaign for the American presidency and change their clothes in order to fit in with the natives of each place they visit.

Why did Cicero make such a fuss about Antonius' dress in this context? First, like Verres' wearing of Greek garb, it was undignified. But returning to Rome at night was an additional disgrace: Antonius did not behave in a way that suited the *dignitas* of a Roman senator. Cicero contrasts this disregard for tradition with his own proper behavior during his return from his aborted journey in late August 44.

A few sections later in this speech, Cicero goes on to criticize the clothing Antonius wore as consul at the Lupercalia on February 15, 44:

Your colleague sat on the rostra, wearing his purple *toga,* on his golden chair, his garland on his head. Up you come, you approach the chair, as a lupercus (you *were* a lupercus, but you should have remembered that you were consul); you display a diadem. Groans all over the Forum! Where did the diadem come from? You had not picked it out of the gutter. No, you had brought it with you, a planned, premeditated crime. You made to place the diadem on Caesar's head amid the lamentations of the people: he kept refusing it, and the people applauded. You had been urging Caesar to make himself king, you wanted him as a master instead of a colleague, so you and only you were found to make this criminal experiment to determine what the Roman People could bear and suffer. Why, you even tried pathos, throwing yourself as a suppliant at his feet. What was your petition? To be a slave? You should have spoken for yourself; from a boy your life had been such as to make everything tolerable and slavery easy. Assuredly you had no such commission from us and from the Roman People. What a marvelously eloquent speech you made—*nudus!*—naked! Disgraceful, loathsome! No punishment could be too bad! (*Phil.* 2.85–86)[25]

A great deal of attention, both ancient and modern, has been paid to the events described in this passage, and yet except for discussions of the controversial "diadem," little has been said about the role clothing plays here. Cicero describes C. Julius Caesar as wearing the toga purpurea and a garland. This was the dress which the

kings had worn, and the right to wear it was one of the honors which the Senate had recently voted him.[26] By contrast, Antonius was naked or *nudus* when he offered Caesar the diadem. This fact is made all the worse, Cicero implies, because Antonius was delivering a speech to the Roman people at that very moment.[27] This claim recurs in the *Third* and *Thirteenth Philippics:*

Indeed, you ought not to have regarded Marcus Antonius as consul after the Feast of Lupercal. On the day when before the eyes of the Roman People he made a public speech *nudus, unctus, ebrius*—naked, anointed, and drunk—and tried to place a diadem on his colleague, on that day he not only abdicated the consulship but his personal freedom as well. (*Phil.* 3.12)

[Antonius wrote to Hirtius and Caesar,] "You took their revenues away from the Julian Luperci." Does he dare make mention of the *luperci*? Does he not shudder at the memory of that day when soaked in wine, smeared with aromatics, and *nudus* he dared to urge a groaning Roman People into slavery? (*Phil.* 13.31)

The question arises as to what is meant by the word *nudus*. Cicero himself provides the answer in the *Second Philippic*. He compares the way Antonius was dressed when he spoke at the Lupercalia with the way his grandfather Marcus Antonius, the great orator, was dressed when he spoke at a public meeting: "I knew your grandfather for a great speaker, but I know you for an even more *open* one. He never addressed a public meeting *nudus,* whereas you, plain honest fellow that you are, have let us see your chest" (*Phil.* 2.111). Clearly, *nudus* in this context means "bare-chested," or, to put it in modern vernacular, "not dressed." This definition makes sense, given what we know about the garb of the participants in the festival of the Lupercalia. They wore loincloths made of goatskin, and it is generally believed that they wore nothing else.[28] If Antonius' genitals had been visible, Cicero surely would not have passed up the opportunity to say so.

Whereas Cicero uses himself as the model of proper dress for political campaigning, he turns to the elder Antonius as the model for speaking at the *contio*. This comparison of the two Antonii works because the grandfather was a renowned orator as well as an ancestor of the consul. The claim that the elder Antonius never gave a speech when *nudus* is juxtaposed with the charge that the younger Antonius exposed his chest to the public. Cicero even employs a pun to humiliate his opponent: Antonius was "more open" in speaking than his grandfather.

Although in this passage Cicero claims to be shocked by Antonius' appearance, he was not always opposed to such displays. In fact, there is evidence from the *Fifth Verrine* to suggest that it was generally considered good rhetorical technique when practiced at the appropriate time, as at the trial of M.' Aquillius: "I remember, in the trial of Manius Aquillius, how impressive, and how decisive, the speech of Marcus Antonius was felt to be. Near the end of it, like the bold and able orator that he was, with his own hands he laid hold of Aquillius, made him stand where all could see him, tore his *tunica* from his chest, that his countrymen might see the scars that he bore on the front of his body; and dwelling at the same time on the wound he had received in his head from the enemy's leader, reduced those with whom the decision lay to a state of trembling agitation" (*Verr.* 5.3). Later in the speech Cicero brings up the subject of Antonius again: "Do you, then, Hortensius, plead that such a man as this was a great military leader? . . . Are we now to fear, as your speech for the defence nears its close, that you will bring into play the impressive methods of argument used of old by Antonius? Will you bid Verres stand up, make his chest *nudus,* show the people of Rome his scars—scars made by women's teeth, the imprinted records of lechery and foulness?" (*Verr.* 5.32).

In both of these passages the act of undressing refers specifically to the baring of a man's chest, and it reveals scars that reflect his character. Aquillius acquired his scars through his military exploits. Verres received his, however, through his erotic adventures. Cicero uses clothing to make two comparisons at the same time: he compares Verres unfavorably with Aquillius, and Hortensius with Antonius. Whereas he uses *abscindere* for Antonius' disrobing of Aquillius (tunicamque eius a pectore abscidit), he uses *denudare* to refer to Verres' disrobing *(ne denudetur a pectore).* Cicero chooses his words carefully. It is Verres, not his lawyer, who removes his tunic; moreover, his action is depicted with a verb related to the term *nudus,* chosen for its connotations of immorality. For Verres to remove his tunic was to make himself *nudus,* that is, not properly dressed for a courtroom, because he had acted immorally when governor of Sicily. By contrast, it was perfectly acceptable for Aquillius' tunic to be removed, because he had served Rome honorably.

It remains for us to ascertain why Cicero criticized Antonius for being a lupercus at the Lupercalia, since this festival was very old and respected and it was well known that the luperci dressed minimally.[29] So Cicero was not objecting to the "nudity" of the luperci. But Antonius was not just a lupercus. He was a consul, and it is implied that he was delivering a speech to the Roman people in this capacity. Lupercalian attire, that is, bare-chestedness, was considered inappropriate for a Roman official, just as Greek dress was inappropriate for Verres while governor of Sicily. This inference helps explain why Cicero twice describes Antonius as *nudus, unctus, ebrius*—undressed, anointed, and drunk. The

luperci did not, as far as we know, engage in drinking during the ceremony, and so a drunk participant would surely not have been acceptable. Therefore, Cicero portrays the consul as someone who had just come from a drinking party, in much the same way as he portrayed Verres. He uses these traits to emphasize the immoral character of the man who went so far as to offer Caesar the diadem. Cicero also stresses Antonius' nakedness for its suggestion of the servility and humiliation he showed before Caesar: hence the numerous references to "slavery" and the loss of his "personal freedom."

The subject of "nudity" appears on three other occasions in Cicero's speeches, each time in the context of banqueting. In the speech *In Pisonem* of 55, he describes the debauched activities of A. Gabinius and L. Calpurnius Piso during their consulship:

What need for me to publish abroad the banqueting that filled those days, your gleeful self-congratulation, and your unbridled potations with your crew of infamous associates? Who in those days ever saw you sober, or engaged in any activity befitting a free man? Who indeed ever saw you in public at all? When the house of your colleague rang with song and cymbals, and when he himself danced *nudus* at a feast at which, when executing those whirling gyrations of his, even then he felt no fear of Fortune and her wheel. Piso meanwhile, neither so elegant nor so artistic a debauchee, lolled amid his tipsy and malodorous Greeks, while amidst all the miseries of his country, his colleague's feast was spoken of as if a sort of banquet of Lapiths and Centaurs; and in it none can say whether that wretch spent more time in drinking or in vomiting or in excreting his potations. (*Pis.* 22)

In this scurrilous passage, there is the same connection between "nudity" and drunkenness that Cicero makes in his portrait of Antonius at the Lupercalia. But Piso and Gabinius are not simply drunk: they have reached the height of intoxication, as is shown by Gabinius' fearless dancing on the one hand, and Piso's association with drunken and foul-smelling Greeks on the other.[30] The analogy of the banquet of the lusty and drunken Centaurs who became embroiled in a brawl with the Lapiths over their wives is a well-chosen one: it suggests that the participants in Gabinius' banquet resembled Centaurs in their appearance, that is, that they were drunk and not wearing any clothes.[31] The use of this myth raises the possibility that the meaning of *nudus* varied with the context. Whereas in a public setting it meant "bare-chested" or "half dressed," in the privacy of one's own home, it may have meant "wearing only underwear" *(perizoma)* or "completely naked," because there is no other Latin word that has this meaning.[32] Although we cannot be certain what the precise meaning of *nudus* was when used in a private context, it is clear that the behavior of the ill-clad consuls, like that of Antonius and Verres, was believed to be detrimental to Rome.

The passages cited here indicate that Cicero usually directed the charge of "nudity" against the holders of the highest offices. Occasionally, however, he used it against lesser officials as well. One prominent target is Apronius, Verres' tax collector, whom Cicero characterizes as the ultimate debaucher. In the *Third Verrine*, after listing a number of Apronius' uncouth activities, he says:

He [Verres] employed this man as his chief man in his debaucheries, in his plundering of sanctuaries, in his filthy banquets: and similarity of character gives rise to such great bonding and friendship that Apronius, who appears savage and barbarous to others, appeared polite and well-spoken to Verres; that everyone else loathed him and shunned the sight of him while he could not live without him; that while others could not take part in the same banquets as Apronius, Verres even drank out of the same cups; finally, that the foulest smell of Apronius' breath and body, which, they say, not even animals could endure, to him and to him alone, seemed sweet and pleasant. Apronius sat next to him on the tribunal, was alone with him in his bedroom, was the leader in the banquet—and just when, with the praetor's son reclining on the dining couch in his *toga praetexta*, he proceeded to dance *nudus* before the company. (*Verr.* 3.23)

Cicero portrays Apronius as Verres' equal, indeed his twin, in debauchery. But the very worst vice of all was his dancing *nudus* in the presence of Verres' son. Cicero's audience would not have failed to miss the irony of the contrast between the outrageous dress and the behavior of Apronius and the decorum of the young man. But there is a more important reason why Cicero mentions Verres' son. He wishes to stress that Apronius' actions were especially objectionable because of the presence of a young man, and because Verres himself encouraged this behavior. Both here and in section 137 of the *Fifth Verrine*, Cicero refers to Verres' son discreetly, so as not to offend the sensibilities of the jurors. He observes the same practice in his account of Antonius' life (*Phil.* 2.76), where he says that Antonius was *praetextatus* as a boy but improperly dressed later in life. Boys were socially protected, and moral charges were reserved for adults.[33]

Once again we have a rule proved by an exception. In the speech *Pro rege Deiotaro* of 45, Cicero defends Deiotarus against the charge of dancing *nudus* and *ebrius* at a banquet:

And what next? What is the next assertion of this gallows rogue? He says that Deiotarus, elated with glee, . . . fuddled himself with wine and danced *nudus* at a banquet. Can the cross inflict adequate torture upon this runaway? Has anyone ever seen Deiotarus either dancing or drunk? This king is an exemplar of all the virtues, as I think you, Caesar, know well enough; but in nothing is he more remarkable and more admirable than in his sobriety. . . . Everyone is free to put what construction he pleases upon my words; none the less I pro-

nounce sobriety, by which I mean moderation and temperance, to be the highest of virtues. . . . As a youth, not yet crowned with the laurels which he was later to win, his every act was exemplary in gravity and dignity; and did he, with his reputation and at his age, dance? (*Deiot.* 26–27)

It is evident from this passage that others besides Cicero accused their opponents of dancing at banquets. Because such behavior was considered completely antithetical to traditional values, Cicero cannot defend it, as he defended Rabirius' wearing of Greek clothes. He can only deny the charge and assert that Deiotarus practiced the traditional Roman virtues of sobriety and moderation.

All of these examples leave little doubt that Romans considered it highly inappropriate, indeed obscene, for any of their officials to be *nudus*. The precise meaning of this word varied with the situation. In the case of the magistrate delivering a speech at a public meeting or the lawyer defending his client in court, it designated a man who was bare-chested. In the private sphere, it could be used of a man who was wearing only his underpants. What remains constant is the association of *nudus* with immoral behavior—drunkenness and dancing. This attitude forms a complete contrast with that of the Greeks, who engaged in athletic competitions in the nude.[34]

## THE TRANSVESTISM OF PUBLIUS CLODIUS

Cicero also criticized the Roman official who wore women's clothes, in particular P. Clodius Pulcher, who became infamous for his infiltration in December 62 of the Bona Dea, a ritual that was closed to men. In the *De haruspicum responsis* of 56, the orator contrasts Clodius' sacrilege with the actions of other demagogues, who took measures that proved harmful to the state but who had legitimate reasons for doing so:

Then came the quaestorship, fraught with disaster for the Commonwealth, for rites and cults, for your collective authority and the public courts, in which he went on to outrage Gods and men, decency and chastity, the Senate's authority, human and divine law, statutes and courts. . . . Each of them [the Gracchi, Saturninus, and Sulpicius Rufus] had a reason—not, indeed, a valid reason, for no reason for doing the Commonwealth disservice can ever be valid; but still a serious reason conjoined with the resentment of a manly spirit. But Publius Clodius—emerging from his *crocata*, his *mitra*, his womanish *soleae* and little purple *fasciae*, his *strophium*, his lute, his act of gross immorality, all of a sudden he became a people's man. If the women had not caught him so attired, and if by the courtesy of the slave girls he had not been let out of the place which he had no right to be in, the Roman People would not have their people's man nor the Commonwealth such a citizen. (*Har. Resp.* 43–44)

The list of men who have a manly spirit (*animi virilis*) is followed by the example of a man in women's clothing. Cicero describes Clodius' outfit from head to toe: the *mitra*, *strophium*, *crocata*, purple *fasciae*, and soleae.[35] Such clothing, in both its style and color, was inexcusable for men. Cicero has truly succeeded in making Clodius look ridiculous. Behind the humor, however, is a serious message that the audience would not have missed. By infiltrating the Bona Dea festival, a very serious rite, Clodius had committed a major sacrilege—one as serious as Alcibiades' infamous profanation of the Mysteries.[36] This act must have upset a great many people. It was only through intimidation and bribery, in fact, that Clodius managed to be acquitted of the charges.[37] With this portrait, therefore, Cicero appeals to his audience's sense of religious propriety.

As we have seen, Cicero generally uses clothing to reflect the character of its wearer. Notably, however, in this speech he does not pursue the sexual implications of Clodius' transvestism. He cannot do so, because he wants to allude to his opponent's well-known *stuprum*, his attempted adultery with Pompeia, Caesar's wife.[38] Describing him in effeminate terms would have obscured that point. Instead, he resorts to sarcasm: these items of clothing and the debauched life-style they represent made Clodius a man of the people and a model of behavior for all of Rome.

Elsewhere, however, Cicero does, indeed, pursue the sexual implications of Clodius' feminine apparel, as fragments of his speech *In P. Clodium et C. Curionem* indicate: "For he must wonder less at us rustic types, who cannot wear a long-sleeved *tunica*, a *mitra*, and purple *fasciae*. Only you indeed are merry, elegant, and urbane, for whom womanly clothing and the gait of a lutist is suitable, you who can make yourself look like a woman, make your voice higher, and make your body smooth." He also says, "When your feet were bound with *fasciae*, when a *calautica* was put on your head, when you put a long-sleeved *tunica* on your arms, when you were properly girded with a *strophium*, in that long period of time, did you never remember that you were a descendant of Appius Claudius?"[39] In these instances, Cicero does charge Clodius with effeminacy. In the first fragment quoted, he does this with a heavy dose of sarcasm: not only is Clodius able to look good in women's clothes, but he can also take on their physical attributes. His appearance reflects his character: he looks like a woman in many respects because of his effeminate nature, just as Verres' immoral character caused him to look like a Greek.

Cicero thus uses clothing of all varieties to comment on the actions and character of the magistrate under discussion. The garb may vary, but all of his subjects have one point in common: they disregarded revered traditions and endangered Rome's authority and reputation. Although Cicero uses clothing most often to characterize key magistrates, on occasion he comments on the life-style of individuals who did not hold a particular office. In the *Second Speech against Catiline* of 63, he describes his opponent's closest associates:

These are the men you see with their carefully combed hair, dripping with oil, some beardless, others with shaggy beards, with long-sleeved and ankle-length *tunicas*, and wearing *vela*, not *togas*. All the activity of their lives and all the efforts of their waking hours are devoted to banquets that last till dawn. In this herd you find all the gamblers, all the adulterers, all the filthy minded lechers. These boys, so dainty and effeminate, have learnt not only to love and to be loved, not only to dance and sing, but also to brandish daggers and sow poison. . . . How will they stand the frosts and snows of the Apennines? Perhaps they think that they will withstand the winter more easily because they have learned to dance *nudi* at banquets. (*Cat.* 2.22)

This passage constitutes a compilation of the invective Cicero uses against Verres, Antonius, Gabinius, and Clodius. The emphasis here is on the effeminacy of Catiline's supporters. Like Verres, they wear ankle-length tunics. These tunicas are said to be "long-sleeved" *(manicatis);* notably, Cicero uses this word elsewhere only twice—both times in the *In Clodium et Curionem*, where he is anxious to stress Clodius' effeminacy.[40] Over their tunics, Catiline's cohorts wear vela, veils of filmy material, rather than proper togas, and they are "beardless." Their actions match their appearance: they dance *nudi* at banquets, like Gabinius. In short, they possess every aspect of immorality that Cicero could conjure up.

One other passage is worth mentioning here. In the *Second Philippic*, Cicero uses clothing imagery to summarize Antonius' career: "Would you like us to examine your record from a boy? Yes, I think that is best. Let us begin from the beginning. Do you recollect that you went bankrupt while wearing the *toga praetexta*? . . . You donned the *toga virilis* [toga of manhood]—and promptly it became the *toga muliebris* [toga of womanhood]. You started out as a common whore. Your shame had a fixed price, and no mean one. But presently along came Curio. He took you out of the prostitute's trade, gave you a *stola* as it were, and settled you down in steady wedlock." (*Phil.* 2.44)[41]

This passage is especially interesting, for it is a rare instance of Cicero speaking of clothing in a metaphorical sense. He begins by referring to Antonius' boyhood as the time when he wore the toga praetexta. As we observed in the case of Verres' young son, Cicero does not wish to charge him with immoral behavior at that age, only bankruptcy. When Antonius reached adulthood, the orator continues, he put on the toga virilis, the toga of manhood. Cicero plays on the meaning of *virilis* in relating Antonius' subsequent behavior: he turned the toga virilis into a toga muliebris, the toga that prostitutes wore. His clothing thus reflects the fact that he sold himself for financial gain.[42] Cicero continues the metaphor with words used of marriage. He gives Curio the credit for making an "honest woman" out of Antonius. They are united in a "stable and honest marriage," and Antonius now wears a *stola,* the garb of the respectable Roman matron.[43] Note the derisive tone here: although Antonius has become respectable again, he is respectable as a woman, not a man. Cicero thus carefully develops a metaphor that everyone would have understood in order to comment generally on Antonius' career and then specifically on his most recent political actions.

The connection Cicero consistently draws between clothing and the character of its wearer helps explain the metaphor as it applies to Antonius. It may also help explain why female prostitutes wore the toga, the symbol of the Roman man: perhaps such women were believed to behave like men, that is, in their promiscuous actions.[44]

THE CLOTHING OF MOURNING RITUALS

Cicero is also an important source for Roman attitudes toward the clothing worn on occasions of mourning. Once again, we can attempt to deduce what his contemporaries considered appropriate garb from his references to those who were inappropriately dressed. In the speech *In P. Vatinium testem interrogatio* of 56, a general attack on P. Vatinius and his tribunate, Cicero criticizes his opponent for wearing mourning clothing at the funeral celebrations which Q. Arrius had held in honor of his father, Q. Arrius, in 59:[45]

I should also like to ask you what design or object you had in view when you took your place at my friend Quintus Arrius' banquet in a *toga pulla.* Have you ever seen or heard of such a thing? Where was your precedent, what usage were you following? You will say that you did not approve of that thanksgiving [*supplicationes*]. . . . Well, suppose there was no thanksgiving: tell me, who ever dined in a black gown [*atratus*]? It was a funeral feast, true; but while the function of such a feast is to celebrate a death, the feast itself is an occasion of good cheer. But I say nothing of the public funeral celebration. . . . Whoever dined when in private mourning for a death in the family? Who was ever handed a *toga pulla* as he came out of the bath, except you? When so many thousands were at their tables, when the master of the feast, Quintus Arrius, was in white, you and Gaius Fidulus (also in black) and the other evil spirits entered the temple of Castor in funeral attire. . . . Who but groaned to see it and grieved for the plight of the commonwealth. . . . Did you not know the custom? . . . Before the banquet you had seen the master and his friends in a *toga pulla,* but you did not see them dressed so at dinner. What fit of lunacy took possession of you to think that unless you committed sacrilege and violated the temple of Castor and the omen of the feast and established custom and the dignity of your host you would have failed to demonstrate sufficiently your opinion that the thanksgiving was invalid? (*Vat.* 30–32)[46]

This passage indicates that Romans considered the toga pulla proper dress for attending the actual burial ceremony but not for partaking in the subsequent banquet. Cicero appears to equate a person who wore the toga pulla with one who was said to be *atratus,* that is, dressed in black. Opinion is divided on whether *pulla* means gray or black. One scholar has suggested the garment was a gray-black toga.[47] This solution, however, does not take into account the role of rhetoric here. Since Cicero calls Vatinius *atratus* in order to create a strong contrast with the white garb of the correctly dressed Arrius, we cannot be certain of the actual hue of the garment.

The actions of Vatinius and his supporters, of course, had been carefully planned: they were a form of political protest, which must have greatly disturbed Arrius and his guests at the funeral feast. In wearing the toga pulla, the tribune had not only offended the host, but had also violated religious custom. This behavior must have upset Romans in much the same way as had Clodius' infiltration of the Bona Dea rites.

Cicero provides some insight into another type of toga that was worn as a sign of mourning. This evidence is unusual in that it consists not of invective, but of straightforward descriptions of clothing worn on particular occasions. In February 58 Clodius as tribune had introduced a bill that would outlaw anyone who had Roman citizens executed without a trial. Clearly this bill was meant to force Cicero into exile for his treatment of the Catilinarian conspirators in 63. Thousands protested, and some of Cicero's supporters went further: P. Sestius and T. Milo tried to block the election of Clodius to the aedileship, and both were charged with *vis* (violence resulting in public danger).[48] In the *Pro Sestio,* Cicero refers to the appearance of Sestius and his supporters at his trial: "I see Publius Sestius, defender, champion, promoter of my restoration, of your authority, and of the public cause, standing trial. I see his son in his *toga praetexta* tearfully gazing at me. I see Milo, vindicator of your freedom, guardian of my safety, help of the prostrate Commonwealth . . . dressed as a man with a charge hanging over his head [*sordidatum*]" (*Sest.* 144–45).

It has often been assumed that the word *sordes* was simply another term for the toga pulla, but scrutiny of the contexts in which the two terms appear suggests that Cicero did not use them interchangeably.[49] Rather, they referred to two distinct types of clothing. The words *squalor* and *sordes* in passages like the one quoted here suggest that these men wore white togas that had been dirtied in some way, most likely with ashes or dirt. As soon as an accusation was launched, the defendant, his family, and his friends put on sullied togas.[50] These garments were probably meant to imitate the toga pulla, which could not be worn in court because it was reserved for religious rituals. The donning of such clothes, therefore, was a very dramatic gesture that was made only in times of legal crisis. The symbolic significance of this ritual is clear: a guilty verdict of a capital charge brought the punishment of exile, which was tantamount to the demise of one's citizenship.[51]

Related to this practice is the ritual of *vestem mutare* (the changing of clothes), in which large numbers of people removed their togas and donned dirtied ones. This was an official protest decreed by the Senate in times of national emergency. In the *Pro Sestio* and the *Post reditum in Senatu,* Cicero vividly recalls how this ritual was observed in protest of his imminent exile:

Suddenly a vast multitude from all over Rome and Italy assembled on the Capitol. All were in favor of practicing *vestem mutare* and defending me by every means possible on private initiative, seeing that the Commonwealth had no official leaders. . . . You, you Roman Knights I mean, and all honest men with you, came to the Senate having practiced *vestem mutare* . . . and the Senate in large numbers voted to practice *vestem mutare* for the sake of my preservation. (*Sest.* 26)[52]

Later on, a vast concourse of honest men came from the Capitol, dressed in *sordes,* as suppliants; young men of the highest birth and the whole company of Roman Knights threw themselves at the feet of the shameless pimp [Gabinius]. How haughtily the ringleted rake rejected his fellow-countrymen's tears, nay, his country's prayers! . . . And when you voted to practice *vestem mutare* and actually all did so (all honest men had already done the same), he appeared bathed in perfume and wearing his *toga praetexta,* which all Praetors and Aediles then in office had discarded, to mock your garb of woe [*squalor*] and the sorrowing of a grateful community. (*Red. Sen.* 12)

It is clear that Romans took the practice of *vestem mutare* very seriously: even officials who normally wore the toga praetexta donned sordes on this occasion. Moreover, the rite apparently could be reversed only by a consular edict, as Cicero indicates:

What consul ever forbade the Senate to obey its own decrees? What tyrant ever prohibited the unhappy from mourning? Is it not enough, Piso (never mind Gabinius), to have so grossly betrayed public expectation? You neglected the authority of the Senate, scorned the advice of its leading members, played traitor to the Commonwealth, brought low the name of consul: would you dare to publish an order forbidding men to mourn my misfortune and theirs and the Commonwealth's and to signify their grief by their clothing? Whether the practicing of *vestem mutare* was an expression of their own sorrow or an appeal on my behalf, who ever had the cruelty to forbid anyone to mourn for himself or to supplicate for others? Is it not customary to practice *vestem mutare* spontaneously when a friend is in jeopardy? (*Sest.* 32–33)

These passages illustrate how a practice associated with religious ritual was converted for use in legal and political contexts. They emphasize how conservative the Romans of the late republic were and how strongly they felt about wearing certain types of clothing on particular occasions. The dress code was so important that it was legally regulated: decrees were enacted to compel people both to don sordes and to change back to togas. There is also the suggestion that dissidents often chose to express their disagreement with popular sentiment by wearing clothing that was inappropriate for the occasion at hand. Gabinius, for example, wore a toga praetexta when most people were wearing sordes. Cicero used invective to criticize him just as he had criticized others: again we see that he chose to attack individuals for inappropriate dress only when the appropriateness of their actions was in question.

Cicero provides evidence concerning another type of changing clothes, that of exchanging the toga for the sagum. The technical term for this ritual is *saga sumere* (to take up the saga).[53] Cicero urges the Senate to take up the saga repeatedly in the *Philippics:* "Therefore, Members of the Senate, in my judgment no mention should be made of envoys. I think the business should be put in hand without any delay and prosecuted at once. I say that a state of tumult should be decreed, suspension of business proclaimed, *saga sumere* be practiced, and a levy held with no exemptions in Rome and in the whole of Italy, Gaul excepted" (*Phil.* 5.31).[54] As with the wearing of sordes in public protest, *saga sumere* was a practice initiated by decree of the Senate only in times of national emergency.[55] The *Fourteenth Philippic* shows that the Senate also determined when togas were to be put on again. In this speech, Cicero asks the Senate not to abandon military garb as long as Decimus Brutus is still under siege in Mutina:

But until the news which the community is so impatiently awaiting arrives, it is enough to enjoy the happy knowledge of a great and glorious battle. Reserve a return to *vestitum* [civic dress] for final victory. . . . As for the proposal that we change our dress for today only and reappear tomorrow in *saga,* I wonder what it means. No, when once we have returned to the dress we want and pray for, let us make sure we keep it forever. Having approached the altars of the Immortal Gods in *togas,* to leave them and put on our *saga* again would be unseemly, nor would it be pleasing to the Gods themselves. I notice, Members of the Senate, that certain persons favor this proposal, and I perceive their purpose and plan. They see that the day we return to normal dress on account of Decimus Brutus' deliverance will be a most glorious day for him. Therefore they wish to deprive him of this gratification and not let it be handed down for posterity to remember that the Roman People put on *saga* because of one citizen's peril and went back into *togas* because of the same citizen's rescue. (*Phil.* 14.1–3)

Cicero refers to the return to togas also in the speech *In Pisonem,* when he discusses Piso's return from his proconsular command in Macedonia: "But why not enumerate those who did *not* come to meet you? Why not assert that scarce a single person came, even of the prospective candidates for office . . . ? At the gate little *togas* were given to the lictors, who took them, laying aside their little *saga*" (*Pis.* 55). This is an account of the normal procedure of exchanging the sagum for the toga, but the orator's use of the diminutive forms of these words *(togulae, sagula)* makes it clear that he was quite disdainful of Piso's triumph.

The wide variety of references examined here reveals much about the attitudes of Cicero's contemporaries toward dress. They believed particular attire was appropriate for particular occasions. Those who did not observe these unwritten rules displayed a defect in character, a defect that was reflected by the type of clothes they wore. Officers of Rome especially were expected to dress in a way respectful of their office and the *dignitas* of Rome. Consequently, when they did not, they were targets of Cicero's harshest criticism. As governor of Sicily, Verres displayed his Greek nature by wearing the dark tunic and purple pallium. Clodius revealed his effeminate nature by wearing women's clothes. Antonius as consul dressed obscenely with his chest exposed during the public Lupercalia; Gabinius and Piso in the same office also crossed the line of obscenity by wearing very little, perhaps nothing at all, at a private banquet. Some individuals wore inappropriate clothing to express political dissent: Vatinius wore mourning dress at Arrius' celebration, and Gabinius continued to wear a toga praetexta after the Senate had decreed that sordes were to be donned. All types of improper dress that Cicero cites had one thing in common: they reflected the immoral character of the individuals who wore them. These were men who had little regard for revered Roman traditions and the *dignitas* of Rome. But in fact, the orator provides us with hints that the rules were not as rigid as he often implies. His defense of Rabirius Postumus' wearing of Greek clothes and the examples of Sulla, L. Scipio, and Rufus suggest that people could and did break the rules; such behavior was condoned, as long as the individuals behaved properly otherwise.

Thanks to Cicero, we can be certain that during the late republic, dressing appropriately was a serious concern, closely connected to Rome's oldest political and religious practices. It showed, in a visible manner, the *gravitas*, or "seriousness," appropriate to a Roman citizen.

## NOTES

1. The significance of uniforms and deviations from them is explored by N. Joseph, *Uniforms and Non-Uniforms: Communication through Clothing* (New York, 1986).

2. For definitions of all items of clothing referred to in this essay, see the Glossary. For the sake of consistency and accuracy, only the original terms will be used here.

3. For the most recent discussion of the artistic representations of togas during the late republic, see Goette, *Togadarstellungen;* and S. Stone, chap. 1 in this volume.

4. For Cicero's attitude to Greeks and things Greek, see M. A. Trouard, *Cicero's Attitude towards the Greeks* (Chicago, 1942), esp. 17–32, 60–71; H. Guite, "Cicero's Attitude to the Greeks," *Greece and Rome* 9 (1962): 142–59. All dates are B.C. unless otherwise indicated.

5. The translations of the *Verrines* quoted here have been taken, in adapted form, from L. H. G. Greenwood, *Cicero: The Verrine Orations*, LCL (Cambridge, Mass., 1935); in the same series are the speeches *Pro C. Rabirio Postumo, Pro Rege Deiotaro,* and *In L. Calpurnium Pisonem,* all translated by N. H. Watts (1935), and *In Catilinam II*, translated by C. MacDonald (1977). The translations of the passages from the *Philippics* are reprinted (also in adapted form) with permission from D. R. Shackleton Bailey, ed., *Cicero Philippics* (Chapel Hill, N.C., 1986); those of *Post reditum in senatu, De haruspicum responsis, Pro P. Sestio,* and *In P. Vatinium testem interrogatio* have been taken from D. R. Shackleton Bailey, ed. and trans., *Cicero Back from Exile: Six Speeches upon His Return* (New Baskerville, 1991).

6. According to Mommsen, the governor wore the toga praetexta; T. Mommsen, *Römische Staatsrecht*, 3d ed., vol. 1 (1889; Graz, 1969), 418. But before the governor left Rome for his province, he and his lictors took part in a ceremony in which they put on military dress (DarSag 3.² 1239, with references; see n. 55 below). We should, therefore, infer that he regularly wore the paludamentum for official occasions.

7. "This workshop . . . golden vases . . . that man's pallium"; "Quis enim est qui de hac officina, qui de vasis aureis, qui de istius pallio non audierit?"

8. The term *praetor* was used both of a governor of praetorian rank and of the magistrate in his year of office.

9. DarSag 4.¹ 295.

10. Aulus Gellius 6.12.1.

11. L & S, s.v. solea II. Plautine characters typically took them off before dining (e.g. *Truculentus* 363, 367).

12. Cf. Cicero's criticism of Piso for leaving his house in soleae (*Pis.* 13). Soleae were considered effeminate in Cicero's day. See *Har. Resp.* 44 and discussion of Clodius below.

13. J. Marquardt and T. Mommsen, *Handbuch der römischen Alterthümer*, 2d ed., vol. 7 (Leipzig, 1886), 124. See also J. Sebesta, chap. 2 in this volume.

14. It appears in 4.54, 5.86 (twice), and 5.137; it is alluded to in 5.31 and 5.40.

15. Plutarch, *Cato Maior* 23. See D. Earl, *The Moral and Political Tradition of Rome* (London, 1967), 36–43; A. E. Astin, *Cato the Censor* (Oxford, 1978); E. S. Gruen, *The Hellenistic World and the Coming of Rome*, vol. 1 (Berkeley, 1984), 260–72; idem, *Studies in Greek Culture and Roman Policy* (Leiden, 1990), 76–77, 171–72.

16. According to Livy, complaints were made about P. Cornelius Scipio Africanus, who is said to have worn a pallium and crepidae at Syracuse (Livy 29.19.12; Valerius Maximus 3.6.1). On crepidae, see N. Goldman, chap. 6 in this volume.

17. See the fragment of Posidonius, which tells of Romans who, after suffering defeat at the hands of Mithridates in 88, became turncoats. They gave up their togas for the Greek himation (i.e., the pallium) in order to escape execution; see F. Jacoby, *Die Fragmente der griechischen Historiker* (Berlin, 1926), 87 F 36.50–L. Edelstein and I. G. Kidd, *Posidonius*, vol. 1, *The Fragments* (Cambridge, Eng., 1972), F 253.21B; Kidd, *Posidonius*, vol. 2, *The Commentary, Fragments 150–293* (Cambridge, 1988), 875.

18. See Plutarch, *Sulla* 36; Appian, *Bellum civile* 1.104.

19. Dio Cassius 28.97.3.

20. See n. 17 above.

21. L. Aemilius Paulus is a prominent example of a magistrate who, despite expertise in Greek, used interpreters to address his Greek subjects (Livy 45.29.3). On this practice, see Gruen, *Hellenistic World*, vol. 1, 267–68.

22. Cic. *Att.* 16.11.1; see J. D. Denniston, ed., *M. Tulli Ciceronis Orationes Philippicae I, II* (Oxford, 1926), xvii.

23. Aulus Gellius 13.22.6. On the gallicus, see N. Goldman, chap. 6 in this volume.

24. Isidore, *Origines* 19.24.6.

25. The Lupercalia was a festival in which its participants, priests known as Luperci, engaged in various rites. These included sacrificing goats and running around the Palatine. For a detailed account of the ritual, see H. H. Scullard, *Festivals and Ceremonies of the Roman Republic* (Ithaca, N.Y., 1981), 76–78.

26. Dio Cassius 44.6.1.

27. Cicero describes Antonius as addressing the people in a *comitium*, i.e., a formal meeting, but in fact it was a *contio*. See L. R. Taylor, *Roman Voting Assemblies* (Ann Arbor, Mich., 1966), 1–33. On nudity, see Bonfante, "Nudity as a Costume," 563 nn. 119–20.

28. See Scullard, *Festivals*, 76f.

29. Cf. *Cael.* 26, where Cicero emphasizes the primitive nature of these priests, but he avoids criticizing them further because Caelius was a Lupercus. Cicero's brother, Q. Tullius Cicero, was very pleased when his son became one (Cic. *Att.* 12.5.1), although apparently it was generally considered no great honor for the son of a senatorial family. See D. R. Shackleton Bailey, ed., *Cicero's Letters to Atticus*, vol. 5 (Cambridge, Eng., 1966), 303.

30. Dancing seems to have been considered the worst of the improprieties that resulted from overly indulgent drinking; accordingly, dancing *nudus* signified complete intoxication. See Cic. *Mur.* 13.

31. For discussion of the myth concerning the Centaurs at the wedding feast of the Lapith King Pirithous, see W. H. Roscher, *Ausführliches Lexikon der griechischen und römischen Mythologie*, 6 vols. (Leipzig, 1884–1937), vol. 2, part 1, pp. 1035–40.

32. On nudity and the wearing of the perizoma, see Bonfante-Warren, "Roman Costume," 609, where she defines *nudus* as "without the toga, wearing only the *perizoma*, or a light tunic."

33. There are, as far as I can determine, virtually no instances in which a boy from a respectable family is criticized, as long as he is *praetextatus*. On obscene or improper lan-guage in the presence of praetextate children, see J. Sebesta, chap. 2 in this volume.

34. Thucydides 1.6 (archaic Sparta); Plato, *Republic* 5.452c; J. Jüthner, "Die athletischen Leibesübungen der Griechen, 1: Geschichte der Leibesübungen," *Sitzungsberichte der Österreichische Akademie der Wissenschaften* 249, no. 1 (1965): 101–2. Cicero implies that Romans found nude athletic competitions offensive (*Tusc.* 4.70). See also Bonfante, "Nudity as a Costume," 563 n. 119.

35. Quintilian, *Institutio oratoria* 11.144. According to Quintilian, fasciae were inexcusable for men, except for those in bad health. For an analysis of Cicero's descriptions of Clodius' clothing in these passages as invective, see K. A. Geffcken, *Comedy in the "Pro Caelio"* (Leiden, 1973), 57–88. (Note p. 84, where Geffcken suggests that Clodius wore fasciae to conceal his hairiness.)

36. Thucydides 6.53, 60–61; Plutarch, *Alcibiades* 18–20.

37. Cic. *Att.* 1.12.3, 1.13.3; Plutarch, *Julius Caesar* 10.5.

38. It was said that Clodius had infiltrated the festival in order to approach Pompeia. Caesar divorced her at once, for he claimed she had to be above suspicion: Plutarch, *Julius Caesar* 10.8–10. The most recent treatment of this incident is D. Mulroy, "The Early Career of P. Clodius Pulcher: A Re-examination of the Charges of Mutiny and Sacrilege," *TAPA* 118 (1988): 155–78. For a list of Cicero's references to Clodius' *stuprum*, see P. Moreau, *Clodiana Religio: un procès politique in 61 av. J.–C.* (Paris, 1982), 24 n. 30.

39. F. Schoell, ed., *M. Tulli Ciceronis Scripta quae manserunt omnia* (Leipzig, 1918), vol. 8, xv. frags. 22, 24; G. Puccioni, *M. Tulli Ciceronis Orationum deperditarum fragmenta* (Milan, 1963), xv. frags. 21, 23.

40. Gellius preserves a quote from a speech of P. Cornelius Scipio Aemilianus against P. Sulpicius Gallus, who apparently was quite effeminate in appearance. In this fragment, Scipio speaks of his opponent's "long-sleeved tunic" (*chiridota tunica*); see E. Malcovati, *Oratorum Romanorum fragmenta liberae rei publicae*, 2d ed. (Turin, 1953), 21.17 (Aulus Gellius 6.12.4–5).

41. "Sumpsisti virilem, quam statim muliebrem togam reddidisti. Primo volgare scortum; certa flagiti merces nec ea parva; sed cito Curio intervenit qui te a meretricio quaestu abduxit et, tamquam stolam dedisset, in matrimonio stabili et certo conlocavit."

42. Supposedly, Antonius was bankrupt. This is difficult to verify, however, since Plutarch, the only other source that says Curio gave Antonius financial support, based his account on the *Second Philippic*. See E. G. Huzar, *Mark Antony: A Biography* (Minneapolis, 1978), 24 n. 19; C. B. R. Pelling, ed., *Plutarch, Life of Antony* (Cambridge, Eng., 1988), 33–36.

43. See J. Sebesta, chap. 2 in this volume.

44. Professor E. Badian suggested this solution to a question that, to my knowledge, scholars have not solved before. The prostitute's wearing of the toga appears to be similar to a ritual engaged in by the Gogo tribe of Tanzania, in which married women wear men's clothing and perform men's tasks. In this symbolic reversal of status, women take on the traits of men; see Joseph, *Uniforms*, 184. On the toga worn by adulteresses, see J. Sebesta, chap. 2 in this volume. On clothing revealing the character of its wearer, see L. Bonfante's introduction to this volume.

45. According to the Scholiast of Bobbio, Vatinius and his friends protested the *supplicationes* held in honor of C. Pomptinus, who as governor of Transalpine Gaul had repressed a revolt of the Allobroges in 61. See T. Stangl, *Ciceronis Orationum scholiastae* (Hildesheim, 1964), Schol. Bob. 149–50 at VAT. 30. See also T. R. S. Broughton, *The Magistrates of the Roman Republic,* vol. 2 (New York, 1952), 191.

46. For discussion of the Thanksgiving, or *supplicatio,* see G. Wissowa, "Supplicationes," RE, 2d ser., vol. 7 (1931), 942–51.

47. G. Herzog-Hauser, "Trauerkleidung," RE, 2d ser., vol. 12 (1937), 2225–31. Wilson, *Clothing,* 37–38.

48. Cic. *Att.* 3.15.5; Velleius Paterculus 2.45.1; Dio Cassius 38.14.4–6. See E. Gruen, *The Last Generation of the Roman Republic* (Berkeley, 1974), 245–46.

49. See DarSag 5.348 n. 42; Wilson, *Clothing,* 37.

50. Quintilian speaks of how useful it was for the defendant and his relatives to wear sordes in court: Quintilian, *Institutio oratoria* 6.1.33.

51. Mommsen, *Staatsrecht* 3:1. 140.

52. In a letter to Atticus, Cicero refers to his taking part in *vestem mutare* himself (*Att.* 3.15.5). According to Dio Cassius, Cicero "changed his clothes" from his senatorial outfit to an equestrian one (Dio Cassius 38.14.7).

53. See n. 6 above.

54. See Mommsen for a list of instances in the *Philippics: Staatsrecht* 3: 2.1247 n. 2.

55. The Romans had last practiced *saga sumere* during the Social War: Velleius Paterculus 2.16.4.

# De Habitu Vestis: Clothing in the *Aeneid*

## 8

HENRY BENDER

Recent articles have focused upon segments of the *Aeneid* in which clothing plays a key part, such as the speech of Numanus Remulus, but no study has as yet examined the role of clothing throughout the epic.[1] Such a study is of special interest in view of the many national groups which fill the landscape of the *Aeneid*. There are the peoples of Tyre, Sidon, and the Near East, northern, southern, and western Greeks, Carthaginians and Numidians, Sicilians, southern Italians, Latins, Rutulians, and, of course, Trojans. Indeed, such a gathering is envisioned in the scene engraved on Aeneas' shield, in which Augustus triumphantly surveys a mass of his conquered peoples: "In long file conquered peoples parade, as varied in their language as in their style of dress and weapons" (8.723–24).[2]

How were these peoples visually distinguished from one another in Vergil's imagination? What perspective and experience inform the poet's portrayal of figures from an unseen, remote past and of individuals closer to his time, yet still from an age which Vergil did not witness? This chapter will attempt to answer these questions but will restrict its investigation to clothing terms which seem significant to the narrative.[3]

Born near Mantua, a "northerner," Vergil has been described by some scholars as "as much Celtic as Italian or Etruscan."[4] Roman citizenship was not extended by Julius Caesar to the region where Vergil's father owned a farm until 49 B.C., when Vergil was twenty-one years old. As a Roman citizen, Vergil himself no doubt wore the short-sleeved, two-piece seamed tunic and received the toga virilis. As an inhabitant of northern Italy, he would have recognized pants (bracae) as the garb of legionaries in winter, a type of apparel shunned by the Romans as Gaulish.

Vergil's education as a young man certainly influenced his perspective on clothing. Reflections of such schooling appear in the delicate and patterned symmetry of paired speeches throughout his poem, Greek rhetorical devices which characterize this masterpiece, left unfinished, we are told, in 19 B.C., the year of the poet's death at the age of fifty-one.[5]

Homeric references and structure inform the *Aeneid*, in which the forty-eight books of Homer's *Iliad* and *Odyssey* are telescoped into twelve books. While Vergil clearly adopts the form of the Homeric epic, he does not adopt Homer's attitude: "What Vergil does is more complicated. His object is not pastiche, but the creation of an illusion—a poem which looks and sounds like Homer, though completely different in attitude and spirit."[6] While Vergilian description rests upon Homeric underpinnings, it is not intended to function solely as narrative ornamentation for a character or action. Rather, it is intended to impart a specific and meaningful nuance. Hornsby remarks that "nothing is said or done or described at any point in the *Aeneid* without having connections throughout the poem."[7]

As an epic poet, Vergil is not preoccupied with details of the personal appearance of his characters as an antiquarian, such as Suetonius, was.[8] The dearth of such detail in the poem may be due to Vergil's belief that "it is the presence of the hero, not his physical appearance that matters" or to his desire for "readers to form an image that suits their own interpretation."[9]

Yet descriptive vignettes stand out in comparison with the great parade of figures who move with controlled rhythm through the poem's narrative landscape. These pictorial surges with their specific detail and visual interest lend high verbal relief to the figures and action involved, placing in low relief those not similarly treated.

The generic word *vestis* (clothing) appears quite frequently throughout the poem, in both singular and plural forms, and most often without any modifiers. On such occasions, it is used in a very general sense, to denote the dress worn by individuals as well as by groups, in contexts where the poet does not seek to be specific about what his characters wear or how they appear. The following is a summary of contextualized references of the word *vestis*: Venus' clothing (1.404) falls to her feet as she walks, revealing her as a true goddess. Aeneas (2.722) puts on the skin of a lion over what he is already wearing as he picks up his father. Clothing (2.765) is part of the spoils collected by the victorious Greeks on the night of Troy's fall. Dido's clothing, torn at her death (4.518), is used by Anna (4.687) to absorb Dido's blood. Dido (4.648) speaks her last words after seeing Trojan clothing. In the athletic games Menoetes (5.179) has soaked his clothes in water, as has Palinurus (6.359). Iris (5.619) flings aside her garment as she becomes Beroe and joins the group of sorrowful Trojan mothers. Aeneas (5.685) takes the cloak from his shoulders as a gesture showing his spontaneous eagerness to cope with the burning ships. The Sibyl (6.406) brings the golden bough from under her clothing. The fury Allecto (7.349) hurls a snake at Amata, which winds its way through her clothing, goading the queen to heightened levels of anger. Under the leadership of Turnus, the Rutulian army advances, resplendent in gold-embroidered garments (9.26). The mother of Euryalus (9.488) mourns his loss and is saddened, since the clothing she has made for him will never be worn by him. Aeneas (10.539) kills the son of Haemon, whose attire gleams. Latinus (12.609) tears his raiment in grief over the suicide of Amata.

Of all of the instances in which *vestis* is used unmodified or undescribed, the most interesting passages for us are two: Augustus (8.723) is depicted surveying the parades of subject peoples, whose clothing is as diverse as their language, and Juno (12.825) urges that the Latins not be forced to lose their ancient name and be called Trojans, changing their language as well as their attire.

*Vestis,* however, does seem to have thematic significance when it is modified by adjectives which relate color, dimension, or condition. Such visual imagery enhances pathos, as when, for example, the garments which Dido gives Aeneas carry tragic overtones as reminders of dashed hopes when they become the funeral wrappings for the young Pallas (11.72).

MITRA, TIARA, INFULA, VITTAE

The mitra, a headdress of Near Eastern origin, was a turban fastened by ribbons tying under the chin. It was used sparingly by Vergil to portray exclusively the barbarian aspects of Greeks or Near Easterners. As an article of clothing, it carries negative connotations which are transferred to the wearer: "She [Dido] has rejected my marriage offers and has welcomed Aeneas as her lord in her realm. And now that Paris with his half-male retinue, with a Maeonian mitra tied below his chin, and with his hair oiled, has won possession of what he has seized" (4.213–17).[10] Thus Iarbas, a suitor rejected by Dido, saw the mitra as characterizing the appearance of Aeneas and his followers as effeminate. Numanus Remulus levels the same accusation at all Trojans: "And your tunics have long sleeves and your mitrae have strings. Oh truly you are Trojan women, not Trojan men!" (616–17).[11]

Through the mention of the mitra, Vergil focuses attention on one piece of wearing apparel which serves to set off the Trojans from the backdrop of Iarbas and the backdrop of their surroundings. Aeneas is silhouetted alongside the Carthaginians whose city he surveys. For the hostile Numanus Remulus, the mitra is an additional visual image by which Trojan can be distinguished from friend in the frenzy of battle. The mitra, then, becomes an effective visual link between two distant scenes in the narrative, between the Trojans, who wear the mitra as they enter the field of battle, and their leader, Aeneas, who had worn the mitra much earlier in the story in a context of peace.

The single appearance of the tiara, an Asiatic and especially Persian type of headdress, consisting of an elaborately decorated felt cone, is as a relic from Troy which is offered as part of the treasure passed to Latinus by Ilioneus. The presentation speech of Ilioneus bears close scrutiny: "Further [our king, Aeneas] gives you these small gifts of our better days, relics snatched from burning Troy. Father Anchises used to pour libation at the altars with this golden cup; this was what Priam wore when he used to give the assembled people laws— his scepter, the sacred tiara and robes, the labor of the Trojan women" (7.243–48).[12] These lines suggest that the tiara is a kind of crown, symbolizing the former ascendancy of Troy. Now, as the possession of Latinus, the future father-in-law of Aeneas, the leader-king of Troy's survivors, the tiara serves as a general acknowledgment of the passage of Troy's power to Italy, a Trojan annexation of Latinus' suzerainty, and the establishment, in particular, of Trojan power in Latium.

The infula was a woolen headband, knotted with ribbons or fillets (vittae), worn by priests, suppliants, or sacrificial animals.[13] Worn exclusively in the poem by priests of Apollo, the infula identifies the Trojan priest Panthus (2.430) as destined for death; his impending destruction, as a victim of the Greeks, is associated with the fall of the city itself. Later on, the infula (10.538) is worn by an otherwise unidentified priest of Apollo, known only as the "son of Haemon," whom Aeneas kills in his enraged grief for the loss of Pallas. The word *infula,* appearing only twice in the entire poem, acts effectively as a visual link between the fates of the two priests, to balance the murder of Panthus by the Greeks with that of Haemon's son by the Trojan Aeneas.

Vittae (fillets, ribbons, streamers) are normally worn by persons involved in a sacral act, such as the Trojan suppliants for peace (7.237) or Aeneas when he offers boughs to Evander in supplicating for an alliance (8.128). Vittae are essential to the costume of priests: King Anius, priest of Apollo on Delos, wears vittae (3.80), Helenus wears vittae when sacrificing (3.37), and animal victims, such as a bullock about to be sacrificed, wear vittae (5.366). In a dreadful parody of an animal sacrifice, Sinon, essentially a victim whom the Greeks have designated for immolation, describes being fed the traditional, sacred salted grain *(mola)* offered to animal victims and being adorned with fillets like a sacrificial animal (2.133, 156).

Both sacrificing priest and sacrificial victim wear vittae, which thus function as a dual, identifying item of costume, a duality which Vergil repeatedly exploits through irony. In the *Aeneid,* vittae are worn by persons involved wittingly or unwittingly in sacrifice: Vergil uses vittae to intimate, ironically, a sacrifice that is yet to happen. As a priest, Laocoon naturally binds his head with vittae, but then he suddenly becomes a victim, sacrificed to ensure the safe passage of the wooden horse through the gates of Troy (2.221). A son of Haemon, a priest of Apollo, also wears vittae, but then he unexpectedly becomes Aeneas' victim (10.538). Dido instructs her nurse, Barce, and her sister, Anna, to go and put vittae on their brows, as preparation for their assisting roles in a sacrifice, which she is planning as an act of atonement for abandoning her pledge of loyalty to her dead husband, Sychaeus (4.637). They return to find that Dido has substituted herself for the sacrificial victim and become victims themselves of sorrow for her suicide.

The goddess Discord wears bloodied fillets *(cruentis vittis),* symbolic of the sacrifice of human life in the impending war between the Trojans and the Rutulians (6.281). As participants in a sacral, Bacchic procession, Amata and the Latin women naturally wear vittae. But as women, they are also natural victims of the war between Aeneas and Turnus, a role Amata ironically urges them to shed with their vittae. She encourages them to run with her to fight in the battle (7.403). Just a few lines before this scene, Allecto has hurled at Amata one of the snakes which she wears in her hair; the black snake creeps to Amata's head and transforms into a ghastly vitta, portending Amata's fate as a victim of Aeneas' advent (7.352). Later Allecto, disguised as a priestess of Juno, wears a vitta as she urges Turnus to resist Aeneas in war—a resistance fated to fail, which also sacrifices Turnus to Juno's hatred of Aeneas (7.418).

Vittae also identify sacral objects, such as the altar of the dead Polydorus (3.64). But Vergil infuses vittae with his own symbolism even when they serve this function. As a sacral object, the Palladium of Troy naturally is adorned with vittae (2.168). When Odysseus and Diomedes steal the Palladium, they remove its sacral protection from Troy and jeopardize the continued existence of the city, which soon after is physically destroyed. In a dream of Aeneas, Hector, however, retrieves the sacred vittae from the shrine of the Trojan Vesta and entrusts them to Aeneas (2.296). Though Aeneas cannot carry with him the Palladium, the image of Troy's existence as a city, the dream symbolically endows him with the mission to refound the Trojan race by means of an essential part of the lost Palladium.

### TUNIC

The tunic is the standard garment worn by both sexes, either by itself or under a toga or stola. It is the simplest garment, worn by workers, hunters, and other active people. The tunic is appropriately worn by those inhabiting the future site of Rome. When Evander meets Aeneas, he puts on a tunic made of panther skin to augment the typical hunter's dress (8.457). Thus, when the king of the community atop the Palatine meets the future founder of the Roman people, he is dressed in the garment of the Roman people who will eventually take over and inhabit the hill. The tunic characterizes the simplicity and moral sternness of the Romans-to-be. That the Trojans must undergo a moral reform is indicated when Numanus Remulus rebukes them because their tunics have long sleeves—a sign of effeminacy (9.616).

The tunic, part of the national costume of the ancestors of the Romans, sometimes becomes an inappropriate garment when worn by other characters in the *Aeneid.* Its moral associations underline the impropriety of the former Cybelean priest Chloreus, when he assumes the role of a war leader while wearing a tunic woven from brightly colored fibers and embellished with embroidery, for such decoration makes the tunic a garment more suitable for a woman than a warrior (11.777). By extolling the beauty of the priest's attire, Vergil attracts the attention of the reader even as the beautiful garment attracts the warrior Camilla and ignites her desire to possess it. But to both the castrated priest and the woman warrior the garment is fatal:

Camilla kills Chloreus but is herself drawn into the line of fire and killed (11.794). In another passage, Aeneas kills the tunic-clad Theron, a Latin, and later on the tunic-clad Lausus, both of whom are resisting the Trojan ancestor of the Romans (11.314, 818). The murder of Lausus, at a moment when Aeneas' violent anger is at its high point, is accentuated by Vergil's brief *ecphrasis* on the tunic made by the loving hands of Lausus' mother, who never intended it to serve as his shroud. In these two scenes, the tunic anticipates the tragic circumstances of death, perhaps suggesting that on all people but those allied with Rome, the garment is inappropriate and brings only death.

### AMICTUS, LAENA, CHLAMYS, PALLA, TOGA

While it is clear that Vergil could not dress Aeneas in a toga, because this would have been a glaring anachronism, he could use a general term for a draped mantle which could substitute for the toga, the distinctive garment so emphasized by Augustus. The word, *amictus*, or "covering," nicely substitutes for *toga*, which is derived from the Latin verb "to cover," *tego*.

One of the least well known of garments, the amictus is mentioned ten times in the *Aeneid*. Since this mantle or draped covering lends its wearer greater importance, it is associated with individuals who have high profiles rather than commonplace roles in the poem. For example, the doctor Iapyx works upon the wounded Aeneas and is described as tying his garment back in an unusual manner *(amictu retorto)*, perhaps reminiscent of the "Gabinian draping," *cinctus Gabinus* (12.401).[14] Being clothed in an amictus links three characters who die wearing it. Aeneas dresses the body of Pallas with one of two garments made by Dido (11.77); the second of these, an amictus, is used to cover the head of Pallas, hiding the hair which is to be burned (11.77). Amata takes her life by hanging herself from a beam with her torn purple cloaks *(amictus purpureos)* (12.602). The river god Tiber also appears veiled with a gray cloak *(glauco amictu)*, for he personifies the landscape of the Rome of the future (8.33). Later, clad in a similarly gray wrapping, which visually links her to the Tiber, Juturna dives to her death *(glauco amictu)* (12.885). These three, Pallas, Amata, and Juturna, are characterized as those who are unable to live in a world with Trojans. They die wrapped in the garment which, as it was worn by Aeneas when he first landed in Italy, symbolizes the arrival and thus, metaphorically, the birth of Trojans in their world.

The amictus is imbued with sacerdotal significance in Book 3 when it is worn by Aeneas at the sacrifice-offering in newly found Italy. This moment is enhanced because it was predicted and then fulfilled: the ritual of such a cycle's completion is accented by the earliest use in the *Aeneid* of the amictus as a real garment which veils the head *(capite velato)*. Helenus had instructed Aeneas on what he must do upon his arrival on Italian shores: he is to dress in a purple cloak *(amictu purpureo)* as he sets up his altar and makes votive offerings and is reverently to cover his head (3.405). By using the word *amictus*, Vergil draws special attention to Aeneas' exact compliance with these directives later in the *Aeneid*.[15] Aeneas' stature as a hero is enhanced by his unique attire for that ritual. Through such a visual detail of costume, Vergil is freed from the need to give attention to the physical appearance of Aeneas, because he wishes his readers to form an image that has been shaped by their own interpretation. The gesture of Aeneas' covering his head with his garment *(capite velato)* during his first moments in his new homeland, Italy, may be seen as foreshadowing just such a gesture as replicated by the figures on the Ara Pacis and the figure of Aeneas himself on the right front panel.

The personified Tiber, attired like Aeneas in Book 3 when he first sacrifices in Italy, is unable to see unfavorable omens in the conflict which will take place, because he wears his amictus drawn over his head *(capite velato)* (8.33). The amictus, when worn in such a way, can be said to signal the onset of a dramatic change.

Two other characters, Entellus and Charon, are also more fully delineated by the amictus which each wears. The amictus singles out the Sicilian fighter Entellus, whose surprising victory over the Trojan fighter Dares warns of the opposition which awaits Aeneas upon his landing in Italy (5.421). Charon is set off from all others in the underworld by wearing an old man's poor garment *(sordidus amictus)*, which underscores his being a deathless god among the innumerable souls of the dead in the Underworld (6.301). The amictus worn by Aventinus further distinguishes him in the landscape of battle, when he, Hercules' son, strides into the fray with his shoulders covered by his father's cloak *(Herculeo amictu)* (7.669).

*Amictus* is also used to denote a natural or supernatural cover, such as the mist or cloud with which Venus surrounds Aeneas and Achates (1.412). This covering is metaphorically linked to the image of a cloak, an amictus made of *nebulae*, which hides the pair throughout their passage from the forest to the palace in Carthage. The word *amicti* (cloaked) again draws our attention to the condition of these two as they await Dido and her meeting with Cloanthus and the other Trojans (1.516).

The laena, a woolen cloak about twice the size of the toga, was the distinctive garment of the priests called flamines. The earliest depiction of these priests is on the Ara Pacis, where they are shown wearing the laena draped over both shoulders along with their characteristic animal-skin cap, the galerus.[16]

*Laena*, however, appears only once in the *Aeneid*, and then as a general term for a huge mantle. Dido fashions a laena for Aeneas which he is wearing as he lays the foundations of Carthage, guiding the inauguration of that city. Sent by Jupiter to command Aeneas to leave Carthage, Mercury is prompted to a sharp rebuke by the sight of the garment and Aeneas' actions: "He [Mercury] caught sight of Aeneas founding the citadel and building new houses. And his [Aeneas'] sword was studded with yellow jasper; his laena was shining with Tyrian dye and hung from his shoulders—gifts which wealthy Dido had made, and with a gold thread she had woven the web. Immediately he confronted Aeneas, saying, 'Are you now establishing the foundations of lofty Carthage?'" (4.260–66).[17]

The scene is critical to the plot of the epic: Mercury's question brings Aeneas to his senses and forces him to realize that he must get on with his fated purpose, the foundation of a new realm in Italy. At this dramatic moment Vergil portrays Aeneas clothed in a garment made for him by the Carthaginian queen; by terming this garment *laena*, which denoted to Romans a specific garment laden with religious significance, Vergil uses the garment as an effective symbol of Aeneas' disorientation. The garment isolates Aeneas uniquely and dramatizes the extent to which he has mentally departed from his mission.

The chlamys, a woolen mantle or cloak, fastened at the shoulder with a fibula, is thought to be the predecessor and rough equivalent of the paludamentum, the cloak of a general. Later, the chlamys became the garment of the emperor, and as a cloak of both a general and an emperor, it adorns the statue of Augustus from Prima Porta.

Thus the role of the chlamys in indicating leadership makes it an appropriate award for Aeneas to give to the winners of the funeral games (5.250). Furthermore, when characters in the *Aeneid* inappropriately assume the role of war leader, Vergil uses the chlamys to accentuate the leadership role associated with those who wear the garment fittingly. For example, the son of Arcens, a young, untried warrior, wears the chlamys in his first battle, and its brilliant color attracts the attention of the seasoned fighter Mezentius, who quickly dispatches him (9.582). Chloreus, originally a priest of Cybele and therefore a eunuch, inappropriately assumes the role of war leader and wears a yellow chlamys (11.777). Since in Roman society yellow was the color appropriate for a woman's wedding veil (flammeum), the garment functions as a visual symbol of his improper role as war leader.[18]

Vergil uses the chlamys to suggest ties which characters have or should have to their past life. In its first appearance in the *Aeneid* (3.484), the chlamys denotes the well-woven Phrygian cloak given to Ascanius by Andromache as a memento of her son Astyanax, who was killed by the Greeks. It is thus a reminder to her of Troy and of the life which she has lost. When Evander explains to Aeneas his willingness to become an ally because of the friendship which he had formed with Anchises, he specifically mentions the gold-embroidered chlamys given to him by Anchises when they met long ago and formed their friendship (8.621). In this context, the chlamys functions as a physical symbol of the importance to Evander of this past relationship, and it is this very garment that Pallas wears as he sets off with Aeneas to war (8.588). The bond between the two fathers is now renewed by their sons, a bond which brings Pallas death and makes Aeneas slay Turnus. Dido, preparing for the hunt with Aeneas, wears a Sidonian cloak, a chlamys, with an embroidered border, brought from her native land on her exile (4.137). It is on this hunt that she, forswearing her love and mourning for her dead husband, Sychaeus, gives in to her love for Aeneas and commits herself physically and emotionally to him. The chlamys effectively symbolizes her love and allegiance to Sychaeus that should have remained paramount to her.

For Vergil's Augustan audience, who associated the chlamys with political and military leadership, Dido's chlamys also symbolizes her leadership and independence as a queen, which she gives up for Aeneas. By having Dido wear the chlamys, Vergil strengthens the notion of *dux femina facti* ("a woman became the leader of the expedition," 1.364). Thus the chlamys signifies the leadership of the person who wears it: the aged Evander, for example, can no longer lead his people to war; his young son, Pallas, dressed in his father's chlamys, takes his place as their general (8.587–88).

The palla was a rectangular mantle worn especially as an outdoor garment by women. Vergil's use of the palla in the *Aeneid* retains its traditional use as an exclusively feminine outdoor garment. He points out that the woman warrior Camilla never wore a real palla, but only the skin of a tiger, an attire more suited to the unwomanly fierceness of her nature (11.576).

Dido's chlamys, a traditionally masculine garment, symbolizes her role as leader of her nation. Vergil ironically underscores her uniqueness in this respect when he has Aeneas present her with a palla: "Furthermore, he [Aeneas] ordered them to bring the gifts saved from the ruins of Troy, a palla stiff with gold and figures and a veil bordered in yellow acanthus, gifts of Argive Helen" (1.647–50).[19] Vergil further endows this palla of gold brocade with a specific and symbolic value, for it symbolizes the fall of the once-elegant Troy. Through the palla, Vergil provides an association between Dido and Helen. The palla, thus, may foreshadow a tragedy in love as well, since Helen also loved a foreigner, with disastrous consequences for herself and her nation. Elsewhere in the *Aeneid,* the fierce and foreboding Tisiphone wears a bloody palla (6.555). Discord is depicted on Aeneas' shield wearing a palla that is symbolically torn (8.702). On Dido and those other females who wear it, the palla is an ominous symbol suggesting doom either to its wearer or to those who, in the case of Tisiphone, must confront the rage of its wearer.

The toga, the formal garment of the Roman male citizen, is not mentioned by name in the *Aeneid.* The adjectival form of *toga,* however, is used in a famous passage which heralds the future glory of the Roman people: "the Romans, masters of the world, the toga-clad race" (1.282).[20] This comment has been interpreted as heralding the endorsement by Augustus, through Vergil, of the toga as the official dress for all Roman men.[21] The togate figures on the Ara Pacis seem to constitute a physical illustration of Augustus' desire to have a "state dress."[22]

Throughout the *Aeneid,* Vergil, unlike Homer, rarely dwells on the details of clothing and ornament. Most descriptions of what characters are wearing are routine and remain nonspecific or unmemorable. The appearance of some garments used in a special, symbolic way in the *Aeneid,* however, such as the laena and the amictus, may be intended to foreshadow the importance of these garments' descendants in Augustan Rome. There are parallels between the dress of the figures on the Ara Pacis and the costume of several important characters in the *Aeneid.* Thus, Aeneas' wearing the laena is significant, and the toga, a garment viewed by Augustus as national dress for Roman citizens, is prefigured by the amictus worn by Rome's founder, Aeneas. This is the only garment with which Vergil can visually fuse the two worlds—epic and present—which he intends to meld: it retains that symbolic, visual force wherever it appears in the narrative and makes more than superficial connections with standard religious dress of the Augustan Age as exemplified by certain figures on the Ara Pacis.

### NOTES

1. For references to earlier work on clothing, see particularly M. Griffith, "What Does Aeneas Look Like?" *CP* 90 (1985): 309–19; M. Dickie, "The Speech of Numanus Remulus (*Aeneid* 9.598–620)," *Papers of the Liverpool Latin Seminar 5* (1985): 165–221. For some interesting interpretations of this scene, see C. R. Phillips, "Italian Landscapes and Peoples in the Aeneid," Ph.D. diss., Brown University, 1974, pp. 140–42,

169. See also N. Horsfall, "Numanus Remulus: Ethnography and Propaganda in *Aeneid*, IX, 598f.," *Latomus* 117 (1971): 1108–16.

2. "Incedunt victae longo ordine gentes / quam variae linguis, habitu tam vestis et armis." This and all other translations of Vergil in this chapter are my own.

3. Excluded from this article are items of jewelry, such as the *circulus, bulla,* and *fibula,* items of military apparel, such as *cingula, apex, balteus, galerus,* and *lorica,* and priestly items, such as the *lituus.* For a basic discussion of clothing terms, see Bonfante-Warren, "Roman Costume," 585–614.

4. R. Fitzgerald, *The Aeneid* (New York, 1984), 411.

5. See G. Highet, *The Speeches in Vergil's "Aeneid"* (Princeton, 1972), particularly 1–96 and 291–343. See also G. N. Knauer, *Die Aeneis und Homer* (Göttingen, 1964).

6. K. Quinn, *Virgil's "Aeneid": A Critical Description* (London, 1968), 300.

7. R. Hornsby, *Patterns of Action in the "Aeneid"* (Iowa City, 1970), 2.

8. See Suetonius, *Augustus* 79–80.

9. Griffith, "Aeneas," 312, 319. While the height, eye color, or complexion of Aeneas may not be of central concern to Vergil, there are several places in the text where some details of a character's personal appearance or garb do receive attention. In such situations Vergil could have drawn on his own creative resources as well as the works of earlier Roman writers. His contemporary Marcus Terentius Varro (116–27 B.C.) provided definitions of words for garments in his *De lingua Latina,* while his *Imagines,* published ca. 39 B.C., may have offered portraits of famous Romans and Greeks accompanied by capsule descriptions. We have no reliable way of knowing, however, what literary sources were used in the *Aeneid.*

10. "Conubia nostra / repulit ac dominum Aenean in regna recepit. / Et nunc ille Paris cum semiviro comitatu, / Maeonia mentum mitra crinemque madentem / subnexus, rapto potitur."

11. "Et tunicae manicas et habent redimicula mitrae, / O vere Phrygiae, neque enim Phryges."

12. "Dat tibi praeterea fortunae parva prioris / munera, reliquias Troia ex ardente receptas. / Hoc pater Anchises auro libabat ad aras, / hoc Priami gestamen erat, cum iura vocatis / more daret populis, sceptrumque sacerque, tiaras / Iliadumque labor vestes."

13. For infula and vittae, see J. Sebesta, chap. 2, and L. La Follette, chap. 3, in this volume.

14. Griffith, "Aeneas," 316. On the *cinctus Gabinus,* see Bonfante-Warren, "Roman Costume," 596–97, 606–7.

15. *Aeneid* 405: "purpureo velare comas adopertus amictu." *Aeneid* 545: "et capita ante aras Phrygio velamur amictu." The second line clearly echoes the earlier; Vergil merely uses a synonym, *Phrygio,* for *purpureo.*

16. The costume of the flamines is described by Suetonius (frag. 167) as "the laena, a double-sized toga, which the flamines wear pinned when sacrificing"; "laena, toga duplex, qua infibulati flamines sacrificant." See Bonfante-Warren, "Roman Costume," 394–95, 607, 608–9. For a summary of the problems in dealing with the identity of the figures of the flamines on the Ara Pacis, see Bender, "Portraits," 1–16; Pollini, "Augustan Historical Reliefs, 88–89, 126–29. For

Gaius and Lucius on the Ara Pacis, see Pollini, *Portraiture of Gaius and Lucius Caesar.*

17. "Aenean fundantem arces ac tecta novantem / conspicit. Atque illi stellatus iaspide fulva / ensis erat, Tyrioque ardebat murice laena / demissa ex umeris, dives quae munera Dido / fecerat, et tenui telas discreverat auro. / continuo invadit: 'tu nunc Karthaginis altae / fundamenta locas . . .'"

18. Pliny the Elder, *H.N.* 21. 46: "I see the most ancient honor of yellow is given entirely to women for their wedding veils"; "lutei video honorem antiquissimum in nuptialibus flammeis totum feminis concessum." The "femininity" of Chloreus as a eunuch is paralleled in poem 63 of Catullus, which describes the self-castration of Attis, who dedicates himself to Cybele. The Latin in the lines following the description of this act uses the feminine forms of adjectives and pronouns in referring to Attis.

19. "Munera praeterea, Illiacis erepta ruinis, / ferre iubet, pallam signis auroque rigentem, / et circumtextum croceo velamen acantho, / ornatus Argivae Helenae . . ."

20. "Romanos, rerum dominos, gentemque togatam."

21. Suetonius, *Augustus* 40.5: "[Augustus] desired to bring back the dress and attire of former generations, and once, seeing a group of citizens clad in dark everyday garments in a public assembly, he became outraged and exclaimed, 'Behold the Romans, masters of the world, the toga-clad race!' He gave the aediles the task of seeing that no one hereafter would be allowed in the Forum or in its vicinity unless they took off their *lacernae* and wore their togas." This text has most recently been cited in Zanker, *Power of Images,* 163.

22. On the toga as "state dress," see Zanker, *Power of Images,* 162–65. On the togate figures on the Ara Pacis, see G. Koeppel, "Die historischen Reliefs der römischen Kaiserzeit, V: Ara Pacis Augustae," part 1, *BJ* 187 (1987): 101–57.

# The Social, Religious, and Political Aspects of Costume in Josephus

DOUGLAS R. EDWARDS

## 9

Josephus betrays the language, attitudes, and assumptions of an aristocratic Jew born in first-century Palestine.[1] Yet his works display a familiarity with Roman concerns that belie a provincial world view. Neither aspect should surprise us; Josephus served both as a client of the Flavian emperors and as an apologist for the Jewish people.[2] Josephus' literary uses of dress or costume reflect his involvement in the status-conscious, symbol-laden world of first-century Roman society and the tradition-laden Jewish world from which he came.[3] This chapter explores the role that costume plays in the works of Josephus with special emphasis on how it reflects the author's political, religious, and social propaganda.[4]

Josephus' world underwent a remarkable if not a traumatic transition.[5] His works disclose a man seeking to come to grips with Roman power by using the language, symbols, and myths available in his world. His effort is not unique. Simon Price, for one, has shown this tendency among urban residents of Asia Minor in their various implementations of the imperial cult.[6] Josephus, like many aristocrats in the provinces under the control of Rome in the first century, sought to integrate Roman imperial power into his own traditions and systems of belief. Josephus' use of dress and ornamentation to create a vivid literary portrait for his audience reveals an important aspect of this integration of Jewish and Roman views and values.

## THE SIGNIFICANCE OF WOMEN'S DRESS

Josephus' account of the story of Paulina offers a clear instance of his implicit understanding of dress in Roman culture and society (*AJ* 18.65–80). Paulina, a Roman matron of good lineage and impeccable social credentials, exhibits the appropriate characteristics of a matron in first-century Roman society, especially during the Flavian period: she is virtuous, wealthy, and attractive, and she lives a life devoted to good conduct.[7] In Josephus' account, Decius Mundus, a knight, becomes infatuated with Paulina and attempts to bribe and seduce her, all to no avail.[8] He does succeed, through a servant, in bribing the priests of Isis in Rome to allow him to sleep with Paulina, a devotee of Isis, under the guise of the god Anubis. After the deed, Mundus informs Paulina of his chicanery. Paulina, upon finding that she has lost her chastity, dramatically rips her stola, indicating her loss of status, and demands that her husband go to the emperor Tiberius and seek immediate lawful redress, which he does.

Josephus recognized that the stola of Roman matrons in imperial Rome symbolized both a woman's married status and her moral character.[9] His depiction of Paulina dramatically ripping her stola is designed to shock and anger his readership. Yet more is at stake here than the loss of one woman's honor, for the scene offered Josephus a chance to denigrate a popular cult that was competing with the Jewish religion, the worship of Isis.[10] With legal and moral justification, Josephus implies, Tiberius redresses the wrong by crucifying the priests of Isis, razing their temple, and having the statue of Isis thrown in the river.

Foreign cults such as that of Isis, Josephus indicates, are fraudulent and governed by corrupt officials. The tearing of the stola, the harsh punishment meted out to Mundus, the crucifixion of the priests, and the destruction of the cult indicate the political, social, and religious ramifications of the rape of Paulina. The deceit of Mundus and, even more dastardly, the complicity of the Isiac priests shook the fabric of Roman society. Here

Josephus taps a reservoir of fundamental attitudes and assumptions in Roman society. As Hallett argues, "the elite Roman family did not merely possess political influence and social significance. It also ranked as a major and stable social, economic, and political institution."[11] Josephus uses dress to emphasize how a foreign religion, the Isiac cult, threatens the broad and deep social networks that bind Roman family and Roman society.

Josephus also uses the stola in his adaptation of biblical tradition. Josephus recounts the story of the Israelite king Jeroboam, whose son was on the verge of death (*AJ* 8.266–73). Josephus' account parallels in large measure the Masoretic and Greek versions of 1 Kings 14:1–18. For our purposes, however, his addition of one detail is of particular interest. Josephus adds that Jeroboam ordered his wife to remove her stola, to dress as a commoner, and to appear before the prophet Achias in order to find out what was to happen to their son. As in the case of the Roman matron, Josephus implies that the removal of the stola reflects Jeroboam's wife's removal of the garments of wealth, status, and royalty; here, however, the woman assumes the role of a petitioner. Josephus' anachronistic addition of this detail would have appealed to a status-conscious audience who recognized the relation of the stola to the social and political status of the Roman matron. Further, the removal of the stola heightens the disguise of Jeroboam's wife, which in turn makes more dramatic the prophet Achias' recognition of her when she appears before him.

Josephus' version of the rape of Tamar, daughter of King David, by her half brother reveals again how Josephus alters his source to appeal to his audience (*AJ* 7.162ff.). Tamar's beauty, Josephus adds to the biblical text, surpassed that of all the fairest women. The motif of the most beautiful virgin was common in the Flavian and Antonine periods.[12] After telling of the rape, the biblical text offers in an aside that virgin daughters of kings wore a long robe with sleeves (2 Samuel 13:18) and that Tamar ripped her long robe in mourning (2 Samuel 13:19). Josephus' account, although it largely parallels the Masoretic and Greek texts, contains subtle alterations. Josephus heightens the modesty of Tamar and the age in which she lived. He adds that all virgins (not just daughters of the kings) wore long-sleeved tunics (chitons) reaching to the ankle "in order not to be exposed" (*AJ* 7.171).[13] Josephus' addition of the final clause appeals to readers in the Flavian era, in which the modesty of women and lawful respect for their status are paramount. Josephus' aside indicates that he addresses an audience that probably assumes that long sleeves depict the normal attire for slaves in the first century. Long sleeves to the wrist generally signified slaves or barbarians. The normal attire of virgins, long-sleeved

robes extending to the ankles, sharply contrasts with the attire Tamar rips, a *chitoniskos,* or short, small tunic. This heightens the shame of Tamar, as she goes through the streets practically naked.[14] As in Josephus' account of Paulina, the ripping of the garment symbolizes not simply the loss of status and purity but also, and more important, the tearing of the fabric of society itself. Indeed, even in Josephus' biblical source, Absalom, another of David's sons and the brother of the defamed Tamar, subsequently kills his brother Amnon, the rapist, continuing the disintegration of the Davidic line and the social fabric of Israel. Here Jewish tradition and Graeco-Roman expectations in the Flavian period coalesce.

Josephus depicts one form of social control for women in first-century Palestinian society when he discusses the measures taken by a man who suspects his wife of adultery (*AJ* 3.270–73). Much of the procedure described draws on Mosaic law in Numbers 5:12–28. Josephus' addition is set amid a number of laws and regulations that he claims are derived from Moses (*AJ* 3.222–23). Thus, he stresses for his audience the antiquity of the Jewish law and the Jews' strong ethical and lawful activity. Josephus' version is illuminating both for what it may tell us about the circumstances of women in first-century Palestine and for what it does tell us about the writer's special concerns.[15]

Josephus adds to the account that the woman whose virtue is being tested must face the Temple. The priest removes her veil (the himation), presumably pulled over the head, inscribes the name of God on a skin, and bids her to declare that she has done her husband no wrong. What does the removal of the veil from the head connote in the Roman world of Josephus? Ramsay MacMullen cites a number of examples that show the importance of veils in both the Roman and Eastern provinces. He notes that Valerius Maximus (6.3.10), writing during the reign of Tiberius, describes a situation in Rome in the second century B.C. in which a woman was divorced by her husband for appearing in public unveiled. MacMullen suggests, however, that in the East women belonging to wealthy families were likely to remain unveiled when they appeared in public. Only women of the humbler class went veiled. MacMullen notes that no pictorial evidence exists that supports the idea that wealthy women wore the veil.[16]

Two sets of evidence, however, suggest that the veil covering the head continued to play a role in Palestine even among wealthy women. In the *Judaea Capta* coin series, displayed so prominently as part of the Flavian propaganda campaign, one often sees a veiled woman seated in a state of mourning, perhaps based on a prototype that goes back to C. Sosius in 37 B.C.[17] The veiled woman probably represents Judaea, as female figures often symbolize nations.[18] At least this suggests that in the first century B.C. the veil was associated with the Jewish woman in a state of mourning. Josephus' remark regarding the test for adultery also suggests that the veiling of married women continued at least up to (and perhaps through) the Flavian period.

Another literary parallel may exist in the Book of Susanna, a Greek addition to the Book of Daniel written in the second or first century B.C. Susanna, a woman of refinement and beautiful appearance, is accused by two elders of committing adultery. They demand that she be uncovered (the Revised Standard Version translates this as "unveiled"). Their secret reason, the text states, is to view her beauty, but one assumes that the legal reason is to make her vulnerable for judgment. The elders lay their hands on her head, after removing her veil, and accuse her of adultery (Susanna 31–34). At a later point in the narrative, the term *head* again shows up, this time when Daniel condemns both elders, saying, "You have lied against your own head" (Susanna 55). In both Susanna and Josephus, the head seems associated with judgment.[19] Literary and numismatic evidence suggests that the veil as head covering did exist, that it had symbolic significance, and that it was associated with issues of law, morality, social responsibility, and mourning.

Josephus' portrayal of the clothing of women reflects issues of purity, social status or its loss, and the continuance of the social fabric of society. In that sense, Josephus' portrait of Jewish women would bolster the impression that proper Jews are just as concerned with appropriate decorum, issues of purity, and the law as any other group in the empire.

ROYALTY AND DRESS:
PRESTIGE AND DESTRUCTION

Josephus uses costume to highlight the wealth, prestige, and power of the Jewish nation in antiquity. In the expansion and adaptation of the biblical account of Solomon's court (1 Kings 10.23f.; 2 Chronicles 9.22f.), he fashions a portrait that elicits the image of a wealthy potentate (*AJ* 8.182–86). In both the biblical and Josephean accounts Solomon's wisdom and virtue are extolled, and the nations send extravagant gifts as a result. Josephus, however, embellishes the biblical account and adds that Solomon's escort included tall young men who dressed in tunics of Tyrian purple and whose long hair was sprinkled with gold dust.[20] The addition heightens the power and prestige of Solomon as well as the glorious past of the Jewish nation. The description fits the glorification of one's past that was common in the provinces during this period, especially among Greek-speaking people.[21] Solomon, Josephus suggests, was a rich and powerful king whose wealth and prestige

rival and perhaps outdo those of any king in the known world, past or present.

Josephus also uses dress to depict the power and prestige of the Flavians and, to a lesser extent, the wealth of the Jewish nation. The Roman triumph of Titus and Vespasian following their defeat of the Jewish nation is portrayed as so magnificent (and by implication the Flavians are so powerful) that even the attendants of the animals wear expensive garments of true purple (*BJ* 7.136f.).

Josephus' portrayal intends to show that the Jewish war was no minor skirmish, but a major military battle between two powerful opponents. This coincides with Josephus' obvious exaggeration of the battles he fought against the Flavians.[22] The portrait Josephus paints serves two purposes. First, it addresses the Flavian propaganda campaign that exploited the Jewish war to great advantage. The *Judaea Capta* series so evident in coins and on breastplates and statuary reveals the importance of the Jewish war for the Flavians.[23] The triumph in the war and its promotion legitimated as well as concretized the Flavian claim to the imperial throne, a necessary move for anyone attempting to supercede the Julio-Claudian line. Josephus' portrait acknowledges this power but subsumes it under the power of the Jewish God. Second, Josephus' description has the added effect of picturing a wealthy, prosperous region tragically destroyed by lawless brigands and those who circumvent the will of God.

One episode in the *Bellum Judaicum* especially illustrates how Josephus uses clothing as a literary device to bolster the power and prestige of the Flavian victory and to depict the tragic destruction of a powerful, prosperous region: the account of Simon ben Gioras (*BJ* 7:26–36). Too often this episode has been accepted as historical reportage. It seems more appropriate to evaluate how Josephus interprets the event within the framework of his narrative rather than to take it as a strictly historical account.

Josephus shows Simon taking his friends, stonecutters, and provisions into secret passages under the Temple complex as the Romans enter Jerusalem, in an attempt to dig out through old collapsed tunnels. When they fail, Simon seeks to outwit (*apatesai*) the Romans by dressing in a white chiton with a purple mantle (*porphura clanis*) over it. His garb, probably a purple cloak with a clasp at the shoulder, sounds very much like a paludamentum, the garb of a Roman general or officer. The onlookers at first draw back, but then they approach him and ask who he is. Simon orders them to send for the general, who puts him in chains and sends him to Rome to participate in the Roman triumph (*BJ* 7.26–36).

Simon is portrayed more favorably by Josephus than are other rebels. He had superior physical attributes and courage (*BJ* 4.503–4) and significant military prowess

(4.529ff.).[24] Josephus avoids using Jewish messianic language to describe his exploits, but the use of kingship imagery is quite common.[25] Throughout his account Josephus stresses Simon's aristocratic lineage and skill as a military general in order to portray him as a worthy opponent of the Romans. Simon's valor heightens both the Flavian conquest and the magnificence of the triumph.[26] Indeed, Simon's dress at the Temple, which depicts him as a general, does not emphasize Simon's martyrdom but rather his appearance as a powerful kingly and military opponent, worthy to be exhibited in the Roman triumph.[27]

PRIESTLY DRESS

For Josephus, the priestly vestment more than any other item of dress symbolized the height of the Jewish nation's power and prestige, as well as the depth of its downfall. The high priest wore sardonyxes on his shoulders, which, Josephus states, in the past had flashed when God assisted in ceremonies. In addition, the twelve stones worn by the high priest on his breast and stitched to his *essen* foretold who would be victorious in battle. The flash of light that had once emanated from the *ephod* or breastplate, however, had stopped two hundred years before, because God was displeased with the transgression of the law (*AJ* 3.215–17). Again the power of the nation and its religion are understood within the context of the nation's apostasy from the law, symbolized in the high priest's garb. In *Antiquitates Judaicae* Josephus emphasizes the fact that the defeat of Israel was not due so much to the power of Rome but rather to the apostasy of the nation.

Josephus' emphasis on the priestly garments and the abrogation of ancestral law finds antecedents in the biblical accounts. On one occasion, Josephus illustrates this in his adaption of 2 Chronicles 26:16–23, the account of Uzziah, the Israelite king. Josephus' version parallels the biblical text in depicting Uzziah as corrupt and as putting on the priestly stola in order to offer sacrifices to God. The high priest and eighty priests try in vain to stop him. Josephus' dramatic rendition, however, adds the story that when Uzziah spoke, an earthquake occurred, and a brilliant shaft of light came through and fell on his face, giving him leprosy. The shaft of light with its resultant disease displays the inappropriateness of Uzziah's assuming divine attributes. The issue does not seem to be Uzziah's attempt to achieve divine status.[28] Rather the account would have impressed Josephus' audience with the power of the Jewish God as well as the ultimate result of apostasy. The apostasy in this case is the presumption of Uzziah to wear the garment of the high priest. Clothing symbolizes the arrogance of Uzziah, his return to civilian status, and his humbling at the behest of God. Indeed, Josephus insists that priests with imperfections should be clad in ordinary clothing during certain festivals (*BJ* 5.228).

Political Significance

The high priest's garments were intimately connected with the political and social fabric of Palestinian society. An instance of such connections occurs, according to Josephus, when Herod the Great kills Jonathan, a youth with the royal Hasmonean bloodlines, because he wears the high priest's garb before a crowd: "Herod had bestowed upon him in his seventeenth year the office of high-priest, and then immediately after conferring this honour had put him to death, because, on the occasion of a festival, when the lad approached the altar, clad in the priestly vestments, the multitude with one accord burst into tears" (*BJ* 1.437). The connection of a descendant from the Hasmonean monarchy with the high priest's garb combined with the enthusiastic reaction of the Jewish population created political repercussions that Herod could not ignore.

Nor could the Romans ignore the political overtones of the high priest's garb. Josephus indicates that a conflict over control of the garments took place intermittently between the Roman administration of Judaea and the priests. In *Antiquitates Judaicae* 15.403–6 Josephus details elaborate procedures used by the high priests to secure the vestments' use from the Romans for festival and holy days. The Romans were concerned about the symbolic import of the garments. The account culminates when Vitellius, the Roman governor, returns control of the stolas to the priests (cf. *AJ* 18.90–95). Later, however, Fadas, procurator of Judaea, orders the high priest's garments returned to Roman custody; this had occurred when Archelaus, the son of Herod the Great, had been replaced by Roman procurators. The response was a Jewish petition to Claudius, who feared "that Fadas' commands would force the Jewish People into rebellion" (*AJ* 20.7). At the intercession of Herod Agrippa II, Claudius relents. Josephus' portrayal of Claudius' rationale emphasizes a key theme in Josephus' work, the Romans' insistence on the maintenance of Jewish religion. Claudius states, "I have given my consent of this measure, . . . because I cherish religion myself and wish to see every nation maintain the religious practices that are traditional with it" (*AJ* 20.13).

The political significance of the high priest's garments is not lost on some of the Jewish rebels either, according to Josephus. The Zealots, for example, set up their own high priest when they take over the Temple area. The unsympathetic Josephus compares the ploy to a farce or a play on a stage. Indeed, the act simply confirms for him the fact that the rebel leaders had become tyrants (*BJ* 4.155–57).[29] The symbolic significance of the garments extends well beyond the religious realm and into the political.

## Cosmic Significance

Josephus leaves no doubt about the cosmic significance of the high priest's garments (*AJ* 3.181ff.). The breast-plate symbolizes the earth (3.185), the sardonyxes on the shoulder represent the sun and the moon (3.185), the twelve stones symbolize the twelve months or the twelve signs of the zodiac (3.186), the vestments of linen symbolize the earth, the blue coloring represents the sky, the pomegranate ornaments are lightning, the bells equal thunder, and the headdress itself symbolizes heaven. In short, the high priest's garb represents the meeting place of heaven and earth. Indeed, although Josephus mentions the symbolism of the twelve tribes of Israel, a political entity (*AJ* 3.165–66), in connection with the garments he prefers to emphasize the cosmic significance of the number twelve.[30] Jewish worship fits into the universal order. Cosmic symbolism reinforces Josephus' point that Judaism follows the universal law codes.[31] His reasons are clear.

> But one may well be astonished at the hatred which men have for us and which they have so persistently maintained, from an idea that we slight the divinity whom they themselves profess to venerate. For if one reflects on the construction of the tabernacle and looks at the vestments of the priest and the vessels which we use for the sacred ministry, he will discover that our lawgiver was a man of God and that these blasphemous charges brought against us by the rest of men are idle. In fact, every one of these objects is intended to recall and represent the universe. (*AJ* 3.179–80)

Josephus also uses the high priest's apparel to contrast starkly the disastrous results of the Jewish revolt with the prior situation. Ananus, a former high priest of the highest integrity, was a lover of "liberty and an enthusiast for democracy" who "on all occasions put the public welfare above his private interests" (*BJ* 4.319–20). He had formerly worn "the sacred vestments, led those ceremonies of world-wide significance and had been reverenced by visitors to the city from every quarter of the earth" (*BJ* 4.324). Now, Josephus says, the naked bodies of Ananus and his colleague Jesus lie thrown by the rebels into the streets of Jerusalem to be eaten by dogs (*BJ* 4.325). The nakedness of the priest makes a striking contrast with the magnificence of the priestly garments he formerly wore.[32] Those in the Jewish nation who had perpetrated the revolt had gone totally mad. Such pollutions caused God to condemn "the city to destruction" and "to purge the sanctuary by fire" (*BJ* 4.323).

### MEN DISGUISED AS WOMEN

Josephus reserves some of his strongest invective for men who dress as women. In particular, he is hostile to those who take on that guise during a battle. In *Antiquitates Judaicae* 4.301, Josephus veers from his biblical source by adding that "above all in battle" men and women should not wear the opposite sex's garb. The following example epitomizes this attitude. In *Bellum Judaicum* Josephus portrays John of Gischala and the Galileans as dressing as women, "plaiting their hair and attiring themselves in women's apparel, drenching themselves with perfumes and painting their eyelids to enhance their beauty. . . . Yet, while they wore women's faces, their hands were murderous, and approaching with mincing steps they would suddenly from under their dyed mantles transfix whomsoever they met" (4.562–64).

This portrayal, of course, serves to bolster Josephus' own position. He, the staid and conservative military leader, contrasts sharply with the likes of John and his Galilean brigands, whom he portrays as a band of effeminate sneaks (*BJ* 4.561). The unflattering portrait would certainly appeal to a Roman audience not sympathetic with effeminate practices. Josephus uses this motif to highlight the rightful end of those who attempt to circumvent the laws of nature, countries, and/or God. All meet a dire end and receive their just reward.[33]

### CLOTHING THE LEVITES
### AND DESTROYING THE NATION

Clothing symbolizes the nation's demise in yet another way according to Josephus. When the Levites, one of the religious orders in the Temple of Jerusalem, lobby for a new style of dress, the linen stola worn by the priests, they abrogate tradition and the religious conformity so necessary for proper order in Jewish society. Herod Agrippa II's granting of the Levite request, according to this view, was a major cause for the defeat of the Jews and the destruction of the nation. "All this was contrary to the ancestral laws, and such transgression was bound to make us liable to punishment" (*AJ* 20.218).[34]

Josephus' use of dress supports his attempt to construct a system to explain Roman power in light of his ideological, social, and political agenda. In his *Bellum Judaicum* he seeks to convince his reading public that the Flavians represent legitimate power and authority in the Roman Empire (a point the Flavians promoted as well). He promotes the view that the Jewish nation is a viable and ancient political institution. Finally, he argues that the Jewish religion is a venerable and legitimate expression of the people of Israel. Costume plays a small but important role in his effort to clarify his position and the position of Jews within a new power situation. The use of clothing reflects the social and cultural mores of Josephus and his society in the first century. Josephus struggles with a world in which Roman power and

Jewish identity must be reinterpreted. No Temple cult existed, Jewish leadership was in disarray, and a new Roman regime was establishing itself in a world fraught with ambiguity and competing claims. Josephus' use of the imagery of clothing highlights one man's attempt to reconcile Jewish identity within that new order.

## NOTES

Translations of Josephus in this chapter are taken from the Loeb Classical Library edition of Josephus' *The Jewish War* (*Bellum Judaicum*, abbreviated *BJ*) and *Jewish Antiquities* (*Antiquitates Judaicae*, abbreviated *AJ*).

1. All dates are A.D. unless otherwise noted. For an extensive bibliography on Josephus, see L. Feldman, *Josephus and Modern Scholarship, 1937–1980* (Berlin, 1984); and idem, *Josephus: A Supplementary Bibliography* (Berlin, 1986).

2. T. Rajak, *Josephus: The Historian and His Society* (Philadelphia, 1984), 185–222.

3. For the importance of costume and status in ancient Rome, see Bonfante-Warren, "Roman Costume," esp. 586f., and L. Bonfante's introduction to this volume; M. T. Griffin, *Nero: The End of a Dynasty* (New Haven, 1985), 222f.

4. Although I discuss at several points the historical veracity of Josephus' descriptions of dress, that is not the main focus of this chapter; rather, my concern is with the reasons for his portrayal of the events in which he includes these descriptions.

5. T. Rajak, "Josephus and the *Archaeology of the Jews*," *Journal of Jewish Studies* 33 (1982): 477.

6. S. Price, *Rituals and Power: The Roman Imperial Cult in Asia Minor* (Cambridge, Eng., 1984). For the military response as well as the cultural resistance to the Romans, see F. Millar, "Empire, Community and Culture in the Roman Near East: Greeks, Syrians, Jews and Arabs," *Journal of Jewish Studies* 28 (1987):143–64.

7. Joseph. *AJ* 18.66. Even though the scene is set during the reign of Tiberius, Josephus' audience was that of the Flavian period. Certainly texts from the republic through late antiquity reflect these virtues in women. Nevertheless, writers during the Flavian and Antonine periods seem to stress "a general return to a love of respectablity"; A. Richlin, "Approaches to the Sources on Adultery at Rome," in *Reflections of Women in Antiquity*, ed. H. P. Foley (New York, 1981), 380. It seems best to imagine how Flavian audiences would "read" this passage.

8. Seduction of a beautiful but chaste woman is a leitmotiv in Greek, Jewish, and Roman literature; see J. P. Hallett, *Fathers and Daughters in Roman Society: Women and the Elite Family* (Princeton, 1984), 110ff.; and T. Hägg, *The Novel in Antiquity* (Berkeley, 1983).

9. See J. P. V. D. Balsdon, *Roman Women: Their History and Habits* (New York, 1962), 252; B. Holtheide, "Matrona Stolata—Femina Stolata," *ZPE* 38 (1980): 127–34; Richlin, "Approaches," 384, 404 n. 42. See also J. Sebesta, chap. 2 in this volume.

10. For the popularity of this cult in the Roman empire, including the Flavian period, see R. E. Witt, *Isis in the Graeco-Roman World* (Ithaca, N.Y., 1971), 222–34.

11. Hallett, *Fathers and Daughters*, 28.

12. The ancient novels offer many examples; see Hägg, *Novel in Antiquity*. For Josephus' portrayal of married and unmarried women and its relation to his age, see J. L. Bailey, "Josephus' Portrayal of the Matriarchs," in *Josephus, Judaism, and Christianity*, ed. L. Feldman and G. Hata (Detroit, 1987), 154–79.

13. Feldman notes that Josephus reflects two textual traditions, one which mentions long sleeves, the other a garment "reaching to the ankle" (*AJ* 7.171, 452–53). Neither tradition has "in order not to be exposed."

14. See M. M. Evans, "Chapters on Greek Dress," in *Ancient Greek Dress*, ed. M. Johnson (Chicago, 1965), 56; Bonfante-Warren, "Roman Costume," 614. On Jewish dress see D. Edwards, "Dress and Ornamentation," in the *Anchor Bible Dictionary*, ed. D. N. Freedman (New York, 1992), 2:232–38.

15. It is notoriously difficult to determine the actual dress of inhabitants of first-century Palestine, in large part because of the prohibition against images. Some clues may be provided from such things as the *Judaea Capta* coin series, which often portrays a veiled Jewish female captive. In addition, Y. Yadin has found a number of early second-century garments of Jews participating in the Bar Kokhba revolt against Rome *(Finds from the Bar Kokhba Period)*. Nikos Kokkinos draws on coin evidence to reconstruct a portrait of Salome, daughter of Herodias; "Which Salome Did Aristobulus Marry?" *Palestine Exploration Quarterly* (Jan.–June 1986): 33–48.

16. MacMullen, "Women in Public," 208. MacMullen lists literary examples that depict women as veiled. Tertullian, MacMullen notes, states that veiling referred to the head only, except in Arabia, where it covered the face as well (208–9 n. 4.; cf. 218). On Roman veiling, see also L. La Follette, chap. 3, and J. Sebesta, chap. 2, in this volume.

17. The veil normally only covers the head. For bibliography and examples of *Judaea Capta* iconography on coins and cuirass statues, see C. Vermeule, "Jewish Relations with the Art of Ancient Greece and Rome: Judaea Capta Sed Non Devicta," *Art of Antiquity*, vol. 4.2 (Boston, 1981). Stone, "Imperial Sculptural Group," 378–91 and esp. 389–90 nn. 68–75. Stone notes that the hooded woman in such iconography of this period seems uniquely Jewish; late Byzantine manuscripts, for example, depict Jews wearing hooded garments. Even earlier evidence exists. A bronze coin of Sosius apparently served as a prototype for Vespasian's *Judaea Capta* series. In 37 B.C., C. Sosius, who was Mark Antony's lieutenant, conquered Jerusalem. His coin commemorating that even displays a bound Jewish prisoner and a veiled or hooded Jewish female captive. See T. Reinach, *Jewish Coins* (London, 1903), 30, 99 n. 3; pl. 3.5. For the *Judaea Capta* coin series, see *British Museum Catalogue of Coins of the Roman Empire* 3, 493–94, pl. 92.1, 3, 6, 8, 9. For a study of head coverings for women in Corinth, see C. L. Thompson, "Hairstyles, Head-Coverings, and St. Paul: Portraits from Roman Corinth," *Biblical Archaeologist* 51 (1988): 99–115. On the *Judaea Capta* motif on cuirassed statues, see R. Gergel, chap. 12 in this volume.

18. See the nations portrayed at Aphrodisias in K. Erim, *Aphrodisias: City of Venus Aphrodite* (London, 1986).

19. I would like to thank Larissa Bonfante for sharing a note

from E. Badian that pointed out the Susanna text. They, of course, are not responsible for my interpretation.

20. Cf. Gallienus, who had gold dust sprinkled in his hair; SHA *Duo Gallieni* 16.4.

21. See D. Edwards, "Acts of the Apostles and Chariton's *Chaereas and Callirhoe*," Ph.D. diss., Boston University, 1987, chap. 2 for bibliography.

22. The *Bellum Judaicum* is replete with examples of Josephus' self-described genius as a military strategist: *BJ* 3.171f., 234f., 258f.

23. For additional references on the triumph, see B. W. Jones, *The Emperor Titus* (New York, 1984), 100–101 n. 5; D. Edwards, "Religion, Power, and Politics: Jewish Defeats by the Romans in Iconography and Josephus," in *Diaspora Jews and Judaism*, ed. J. Overman and R. MacLennen, University of South Florida Series in Ancient Judaism, 1992, 293–310. See also R. Gergel, chap. 12 in this volume.

24. Cf. *BJ* 2.444: Menahem, a rebel who arrays himself in royal robes, is viewed as a tyrant and killed by a mob.

25. R. A. Horsley and J. S. Hanson, *Bandits, Prophets, and Messiahs: Popular Movements in the Time of Jesus* (Minneapolis, 1985), 119; Rajak, *Josephus: The Historian and His Society*, 141.

26. M. Goodman, *The Ruling Class of Judaea: The Origins of the Jewish Revolt against Rome, A.D. 66–70* (Cambridge, Eng., 1987), 202–7.

27. Those who focus on the question of the martyrdom or on the messianic issue stress the question of the historical accuracy of the account and Simon's own agenda, rather than the redactional issue that is Josephus' reason for reporting or telling the story in the way that he does. It is the latter that interests us. Also compare Josephus' attitude toward Simon as kingly (*BJ* 4.557), toward the official governor of Acrabatene (Goodman, *Ruling Class,* 163), and toward a tyrant (*BJ* 1.10, 11, 24, 27, 28; 2.564; 4.508).

28. Contra J. Morgenstern, "The King God among the Western Semites and the Meaning of Epiphanes," *Vetus Testamentum* 10 (1960): 138–97.

29. For Josephus' portrayal of the rebel leaders as tyrants, see D. J. Ladouceur, "Josephus and Masada," in *Josephus, Judaism, and Christianity*, ed. Feldman and Hata, 95–113.

30. Cf. *BJ* 5.5.7f. "The conception that the whole cosmos is the robe of God is Platonic and Stoic; the whole train of thought is alien to Judaism, but it is introduced to show that Judaism is aware of the truth that God is immanent in the whole of creation" (Feldman, *Bibliography,* 417). Cf. J. P. Brown, "The Sacrificial Cult and Its Critique in Greek and Hebrew, II," *Journal of Semitic Studies* 25 (1980): 1–21.

31. C. R. Holladay, *Theios Aner in Hellenistic Judaism: A Critique of the Use of This Category in New Testament Christology* (Missoula, Mont., 1977), 86f. On the religious significance of costume, see L. Bonfante's introduction to this volume.

32. On the symbolism of nakedness in the Old Testament, see Bonfante, "Nudity as a Costume," 546, and nn. 17 and 20.

33. Cf. also Josephus' negative portrayals of Gaius Caligula, who put on women's stolas (*AJ* 19.30), and his account of Ammonius, who, having committed reckless crimes, was "cut down shamefully as a woman, for he had made an effort to conceal himself in a woman's dress [*stola*]" (*AJ* 13.108).

34. Cf. *AJ* 4.208, which quotes the admonition that none were to wear raiment of wool and linen except the priests.

# PART III
# ROMAN COSTUME AND
# GEOGRAPHIC QUESTIONS

# Graeco-Roman Dress in Syro-Mesopotamia

## 10

BERNARD GOLDMAN

After the collapse of the Hellenistic kingdoms, a central Asian people of Iranian stock became the dominant power in Western Asia, ruling from the first century B.C. to the beginning of the second quarter of the third century A.D. These Iranian Parthians (of the old Persian Empire satrapy of Parthava) under the Arsacid dynasty integrated into their society from their Macedonian Seleucid predecessors various cultural traits, not the least of which was Greek costuming. Then came the Romans, the next major Western intruders from the Mediterranean appropriately habited in their Western fashions. How were they accepted? Here I attempt an estimate, based on the monumental remains, of the reaction of the Syro-Mesopotamian communities to the costuming brought by this wave of interlopers from overseas.

Asia was well familiar with Mediterranean gods and goods long before the Roman merchants and commercial travelers stepped onto Syrian and Phoenician docks with their Romanized version of the gods of the old Greek pantheon clothed in adaptations of Greek dress. As Rome's interests in the East expanded, the entrepreneurs were followed by the cumbersome panoply of high-level functionaries, civil servants, and soldiery endemic to the realization, expansion, and protection of empire. They brought to Syro-Mesopotamia Roman gold and Roman law, as well as architects and, inevitably, the Roman sword. But here I confine myself to a modest aspect of the Roman intrusion, that of the reception given Roman dress in an area where Hellenism had left an indelible mark, where Parthian influence was strong, and where Iranian costume was fashionable.[1]

The extent and depth of Roman influence in Western Asia from the first century B.C. through the fourth century A.D. have been the subjects, of course, of close monitoring and are commonly argued. The British historian Fergus Millar concluded that Roman westernization of the region was mainly the creation of a political framework, that "Rome contributed only indirectly to the social and cultural history of the area." What the monuments show us of the fashion-conscious women and their well-to-do spouses in the more cosmopolitan centers of Syro-Mesopotamia seems to support Millar's generalization. Certainly the remains indicate an official enthusiasm for Roman imports, albeit adapted to fit Asian taste, which, it must be remembered, was preconditioned by things Greek during the resident reign of the Seleucid court.[2]

As one would expect, the closer an Asian city was to the Mediterranean coast, and the nearer its location to a major commercial highway, the more apparent were its Graeco-Roman features. Antioch, located inland some eighteen miles from the sea, was settled by Greeks and Macedonians and became the capital of Roman Syria, a magnet drawing tourists and summer residents from the Mediterranean West. Geographically a part of Syria, Antioch fell into the orbit of the Graeco-Roman world. To a lesser extent, Baalbek-Heliopolis, in the valley between the Lebanon and Anti-Lebanon ranges, was dominated first by the Macedonians and then by the Romans, as evidenced, for example, in the lavish building programs they undertook. But further inland the proportions of the East-West mix shift as we enter an Arab-Semitic cultural landscape with Parthian Iran looming on the horizon. In this area, three cities with markedly different backgrounds, each one further removed than the next from Rome and each more distant than the next from the well-traveled roads leading to the sea, illustrate some of the varying uses of Graeco-Roman dress in Syro-Mesopotamia during the Roman era.

Although not typical of Syro-Mesopotamian cities, Palmyra (ancient Tadmor), the wealthy commercial Arab center located in the heart of the Syrian desert, deserves first consideration because it best illustrates the manner in which Graeco-Roman fashion was incorporated into the Roman East. Roman presence is evident in Palmyra probably as early as the first decade of the first century A.D., but the city retained a jealously guarded measure of political independence from both the Roman West and the Iranian East until finally put to the sword by Aurelian's troops in A.D. 272/273. The second center, Dura-Europos, lies east of Palmyra, perched on the lip of the desert shelf overlooking the Euphrates. This fortified town, founded by a Macedonian general, later fell to the Parthians and in the second century came under a Roman governor. In the middle of the third century, its Roman garrison unsuccessfully defended the city walls against a Persian Sasanian siege, and the town was given back to the desert sands. Still further removed, northeast across the Euphrates in Upper Mesopotamia, stood Hatra, the last of our three cities. Hatra was an independent Semitic metropolis, and its streets did not echo to the tramp of Roman boots until the time of Severus Alexander. It fell, like Dura-Europos, however, to the Sasanians about a dozen years later.

The basic Iranian dress of Parthian men is easily distinguished from Graeco-Roman styling. The Iranian costume is based on tailoring: weaving and cutting material to patterns and sewing the various parts together. Graeco-Roman costuming is primarily a display of lengths of material draped, pinned, and belted, with a minimum of fitting. It is the variable mix of these two manners of dress that was worn at Palmyra, Dura-Europos, and Hatra during the Roman period and which may give some insight into the pervasiveness of Roman ways and taste in urban areas.

This integration (rather than synthesis) of East and West in the Orient is neatly epitomized by an inscription from Coptos in the Egyptian Thebaid. There, in A.D. 216, one Marcus Aurelius Bel 'aqab, an officer of the Hadrianic Palmyrene Antonian archers, offered a dedication in Greek "to the greatest god Hierabolus."[3] Here we have a soldier serving with Syrian archers whose unit is named in honor of the Roman emperor who had visited Palmyra. Bel 'aqab and his Asian troops are stationed far from home on a well-traveled trade route linking Rome, Egypt, Arabia, and India. As his cognomen indicates, Bel 'aqab has Semitic forebears but also carries the Roman family name of Aurelius with the Latin praenomen of Marcus. Yet he honors in Greek, rather than in an Aramaic dialect or Latin, the radiant Iarhibol, Semitic solar god of Palmyra, a deity assimilated with the Greek Helios!

Little imagination is needed to picture Marcus Aurelius Bel 'aqab: very probably a native Palmyrene, he would be clad in the standard Parthian-Palmyrene tunic and trousers on ceremonial occasions, a Greek short riding cloak (chlamys) pinned on his shoulder, his feet encased in soft chukker boots, and a short Persian dagger (akinakes) in its lobbed sheath strapped to his right thigh (fig. 10.1). This is the male portrait repeated over and over again in the painting and sculpture of the Palmyrene.

## PALMYRA

Founded in ancient times on an oasis in the Syrian desert, Palmyra was a major, and hence wealthy, entrepôt on the trade routes that linked East and West.[4] Goods from Central Asia, Persia, India, and Arabia left Palmyra for transshipment or resale to Roman customers at Antioch and other port cities on the Syro-Lebanese coast. Palmyrene caravan chiefs hauled their merchandise along the Tigris and Euphrates valleys; at Charax, at the head of the Persian Gulf (now the Shatt el-Arab), goods were brought in from or shipped out through the Gulf. Chinese silk and Indian spices, Arabian aromatics and Asian furs, and African animals and Persian Gulf pearls headed west from Palmyra's *suq* to deplete the purses of the boulevardiers of Rome. The donkey and camel caravans plodding toward the Mediterranean littoral across the gravelly desert saluted the merchant trains eastbound with goods as cumbersome as marble from quarries in the eastern Mediterranean lands destined to embellish Palmyrene buildings.[5] The importance of the oasis as a profitable commercial link was not lost on the Roman Senate. Imperial interest is indicated during the reign of Tiberius, for example, in his dedication in Palmyra of a magnificent temple to the Asian Bel in A.D. 32. Although Pompey had annexed Syria in 63 B.C., the city of Palmyra was not absorbed into the Roman structure until the first century A.D. Hadrian visited the city, which he renamed in his own honor Hadriana Palmyra.[6] Its basic population was Aramean and Arab. Among its foreign population, a Jewish enclave was sufficiently affluent and traditionally observant to carry some of its deceased members to the Galilee for burial in the catacombs at Beit She 'arim.[7]

Fortunately, the enthusiasm of Palmyrene burghers to have their families and themselves immortalized in mortuary portrait sculpture has provided us with a wealth of evidence—although composed of artists' representations of realia only—for the clothes they wore and the jewelry they affected. Of course, one must be mindful of the caveat that representations of dress in painting and sculpture need not necessarily reflect current styles. The depersonalized images of gods and heroized figures may be portrayed in the sort of traditional dress deemed appropriate to the figures' statures and roles rather than in the style current in the streets.[8] Horatio Greenough's civic statue of George Washington, for example, has him draped as if he were the Olympian Zeus, seated half naked in the city bearing his name, in a manner that would have shocked the first president's eighteenth-century sense of propriety. On the other hand, it is fair to assume that the humbler, personal memorial portrait most probably illustrates the sitter's Sunday best. True, the costuming may be resplendent beyond the status of the wearer (vanity is no less a historical constant than are death and taxes), but yet it is of its time and place rather than a product of the artist's imagination.

In general, the Iranian tunic and trousers (short caftan and anaxarides) seem to have served as the optional formal dress of the men of Palmyra, sometimes worn with a mantle (himation or pallium) or the short riding cape (chlamys). The trousers of the European barbarians (bracae) are visibly different from the Iranian: they are cut narrower and pulled tight, held by a cord tied around the ankle. Typical Iranian trousers are much fuller and looser than the European version, falling in parallel looping or horizontal folds, probably indicating a finely woven material. They are either bloused over or tucked into the boot. Herodian, the historian of Rome of the early third century A.D., himself perhaps from Antioch and writing in Greek, refers to the basic costume as a Phoenician style: the long-sleeved tunic of gold and purple that reached the feet ornamented with a median purple stripe, legs covered from the waist down to the toes (5.3.6, 5.5.10).

A knee- or full-length tunic with mantle was worn in the Graeco-Roman manner, probably as everyday dress. Mortuary reliefs illustrate the continuation of the classical theme of the deceased reclining on his couch accompanied by members of his family and servants, but all else is Eastern (fig. 10.1): the tunic with side vents is worn over loose trousers tucked into strapped boots. The short riding cloak pinned on the right shoulder is a nod to the West, as is the curtain (dorsalium) behind the deceased, which also designates the sepulchral setting on Roman sarcophagi.[9] The same Iranian dress is worn outdoors as a riding costume (fig. 10.2), for which it is particularly suited. The addition of leggings, baggy overpants pulled up at the thigh (usually referred to in the literature as jambières), no doubt originated as a sort of chaps, as worn by our Western cowhands, the protective chaparreras. At urbanized Palmyra, however, the chaps are also worn indoors, for they have become vestigial, à la mode accessories made of fine, thin material.

A variant dress worn by laymen as well as by desert deities seems to be of local origin. It consists of an ample tunic and a length of cloth rolled and knotted about the hips and dropping to the ankles, with an optional riding cloak. An early third-century A.D. relief (figs. 10.3a–b) of a dedicant making his offering to five tutelary gods shows two of the spear-bearing deities clad in this local dress along with two Western armored companions and a goddess in long chiton and palla. The worshiper, as is customary, wears neither the Iranian nor the local dress, but rather the simple tunic and mantle probably traditional to the occasion.

Palmyrene women preferred the long full gown with a broad veil covering the head and draped over the back and shoulders in the old Asian manner. Their more formal costume is clearly derived from Graeco-Roman fashions. There are several variations that combine local and Graeco-Roman elements. A woman's second-century A.D. mortuary portrait (fig. 10.4) in a hypogeum (that of Ta'ai) is clad in an Eastern tunic, the long sleeves gathered in folds and ornamented with decorated cuffs and armbands; similar broad strips of decoration run like clavi down the front. Over this she wears a chiton, wrapped around her body under the right arm, pinned on the left shoulder and bloused over a waist-belt to drop to floor length; the Graeco-Roman styling of the garment is obvious despite the heavy Eastern anklets and brooch. She has drawn her mantle over her head and shoulders, holding it in either hand along with her symbols as mistress of her household. Greek and Roman matrons similarly wore the palla, no doubt the source of the Palmyra mannerism, but covering the head with a mantle is also an ancient fashion in Mesopotamia and Iran. The manner in which Syrian matrons draped their mantle, however, is part of Western fashion.

Thus the comparatively modest Graeco-Roman costume was increasingly embellished and ornately accessoried in Palmyra in the second and third centuries A.D. Women bound their full, curled, and waved hairstyles in decoratively knotted turbans and patterned snoods over embroidered headbands and draped the arrangements with gold chains, ropes of beads, and jeweled pendants (fig. 10.5). Those who could afford it festooned their ears, necks, and bosoms with a wealth of jewelry and clasped their wrists in thick twisted gold bracelets, but they wore surprisingly modest finger rings. Much of the jewelry has Hellenistic parallels, but the elaborate combinations are Eastern.[10] Such opulent display, while anticipating Byzantine splendor, separates the Palmyrene matron from her Roman contemporary, who often was enjoined officially against too ostentatious dress.

Two reliefs from rural Syria are well within the old Asiatic tradition that is hardly concealed by the thin veneer of Western dress. The Asiatic storm god (Zeus-Hadad or Jupiter Dolichenos?) in his hieratic pose wears an Asian horned, high tiara and the Assyrian square beard as he brandishes Zeus-Jupiter's thunderbolts in one hand and his ax in the other (fig. 10.6). He is encased in the Hellenistic cuirass that continued to be used during Roman times and armed with the broad Roman sword (gladius) swung from a baldric. Similarly from an Asian family is a stocky goddess, perhaps a product of the same stone carver's workshop (fig. 10.7). Her thick plait bound with a ribbon falls to her back; so Asian ladies had their hair dressed since the third millennium B.C. Except for her stiff, frontal pose with head in profile, an Eastern mannerism, she holds herself and her garment in the classical manner. The floor-length chiton is pinned at either shoulder with the overfold secured by a cord tie under the bosom; her robe draped over one shoulder is worn low on her hip in the late Roman manner.

The visual richness of the Iranian suit and the opportunities it presented for decorative touches—couched embroidery or brocade, woven patterns, applied strips, rows of beading, shirring—makes the Roman tunic and mantle conservative and modest by comparison. That fact may be partially responsible for the affectation of a working Iranian riding suit's losing its utility and becoming high style and hence the expensive wear of the upper-class layman or priest reclining in elegant leisure on his upholstered couch. (Comparison with our contemporary transformation of workmen's blue denims into designer jeans is inevitable.)

When portraying their gods, the Palmyrenes clothed the Western deities in their traditional Western robes, taken directly from Graeco-Roman prototypes. Nike may be portrayed in an Eastern manner, but her chiton is unmistakable (fig. 10.8), even if the local artist nodded in this case, baring one leg in the usual fashion but then incongruously continuing the border of the garment across the figure's ankle (cf. the Dura-Europos Nike, fig. 10.14). Major Semitic deities and those that have been assimilated with their Graeco-Roman equivalents also wear Western garments, but often with additions from Iranian clothiers. Ba'al Shamin, flanked by Palmyra's solar and lunar gods, wears Greek lamellar armor with the double row of Roman tabs (pteryges) over a tunic with the Iranian loose sleeves. He carries the Roman sword (gladius), but unlike his companions of lesser status, he also wears Parthian trousers. The trim of beard, flowing hair, and crown with diadem are of the Eastern tradition.

Gods in military dress probably are a Roman contribution.[11] Lamellar armor and chain mail appear in Iranian battle garb. In the Palmyrene, we find gods posed beside each other, some in Hellenistic segmented cuirasses and others in Roman anatomical cuirasses with long and rounded leather tabs. An Asian god (possibly Shadrafa, known in Palmyra, perhaps of Canaanite origin) appears in a relief clad in full Roman anatomical cuirass, but his legs are thrust into Parthian trousers enriched with strings of pearls. Although the martial costuming for the divinity was most likely borrowed from the West, there is, of course, no want of bellicose gods brandishing weapons in Western Asian history. But they make their appearance in regal dress, rather than in clanking armor. The source of the tradition in the West, it has been reasoned, may be that deified warrior Alexander the Great, the consummate symbol of imperial might, raised to the status of a god in Egypt and even sufficiently revered in the East to be gratuitously burdened with a fictitious Persian heritage in one of the popular tales that circulated in Asia. It has been suggested that the Roman emperors displayed themselves in full armor as new Alexanders, a tradition then adopted from Rome for the tutelary gods in Syria.

It appears that the West had more influence in women's fashions at Palmyra than in men's, whose dress varies among the local, Iranian, and Graeco-Roman, depending upon occasion and social role. Heroes, men of status, and deities with Iranian connections (viz. Mithras) dressed in the Parthian Iranian manner. Servants and youngsters usually wear a plain, knee-length belted tunic, sometimes with an undergarment just visible below the hem. But young boys of well-to-do families also copied their elders, wearing richly decorated tunic, trousers, and chaps. Members of the priestly class may wear Iranian garb in formal portraits, but when they officiate, dropping incense into the ritual burners, they clothe themselves in Western or local robes. The only specific indication of the priestly status in the various sculptured portraits is a flat-topped cylindrical hat (modius) either worn by the sitter or placed beside him (figs. 10.9a–b).[12] The hat is usually encircled by a wreath that carries a central rosette or a portrait medallion-tondo of Western design. At Dura-Europos, a different type of hat, tall and conical, was worn by the Eastern clergy clothed in their unadorned, long-sleeved white caftans. Thus, the Palmyrene priests in Parthian and westernized dress, capped with the modius, had assimilated to the non-Semitic world to a greater extent than had their counterparts in the more Eastern reaches.

In the heyday of the city, honorific statues in bronze and stone decorated the main thoroughfares. Almost all have long since disappeared, but remaining examples are instructive. A male fragmentary portrait (fig. 10.10) clearly wears the Roman toga, and the female figure is clad in the equally Roman tunic and palla. It would seem, then, that the comparatively new fashion of Roman dress (fig. 10.11) may have played a limited role in the social scene of Palmyra, perhaps for public, community viewing. Any conclusion, however, is at the mercy of the odds and ends that time and chance have preserved from the past. The more private dress, that of the intimate familial and cult gatherings, of sepulcher and chapel, may have been consciously conservative, holding to older patterns.

It is difficult to resist the impression that, while a certain elegant cachet was associated with appareling oneself in Iranian dress, neither it nor more Western styles necessarily signified caste, rank, or office. That task was well served by the quality of fabric, elaboration of jewelry, and wealth of ornamentation. Palmyrene women and their goddesses (fig. 10.12) were more conscious of Western fashion, in the draping and wearing of their robes, in their sandals, hairstyles, and jewelry. They may sit in Roman wicker chairs or on Roman bolsters, perhaps keeping up with their Hellenized Antiochene sisters across the desert waste. But they also were given to wearing richly brocaded, fur-lined (perhaps fur-trimmed) caftans and a profusion of decorative accessories, characteristic orientalizing traits.

It is doubtful that a matron and her husband strolling along the columned boulevards of Palmyra would be mistaken for a Roman couple. In fact, Palmyra's basic Eastern character is always visible under its fashionable Hellenized gloss. Certainly Roman sensibilities were sharply attuned to the extravagance of foreign dress, which, as Herodian reports, "is not admired by the Roman troops, appearing to be more appropriate to barbarians and women" (5.2.4). The mortuary portrait slabs are conceptually Roman, but their arbitrary formalism and fairly uncompromised sense of abstraction are Asian to the core. Hence, one is unprepared to find a portrait (carrying the name [M]LKW in Palmyrene) that is distinctively Roman in its modeling and dramatic realism (fig. 10.13). But the fact that it is so different from the dozens of Palmyrene portraits scattered through the museums of the world is perhaps a measure of the fragility of Roman influence in the city.

### DURA-EUROPOS

Somewhat the country cousin of lordly Palmyra, Dura retained much of its Macedonian inheritance during its more than five hundred years.[13] In addition to its military importance on the Roman eastern *limes* (as it had previously served the Parthians, guarding their western flank), it was well placed astride the caravan route that followed the west bank of the Euphrates. The main city gate faced west, a door open to the desert traffic. Newly founded in 300 B.C. as part of the Seleucid Hellenization

of Syria, Dura came under Parthian military control in 113 B.C. and a few generations later served as the seat of the Parthian provincial governor. Trajan's legions attacked and perhaps held Dura for a year, but the city was not made part of the Roman *limes* until Verus took it in A.D. 164, and in less than fifty years it was designated a Roman colony. The Roman units, which reinforced the authority of the Dux Ripae, established their military quarters in the northern sector of the walled city.

The evidence for the dress worn by the local residents of Dura during this Roman period is not as straightforward as that from Palmyra. The use of different types of clothing is complicated, but also made interesting, by the fact that much of the figural painting and sculpture was either imported or came from the hands of artists brought to Dura for the purpose.

Unlike Palmyra, Dura was controlled by the Seleucids for almost two hundred years, providing an orientalized Greek substructure for the ensuing Parthian and Roman periods. As at Palmyra, traditional figures of Western origin, such as the wreath-bearing Nike (fig. 10.14), usually appear in classical costume with minor modifications or in nothing but the revealing mantle, while Arab deities wear the local dress found at Palmyra: the tunic covered by the bunched and draped mantle over the lower torso and legs. But some gods, such as the Lord Zeus (Zeus-Kyrios), are orientalized in appearance as well as in dress, clad in the draped, long-sleeved, full-length tunic with a mantle thrown over shoulder and arm, accompanied by conventionally dressed attendants (fig. 10.15).

Some of the monuments in Dura provide information on the function of Graeco-Roman dress that is not available at Palmyra. The murals of the Dura synagogue, of extraordinary importance because they are unique in the ancient as well as in the modern world, provide a review of dress in Syro-Mesopotamia in the third century A.D.[14] Although we do not know the home of the artist who painted the walls, it is unlikely that he was a local man; the small Jewish community could not have provided sufficient work for their painter to remain a permanent resident of Dura. Most likely, the master painter was brought in from Palestine; southern Mesopotamia has also been suggested, but there is no preserved contemporary painting from either region with which to compare or identify the style. Therefore the dress portrayed in the paintings may be representative of local garb but also of the *koine* of Syro-Mesopotamian fashions.

The murals show the same mixture of Graeco-Roman and Parthian Iranian dress as that found at Palmyra, although with differences in styling. The religio-historical content of the individual panels had some influence

Fig. 10.1. Palmyrene mortuary relief. Courtesy of The University Museum, University of Pennsylvania, Philadephia, neg. 8902.

Fig. 10.2. Palmyrene relief of cameleers and equestrians. Cleveland Museum of Art, inv. 70.15, purchase from the J. H. Wade Fund. Photo courtesy of The Cleveland Museum of Art.

Fig. 10.3a. Palmyrene relief of gods and dedicant. National Museum, Damascus. From Colledge, *Art of Palmyra,* fig. 41.

Fig. 10.3b. Detail of the gods Ashur, Ashu, and Astarte-Belti.

Fig. 10.4. Palmyrene mortuary relief. National Museum, Damascus.

Fig. 10.5. Palmyrene mortuary relief. British Museum, London. Reproduced by courtesy of the Trustees of the British Museum.

Fig. 10.6. Basalt relief from Khaltan, Syria. From Will, "Nouveaux monuments," pl. 5.

Fig. 10.7. Basalt relief from Khaltan, Syria. From Will, "Nouveaux monuments," pl. 5.

Fig. 10.8. Palmyrene fragment of arch with Victory. National Museum, Damascus.

Fig. 10.9a. Relief of the Gad of Dura. Yale University Art Gallery, New Haven. Photo by C. Hopkins.

Fig. 10.9b. Detail of head of priest.

Fig. 10.10. Palmyrene male togate figure. National Museum, Damascus.

Fig. 10.11. Palmyrene woman in palla. National Museum, Damascus.

Fig. 10.12. Palmyrene relief of the Ashtarte(?) and the Tyche of Palmyra. National Museum, Damascus.

Fig. 10.13. Palmyrene mortuary bust. Palmyra Museum.

on the choice of costume. In general, the painter seems to have kept to the plan that the male actors in narrative scenes set in the historical context of the East, having to do with activities and events worldly in theme, should be appropriately clothed in identifiable Eastern costume. Thus, the participants in scenes of the court, regardless of religion or nationality—Jewish Mordecai and King David, Egyptian Pharaoh and Persian Ahasuerus—wear Iranian tunic and trousers. So also dressed are the mounted fighters in the battle of Eben Ezer, David and Saul in the wilderness, the high priest Aaron standing before his Temple with his retinue engaged in the Temple ceremonies, and others. When the painter applied his brush to significant spiritual acts and hieratic figures, as well as to the crowds of "witnesses," he painted them in classical garb: Moses parting the waters, the full-length portraits flanking the ark (variously identified as spiritual leaders or symbolic of religious concepts), the anointing of David, Elijah healing the infant, and so forth (fig. 10.16). The artist also adhered to a flexible rule of thumb that ordered a short haircut, a more Western styling, for the men in westernized dress; the hair of those in Iranian garb is barbered in the Parthian manner—fuller, puffed out, and touching the shoulders.

If this premise is correct, it provides an estimate of the painter's intention, based on the identification of those figures generally agreed upon by students of the Dura panels. It would reveal an attitude toward dress not entirely unexpected: the earlier form of dress is associated with the mythical past (however inaccurately) when the heroes of biblical stories walked the earth and God's plan for his people was clearly articulated by him (fig. 10.17). Should one or another figure in the panels seem to be forced, Procrustean-like, into this scheme of costuming, it is well to remember that painters are rarely, if ever, consistent theologians. Alternate propositions have been advanced to account for the use of two distinctive dress types. The selection of different costumes has been put forward to buttress arguments for identifying the figures in the panels, all part of very complex and detailed iconographic interpretations given for the scenes and the overall program. Such is possible, but the ever-present question is whether this small Jewish enclave in the back country, or the artist it hired, would have been sufficiently knowledgeable of and schooled in the erudite niceties of Judaism, biblical exegesis, and Talmudic interpretations attributed to them by modern scholarship. One way to avoid, if not to answer, this concern is to regard the panels as copies of preexisting illustrations, though no such prototypes have been found.

Women's dress in the synagogue murals is also of two types, but both are variations of Graeco-Roman costume. The floor-length tunic–chiton has an oval neckline and loose half sleeves with the palla wrapped around the torso, under the arms, and just beneath the bosom, with an edge or corner of the material brought over the left shoulder and pinned in front (see the women at the extreme left and right of fig. 10.18). It appears to be wound again around the hips with a thick roll and falls just short of the bottom edge of the chiton: the free end is drawn over the head as a covering veil. Whatever the origin of this manner of draping, it differs from the way Palmyrene women wore their mantles.

The second type of women's wear is found in only two of the paintings (though only about half of the synagogue's panels are preserved, and hence, one must be cautious in seeing the costume's apparent rarity as particularly significant). It is difficult to identify the style worn here (fig. 10.18) by the three maidens in the center modeled on the classical nymphs. The dress may be a misunderstood rendering of the peplos made from a length of material woven in two colors: one color bands the lower and upper hems, and a broader band of the same color is on that part of the material forming the overfold on the bosom, above the belt. The costume is completed with an Eastern napkin veiling the head.

The affluent community of Palmyrenes in Dura-Europos imported works of art and, in all probability, its artists also. Hence, several of the monuments illustrate the characteristic dress of Palmyra, both civil and military (fig. 10.11).[15] Asian dress had a tighter grip on Dura, however, perhaps marking the greater provincialism of the border town as well as the loose hold of Rome, which was, after all, primarily that of the military. The gods worshiped at Dura signal heterogeneous tastes and attitudes: Babylonian Bel, Nanaia, and Shamash; Syrian Hadad and Atargatis; Phoenician Adonis; Arab Arsu; Macedonian Zeus Olympus, Apollo, and Artemis; Rome's adopted Mithras and Jupiter Dolichenus; and the Christian and Jewish God.[16]

The wall paintings in the Temple of the Palmyrene Gods (or Temple of Bel) show sacrificing priests in their plain long, belted caftans and conical caps, all in white and with their feet bare.[17] An acolyte wears a caftan and red turban with a short decorated mantle over one shoulder and wrapped around the waist. He is shod in Palmyrene-style shoes. The women, now only dimly visible in this cult scene, are robed and abundantly veiled, wearing elaborate tiaras, all belonging to the Orient. When the Roman officer Terentius offers incense in a wall painting, he and his retinue wear the short military tunic and long cloak before the receptive, cuirassed gods posed in Roman high boots.[18] An ill-proportioned relief of Iarhibol shows him in full Roman dress—high open-toed boots, anatomical cuirass with tabs and lappets over a chiton, and cloak. But no matter his costume, his

Asian ancestry is announced in the mass of hair, parted in the center and puffed out shoulder length to form a broad frame around his head in the Parthian manner.

HATRA

Ever since its founding in the first century B.C., Hatra had maintained successfully, despite military pressure, its nominal independence within the sphere of Parthian control, at least until shortly before its last days, at which time a Roman presence was evident.[19] Excavations in the antecella of Temple IX at Hatra (in upper Mesopotamia, some ninety-three miles southwest of modern Mosul) produced fragmented remains of the inscribed statues. One of these had been "Consecrated to Hercules for the health of our lord the emperor; Petronius Quintianus, military tribune of the first Parthian legion, tribune of the IXth Gordion cohort, [set up this statue] to the patron deity of the cohort after the victory over Media." Hence, at least by A.D. 235, the suggested date for the statue, Roman troops were in Hatra, either uninvited or now as allies against the common enemy, the Sasanian invaders. The years of residence by Roman troops in Hatra were few, however. The Sasanian king Ardashir took the city, perhaps in the month of April, in A.D. 240 and destroyed it.[20] Earlier in Hatra's history, Trajan (probably in A.D. 117) and then Septimius Severus (in A.D. 198 or 200 and again in the following year) were thwarted in their sieges by the double circuit of walls protecting the city as well as by unfavorable weather and short supplies, so Dio Cassius reports. The impact of Roman culture in general and Roman dress in particular was, as might be guessed, much less evident at Hatra than at Palmyra or Dura.

The ongoing excavations have uncovered the expected material evidence of Graeco-Roman influence, such as that employed in the ornament and decoration of the architecture, in the representations of Semitic gods syncretized with their Western counterparts, and in small statuary that is Western in both theme and execution. These figures wear conventional classical dress or, as in the many statuettes of Heracles with lion skin and club, are naked. (Nakedness had long been alien to old oriental official tradition except for a few revealing goddesses.) Some of this sculpture obviously was imported from the West, while other examples were made locally, based on Western models.

The large-scale works—civic portraits and cult figures—are clad in some articles of dress that originally came from the West but were well integrated into an Asian costume.[21] This transformation of parts of Graeco-Roman clothing gives one the impression that the Hatrenes were, at best, getting secondhand their ideas about Western dress. The Parthians are the best

Fig. 10.14. Dura-Europos Victory panel, excavation photo. National Museum, Damascus.

Fig. 10.15. Dura-Europos relief of Zeus-Kyrios, excavation photo. Yale University Art Gallery, New Haven.

Fig. 10.16. Dura-Europos synagogue mural detail of "witnesses" before Ahasuerus and Mordecai, excavation photo. National Museum, Damascus.

Fig. 10.17. Dura-Europos synagogue mural detail, excavation photo. National Museum, Damascus.

Fig. 10.18. Dura-Europos synagogue mural detail of the finding of the infant Moses. National Museum, Damascus.

Fig. 10.20. Hatra, graffito. After Safar and Mustafa, *Hatra*, 203.

Fig. 10.19. Hatra, statue of Ubal. Iraqi National Museum, Baghdad.

Fig. 10.21. Relief of solar deity. Iraqi National Museum, Baghdad.

candidate as the intermediary. Belonging to the Parthian milieu are various Hatrene features, in addition to beards, hairstyles, and the standard costume, which is an ornate version of Iranian trousers and tunic. Heracles, well represented in Hatra, was a Western mythological figure (although myth puts his birthplace as Asian Nisa), but he had also long been established as a popular cult figure in Parthian Iran. Some of the minor finds and ornamentation at Hatra are strikingly similar in style to Gandharan works.[22] Trade between Gandhara (roughly modern Pakistan and southern Afghanistan) and Hatra is not unexpected: a historiated "cosmetic" tray from Hatra, for example, is of a type popular in contemporary Gandhara and may even be an import. And both Gandhara and Hatra show similar Iranian influences. There is good reason, then, to suggest that Hatra received Western dress via the Parthians rather than directly from the West.

Whereas the Palmyrene woman wore a version of Western dress with Eastern elements, the clothing of her sister from Hatra is fundamentally Asian with a faint echo of classical influence. The basic garment is the Asian ample, floor-length robe with long, heavily patterned sleeves. Over this robe sometimes is worn an Asian version of the sleeveless chiton of thin material pinned at the shoulder and falling to midcalf; one side is left open and draped, and the whole is unbelted. A tall, jewelry-bedecked headdress is covered with a veil that drops down the back. Heavy necklaces, large pendants on braided chains, earrings, and twisted bracelets complete the inventory. The standard, genteel pose was to have the left hand gather a few folds of the chiton to raise it a bit, an affectation of no help in walking because the bottom of the underrobe still swept the floor (fig. 10.19). The Semitic goddess Atargatis wears a short-sleeved, belted tunic over the basic robe. But the syncretic Athena-Allat, armed and helmeted with the aegis on her breast, wears a belted peplos. Her fully Asian goddesses, Al ʿuzza and Manat, wear the sleeved long robe with draped mantle fastened on one shoulder and the Hatrene tall headdress and veil. A graffito of a statue of an unnamed goddess is clearly dressed and posed in the Western manner (fig. 10.20). Hence, the pattern found at both Palmyra and Dura-Europos of Western and westernized deities being clothed in fashions befitting their Mediterranean background and the Semitic gods of Asia in oriental garb is maintained at Hatra also.

The male gods and men of Hatra almost uniformly wear the local version of Iranian dress, the caftan sometimes draped with the Greek mantle. The male gods who spring from the syncretism of East and West wear, as do the goddesses, equally mixed costumes. A solar god is clad in the loose, sleeved tunic worn under a relative of the Greek chiton pinned at the shoulder with exaggerated, eagle-embossed clasps (fig. 10.21).

Can we find, then, a general pattern in the use of dress emerging from these three cities that holds some implications for the cultural context of Roman Syro-Mesopotamia? How one chose to dress in this ancient region was not circumscribed by national boundaries, competing political systems, or institutionalized enmities. Iranian dress flourished well beyond the state's borders and in areas aggressively opposed to being incorporated into the Parthian Empire. The Parthians themselves, having wrested their territories from their erstwhile foes, the Seleucids, included Greek dress in their clothes chests, even as they incorporated Greek gods into their shrines and assumed a Greek heritage as self-described Philhellenes. While Dura-Europos became for many, many years a far-western holding of the Parthian Empire, neither Palmyra nor Hatra was similarly occupied. But all three centers adopted Iranian dress as a highly fashionable and expensive style.

The fact that the Romans came to these three cities primarily as soldiers rather than as settlers would seem to go a long way toward explaining the continuation of Hellenistic styles, largely at the expense of Roman ones. The Asian East simply continued to be more familiar with the Greek himation than with the Roman toga, as it was more comfortable with the Greek language than the Latin. Yet another factor explains the persistence of the himation (the pallium and palla) and the draping of cloak and mantle in the Greek manner. Margarete Bieber, the doyen of classical costuming, has extensively documented the continued popularity of the Greek himation in republican and imperial Rome and on into the fourth century.[23] Not only was it particularly appropriate dress for funerary, commemorative, and honorary monuments, but it was also more convenient to wear than the toga.

The situation is much the same if we look at contemporary dress far to the east, beyond Syro-Mesopotamia. At Old Nisa in Turkmenistan the women dress in the Greek manner, while the men follow Parthian fashions.[24] There can be no question but that where trade with the West was most active, so also was the importing of Roman goods and fashions. The Palmyrene mortuary portrait busts are a case in point. Because Hatra was not a way station on the more popular caravan routes and did not house Roman troops until its last years, and also because it was probably not founded until late in the first century B.C., the evidence of Graeco-Roman influence generally, and costume in particular, is superficial and spotty.

The impression one gains is that the Roman manner

of dress, like Rome's art styles and aesthetics, remained a foreign, though not unacceptable, fashion in the East. Hellenistic wear retained—as Dura-Europos well illustrates—an aura of the respected past, part of the Asian's inheritance. A similarly conservative attitude is evident in Attica, where the preferred costume in the tombstone reliefs remained steadfastly Greek during the Roman period. May one speculate whether the Syro-Mesopotamian diffidence concerning Roman dress is a reflection of the Asian's view of Rome in the larger context?

## NOTES

Translations of Herodian are from E. C. Echols, *Herodian*, LCL (Cambridge, Mass., 1961).

1. If the close examination of Roman dress is now entering early maturity, then the story of Graeco-Roman costume in post-Alexander Western Asia is but a gleam in the historian's eye. The appearance of Western dress in Asia is mentioned by classical historians in discussion of the monuments; no better example comes to mind than in the encyclopedic volumes on the social and economic histories of the Hellenistic and Roman periods by M. I. Rostovtzeff. Students of Asian history sometimes identify the specifics of oriental dress but only notice the Western intrusion in passing, except for the few specialized studies noted below.

There are no historical narratives by ancient Asian authors before Islamic times that fill a role comparable to that of Western writers whose horizon included Asia: Arrian, Pliny, Cassius Dio, Strabo, and Ammianus Marcellinus. These write about an alien, strange land, of course, their information gained mainly second- and third-hand, viewed through the distorting lenses of Graeco-Roman historical preconceptions. In all, they are of modest use in supplementing or reinforcing that which the monuments themselves have to tell of Asian dress. For the trustworthiness of Western literary sources for Asian history, see H. Sancisi-Weerdenburg, ed., *Achaemenid History*, vol. 1, *Sources, Structures and Synthesis* (Leiden, 1987), and H. Sancisi-Weerdenburg and A. Kihrt, eds., *Achaemenid History*, vol. 2, *The Greek Sources* (Leiden, 1987).

2. The most accessible reviews of the Hellenic intrusion into post-Alexander Western Asia based on the monuments are D. Schlumberger, *L'Orient hellénisé: L'art grec et ses héritiers dans l'Asie Méditerranéenne* (Paris, 1970); and idem, "Descendants non-Méditerranéens de l'art grec," *Syria* 37 (1960): 130–318. E. Will examines Graeco-Roman, Parthian, and local aspects in "La Syrie romaine entre l'Occident gréco-romaine et l'Orient parthe," in *Le rayonnement des civilisations grecque et romaine sur les cultures périphériques* (Paris, 1965), 511–26.

3. *IGR* 1: 1169.

4. Of the several summary histories of Palmyra, I mention four that offer a good introduction: J. Starcky, *Palmyre* (Paris, 1952); M. A. R. Colledge, *The Parthians* (London, 1967); H. Drijvers and M. Versteegh, "Hatra, Palmyra, und Edessa", *ANRW* 2.8 (1977): 799–906; J. Teixidor, *Un port romain du désert: Palmyre et son commerce d'Auguste à Caracalla*, Semitica 34 (Paris, 1984). The most recent, detailed review of Palmyrene art with descriptions of dress is M. A. R. Colledge, *The Art of Palmyra* (London, 1976). Two volumes of the *Sculptures of Palmyra* are edited by K. Tanabe (Tokyo, 1986). For monuments in the region of Palmyra, see D. Schlumberger, *La palmyréne du nord-ouest* (Paris, 1951).

5. H. Dodge, "Palmyra and the Roman Marble Trade," *Levant* 20 (1988): 215–30, locates the sites; concerning imported statuary, see *CISem* II.iii, fasc. 1, no. 3913.1.

6. For concise reviews of the Roman presence in Syro-Mesopotamia, see I. A. Richmond, "Palmyra under the Aegis of the Romans," *JRS* 53 (1963): 43–54; pertinent chapters in F. Millar, *The Roman Empire and Its Neighbors* (London, 1967); and J. Wagner, "Die Römer an Euphrat und Tigris," *Antike Welt* 16 (1985): 3–72. On Palmyra's eastern extension to the Euphrates, see M. Gawlikowski, "Palmyre et l'Euphrates," *Syria* 60 (1983): 53–68. For trade to the Persian Gulf and beyond, see J. P. Rey-Coquais, "Syrie romaine de Pompée à Dioclétien," *JRS* 68 (1978): 44–73; and J. Schwartz, "Les palmyréniens et l'Egypte," *Bulletin Société archéologique d'Alexandrie* 40 (1953): 64–66.

7. The slight evidence for the Jewish community is in the form of short inscriptions: J. B. Chabot, *Choix d'inscriptions de Palmyre* (Paris, 1922), 106; B. Mazar, *Beth She'arim*, vol. 1 (New Brunswick, N.J., 1973).

8. H. Seyrig published the first and still only essay on the subject: "Armes et costumes iraniens de Palmyre," *Syria* 18 (1937): 4–31. The fragments of textiles recovered are fully described in R. Pfister, *Textiles de Palmyre*, 3 vols, (Paris, 1934–40); D. DeJonghe and M. Tavernier, "Les damassés de Palmyre," *Annales archéologiques arabes syriennes* 32 (1982): 99–116.

9. On Roman sarcophagi with the dorsalium *(parapetasma)*, see I. I. Saverkina, *Römische Sarkophage in der Ermitage* (Berlin, 1979).

10. For Palmyrene jewelry, see Mackay, "Jewellery of Palmyra," 160–87; M. Gawlikowski, "Remarques sur l'usage de la fibule à Palmyre," in *Mélanges K. Michalowski* (Warsaw, 1966), 411–19; and the catalog of Palmyrene jewelry in B. Musche, *Vorderasiatischer Schmuck zur Zeit der Arsakiden und der Sasaniden*, Handbuch der Orientalistick VII, Abt. i, Bd. 2-b, Lief. 5 (Leiden, 1988).

11. Gods in armor have been taken up in H. Seyrig, "Les dieux armés et les Arabes en Syrie," *Syria* 47 (1970): 77–99; idem, "Les dieux syriens en habit militaire," *Annales archéologiques arabes syriennes* 21 (1971): 67–70; idem, "Antiquités syriennes 94," *Syria* 48 (1971): 115–16. For the Roman genre, see Kantorowicz, "Gods in Uniform," 368–93.

12. On the Eastern modius, see H. Ingholt et al., *Recueil des tesséres de Palmyre* (Paris, 1955).

13. Three readable surveys of the history and the monuments, with sufficient bibliographies, are M. I. Rostovtzeff, *Dura-Europos and Its Art* (Oxford, 1938); A. Perkins, *The Art of Dura-Europos* (Oxford, 1973); and C. Hopkins, *The Discovery of Dura-Europos* (New Haven, 1979). For Iranian dress at Dura, see B. Goldman, "The Dura Synagogue Costumes and Parthian Art," in *The Dura-Europos Synagogue: A Re-evaluation, 1932–1972*, ed. J. Gutmann (Missoula, Mont., 1973), 53–78.

14. The synagogue murals have been extensively treated and illustrated in C. Kraeling, *The Synagogue*, The Excavations of Dura-Europos, final report 8.1 (New Haven, 1956); E. R. Goodenough, *Jewish Symbols in the Greco-Roman Period*, vols. 9–11 (New York, 1964). Concerning the possible sources, iconography, and relation with later Christian manuscript illumination, see K. Weitzmann and H. L. Kessler, *The Frescoes of the Dura Synagogue and Christian Art* (Washington, D.C., 1990).

15. On the Palmyrene community of Dura, see R. du Mesnil de Buisson, *Inventaire des inscriptions palmyréniennes de Doura-Europos*, Revue des études sémitiques 2 (Paris, 1936); for other visitors and travelers identified by their dress, see B. Goldman, "Foreigners at Dura-Europos: Pictorial Graffiti and History," *Le Muséon* 103 (1990): 5–25.

16. See C. B. Welles, "The Gods of Dura-Europos," in *Beiträge zur alten Geschichte und deren Nachleben*, ed. R. Stiehl and H. E. Stier (Berlin, 1970), 50–65.

17. The first substantial evidence for the archaeological importance of the site and its identification with the discovery of the Palmyrene Temple is detailed in J. H. Breasted, *Oriental Forerunners of Byzantine Painting* (Chicago, 1924), followed by F. Cumont, *Fouilles de Doura-Europos*, 1922–1923, 2 vols. (Paris, 1926).

18. The Roman detachments stationed at Dura are discussed in R. O. Fink, "The Cohors XX Palmyrenorum, a Cohors Equitata Miliaria," *TAPA* 78 (1947): 159–70; and in J. F. Gilliam, "The Roman Army in Dura," in *The Parchments and Papyri*, ed. C. B. Welles, R. O. Fink, and J. F. Gilliam. The Excavations of Dura-Europos, final report 5.1 (New Haven, 1959), 22–27.

19. Beyond Walter Andrae's two-volume reports of 1908 and 1912 on the German excavations, descriptions of Hatra's monuments have been relegated mainly to the periodical literature; the important exception is the heavily illustrated volume in Arabic by F. Safar and M. A. Mustapha, *Hatra, city of the sun god* (Baghdad, 1974). Iraqi archaeologists are continuing excavations of the city.

20. On the Roman and Persian battles at Hatra, Tacitus (*Annals* 13.35) and Dio Cassius (*Romaika* 75.11–13) record the events associated with the Roman military adventures in the region; Herodian the Syrian (died sometime after A.D. 238) provides additional information on the unsuccessful Roman campaigns against Hatra; Ammianus Marcellinus recalls (25.8.5) that "at different times those warlike emperors, Trajan and Severus, had attacked it with a view to its destruction, but had been almost destroyed with their armies."

On the Roman detachments stationed at Hatra, see D. Oates, "A Note on Three Latin Inscriptions from Hatra," *Sumer* 11 (1955): 39–43; A. Maricq, "Les dernières années de Hatra: L'alliance romaine," *Syria* 34 (1957): 291f. For the Sasanian taking of the city, see M. L. Chaumont, "A propos de la chute de Hatra et du couronnement de Shapur Ier," *Acta Antiqua Academiae Scientiarum Hungaricae* 27 (1979): 207–37. The date of Hatra's fall is recovered from a biography of Mani in a Greek codex, probably fifth century; see A. Henrichs and L. Koenen, "Ein griechischer Mani-Codex (P. Colon. inv. nr. 4780)," *ZPE* 5 (1970): 120.

21. Two slender volumes include Hatrene dress: H. Ingholt, *Parthian Sculpture from Hatra*, Memoirs of the Connecticut Academy of Arts and Sciences 12 (New Haven, 1954); D. Homès-Fredericq, *Hatra et ses sculptures parthes: Etude stylistique et iconographique* (Istanbul, 1963). J. M. C. Toynbee suggests that Hatrene dressmakers used "pattern books" of Graeco-Roman designs; Toynbee, "Some Problems of Romano-Parthian Sculpture at Hatra," *JRS* 62 (1972): 106–10.

22. On commerce with the Persian Gulf region, see A. Caquot, "Nouvelles inscriptions araméennes de Hatra," *Syria* 30 (1953): 234–46. For material that raises the probability of connections with Gandhara in the second century A.D., see H. P. Francfort, *Les palettes du Gandhara*, MDAFA 23 (Paris, 1979); and E. Quarantelli, ed., *The Land between the Rivers: Twenty Years of Italian Archaeology in the Middle East* (Turin, 1985).

23. On the popularity and role of the Greek himation in Roman Italy and Asia Minor, see M. Bieber, "Roman Men in Greek Himation (Romani Palliati): A Contribution to the History of Copying," *PAPhS* 103 (1959): 347–417. "Roman dress seems never to have been accepted in Athens" during the Roman period, concludes A. Muehsam in "Attic Grave Reliefs from the Roman Period," *Berytus* 10 (1953): 73.

24. For dress in the sculpture at Old Nisa, see G. A. Koshelenko, *Rodina Parfjan* (Moscow, 1977).

# Costume in Roman Palestine: Archaeological Remains and the Evidence from the Mishnah

## 11

LUCILLE A. ROUSSIN
*In Memoriam Morton Smith*

"The glory of God is man, the glory of man is dress," we read in an ancient Jewish text.[1] Today it is difficult to reconstruct the ancient dress to which this text refers. The fragments of clothing and shoes found in one of the caves in the Judean desert and published by the late Yigael Yadin are among the only material remains of the clothing worn by the Jews in Roman Palestine. Jewish costume of the postbiblical era has been the subject of several studies, and in his study of the textiles and clothing found in the Judean desert Yadin does relate many of the items to specific Jewish texts.[2] It is my intention to see if we can go further in examining these clothing fragments in the broader context of Roman costume, in their relationship to Jewish religious traditions, and against the social and economic background of Roman Palestine during the Mishnaic and Talmudic period.

The Cave of Letters, located near ʿEn-Gedi, is the largest and most important of the caves in the Judean desert occupied by the followers of Bar Kokhba during the second Jewish war against Rome. Letters in Hebrew and Aramaic found in the cave appear to have been dictated by Simeon Bar Kokhba himself; one of the letters seems to have been written on the eve of the festival of Succoth in A.D. 135. The burials in the cave indicate that it was the last refuge of some families who participated in the rebellion at ʿEn-Gedi.[3] Assuming that the garments and textiles were brought into the cave and not manufactured there during the period of residence in it, we thus have a *terminus ad quem* of ca. A.D. 100 to 135 for the manufacture of the garments, many of which were reused as burial cloths.

There are no preserved representations of Jewish life of this period with which to compare these garments—as there are for other areas of the Roman Empire—no

statuary or wall paintings to reconstruct contemporary costume. The third-century A.D. frescoes from the synagogue of Dura-Europos provide the earliest pictorial evidence of Jewish dress in the late Roman world.[4] We do, however, have a wealth of contemporary literary evidence from the Mishnah, the collection of oral laws concerning Jewish religious life and customs in Palestine compiled by Rabbi Judah the Prince in A.D. 200. The Jerusalem and the Babylonian Talmuds, the commentaries on the law contained in the Mishnah, completed ca. A.D. 500–600, also provide many enlightening references to Jewish costume.[5] Early Christian written sources contain only two references to Jewish costume. In Mark 9:3 we learn that Jesus wore white, because in the Transfiguration "his clothes turned dazzling white, with a whiteness no bleacher on earth could equal." The only other Jewish citizen about whom we have any evidence concerning costume is St. Paul, who instructs his followers to bring his paenula to him (2 Timothy 4:13).

There is ample evidence that weaving and dyeing were a Jewish specialty in the ancient world. The village of Kfar Namra is said to have had three hundred weaving shops.[6] The villages of Sarepta, Neapolis, and Lydda, and Arbela in Galilee, were known as centers of weaving and dyeing.[7] Ancient authors attest to the fine quality of the cloth woven in Palestine. Clement of Alexandria laments the fact that coarse linen garments woven in Egypt are rejected in favor of fabrics imported from "the land of the Jews," and Pausanias declares that "for its fineness Elean linen flax is just as good as Jewish, though not so tawny."[8] Beth Shean was one of the cities that supplied textiles to the entire world and was especially famous for the fine quality of its linens. Because of their quality, the linens and finished clothing from Beth

Shean are listed among the most expensive goods of their type in the *Edict of Diocletian*, issued in A.D. 301.[9]

Sources indicate that in some towns weavers were so numerous that they formed guilds. At Hieropolis, in Phrygia, purple dyers even formed a guild that was entirely Jewish. There is also evidence that those engaged in the same craft not only inhabited separate quarters of the towns and cities but also had their own synagogues.[10] A second-century A.D. text relates that in the Great Synagogue of Alexandria, "the people did not sit at random, but rather grouped by trades: goldsmiths in their own sections, silversmiths in theirs, blacksmiths in theirs, weavers in theirs. So when a newcomer entered, he sought out the members of his own craft"[11]

Other references in the Mishnah indicate that weaving was also a task done at home by women. In Mishnah Kethuboth 5:5 we read:

These are the tasks that the wife must carry out for her husband: she must grind corn and bake and do washing, cooking, and suckle her child, make his bed for him, and work in wool. If she brought him one bondswoman, she need not grind or bake or wash; if two, she does not have to cook or give suck to her child; if three, she is not required to make his bed or work in wool; if four, she may sit on a raised seat. Rabbi Eliezer says, "Even if she brought him a hundred bondswomen, he can compel her to work in wool, since idleness leads to lewdness."

The wife's duties as a weaver are again mentioned in Kethuboth 5:9: "And how much does she have to work for him? She must weave five selas' weight of warp in Judea, which are equivalent to ten selas in Galilee."

A passage in the Babylonian Talmud indicates that the basic items of clothing worn by Jews did not differ significantly from those worn by other inhabitants of the Graeco-Roman world. Indeed, almost all of the Hebrew words for the clothing mentioned here are transliterations of Greek and Latin words.[12] "Rabbi Jose said: only eighteen garments [may be carried from a burning house on the Sabbath]. And these are the eighteen garments: a cloak [amictorium], undertunic [anakolos], a money belt, linen tunic [colobium], shirt [haluq], a felt cap, a cloak [pallium], an apron, a pair of trousers [bracae], a pair of shoes, a pair of felt slippers [impilia], a pair of breeches, the girdle round his loins, the hat on his head, and the scarf [sudarium] around his neck."[13]

We get an idea of the daily costume from the rules for the order of removing clothes at a bath recorded in the Tosefta Derech Eretz: "On entering the bathhouse, what is the order of procedure? First he removes his shoes, then the hat, then the mantle [tallit], then he unfastens the girdle, then his shirt [haluq], and after that he unties the *epikarsion* of the undergarment."[14]

Although the basic items of clothing are the same, there are two traditions about Jewish garments that are distinctive: the laws of *shaatnez* and *tzitzit*. Shaatnez is set forth in Deuteronomy 22:11: "You shall not wear clothes woven with two kinds of yarn, wool and flax together." The exception to this rule was the garment of the high priest. The reason for this prohibition may, indeed, have been to reserve this privilege to the high priest and differentiate him from the people.[15] The other distinctive ruling about Jewish clothing is requiring the application of tassels, tzitzit, at each corner of the mantle. This law is found in Deuteronomy 22:12: "You shall make twisted tassels on the four corners of your cloaks which you wrap around you."[16]

All the textiles found in the Cave of Letters conform to the Halachic injunction against mixing woolen and linen fibers in the same garment. Among the finds were also separate balls of spun woolen and linen threads, and a ball of unspun wool. Because of the injunction against the mixing of fibers, some Jewish weavers made wool their specialty.[17] The complex preparation of woolen garments is noted in the Tosefta: "How much did the first man toil: another [example]: He did not put on a tunic until he sheared and bleached and combed and dyed and spun and wove and sewed; and only then he wore it."[18] The Mishnah sheds more light on the process in the list of work forbidden on the Sabbath: "The main labors [prohibited on the Sabbath] are shearing wool and washing and combing or dyeing it, spinning, weaving, making two loops, weaving two threads, separating the warp from the woof or weft, tying a knot or loosening one, sewing two stitches."[19]

The tunic, the main garment worn by all, consists of a large rectangular sheet woven with two parallel bands of decoration of a different color that run from selvage to selvage and are spaced widely apart. The tunics and tunic sheets found in the Cave of Letters are among the only ancient garments found in a dated context and known to have been worn by Jews.[20] While most Greek and Roman tunics were woven in a single piece, the tunics from the Cave of Letters were woven in two pieces and joined at the shoulders, leaving an opening for the neck (fig. 11.1). The Hebrew word for the tunic, haluq, may be derived from this method of weaving the garment in two pieces (heleq).[21] Jewish sources provide evidence for this method of weaving: "Rabbi Jose said: At the opening of a haluq which is made like two leaves."[22]

Although this method of weaving a tunic may not be unique to Jews, it had for the Jews a major advantage: it facilitated adherence to the laws of purity. The Mishnah states: "And so two leaves of a haluq on one side of which is a visible defect, the other is ritually clean." The ritually unclean half of the tunic could therefore be removed and replaced without defiling the other half. For purposes of ritual cleanness, the garment was considered finished when one sewed the two pieces together and finished the neck hole. The Tosefta says, "A haluq of linen, when does it become susceptible? When the work for it is completed. And when is the completion of the work? When its neck hole will be formed."[23]

The narrow stripes woven into the tunics so that they descend from the shoulders characterize all tunics of the Roman period. Called *clavi* in Latin, and usually woven in shades of purple, these stripes defined the rank of the wearer: the wide *latus clavus* was the mark of senatorial rank, the narrower *angustus clavus* was worn by the equites, the upper ranks of officials, and the narrowest stripe adorned the tunics of boys. Most of the tunics found in the Cave of Letters are decorated with narrow or medium-width clavi.[24] Yadin has demonstrated that the Hebrew term for *clavus* is *'imrah*. The Talmud provides several references to this feature of the tunic. "An unskilled tailor . . . Rabbi Jose ben Hanina said, means anyone who cannot sew an even *'imrah*."[25] In the same tractate of the Talmud we find: "Which is the unskilled and which is the skilled tailor? Said Rabbi Jose ben Hanina: He who matches the *'imrahs* is the skilled one, and he who does not match the *'imrahs* is unskilled." Further, the *'imrahs* seem to be reusable: "A haluq in which a defect is visible, the *'imrahs* on it may be saved even if they are purple."[26]

Worn over the man's tunic was a mantle, the tallit, equivalent to the Roman pallium and the Greek himation. The sources describe proper dress for going out in public: "Dressed in a haluq and wrapped in a tallit."[27] The tallit consisted of one rectangular sheet with the selvages longer than the borders.[28] It is to the four corners of the tallit that the tzitzit were attached, and these are the only way in which the mantle differed from non-Jewish mantles. The tallit worn as a prayer shawl by Jewish men during synagogue services today is a descendant of the ancient tallit; similarly, the Roman mantle has survived as the pallium, or scarf, worn by Catholic priests. That the tallit was the outer garment of Jewish men and not the distinctive Roman toga is indicated by a passage in Sifre Deuteronomy 81: "So that you might not do as they do, causing others to come and destroy you . . . you should not say, 'Since they go out clad in a toga, so will I go out clad in a toga; since they go out wearing purple, so will I go out wearing purple.'"

The tallit was worn by all men, but those worn by scholars, distinguished persons, and those who led in prayers were of finer materials and larger than those worn by the common people.[29] The scholar's tallit completely covered his tunic, so that the latter, with its *'imrahs*, was not visible. Thus we read in the Babylonian Talmud, "How should the upper garment of a *talmid hakham* be worn? So long that not more than a hand-

breadth of his undergarment should be visible underneath." That the tallit covers the entire tunic is made clear by Rabbi Jose, who says, "The beams of my house have never seen the *'imrahs* of my haluq."[30]

"A man's dignity is seen in his costume," and therefore one must put on clean clothing to honor the Sabbath.[31] Even the common man who can afford it must have two sets of clothing, one for weekdays and a clean set for the Sabbath.[32] If the commoner cannot afford two sets of clothing, he must at least turn his garments inside out on the Sabbath so that they appear clean.[33] The scholar must change his clothes even if only one side is soiled: "The garments of a *banna'im* [literally, builder] a stain even on one side interposes; of uncultured persons only a stain on both sides interposes."[34]

The ancient sources give us some information on the cost of clothing, but they are difficult to interpret. A very cheap haluq or tallit could be bought for one dinar, a more expensive haluq could cost between twelve and twenty-five dinars, and a rich man's cloak might cost up to a hundred dinars.[35]

The mantles found in the Cave of Letters are decorated by notched bands, checkerboard patterns, and gamma-shaped designs, in addition to the clavi. The notched bands are all the same shape, although the width varies (fig. 11.2). The gamma-shaped patterns are composed of two notched bands at right angles, woven into the four corners of the mantle about thirty centimeters from the edge (fig. 11.3).[36] The gamma-shaped ornament is mentioned in a passage in the Jerusalem Talmud: "There is a colored bent place like a Greek gamma, one thread to this direction, the other to the other direction, which forms a sign . . . that is to say, that [the weaver] when he weaves, he forms ornaments like letters . . . as if he is found to be writing." Yadin tends to believe that these designs originally carried no symbolism and were merely decorative: the notched bands resemble the weaver's shuttle, and the gamma form is merely two notched bands joined to fit the corners of the cloth.[37]

Three of the mantles also have small designs which appear to be weaver's marks, small signs enclosed in square borders (fig. 11.4). Here, too, an ancient text enlightens us about these small symbols: the Mishnah, in a passage regarding lost property to be returned to the owner, states: "A garment was also included among all these things. Why was it mentioned separately? To compare other things to it: to teach you that as a particular garment has both special marks and them that lay claim to it, so everything must be proclaimed which has both special marks and them that lay claim to it."[38]

There seems to be a correlation between the type of mark on the mantle and the color of the garment. The entire range of colors on all the textiles comprises about

Fig. 11.1. Tunic with purple clavi. From Yadin, *The Finds from the Bar Kokhba Period in the Cave of Letters*, pl. 66.

Fig. 11.3. Gamma-shaped design from a mantle. From Yadin, *The Finds from the Bar Kokhba Period in the Cave of Letters*, pl. 67.

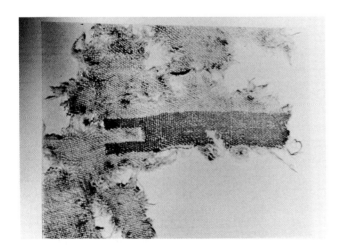

Fig. 11.2. Notched decoration from a mantle. From Yadin, *The Finds from the Bar Kokhba Period in the Cave of Letters*, pl. 68.

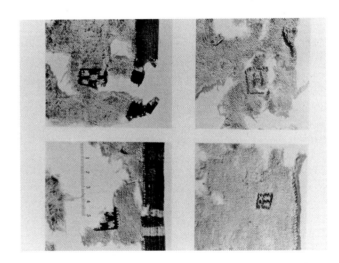

Fig. 11.4. Weavers' marks from mantles. From Yadin, *The Finds from the Bar Kokhba Period in the Cave of Letters*, pl. 69.

thirty-four colors, mostly shades of red, yellow, brown, blue, purple, and green. The mantles with notched bands are dyed in light colors obtained from saffron. The mantles with gammas are dyed in a variety of deep colors, such as reddish brown.[39] Color differentiated women's garments from men's. Sifre Deuteronomy 115b states explicitly that "a woman shall not wear a man's white garments and a man shall not wear colored garments." There is, however, some evidence that this prohibition was not always strictly obeyed. A discussion in the Babylonian Talmud about what someone in mourning may or may not wear relates the following incident: "[During the whole] thirty days the mourner is debarred from donning pressed clothes: it makes no difference whether they be old or new clothes. . . . Rabbi Eleazar, son of Rabbi Simeon, says, 'They only forbade new white linen clothes'. . . . Rabba went out [during the thirty-day mourning period] in a new Roman red tunic, in accordance with Rabbi Eleazar, son of Rabbi Simeon."[40]

Women wear colored clothing to camouflage possible menstrual stains. The Talmud says: "Our rabbis taught: A dyed garment is susceptible to the uncleanness of a bloodstain. R. Nathan ben Joseph ruled: It is not susceptible to the uncleanness of a stain, for dyed garments were ordained for women only in order to relax the law in regard to their bloodstains." Jewish women are forbidden to wear red, however, which signifies the menstrual blood and is considered the color of non-Jewish women.[41] Several passages in the Talmud also indicate that women wear colored garments because they are considered attractive by men; married women are thus permitted to wear colored garments to please their husbands.[42]

It was, incidentally, the duty of a husband to provide clothing for his wife. Mishnah Ketuboth 5:8 states that a husband "must give her a cap for her head and a girdle for her loins, and shoes at every holy day, and clothing worth fifty zuz every year. And he may not give her new garments for summer nor threadbare clothes for winter; but he must give her clothing worth fifty zuz for winter, and she may cover herself with the worn-out ones in summer, and the threadbare ones belong to her."[43]

The differentiation between men's white garments with notched bands and women's colored garments with gamma-form decoration is borne out by the clothing depicted in the paintings of the synagogue of Dura-Europos, which provide the earliest pictorial evidence for Jewish dress (or at least for the dress with which the Jews of the synagogue or the artists they hired clothed biblical figures).[44] In these paintings the Jewish men wear white or off-white mantles with notched bands visible at the lower edges; under the mantle the tunic with clavi is clearly visible (fig. 11.5).[45] The women in the

Dura-Europos paintings all wear colored garments, many in shades of pink or reddish brown and decorated with the gamma shape. In the scene depicting the infancy of Moses on the west wall, the Dura muralist uses differences in costume to characterize the participants. Pharoah and his attendants wear the trousers and long-sleeved tunics characteristic of Persian dress. All the Jewish women—the midwives and the mother and sister of Moses—are dressed in long-sleeved tunics covered by mantles with the gamma-shaped design clearly visible; the maidens who walk beside the river with Pharoah's daughter wear the Greek peplos (fig. 11.6).[46]

Other than the pieces of colored mantles, the only items of women's clothing found in the Cave of Letters are two remnants of hairnets. One of these is black and may have been worn for mourning. The other, of two-ply wool about one millimeter in diameter and firmly twisted, is yellow. Mishnah Kelim 24:16 tells us: "There are three kinds of hairnet: that of a girl, which is susceptible to uncleanness; that of an old woman, which is susceptible to corpse uncleanness; and that of a harlot, which is not susceptible to any uncleanness."[47]

The importance of a woman's head covering is stated unequivocally in the Babylonian Talmud. A woman may be divorced without payment of her marriage contract if she goes out with her hair fully or partially uncovered. The discussion is enlightening.

And what is deemed to be a wife's transgression against Jewish practice? Going out with an uncovered head. Is not the prohibition against going out with an uncovered head Pentateuchal; for it is written, "And he shall uncover the woman's head" (Num. 5:18). And this, it was taught at the school of Rabbi Ishmael, was a warning to the daughters of Israel that they should not go out with uncovered head. Pentateuchally it is quite satisfactory [if her hair is covered by] her work basket. According to traditional Jewish practice, however, she is forbidden to go out uncovered even with her basket on her head.[48]

The question of a head covering is therefore Jewish practice and not mandated by Jewish law. A statement in the Midrash Rabba further elucidates this practice as custom, not law; in discussing the fate of an adulteress, it says, "You have departed from the way of the daughters of Israel, whose habit it is to have their heads covered, and you have walked in the ways of the idolatrous women, who walk about with heads uncovered." The Mishnah, however, also allows for local customs: "Women of Arabia may go out veiled, and women of Medea with their cloaks looped over their shoulders."[49]

The custom of a head covering for a married woman, however, was not limited to the Jews. A passage from Valerius Maximus (6.3.10) describes "the frightful marital severity of Sulpicius Gallus, who dismissed his wife because, as he learned, she had gone about in public

Fig. 11.5. Samuel anointing David, west wall of the synagogue of Dura-Europos. Yale University Art Gallery, The Dura Europos Collection.

Fig. 11.6. The infancy of Moses, west wall of the synagogue of Dura-Europos. Yale University Art Gallery, The Dura Europos Collection.

187

unveiled."[50] Plutarch (*Moralia* 267A) also informs us that it was the custom in the Greek East for women to be veiled. Although this custom among Roman women gradually disappeared, Jewish women maintained the practice; the practice survives today among orthodox Jewish women. Tertullian, writing in Carthage in the mid–second century A.D., says, "Among the Jews, it is so usual for their women to have the head veiled that this is the means by which they may be recognized."[51] The veiling of the head as a sign of modesty was also encouraged for Christian women. Paul writes that "a woman brings shame on her head if she prays or prophesies bareheaded; it is as bad as if her head was shaved. If a woman is not to wear a veil she might as well have her hair cut off; but if it is a disgrace for her to be cropped and shaved, then she should wear a veil" (1 Corinthians 11:5–6).

Only one garment from the Cave of Letters, a small child's shirt, was found nearly intact. Several small sacks tied off with string are attached to the shirt. These sacks were filled alternately with seeds, a large salt crystal, a lump of rat dung, and an assortment of other unidentifiable materials. The sacks indicate a type of custom that has lasted into the twentieth century, that of wearing a garlic clove or a mustard seed to ward off illness. Mishnah Shabbat 6:9 tells us: "Children may go out with bindings. . . . Abaye said, 'Mother told me: three qesharim [bindings] arrest illness before it starts; five cure it; seven are effective even against witchcraft.'"[52]

Among the most interesting items of clothing found in the Cave of Letters are the leather sandals—men's, women's and children's. The sandals are constructed with several layers of leather fastened by means of leather thongs; none bear any trace of the hobnails that characterized the sandal of Roman soldiers.[53] One text, Mishnah Shabbat 6:2, states an injunction regarding the construction of sandals made entirely of leather, as opposed to the Roman hobnailed caligae: "A man may not go out with his sandals shod with nails [on the Sabbath]." Lieberman has pointed out that this prohibition is not necessarily concerned with the Sabbath alone, but the rabbis ascribe it to the Sabbath in order to avoid explaining its true nature.[54] Since most people did not have more than one pair of sandals and the pair they had would have had to have been worn on the Sabbath, the result was that sandals were nailless. A passage in the Babylonian Talmud suggests that the true purpose of the law was probably security:

A nail-studded sandal, what is the reason? Said Samuel: "It was at the end of a period of persecution, and they [some fugitives] were hiding in a cave. They proclaimed, 'He who would enter, let him enter, but he who would go out, let him not go out.' Now, the sandal of one of them became reversed, so that they thought one of them had gone out and had been seen by the enemies, who would now fall upon them. Thereupon they pressed against each other, and they killed more of each other than their enemies slew of them. . . . In that hour it was enacted, A man must not go out with a nail-studded sandal."[55]

This prohibition enabled the Jews to know in advance by the clatter of nail-studded sandals that Roman soldiers were approaching. The injunction against hobnailed sandals remained in the texts even after the danger was over. The Jerusalem Talmud says: "Now, did they not rule this in the time of persecution? Thus since the persecution has passed, it should be permitted [i.e., the wearing of hobnailed sandals]. No Beth-Din [Jewish court] rose to void the previous ruling. If so, it should be forbidden even on weekdays."[56] Thus a custom begun of political necessity became Jewish law.

The material evidence from the Cave of Letters indicates that although the Jews of Palestine did not have any distinctive national costume, the customary dress of tunic and mantle was altered to conform with Jewish law. While some of these alterations might not have been immediately apparent to foreigners, such as the use of a single fiber or the fact that the garments were woven differently, other aspects of the costume were visible enough so that one could identify the wearer as a Jew. The religious injunction requiring the application of tassels, the tzitzit, to the corners of the man's mantle is unique to Jewish costume.[57] Jews who traveled from Palestine to Babylonia were recognized as foreigners by their clothes: "Why are the scholars of Babylonia distinguished in dress? Because they are not in their original homes, as people say, 'In my own town my name is sufficient; away from home, my dress.'"[58] The color restrictions may also have been a distinguishing factor, although this is more difficult to judge from the extant texts.[59] Except for the prohibition against wearing red, Jewish women's garments seem to have been much the same as those worn by other women in the eastern Mediterranean. For both men and women, however, the emphasis on the ritual purity of garments not only for the Sabbath but also in daily usage is a distinguishing feature of Jewish costume. What we can conclude from a comparison of the material remains with the literary sources is that the daily dress of the Jews during the Mishnaic and Talmudic periods reflected a fusion of Graeco-Roman costume and Jewish religious traditions. The elements required by Jewish law made Jewish costume distinctive.

## NOTES

I am deeply indebted to Professor Morton Smith, who was always more than generous in sharing with me his vast knowledge of the history of Palestine and who, with unfailing generosity, assisted me in the preparation of this chapter and other papers and articles I have written. I would also like to thank

Leonard Rutgers of the Center of Judaic Studies of Duke University for his careful reading of the manuscript and for his helpful comments and Rabbi Miriam Shapero for allowing me to see a copy of her unpublished rabbinic thesis, "The Dress System of Traditional Jewry." In the following notes BT is Babylonian Talmud and JT is Jerusalem Talmud. Translations of the Babylonian Talmud are from I. Epstein, ed., *Babylonian Talmud* (London, 1938). Translations of the Mishnah are from P. Blackman, ed., *Mishnayoth*, 6 vols., 2d ed. (Gateshead, 1983). All other translations are my own.

1. Derech Eretz Zuta 10. Only items of clothing will be discussed here; for some of the problems of dealing with jewelry, see E. E. Platt, "Jewelry of Bible Times and the Catalog of Isa. 3: 18–23," *Andrews University Seminaary Studies* 17 (1979): 71–84, 189–201. I would like to thank Professor Marvin Sweeney of the University of Miami, Coral Gables, for bringing this reference to my attention.

2. Yadin, *Finds from the Bar Kokhba Period*, 240f. A number of textiles and items of clothing were found during the Masada excavations, but these remain unpublished. For other studies of Jewish textiles and clothing, see A. Brüll, *Trachten der Juden im nachbiblischen Alterthume* (Frankfurt, 1873); A. Rosenzweig, *Kleidung und Schmuck im biblischen und talmüdische Schrifttum* (Berlin, 1905); M. Shapero, "The Dress System of Traditional Jewry," rabbinic thesis, Hebrew Union College, Jewish Institute of Religion, New York, 1987.

3. Y. Yadin, *Bar Kokhba: The Rediscovery of the Legendary Hero of the Last Jewish Revolt against Imperial Rome* (London, 1971), 124–33, 8.

4. Kraeling, *Synagogue*.

5. E. Schürer, *The History of the Jewish People in the Age of Jesus Christ*, 175 B.C.–A.D. 135, 3 vols., rev. and ed. G. Vermes, F. Millar, and M. Goodman (Edinburgh, 1986) 1:70–78.

6. Mishnah Baba Qamma 10:9.

7. I. Mendelsohn, "Guilds in Ancient Palestine," *Bulletin of the American Schools of Oriental Research* 80 (1940); 17–21; J. Juster, *Les Juifs dans l'empire romain*, vol. 2 (Paris, 1914), 307.

8. Clement of Alexandria, 2.20.116, ed. 0. Stählin, vol. 1, 170; Pausanias 5.5.2.

9. M. Avi-Yonah, "Scythopolis," *Israel Exploration Journal* 12 (1962): 123–36, 132.

10. G. Alon, *The Jews in Their Land in the Talmudic Age*, vol. 1 (Jerusalem, 1980), 170; Juster, *Juifs* 2: 307; Mendelsohn, "Guilds," 20 and n. 41.

11. Tosefta Sukka 4:6; BT Sukka 51b: JT Sukka 5:55b. Translation in Alon, *Jews*, 171.

12. Brüll, *Trachten*, 31–64, S. Krauss, *Griechische und lateinishe Lehnwörter im Talmud, Midrasch und Targum*, vol. 2 (Berlin, 1899), 641–43; idem, *Talmüdische Archäologie*, vol. 1 (1910; New York, 1979), 159–60; Schürer, *History of the Jewish People* 2: 70–71.

13. BT Shabbat 120a; Brüll, *Trachten*, 31–40; Krauss, *Talmüdische Archäologie* 1: 164–75. Rabbi Jose lived ca. A.D. 130. *Bracae* here probably refers to any type of trousers and not specifically to the military trousers worn by Roman equestrian soldiers. The only illustration of a Jew wearing trousers is that on the Sabratha Vespasian cuirass statue, where a Jewish pris-

oner is wearing long trousers. No trousers are mentioned in the list of clothing removed from a bath which is recorded in the Tosefta Derech Eretz.

14. Tosefta Derech Eretz, Perek Ha Niknas 1. A shorter variation is found in Derech Eretz Rabba 2:3, where the order is given as the head covering, shoes, trousers or undergarments, and the haluq. The undergarment listed as an epikarsion is mentioned in other Jewish texts: see Krauss, *Talmüdische Archäologie* 1: 165, and esp. 597 n. 504; and idem, *Lehnwörter* 2:113. Liddell and Scott's *Greek-English Lexicon* defines *epikarsion* as a striped garment known only from the eastern provinces. The Greek examples cited are found in U. Wilcken, *Griechische Ostraka aus Ägypten und Nubien* (Leipzig, 1899), 64 (dating to the second century A.D.); and B. Grenfell and A. S. Hunt, eds., *Oxyrhynchus Papyri* (London, 1898), 921.14 (dating to the third century A.D.).

15. A Rubens, *A History of Jewish Costume* (New York, 1973), 8. The prohibition against the mixing of fibers also reflects the general Mediterranean regard of wool as a holy fiber not to be mixed with other fibers; see Pley, "De lanae." I would like to thank Professor Judith Sebesta for bringing this reference to my attention. On the costume of the high priest, see D. Edwards, chap. 9 in this volume.

16. Cf. Numbers 15:38.

17. Yadin, *Finds from the Bar Kokhba Period*, 170, pl. 59.

18. Tosefta Berachot 7:5.

19. Mishnah Shabbat 7:2.

20. Yadin, *Finds from the Bar Kokhba Period*, 205, pls. 63–66, 73–79. We look forward to the publication of the Masada textiles.

21. Ibid., 209.

22. JT Shabbat 15a, 209.

23. Mishnah Negaim 11:9; Tosefta Kelim 5:1.

24. Bonfante-Warren, "Roman Costume," 614, s.v. "tunica"; Yadin, *Finds from the Bar Kokhba Period*, 209.

25. BT Mo'ed Katan 10a.

26. JT Mo'ed Katan 80d: JT Negaim 11:10.

27. Tosefta Tohoroth 8:13.

28. Yadin, *Finds from the Bar Kokhba Period*, 221, pls. 78, 80.

29. Tosefta Tohoroth 8:12; Shapero, "Dress System," 49.

30. BT Baba Bathra 57b; BT Shabbat 118b.

31. Exodus Rabbah 18:5. For a comparable, Roman view that clothing revealed one's character, see L. Bonfante's introduction and J. Heskel, chap. 7, in this volume.

32. JT Peah 8:7; cf. Genesis Rabbah 12:2 and BT Shabbat 119a.

33. Mishnah Mikvaoth 9:6; Shapero, "Dress System," 50f.

34. BT Shabbat 114a; Mishnah Mikvaoth 9:6.

35. Mishnah Me'ila 6:4; BT Shabbat 128a and Baba Metzia 86b. See D. Sperber, *Roman Palestine, 200–400: Money and Prices* (Ramat Gan, Israel, 1974), 103–6. A dinar is one silver denarius, see Schürer, *History of the Jewish People* 2: 65.

36. Yadin, *Finds from the Bar Kakhba Period*, 222f.

37. JT Shabbat 105a; Yadin, *Finds from the Bar Kokhba Period*, 231, pls. 67–69, 81–85. In later Christian art the gamma-shaped ornament becomes the *gammadia*, which decorates the mantles of the Apostles and the altar cloth.

38. Yadin, *Finds from the Bar Kokhba Period*, 225; Mishnah Baba Metziah 2:5.

39. Yadin, *Finds from the Bar Kokhba Period*, pl. 58 and p. 225.

40. BT Mo'ed Katan 23a. Rabbi Eleazar, son of Rabbi Simeon, who lived ca. A.D. 160–200, forbade new pressed clothes only if they were white.

41. BT Nidda 61b; Shapero, "Dress System," 45.

42. BT Ketuboth 71a; BT Pesah 109a; Shapero, "Dress System," 42f.

43. *Zuz* is the Semitic word for a silver denarius; see Schürer, *History of the Jewish People* 2: 65f.

44. See Kraeling, *Synagogue*, and Goodenough, *Jewish Symbols*, vols. 9–11, on the Dura-Europos synagogue. On the synagogue and the costumes depicted in its paintings, see B. Goldman, chap. 10 in this volume.

45. Kraeling, *Synagoge*, pls. 52–53. Goodenough, *Jewish Symbols* 9: 187; the tzitzit on the corners of the tallit are clearly visible only on Moses' mantle in the scene of the crossing of the Red Sea (11: pl. 14).

46. Kraeling, *Synagogue*, pl. 67; Goodenough, *Jewish Symbols* 9: 199–204; 11: pl. 9.

47. Yadin, *Finds from the Bar Kokhba Period*, 248, pl. 100. Netting of this or a similar type apparently had other uses. Further along, in Mishnah Kelim 28:9, we read, "A harlot's shift that is made like net work is not susceptible to uncleanness."

48. BT Ketuboth 72b. Rabbi Ishmael lived ca. A.D. 90–130. On the veiling of Roman women, see L. La Follette, chap. 3, and J. Sebesta, chap. 2, in this volume.

49. Midrash Rabba Numbers 9:16; cf. 9:33. Mishnah Shabbat 6:6.

50. F. Münzer, "Sulpicius," n. 66, *RE*, 2d ser., vol. 7 (1931), 808–11. MacMullen, "Women in Public," 208–18. The incident, although reported in the second century A.D., took place in the second century B.C. I would like to thank Professor Judith Sebesta for bringing this reference to my attention.

51. Tertullian, *De corona militis* 4. E. Noeldechen, "Tertullian von dem Kranze," *Zeitschrift für Kirchengeschichte* 11 (1890): 377–78.

52. See Yadin, *Finds from the Bar Kokhba Period*, 256, pl. 89.

53. Ibid., 165–68, pl. 57. A nail-studded sandal was found recently in a cave at Ketef Jericho, along with other objects that date to the period of the Bar Kokhba revolt A.D. 132–35: see H. Eshel, "Finds and Documents from a Cave at Ketef-Yeriho," *Qadmoniot* 21 (1988): 22 (Hebrew); and idem, "How I Found a Fourth-Century B.C. Papyrus Scroll on My First Time Out!" *Biblical Archaeology Review* 15.5 (1989): 50–51. Eshel points out that this newly discovered nail-studded sandal indicates that Yadin's assumption that the passages in the Talmud concerning the prohibition against such sandals referred to the first Jewish revolt against Rome (A.D. 66–73) is erroneous.

54. S. Lieberman, *Hellenism in Jewish Palestine* (New York, 1962), 139f.

55. BT Shabbat 60a. On nail-studded shoes, see N. Goldman, chap. 6 in this volume.

56. JT Shabbat 8a.

57. Tassels and fringes applied to the corners of a man's mantle are known in other civilizations, but it is not clear whether they have any meaning or are merely decorations. On Etruscan tassels, see Bonfante, *Etruscan Dress*, 2–132 passim. On tasseled garments of Eastern peoples, see S. Bertman, "Tasseled Garments in the Eastern Mediterranean," *Biblical Archaeologist* 24, no. 4 (1960); 119–28.

58. BT Shabbat 146b.

59. See quotation of BT Mo'ed Katan 23a, above, where the tunic is explicitly referred to as a Roman red tunic.

# Costume as Geographic Indicator: Barbarians and Prisoners on Cuirassed Statue Breastplates

## 12

RICHARD A. GERGEL

The Roman imperial cuirassed statue depicts its subject dressed in the full military parade costume of a triumphant general.[1] Erected throughout the Roman world in honor of reigning and deceased emperors, members of the imperial family, victorious generals, local heroes, and also in honor of Mars, the god of war, the Roman imperial cuirassed statue portrait functioned as an important form of honorific dedication. Approximately six hundred complete and fragmentary examples attest to the popularity of this statue type, and the list of known works increases annually through the discovery of additional examples at archaeological sites in Europe, North Africa, and the Near East.[2] Through the iconography of its breastplate composition and lappet motifs, the cuirassed statue not only provides a rich visual medium for celebrating the military victories of the Roman emperor but also documents the course of Roman territorial expansion throughout the Mediterranean world.

This chapter deals with the costume and iconography of the Roman imperial cuirassed portrait statue. Emphasis will be placed, however, on the iconographic embellishment of the cuirassed statue breastplate. Examining six principal types, ranging in date from the age of Augustus through the reign of Trajan, the discussion will focus on the use of costume to identify the national origin of barbarians and captives depicted on breastplate compositions. Depending largely on *comparanda* drawn from numismatic sources, this chapter will identify the attributes used in the representation of foreign peoples in cuirassed statue iconography. It will be shown that cuirassed statue iconography relies on standardized types, characterized by readily identifiable features, rather than on actual appearance in the representation of vanquished nations and foreign peoples. It is, however, first

necessary to familiarize the reader with the different costume elements of the cuirassed portrait statue.

The full costume of the cuirassed portrait statue comprises several garments. The cuirass itself is made in two main sections, the breastplate (front plate) and the dorsal plate (back plate), which usually join together with a hinge along the right side of the torso and fasten at the left side through a system of pins and hooks. In addition, shoulder straps (epomydes) help to secure the front and back plates of the cuirass together. The epomydes, which are permanently attached to the dorsal plate, pass over the shoulders and fasten to the breastplate through a system of leather thongs and ring hooks.

Beneath the cuirass the figure wears two garments. Nearer to the body is a short-sleeved linen tunic which falls over the legs to just above the knees. Over this the figure wears a protective vestlike jacket made of quilted wool or leather material. A single row of long leather straps falls over the upper legs from the lower edge of the vest, and short leather straps trim the armholes. Over the cuirass the figure customarily wears the large rectangular paludamentum, or military cloak. Clearly distinguishable from the sagum of the common foot soldier by its greater size and distinctive purple-red color, the paludamentum is a requisite element of the cuirassed statue costume. Although several rare examples, such as the Augustus of Prima Porta (see fig. 12.1), show the paludamentum wrapped around the hips, the garment is usually worn draped over the upper torso and fastened at either the left or right shoulder by means of a fibula, or pin.

Additional costume elements frequently associated with the cuirassed portrait statue include the cingulum and the balteus. The cingulum is a ceremonial sash or

Fig. 12.1. Augustus of Prima Porta. Vatican Museums, inv. 2290. Photo: Alinari/Art Resource, New York, 1318.

Fig. 12.2. Augustus of Prima Porta, detail. Photo from DAI, Rome, neg. 62.1788.

Fig. 12.4. Augustus of Prima Porta, detail showing the province of Hispania on the breastplate. Photo: Musei Vaticani, Archivio Fotografico XXXI.2.96.

Fig. 12.3. Augustus of Prima Porta, detail showing the principal scene at the center of the breastplate. Photo: Musei Vaticani, Archivio Fotografico XXXI.2.98.

Fig. 12.5. Augustus of Prima Porta, detail showing the province of Gaul on the breastplate. Photo: Musei Vaticani, Archivio Fotografico XXXI.1.103.

military belt which is wrapped once, but sometimes twice, around the waist and tied at the front with an elaborate Hercules knot, or square knot, to protect the bearer from evil. In addition, a number of figures also wear a balteus, or baldric, which is slung diagonally across the torso from the right shoulder to support a scabbard over the left hip.

It should be noted that the Romans employed two basic armor types in the design of their cuirassed portrait statues: the so-called classical and Hellenistic cuirasses.[3] The Roman imperial "classical" cuirass is based on an armor type that developed in Greece in the fifth and fourth centuries B.C. Its principal characteristics include a modeled surface, which imitates the musculature of the human figure, and a curved lower edge (see figs. 12.6, 12.7, 12.10, 12.11, 12.13, and 12.19). In addition, one or more rows of round or long tongue-shaped hinged lappets (also known as tabs, or pteryges) are fastened to the lower edge of the cuirass. The characteristic appearance of the Roman "classical" cuirass shows, therefore, one or more rows of hinged lappets which hang over the single row of long leather straps attached to the lower edge of the underlying vest. The Roman imperial "Hellenistic" cuirass, on the other hand, developed in the late first century B.C. Its origins can be traced back, however, to a bell-shaped cavalry-style cuirass which had been popularized in the late fourth century B.C. by Alexander the Great.[4] Although the Alexandrian cavalry-style cuirass remained in use well into the late empire, the late first century B.C. witnessed the evolution of a variant "Hellenistic" cuirass type which emulated the greater length, modeled surface, and curved lower edge of its "classical" counterpart. The two predominant cuirassed statue armor types differ actually in only one fundamental aspect. Instead of having hinged lappets, the Roman imperial "Hellenistic" cuirass has a single row of short leather straps attached to its lower edge. The characteristic appearance of the "Hellenistic" cuirass shows, therefore, a single row of short leather straps which hang over the single row of long leather straps attached to the lower edge of the underlying vest (see figs. 12.1, 12.12, and 12.18).

While most cuirassed statue breastplates are decorated with standardized subjects such as pendant griffins, griffins facing candelabra, or winged Victories lighting incense burners, approximately 150 examples bear more complex compositions which can be associated with specific military victories and events in Roman history. Many of these depict barbarian prisoners and captives whose identity can be established only on the basis of costume. The result is a form of narrative, similar to that found on Roman numismatic reverse types, which employs a combination of allegorical symbols, geographic personifications, and visual references to relay its message of imperial victory to the observer.

The representation of barbarians and captives on cuirassed statue breastplates begins with the Augustus of Prima Porta in the Vatican Museum (figs. 12.1–5).[5] This important work, which was discovered on April 20, 1863, at the Villa of Livia at Prima Porta outside Rome, preserves not only one of the earliest but also the most elaborate of all Roman imperial cuirassed statue breastplate compositions. The breastplate employs a combination of mythological figures, symbolic representations, and allegorical personifications to convey its message of imperial victory to the observer. It celebrates the return, negotiated by Augustus in 20 B.C., of Roman military standards which previously had been lost to the Parthians by Crassus in the battle of Carrhae in 53 B.C. and by L. Decidius Saxa and Marcus Antonius in later encounters with the Parthians in 40 and 36 B.C. Augustus considered the return of these standards, achieved without recourse to war, to be one of his greatest accomplishments. In his own *Res gestae*, Augustus wrote: "From Spain, Gaul, and the Dalmatians, I recovered, after conquering the enemy, many military standards which had been lost by other generals. The Parthians I compelled to restore to me the spoils and standards of three Roman armies, and to seek as suppliants the friendship of the Roman people. These standards I deposited in the inner shrine which is in the Temple of Mars Ultor."[6] The center of the breastplate (fig. 12.3) allegorizes this event and shows a representative of the Parthian nation handing an eagle-crested standard to a Roman dressed in military costume.

The thematic focus of this breastplate, however, is not on military victory, but on pacification. The iconography of the principal scene makes this clear. The main subject occurs under the watchful protection of Caelus, the sky god, who draws a blanket of protective clouds over the scene from above. At the lower edge of the breastplate reclines a female figure who personifies the wealth and abundance of the earth. She wears a chiton and a himation, has a wreath on her head, and balances a cornucopia over her lap with her right arm. Two infant children play at her side, a grain stalk and a poppy flower grow at her feet, and a tambourine rests against her right foot. She has variously been identified as Tellus, the earth goddess, Italia, the personification of Italy, Terra Mater, the earth mother, Magna Mater, the great mother, Ceres, goddess of the grain harvest, and Cybele, the Eastern earth goddess.[7] Whichever identification is preferred, the essential meaning remains clear: the Golden Age of Augustus has brought peace and prosperity to the Roman world.

The iconography of the breastplate also proclaims the

dawning of a new day for Rome. Across the upper left and center of the breastplate appears Sol, the sun god, driving a chariot pulled by four horses. He is dressed in a long chiton and wears his himation tied around his waist. Before him flies the winged dew goddess. She carries a pitcher and wears a long chiton belted high above her waist. On her back she carries Aurora, the goddess of the morning light. Aurora carries a torch with her left hand and wears a mantle which billows out over her head. To the left and right of the main scene appear Apollo and Diana, the patron deities of Augustus. Apollo, who is at the left, sits on a griffin, his symbol, and holds a lyre. At the right is Diana, who holds a torch and rides a stag. Slightly above these two deities and immediately to the left and right of the principal scene are two seated female figures who personify provinces already pacified by Augustus. A decorated trophy and the left wing of a Victory also appear on the back of the cuirass over the right hip. The visual references to Apollo and Diana, to Sol in his chariot, to the earth and prosperity, and to the triumph over the Parthians evoke a striking visual parallel to the Golden Age imagery of the *Carmen saeculare* composed by Horace in 17 B.C.[8]

A full understanding of the breastplate composition depends, however, on the identification of the two figures of the principal scene (fig. 12.3) and on the identity of the accompanying provincial personifications who appear slightly above and to the left and right of the central group (figs. 12.4–5). The left figure of the central group is clearly a Roman. Dressed in the full military costume of a Roman officer, he wears an undecorated "classical" cuirass embellished with a double row of large, plain tongue-shaped lappets. Beneath the cuirass he wears a short-sleeved tunic and a quilted wool or leather vest trimmed with a single row of leather straps at the shoulders and below the waist. He also wears a paludamentum fastened over his left shoulder, a narrow cingulum wrapped once around his waist, military boots, and a helmet. Since he is engaged in a peaceful mission, his sword, which he holds by its pommel, remains sheathed in its scabbard.

The identity of this figure has been much discussed. He has often been identified as the youthful Tiberius, but the figure is much too generalized to be a portrait, nor is there any evidence that Tiberius played a role in the return of the standards.[9] Identifications with Mars, Aeneas, and Romulus have also been proposed, but the figure does not conform to any of the standard iconographic types associated with these individuals.[10] Any attempt at identifying the military officer on the breastplate as a particular historical figure is, moreover, doomed to failure. This would run counter to standard breastplate iconographic practice, which customarily relies on symbol and allegory to relay its message to the viewer. The military figure can only be understood, therefore, as a symbol of Roman strength or as a personification of Roman military might.[11] The presence of the camp dog at the figure's side supports this view. As an allegorical personification of the Roman army, the military figure accepts the symbolic return of a captured standard from his barbarian counterpart.

The figure returning the standard typifies the Roman conception of an Eastern barbarian in costume and appearance. The figure is bareheaded and has medium-length hair and a full beard. He wears a loose-fitting tunic girt at the waist. He also wears the loose-fitting trousers customarily worn by all Eastern barbarians, whether they are Parthian, Armenian, or Dacian. His identification as a Parthian, rather than as an Armenian, can be verified, however, on the basis of numismatic evidence. On contemporary reverse types of the Augustan Age, Parthians are always shown wearing short tunics and appear bareheaded, while Armenians are customarily depicted wearing loose-fitting trousers, long, flowing robes, and either a tiara or a round cap.[12] As for the Dacians, although they are always shown wearing loose-fitting trousers, they are also customarily represented wearing tight-fitting long-sleeved jackets and Phrygian caps.

The possible identity of the Parthian figure has also been much discussed. If the Roman is Tiberius, then it is thought that the Eastern barbarian must be Phraates IV, the Parthian king who returned the standards to the Romans. If the figure in military costume represents Mars or Romulus, it has been suggested that the barbarian should be Mithridates I, the founder of the Parthian nation.[13] Since all of the proposals are purely speculative, it is best simply to identify the Eastern barbarian on the breastplate as an allegorical personification of Parthia.[14]

The identification of the two female provincial personifications flanking the central scene is also problematic, since no exact counterparts to these figures exist either in numismatic reverse imagery or in the plastic arts to aid in their identification. By their attitudes, their lowered heads and dejected looks, it is clear that they represent pacified peoples, but they lack the customary crowns and associative symbols of prosperity and cultural assimilation that usually accompany provincial personifications. They are, it appears, unique to the Prima Porta breastplate.

Differing opinions have been offered on their identification, but, considering their placement in direct association with the principal scene on the breastplate, they can only be understood in the context of the return of the captured standards. The figure on the left (fig. 12.4) sits in deep sorrow, resting her head against her left hand.

She has her long hair gathered together at the back of her head and wears a long-sleeved tunic, a fringed mantle, and open-toed sandals. With her extended right hand she holds a short sword embellished with an eagle-headed handgrip. Her weapon has been identified as a *gladius Hispaniensis,* and hence she probably represents the province Hispania, which has been conquered by Augustus and Agrippa but not yet fully pacified.[15] The female personification on the right (fig. 12.5) sits with downcast eyes. She has her long hair held in place by a fillet and wears a long-sleeved tunic, a long mantle, and open-toed sandals. She holds an empty sworth sheath in her left hand and a dragon-headed trumpet in her right. On the ground before her lies a Celtic military standard decorated with a wild boar. Based on the dragon trumpet, the empty sword sheath, and the boar standard, she probably represents Gaul, recently pacified and fully disarmed.[16] The trophy on the back of the cuirass is often associated with the adjacent personification of Gaul on the breastplate, but it may refer to Dalmatia, since in his *Res gestae* Augustus boasted that he obtained the return of previously lost standards from Spain, Gaul, Dalmatia, and Parthia.[17]

Augustus obtained the return of the lost standards from the Parthians in 20 B.C. and celebrated his victory with a triumph in Rome the following year. Thus, the Vatican statue reflects a portrait type which can date no earlier than 20 B.C., and it may, in all likelihood, have been commissioned at the time of the Parthian triumph in 19 B.C. If, however, the Prima Porta Augustus is a copy of a lost original, as has often been suggested, it may actually date much later during the emperor's reign or may even be a posthumous dedication made specifically for display at Livia's villa at Prima Porta. Nevertheless, the original which it copies can only have been made around 19 B.C. or shortly thereafter.

The Prima Porta Augustus occupies a unique position in the development of the Roman imperial cuirassed portrait statue. It preserves the earliest example of a decorated breastplate used to celebrate a specific event from Roman history, and it does this, moreover, through a complex iconographic program. Gods, mythological figures, provincial personifications, allegorical representations, and visual symbols are combined to present a complicated allegory of imperial victory to the observer. Later breastplates, however, rely on less sophisticated means to relay their messages to the observer. In this respect, the complex iconographic program of the Prima Porta statue had little influence on the development it initiated.

Subsequent works of the Julio-Claudian period employ a simpler means of expression to achieve more direct visual impact by eliminating the multiple levels of imagery of the Augustan example in favor of a more

economical use of symbol and allegory. Costume and attributes remain, however, the primary means for establishing the identity of the pacified peoples and conquered territories represented on breastplate compositions. The results, although still often quite complex, may appear less impressive, but they produce a didactic message of greater clarity. A well-known example in the Lateran collection of the Vatican Museum (fig. 12.6) exemplifies the somewhat more simplified, but refined, iconography of the cuirassed statue breastplate during the Julio-Claudian period.[18]

A complex composition decorates the breastplate of the Lateran statue. Helios, in a four-horse chariot, rises forward over a stylized sea. The horses of the *quadriga* flare out, two to each side, to reveal the sun god in frontal view within the car of his chariot. He is shown radiate, with rays of light emanating from his head, and wearing a tunic and mantle. Below Helios, at the center of the breastplate, appear two Arimaspes positioned back-to-back to either side of an acanthus stalk. The Arimaspes have full beards and medium-length hair. Both wear Phrygian caps (symbols of their Eastern origin), loose-fitting trousers, and short-sleeved chitons girt low across the waist with an ample overfold. The Arimaspes bend down on one knee to offer drinks, in libation dishes (omphaloid *phialai*), to pendant griffins. The Arimaspes were a legendary one-eyed people who lived north of the Scythians in central Asia, in the region of the Ural Mountains and north of Baktria (modern Iran).[19] According to some accounts, the Arimaspes lived near a river rich with gold sand, from which they obtained their great wealth, but according to a Scythian legend recorded by Herodotus, they obtained their vast treasure by secretly stealing the gold guarded by the griffins.[20] Clearly it is the latter account that inspires the iconography of the Lateran breastplate. The meaning of this composition is clear: the Romans have gained control over the wealth of the East, just as the Arimaspes obtained possession of the gold of the griffins. The Lateran breastplate exemplifies, moreover, a purely symbolic approach to cuirassed statue iconography. References to Helios rising over the sea in his chariot and to Arimaspes giving drinks to griffins establish a dual topographic reference to the East, and the wealth of the Arimaspes provides a fitting corollary to Roman control over the riches of the Orient.

Based on the criteria of style and execution, the Lateran statue dates between A.D. 40 and 60 and must therefore commemorate an Eastern victory celebrated either during the reign of Claudius (31–54) or Nero (54–68). The most likely historical association for the subject of the Lateran breastplate is with the Eastern campaign undertaken by Domitius Corbulo against the

Armenians and Parthians during the middle years of Nero's reign. After several years of conflict, Corbulo brought the problematic situation in the East to a satisfactory resolution in 60. Although Nero declined to take a new title to celebrate Corbulo's Armenian victory, a numismatic reverse type bearing the legend ARMENIAC was issued at Caesarea.[21] The Lateran breastplate, with its strictly symbolic use of visual vocabulary, demonstrates the viability of the cuirassed statue breastplate as a primary didactic vehicle for commemorating the course of Roman territorial expansion.

Although barbarians and captives appear frequently on Julio-Claudian statues, the full exploitation of their use on breastplate compositions first occurs during the Flavian period (A.D. 69–96) and commences with the celebration of the Flavian conquest of Judaea under Vespasian and Titus. Settlement of the military situation in Judaea had been placed in the capable hands of Vespasian during the last years of Nero's reign, and fighting continued through the brief reigns of Galba, Otho, and Vitellius. Soon after his nomination to the rank of Augustus by the Eastern legions in the spring of 69, Vespasian departed from Judaea to lay claim to the throne in Rome and placed his son Titus in charge of military activities in the East. Titus completed the conquest of Judaea in 70 and returned to Rome to celebrate a joint triumph with his father in September 71. The success of the Jewish war provided Vespasian (69–79) with the military victory he needed to legitimate his seizure of imperial authority and to secure his dynastic ambitions that his sons Titus (79–81) and Domitian (81–96) should succeed him. Vespasian took, therefore, great care to advertise the military successes which he and his son had achieved in Judaea.

A remarkable cuirassed statue from Sabratha in Libya (fig. 12.7) celebrates the Flavian conquest of Judaea.[22] The Sabratha statue was found in the exedra of the basilica in the forum of this city along with a second cuirassed statue with a head of Titus.[23] Both statues appear to be products of the same workshop, and since the better-preserved example of the two has survived with a head of Titus, it has logically been assumed that the headless second statue must be a portrait of Vespasian. As the reigning emperor, Vespasian celebrates, along with Titus, the overseas Roman conquest of Judaea. The Sabratha statue can date no earlier than the celebration of the Judaean triumph in 71 but may have been set up as late as the death of Titus in 81.

The breastplate of the Sabratha statue proclaims its subject through a combination of symbol and allegory. A Medusa head, which serves as a talismanic device to protect the wearer, decorates the chest of the cuirass. Near the center of the breastplate appears a date palm.

Although palm trees are cultivated throughout the Mediterranean region, Flavian iconographers employ the date palm as a specific topographic symbol for Judaea. To the left of the palm tree stands a winged Victory. Nude from the waist up, she wears her mantle draped about her hips as she leans forward to inscribe a victory slogan on a shield, which she hangs on the trunk of the palm tree. The inscription, which would have been added in colored pigment, has not survived, but probably echoed the IUDAEA CAPTA or IUDAEA DEVICTA slogans of contemporary numismatic reverse types.[24]

To the right of the palm tree stands a single male Jewish captive. Defeated but proud, he stands with his hands bound behind his back. Stripped of his clothing, he wears only a simple sagum, the military cloak of the common foot soldier, which he wears wrapped around the left side of his body and fastened over his right shoulder with a fibula. Unfortunately, the head of this figure has not survived. A second male captive appears seated below on a pile of oval shields. Defeated but not yet bound and stripped like the figure above, he raises his right hand in vain supplication to the goddess Victoria as he leans back slightly, supporting the weight of his upper torso with his left hand. Perhaps meant to represent a youth, the figure is clean shaven and has medium-length hair brushed straight down to the sides and back of his head. The seated figure also wears a sagum wrapped around his torso and fastened at the right shoulder. Surprisingly, he also wears bracae, the tailored leggings, which the Romans understood as the costume of barbarian peoples. In this particular instance, the costume worn by the two captives on the Sabratha breastplate is principally the product of artistic license and bears no correspondence to actual Jewish costume: Jewish males do not wear trousers. The nude torso of the standing figure and the bracae of the seated figure have been employed for the sole purpose of identifying the Jewish people as yet another Eastern nation which has been humiliated and subdued by Roman might.

Numismatic evidence verifies, nevertheless, the identification of these two figures as Jewish captives. The representation of the standing figure corresponds exactly to representations of male Jewish prisoners on numismatic reverse types issued during the reigns of Vespasian and Titus (fig. 12.8).[25] Accompanied by the legend IUDAEA CAPTA, the variant issues of this well-known reverse type generally show a standing male captive and a seated female prisoner flanking a palm tree. The male captive stands to one side of the palm tree with his hands bound behind his back. He has a full beard and medium-length hair. His only garment is a sagum, which he wears wrapped around the left side of his body and fastens with a fibula over his right shoulder. The accompanying

Fig. 12.6. Julio-Claudian cuirassed statue, detail. Museo Profano, Vatican Museums, inv. 348. Photo from DAI, Rome, neg. 62.1775.

Fig. 12.7. Early Flavian cuirassed statue. Museum of Antiquities, Sabratha, inv. 659. Photo from DAI, Rome, neg. 61.2145.

Fig. 12.8. Sestertius of Vespasian (reverse), A.D. 71. American Numismatic Society, New York. Photo: R. Gergel.

Fig. 12.9. Sestertius of Domitian (reverse), A.D. 85. American Numismatic Society, New York. Photo by D. Darst, from a cast.

female prisoner sits on a pile of polygonal shields in a pose of mourning with her left arm bent up at the elbow to support her lowered head. She is fully draped and wears her mantle drawn up over her head. Her costume, unlike that of the male prisoner, reflects the actual appearance of Jewish women, who were customarily veiled. The hooded figure remains a standard iconographic type in later representations of Jewish captives in Roman art.

Domitian (81–96) employed a modified version of this same coin type to celebrate his various victories against the German tribes (fig. 12.9). Bearing the inscription GERMANIA CAPTA, the new Domitianic reverse type substitutes a decorated trophy for the palm tree of the early Flavian issues.[26] A helmet, sagum, and rectangular shields decorate the trophy. A single male German prisoner stands with his hands bound behind his back to the right of the trophy. He wears a full beard and shoulder-length hair. He is bare-chested but wears tight-fitting trousers and also a mantle, which is fastened around his neck and draped over his left shoulder. The seated mourning female captive wears only a single, long, trailing sleeveless garment and is shown with her head bare. It is interesting to note, moreover, that while Jewish female prisoners are customarily depicted with their heads veiled, German female captives are always shown bareheaded.

To fulfill Vespasian's ambition of establishing a secure northern border along the natural line of the Rhine-Danube frontier, Domitian initiated a series of controversial campaigns against the Germans, Dacians, and Sarmatians. He waged the first of these against the Chatti, a German tribe which threatened Roman interests in the border area north of Mogontiacum (Mainz). In the spring of 83 Domitian entered Gaul on the pretext of undertaking a census of that province, but then he moved into Germany to launch a quick excursion into Chatti territory. He returned to Rome later that year and celebrated his triumph over the Chatti in October 83.

A cuirassed statue in the Musée du Louvre, Paris, probably commemorates the triumph of 83 (fig. 12.10).[27] Although presently restored with a head of Trajan, this statue most likely represents a portrait type set up in 83 to honor Domitian as the new conqueror of Germany. In October of that same year, Domitian assumed the title Germanicus for the first time, and he retained it as an official title for the duration of his reign. Stature, body sway, proportions, shoulder straps, and height of relief all indicate a late Flavian date for this work, and the two rows of lappets are decorated with standard Flavian motifs such as single and double rosettes, palmettes, lion heads, and elephant heads. The head of a bearded water deity, probably Rhenus, the personification of the Rhine River, appears on the chest of the cuirass and provides a topographic reference for identifying the locale of the victory commemorated on the breastplate below. At the center of the breastplate appears a trophy draped with a sagum and crowned with a helmet. Two dancing Victories, wearing long-belted chitons, raise oblong shields with both hands to decorate the trophy. The two bound male captives huddled together at the foot of the trophy are Germans. They wear the tight-fitting trousers customarily worn by Germans and have long hair.

A torso in the Art Museum, Princeton (fig. 12.11), and a statue restored with a head of Trajan in Auch (fig. 12.12), also probably represent Domitian as Germanicus and also probably celebrate his Chatti triumph of 83.[28] The Princeton breastplate shows a single, bound male German captive tied to a trophy flanked by winged Victories carrying shields.[29] The captive, who survives in poor condition, has been stripped of his cloak and wears only the tight-fitting trousers which help to identify him as a German prisoner. He sits on the ground line at the foot of the trophy, bent forward with his knees drawn up to his chest and with his hands tied behind his back. A Medusa head appears on the chest of the cuirass. The Auch statue, which has a "Hellenistic" cuirass, shows two bound captives tied to the foot of the trophy on the breastplate. The left captive wears only bracae, while the right captive wears bracae and a sagum draped over the left side of his body and fastened at his right shoulder with a fibula. A head of the goddess Luna, above a crescent moon, appears on the chest of the cuirass. The Paris, Princeton, and Auch statues illustrate variations on a breastplate type used by Domitian to celebrate his Chatti triumph in 83; all show one or two bound prisoners in German costume tied to the base of a single trophy.

Domitian's iconographers, however, developed a more elaborate breastplate type to celebrate the emperor's double triumph over the Marcomanni and the Dacians in 89. An example of one of the important statue types set up by Domitian to celebrate his double triumph is preserved in the Vatican Museum (fig. 12.13).[30] Restored with a head of Lucius Verus, the Vatican statue has a "classical" cuirass embellished with two rows of richly decorated lappets. Two important lappets of the upper row depict an eagle clutching the underbelly of a hare and provide a basis for associating the Vatican statue with a number of related works that celebrate Domitian's northern wars.[31] The breastplate, which also displays an elaborate iconographic program, employs a combination of barbarian captives and allegorical figures to relay its message of imperial victory to the spectator.

A talismanic Medusa head decorates the chest of the cuirass. At the center stands a winged female (fig. 12.14). She wears a long, sleeveless chiton, which has fallen from her left shoulder to reveal her left breast, and

Fig. 12.10. Late Flavian cuirassed statue. Musée du Louvre, Paris, inv. 1150. Photo: Giraudon/
Art Resource, New York.

Fig. 12.11. Late Flavian cuirassed torso. Art Museum, Princeton University, acc. no. 84-2. Photo: The Art Museum, Princeton University. Museum purchase, Caroline G. Mather Fund.

Fig. 12.12. Late Flavian cuirassed statue, detail. Cliché Samuel, dépôt du Musée du Louvre au Musée des Jacobins, Auch. Photo: Samuel, by courtesy of the Musée des Jacobins, Auch.

Fig. 12.13. Late Flavian cuirassed statue. Galleria delle Statue, Vatican Museums, inv. 420. Photo: Alinari/Art Resource, New York, 1399.

Fig. 12.14. Late Flavian cuirassed statue, detail showing Victoria Augusta and Tellus on the breastplate. Photo from DAI, Rome, neg. 37.747.

Figs. 12.15a and b. Sestertius minted by Domitian under Titus, both sides, A.D. 80–81. American Numismatic Society, New York. Photo by D. Darst, from a cast.

Fig. 12.15b.

also a mantle, which is draped around her right hip and over her left arm. With her left arm she cradles a cornucopia, and with her right hand she holds a palm of victory. While the cornucopia suggests an identification with Fortuna, the palm of victory clearly indicates an association with some aspect of the goddess Victoria. Indeed, based upon a comparison with a sestertius reverse type (see figs. 12.15a and b), which was minted by Domitian under Titus and which bears the legend VICTORIA AVG, it is relatively certain that she represents Victoria Augusta, the goddess of imperial victory.[32] Below this figure reclines a semidraped nymph bearing fruit within the folds of her mantle. As on the breastplate of the Prima Porta Augustus, she represents Tellus, the earth goddess, or Terra Mater, the earth mother, or, perhaps, Italia, the personification of Italy. Her axial juxtaposition to the figure of Victoria Augusta has a twofold meaning. First, her presence suggests the prosperity which Domitian has brought to the Roman world through his military triumphs, and second, her close proximity to Victoria Augusta indicates that the breastplate composition celebrates a military victory on land. At either side of the central group appears a single barbarian captive tied to a trophy. The two trophies provide a definite allusion to the double triumph celebrated by Domitian in 89, and a differentiation between captive types establishes the identities of the vanquished peoples.

The captive on the left (fig. 12.16) is a mature male with a full beard. He is bare-chested but wears shoes, bracae, and a sagum fastened across his chest. He is bound, with his hands tied behind his back, to a trophy that has been draped with a tunic and decorated with a round shield and a helmet with large cheek pieces. A comparison with the standing male captive on the previously discussed Domitianic GERMANIA CAPTA sestertius reverse type (fig. 12.9) demonstrates clearly that the bound prisoner on the left is a German. These representations also correspond with the description Tacitus gives of the Germans, who "all wrap themselves in a cloak which is fastened with a clasp or, if this is not forthcoming, with a thorn, leaving the rest of their persons bare."[33] In this same passage Tacitus describes the tight-fitting undergarments—presumably he means trousers—that are worn by the Germans. These clearly are depicted both on the German prisoner on the sestertius reverse type and on the Marcomanni prisoner on the breastplate.

The barbarian captive on the right (fig. 12.17) is a youth. He wears shoes, bracae, a long-sleeved tunic, a sagum, and a Phrygian-style soft wool cap, or pilleus. His hands are bound beneath his right leg and presumably tied to the adjacent trophy, which has been decorated with a round shield, a polygonal shield, a cuirass, and a helmet. The captive on the right is a Dacian. The identification can be verified on the basis of comparisons with later representations of Dacian captives on Trajanic monuments and by the presence of the Phrygian-style cap, which the Romans recognized as an identifying characteristic of the Dacian people.[34]

A replica of the Vatican statue is in the collection of the British Museum, London (fig. 12.18).[35] Currently restored with a head of Hadrian, the London example displays practically the same breastplate composition as the Vatican statue. The two figures wear, however, different cuirass types. Whereas the Vatican statue perfectly exemplifies the "classical" cuirass embellished with two rows of decorated lappets hanging over a single row of long leather straps, the London statue has a "Hellenistic" cuirass with two rows of overlapping short and long leather straps hanging from its lower edge. Otherwise, the two breastplate compositions differ only in minor details. For example, the palm branch carried by Victoria Augusta on the Vatican example is slightly longer, and the folds of her chiton fall differently across her torso.

Because of similarities between this breastplate and the cuirass relief on the Augustus of Prima Porta, such as the representation of Terra Mater at the lower edge of the breastplate, the visual references to multiple victories, and a comparably ambitious iconographic program, previous scholarship proposed to assign both of these statues to an early imperial context.[36] The style of the breastplate is, however, clearly Domitianic, and the reference to a dual victory over a combination of German and Dacian adversaries can only relate to the celebration of Domitian's double triumph of 89. A comparative analysis of the Augustan and late Flavian breastplate compositions reveals, moreover, a fundamental philosophical difference. Whereas the general theme of the Prima Porta breastplate focuses on victory achieved as the result of peaceful negotiations, the Domitianic examples attest to the overall program of the Flavian dynasty for peace achieved through military conquest and territorial acquisition. The iconography of Victoria Augusta, the Flavian goddess of imperial victory, makes this clear: she carries both the cornucopia and the palm of victory.

Domitian waged one last campaign along the northern border of the empire, against the Sarmatians in 92, before his reign was cut short by an assassin's knife in 96. After his death the Senate proclaimed a *damnatio memoriae* against him.[37] Consequently, nothing substantial survives of the statues and monuments which Domitian undoubtedly erected to celebrate his Sarmatian victory of 92. The majority of his monuments were either dismantled or rededicated by later rulers, and most of his statues were either destroyed or had their

Fig. 12.16. Late Flavian cuirassed statue, detail showing the German captive on the breastplate. Photo from DAI, Rome, neg. 37.745.

Fig. 12.17. Late Flavian cuirassed statue, detail showing the Dacian captive on the breastplate. Photo from DAI, Rome, neg. 37.746.

heads replaced with portraits of his successors. Several years later, the military situation necessitated that Trajan (98–117) lead his troops through much of the same terrain traveled by Domitian in his wars against the Dacians and the Sarmatians. Consequently, it was only natural for Trajan to usurp the victory monuments and statues of his unpopular predecessor for his own use. Many of the statues which we now recognize as Domitianic, on the basis of their execution in a characteristically late Flavian style, may have survived only because they were appropriated for reuse by Trajan.

With the reign of Trajan a significant transformation occurs, moreover, in cuirassed statue breastplate iconography. The specific rendering of barbarian captives which played so prominent a role in documenting the territorial expansion of the Roman Empire during the Flavian period disappears. Instead, the few Trajanic breastplate types which have historical associations employ either a strictly symbolic or a purely allegorical use of topographic reference to relay their message to the viewer, and those examples which do survive date

mainly to the later years of Trajan's reign. Indeed, only two cuirassed statues with portraits of Trajan have survived from the time of the Dacian wars (101–2 and 105–6), and both are decorated with standardized representations of pendant griffins flanking a candelabrum.[38] The absence of a specific breastplate type that can be associated with the conquest of Dacia is unfortunate. Perhaps none was made, perhaps a surplus of available Domitianic statues awaiting reuse satisfied the need for such works, or perhaps Trajan desired to avoid the lavish excess for which his predecessor would be so severely censored by second-century historians. Whatever the reason, it is quite unusual that, thus far, no recognizable breastplate type has been identified that can be associated with the celebration of Trajan's Dacian wars. The situation is quite different, however, with respect to Trajan's Parthian victory and his posthumously awarded triumph, celebrated by Hadrian (117–38), his successor, in 118.

The circumstances which called for Trajan's presence in the East were precipitated by serious political con-

Fig. 12.18. Late Flavian cuirassed statue, detail. British Museum, London, inv. 1895 (currently displayed at Hampton Court). Courtesy of the British Museum.

cerns. A disagreement between Rome and Parthia over the Armenian succession in 113 led to Trajan's expedition to the East and to a series of spectacular military victories which by 117 brought him as far as the shores of the Persian Gulf. These successes also brought him great honors. After Trajan captured Armenia in 114, "the Senate voted to him all the usual honors in great plenty and furthermore bestowed upon him the title of *optimus*, or Most Excellent."[39] After he captured the Parthian cities of Nisibis and Batnae, the Senate, on February 12, 116, rewarded him with the title Parthicus, "Conqueror of Parthia."

A small group of closely related statues appear to celebrate Trajan's Parthian victory and posthumous triumph. The most important of these is a cuirassed statue of Trajan in the Sackler Museum (figs. 12.19–20).[40] The Sackler breastplate shows a female Arimaspe fighting two griffins. The Arimaspe, shown moving to her right, falls to her knees as she wards off the coordinated attack of two rampant griffins. In self-defense, she grabs the throat of the right griffin with her left hand as she plunges a knife, which she wields with her right hand, into the breast of the griffin on the left. She wears a high-girded short chiton which has fallen down from her shoulders to expose her upper body, and a Phrygian cap, which provides a topographic reference to her Eastern origins. While standardized Trajanic motifs and floral subjects decorate the majority of the rectangular lappets which hang in two rows from the lower edge of the cuirass, several are embellished with representations of bovine skulls. Cornelius Vermeule, noting that this motif appears on no other cuirassed statue, has interpreted its presence as a sign of Trajan's apotheosis.[41] The statue must date, according to Vermeule, shortly after 117 and would have been set up as a posthumous dedication in honor of Parthicus Divus Trajanus Augustus, the "divine Trajan Augustus, conqueror of Parthia." The use of the motif of an Arimaspe fighting griffins to celebrate Trajan's Parthian victory echoes the use of male Arimaspes giving drinks to griffins on the previously examined late Julio-Claudian statue (fig. 12.6) which celebrated an earlier resolution of the Armenian problem during the reign of Nero. To Romans of both ages, the victory of the Arimaspes over the griffins symbolized Roman control over the wealth and political fortunes of the East.

For almost a century and a half, from Augustus through Trajan, the cuirassed statue breastplate documented the acquisition of new territories and the assimilation of new peoples within the expanding borders of the empire. The use of costume played an important role in identifying the barbarian nations and captives represented on these breastplates. With the reign of Trajan,

Fig. 12.19. Cuirassed statue of Trajan. Courtesy of The Arthur M. Sackler Museum, Harvard University, Cambridge, Massachusetts, Alpheus Hyatt Fund.

however, the Roman Empire reached its greatest territorial expansion. Under Hadrian this expansion came to an end, and the cuirassed statue breastplate ceased to play an important role in documenting the military victories of the reigning house. Cuirassed statues continued to be made, and often in great numbers, well into the late empire, but breastplate compositions lose their sense of specificity. No longer embellished with references to particular victories, breastplate iconography resorts, more and more, to standardized types that celebrate in generalized fashion the military successes of the ever-victorious emperor and the eternal glory of Rome.

Fig. 12.20. Cuirassed statue of Trajan, detail. Courtesy of The Arthur M. Sackler Museum, Harvard University, Cambridge, Massachusetts, Alpheus Hyatt Fund.

## NOTES

1. Fundamental to the study of Roman imperial cuirassed statues are C. C. Vermeule, "Hellenistic and Roman Cuirassed Statues," *Berytus* 13 (1959): 1–82, with supplements in *Berytus* 15 (1964): 95–110; 17 (1966): 49–59; 23 (1974): 5–26; and 26 (1978): 85–123; and K. Stemmer, *Untersuchungen zur Typologie, Chronologie und Ikonographie der Panzerstatuen* (Berlin, 1978).

2. For lists of known works, see Stemmer, *Untersuchungen,* 168–80; and C. C. Vermeule, *Concordance of Cuirassed Statues in Marble and Bronze* (Boston, 1980).

3. For a concise discussion on the development of cuirassed statue types, see Vermeule, in *Berytus* 13 (1959): 3–31.

4. See C. M. Havelock, *Hellenistic Art,* rev. ed. (New York, 1981), 252–3, pl. 11.

5. The bibliography on the Augustus of Prima Porta is extensive. For references to the earlier writings on this subject, see H. Kähler, *Die Augustusstatue von Primaporta,* Monumenta Artis Romanae 1 (Cologne, 1959), 29–30; and H. G. Niemeyer, *Studien zur statuarischen Darstellung der römischen Kaiser,* Monumenta Artis Romanae 7 (Berlin, 1968), 91–92. See also H. Ingholt, "The Prima Porta Statue of Augustus," *Archaeology* 22 (1969): 176–87, 304–18. For recent discussion on this work and additional bibliography, see G. Daltrop, in *The Vatican Collection: The Papacy and Art* (New York: 1983), 208–9; Zanker, *Power of Images,* 188–92; and J. Pollini, "The Findspot of the Statue of Augustus from Prima Porta," *BCAR* 92 (1987–88): 103–8.

6. *Res Gestae Divi Augusti* 5.29, trans. F. W. Shipley, LCL, (Cambridge, Mass., 1924).

7. For an association with Tellus, see W. Amelung, *Die Sculpturen des Vaticanischen Museum I* (Berlin, 1907), 27; H. von Heintze, "Augustus Prima Porta," in Helbig, 315 (No. 411); F. L. Bastet, "Feldherr mit Hund auf der Augustusstatue von Prima Porta," *BABesch* 41 (1966): 77–90, esp. 79; and Hannestad, *Roman Art,* 56. For Italia, see L. A. Holland, "Aeneas-Augustus of Prima Porta," *TAPA* 22 (1969): 276–84, esp. 280. For Terra Mater, see E. Strong, "Terra Mater or Italia?" *JRS* 27 (1937): 114–26, esp. 115. For Magna Mater, see Kähler, *Augustusstatue,* 19; W. H. Gross, "Zur Augustusstatue von Prima Porta," *Nachrichten der Akademie der Wissenschaften in Göttingen I: Philologisch-historische Klasse* 8 (1959): 143–68, esp. 152 n. 30. For Ceres-Cybele, see E. Simon, *Der Augustus von Prima Porta,* Opus nobile 13 (Bremen, 1959), 10.

8. M. Reinhold and P. T. Alessi, *The Golden Age of Augustus* (Toronto, 1978), 44–45. Except where otherwise noted, the designations *left* and *right* refer to the perspective of the viewer.

9. See F. Studniczka, "Zur Augustusstatue der Livia," *RM* 24 (1916): 27–55, esp. 48; E. Löwy, "Zum Augustus von Prima Porta," *RM* 42 (1927): 203–22, esp. 203; L. Polacco, *Il volto di Tiberio* (Rome, 1955), 160; G. C. Picard, *Les trophées romains* (Paris, 1957), 279; Kähler, *Augustusstatue,* 17–18; Gross, "Zur Augustusstatue," 151; Simon, *Der Augustus,* 8; G. Zinserling, "Der Augustus von Primaporta als offiziöses Denkmal," *Acta Antiqua* 15 (1967): 327–39, esp. 335; Niemeyer, *Studien zur statuarischen Darstellung,* 92; and Hannestad, *Roman Art,* 55.

10. For Mars, see Amelung, *Die Sculpturen,* 22; A. von Domaszewski, "Der Panzerschmuck der Augustusstatue von Primaporta," in *Strena Helbigiana* (Leipzig, 1900), 51–53; A. Alföldi, "Der Panzerschmuck der Augustusstatue von Primaporta," *RM* 52 (1937): 48–63, esp. 54. For Aeneas, see Bastet, "Feldherr," 88–90; and Holland, "Aeneas-Augustus," 279–80. For Romulus, see Ingholt, "Prima Porta Statue," 185–87.

11. Pollini, "Augustan Historical Reliefs," 13–24, provides convincing evidence for identifying the military figure as Exercitus Romanus, the personification of the Roman army. See also von Heintze, in Helbig 316, where the figure is identified as a representative of the Roman Senate and people; and J. P. A. van der Vin, "The Return of Roman Ensigns from Parthia," *BABesch* 56 (1981): 117–39, where it is identified as "a Roman official" (121).

12. For Augustan numismatic reverse types showing Parthians, see H. Mattingly, *Coins of the Roman Empire in the British Museum,* vol. 1, *Augustus to Vitellius* (London, 1983), 3–5, nos. 10–21, pl. 1, figs. 7–9; 8, nos. 41–42, pl. 2, fig. 2; 11, nos. 56–58, pl. 2, fig. 11. For Armenians wearing the tiara, see 5–6, nos. 18–21, pl. 1, figs. 10–11; 8, nos. 43–44, pl. 2, figs. 3–4. For those wearing the round cap, see 109, nos. 676–78, pl. 16, figs. 18–19 (from an Eastern mint).

13. For an association with Phraates IV, see Studniczka, "Zur Augustusstatue," 40; Löwy, "Zum Augustus," 203; Polacco, *Il volto,* 110; Picard, *Trophées romains,* 279; Kähler, *Augustusstatue,* 17–18; Gross, "Zur Augustusstatue," 151; Simon, *Der Augustus,* 8; and Hannestad, *Roman Art,* 55. For Mithridates I, see Domaszewski, "Der Panzerschmuck," 52; and Ingholt, "Prima Porta Statue," 181–85.

14. Pollini, "Augustan Historical Reliefs," 35, identifies the barbarian figure as Parthus, the personification of Parthia. See also Amelung, *Die Sculpturen,* 34; Kähler, *Augustusstatue,* 316; Vin, "Return of Roman Ensigns," 121.

15. For an association with Hispania, see Amelung, *Die Sculpturen,* 24; Domaszewski, "Der Panzerschmuck," 52; K. Woelcke, "Beiträge zur Geschichte des Tropaions: Der Tropaion am Panzer der Augustusstatue von Primaporta," *BJ* 120 (1911): 180–91, esp. 191; Picard, *Trophées romains,* 279; Simon, *Der Augustus,* 9; Pollini, "Augustan Historical Reliefs," 38; Hannestad, *Roman Art,* 555. For an alternate association with Germania, see Alföldi, "Der Panzerschmuck," 48–52; Polacco, *Il volto,* 161; Kähler, *Augustusstatue,* 17; Gross, "Zur Augustusstatue," 152; Zinserling, "Augustus von Primaporta," 334; Niemeyer, *Studien zur statuarischen Darstellung,* 92. H. von Heintze (Helbig 316) proposes Dalmatia or Pannonia. Ingholt, "Prima Porta Statue," 315–17, proposes Armenia.

16. For an association with Gaul or Gallia, see Amelung, *Die Sculpturen,* 24; Domaszewski, "Der Panzerschmuck," 52; Woelcke, "Beiträge zur Geschichte," 191; Picard, *Trophées romains,* 279; Simon, *Der Augustus,* 9; von Heintze, Helbig 315; Pollini, "Augustan Historical Reliefs," 38; Hannestad, *Roman Art,* 55. For an alternate association with Pannonia, see Alföldi, "Der Panzerschmuck," 52; Polacco, *Il volto,* 161. Kähler (*Augustusstatue,* 17) and Gross ("Zur Augustusstatue," 152) propose Dalmatia; H. von Heintze (Helbig 315) proposes Dalmatia or Pannonia. Zinserling ("Augustus von

Primaporta," 334) offers an association with the Danube peoples; Niemeyer (*Studien zur statuarischen Darstellung*, 92) proposes Dalmatia or Dacia; and Ingholt ("Prima Porta Statue," 314–15) proposes Galatia.

17. *Res Gestae Divi Augusti* 5.29. For an association of the trophy with Gaul or Gallia, see G. Loeschke, "Zur Augustusstatue von Prima Porta," *BJ* 114–15 (1906): 470–72; Woelcke, "Beiträge zur Geschichte," 180–91; Picard, *Trophées romains*, 279; Ingholt, "Prima Porta Statue," 312. Gross ("Zur Augustusstatue," 153) and Simon (*Der Augustus*, 9) identify the trophy as Celtic. Zinserling ("Augustus von Primaporta," 335) associates it with the 7–6 B.C. Augustan Trophy of the Alps. Kähler (*Augustusstatue*, 14) and von Heintze (Helbig 17) interpret the trophy as simply a space-filling device added by the copyist.

18. A nonbelonging head, long shown with this statue, has been removed. See Vermeule, in *Berytus* 13 (1959): 38–39, no. 41; and Stemmer, *Untersuchungen*, 96–99, no. VIIa 2, pl. 65, figs. 1–2. A related example is in the Museo di Antichità, Turin. See Vermeule, 39, no. 42, and Stemmer, 96, no. VIIa 1, pl. 65, figs. 1–2.

19. On the Arimaspes, see K. Wernicke, "Arimaspoi," *RE*, vol. 2 (1895), 826–27.

20. Herodotus 3.116; 4.13, 27.

21. See Mattingly, *Coins 1:* 281, nos. 405–8, pl. 40, figs. 16–17.

22. See Vermeule, in *Berytus* 13 (1959): 44, no. 85, pl. 8, fig. 25; and Stemmer, *Untersuchungen*, 62, no. V 10, pl. 38, figs. 1–2.

23. Sabratha, Museum of Antiquities, Statue of Titus. See Vermeule, in *Berytus* 17 (1966): addendum, 59, no. 92A; and Stemmer, *Untersuchungen*, 63, no. V 11, pl. 39, fig. 1.

24. E. Bianco, "Indirizzi programmatici e propagandistici nella monetazione di Vespasiano," *Rivista Italiana di Numismatica* 70 (1968): 158–65.

25. For examples of this reverse type from the mint in Rome, see H. Mattingly, *Coins of the Roman Empire in the British Museum*, vol. 2, *Vespasian to Domitian*, 2d ed. (London, 1976), 115–17, nos. 532–42, pl. 20, figs. 4–7; 256–57, nos. 161–70, pl. 48. figs. 8–10. On the costume of Jews, see L. Roussin, chap. 11 in this volume.

26. For the GERMANIA CAPTA reverse type, see Mattingly, *Coins 2:* 362, no. 294, pl. 70, fig. 8; 369, nos. 325–26, pl. 72, fig. 8; 376, no. 361, pl. 74, fig. 2; 380, no. 372, pl. 75, fig. 4; and 385, no. 395, pl. 76, fig. 6.

27. See Vermeule, in *Berytus* 13 (1959): 46, no. 101; Stemmer, *Untersuchungen*, 14–15, no. I 9, pl. 6, figs. 1–2; and R. A. Gergel, "A Late Flavian Cuirassed Torso in the J. Paul Getty Museum," *GMusJ* 16 (1988): 14 and fig. 6.

28. See R. A. Gergel, "An Allegory of Imperial Victory on a Cuirassed Statue of Domitian," *Record of the* (Princeton) *Art Museum* 45.1 (1986): 3–15; idem, "Late Flavian Cuirassed Torso," 11–12, and figs. 2a–e. See Vermeule, in *Berytus* 13 (1959): 46, no. 100; and R. A. Gergel, "A Julio-Claudian Torso in the Walters Art Gallery," *JWAG* 45 (1987): 26 and fig. 17.

29. See Gergel, "Allegory of Imperial Victory," 9, fig. 9.

30. See Vermeule, in *Berytus* 13 (1959): 45, no. 88; Stemmer, *Untersuchungen*, 61–62, no. V 9, pl. 37, figs. 1–4; Gergel, "Late Flavian Cuirassed Torso," 15–16, fig. 9.

31. On the significance and development of the lappet motif depicting an eagle vanquishing a hare, see Gergel, "Late Flavian Cuirassed Torso," 14–22.

32. See Mattingly, *Coins 2:* 272, no. 235.

33. Tacitus, *Germania* 17, trans. M. Hutton, in *Tacitus*, vol. 1, LCL (Cambridge, Mass., 1970).

34. For a discussion of Dacians wearing the pilleus on Trajanic monuments, see A. -M. L. Touati, *The Great Trajanic Frieze* (Stockholm, 1987), 39 n. 146 and 73, pls. 1–4, 33; and L. Rossi, *Trajan's Column and the Dacian Wars*, trans. J. M. C. Toynbee (Ithaca, N.Y., 1971), 121.

35. See Vermeule, in *Berytus* 13 (1959): 45, no. 89: Gergel, "Allegory of Imperial Victory," 10, fig. 10; idem, "Late Flavian Cuirassed Torso," 16 and fig. 10.

36. Amelung, *Die Sculpturen 2:* 661; Strong, "Terra Mater," 118–19.

37. Suetonius, *Domitianus* 23: "The senators . . . finally . . . passed a decree that his [Domitian's] inscriptions should everywhere be erased, and all record of him obliterated"; trans. J. C. Rolfe, in *Suetonius*, LCL (Cambridge, Mass., 1951). See also Pliny the Younger, *Panegyricus* 52.4.

38. Copenhagen, Ny Carlsberg Glyptotek, Cuirassed Statue of Trajan, inv. 1584: see Vermeule, in *Berytus* 13 (1959): 49, no. 126, pl. 11, fig. 34; and Stemmer, *Untersuchungen*, 113, no. XI 3, pl. 76, figs. 1–2. Leiden, Rijksmuseum von Oudheden, Cuirassed Statue of Trajan, inv. H II BB 1: see Vermeule, 49, no. 130, pl. 12, fig. 36; and Stemmer, 36–37, no. III 10, pl. 20, fig. 3 and pl. 21, fig. 1.

39. *Epitome* of Dio Cassius 68.23.1, trans. E. Cary, in *Dio Cassius*, LCL (Cambridge, Mass., 1951).

40. See G. M. A. Hanfmann and C. C. Vermeule, "A New Trajan," *AJA* 61 (1957): 223–53, pls. 68–75; Vermeule, in *Berytus* 13 (1959): 53, no. 168, pl. 13, fig. 42; Stemmer, *Untersuchungen*, 58–59, no. V 4, pl. 36, fig. 3; and C. C. Vermeule and A. Brauer, *Stone Sculptures: The Greek, Roman and Etruscan Collections of the Harvard University Museums* (Cambridge, Mass., 1990), 150–51. An Arimaspe fighting griffins also appears on breastplates in Centuripe (Antiquarium Comunale: see Vermeule, in *Berytus* 17 [1966]: 54, no. 170A; and Stemmer, 32, no. III 1, pl. 17, fig. 1); in Mentana (coll. Zeri: see Vermeule, in *Berytus* 13 [1959]: 53, no. 170; and Stemmer, 12–13, no. I 6, pl. 4, fig. 1); in Orange (Musée Municipal d'Orange: see Vermeule, in *Berytus* 13 [1959]: 53, no. 169; and Stemmer, 59–60, no. v 5, pl. 36, fig. 1); in Palma de Mallorca (Museo de Mallorca: see Vermeule, in *Berytus* 13 [1959]: 54, no. 174; and Gergel, "Julio-Claudian Torso," 27); in Sabratha (Museum of Antiquities: see Stemmer, 19–20, pl. 20, fig. 2; and Vermeule, *Concordance*, 20); in Volubilis (Musée des Antiquités: see Vermeule, in *Berytus* 13 [1959]: 54, no. 175; and Gergel, "Julio-Claudian Torso," 270); and on two breastplates in Rome (Villa Torlonia-Albani, no. 82: see Vermeule, in *Berytus* 13 [1959]: 56, no. 194; also Garimberti Coll.: see Vermeule, in *Berytus* 13 [1959]: 53, no. 171).

41. Hanfmann and Vermeule, "New Trajan," 236–43.

# PART IV
# RECONSTRUCTIONS

# Reconstructing Roman Clothing

NORMA GOLDMAN

## 13

The National Endowment for the Humanities Summer Seminar, directed by Professor Larissa Bonfante in 1988 and held at the American Academy in Rome, allowed me the opportunity to construct eighteen costumes, based on paintings, sculpture, and mosaics from Roman antiquity. The seminar consisted of field research, as we visited sites and monuments from the tombs at Tarquinia to the Villa of the Mysteries at Pompeii, from the Ara Pacis to the Arch of Constantine in Rome, and of course as we visited the museums at sites and in Rome. Academic research was pursued in the libraries of Rome as we searched for literary evidence. In each endeavor we were trying to discover what the Romans wore at different periods and for different occasions, and the historical, social, and religious significance of the costumes became apparent in the visual and literary evidence. I used both kinds of evidence to form patterns on which I based the costumes that I designed and sewed.

Two fashion shows were held on the front steps of the American Academy with the NEH participants as models (fig. 13.1). As far as possible the costumes were matched to the interests of the participants: Laetitia La Follette wore the flammeum of the bride, Shelley Stone wore the toga, and Richard Gergel wore military garb. The participants in the seminar continued wearing the Roman costumes long after the show, and the colonnaded *cortile* of the American Academy in Rome was a perfect setting. The garments were elegant and comfortable, despite the 100-degree weather in Rome. The ancient Romans knew how to dress suitably for their climate. Because the tunics and mantles were adaptations of basic rectangles, the costumes could be folded afterward into flat packets, smoothed, and stored easily in chests or drawers, an advantage in both the ancient and modern worlds.

Working out practical solutions to problems of constructing the ancient garments gave insights that became apparent once the fabric was cut, draped, and sewn. There is no substitute for repeating the actual process of making the costumes to find out how they were constructed, and lessons were learned from each experience, from cutting and sewing the simple tunic to riveting together the complex armor of the soldier. Although my original proposal called for using pure wool, linen, cotton, and silk, the price of fabric in Rome caused a revision in the plan, and synthetic fabrics that would drape in the same way that the cloth in the monuments was draped were substituted where necessary. Several of the costumes, such as the flammeum for the bride, were made of pure silk, and some tunics were made of pure cotton. Modern linen is much too expensive and too stiff to drape properly for a reconstruction of an ancient garment. It would have to be softened, like "handkerchief linen," before it would be usable. Modern wool would have been much too expensive and much too thick and heavy to serve my purpose. The Office of Research and Sponsored Programs at Wayne State University granted me seven hundred dollars toward the purchase of fabric and materials for the costumes, and all of the money was spent, despite my shopping at the discount fabric stores on or near the Largo Argentina. I found a small shop on the Via Torre Argentina, a half block up from the Largo, which sold a fine collection of trims and accessories, colored satin cord for belts, embroidered edgings in gold threads, and fringes. These were expensive, and I spent the entire seven hundred

Fig. 13.1. The 1988 NEH Summer Seminar: *front row,* Larissa Bonfante, Gerhard Koeppel (director of the Academy summer session), Hugh Witzmann, Beri Goor (guest model); *second row,* Judith Sebesta, Mary Edwards holding Sam Edwards (both guest models); *third row,* Norma Goldman, Pamela Starr (guest model), Fredrick Biele (guest model); *fourth row,* Douglas Edwards, Ann Stout, Lucille Roussin, Julia Heskel, Shelley Stone; *fifth row,* Stefania Del Papa (seminar assistant), Laetitia La Follette, Richard Gergel. Photo: Barbara Bini.

Fig. 13.2a. Etruscan priestess wearing palla with a high tutulus headdress and pointed soft felt calcei repandi. Tomb of the Baron, Tarquinia.

214

Fig. 13.2b. Larissa Bonfante wearing the costume of the Etruscan priestess from the Tomb of the Baron. Soft felt calcei repandi loaned by E. H. Richardson. Photo: B. Goldman.

Fig. 13.3. Hugh Witzmann as Agrippa and Sebastian Raditsa as the barbarian child. Photo: Barbara Bini.

Fig. 13.4. Costumes based on the Ara Pacis relief: Gerhard Koeppel as the Flamen Dialis wearing the apex-pointed helmet cap and laena mantle; Henry Bender as the Rex Sacrorum wearing toga, *capite velato*, and carrying the sacred ax. Photo: Barbara Bini.

for a similar project twenty years earlier. Included were the imperial toga, which had been sewn by Isabelle Baade, and two costumes, that of Tarquin in triumph and the late Byzantine emperor, both with gold stenciling to simulate woven or embroidered gold threads. In the first show, Professor Bonfante's son, Sebastian, wore the costume of the barbarian child holding on to the toga of Agrippa in the Ara Pacis relief (fig. 13.3). Illness prevented his appearing in the second show, and another child, Beri Goor, the daughter of participant Lucille Roussin, substituted. Gerhard Koeppel, who was directing the Academy summer session, wore the costume of the Flamen Dialis, and Henry Bender wore that of the Rex Sacrorum: these were appropriate roles, since both scholars have published articles concerning the Ara Pacis reliefs (fig. 13.4; fig. 6.22). Barbara Bini photographed the second NEH fashion show, and her photographs appear here.

The NEH Summer Seminar provided us the opportunity to study the visual and literary evidence for the garments and to reconstruct them as accurately as possible.

Styles of clothing, hair, and footwear represent a sort of language, sometimes subtle and unintelligible, sometimes loud and blatant. There is no dictionary for this language, no grammar or syntax, but its style is the conscious or unconscious expression of what is appropriate for certain times and occasions. Certain kinds of activity are associated with special kinds of garments: clerical, judicial, or medical gowns; uniforms for the military, for musical bands, for athletes, for students whose schools have dress codes. Even the now-ubiquitous blue jeans have become the uniform in the schools and colleges for the young who want to "go with the crowd." In the same manner, special garments in Roman antiquity also designated different groups in occupation and status. They separated the patrician from the plebeian, the priest from the layman, the various ranks of the military, the citizen entitled to wear the toga from the freedman.

Clothing of fine fabric and quality construction has always sent an immediate message about the wealth of the wearer. The ancient Romans had still other means of letting the rest of the world know exactly the social status of the wearer. This language was communicated in symbols, apparent in the width of the stripes that decorated the garments, as well as in the richness of the fabric, in the choice of colors achieved by expensive dyes, and in the elegant shoeboots reserved for senators and patricians.

The robes of the ancient Romans display a consistency in styling during almost a thousand years, as the Romans inherited the clothing traditions of the Etruscans and Greeks and adapted them to the environment of

dollars for yard goods and trims. Had I gone to the regular fabric shops, the price would have tripled.

The two fashion shows on the front steps of the Academy were held first for the summer school students and two weeks later for the entire Academy community. Professor Bonfante herself was attired as the Etruscan priestess, based on the figure from the Tomb of the Baron, complete with tutulus and pointed calcei repandi (figs. 13.2a–b; see fig. 13.1). The pointed-toed shoes were part of the generous loan from Professor Emeline Hill Richardson of the University of North Carolina, who graciously sent some of the costumes that had been created

Italy. The basic Greek garment put on over the head, the chiton, and the mantle wrapped around the body, the himation, became the Roman tunic and toga. The garment "put on" was referred to as *indutus* (worn); the garment wrapped around the body was described as being *amictus* (girt, wrapped). Lillian Wilson says that the latter garment was developed from the "simple blanket common to all primitive peoples," like the American Indian blanket.[1] It could be wrapped around the body as costume but at night could serve as both blanket and sheet.

Roman clothing was simple and elegant, practical and comfortable. Based on the rectangles that came directly from the loom, first in wool and linen, then in cotton, in silk, and in combinations of fibers, the basic garments for men, women, and children were the tunic, toga, peplos, stola, palla, and pallium. They differed little in shape from garments that had existed in the Greek world. They could be modified in color, in pleating, in draping, in embroidery, and in fabric to provide all of the variety that men and especially women demanded in their costumes, but the basic garments did not change in nearly a millennium. There were slight modifications in sleeve extensions, either woven into the cloth on the loom or added along the side, selvage to selvage. Edges could be rounded, as in the Etruscan tebenna, an early form of the toga, and in later Roman republican and imperial togas. The tunic developed from the Greek or early Etruscan chiton, and the Roman peplos was an adaptation of the same garment from the Greek original. The large imperial toga with its wide expanse of cloth and elliptical shape may have been woven on the loom in that shape, but since it became such a wide garment, it probably was pieced from several widths sewn to each other. The curve could have been achieved by alternately increasing and then decreasing the width of the woven fabric, or it could have been cut to shape, although ancient scissors were not designed for heavy or extensive work. The rectangular women's palla and men's pallium were used as everyday mantles. Elliptical, rectangular, circular, or half-circular garments were used as cloaks: the paenula, the cucullus, the laena, the lacerna, and the sagum for military wear. Also for military wear was the paludamentum, the cloak for the general or emperor.

Costumes were enhanced by the addition of jewelry: fibulae of all kinds, including brooches to hold the garments together at the shoulder, as well as to decorate and complement the design of the cloth, and, mostly for women, necklaces, earrings, finger rings, bracelets, and pendants to increase the effect. These were made of a variety of metals, including iron, copper, bronze, silver, and gold, with precious stones and pearls to decorate the wearer and dazzle the beholder. Some of the tunics in sculpture and painting are held together along the shoulder and down the arm by a series of buttons which could have been made of stone, shell, wood, metal, ivory, ceramic, or knotted fibers (fig. 13.5). Some garments are depicted as being sewn together, the seam reinforced by a colored band, as seen on Etruscan paintings such as those in the Tomb of the Leopards in Tarquinia, dated 500 B.C. (figs. 13.6a–b).

Women's garments could also be held together by fibulae or brooches, and the costume of the dancing girls from Herculaneum, the traditional Greek peplos, is constructed in just that manner with a round brooch holding the back cloth over the front at each shoulder (fig. 13.7).[2] The Karyatids on the Porch of the Maidens of the Erechtheum on the Acropolis in Athens, dated to the late fifth century B.C., were dressed in these same handsome peploi, with the blousing *(kolpos)* showing under the overhanging panel in front and back. The same garment appears on the Karyatids along the upper register of the Forum of Augustus and on the Karyatids along the Canopus pool in Hadrian's Villa, indicating that the graceful and practical costume had continued as a style for well over six hundred years (figs. 13.8a–b).

Costumes could also be modified by embroidered edges, either woven into the fabric on the loom, in colored or metallic gold or silver threads, or embroidered after the cloth was taken from the loom. The decorative edgings could be appliquéd along the edges or added to seams and along necklines. Vase paintings from the ancient world, on which Hope bases most of his costumes in the drawings for his book on ancient Greek and Roman costume, show some cloth woven with delightful designs over the entire cloth, but more often "border patterns" add a new dimension as they dip and curve at the edges of the garment. Both men and women desired a variety of cloth in different colors and with decorative edgings. Women in particular, however, seem to have delighted in the novelty of new sheer fabrics, like Coan silk, that revealed the body, in cloth shot through with gold thread, and in the luxury of soft, lustrous silk that could be dyed many colors.

There was a minimum of cutting and sewing. Tools were not so precise as they are today. Even needles, some of which have been preserved, are not so fine or pointed as the modern "sharps," and thread was probably the same thread that was used on the loom for the fabric itself. On the Arringatore in the Archaeological Museum in Florence, it is possible to see under the orator's raised arm the stitching holding the two selvages (self-edges) together (see fig. 1.1).

Since the garments were often woven so that the selvages could be connected, there would have been no need for seam allowances. The selvages could be at-

Fig. 13.5. Tunic of Roman matron, held together by buttons along the sleeve at the shoulder. This female figure, from the Capitoline Museum in Rome, is variously identified as Venus or the wife in the "Married Couple." Photo courtesy of the Capitoline Photo Archive, inv. 652.

Fig. 13.6a. Female banqueter wearing a tunic in striped fabric, outlined along the shoulder by a band of color. Plaid fabric covers the couch. Tomb of the Leopards, Tarquinia. Photo: N. Goldman.

Fig. 13.6b. Mary Edwards wearing the costume of the banqueter from the Tomb of the Leopards. Photo: Barbara Bini.

Fig. 13.7. The peplos worn by the dancing girl from the Villa of the Papyri at Herculaneum, now in the Museo Nazionale Archeologico, Naples. Photo courtesy of the Museo Nazionale Archeologico, Naples.

Fig. 13.8a. The peplos worn by the Karyatid from the Canopus pool at Hadrian's Villa in Tivoli. Photo from DAI, Rome, neg. 61.2993.

Fig. 13.8b. Reverse of Karyatid, showing hairstyle and back of peplos. Photo from DAI, Rome, neg. 61.2970.

tached by overcasting the abutting edges. In modern reconstructions, seams have been allowed where necessary, and we have made allowances for hems where there are no selvages. It is possible to fringe garments for an easy and practical hem at the bottom. Doubtless this could have been done in antiquity as well. Following are descriptions of the basic garments and directions for their construction. Lillian Wilson's two works on reconstructing Roman clothing, *The Roman Toga* and *The Clothing of the Ancient Romans*, have proved invaluable.

### GARMENTS PUT ON OVER THE HEAD

## Tunic

The basic garment for both men and women was the tunic, for men ending about midcalf (or higher for children, young men, or male servants), for women of all classes full or ankle length. In Etruscan times it was worn loose or belted; in Roman times it seems more commonly to have been belted, except for special occasions when the unbelted garment indicated grief, mourning, or religious observance. This garment is easily reproduced from rectangles of cloth attached at the shoulders and sewn from the underarm to the bottom of the cloth. Originally the cloth was woven at home on upright looms by the women of the household; during the empire the women seem usually to have been otherwise occupied, and weaving became the work of guilds of skilled laborers, although more conservative women seemed still to have taken pride in the "old-fashioned virtues," which included weaving garments for themselves and for members of their family. The rectangles could be attached in several ways, depending on how the cloth was woven and how it was folded.

If the cloth was folded with the long edge horizontal, then extra cloth would be allowed at the front edge along the top to produce the attractive V-shaped neckline which was practical for comfort and fit, also allowing extra cloth in front for the woman's bosom (figs. 13.9a–c). The only seam needed was along *GB* to *G'B'*, since fibulae or brooches could hold the garment together at *CC'* and *DD'*, or buttons along the shoulder on each side could also hold the garment together. Tiny gathers at each button make the cloth gap to show the arm beneath. The cloth would have to be cut at *EF* to allow the arm to go through, if the seamstress decided to sew the shoulders together, *AC* to *A'C'* and *DE* to *D'E*. If the garment was pinned at the shoulders with fibulae, the cloth would fall on each side, and cutting an armhole would not be necessary. A solid-color twin-size sheet (90″ × 62″) can easily be draped with pins fastening the

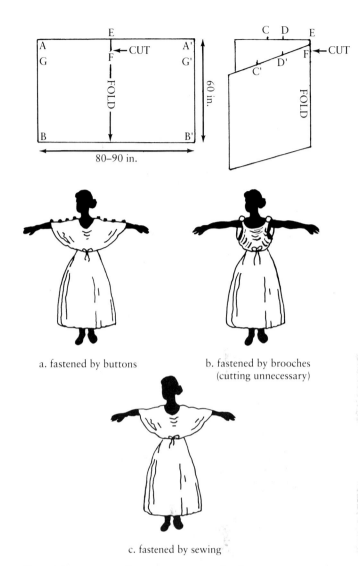

a. fastened by buttons      b. fastened by brooches (cutting unnecessary)

c. fastened by sewing

Figs. 13.9a–c. Patterns for woman's tunic and palla.
Fabric: cotton, muslin, polyester, blends, jersey, shantung, lightweight twill
Color: any solid color except brown or black
Dimensions: length, 80–90 in.; width, 60 in. (less if under 5 ft. 4 in.)

back over the front at the shoulders. It requires only two decorative pins and a belt to produce a realistic tunic. If the wearer is under 5′5″, double belting at both waist and hips is recommended, as in figure 13.14.

A man's tunic, requiring no extra fabric in front, was made by folding the long rectangle in half with the long side held vertically. Fifth-century A.D. Coptic garments from Egypt verify this method of weaving and construction. The neck allowance was left open in the weaving on the loom as selvages in the center *C* to *D* (fig. 13.10).[3] The stripes (clavi) for equestrian and senatorial orders, in purple against natural, beige, or white cloth, were probably woven on each side of the cloth: a clavus was about one inch wide *(angustus clavus)* for the equestrian and about three inches wide *(latus clavus)* for the senator, patrician, or emperor. There is literary evidence for a central stripe on Eastern garments, but all of the visual evidence in Italy points to stripes on either side for the male tunic.[4] Extra material for the sleeves could have been woven as part of the garment, but sleeves could also have been sewn onto each side (*H* additions). For our modern reconstructions, the stripes, both narrow for the Arringatore and wide for the imperial tunic, were appliquéd. The former was done by hand, and the latter was done by machine stitching when I saw that I would never have finished in time sewing by hand. With the neckline already established, by cutting a hole for the head (*C* to *D*) about eleven or twelve inches in length and carefully rolling a slender hem, one simply achieves the fold at the shoulder, as well as also the armhole openings along the selvages above the seams *G'B* on each side, and no shoulder seam is necessary.

The additional material to extend the sleeve is optional, but it was used in the *tunica picta* of the Tarquin costume sent by Emeline Hill Richardson. This tunic had no stripes but was decorated with gold stencils to imitate embroidery. A tebenna cut in a half-moon shape, also with gold stenciling, completed the body costume. A triumphal wreath of gold, red, and green oak leaves and acorns, sewn onto a band or fillet, decorated the head. Following this vertical folded pattern and attaching appliquéd stripes is the ideal way to reconstruct a male tunic, and the pattern was used for the Arringatore costume without adding the sleeve extensions (fig. 13.11). In making reproductions, one can allow a seam of 1/2 to 5/8 inch, with the seam allowance pressed open on the inside. Since modern cloth is cut from a bolt at a fabric store, the bottom edges need to be hemmed to finish the garment and to prevent fraying. A caftan from any decorative fabric, like those shot through with gold thread, can easily be made in just this manner without extra sleeve extensions.

A third method of construction for the tunic would be attaching two separate rectangles of cloth, by adding buttons over the shoulder and down the arm, by using decorative pins as fibulae, or by sewing the shoulder seams together. The side seams would be sewn down from under the arms to the hem (fig. 13.12). The width of the cloth would determine the length of the sleeve. Again, the V of the front neckline must be achieved by allowing about three or four inches extra at the neck between shoulder attachments, whether pinned, buttoned, or sewn. That means that the front fabric would be three or four inches wider than the back to allow for the extra cloth at the neckline in front.

A tunic for a slave was probably made of coarse cloth

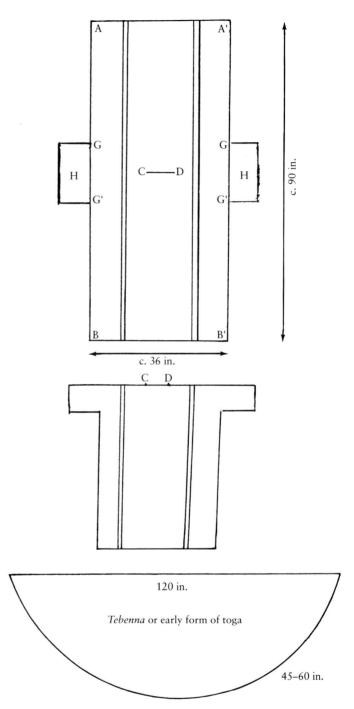

Fig. 13.10. Patterns for man's tunic and tebenna or toga.
Fabric: cotton, lightweight wool, linen, muslin, twill
Color: white, natural, cream, or red-purple
Dimensions: length, 90 in.; width, 36 in. (more for over 5 ft. 7 in.)

and fastened with a cheap pin or even a thorn at the top. It was bloused so that the thighs were exposed for men, but it fell full length to the ankle for women. For any man performing heavy physical work, perhaps only the sections at the left shoulder would have been fastened to

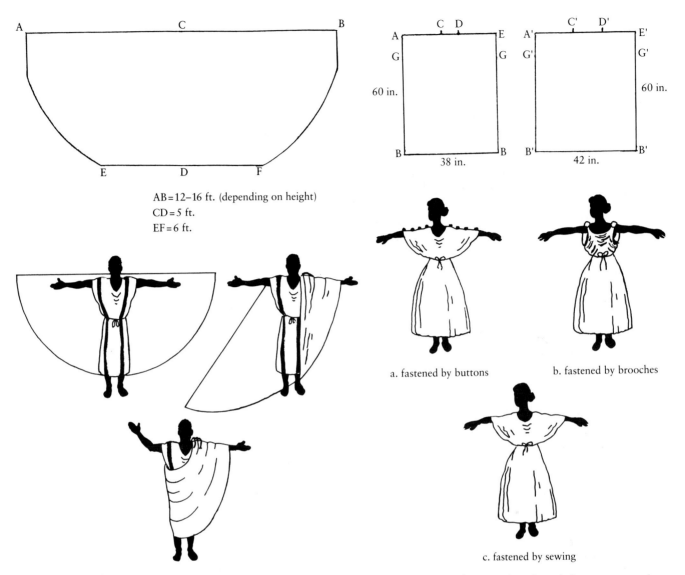

AB = 12–16 ft. (depending on height)
CD = 5 ft.
EF = 6 ft.

60 in.

38 in.

60 in.

42 in.

a. fastened by buttons

b. fastened by brooches

c. fastened by sewing

Fig. 13.11. Pattern for Arringatore tunic and toga.

Fig. 13.12. Pattern for woman's tunic made from two rectangles of pleated cloth. The Romans often used fabric pleated into tiny folds, as is apparent in fig. 13.14.

allow for more right-arm freedom, or the right arm could have been taken out of the garment, leaving the shoulder bare. Household slaves would have worn better clothing that would slaves on farms or those doing heavy labor. The wealthy would have wanted to show off the livery of slaves carrying litters or the garments of those employed in serving guests.

### Peplos

The peplos, originally a Greek garment, popular in sculpture, was probably also popular for women in Roman times as well. The dancing girls from Herculaneum wear the peplos. It consisted of a garment related to the tunic but with an overblouse or overpanel front and back, created by folding the top of the material over to a desired

length (see fig. 13.7). The overpanels could be of varying lengths, from shoulder to waist or shoulder to knee, and the garment itself could be either sewn or pinned at the shoulder. The overpanels could hang free to the waist, or, when longer, they could be belted, either at the waist or, as in the time of the empire, high under the breasts (figs. 13.13a-b).[5] The panels could be embroidered along the edge, or they could have bordered patterns woven into the cloth. If pinned at the shoulder, the arms would go through the top of the garment, which would fall under the arms in soft, graceful folds. The dancing girls from Herculaneum in the Naples Museum wear such garments, with round brooches to hold the back cloth over the front at a single point on each shoulder. Sometimes both tunic and peplos were belted twice, once at

Fig. 13.13a. Peplos, with overfold to the waist with kolpos showing, belted under the overfold, worn by the dancing girl in bronze from the Villa of the Papyri at Herculaneum. Photo courtesy of the Museo Nazionale Archeologico, Naples.

Fig. 13.13b. Longer overfold peplos belted at the waist (could also be belted high under the breasts), worn by Julia Heskel. Photo: Barbara Bini.

the waist and again at the hips, giving a double-bloused effect (fig. 13.14). It is possible to construct the peplos from a solid-color regular or queen-size sheet, allowing for the overblouse panels by making a fold along the longer side, and pinning the garment, back over front, at the shoulders, allowing extra fabric in front for the V-shaped neckline. The garment can then be belted underneath the fold, which should fall just to the waist (figs. 13.15a–b). Decorative matching pins at the shoulders can provide the desired effect. Professor Phillip G. Fike, metalsmith from the Department of Art and Art History at Wayne State University, has been experimenting making

Etruscan and Roman fibulae, and he has re-created many of the ancient pins to be used for the final versions of the costumes reconstructed during the NEH seminar.

## Stola

The stola, an overgarment giving the "layered look," prized both in antiquity and today, is a full-length garment worn over the woman's tunic (fig. 2.1). It was usually sleeveless, and it was fastened back to front by pins or brooches or sewn together at the shoulders. It could be made by bunching the cloth at the place where it was to be joined, or it could have been cut or woven into a

Fig. 13.14. Double belted tunic with palla around hips, worn by the female
figure in the "Married Couple" (also identified as Venus and Mars). Male
figure wears only a lacerna mantle caught at his right shoulder by a round
brooch. Capitoline Museum, Rome. Photo courtesy of the Capitoline
Museum Photo Archive.

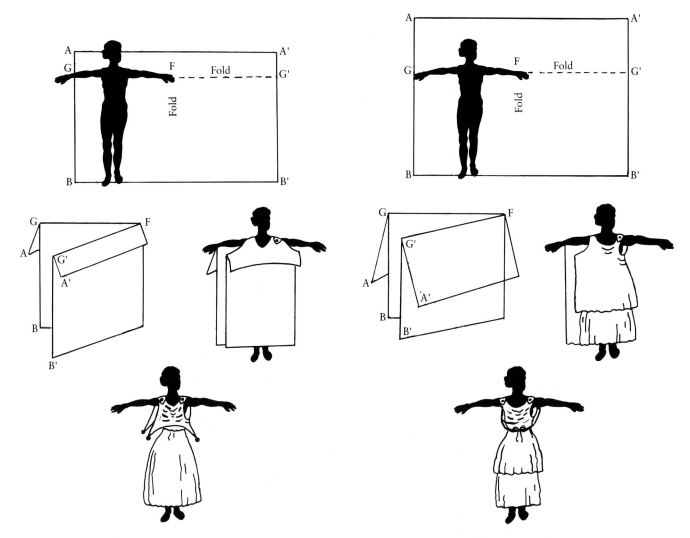

Fig. 13.15a. Pattern for peplos with overfold to waist, made from a queen-size sheet, belted at the waist under the overfold panels with kolpos showing.

Fig. 13.15b. Pattern for peplos with overfold, made from a queen- or king-size sheet, belted under the breasts.

narrow shape at each shoulder to be joined by a fibula or by a small seam. It could also have been suspended by straps from the shoulder: Margarete Bieber interpreted the *instita* as the strap of a stola, not as a pleated or flounced panel at the bottom of the garment.[6] The stola was a garment worn when the woman became a matron, and it signaled her change in status to being a married woman. The stola could have been made of any kind of cloth—wool, linen, cotton, or silk—and probably was chosen in a color that complemented or contrasted with the tunic underneath.

Wearing an extra garment was probably a very practical solution to two needs familiar to all women. One was the need for warmth, and the other was the need for modesty. Diaphanous cloth for the tunic would require

an overgarment or stola to make the costume acceptable in mixed society. Some of the cloth purchased in Rome for the reconstructed costumes was transparent, and a stola made the costume "proper." Many of the statues of women wearing the stola show the cloth over the breasts that narrows at the shoulder, where it is then attached to the fabric at the back by being pinned or connected to thin straps of cloth (fig. 13.16). This effect without straps can be achieved by the soft material being pinned back over front, the straight full fabric falling into the V at the center of the front and to the side deep under the arm. Underneath the stola, the long-sleeved tunic, buttoned down the shoulder to form the sleeve, is often visible. Wilson refers to a *tunica interior* and a *tunica exterior*. I interpret the stola to be the lat-

Fig. 13.16. Hellenistic marble sculpture showing an inebriated old woman wearing garment with straps over the shoulders. This is not a stola, since it is not worn over a tunica. Capitoline Museum, Rome. Photo courtesy of the Capitoline Museum Photo Archive.

ter. Side seams could make the stola into the "outer tunic," which could be belted along with the "inner tunic," or left hanging loose.

### MANTLES DRAPED AROUND THE BODY

#### Palla

The palla was a long rectangular piece of cloth used by Roman women as a covering when they left the house. Like women in the Near East today, women in ancient Rome did not go outdoors without being modestly covered by a mantle. The woman outdoors covered her body, and probably her head as well, with the palla, both to protect herself against the cold or improper display and against any evil eye or improper advance. Naturally the palla would have been of heavy woolen cloth in cold weather and of thinner cloth (linen, cotton, or silk) in warm weather. Roman women had all colors of cloth available, and the color of the palla was probably chosen with great care to complement or contrast with the tunic and stola worn underneath. The garment was worn in a variety of ways, either over the head and enveloping the body entirely, or loosely draped over the arm when the woman was seated or in a more relaxed pose (fig. 13.17). Our modern reproductions were usually ten or eleven feet in length and sixty inches wide.

Only women in disgrace for adultery or prostitutes wore the toga, and we do not know whether it was a white garment or a colored one.[7]

#### Flammeum

The bridal costume is discussed by Laetitia La Follette in chapter 3 of this book, but a word about the reconstruction used for the NEH seminar might help those who would like to duplicate the materials. I made the *tunica recta* of a softly draping cotton-polyester jersey, with the front panel about four inches wider than the back, following the pattern for the woman's tunic (figs. 13.9a-c). It was tied with a white cord with the Herculean knot, which resembles the knot worn by the Vestal Virgins on their statues. The width (thirty-six to forty-five inches) and length (about four inches longer than the height of the wearer from shoulder to floor, to allow for blousing of the garment) vary with individuals but are easily adjustable. Covering the tunic is the flammeum, a flame-colored veil, which was constructed based on the Domina painting from the Villa of the Mysteries in Pompeii. It was a long rectangle of silk, a little over double the height of the wearer from head to toe, and fifty-four inches wide. Along the length of the entire veil was added a purple edging, also of silk, about six inches in width. Wilson suggests that the veil might have been transparent, and when single width, it is indeed transparent. The veil would be opaque when folded lengthwise. The various interpretations for the "seni crines" in reproducing the hairstyle for the bride have been discussed in the chapter on the bride, but the flammeum would have covered the head as the modestly draped bride stood beside her husband in the ceremony.

#### Tebenna, Toga, Pallium

The toga is the uniquely Roman mantle for males, and its history shows a garment of great variety, from the Etruscan tebenna, from which it descended, to the voluminous imperial garment that required two to three slaves for proper draping. Its complex draped folds, along with the sinus and the umbo, appear in togate figures both sculpted and painted. One can follow the historical descent of the sinus from a small graceful drapery across the chest and stomach to the deep folds of the knee-length drapery. The later phase required an extra pouch, the umbo, for carrying a drawstring purse or document (see chapter 1). No matter what its size, however, the half-moon or elliptical-shaped toga differs from the rectangular pallium, which is another, more Greek mantle for a male, also wrapped around the body.

The tebenna loaned by Professor Emeline Hill Richardson to accompany the costume of Tarquin is a half-moon–shaped cloth with a stenciled gold design to resemble embroidery. A toga similar to that worn by the Arringatore (fig. 1.1) was also made from a half-moon–shaped piece of cloth, which can be formed by curving the two bottom corners of a rectangle. Using fabric sixty inches in width necessitates leaving part of the bottom curve straight, and the curves can blend into the straight edge. The garment is about ten feet in length at the straight edge for a man about 5′9″. If he is over 6′2″, add another six inches to the length. Fold the cloth in half, cutting both curves at one time. Begin the curves at the bottom, about two feet from the center fold, and cut up to about a foot from the top. Because the toga on the statue has a band around the bottom, the reconstruction duplicated that band by adding parallel welting about three inches wide to the curved edge of the garment, including the straight edge at the bottom. There were Etruscan letters in the band along the curve in the original sculpture, giving the name of Aule Meteli as the orator. Note that in draping this version of the toga, the extra width of cloth is accommodated by bunching the two sections together along the neckline and over the chest. It would not slip down or come apart when held together so securely (fig. 13.11).

The toga worn by the male figures on the Ara Pacis is a larger garment with the edges curved both at the bottom and the top of the rectangle of cloth, creating an elliptical shape. The top half of the ellipse is folded down and can be raised up over the head as a covering when the wearer (e.g., Agrippa) is *capite velato*. Note that Agrippa's toga has weights at the ends to help hold it in place. The imperial toga is even larger—wider and longer than the garment worn by the figures on the Ara Pacis. Its dimensions vary during the empire, but the one we reconstructed is eighteen feet in length and about eight feet wide, with curved edges, again producing an irregular ellipse (figs. 13.18, 13.19). The border of red-purple, about three inches wide, runs along the top curved edge. Underneath the toga, the tunic is decorated with straight three-inch stripes in the same color running shoulder to hem, front and back.

The draping of both togas is the same: fold the cloth in half top to bottom (for the imperial toga, fold the top half of the ellipse first); place the midpoint at the top under the right arm of the wearer, asking him to hold it in place by dropping his arm; and bring the back cloth around the back of the wearer and up over the left shoulder, allowing the cloth to hang evenly over the extended left arm to the wrist. The point in front should extend to the floor but not touch it. Bring the front cloth across the body and up over the left shoulder, again allowing the cloth to hang evenly over the left arm on top of the cloth from the back; again the tip of the fabric should not touch the floor in the back. The sinus will fall in front deeply over the right knee; the longer the length of the toga, the deeper the sinus. Pull out a pouch of cloth just below the waist from the inside to form the umbo, which serves not only a decorative function but a practical one as well. When the sinus was small, it served as the pouch for carrying valuables—a drawstring leather or fabric purse or a scroll. When it became so deep that it could no longer function as a pouch, the umbo took over that role. The toga was the formal robe worn by citizens all over the empire, and it was to be worn outdoors with calcei, not with sandals. The toga was the appropriate garb for a Roman citizen, but the pallium (the equivalent of the Greek himation) was also worn by Romans abroad, at less formal occasions, and at home in the country.

## Paenula and Cucullus

The paenula was a cloak of varied length, made of heavy wool, leather, or even fur. It was often hooded and could be made of two shaped pieces of material with the hood as part of the fabric or added (fig. 13.20). Our reconstruction has an added hood based on the pattern given by Wilson. The face was framed by the peaked hood, but since the cloak had no sleeves, it hampered movement, especially if it was narrow. It was very practical for severe weather, and soldiers were issued paenulae when stationed on the northern frontiers. Because travelers often needed warm garments, the paenula became a garment for any citizen of any class going on a trip, especially into cold climates. But since the paenula restricted the arms, the loose lacerna became a more popular cloak. The wider paenula has continued in use as a priestly robe and is the predecessor of the chasuble in Christian church vestments.[8]

The cucullus is a variant of the hooded paenula, but it seems to be a close-fitting short cape extending only over the shoulders or at most to the waist. Representations on sarcophagi show figures of shepherds or hunters wearing the cucullus. The cucullus has a peaked hood like that of the paenula. Its design seems to recommend it as extra protection from rain or cold weather. Sometimes it is shown closed in front and would have had to have been put on over the head; sometimes it is open in front and would have been held together by brooch, fibula, clasp, or string tie.

## Lacerna

The lacerna was a cloak first worn by soldiers but then adopted by civilians because of its practicality. Writers did not refer to it until the end of the republic, and it was in use at the time of Cicero. Citizens wore it over the toga to prevent the garments worn underneath from becoming dusty or wet. It was made originally of wool and was open at the side and fastened with a brooch or buckle on the right shoulder (fig. 13.21). The arms could extend freely, and the cloak could be thrown back over the shoulders as well. Originally of dark colors for the soldiers, the lacernae eventually were made of bright colors and lighter cloth for upper-class men and women, although the poor usually wore dark colors. The lacerna is usually considered hoodless, although a hood could have been added as an attached piece of cloth sewn along the top of the neckline. Martial mentions a white lacerna covering the toga used in the chilly amphitheater (14.137: "the chilly toga"). Obviously in late fall, winter, and early spring, a warm cape such as this would have been a necessity, even over the woolen toga. The *trabea*, referred to in literature as being either purple or striped with purple, was a mantle worn by equites or by those engaged in some ritual.

## Laena

The laena, a priestly mantle, is often referred to as *duplex,* and there are many interpretations of the term. It could mean that the garment was double or doubled over, or perhaps made of two pieces of cloth sewn together. It was semicircular in shape and was worn by the *flamines;* according to Vergil, it was also worn by Aeneas (*Aeneid* 4.262). It was held together by a brooch or fibula at the shoulder or in the back. The Flamen Dialis

Fig. 13.17. Palla worn fully covering figure. Capitoline Museum, Rome, inv. 99. Photo courtesy of the Capitoline Museum Photo Archive.

Fig. 13.18. Togate figure, showing imperial toga with deep sinus and umbo. Photo from DAI, Rome, neg. 61.1747.

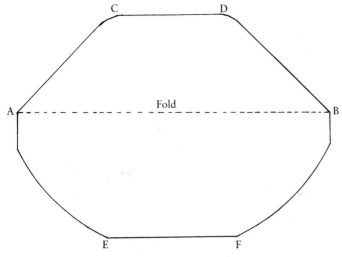

Use blanket bias tape 3 in. wide for trim along ACDB.

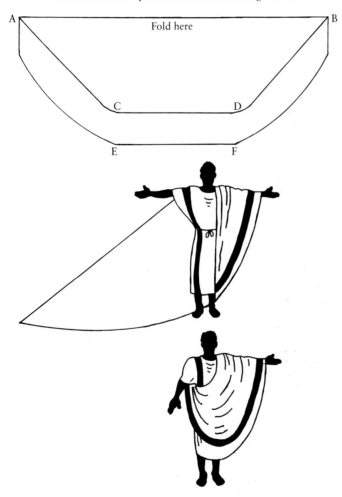

Fig. 13.19. Pattern for imperial toga.
Fabric: cotton, muslin, polyester, jersey, gabardine, twill
Color: white or cream
Dimensions: length, 12–18 ft., depending on how full toga is to be and height of wearer; width, 8–9 ft., depending on height of wearer
Trim: band of red-purple to be attached to ACDB, covering both sides of cloth

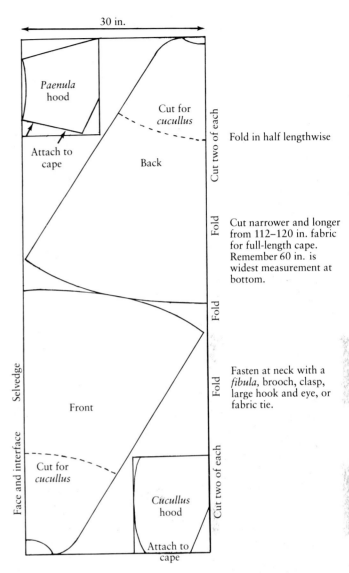

Fig. 13.20. Patterns for paenula and cucullus.
Fabric: heavy wool, linen, gabardine, twill, fake leather, fake fur
Dimensions: length, 80 in. for short paenula (for man 5 ft. 6 in; longer for taller man); 40–60 in. for cucullus (depending on desired length); 112–120 in. for full-length paenula; width, 60 in.

on the Ara Pacis wears his garment with the curves of the cloak coming across the front, indicating a fastening in the back (figs. 13.4, 13.22, 6.22). This ritual garment of priests was purple in color. The laena also continued in use as a form of priestly robe in the Christian church, anticipating some forms of the casula.[9]

### Sagum

The sagum was a short military cloak of Gallic origin, and although the word has a masculine form *sagus*, it is most commonly known in the neuter, both for the sagum worn by the Gauls and Germans and for a smaller garment called the *sagulum*, which, according to Vergil,

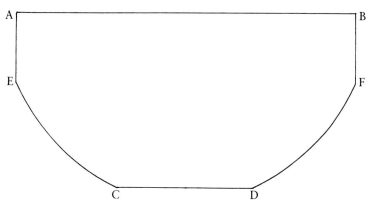

Cut curve at EC and FD by folding material and cutting double at one time.

Fig. 13.21. Pattern for lacerna.
Fabric: any heavy weight wool, linen, cotton, twill, gabardine
Color: dark—preferably brown or purple-brown
Dimensions: length, 10 ft.; width, 5 ft.

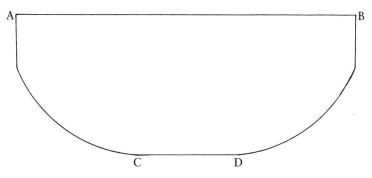

*Laena* (to be accurate) should be double, and you might wish to cut two from the same pattern. They can be seamed easily along the straight edge. Leave the curved edge open, and hem each.

Fig. 13.22. Pattern for the laena.
Fabric: any medium weight blend of wool polyester, twill, gabardine, linen
Dimensions: length, 100 in.; width, 50–60 in.

was striped (*Aeneid* 8.660). Woven of rough warm wool, it became so popular with the Roman soldiers that "to put on the sagum" became idiomatic for "going to war," and "laying aside the sagum" meant "making peace." Strabo says that a Spaniard sleeps in his sagum, confirming the blanket as the basis for all wrapped garments. Tacitus says that the Germans held it together with a fibula or a thorn.[10] Whatever its origin, the sagum or sagulum (the short cloak) as the basic military cloak is represented on many of the soldiers on Trajan's Column. It can be easily duplicated in modern reconstruction, since

Fig. 13.23a. Soldiers from Trajan's Column, Rome, wearing the sagum. Photo courtesy of Editura Meridian, *Decibal si Traian* (Bucharest, 1980), fig. 39.

it is merely a rectangle of heavy cloth (figs. 13.23a–b). It was probably of dark color, gray or brown, practical for the long march with no cleaners or fullers available. Columella recommends it for farm laborers in bad weather. It appears in many forms on the Column of Trajan, doubled over in front but longer in the back. When Marcus Aurelius returned from his military campaigns, he donned the toga and ordered his soldiers to do likewise.[11] Perhaps that is the reason why the sagum does not appear on the Column of Marcus Aurelius.

Paludamentum and Military Costume
The paludamentum was the military cloak for the general, and it is represented on many of the statues of cuirassed military men, especially the emperor figures. Whether it is a rectangle of cloth, as Richard Gergel recommends, or a half-moon with curved edges, according to Lillian Wilson's pattern, is open to interpretation. It can be made in either shape, since most paludamenta are rolled up or tossed over the shoulder, making the exact

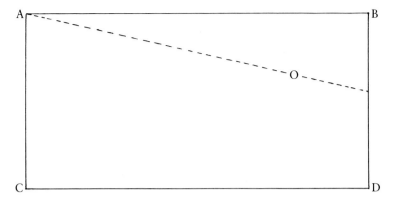

The rectangle pattern can be used for the *sagum*, but it must be folded at a sharp triangle at the top. The folded edge is brought around to the front. The fully extended corner is brought over the right shoulder and attached to the doubled edge about a foot and a half from the end of the fold. Thus the *sagum* can be short in front, but long in back. The folded part in the back can be pulled over the head in foul weather.

Attach A to O with a round brooch or a *fibula.*

Fig. 13.23b. Pattern for the sagum.

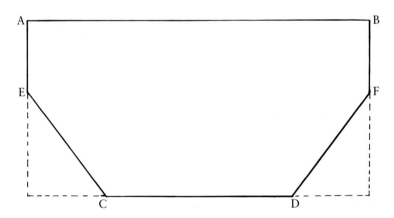

Wilson's pattern begins with a rectangle, but has both corners at one end angled sharply. Gergel prefers the pattern with the rectangle preserved intact. Since the *paludamentum* is usually represented rolled or bunched, there is no hard evidence for one idea or the other.

Fig. 13.24. Pattern for the paludamentum.
Fabric: Any heavy-weight twill, wool-polyester blend, wool, gabardine
Color: Purple-brown
Dimensions: length, 120 in.; width, 60 in.

shape impossible to determine. It can vary in length and width also, but our reconstruction is nine feet long and five feet wide (fig. 13.24). It is made of purple wool, and purple is appropriate for the role it plays in imperial costume. In sculpture, the paludamentum usually appears caught by a round brooch on the right shoulder of the wearer, and naturally the sculptor often represents it

thrown back so that the symbolism documented on the cuirass on the upper torso of the general or emperor can be seen completely.

We have not attempted to construct the cuirass, although stiff plastic cuirasses can be purchased, along with greaves, at costume shops. Our costume for the legionary soldier consists of a short, knee-length tunic, over which the soldier would have worn a leather jerkin to protect his skin from the metal armor. The armor could have been made of solid or attached strips of leather, which would have required no underjerkin, but our armor was made of strips of metal riveted together down the center back, down each side of the front, and over the shoulders. Leather thongs attached through holes on each side of the front held the armor together. A triangular scarf at the neck completed the undercostume. Around the waist the soldier wore a leather belt, to which was fastened his sword. From the center of the belt hung four short leather strips, each covered with metal bosses to protect the lower torso. A mantle was draped over the military costume.

UNDERGARMENTS: SUBLIGACULUM,
STROPHIUM, INDUSIUM

Questions about undergarments for the Romans cannot easily be answered from visual evidence. Few monuments from Roman antiquity depict the Romans without their outer garments. They evidently did not have the same attitude toward nudity that was exercised by the Greeks, and they displayed a modesty in representing the human body, both male and female. Even depictions of the lower classes represent them dressed. Gladiators, like the *retiarii,* appear with some kind of apron or loincloth, as do wrestlers. This loincloth is a kind of shaped, diaperlike cloth that was tied underneath, perhaps explaining the name *subligaculum (subligar, subligaria),* used in literary passages. Bonfante calls this a form of the diaper-shaped perizoma (fig. 13.25), which could have many types, even to a kind of shorts.[12] One wonders whether workmen and soldiers, who wore the tunic quite short, wore undergarments for modesty and protection. Slaves doing very heavy labor perhaps wore only the subligaculum. The visual evidence is lacking; the literary evidence is scant. There is reference in literature to *feminalia* and *tibialia,* covering for the thighs and legs, mentioned by Suetonius as worn by Augustus in winter (*Augustus,* 82). These may have been wrappings, in the style of bandagelike puttees, worn for warmth. Winter in unheated areas must have been hard on everyone.

The exercising bikini-clad girls from Piazza Armerina (fig. 13.26) wear scanty "briefs," which could have been made in a dainty version of the man's loincloth, and a

Regular Diaper-style pattern       Fitted Diaper-style pattern

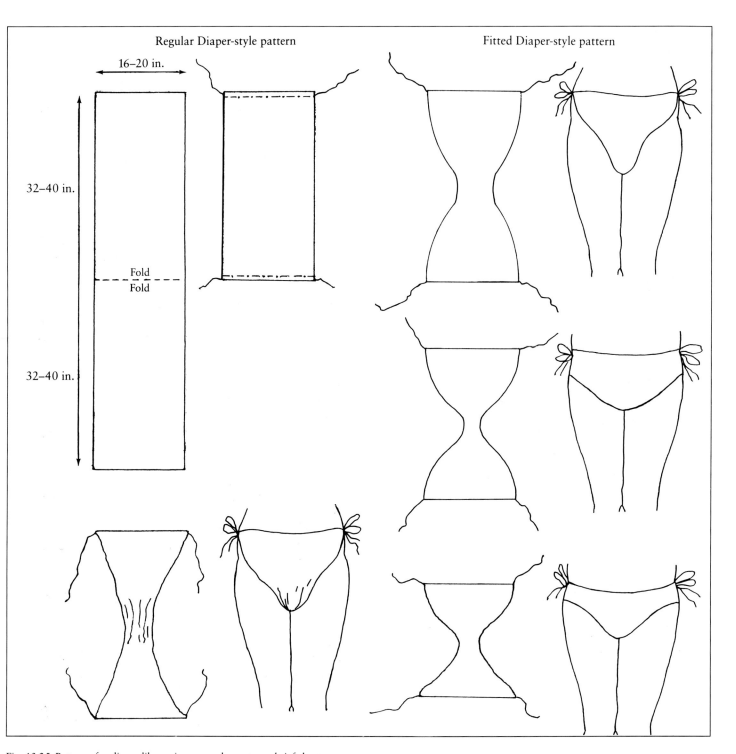

16–20 in.

32–40 in.

Fold
Fold

32–40 in.

Fig. 13.25. Patterns for diaper-like perizoma, underpants, or brief shorts.

Fig. 13.26. Exercising girl clad in bikini-style garments. Piazza Armerina, Sicily. Photo: N. Goldman.

Fig. 13.27. Terracotta Roman lamp showing Cupids helping Venus tie her strophium. Deneauve, *Lampes de Carthage*, no. 415.

band about the breasts, referred to in literature as a *strophium* or *fascia* (any kind of bandage). There are many depictions on the discus scenes of ancient Roman terracotta lamps of Cupids helping Venus to tie her strophium (fig. 13.27), and it seems that the bandagelike cloth is wound several times around and beneath the breasts. It does not seem to have any shaping to cup the breasts, and it either flattened them or merely held them in place. Experiments with wrapping a band of cloth eight inches wide and seventy inches long taught me that the band would be most efficiently used as a brassiere by bringing the ends around the body from the back so that each long end crossed in front, supporting the breasts. These ends then continue around to the sides to the back, where they are tucked inside the wrapping to be held securely in place. The Cupids assisting Venus on the discus scene of the lamp in figure 13.27 seem to be helping in the back-to-front wrapping. Any shorter length of cloth or wrapping beginning at one end merely flattened the breasts, a style popular in the "flapper" days of the 1920s and apparent in the costume of the "bikini girls" from Piazza Armerina. Roman statues do not seem to show any such popularity in style. Some even show the "braless" look of the late twentieth century.

There are words for a "slip" or undergarment for the tunic, which itself could be an undergarment in thin cloth, such as *supparum*, *subucula*, and *camisia*, which Wilson cites as used by Festus, quoting Afranius, and by Nonius, referring to linen coverings for the thighs of girls down to the ankles. *Camisia* is a late Latin word applied to a nightgown (Isidore, *Origines* 19.22, 29). The sliplike garment equivalent to the supparum or subucula for a matron seems to have been called by another name, *indusium*.

### SYNTHESIS

Although the word *synthesis* has many meanings of things "put together" besides its meaning as a garment, the use of the word to refer to the dinner costume of a man is evident in many literary passages. Martial makes fun of a man who changes his *synthesis* many times during a dinner on the pretext of perspiring (5.79), and he describes a friend who owns many lacernae and *syntheses* in beautiful colors. The idea of the costume being put together seems to evolve from the idea that the garb was a combination of other garments. The *synthesis* seems to be a rich costume worn by the wealthy, a costume to be shown off for its rich fabric and expensive color and embroidery. Martial indicates that it was worn also at the time of the Saturnalia (14.1 and 141), in winter when the toga was not appropriate. In white, it was worn by the Arval brothers for a certain feast.[13] Otherwise it was not a costume to be worn in public.

Fig. 13.28a. Distinctive Flavian hair style with a high tiara facade of curls framing the face and a braided coil in the back. Photo courtesy of the Capitoline Museum Photo Archive.

Fig. 13.28b. Conservative Roman hair style parted in the middle, with waves and curls down the sides. Photo courtesy of the Capitoline Photo Archive.

ROYAL BYZANTINE COSTUME:
JUSTINIAN AND THEODORA

The mosaics showing Justinian and Theodora on the walls of San Vitale in Ravenna (see figs. 5.8 and 5.9) are so explicit in detail that an attempt has been made to duplicate the jeweled garments as closely as possible, substituting fabric for *tesserae* and using artificial gems and pearls for adornment. For the costume of Justinian, I made a belted white tunic decorated with gold lamé down the sides from waist to knee and at the edges of the sleeves. His spectacular purple robe is a large half-moon–shaped garment, like a huge lacerna, caught at his left shoulder by a jeweled brooch ending in a three-drop pendant.[14] The curious angle of the inserted golden panel, the tablion, embroidered with rows of green ducks inside red circles, is explained by the panels added to the straight edge of the half-moon–shaped cloak. When the cloak is put around the neck, with the panels matching, the tablion falls at about a 45-degree angle,

and all of these panels on the cloaks of the male figures in the mosaics fall in this manner at parallel angles. An end of the tablion is pulled through the jeweled three-drop pendant brooch. Justinian wears tight hose and flowered or jeweled slippers or shoes. His crown is jeweled, and long, pearl-tipped pendilia are draped, for convenience, over his ears.

Theodora wears a white, belted, floor-length tunic with deep gold lamé edging at the bottom and also at the ends of the sleeves. Her matching purple mantle is made of fabric cut into a large half-moon, and it has golden embroidery along the edges and above a gold-embroidered representation of the three magi bearing gifts. Over the mantle from neck to midchest, Theodora's lavish display of jewelry, which I affixed to a short felt cape, attaching a combination of jewels and pearls, allows her own long pearl earrings to fall into place among the pearls of the pectoral decoration. Her crown, appropriately ornate, has been altered to allow the high green (emerald?) center stone to be incorporated into the crown, so that it can be packed in a suitcase without being damaged. The jewels were either sewn onto the fabric of the crown and cape or were attached by using a glue gun. There are bead shops which sell all kinds of colored stones and artificial pearls for such a project.

When teachers have their students attempt to reconstruct ancient Roman costumes, the results many times are last-minute frantic efforts pinning sheets that bear little or no resemblance to the costumes of antiquity. Teachers may wish to construct garments that can be used for many occasions. Students generally are more interested in adapting sheets with pins and belts for a single occasion. Pinning and belting solid-colored sheets will result in quite authentic-looking garments. For those who wish to construct more permanent garments, we recommend shopping for opaque, solid-colored cloth that will not wrinkle—either cotton, muslin, or polyester blend—and putting together, for the women, complementary or contrasting colors for tunic and palla to make an attractive ensemble. Adjust measurements to accommodate the width and height of the wearer, allowing for blousing of tunics. For the male costumes, use white or beige-white cloth and red-purple for the stripes. Add vine leaves for wreaths for both sexes, jewelry and flowers for the women. The women may even want to arrange their hair in the styles evident on sculpture: most female figures have long hair, usually parted in the center and arranged in long curls or pulled back into buns or "Psyche knots," or braided and arranged in coils at the nape of the neck. In front, bangs cut short can be arranged into forehead curls or kept straight to cover the forehead. The more adventuresome may even want to try the complicated Flavian hairstyle with its high tiara of snail curls in front and braided coils in back (figs. 13.28a-b). Most important, enjoy re-creating the roles you are playing.

## NOTES

1. Wilson, *Clothing*, 36.
2. Whether the six dancing girls were originally Greek bronzes, bronzes executed by Greeks working in the area of the Bay of Naples, or bronzes executed by Romans working in the style of Greek sculptors, these are sculptures from the destroyed city of Herculaneum (A.D. 79) and therefore can be considered Roman.
3. Wilson, *Clothing*, pl. 41, Coptic weaving from the Victoria and Albert Museum, London. Such a tunic is referred to as a Coptic tunic.
4. A single wide stripe in the center of the garment was used in Phoenician garments, according to Herodian, 5.5.10.
5. A statue in the Norwegian Institute in Rome, identified by L'Orange ("Statua di un'imperatrice") as an imperial personage on the basis both of her mantle and her pearl-studded calcei, wears the peplos belted high under the breasts.
6. Bieber, *Ancient Copies*, 23.
7. T. McGinn, lecture to the NEH summer session, American Academy in Rome, 1988. See also J. Sebesta, chap. 2 in this volume.
8. See J. Mayo, *A History of Ecclesiastical Dress* (London, 1984), 13-15. Mayo calls the cucullus the hood of the paenula.
9. Wilson, *Clothing*, 112-13, 115.
10. Cicero, *Philippics* 5.12; 7.2, 11; 14.1. Strabo 3.3, 4; Tacitus, *Germania* 17.
11. Columella 1, 8, 9; SHA *Marcus Aurelius* 27.3.
12. Bonfante, *Etruscan Dress*, 19-29, 164.
13. W. Henzen, *Acta fratrum arvalium* (Berlin, 1874), 15.
14. B. Goldman discusses such a crossbow-type of fibula with the royal three-drop pendant in his article "Imperial Jewel," 834–35.

GLOSSARY
BIBLIOGRAPHY
INDEX

# GLOSSARY

This is not a complete glossary of dress terms, but is an explanation of terms used in this book.

## COLORS

Color terms are given in masculine adjectival form. Where an ancient author describes a color only in relation to a noun, such as "the color of almonds," the noun in nominative form is printed in bold type. In a few instances the noun form of an adjective is found in a Latin text, and this form is indicated by parentheses.

**Aer:** Light blue.
**Albens rosa:** Pale gray, or possibly pale pink.
*Albus:* White.
*Amethystinus* (**purpura amethystina**): Amethyst purple
**Amygdala:** Almond, light tan.
*Aureus:* Golden yellow.
*Caesicius:* Sky blue.
*Callainus:* Green-turquoise.
*Calthulus:* Marigold yellow.
*Carinus:* Walnut brown, dark brown with red overtones.
*Cerasinus:* Cherry red.
*Cereus:* Wax yellow, brownish yellow, perhaps identical to *cerinus*.
*Cerinus:* Brownish yellow.
*Coccinus, coccineus (coccum):* Scarlet.
*Conchyliatus (conchyliatum):* Pale lavender.
*Coracinus:* Deep black.
*Crocotulus:* Reddish orange.
*Croceus:* Saffron yellow, red-orange or yellow with orange overtones, perhaps identical to *crocotulus*.
*Cumatilis:* Sea blue.
*Erythraeus:* A natural reddish hue of wool.
*Ferrugineus:* A somewhat purplish red.
*Flammeus:* Reddish orange.
*Fuscus:* Brown with a reddish tinge.
*Galbinus:* Yellow-green.
**Glandes:** Chestnut brown.
**Heliotropium:** Reddish blue-red.
*Hyacinthinus:* Reddish violet.
*Hysginus (hysginum):* Scarlet.

*Ianthinus:* Violet.
*(Indicum):* Indigo blue.
*Luteus:* Yellow-red.
**Malva:** Mauve.
*Molocinus:* Mauve.
*Niger:* Black, or very dark brown.
*Ostrinus (ostrum):* Reddish purple. That the color had a red tinge is indicated by descriptions of the hue as *rubens*, red; *sanguineus*, bloody; and *puniceus*, scarlet.
**Paphiae myrti:** Dark green.
*Prasinus:* Bluish green, pea green.
*Pullus:* Gray, according to Ovid; also black or a very deep brown-black, the color of mourning.
*Puniceus, phoenicius, poenicius:* Scarlet.
*(Purpura):* Purple. The four major shades were *ater*, dark; *lividus*, pale; *ruber*, red; and *violaceus*, blue.
*Purpureus laconicus:* Dark rose purple.
*Purpureus Tyrius (purpura dibapha Tyria):* Light rose purple.
*Ruber Tarentinus:* Reddish violet.
*Russus, russeus, russatus:* Bright red.
*Thalassinus:* Purple of undetermined hue.
**Threicia grus:** Gray.
*Tyrianthinus:* Violet purple.
**Undae:** Sea blue? darker blue?
*Venetus:* Dark blue.
*Violaceus:* Violet.
**Viola serotina:** Blue-red.
*Violeus:* Violet.
*Viridis:* Green.

## GENERAL TERMS

Modern terms appear in bold type.

*Akinakes:* A short Persian sword.
*Amictorium:* Jewish word for a cloak.
*Amictus* (Latin, *amicire*, "to wrap"): Generally, a covering.
*Amiculum:* A mantle, worn by prostitutes according to Isidore (*Origines* 19.25.5).

*Amphimallium:* A cloak which was shaggy on both sides.

*Anakolos:* Jewish word for an undertunic.

*Anaxarides:* Iranian trousers of somewhat full cut.

**Ankle shoe:** A shoe covering the foot up to the ankle joint. See *boot.*

**Ankle strap:** A strap fastening around the ankle with a tie, knot, or buckle.

*Auratus:* Woven with gold thread.

*Babylonica hypodemata:* Elegant Babylonian sandals made of excellent quality leather (see the *Edict of Diocletian* 9.7). They were considered luxurious and worn by both men and women.

**Baldric:** A belt worn diagonally from shoulder to hip to support a sword.

*Balteus:* A term borrowed by modern scholars from Quintilian, *Institutio oratoria* 11.3.140, where it is used to describe the appearance of the rolled cloth of the toga which extended diagonally from the right armpit to the left shoulder, and which thus resembled a sword belt. The term was not used in antiquity.

*Bardocucullus* (Celtic loan word): A very thick, heavy *cucullus* which retained much of the natural grease of wool to make itself waterproof. See *cucullus.*

*Baucides* (from Greek, *baukos,* "prudish, affected"?): Expensive saffron-colored footwear especially popular among courtesans (Athenaeus, *Epitome* 13.23.568). Some had cork soles to increase the wearer's height.

*Bombycina:* Silk.

**Boot:** A kind of footwear extending above the ankle joint.

*Bracae (braccae):* Loose or baggy trousers tied by a cord at the ankle and worn by European barbarians.

**Brocade:** A fabric woven with a raised overall pattern.

**Brodequin:** Stout, laced ankle boot or sock.

*Bulla:* The boy's rounded, convex locket enclosing an amulet, often phallic in nature. The bulla was adopted by the Romans from the Etruscans. It could be gold, silver, bronze, or even leather.

**Buskin:** A soft, high-laced leather boot which apparently developed from the *cothurnus* worn by tragic actors. See *cothurni.*

**Butted seam:** A seam joining two edges of the leather of uppers, usually at the back of the heel or the toe front, with no lapping of the leather.

*Calautica:* A woman's headdress. According to Servius (*In Aeneadem* 9.613), it was a woman's *mitra.* See *mitra.*

*Calcamen:* Roman shoe or boot that reached to the midcalf.

*Calceamentum:* Any kind of shoe, and footwear in general. It also designated a Roman shoe or boot that reached to the knee.

*Calceare:* To put on shoes.

*Calceatus:* Wearing shoes.

*Calcei muliebres* (Latin, *mulier,* "woman"): Shoes for women; a term identical to *calceoli.*

*Calcei patricii:* Boots for Roman nobles which had closed uppers and a long tongue (*Edict of Diocletian* 9.7). They were bound to the leg with four thongs *(corrigiae),* two on each side attached between the sole and the uppers, front and back. The thongs tied around the upper ankle and the

middle of the leg. These *calcei* were perhaps distinguished from the senatorial boot *(calcei senatorii)* by the distinctive red color of the patrician shoe *(mulleus).* The senatorial boot seems to have remained black.

*Calcei repandi:* Pointed-toed shoes, curving upward at the toe, that were worn by Etruscans in the sixth century B.C. These, in theory, were the model for the later Roman senatorial *calcei* with lacing and straps. Cicero says that only statues of Juno Sospita continued to use the pointed-toe *calcei repandi,* but a rounded-toe version may have been in use as late as the third century A.D.

*Calcei senatorii:* Boots for Roman senators, which were perhaps distinguished by their black color from the patrician boot. When members of the equestrian class began to enter the ranks of the senators, patricians might then have been distinguished by the color of their boots. The style of the senatorial boot seems to have been identical to that of the *calceus senatorius;* in the *Edict of Diocletian,* however, the *calcei patricii* cost 150 sesterces, while the *calcei senatorii* cost only 100 sesterces, which indicates some substantial difference.

*Calceoli* (diminutive of *calcei*): Small shoes, half boots, usually for women.

*Calceus* (pl. *calcei*): Shoes that came up over the ankle; the term comes from the Latin *calx,* "heel." This shoe was the major contribution of the Romans to footwear, since the Greeks relied mostly on varieties of sandals or boots. *Calcei* were formal shoes worn with the toga outside the house, while sandals were worn with the tunic inside the house. Slaves were not allowed to wear *calcei.* Bonfante-Warren ("Roman Costume," 605) adds, "Though the word was used for high closed shoes in general, cf. *calceamentum,* in contrast to *soleae* or sandals, it meant especially the official Roman shoe worn with the toga *(toga et calcei).* A special type, *mulleus,* was believed to have been the shoe of the kings of Rome, specifically the Etruscan kings. . . . The Roman senatorial *calcei,* derived from Etruscan shoes . . . were high-topped, laced with black *corrigiae* . . . and fastened with a buckle called a *luna.*"

*Calicae:* Shoes, differentiated in the *Edict of Diocletian* (9.9) as shoes for senators and for equites *(calicae equestres).*

*Caligae:* Army boots with hobnailed soles and cutwork straps. These straps formed a complex network on the uppers; there were also two or more straps tying at the upper ankle. *Caligae* are also referred to in the *Edict of Diocletian* (9.5–6) as "boots for mule drivers or farm workers, first quality, without hobnails."

*Caligae muliebres:* Boots for women, similar to those worn by soldiers, but without hobnails. *Caligae muliebres* cost only 60 sesterces in the *Edict,* but those for soldiers, without nails, cost 100 sesterces.

*Camisia* (Gallic loan word): An undertunic.

*Campagi imperiales:* A shoe, similar to that of the soldiers, worn by emperors in the late empire (e.g., Maximinus and Gallienus) and by Byzantine emperors.

*Campagus* (pl. *campagi*): Soldiers' shoes, also called *campagi militares.* In the *Edict of Diocletian* (9.14), these cost 75 denarii.

*Capite velato:* The action of pulling the toga over the head for certain types of sacrificing.

*Carbasina:* Heavy, durable linen-cotton cloth.

*Carbasus* (Hebrew loan word): Cotton.

*Carbasus lina:* Linen-cotton mixture.

*Carbatina* (pl. *carbatinae*): One-piece shoes with soles and uppers cut from a single piece of leather. The edges were cut into loops through which a lacing pulled the uppers together.

*Centonarius:* Patchworker, dealer of patchwork.

**Chain mail:** Flexible armor made of interlocked metal rings.

**Chaps:** A contraction of *chaparreras*, referring to leather overalls which are usually open at the back and worn by Mexican and American horsemen for protection against thorns and brush.

*Chiridota tunica* (Greek, *cheir*, "hand"): A long-sleeved tunic, also called the *tunica manicata* (Latin, *manus*, "hand").

*Chiton:* A Greek dress made of two rectangular lengths of material which were sewn along the sides up to the arms. The rectangles were pinned together at intervals along the top with a space left for the head and neck. Josephus also uses the word to denote the long-sleeved woman's dress worn by unmarried Jewish women and the sleeved tunic worn by Jewish men.

*Chitoniskos:* A short, long-sleeved woman's dress worn by unmarried Jewish women, according to Josephus.

*Chlamys:* A long cloak reaching the ankles and worn by the emperor and empress as part of their civil costume in the sixth century A.D.

*Chlanis:* A man's mantle. The word is a derivative of *chlamys.*

**Chukker boot** (Hindi): An ankle-high shoe, laced through two pairs of eyelets and often made of soft leather.

*Cilicium:* Cloak of Cilician goats' hair (Varro, *De re rustica* 2.11.12).

*Cinctus Gabinus:* The "Gabinian" girding, a way of tucking up the toga while the wearer performs a ritual. The wearer threw one end of the toga over his shoulder and then knotted the garment around his waist.

*Cingulum:* A belt. The bride's *cingulum* was in the form of a cord of woolen fibers twisted together.

*Clavus:* The woven, vertical stripe of reddish purple on the tunic extending from each shoulder to the hem.

**Clogs:** Wooden-soled shoes which had broad leather straps over the insteps. The toes were left bare.

*Colobium* (Greek, *kolobion,* "curtailed"): Jewish term for a linen tunic.

*Confarretio:* The oldest form of marriage among the patricians. It was a binding religious ceremony rather than a civil contract.

*Corolla:* The small bridal wreath of herbs, flowers, and sacred branches *(verbenae),* worn by the bride under her veil.

*Corona:* Generally, a wreath or crown. Specifically, the highest distinction awarded for valor in war, as in *corona civica,* a wreath of oak leaves for saving a citizen's life in battle, or *corona muralis,* a golden circle in the form of a city wall for the soldier who first climbed the wall of an enemy's camp. See *crown.*

*Corrigia* (pl. *corrigiae*): Straps on the *calcei,* two on each side. These were wrapped around the ankle, and each pair was tied in front with a knot. The *corrigiae* may have been formed by two continuous, long straps which were inserted between the inner sole and the outer sole of the shoe.

*Cothurni* (possibly a Lydian loan word; see Herodotus 1.155): The tragic actor's shoes or boots which had high platform soles to increase his height and stage presence. See *buskin.*

**Couched embroidery:** A method of embroidering in which heavy threads, laid out on the material, are stitched down at intervals with another thread.

*Crepidae* (Greek *krepis, krepides*): Greek shoes which covered more of the foot than did the simple thonged *soleae.* The *crepidae* sometimes had straps but most often sported high up on the foot or ankle a complex network of cutwork designs, on the order of modern huaraches.

**Crown:** A circlet for the head. In the third century A.D. the radiate crown of the sun god was commonly worn by Roman emperors. Religious crowns worn by priests frequently had images of deities engraved on them. See *corona.*

*Cucullus:* Hooded cape or cloak. See *bardocucullus.*

**Cuirass:** Defensive armor for the torso, consisting of a breastplate and back plate (dorsal plate) and worn over a cloth, leather, or padded vest. Originally they were made from leather, as the etymology of *cuirass (corium)* indicates, but Roman generals came to wear iron breastplates which were often molded to replicate musculature; these are also called "classical" or "anatomical" cuirasses. The lower edge of the cuirass was curved and had one or more rows of round or long tongue-shaped lappets *(pteryges).* The Roman imperial or "Hellenistic" style of cuirass, which appeared in the late first century B.C., developed from the Greek cavalry cuirass. It was also modeled to represent the musculature of its wearer but had a single row of short leather straps attached to its lower edge. These short straps are distinct from the longer leather straps attached to the lower edge of the underlying vest. Cuirasses of Roman generals, and especially of Roman emperors, also were decorated with embossed historical, allegorical, or mythological figures and symbols of victories.

*Cyclas* (Greek, "circular"): A woman's mantle with a border running all around it. The mantle could be luxurious. Propertius (4.7.40) mentions a gilded border, while Juvenal (6.259) states that the mantle was made of a light (gauzy?) material.

**Delamination:** The separation of the leather into grain and flesh layers when leather lies underground or in a watery environment.

*Dextrarum iunctio:* Joining of the right hands, which marks the union in Roman marriage.

*Diadem* (Greek, "to bind around"): Originally a simple band or fillet tied at the back of the head and visible in coin portraits of Alexander the Great, where it symbolized absolute monarchy. It was rarely worn by Roman emperors until the time of Constantine the Great, who wore one decorated with jewels and laurel leaves. The ties in the back of the emperor's diadem were usually adorned with jewels. In the fourth century, a large central jewel adorned the diadem above the forehead, giving it a more massive appearance.

*Dorsalium*: A curtain which hangs behind the deceased in mortuary sculpture.

*Embades*: Any enclosed boots which had to be "put on" with a foot stepping into them (Greek *embainein*, "to step into"). The long leather tongue came down over the top in front of the lacing, and the boots could have been lined with felt or fur. Dionysus is depicted wearing these, and so they came to be used in tragic drama. The woman's version, *Sikyonia embas* (from the island Sikyon), was a fancy shoe made of white felt.

*Endromides*: High boots worn by runners or hunters. They were split vertically up the inside middle to make them easier to put on.

*Ephod*: The jeweled breastplate worn by the Jewish high priest (Exodus 28:6). Its shape and the kind and number of its jewels, like those of the other garments of the high priest, had cosmological symbolic meaning.

*Epikarsion*: A type of shirt worn in Palestine under a tunic.

*Epomydes*: Shoulder straps which tie the front and back plates of a cuirass together.

*Essen*: The long robe worn by the Jewish high priest.

**Eyelets**: Holes for lacing. Some were bound or reinforced.

*Fasciae*: Bands wrapped around the legs. They were appropriately worn by men only in ill health.

*Feminalia* (*femur*, "thigh"): Short, tight-fitting pants covering the thighs to the knees, worn in cold weather.

*Fibula*: A pin or brooch fastening a person's mantle, or *chlamys* of the emperor, at the shoulder. Beginning in the third century A.D., the emperor wore a more elaborate jeweled brooch to signify his status over military tribunes, who began to be awarded jeweled brooches. Under Constantine the Great, the emperor's jeweled brooch became conspicuously larger, and by the reigns of his three sons, three pendant jewels hanging from the brooch were consistently part of the imperial insignia.

*Flammeum*: The bride's rectangular, enveloping veil, dyed with yellow *luteum* pigment. Though the word is cognate with the Latin *flamma* ("flame"), literary sources make clear that the veil was a deep yellow, like the flame of a candle.

**Flesh**: In tanners' terminology, the inner surface of the leather, made from the inner surface of the hide.

*Forma*: The wooden last on which a leather shoe was made.

*Galerus*: The helmet-shaped cap made of animal skin worn by Roman priests. The higher-ranking priests' *galerus* had a spike (*apex*) attached to the top; lower-ranking priests' had a knob.

*Gallicae*: Informal sandals worn with tunics and *lacerna*, but not with the toga. There were various kinds of *gallicae*: for men, *gallicae biriles*; for runners, *gallicae cursuriae*; and for farm workers, *gallicae rusticanae*.

*Gausapa* (loan word, possibly from a Balkan language): A felt waterproof cloak.

**Gemara**: The rabbinic commentary on and interpretation of the Mishnah.

*Gladius*: The Roman short sword. The *gladius Hispaniensis*, its progenitor, had an eagle-headed pommel on its hilt.

**Grain**: The outer surface of the leather, made from the hide of the animal. The hair, fur, or wool forms a characteristic pattern on the grain side, which enables identification of the kind of hide used in a shoe.

**Halacha**: Jewish law as set forth in the Mishnah and Torah.

*Haluq*: A Jewish garment identical to a tunic.

*Hasta caelibaris*: The spear used to part the bride's hair in the *seni crines* style.

*Himation*: A rectangular mantle worn by either men or women. It was essentially identical to the *pallium* and *palla*.

**Hobnails**: Iron nails nailed through the soles of shoes or boots to keep the footwear together and to prevent the soles from wearing out. The nails were placed all around the edge of the sole and in various designs on the surface of the sole.

*Holosericus* (Greek, *holos*, "wholly"): Made of pure silk. See *serica*.

*Hosae*: Hose, boots, or gaiters; in general, leg coverings.

*Impilia*: Liners of wool or felt for boots or sandals. Also, a Jewish word for felt slippers.

*'Imrah*: Hebrew term for the *clavus* or purple stripe of a tunic.

*Indusium*: An undertunic.

*Infula*: Woolen fillet or ribbon, either white or red, worn around the head by priests and priestesses, especially Vestals, and also by sacrificial victims and suppliants.

*Insignia*: Distinguishing marks of authority, office, or honor, such as the imperial jeweled brooch with three hanging pendants and the *pendilia* hanging from the diadem.

*Institae*: The shoulder straps of the *stola*.

*Interrasile*: Elaborate openwork settings for medallions and coins hung on chains, bracelets, or necklaces.

**Jambières**: A modern French term designating the leggings worn by Palmyrene men over their trousers (*anaxarides*) as part of their riding costume. Palmyrene men also wore such leggings, made of fine material, indoors.

*Lacerna*: A cloak or mantle worn by both men and women, originally over the tunic and toga, but then just over the tunic.

**Lacing**: Thin lengths of leather or fabric inserted through loops or eyelets to fasten shoes to the foot.

*Lacinia*: A term possibly used to designate the hem of a toga, which was placed against the lower left leg between the knee and ankles (see Suetonius, *Caligula* 35.3). It may, however, merely designate the lower border of any garment.

*Laena*: The heavy rounded mantle, Etruscan in origin, worn by the augurs and flamines during sacrifices. It was shaped like a toga but was draped over both shoulders and hung in a curve, front and back, and was fastened with a pin in back.

**Lamé**: An ornamental material in which metallic threads are interwoven with silk, wool, linen, or cotton.

**Lamellar armor**: A type of armor composed of small, overlapping plates (*lamellae*) laced together.

*Lana*: Wool.

**Lappet:** A small flap or loosely hanging decoration of a garment.

**Last:** A wooden block (*forma*) shaped like a foot on which a shoe was made. The Romans also used an iron block on which to hammer the hobnails, since the points had to be turned or flattened.

**Latchet shoe:** A late Roman style of a low shoe with a strap or straps across the instep.

*Limbus:* A purple band sewn onto the edge of a woman's mantle or the hem of a woman's garment (Nonius M541, Servius, *In Aeneadem* 2.616, 4.137).

*Limes:* The frontier area of a province where troops were stationed.

*Lingula:* The tongue of a shoe.

*Linteo* (pl. *linteones*): Linen weaver and seller.

*Lodex:* A specialty weave of Laodicea, made of wool or flax.

*Loramentum:* A fastener, thong, or strap for tying the shoe.

*Luna:* A crescent-shaped decoration tied to the top of the senatorial *calceus* as a buckle.

*Lunula:* An amuletic necklace worn by girls and women. The amulet was shaped like the crescent moon (*luna*).

*Luteum soccum:* The yellow bridal slipper, dyed the same color as the bridal veil (*flammeum*) and the hairnet (*reticulum*).

*Mafortium:* A short *palla* worn by women.

*Margarita:* The pearl.

*Mater familias:* The wife of a *pater familias*, a man no longer subject to his father's power. As such he was able to have children under his own paternal power (*patria potestas*).

*Matrona:* A female Roman citizen who was married to a Roman citizen.

*Melanteria:* Copper-vitriol solution containing iron, used to blacken leather.

*Metaxa* (loan word of uncertain origin): Silk.

**Mishnah:** The collection of Jewish oral laws compiled by Rabbi Judah the Prince ca. A.D. 200.

*Mitra:* An Asiatic headdress resembling a turban and worn by the Trojans in the *Aeneid*. Romans considered it effeminate dress for a man. See *calautica*.

*Modius:* A flat-topped cylindrical hat worn by Palmyrene priests. The term applied to this type of hat is a modern one: it is owing to the hat's resemblance to the Roman corn measure or bushel basket called the *modius*.

**Mordant:** A substance used in dyeing to fix the coloring matter.

*Mulleus:* A shoe dyed red, named after the mullet fish (*mullus*), which is red in color. The *calceus patricius* probably differed from the *calceus senatorius* or *equestris* by being made of leather dyed red.

*Nimbus:* A halo around the emperor's head in coin portraits, indicating his divinity.

*Nodus Herculaneus (Herculeus):* The ritual knot of the bride's belt, symbolizing the virility of Hercules, who fathered seventy children.

*Nudus:* When used in a public setting, "bare-chested." The priests called Luperci, for example, were bare-chested above their loincloths of goatskin. Used in a home setting, *nudus* could mean "wearing underpants," "completely naked."

*Paenula:* A short, hooded cloak of heavy wool, leather, or fur.

*Palla:* The rectangular mantle of a woman.

*Pallium:* A large rectangular mantle worn by non-Romans and especially by Greeks.

*Paludamentum:* The long mantle worn by a Roman army officer or the emperor in military garb.

*Patagium:* A gold band. A tunic with a neckline decorated by a *patagium* was called a *tunica patagiata*.

*Pellytra:* A Greek word denoting leather "socks" worn to protect the foot against chafing and cold.

*Pendilia:* Chains, beads, gold wires, or pearls to which pearls or other precious stones were attached like pendants. Beginning in the early fifth century, they hung down from the sides of the emperor's diadem and were part of the imperial insignia. The emperor's *pendilia* were short and fell behind his ears, while the empress' *pendilia* were long and hung in front of her ears. The *pendilia* are not to be confused with the jeweled ties of the imperial diadem, which hung behind the head.

*Peplos:* A dress worn by Greek women. The upper third of the material was folded over to form an overblouse. The folded edges of the material were pinned together along the upper arm.

*Perizoma:* Short pants worn by men under the tunic.

*Pero* (pl. *perones*): A soft leather shoe covering the entire foot and ankle. Originally *pero* was a generic term for "shoe," but J. Pollini has used it to denote the type of shoe worn by figures on the Ara Pacis.

**Phrygian cap:** See *pilleus*.

*Pilleus:* A felt or soft wool cap which rises to a forward curving point at its top and was worn by Phrygians and Dacians.

*Piloi:* The name derives from the Greek word for felt (*pilos*) and denotes felt socks used with leather sandals to protect the flesh of the foot from chafing and to keep the foot warm. The *piloi* were commonly worn with the *embas* or *endromis*.

*Pissyrgos:* Pitch worker, a Greek slang word for "shoemaker," who frequently used pitch to blacken shoes.

*Plumatilis:* Pilelike down.

*Plumeus:* Downy, having a pile similar to down.

*Polymita:* A many-threaded damask made in Alexandria.

*Praetexta:* The woven reddish purple border on a garment.

*Pteryges:* Rounded or scalloped leather lappets hanging from the bottom of the Roman, "classical" style of cuirass.

**Quarters:** The four sides of the uppers of shoes.

**Radiate:** A depiction of the head of an emperor from which the sun's rays burst forth as a sign of his divinity.

*Ralla:* A gauzy, open weave.

**Rawhide:** The hide or skin of an animal scraped on the flesh side and made pliable by flexing, not by tanning, leather.

*Reticulum:* Hairnet. Traditionally brides wove their own from wool dyed with *luteum*.

*Ricinium (recinium):* The square mantle worn by women during mourning. It had a woven reddish purple border (*praetexta*) and is likely to have been dark colored like the man's *toga pulla*.

*Rugae:* The folds ("wrinkles") of the skirt of the *stola*.

*Sagum* (Celtic loan word): The soldier's cloak of rough wool. It could be short or midleg length. *Sagum sumere* meant to exchange the toga for the military cloak, that is, to prepare for war.

*Sandalia:* Sandals consisting of a sole and strap or thong to tie the sole to the foot.

*Sculponeae:* See *clogs*.

**Selvage:** The edge of a woven garment finished off to prevent raveling.

*Seni crines:* The ritual hairstyle of brides and Vestals which was made by dividing the hair into six braids.

*Serica:* Silk. The Chinese were called the Seres.

**Shaatnez:** The Jewish prohibition against the mixing of fibers contained in Deuteronomy 22:11.

**Shirr:** To gather material by drawing it up along two or more parallel lines of stitching or encased cords.

**Sifre Deuteronomy:** A commentary on Deuteronomy.

*Sikyonia embas:* See *embades*.

*Sinus:* An overfold which extended down from the diagonal roll of the cloth of the toga which ran from beneath the right arm to the left shoulder. It extended down across the torso like an apron. The *sinus* first became popular during the reign of Augustus and survived into the fourth century A.D. Its length varied according to fashion, although it generally extended to the region of the right knee. When the banded toga became popular during the third and fourth centuries, its *sinus* became very long, extending to the ankle, and its lower portion was generally carried over the left arm.

**Snood:** A clothlike covering for the hair of women in the fifth and sixth centuries. Sometimes the empress wore it under an elaborate jeweled diadem.

*Soccus:* A low, light shoe worn by Greeks and, among the Romans, by women, effeminate men, and actors. The *Edict of Diocletian* lists four colors of *socci*: purple, Phoenecian purple, white, and gilded (9.17-23).

*Solea:* A sandal fastened to the sole, (*solum,* "ground") by leather straps. Greeks wore sandals outdoors, but the Romans wore them mostly indoors; outdoors Roman men wore *calcei*. Sandals were worn to dinner parties, where they were removed before reclining on the couches; "to ask for one's sandals" (*poscere soleas*) was an idiom for "to leave the party."

*Solo alto:* A phrase describing the high platform shoe of the actor. See *buskin, cothurni*.

*Sordes:* Dirtied clothing worn as a symbol of sorrow, as, for instance, when a family member or friend was accused of a crime.

*Spissa:* A closely woven fabric.

*Stephane:* A Hellenistic crownlike headpiece worn by goddesses and Hellenistic and Roman women. It was in the form of a high, triangular-shaped headpiece, sometimes made of gold and embossed, and rose to a point above the forehead.

*Stola:* The dress worn by married Roman women. It was suspended from the shoulders by straps (*institae*) and was long enough to cover the feet. As this dress, distinctive in

form, symbolized its owner's chastity, Josephus anachronistically describes King Jeroboam's wife as wearing it. Josephus also used the Greek word "stola" ("garment") to refer to the robes of Jewish priests.

*Strophium:* A type of bra in the form of a band, made of linen or cotton, worn by women around their breasts for support.

*Subligaculum:* A loincloth.

*Subligar:* A loincloth.

*Subucula:* A linen undertunic worn by both sexes.

*Sudarium:* Jewish term denoting a scarf worn around the neck.

*Suffibulum:* The veil worn by the Vestals, especially while sacrificing. It was short and white with a purple border.

*Supparum:* A linen undertunic worn by girls.

*Synthesis:* A costume for banquets and parties. Its exact form is uncertain, but the word means "a combination."

*Tablion:* A rectangle of elaborately woven decorated cloth on the emperor's *chlamys*.

*Tallit:* Jewish word for "mantle."

*Talmid hakham:* The *tallit* or mantle of a Jewish scholar or distinguished person. It was longer than the average *tallit* and completely covered the tunic.

**Talmud:** The collection of Jewish laws and teachings, comprising the Mishnah and the Gemara. There were two Talmuds. The Jerusalem Talmud was completed in the mid-fifth century A.D. and the Babylonian Talmud in the mid-sixth century A.D.

**Tanning:** Conversion of hides into leather by steeping them in a solution of tannin, an acid solution often brewed out of oak bark or gall.

**Tapestry:** A fabric in which colored threads are woven by hand to produce a design or picture.

*Taurina:* An oxhide sandal for women which could be made single- or double-soled, according to the *Edict of Diocletian* (9.16).

*Tiara* (Eastern loan word): A high turban, worn in the *Aeneid* by the Trojan king. Palmyrene gods also wore a *tiara*, or turban, which was often decorated with horns. A plain *tiara* was worn by Armenians depicted on Roman coinage.

*Tibiale* (*tibia,* "shinbone"): Bandage or wrapping for the legs below the knees, worn in cold weather.

*Toga:* A rounded, woolen garment, adapted from the semicircular Etruscan mantle. It originally was worn without an undergarment by all Romans. From the second century B.C. on, it was generally worn over a tunic by adult males. It was the garment worn by the Roman man during business, governmental, and religious affairs. The toga was draped by placing an edge on the left side of the body which extended from the lower legs (see *lacinia*) up over the shoulder, then around the back and beneath the right arm. The loose end of cloth which remained was then thrown over the left shoulder. The toga extended to the lower legs on all sides. The toga was also worn by a wife divorced for adultery, to signify her dishonorable status.

*Toga candida:* A toga specially whitened by bleaching or chalking, which was worn by candidates for a magistracy.

*Toga contabulata:* A term often used by modern scholars to

designate the banded toga which developed in the later second century A.D. and which remained popular throughout the third and fourth centuries. The term *contabulata* is derived from Apuleius, *Metamorphoses* 11.3, where it is used to describe the complex folds of Isis' *palla*.

*Toga exigua:* A term borrowed from Horace, *Epistles* 1.19.13, and used by modern scholars to describe the short toga worn until the midfirst century B.C.

*Toga muliebris:* A term used by Cicero to denote the toga worn by a prostitute.

*Toga praetexta:* A toga with a reddish purple band woven along its lower edge. It was worn by freeborn children of both sexes and by consuls and priests when presiding at official functions. Upon puberty boys assumed the *toga virilis;* upon marriage girls assumed the *stola* and the *palla*.

*Toga pulla:* A dark-colored toga worn during mourning.

*Toga pura:* The toga in the natural, off-white color of wool.

*Toga purpurea:* A toga woven of purple-dyed wool worn in the early triumphs and by the emperor.

*Toga rasa:* A toga with a closely clipped, smooth pile.

*Togati:* Clothed in a toga.

*Toga virilis:* The plain white toga which boys assumed upon maturity. It was identical to the *toga pura*.

*Torque:* A massive metal, circular necklace, often made of gold. Sometimes it was fashioned of metal wires twisted around each other. A favorite form of jewelry among the Gauls, it was also worn by Persians, and Etruscans and Romans.

**Tosefta:** A "supplement" to the Mishnah.

**Tractate:** A section or chapter of the Talmud, such as the Tractate Shabbat.

*Trochades:* Greek sandals worn by runners.

*Tunic:* The Roman garment worn by men and children under the toga and by women under the stola. It was a sleeved garment, unlike the Greek archaic chiton. Both chiton and tunic are derived from the Phoenician word for the prototype of this garment; possibly *tunica* came into Latin indirectly through Etruscan.

*Tunica pulla:* A dark-colored (gray or black) tunic worn by Verres. Its color made it inappropriate for a Roman governor to wear.

*Tunica recta:* The straight tunic, worn for initiation ceremonies, such as marriage for girls and the coming of age for boys. It was woven on a warp-weighted loom on which the weft was beaten upward. *Recta* ("straight") presumably indicates that the garment was woven as a single, straight piece of material.

*Tunica talaris* (Latin, *talus,* "ankle"): An ankle-length tunic. According to Cicero (*Second Verrine* 2.5.13.31), it was an effeminate garment for a Roman man to wear.

*Tutulus:* Traditionally the ritual form of a woman's hairstyle, it was adopted from the Etruscan hairstyle worn in the late sixth and early fifth centuries B.C. The hair was sectioned and piled high on the head and fastened with *vittae*.

*Tzitzit:* The twisted tassels attached to the four corners of the Jewish mantle as ordained in Deuteronomy 22:12.

*Udo* (pl., *udones*): A woolen sock made from African goat's hair.

*Umbo:* A term used to designate the bunching of cloth pulled from the portion draped over the left side of the body over the *sinus*. It apparently helped to hold the garment in place; see Macrobius, *Saturnalia* 3.13.4. Tertullian (*De pallio 5*) used the term to designate the folded band of the banded toga of the third century A.D.

**Upper:** The portion of the shoe which covers all but the sole of the foot.

**Vamp:** The portion of the shoe which covers the instep and toes.

*Velum:* A woman's veil.

*Vestem mutare:* To change one's clothing to mourning clothing; also, generally, to change one's clothing.

*Vestiarius:* Dealer in ready-made clothing.

*Vestis:* The generic word for "clothing."

*Vestis Coa:* Garment made of wild Coan silk.

*Vincula (vincla):* Straps or shoe strings. In poetry, the term was used as a metaphor for sandal or shoe.

*Vitta:* A woolen band used in women's hairstyles and in decorating altars, victims, graves, and so on. Those used by priests were colored reddish purple *(purpurea)*.

**Welt:** In shoemaking, a strip of leather placed between the outsole of a shoe and the edges of the insole and the upper, through which these parts are stitched.

# BIBLIOGRAPHY

A list of the abbreviations used herein appears on pages xiii-xiv.

### ANCIENT SOURCES

Adhelmus. *De laudibus virginitatis* (In praise of chastity).

*Aetna.* Anonymous poem on Mt. Etna.

Ammianus Marcellinus. *Rerum gestarum* (History).

Appian. *Bellum civile* (The civil war).

Asconius. *Pro Cornelio de maiestate* (Commentary on Cicero's speech on behalf of Cornelius).

Athenaeus. *Deipnosophistai* (The learned banqueters).

Aulus Gellius. *Noctes Atticae* (The Attic nights).

Babylonian Talmud.

Caesar. *Bellum civile* (The civil war).

Cassiodorus. *Variae epistulae* (Various letters).

Catullus. *Carmina* (Poems).

Cicero. *De amicitia* (On friendship).

Cicero. *De finibus bonorum et malorum* (On the limits of good and evil).

Cicero. *De haruspicum responsis* (On the responses of the haruspices).

Cicero. *De legibus* (On the laws).

Cicero. *De oratore* (On the orator).

Cicero. *De reditu* (Upon his return from exile).

Cicero. *Epistulae ad Atticum* (Letters to Atticus).

Cicero. *In Catilinam* (Against Catiline).

Cicero. *In Pisonem* (Against Piso).

Cicero. *In Vatinium* (Against Vatinius).

Cicero. *In Verrem* (Against Verres).

Cicero. *Philippicae* (Philippics).

Cicero. *Post reditum in Senatu* (Following his return to the Senate).

Cicero. *Pro Murena* (On behalf of Murena).

Cicero. *Pro Rabirio Postumo* (On behalf of Rabirius Postumus).

Cicero. *Pro rege Deiotaro* (On behalf of Deiotarus).

Cicero. *Pro Sestio* (On behalf of Sestius).

Cicero. *Pro Sulla* (On behalf of Sulla).

Cicero. *Tusculanae disputationes* (Tusculan disputations).

*Codex Theodosianus.*

Columella. *De re rustica* (On agriculture).

*The Digest of Justinian.*

Dio Cassius. *Romaika* (Roman history).

Diodorus Siculus. *Bibliotheca* (World history).

Dionysius of Halicarnassus. *Antiquitates Romanae* (Roman antiquities).

*Edict of Diocletian on Maximum Prices.*

Festus. *De verborum significatu* (On the meaning of words).

Florus. *Epitome* (Summary).

Frontinus. *Strategemata* (Stratagems).

Herodian. *Meta Markon basileias historiae* (History after Marcus Aurelius).

Horace. *Epistles.*

Horace. *Odes.*

Horace. *Satires.*

Isidore of Seville. *Origines* (Etymologies).

Jerusalem Talmud.

John the Lydian. *De magistratibus* (On the magistrates).

Josephus. *Antiquitates Judaicae* (Jewish Antiquities).

Josephus. *Bellum Judaicum* (The Jewish war).

Julian. *Epistulae* (Letters).

Juvenal. *Saturae* (Satires).

Livy. *Ab urbe condita* (History of Rome from its founding).

Lucan. *Pharsalia* (The battle of Pharsalia).

Lucretius. *De rerum natura* (On the nature of the universe).

Macrobius. *Saturnalia.*

Martial. *Epigrammaton libri* (Epigrams).

Mishnah.

Nonius Marcellus. *De compendiosa doctrina* (Dictionary of republican Latin).

Ovid. *Ars amatoria* (The art of love).

Ovid. *Epistulae ex Ponto* (Letters from the Pontus).

Ovid. *Fasti* (The calendar).

Pausanias. *Hellados periegesi* (Guide to Greece).

Persius. *Saturae* (Satires).

Plato. *Politeia*. (The republic).

Plautus. *Aulularia* (The pot of gold).

Plautus. *Epidicus*.

Plautus. *Miles Gloriosus* (The braggart soldier).

Plautus. *Mostellaria* (The haunted house).

Plautus. *Rudens* (The rope).

Plautus. *Truculentus* (The savage).

Pliny the Elder. *Historia naturalis* (Natural history).

Pliny the Younger. *Epistulae* (Letters).

Pliny the Younger. *Panegyricus* (Panegyric on the emperor Trajan).

Plutarch. *Bioi paralleloi* (Lives of Greeks and Romans).

Plutarch. *Moralia* (Moral essays including Roman questions).

Pollux. *Onomasticon* (Dictionary).

Polybius. *Historiae* (The histories).

Posidonius. *Historiae* (The histories).

Procopius. *Bellum Gothicum* (The Gothic war).

Procopius. *De aedificiis* (On buildings).

Propertius. *Elegiae* (Elegies).

Prodentius. *Contra Symmachum* (Against Symmachus).

Prudentius. *Hamartigenia* (On the origin of sin).

Quintilian. *Institutio oratoria* (On the education of the orator).

*Res gestae divi Augusti* (The achievements of Augustus).

Seneca. *Apocolocyntosis* (The pumpkinification of Claudius).

Seneca. *Epistulae* (Letters).

Seneca. *Medea* (The tragedy of Medea).

Servius. *In Aeneadem* (Commentary on the *Aeneid*).

Sidonius Apollinaris. *Epistulae* (Letters).

Solinus. *Collectanea rerum memorabilium* (A collection of notable events).

Statius. *Thebais* (The Theban war).

Suetonius. *De vita Caesarum* (On the lives of the Caesars).

Suidas. *Lexicon*.

Tacitus. *Agricola* (The life of Agricola).

Tacitus. *Annals*.

Tacitus. *Dialogus de oratoribus* (On oratory).

Tacitus. *Germania*.

Tacitus. *Historiae* (The histories).

Tertullian. *Apologeticus* (Apology).

Tertullian. *De corona militis* (On the crown of the soldier).

Tertullian. *De pallio* (On the pallium).

Thucydides. *Historiai* (The Peloponnesian war).

Tibullus. *Elegiae* (Elegies).

Valerius Maximus. *Factorum ac dictorum memorabilium libri* (Books on memorable deeds and sayings).

Varro. *De lingua Latina* (On the Latin language).

Varro. *De re rustica* (On agriculture).

Vegetius. *De re militari* (On war).

Velleius Paterculus. *Historiae Romanae* (Roman history).

Vergil. *Aeneid*.

Vitruvius. *De architectura* (On architecture).

Zosimus. *Historia nova* (Recent history).

## MODERN WORKS

Acuña Fernandez, P. *Esculturas militares romanas de España y Portugal*. Rome, 1975.

Adrosko, R. J. *Natural Dyes in the United States*. U.S. National Museum Bulletin 281. Washington, D.C., 1968.

Alföldi, A. "Der Panzerschmuck der Augustusstatue von Primaporta." *RM* 52 (1937): 48–63.

Alföldi, A. "Hasta-Summa Imperii." *AJA* 63 (1959): 1–27.

Alföldi, A. "Insignien und Tracht der römischen Kaiser." *RM* 50 (1935): 1–171.

Alföldi, M. *Die constantinische Goldprägung*. Mainz, 1963.

Allason-Jones, L. *Women in Roman Britain*. London, 1989.

Alon, G. *The Jews in Their Land in the Talmudic Age*. 2 vols. Jerusalem, 1980.

Amelung, W. *Die Sculpturen des Vaticanischen Museum I*. Berlin, 1907.

Amorelli, M. "Bulla." In *Enciclopedia dell' Arte Antica Classica e Orientale*. Vol. 2. Rome, 1959.

Anderson, J. C. "Diptych of Probianus." In *The Age of Spirituality: Late Antique and Early Christian Art, Third to Seventh Centuries*, ed. K. Weitzmann, 55–56. New York, 1979.

André, J. *Études sur les termes de couleur dans la langue latine*. Paris, 1949.

Andreae, B. *The Art of Rome*. New York, 1977.

Andreae, B. "Igni et aqua accipi." *Römische Quartalschrift* 57 (1962): 1–16.

Andrews, A.C. "Marjoram as a Spice in the Classical Era." *CP* 56 (1961): 73–82.

Angelocoussis, E. "The Panel Reliefs of Marcus Aurelius." *RM* 91 (1984): 141–205.

Archer, W. "The Paintings in the Alae of the Casa dei Vettii and a Definition of the Fourth Pompeian Style." *AJA* 94 (1990): 95–123.

Ashmole, B. *A Catalogue of the Ancient Marbles at Ince Blundell Hall*. Oxford, 1929.

Astin, A. E. *Cato the Censor*. Oxford, 1978.

Aurigemma, S. *L'arco quadrifronte di Marco Aurelio e di Lucio Vero in Tripoli*. Suppl. 3, *Libya Antiqua*. Rome, [1970].

Avi-Yonah, M. "Scythopolis." *Israel Exploration Journal* 12 (1962): 123–36.

Baatz, D. "Carbatina—ein lateinischer Schuhname?" *Saalburg-Jahrbuch* 42 (1986): 64–67.

Bahn, P. G. "Letters from a Roman Garrison." *Archaeology* 45.1 (1992): 60–65.

Bailey, C., ed. and trans. *Titi Lucreti Cari de rerum natura libri sex*. 3 vols. Oxford, 1947–63.

Bailey, D. R. Shackleton, "Antiquités syriennes 94." *Syria* 48 (1971): 115–16.

Bailey, D. R. Shackleton, ed. and trans. *Cicero Back from Exile: Six Speeches upon His Return*. New Baskerville, 1991.

Bailey, D. R. Shackleton, ed. *Cicero, Philippics*. Chapel Hill, N.C., 1986.

Bailey, D. R. Shackleton, ed. *Epistulae ad Atticum*. Cambridge, Eng., 1966.

Bailey, J. L. "Josephus' Portrayal of the Matriarchs." In *Josephus, Judaism, and Christianity*, ed. L. Feldman and G. Hata, 154–79. Detroit, 1987.

Balsdon, J. P. V. D. *Roman Women: Their History and Habits*. New York, 1962.

Barber, E. J. W. "The PIE Notion of Cloth and Clothing." *JIES* 3.4 (1975): 294–320.

Barber, E. J. W. *Prehistoric Textiles*. Princeton, 1991.

Bardon, H. *La littérature latine inconnue*. Paris, 1956.

Barini, C. *Ornatus muliebris*. Turin, 1956.

Barnes, T. D. *Tertullian: A Historical and Literary Study*. Oxford, 1971.

Bastet, F. L. "Fabularum dispositas explicationes." *BABesch* 49 (1974): 206–40.

Bastet, F. L. "Feldherr mit Hund auf der Augustusstatue von Prima Porta." *BABesch* 41 (1966): 77–90.

Baur, P. V. C., and M. I. Rostovtzeff, eds. *The Excavations at Dura-Europos: Preliminary Report of Second Season of Work*. New Haven, 1931.

Bayet, J. *Croyances et rites dans la Rome antique*. Paris, 1971.

Beard, M. "The Sexual Status of the Vestal Virgins." *JRS* 70 (1980): 12–27.

Bendazzi, W., and R. Ricci. *Ravenna: Mosaics, Art History, Archaeology, Monuments, Museums*. Ravenna, 1987.

Bender, H. V. "Portraits on the Ara Pacis: A Comparison of Current Theories." *The Augustan Age* 4 (1985): 1–16.

Benoît, F. "Recherches sur l'hellénisation du Midi de la Gaule." *Annales de la Faculté des Lettres, Aix-en-Provence*, n.s., 43 (1965): 195–211.

Bertman, S. "Tasseled Garments in the Eastern Mediterranean." *Biblical Archaeologist* 24, no. 4 (1961): 119–28.

Bianchi Bandinelli, R. *Rome: The Center of Power*. New York, 1970.

Bianchi Bandinelli, R. *Rome: The Late Empire*. New York, 1971.

Bianco, E. "Indirizzi programmatici e propagandistici nella monetazione di Vespasiano." *Rivista Italiana di Numismatica* 70 (1968): 158–65.

Bidez, J., ed. and trans. *L'empereur Julien: Oeuvres complètes*. 2 vols. Paris, 1932–42.

Bieber, M. *Ancient Copies: Contributions to the History of Greek and Roman Art*. New York, 1977.

Bieber, M. "Charakter und Unterschiede der Griechische Kleidung." *AA* (1973): 425–47.

Bieber, M. "Costume, Historical Development, the Ancient World." In *Encyclopedia of World Art*, vol. 4, 19–26. New York, 1961.

Bieber, M. "Der Mysteriensaal der Villa Item." *JDAI* 43 (1928): 298–330.

Bieber, M. "Roman Men in Greek Himation (Romani Palliati): A Contribution to the History of Copying." *PAPhS* 103 (1959): 347–417.

Bieber, M. *The Sculpture of the Hellenistic Age*. 2d ed. New York, 1961.

Bieber, M. "Stola." *RE*, 2d ser., vol. 7 (1931), 56–62.

Biel, J. *Catalogue of the Exhibition Held at Stuttgart*. Stuttgart, 1985.

Biel, J. *Der Keltenfurst von Hochdorf*. Stuttgart, 1985.

Bilde, P. *Flavius Josephus Between Jerusalem and Rome*. Sheffield, 1988.

Birley, R. *Vindolanda: A Roman Frontier Post on Hadrian's Wall*. London, 1977.

Blackman, P., ed. *Mishnayoth*. 6 vols. Gateshead, 1983.

Blanck, H. "Wiederverwendung alter Statuen als Ehrendenkmäler bei Griechen und Römern." Ph.D. diss., University of Cologne, 1963.

Blanckenhagen, P. H. von, and B. Green. "The Aldobrandini Wedding Reconsidered." *RM* 82 (1975): 93–98.

Blümel, C. *Katalog der Sammlung antiker Skulpturen*. Suppl. vol., *Römische Bildnisse*. Berlin, 1933.

Blümner, H. *Die römischen Privataltertümer*. Handbuch der klassischen Altertumswissenschaft 4.2.2. Munich, 1911.

Boardman, J. *Greek Sculpture: The Classical Period*. London, 1985.

Boatwright, M. T. *Hadrian and the City of Rome*. Princeton, 1987.

Boels, N. "Le statut religieux de la Flaminica Dialis." *REL* 51 (1973): 77–100.

Böhme, A. "Frauenschmuck der römischen Kaiserzeit." *Antike Welt* 9 (1978): 3–16.

Böhme, A. "Tracht und Bestattungssitten in den germanischen Provinzen und der Belgica." *ANRW* 2.12.3 (1985): 423–55.

Bonfante, G. "I nomi dei colori in indoeuropeo." *Archivio Glottologico Italiano* 73 (1988): 153–54.

Bonfante, L. *Etruscan Dress*. Baltimore, 1975.

Bonfante, L. "Human Sacrifice on an Etruscan Urn." *AJA* 88 (1984): 531–39.

Bonfante, L. "Nudity as a Costume in Classical Art." *AJA* 93 (1989): 543–79.

Bonfante, L., ed. *Etruscan Life and Afterlife*. Detroit, 1986.

Bonfante, L. *Essays on Nudity in Antiquity in Memory of Otto Brendel*. Source 12 (1993), Special Issue.

Bonfante, L., and E. Jaunzems. "Clothing and Ornament." In *Civilizations of the Ancient Mediterranean: Greece and Rome*, vol. 3, ed. M. Grant and R. Kitzinger, 1385–413. New York, 1988.

Bonfante-Warren, L. "Emperor, God and Man in the IV Century: Julian the Apostate and Ammianus Marcellinus." *PdP* 99 (1964): 401–27.

Bonfante-Warren, L. "Roman Costume: A Glossary and Some Etruscan Derivations." *ANRW* 1.4 (1973): 584–614.

Bonfante-Warren, L. "Roman Triumphs and Etruscan Kings: The Changing Face of the Triumph." *JRS* 60 (1970): 49–66.

Bouvrie, S. des. "Augustus' Legislation on Morals: Which Morals and What Aims?" *Symbolae Osloenses* 59 (1984): 93–113.

Bracker, J. "Das Frauengrab Köln, Severinstrasse 129." *Gymnasium* 79.5 (1972): 389–95.

Bradley, K. R. "Roman Slavery and Roman Law." *Historical Reflections / Réflexions Historiques* 15 (1988): 477–95.

Brailsford, J. W. *Guide to the Antiquities of Roman Britain*. London, 1951.

Breasted, J. H. *Oriental Forerunners of Byzantine Painting*. Chicago, 1924.

Breckenridge, J. D. "Head of Constantine I," "Head of Ariadne," "Diptych Leaf with Ariadne," and "Medallion of Justinian I." In *The Age of Spirituality: Late Antique and Early Christian Art, Third to Seventh Centuries*, ed. K. Weitzmann, 16–18, 30–31, 31–32, 45. New York, 1979.

Brendel, O. "The Great Frieze of the Villa of the Mysteries." In *The Visible Idea*, 90–138. Washington, D.C., 1980.

Brenk, B. *Spätantikes und frühes Christentum: Propyläen Kunstgeschichte*. Suppl. vol. 1. Berlin, 1977.

Brilliant, R. "Scenic Representations." In *The Age of Spirituality: Late Antique and Early Christian Art, Third to Seventh Centuries*, ed. K. Weitzmann, 60–108. New York, 1979.

British Museum, Department of British and Medieval Antiquities. *Guide to the Antiquities of Roman Britain*. London, 1951.

Broughton, T. R. S. *The Magistrates of the Roman Republic*. 2 vols. New York, 1952.

Brown, J. P. "The Sacrificial Cult and Its Critique in Greek and Hebrew, II." *Journal of Semitic Studies* 25 (1980): 1–21.

Brown, K. R. "Necklace," "Pectoral" (no. 295), and "Pectoral" (no. 296). In *The Age of Spirituality: Late Antique and Early Christian Art, Third to Seventh Centuries*, ed. K. Weitzmann, 310–11, 318–9, 319–21. New York, 1979.

Brown, P. *The World of Late Antiquity*, A.D. 150–750. London, 1971.

Brüll, A. *Trachten der Juden im nachbiblischen Alterthume*. Frankfurt, 1873.

Brunello, F. *The Art of Dyeing in the History of Mankind*. Vicenza, 1973.

Busch, A. L. "Die römerzeitlichen Schuh- und Lederfunde der Kastelle Saalburg." *Saalburg Jahrbuch* 22 (1965): 158–210.

Butler, T. F. *Roman Galley beneath the Sea*. Leicester, 1964.

Calza, R. *Iconografia Romana Imperiale da Carausio a Giuliano, 287–363 d.C.* Rome, 1972.

Calza, R. *Scavi di Ostia*. Vol. 5, *I Ritratti*, part 1. Rome, 1964.

Calza, R., ed. *Antichità di Villa Doria Pamphili*. Rome, 1977.

Caputo, G. *Il teatro di Sabratha*. Monografie di Archeologia Libica 6. Rome, 1959.

Caputo, G. "Sculture dallo scavo a sud del Foro di Sabratha." *Quaderni di archeologia della Libia* 1 (1950): 1–58.

Caquot, A. "Nouvelles inscriptions araméennes de Hatra." *Syria* 30 (1953): 234–46.

Carcopino, J. *Daily Life in Ancient Rome*. New Haven, 1940. (Trans. of *La vie quotidienne à Rome*. Paris, 1939).

Carney, T. F., ed. *De magistratibus*. Lawrence, Kans., 1971.

Cary, M., and A. D. Nock. "Magic Spears." *CQ* 21 (1927): 122–27.

Cary, M., and H. H. Scullard. *A History of Rome*. New York, 1978.

Casson, L. *The Periplus Maris Erythraei*. Princeton, 1989.

Chabot, J. B. *Choix d'inscriptions de Palmyre*. Paris, 1922.

Chantraine, P. *Dictionnaire étymologique de la langue grecque: Histoire des mots*. 2 vols. Paris, 1968.

Charlesworth, D. "The Aesica Hoard." *Archaeologia Aeliana*, 5th ser., 1 (1973): 225–34.

Charlesworth, D. "Roman Jewellery Found in Northumberland and Durham." *Archaeologia Aeliana*, 4th ser., 39 (1961): 1–36.

Charlesworth, D., and J. H. Thornton. "Leather Found in Mediobogdum, the Roman Fort of Hardknott." *Britannia* 4 (1973): 141–52.

Charlesworth, M. P. *Trade-Routes and Commerce of the Roman Empire*. Cambridge, Eng., 1924.

Chaumont, M. L. "A propos de la chute de Hatra et du couronnement de Shapur 1er." *Acta Antiqua Academiae Scientiarum Hungaricae* 27 (1979): 207–37.

Coarelli, F. *Greek and Roman Jewelry*. London, 1970.

Colledge, M. A. R. *The Art of Palmyra*. London, 1976.

Colledge, M. A. R. *The Parthians*. London, 1967.

Comarmond, A. *Description de l'écrin d'une dame romaine trouvé à Lyon en 1841*. Lyon, 1844.

Courtney, E. *A Commentary on the Satires of Juvenal*. London, 1980.

*Creperia Tryphaena: Le scoperte archeologiche nell' area del Palazzo di Giustizia*. Rome, 1983.

Cristofani, M., and M. Martelli. *L'oro degli Etruschi*. Novara, 1983.

Cumont, F. *Fouilles de Doura-Europos, 1922–1923*. 2 vols. Paris, 1926.

Curtius, L. "Zur Aldobrandinischen Hochzeit." In *Vermächtnis der antiken Kunst*, ed. R. Herbig, 119–40. Heidelberg, 1950.

Cyprus Museum. *Jewellery in the Cyprus Museum*. Nicosia, 1971.

Daltrop, G. In *The Vatican Collection: The Papacy and Art*, 208–9. New York, 1983.

Daltrop, G., U. Hausmann, and M. Wegner. *Die Flavier: Römische Herrscherbild* 2.1. Berlin, 1966.

Dandy, H., ed. *The Mishnah*. Oxford, 1933.

Debevoise, N. *Political History of Parthia*. Chicago, 1938.

Deer, J. *Der Kaiserornat Friedrichs II*. Bern, 1952.

Deichmann, F., G. Bovini, and H. Brandenburg. *Repertorium der christlich-antiken Sarkophage Rom und Ostia*. Wiesbaden, 1967.

DeJonghe, D., and M. Tavernier. "Les damassés de Palmyre." *Annales archéologiques arabes syriennes* 32 (1982): 99–116.

Delbrueck, R. *Antike Porphyrwerke*. Leipzig, 1932.

Delbrueck, R. *Die Consulardiptychen und verwandte Denkmäler*. Berlin, 1929.

Delbrueck, R. "Porträts byzantinischer Kaiserinnen." *RM* 28 (1913): 310–57.

Delbrueck, R. *Spätantike Kaiserporträts von Constantinus Magnus bis zum Ende des Westreichs*. Berlin, 1933.

Delvoye, C. Review of H. I. Marrou, *Décadence romaine ou antiquité tardive?* In *L'Antiquité Classique* 47 (1978): 352–54.

Deneauve, J. *Lampes de Carthage*. Paris, 1969.

Denniston, J. D., ed. *Philippicae*. Oxford, 1926.

Devoto, G. *Origini indoeuropee*. Florence, 1962.

Devoto, G. *Storia della lingua di Roma*. Vol. 1. 1939; Bologna, 1983.

Dickie, M. "The Speech of Numanus Remulus (*Aeneid* 9.598–620)." *Papers of the Liverpool Latin Seminar* 5 (1985): 165–221.

Di Mino, M. R., and M. Bertinetti. *Archeologia a Roma: La materia e la tecnica nell'arte antica*. Rome, 1990.

Dinkler, E. "Abbreviated Representations." In *The Age of*

*Spirituality: Late Antique and Early Christian Art, Third to Seventh Centuries,* ed. K. Weitzmann, 74–76. New York, 1979.

Dixon, S. *The Roman Mother.* London, 1988.

Dodge, H. "Palmyra and the Roman Marble Trade." *Levant* 20 (1988): 215–30.

Dohrn, T. *Der Arringatore.* Monumenta Artis Romanae 8. Berlin, 1968.

Domaszewski, A. von. "Der Panzerschmuck der Augustusstatue von Primaporta." In *Strena Helbigiana.* 51–53. Leipzig, 1900.

Dragendorff, H. "Die Amtstracht der Vestalinnen." *RhM* 51 (1896): 281–302.

Driel-Murray, C. van. "The Leatherwork." In "Funde aus der Fabrica der Legion I Minervia am Bonner Berg," by C. van Driel-Murray and M. Gechter. *Beiträge zur Archäologie des römischen Rheinlandes* 4, *Rheinische Ausgrabungen* 23 (1984): 5–83.

Driel-Murray, C. van. "Leatherwork in the Roman Army." In *Exercitus Institute for Pre- and Protohistory* 2.2., 6–11. Gloucester, n.d.

Driel-Murray, C. van. "The Production and Supply of Military Leatherwork in the First and Second Centuries A.D." In *The Production and Distribution of Roman Military Equipment,* ed. M. C. Bishop, 43–81. BAR 275. Oxford, 1985.

Driel-Murray, C. van. "Roman Footwear: A Mirror of Fashion and Society." In *Recent Research in Archaeological Footwear,* 32–42. Association of Archaeological Illustrators and Surveyors Technical Paper 8. N.p., 1987.

Driel-Murray, C. van. "Roman Footwear from a Well in the Ostkastell Welzheim." Forthcoming.

Driel-Murray, C. van. "Shoes in Perspective." *Studien zu den Militärgrenzen* 3 (1986): 139–45.

Drijvers, H., and M. Versteegh. "Hatra, Palmyra, und Edessa." *ANRW* 2.8 (1977): 799–906.

Druesedow, J. L. "In Style: Celebrating Fifty Years of the Costume Institute." *The Metropolitan Museum of Art Bulletin* (Fall 1987).

Dumézil, G. *Archaic Roman Religion.* vol. 1. Chicago, 1970.

Earl, D. *The Moral and Political Tradition of Rome.* London, 1967.

Edwards, D. "Acts of the Apostles and Chariton's *Chaereas and Callirhoe.*" Ph.D. diss, Boston University, 1987.

Edwards, D. "Dress and Ornamentation." In *Anchor Bible Dictionary,* ed. D. N. Freedman, 2:232–38. New York, 1992.

Edwards, D. "Religion, Power, and Politics: Jewish Defeats by the Romans in Iconography and Josephus." In *Diaspora Jews and Judaism,* ed. J. Overman and R. MacLennen, 293–310. University of Southern Florida Series in Ancient Judaism. Atlanta, 1992.

*Ephemeris epigraphica: Corporis Inscriptionum Latinarum supplementum.* Vol. 8. Berlin, 1899.

*Epigrammata ad codices parisinos accurate recensita.* Paris, 1825.

Epstein, I., ed. *Babylonian Talmud: Seder Moʿed.* London, 1938.

Erbacher, K. *Griechische Schuhwerk.* Würzburg, 1914.

Erim, K. *Aphrodisias: City of Venus Aphrodite.* London, 1986.

Ernout, A., and A. Meillet. *Dictionnaire étymologique de la langue latine.* 4th ed. Paris, 1959.

Eshel, H. "Finds and Documents from a Cave at Ketef-Yeriho" (in Hebrew). *Qadmoniot* 21 (1988): 22.

Eshel, H. "How I Found a Fourth-Century B.C. Papyrus Scroll on My First Time Out!" *Biblical Archaeology Review* 15.5 (1989): 44–53.

Evans, M. M. "Chapters on Greek Dress." In *Ancient Greek Dress,* ed. M. Johnson, 1–78. Chicago, 1965.

Feldman, L. *Josephus: A Supplementary Bibliography.* Berlin, 1986.

Feldman, L. *Josephus and Modern Scholarship, 1937–1980.* Berlin, 1984.

Feldman, L., and G. Hata, eds. *Josephus, Judaism and Christianity.* Detroit, 1987.

Felletti Maj, B. M. *Iconografia Romana Imperiale da Severo Alessandro a M. Aurelio Carino, A.D. 222–285.* Rome, 1958.

Fernea, E. W., and R. A. Fernea. "Symbolizing Roles: Behind the Veil." In *Conformity and Conflict: Readings in Cultural Anthropology,* ed. J. P. Spradley and D. W. McCurdy, 104–12. Boston, 1987.

Fettich, N. *Der zweite Schatz von Szilágy Somlyó.* Budapest, 1932.

Fink, R. O. "The Cohors XX Palmyrenorum, a Cohors Equitata Miliaria." *TAPA* 78 (1947): 159–70.

Fittschen, K. *Die Bildnistypen der Faustina Minor und die Fecunditas Augustae.* Göttingen, 1982.

Fittschen, K. Review of H. G. Niemeyer, *Studien zur statuarischen Darstellung der römischen Kaiser. BJ* 170 (1970): 541–52.

Fittschen, K., and P. Zanker. *Katalog der römischen Porträts in den Capitolinischen Museen und den andern kommunalen Sammlungen der Stadt Rom.* Vol. 1, *Kaiser- und Prinzenbildnisse.* Mainz, 1985.

Fitzgerald, R. *The Aeneid.* New York, 1984.

Flügel, J. C. *The Psychology of Clothes.* London, 1966.

Foley, H. P., ed. *Reflections of Women in Antiquity.* New York, 1981.

Forbes, J. R. *Studies in Ancient Technology.* 6 vols. Leiden, 1955–60.

Fowler, W. W. *Religious Experience of the Roman People.* London, 1922.

Francfort, H.-P. *Les palettes du Gandhara.* MDAFA 23. Paris, 1979.

Franciscis, A. de. *The National Archaeological Museum of Naples.* Naples, n.d.

Frank, T., et al. *An Economic Survey of Ancient Rome.* 5 vols. Baltimore, 1933–40.

Frayn, J. M. *Sheep-Rearing and the Wool Trade in Italy during the Roman Period.* ARCA 15. Liverpool, 1984.

Frédouille, J. C. *Tertullien et la conversion de la culture antique.* Paris, 1972.

Fremersdorf, F. "Ein Fund römischer Ledersachen in Köln." *Germania* 10 (1926): 44–56.

Frenz, H. G. "Untersuchungen zu den frühen römischen Grabreliefs." Ph.D. diss., University of Frankfurt, 1977.

Fröhlich, T. *Lararien- und Fassadenbilder in den Vesuv-städten.* RM-EH 32. Mainz, 1991.

Fujii, H. "Roman Textiles from At-Tar Caves in Mesopotamia." *Mesopotamia* 27 (1987): 214–31.

Fussell, P. *Class: A Guide through the American Status System.* New York, 1983.

Gabelmann, H. "Die Frauenstatue aus Aachen-Burtscheid." *BJ* 179 (1979): 209–50.

Gabelmann, H. "Römische Kinder in *Toga Praetexta.*" *JDAI* 100 (1985): 497–541.

Garbsch, J. "Die norisch-pannonische Tracht." *ANRW* 2.12.3 (1985): 546–77.

Garside, A., ed. *Jewelry: Ancient to Modern.* New York, 1979.

Gawlikowski, M. "Palmyra et l'Euphrates." *Syria* 60 (1983): 53–68.

Gawlikowski, M. "Remarques sur l'usage de la fibule à Palmyre." In *Mélanges K. Michalowski*, 411–19. Warsaw, 1966.

Gebühr, M. *Der Trachtschmuck der älteren römischen Kaiserzeit im Gebiet zwischen unterer Elbe und Oder und auf den westlichen dänischen Inseln.* Göttingen Schriften zur Vor- und Frühgeschichte, Band 18. Neuminster, 1976.

Geffcken, K. A. *Comedy in the "Pro Caelio."* Leiden, 1973.

Gelzer, M. *Caesar.* Oxford, 1968.

Gercke-Voss, W. *Untersuchungen zum römischen Kinderporträt.* Hamburg, 1969.

Gergel, R. A. "An Allegory of Imperial Victory on a Cuirassed Statue of Domitian." *Record of the (Princeton) Art Museum* 45.1 (1986): 1–18.

Gergel, R. A. "A Julio-Claudian Torso in the Walters Art Gallery." *JWAG* 45 (1987): 19–31.

Gergel, R. A. "A Late Flavian Cuirassed Torso in the J. Paul Getty Museum." *GMusJ* 16 (1988): 5–24.

Ghirshman, R. *Parthians and Sasanians.* London, 1962.

Giacosa, G. *Women of the Caesars: Their Lives and Portraits on Coins.* Trans. R. Holloway. Milan, 1977.

Giannecchini, G. "Seni Crines." In "Ornatus e status sociale delle donne romane," by L. Sensi. *ALFPer*, n.s., 4 (1980–81): 91–92.

Gibbon, E. *Decline and Fall of the Roman Empire.* 6 vols., 1776–88. New York, 1981.

Gies, F., and J. Gies. *Marriage and the Family in the Middle Ages.* New York, 1987.

Gilliam, J. F. "The Roman Army in Dura." In *The Parchments and Papyri*, ed. C. B. Welles, R. O. Fink, and J. F. Gilliam, 22–27. The Excavations of Dura-Europos. Final Report 5.1. New Haven, 1959.

Giuliano, A. *Catalogo dei ritratti romani del Museo Profano Lateranense.* Vatican City, 1957.

Giuliano, A., ed. *Museo Nazionale Romano: Le Sculture.* Rome, 1984.

Goethert, F. W. "Studien zur Kopienforschung, 1: Die stil- und trachtgeschichtliche Entwicklung der Togastatue in den beiden ersten Jahrhunderten der römischen Kaiserzeit." *RM* 54 (1939): 176–219.

Goethert, F. W. "Toga." *RE*, 2d ser., vol. 6 (1937), 1651–60.

Goette, H. R. "Corona Spicea, Corona Civica und Adler: Bemerkungen zu drei römischen Dreifussbasen." *AA* (1984): 573–89.

Goette, H. R. "Mulleus—Embas—Calceus." *JDAI* 103 (1988): 401–64.

Goette, H. R. *Studien zu römischen Togadarstellungen.* Mainz, 1990.

Goldman, B. "The Dura Synagogue Costumes and Parthian Art." In *The Dura-Europos Synagogue: A Re-evaluation, 1932–1972*, ed. J. Gutmann, 53–78. Missoula, Mont., 1973.

Goldman, B. "Foreigners at Dura-Europos: Pictorial Graffiti and History." *Le Muséon* 103 (1990): 5–25.

Goldman, B. "The Imperial Jewel at Taq-I Bustan." In *Archaelogia Iranica et Orientalis*, ed. L. De Meyer and E. Haeriuck, 2: 831–46. Ghent, 1989.

Goodenough, E. R. *Jewish Symbols in the Greco-Roman Period.* 13 vols. Princeton, 1953–68.

Goodman, M. *The Ruling Class of Judaea: The Origins of the Jewish Revolt against Rome, A.D. 66–70.* Cambridge, Eng., 1987.

Göpfrich, J. "Römische Lederfunde aus Mainz." *Saalburg Jahrbuch* 42 (1986): 5–67.

Gow, A. S. F. "Notes on the *Persae* of Aeschylus." *JHS* 48 (1928): 143–52.

Grant, M. *The Art and Life of Pompeii and Herculaneum.* New York, 1979.

Grant, M., and R. Kitzinger. *Civilizations of the Ancient Mediterranean.* New York, 1988.

Grenfell, B., and A. S. Hunt, eds. *Oxyrhynchus Papyri.* London, 1898.

Grierson, P. *Byzantine Coins.* London, 1982.

Griffin, M. T. *Nero: The End of a Dynasty.* New Haven, 1985.

Griffith, M. "What Does Aeneas Look Like?" *CP* 90 (1985): 309–19.

Groenman–Van Waateringe, W. *Romeins Lederwerk uit Valenburg Z. H.* Groningen, 1967.

Groenman–Van Waateringe, W. "Society Rests on Leather." In J. G. N. Renaud, ed., *Rotterdam Papers* 2 (1975): 23–34.

Gross, W. H. "Zur Augustusstatue von Prima Porta." *Nachrichten der Akademie der Wissenschaften in Göttingen I: Philologisch-historische Klasse* 8 (1959): 143–68.

Gruen, E. S. *The Hellenistic World and the Coming of Rome.* Vol. 1. Berkeley, 1984.

Gruen, E. S. *The Last Generation of the Roman Republic.* Berkeley, 1974.

Gruen, E. S. *Studies in Greek Culture and Roman Policy.* Leiden, 1990.

Grummond, N. de. "Rediscovery." In *Etruscan Life and Afterlife*, ed. L. Bonfante, 18–46. Detroit, 1986.

Grummond, N. de. "The Study of Classical Costume by Philip, Albert and Peter Paul Rubens." *Ringling Museum of Art Journal, International Rubens Symposium* (1983): 78–93.

Grummond, N. de, ed. *Guide to Etruscan Mirrors.* Tallahassee, Fla., 1982.

Guarducci, M. "Il *conubium* nei riti del matrimonio etrusco e di quello romano." *BCAR* 55 (1929): 205–24.

Guite, H. "Cicero's Attitude to the Greeks." *Greece and Rome* 31 (1962): 142–59.

Guizzi, F. *Aspetti giuridici del sacerdozio romano: Il sacerdozio di Vesta.* Pubblicazioni della facoltà giuridica dell'università di Napoli 62. Naples, 1968.

Gullberg, E., and P. Åström. *The Thread of Ariadne.* Studies in Mediterranean Archaeology 21. Göteborg, 1979.

Gutmann, J., ed. *The Dura-Europus Synagogue: A Re-evaluation, 1932–1972.* Missoula, Mont., 1973.

Hafner, G. "Etruskische Togati." *AntPl* 9 (1969): 25–44.

Hägg, T. *The Novel in Antiquity.* Berkeley, 1983.

Hallett, J. P. *Fathers and Daughters in Roman Society: Women and the Elite Family.* Princeton, 1984.

Hanfmann, G. M. A. "Daedalos in Etruria." *AJA* 39 (1935): 189–94.

Hanfmann, G. M. A. *Roman Art.* Greenwich, Conn., 1964.

Hanfmann, G. M. A., and C.C. Vermeule. "A New Trajan." *AJA* 61 (1957): 223–53.

Hannestad, N. *Roman Art and Imperial Policy.* Aarhus, 1986.

Harden, D. B. *Glass of the Caesars.* Catalogue of Glass from the Corning Museum Exhibition of Ancient Roman Glass. Corning, N.Y., 1987.

Harder, F. "Über die Fragmente des Maecenas." *Wissenschlaftliche Programm, Berlin* 63 (1889): 1–23.

Harrison, E. B. "Notes on Daedalic Dress." *JWAG* 36 (1977): 37–48.

Harrison, E. B. "The Shoulder-Cord of Themis." In *Festschrift Brommer,* ed. U. Höckmann and A. Krug, 155–61. Mainz, 1977.

Hassel, F. J. *Der Trajansbogen in Benevent: Ein Bauwerk des römischen Senates.* Mainz, 1966.

Havelock, C. M. *Hellenistic Art.* Rev. ed. New York, 1981.

Heintze, H. von. "Augustus Prima Porta." In Helbig 314–19, no. 411.

Heintze, H. von. "Drei spätantike Porträtstatuen." *AntPl* 1 (1962): 7–32.

Hekker, A. "Beiträge zur Geschichte der antiken Panzerstatuen." *Jahreshefte des Österreichischen Archäologischen Instituts in Wien* 19–20 (1919): 190–241.

Helbig, W. *Führer durch die öffentlichen sammlungen klassischer Altertümer in Rom.* Vol. 1. 4th ed. Ed. H. Speier. Tübingen, 1963.

Helbig, W. "Über den Pileus der alter Italiker." *SBAW* (1880): 487–554.

Henig, M. "Continuity and Change in the Design of Roman Jewellery." In *The Roman West in the Third Century,* 127–43. BAR 109. Oxford, 1981.

Henrichs, A., and L. Koenen. "Ein griechischer Mani-Codex (P. Colon. inv. nr. 4780)." *ZPE* 5 (1970): 97–216.

Henzen, W. *Acta fratrum arvalium.* Berlin, 1874.

Herbig, R. *Vermächtnis der antiken Kunst Gastvortrage zur Jahrhundertfeier der Archäologischen Sammlung der Universität Heidelberg.* Heidelberg, 1950.

Herzog-Hauser, G. "Trauerkleidung." *RE,* 2d ser., vol. 12 (1937), 2225–31.

Heurgon, J. *La vie quotidienne chez les étrusques.* Paris, 1961.

Heuzey, L. *Histoire du costume antique.* Paris, 1922.

Higgins, R. *Greek and Roman Jewelry.* Berkeley, 1980.

Highet, G. *The Speeches in Vergil's "Aeneid."* Princeton, 1972.

Hill, D. Kent. "An Unknown Roman Togatus." *Antike Kunst* 15 (1972): 27–32.

Himmelmann-Wildschutz, N. "Sarkophag eines gallienischen Konsuls." In *Festschrift für Friedrich Matz,* 110–24. Mainz, 1962.

Hofter, M. "Porträt." in *Kaiser Augustus und die verlorene Republik,* 291–343. Berlin, 1988.

Holladay, C. R. *Theios Aner in Hellenistic Judaism: A Critique of the Use of This Category in New Testament Christology.* Missoula, Mont., 1977.

Holland, L. A. "Aeneas-Augustus of Prima Porta." *TAPA* 22 (1969): 276–84.

Holland, L. A. *Janus and the Bridge.* Rome, 1961.

Hollander, A. *Seeing through Clothes.* New York, 1978.

Holliday, P. J. "Processional Imagery in Late Etruscan Funerary Art." *AJA* 94 (1990): 73–93.

Holliday, P. J. "Time, History and Ritual on the *Ara Pacis Augustae.*" *ABull* 72 (1990): 542–57.

Hölscher, T. "Historische Reliefs." In *Kaiser Augustus und die verlorene Republik,* 351–400. Berlin, 1988.

Holtheide, B. "Matrona Stolata—Femina Stolata." *ZPE* 38 (1980): 127–34.

Holum, K. G. *Theodosian Empresses: Women and Imperial Dominion in Late Antiquity.* Berkeley, 1982.

Homès-Fredericq, D. *Hatra et ses sculptures parthes: Étude stylistique et iconographique.* Istanbul, 1963.

Hope, T. *Costumes of the Greeks and Romans.* 1812; New York, 1962.

Hopkins, C. *The Discovery of Dura-Europos.* New Haven, 1979.

Hornsby, R. *Patterns of Action in the "Aeneid."* Iowa City, 1970.

Horsfall, N. "Aeneas the Colonist." *Vergilius* 35 (1989): 8–26.

Horsfall, N. "Barbara tegmina crurum." *Maia* 41 (1989): 251–54.

Horsfall, N. "I pantaloni di Cloreo." *Rivista di Filologia e di Istruzione Classica* 117 (1989): 57–61.

Horsfall, N. "Numanus Remulus: Ethnography and Propaganda in *Aeneid,* IX, 598f." *Latomus* 117 (1971): 1108–16.

Horsley, R. A., and J. S. Hanson. *Bandits, Prophets, and Messiahs: Popular Movements in the Time of Jesus.* Minneapolis, 1985.

Houston, M. G. *Ancient Greek, Roman and Byzantine Costume and Decoration.* London, 1963.

Hula, E. "Die Toga der späteren Kaiserzeit," *XXIV. Jahresbericht des k.k. zweiten Obergymnasiums in Brunn* (1895): 7–13.

Huzar, E. G. *Mark Antony: A Biography.* Minneapolis, 1978.

Hyde, N. "Wool: The Fabric of History." *National Geographic* 173 (May 1988): 552–91.

Inan, J., and E. Rosenbaum. *Roman and Early Byzantine Portrait Sculpture in Asia Minor.* London, 1966.

Ingholt, H. *Parthian Sculpture from Hatra.* Memoirs of

the Connecticut Academy of Arts and Sciences 12. New Haven, 1954.

Ingholt, H. "The Prima Porta Statue of Augustus." *Archaeology* 22 (1969): 176–87, 304–18.

Ingholt, H., et al. *Recueil des tessères de Palmyre*. Paris, 1955.

Jacobi, L. *Der Römerkastell Saalburg*. 1897.

Jacoby, F. *Die Fragmente der griechischen Historiker*. Berlin, 1926.

Jahn, O., ed. *A. Persii Flacci Saturarum libri cum scholiis antiquis*. Leipzig, 1844.

Jenkins, I. *Greek and Roman Life*. Cambridge, Mass., 1986.

Johnston, M. *Ancient Greek Dress*. Chicago, 1965.

Johnston, M. *Roman Life*. Glenview, Ill., 1957.

Jones, B. W. *The Emperor Titus*. New York, 1984.

Jones, C. P. "Stigma: Tattooing and Branding in Greco-Roman Antiquity." *JRS* 77 (1987): 139–55.

Jordan, H. *Der Tempel der Vesta und das Haus der Vestalinnen*. Berlin, 1886.

Joseph, N. *Uniforms and Non-Uniforms*. New York, 1986.

Jucker, H. "Bildnis einer Vestalin." *RM* 68 (1961): 93–113.

Jucker, H. *Das Bildnis im Blätterkelch*. Lausanne, 1961.

Jucker, H. "Die Prinzen des Statuenzyklus aus Velleia." *JDAI* 94 (1979): 204–40.

Junkelmann, M. *Die Legionen des Augustus: Der römische Soldat im archäologischen Experiment*. Mainz, 1986.

Juster, J. *Les Juifs dans l'empire romain*. 2 vols. Paris, 1914.

Jüthner, J. "Die athletischen Leibesübungen der Griechen, 1: Geschichte der Leibesübungen." *Sitzungsberichte der Österreichische Akademie der Wissenschaften* 249, no. 1 (1965): 1–209.

Kähler, H. *Das Fünfsaulendenkmal für die Tetrarchen auf dem Forum Romanum*. Monumenta Artis Romanae 3. Cologne, 1964.

Kähler, H. *Die Augustusstatue von Primaporta*. Monumenta Artis Romanae 1. Cologne, 1959.

*Kaiser Augustus und die verlorene Republik*. Berlin, 1988.

Kaltwasser, U. *Die Kölner in der Römerzeit*. Cologne, 1977.

Kampen, N. "Biographical Narration and Roman Funerary Art." *AJA* 85 (1981): 47–58.

Kampen, N. *Image and Status: Roman Working Women at Ostia*. Berlin, 1981.

Kantorowicz, E. H. "Gods in Uniform." *PAPhS* 105 (1961): 368–93.

Kent, J. P. C. *Roman Coins*. New York, 1978.

Kent, J. P. C., and K. S. Painter. *Wealth of the Roman World, A.D. 300–700*. London, 1977.

Kidd, I. G. *Posidonius*. Vol. 2, *The Commentary*. Cambridge, Eng., 1988.

King, A., and M. Henry. *The Roman West in the Third Century: Contributions from Archeology and History*. Vols. 1 and 2. BAR 109. Oxford, 1981.

Kiss, A. "Der Zeitpunkt der Verbergung der Schatzfund I und II von Szilágysomlyó." *Acta Antiqua Academiae Scientiarum Hungaricae* 30 (1988): 401–16.

Kitto, H. D. F. *The Greeks*. Baltimore, 1957.

Kitzinger, E. *Byzantine Art in the Making*. Cambridge, Mass., 1977.

Klauner, F., et al. *Das Kunsthistorisches Museum in Wien*. Vienna, 1978.

Kleiner, D. E. E. "The Great Friezes of the *Ara Pacis Augustae*." *MEFRA* 90 (1978): 753–85.

Kleiner, D. E. E. *The Monument of Philopappos in Athens*. Rome, 1983.

Kleiner, D. E. E. "Private Portraiture in the Age of Augustus." In *The Age of Augustus*, ed. R. Winkes, 107–35. Louvain, 1985.

Kleiner, D. E. E. *Roman Group Portraiture: The Funerary Reliefs of the Late Republic and Early Empire*. New York, 1977.

Kleiner, D. E. E., and F. S. Kleiner. "Early Roman Togate Statuary." *BCAR* 87 (1980–81): 125–33.

Knauer, G. N. *Die Aeneis und Homer*. Göttingen, 1964.

Koch, G., and H. Sichtermann. *Römische Sarkophage*. Handbuch der Archäologie 3. Munich, 1982.

Koch, R. "Die Kleidung der Alemannen in der Spätantike." *ANRW* 2.12.3 (1985): 456–545.

Koeppel, G. "Die historischen Reliefs der römischen Kaiserzeit, V: Ara Pacis Augustae," part 1. *BJ* 187 (1987): 101–57.

Köhler, C. *A History of Costume*. Ed. and augmented by E. Sichart. 1928; New York, 1963.

Kokkinos, N. "Which Salome Did Aristobulus Marry?" *Palestine Exploration Quarterly* (Jan.–June 1986): 33–48.

Kolb, F. "Römische Mäntel: Paenula, Lacerna, Mandye." *RM* 80 (1973): 69–167.

Kollwitz, J. *Oströmische Plastik der theodosianischen Zeit*. Berlin, 1941.

Koshelenko, G. A. *Rodina Parfjan* (The cradle of the Parthians). Moscow, 1977.

Kraeling, C. *The Synagogue*. The Excavations of Dura-Europos. Final report 8.1. New Haven, 1956.

Kraus, T. *Das römische Weltreich*. Propyläen Kunstgeschichte 2. Berlin, 1967.

Krauss, S. *Griechische und lateinische Lehnwörter im Talmud, Midrasch und Targum*. 2 vols. Berlin, 1899.

Krauss, S. *Talmüdische Archäologie*. 3 vols. 1910; New York, 1979.

Krueger, P., and T. Mommsen, eds. *The Digest of Justinian*. Trans. A. Watson. 4 vols. Philadelphia, 1985.

Kunckel, H. *Der römische Genius*. RM-EH 20. Heidelberg, 1974.

Ladoceur, D. J. "Josephus and Masada." In *Josephus, Judaism, and Christianity*, ed. L. Feldman and G. Hata, 95–113. Detroit, 1987.

Lanciani, R. "L'atrio di Vesta." *NSc* (1883): 434–87.

La Rocca, E., et al. *Guida archeologica di Pompei*. Rome, 1976.

Lau, O. "Schuster und Schusterhandwerk in der griechisch-römischen Literatur und Kunst." Ph.D. diss., University of Bonn, 1967.

Laver, J. *Costume and Fashion*. London, 1982.

Laver, J. *Costume in Antiquity*. New York, 1964.

Leary, T. J. "That's What Little Girls Are Made Of: The Physical Charms of Elegiac Women." *Liverpool Classical Monthly* 15.10 (1990): 152–55.

Le Bonniec, H. "Le témoignage d'Arnobe sur deux rites archaïques du mariage romain." *REL* 54 (1976): 110–29.

Leeper, F. A. *Trajan's Parthian War.* Oxford, 1948.

L'Hoir, F. "Three Sandalled Footlamps." *AA* 98 (1983): 225–37.

Lieberman, S. *Hellenism in Jewish Palestine.* New York, 1962.

Liebman, S. "Contact between Rome and China." Ph.D. diss., Columbia University, 1953.

Lindsay, W. M., ed. *Isidori Origines.* Oxford, 1911.

Lindsay, W. M., ed. *Nonii Marcelli De compendiosa doctrina.* Leipzig, 1903.

Lindsay, W. M. *Sexti Pompei Festi: De verborum significatu cum Pauli epitome.* Leipzig, 1913.

Loane, H. J. *Industry and Commerce of the City of Rome, 50 B.C.–200 A.D.* Baltimore, 1938.

Loeschcke, G. "Zur Augustusstatue von Prima Porta." *BJ* 114–15 (1906): 470–72.

L'Orange, H. P. *Romerske Keisere.* Oslo, 1967.

L'Orange, H. P. "Statua di un'imperatrice." *AAAH* 4 (1969): 93–99.

Löwy, E. "Zum Augustus von Prima Porta." *RM* 42 (1927): 203–22.

McCann, A. M. *Roman Sarcophagi in the Metropolitan Museum of Art.* New York, 1978.

Macchiaroli, G., ed. *Domiziano-Nerva, la statua equestre: Una proposta di ricomposizione.* Naples, 1987.

MacConnoran, P. "Footwear." In *The Roman Quay at St. Magnus House,* ed. L. Miller, J. Schofield, and E. M. Rhodes, 218–25. London, 1989.

McCormack, S. *Art and Ceremony in Late Antiquity.* Berkeley, 1981.

Mackay, D. "The Jewelery of Palmyra and Its Significance." *Iraq* 11 (1949): 160–87.

MacMullen, R. "Women in Public in the Roman Empire." *Historia* 29 (1980): 208–18.

Magi, F. *I rilievi del palazzo della Cancelleria.* Rome, 1945.

Maiuri, A. *La casa del Menandro e il suo tesoro di argenteria.* Rome, 1932.

Maiuri, A. *La Villa dei Misteri.* Rome, 1960.

Maiuri, A. *Roman Painting.* Skira, N.Y., 1953.

Malcovati, H. *Oratorum Romanorum Fragmenta.* 2d ed. Turin, 1955.

Mancini, G. "Le statue loricate imperiali." *BCAR* 50 (1922): 151–204.

Mansuelli, G. *Galleria degli Uffizi: Le sculture, parte 2.* Rome, 1961.

Maricq, A. "Les dernières années de Hatra: L'alliance romaine." *Syria* 34 (1957): 288–96.

Marquardt, J. *Das Privatleben der Römer.* Leipzig, 1886.

Marquardt, J., and T. Mommsen. *Handbuch der römischen Alterthumer.* 2d ed. Vol. 7. Leipzig, 1886.

Marrou, H. I. *Décadence romaine ou antiquité tardive?* Paris, 1977.

Marshall, F. H. *Catalogue of the Finger Rings: Greek, Etruscan, and Roman.* Oxford, 1968.

Marshall, F. H. *Catalogue of the Jewellery: Greek, Etruscan, and Roman.* Oxford, 1969.

Matthews, K. D. "The Imperial Wardrobe of Ancient Rome." *Expedition* 12 (1970): 2–13.

Mattingly, H. *Coins of the Roman Empire in the British Museum.* Vol. 1, *Augustus to Vitellius.* Vol. 2, *Vespasian to Domitian.* London, 1983 and 1976.

Mau, A. "Bulla." *RE,* vol. 3.1 (1897), 1047–51.

Mayo, J. *A History of Ecclesiastical Dress.* London, 1984.

Mazar, B. *Beth She'arim.* Vol. 1. New Brunswick, N.J., 1973.

Mendelsohn, I. "Guilds in Ancient Palestine." *Bulletin of the American Schools of Oriental Research* 80 (1940): 17–21.

Mesnil de Buisson, R. du. *Inventaire des inscriptions palmyréniennes de Doura-Europos. Revue des études sémitiques 2.* Paris, 1936.

Metcalfe, A. C., and R. B. Longmore. "Leather Artefacts from Vindolanda." *Transactions of the Museum Assistants' Group* (1973): 38–43.

Millar, F. "Empire, Community and Culture in the Roman Near East: Greeks, Syrians, Jews and Arabs." *Journal of Jewish Studies* 28 (1987): 143–64.

Millar, F. *The Roman Empire and Its Neighbors.* London, 1967.

Miller, J. I. *The Spice Trade of the Roman Empire, 29 B.C. to A.D. 641.* Oxford, 1969.

Miller, L., J. Schofield, and M. Rhodes, eds. *The Roman Quay at St. Magnus House.* London, 1986.

Miller, L. M. B., and M. Rhodes. "Leather." In *Excavations at Billingsgate Buildings: 'Triangle', Lower Thames Street, 1974,* 95–128. London and Middlesex Archaeological Society 4. London, 1980.

Mitchell, M., ed. *Objects of Adornment: Five Thousand Years of Jewelry from the Walters Art Gallery.* Baltimore, 1984.

Möhring, A. "Sonderformen römischer Lampen." *Kölner Jahrbuch* 22 (1989): 803–73.

Mommsen, T. *Römische Staatsrecht.* 3d ed. Vol. 1. 1889; Graz, 1969.

Morandi, A. *Epigrafia Italica.* Rome, 1982.

Moreau, P. *Clodiana Religio.* Paris, 1982.

Morgenstern, J. "The King God among the Western Semites and the Meaning of Epiphanes." *Vetus Testamentum* 10 (1960): 138–97.

Morrow, K. D. *Greek Footwear and the Dating of Sculpture.* Madison, Wis., 1985.

Mottadeh, P. E. "The Princeton Bronze Portrait of a Woman with Reticulum." In *Festschrift Leo Mildenberg,* ed. A. Houghton et al., 203–8. Wetteren, Belgium, 1984.

Muehsam, A. "Attic Grave Reliefs from the Roman Period." *Berytus* 10 (1953): 51–114.

Mulroy, D. "The Early Career of P. Clodius Pulcher: A Re-examination of the Charges of Mutiny and Sacrilege." *TAPA* 118 (1988): 155–78.

Münzer, F. "Sulpicius," n. 66, *RE,* 2d ser., vol. 7 (1931), 808–11.

Murga, J. L. "Tres leyes de Honorio sobre el modo de vestir los romanos." *Studia et Documenta Historiae et Iuris* 39 (1973): 129–86.

Muscettola, S. "Nuove letture borboniche: I Nonii Balbi ed il Foro di Ercolano." *Prospettiva* 28 (1982): 2–16.

Musche, B. *Vorderasiatischer Schmuck zur Zeit der Arsaki-*

den und der Sasaniden. Handbuch der Orientalistik. VII, Abt. i, Bd. 2-b, Lief. 5. Leiden, 1988.

Napoli, M. "Statua ritratto di Virio Audenzio Emiliano consolare della Campagna." *BA* 44 (1959): 107–13.

Nash, E. *Pictorial Dictionary of Ancient Rome*. Vol. 1. London, 1968.

Nazzaro, A. *Il 'de pallio' di Tertulliano*. Naples, 1972.

Newbold, R. F. "Polysemy and Authority in the Late Roman Empire." *Semiotica* 71 (1988): 227–42.

Niemeyer, H. G. *Studien zur statuarischen Darstellung der römischen Kaiser*. Monumenta Artis Romanae 7. Berlin, 1968.

Noeldechen, E. "Tertullian von dem Kranze." *Zeitschrift für Kirchengeschichte* 11 (1890): 377–78.

Noll, R. *Vom Altertum zum Mittelalter: Kunsthistorisches Museum*. Vienna, 1958.

Oakley, J. "The *Anakalypteria*." *AA* 97 (1982): 113–18.

Oakley, J., and R. Sinos. *The Wedding in Ancient Athens*. Madison, Wis., 1993.

Oates, D. "A Note on Three Latin Inscriptions from Hatra." *Sumer* 11 (1955): 39–43.

Oehler, H. *Untersuchungen zu den mannlichen römischen Mantelstatuen: Der Schulterbauschtypus*. Berlin, 1961.

Overman, J., and R. MacKennan, ed. *Diaspora Jews and Judaism*. University of Southern Florida Series in Ancient Judaism. Forthcoming.

Pappalardo, U. "Die Villa Imperiale in Pompeij." *Antike Welt* 16.4 (1985): 3–15.

Patrick, J. "Hideouts in the Judean Wilderness." *Biblical Archeology Review* 5 (1989): 50–51.

Pelling, C. B. R., ed. *Plutarch, Life of Antony*. Cambridge, Eng., 1988.

Perkins, A. *The Art of Dura-Europos*. Oxford, 1973.

Pertegato, F. "Tecniche di lavorazione delle calzature rinascimentali." In *Il costume nell'età del Rinascimento*, 347–49. Florence, 1988.

Peruzzi, E. *Le origini di Roma I*. Florence, 1970.

Peyre, Ch. "L'ornement . . . Gaulois." *Studi Romagnoli* 14 (1963): 255–57.

Pfeiler, B. *Römischer Goldschmuck des ersten und zweiten Jahrhunderts n. Chr. nach datierten Funden*. Mainz, 1970.

Pfister, R. *Textiles de Palmyre*. 3 vols. Paris, 1934–40.

Pfister, R., and L. Bellinger. *The Textiles*. The Excavations of Dura-Europos. Final report 4.2. New Haven, 1945.

Philipp, H. "A Pair of Gilded Slippers." *Journal of the American Research Center in Egypt* 7 (1968): 73–77.

Phillips, C. R. "Italian Landscapes and Peoples in the *Aeneid*." Ph.D. diss., Brown University, 1974.

Picard, G. C. *Les trophées romains*. Paris, 1957.

Platt, E. E. "Jewelry of Bible Times and the Catalog of Isa. 3:18–23." *Andrews University Seminary Studies* 17 (1979): 71–201.

Pley, J. "De lanae in antiquorum ritibus usu." *RVV* 11.2 (1911): 1–114.

Pokorny, J. *Indo-germanisches etymologisches Wörterbuch*. Bern, 1959.

Polacco, L. *Il volto di Tiberio*. Rome, 1955.

Pollini, J. "Ahenobarbi, Appuleii and Some Others on the *Ara Pacis*." *AJA* 90 (1986): 453–56.

Pollini, J. "The Findspot of the Statue of Augustus from Prima Porta." *BCAR* 92 (1987–88): 103–8.

Pollini, J. *The Portraiture of Gaius and Lucius Caesar*. New York, 1987.

Pollini, J. "Studies in Augustan Historical Reliefs." Ph.D. diss., University of California, Berkeley, 1978.

Pollitt, J. J. *Art in the Hellenistic Age*. Cambridge, Eng., 1986.

Price, S. *Rituals and Power: The Roman Imperial Cult in Asia Minor*. Cambridge, Eng., 1984.

Puccioni, J. M. *Tulli Ciceronis Orationum deperditarum fragmenta*. Milan, 1963.

Quarantelli, E., ed. *The Land between the Rivers: Twenty Years of Italian Archaeology in the Middle East*. Turin, 1985.

Quinn, K. *Catullus' Poems*. New York, 1973.

Quinn, K. *Virgil's "Aeneid": A Critical Description*. London, 1968.

Rabbinowitz, J., ed., *The Jerusalem Talmud: Talmud Yerushalmi Bikkurim*. London, 1975.

Rackham, H., ed. *Pliny: Natural History*. Vol. 9. Cambridge, Mass., 1961.

Radice, B. *Who's Who in the Ancient World*. New York, 1980.

Raditsa, L. "The Appearance of Women and Contact: Tertullian's *de habitu feminarum*." *Athenaeum* 73 (1985): 297–326.

Rajak, T. *Josephus: The Historian and His Society*. Philadelphia, 1984.

Rajak, T. "Josephus and the *Archaeology of the Jews*." *Journal of Jewish Studies* 33 (1982): 456–97.

Redfield, J. "Notes on the Greek Wedding." *Arethusa* 15 (1982): 181–201.

Reed, R. *Ancient Skins, Parchments and Leathers*. London, 1972.

Reekmans, L. "La *dextrarum iunctio* dans l'iconographie romaine et paléochrétienne." *BIBR* 31 (1958): 23–96.

Reinach, T. *Jewish Coins*. London, 1903.

Reinhold, M. "History of Purple as a Status Symbol in Antiquity." *Latomus* 116 (1970): 37–47.

Reinhold, M., and P. T. Alessi. *The Golden Age of Augustus*. Toronto, 1978.

Rey-Coquais, J.-P. "Syrie romaine de Pompée à Dioclétien." *JRS* 68 (1978): 44–73.

Rheinisches Landesmuseum Trier. *Trier Kaiserresidenz und Bischopssitz*. Mainz, 1984.

Richardson, E. H. "The Etruscan Origin of Early Roman Sculpture." *MAAR* 21 (1953): 110–16.

Richardson, E. H. *The Etruscans: Their Art and Civilization*. Chicago, 1964.

Richardson, E. H. *Etruscan Votive Bronzes*. Mainz, 1983.

Richardson, E. H. and L. Richardson, Jr., "*Ad Cohibendum Bracchium Toga*: An Archaeological Examination of Cicero, 'Pro Caelio' 5.11." *YCS* 19 (1966): 251–68.

Richlin, A. "Approaches to the Sources on Adultery at Rome." In *Reflections of Women in Antiquity*, ed. H. P. Foley, New York, 1981.

Richmond, I. A. "Palmyra under the Aegis of the Romans." *JRS* 53 (1963): 43–54.

Richter, G. M. A. *Catalogue of Greek and Roman Antiquities in the Dumbarton Oaks Collection*. Cambridge, Mass., 1956.

Ridgway, B. S. "The Fashion of the Elgin Kore." *GMusJ* 12 (1984): 29–58.

Ridgway, B. S. "The Peplos Kore, Akropolis 679." *JWAG* 36 (1977): 49–61.

Riegl, A. *Late Roman Art Industry*. Trans. R. Winkes. Rome, 1985.

Rohden, H. von. "Die Panzerstatuen mit Reliefverzierung." In *Bonner Studien R. Kekulé gewidmet*, 1–20. Leipzig, 1893.

Rolfe, J. C., ed. *Ammianus Marcellinus*. LCL. Cambridge, Mass., 1935.

Roscher, W. H. *Ausführliches Lexikon der griechischen und römischen Mythologie*. 6 vols. Leipzig, 1884–1937.

Rose, A. "Clothing Imagery in Apollonius' *Argonautica*." *Quaderni urbinati di cultura classica* 50 (1985): 29–44.

Rose, B. "Princes and Barbarians on the Ara Pacis." *AJA* 94 (1990): 453–67.

Rosenzweig, A. *Kleidung und Schmuck im biblischen und talmüdische Schrifttum*. Berlin, 1905.

Ross, C. F. "The Reconstruction of the Later Toga." *AJA* 15 (1911): 24–31.

Ross, M. C. *Byzantine and Early Mediaeval Antiquities in the Dumbarton Oaks Collection*. Vol. 2, *Jewelry, Enamels, and Art of the Migration Period*. Washington, D.C., 1965.

Rossi, L. *Trajan's Column and the Dacian Wars*. Trans. J. M. C. Toynbee. Ithaca, N.Y., 1971.

Rostovtzeff, M. I. *Dura-Europos and Its Art*. Oxford, 1938.

Rubens, A. *A History of Jewish Costume*. New York, 1973.

Rubenius, A. *De re vestiaria*. Vol. 2. Antwerp, 1655.

Rüdiger, U. "Die Anaglypha Hadriani." *AntPl* 12 (1973): 161–73.

Ryberg, I. S. *Panel Reliefs of Marcus Aurelius*. AIA Monographs 14. New York, 1967.

Ryberg, I. W. "Rites of the State Religion in Roman Art." *MAAR* 22 (1955).

Ryder, M. L. "Skin and Wool-Textile Remains from Hallstatt, Austria." *Oxford Journal of Archaeology* 9 (1990): 37–49.

Safar, F., and M. A. Mustapha. *Hatra, City of the Sun God* (in Arabic). Baghdad, 1974.

Saletti, C. *Il ciclo statuario della basilica di Velleia*. Milan, 1968.

Samter, E. *Familienfeste der Griechen und Römer*. Berlin, 1901.

Sancisi-Weerdenburg, H., ed. *Achaemenid History*. Vol. 1, *Sources, Structures and Synthesis*. Leiden, 1987.

Sancisi-Weerdenburg, H., and A. Kuhrt, eds. *Achaemenid History*. Vol. 2, *The Greek Sources*. Leiden, 1987.

Sande, S. "Zur Porträtplastik des sechsten nachchristlichen Jahrhunderts." *AAAH* 61 (1975): 65–106.

Saverkina, I. I. *Römische Sarkophage in der Ermitage*. Berlin, 1979.

Schleiermacher, M. "Römische Leder- und Textilfunde aus Köln." *Archäologisches Korrespondezblatt* 12 (1982): 205–16.

Schlumberger, D. "Descendants non-Méditerranéens de l'art grec." *Syria* 37 (1960): 130–318.

Schlumberger, D. *La palmyréne du nord-ouest*. Paris, 1951.

Schlumberger, D. *L'Orient hellénisé: L'art grec et ses héritiers dans l'Asie Méditerranéenne* Paris, 1970.

Schramm, P. E. "Von der Trabea Triumphalis des römischen Kaisers über das byzantinische Lorum zur Stola des abendländischen Herrscher." In *Herrschalfzeichen und Staatssymbol* 1: 26–30. Stuttgart, 1954.

Schumacher, L. "Das Ehrendekret für M. Nonius Balbus aus Herculaneum (AE 1947, 53)." *Chiron* 6 (1976): 165–84.

Schürer, E. *The History of the Jewish People in the Age of Jesus Christ, 175 B.C.–A.D. 135*. 3 vols. Rev. and ed. G. Vermes, F. Millar, and M. Goodman. Edinburgh, 1986.

Schwartz, J. "Les palmyréniens et l'Egypte." *Bulletin Société archéologique d'Alexandrie* 40 (1953): 64–66.

Scullard, H. H. *Festivals and Ceremonies of the Roman Republic*. Ithaca, N.Y., 1981.

Seaford, R. *Pompeii*. New York, 1978.

Seligman, C. G. "The Roman Orient and the Far East." *Smithsonian Report* (1930): 547–68.

Sensi, L. "Ornatus e status sociale delle donne romane." *ALFPer*, n.s., 4 (1980–81): 55–102.

Settis, S. "Die Ara Pacis." In *Kaiser Augustus und die verlorene Republik*, 400–425. Berlin, 1988.

Seyrig, H. "Antiquités syriennes 94." *Syria* 48 (1971): 115–16.

Seyrig, H. "Armes et costumes iraniens de Palmyre." *Syria* 18 (1937): 4–31.

Seyrig, H. "Les dieux armés et les Arabes en Syrie." *Syria* 47 (1970): 77–99.

Seyrig, H. "Les dieux syriens en habit militaire." *Annales archéologiques arabes syriennes* 21 (1971): 67–70.

Shams, G. P. *Some Minor Textiles in Antiquity*. Göteborg, 1987.

Shapero, M. "The Dress System of Traditional Jewry." Rabbinic thesis, Hebrew Union College, Jewish Institute of Religion, New York, 1987.

Shaw, B. "The Age of Roman Girls at Marriage: Some Reconsiderations." *JRS* 77 (1987): 30–46.

Shelton, K. J. "Missorium of Theodosius." In *The Age of Spirituality: Late Antique and Early Christian Art, Third to Seventh Centuries*, ed. K. Weitzmann, 74–76. New York, 1979.

Shore, A. F. *Portrait Painting from Roman Egypt*. London, 1962.

Sieveking, J. "Eine römische Panzerstatue in der Münchner Glyptothek." *Berlin Winckelmannsprogram* 91 (1931): 3–34.

Simon, E. *Ara Pacis Augustae*. Greenwich, Conn., 1967.

Simon, E. *Der Augustus von Prima Porta*. Opus nobile 13. Bremen, 1959.

Simon, E. "Zur Fries der Mysterienvilla bei Pompeji." *JDAI* 76 (1961): 111–72.

Simson, O. G. von. *Sacred Fortress: Byzantine Art and Statecraft in Ravenna*. Chicago, 1988.

Smith, E. Baldwin. *The Dome: A Study in Architectural Symbolism*. Princeton, 1950.

Smith, R. R. R. *Hellenistic Sculpture*. Harmondsworth, Eng., 1991.

Smith, R. R. R. "Simulacra Gentium: The Ethna from the Sebasteion at Aphrodisias." *JRS* 78 (1988): 50–77.

Smith, W., et al. *A Dictionary of Greek and Roman Antiquities.* London, 1901.

Spain, S. "The Promised Blessing: The Iconography of the Mosaics of S. Maria Maggiore." *ABull* 61 (1979): 518–40.

Sperber, D. *Roman Palestine, 200–400: Prices and Money.* Ramat Gan, Israel, 1974.

Spradley, J. P., and D. W. McCurdy. *Conformity and Conflict: Readings in Cultural Anthropology.* Boston, 1987.

Spriggs, J. A. "Aspects of Leather Conservation at York." In *Recent Research in Archaeological Footwear,* 43–46. Association of Archaeological Illustrators and Surveyors Technical Paper 8. N.p., 1987.

Stangl, T. *Ciceronis orationum scholiastae.* Hildesheim, 1964.

Starcky, J. *Palmyre.* Paris, 1952.

Stemmer, K. *Untersuchungen zur Typologie, Chronologie und Ikonographie der Panzerstatuen.* Berlin, 1978.

Stewart, A. *Greek Sculpture.* New Haven, Conn., 1990.

Stiehl, R., and H. E. Stier. *Beiträge zur alten Geschichte und deren Nachleben.* Berlin, 1970.

Stone, S. C. "The Imperial Sculptural Group in the Metroon at Olympia." *AA* 100 (1985): 378–91.

Strong, D. *Catalogue of the Carved Amber in the Department of Greek and Roman Antiquities.* London, 1966.

Strong, D. *Roman Art.* New York, 1976; 2d ed., Harmondsworth, Eng., 1988.

Strong, D. *Roman Imperial Sculpture.* London, 1961.

Strong, D., and D. Brown, eds. *Roman Crafts.* New York, 1976.

Strong, E. "Terra Mater or Italia?" *JRS* 27 (1937): 114–26.

Studniczka, F. "Zur Augustusstatue der Livia." *RM* 24 (1916): 27–55.

Syme, R. "Neglected Children on the *Ara Pacis.*" *AJA* 88 (1984): 583–89.

Talamo, E. In *Museo Nazionale Romano: Le sculture.* Vol. 1.1, by A. Giuliano, 274–77. Rome, 1979.

Tanabe, K., ed. *Sculptures of Palmyra.* 2 vols. Tokyo, 1986.

Taylor, L. R. *Roman Voting Assemblies.* Ann Arbor, Mich., 1966.

Teixidor, J. *Un port romain du désert: Palmyre et son commerce d'Auguste à Caracalla.* Semitica 34. Paris, 1984.

Thompson, C. L. "Hairstyles, Head-Coverings, and St. Paul: Portraits from Roman Corinth." *Biblical Archaeologist* 51 (1988): 99–115.

Thompson, D. L. *Mummy Portraits in the J. Paul Getty Museum.* Malibu, 1982.

Tilke, M. *Entwicklungsgeschichte des orientalischen Kostüm.* Berlin, 1923.

Tilke, M. *Oriental Costumes: Their Designs and Colors.* London, n.d.

Tingay, G. I. F., and J. Badcock. *These Were the Romans.* 2d ed. Chester Springs, Penn., 1989.

Torelli, M. *Lavinio e Roma: Riti iniziatici e matrimonio tra archeologia e storia.* Rome, 1984.

Torelli, M. *Typology and Structure of Roman Historical Reliefs.* Ann Arbor, Mich., 1982.

Touati, A.-M. L. *The Great Trajanic Frieze.* Stockholm, 1987.

Toynbee, J. M. C. *Art in Roman Britain.* London, 1962.

Toynbee, J. M. C. "Some Problems of Romano-Parthian Sculpture at Hatra." *JRS* 62 (1972): 106–10.

Toynbee, J. M. C. "The Villa Item and a Bride's Ordeal." *JRS* 19 (1929): 67–87.

Treggiari, S. "Roman Marriage." In *Civilizations of the Ancient Mediterranean,* vol. 3, ed. M. Grant and R. Kitzinger, 1343–54. New York, 1988.

Trouard, M. A. *Cicero's Attitude towards the Greeks.* Chicago, 1942.

Van Deman, E. B. "The Value of the Vestal Statues as Originals." *AJA* 12 (1908): 324–42.

Vercoutter, J. *L'Egypte et le monde égéen préhellénique.* Cairo, 1956.

Vermeule, C. C. *Concordance of Cuirassed Statues in Marble and Bronze.* Boston, 1980.

Vermeule, C. C. "Hellenistic and Roman Cuirassed Statues." *Berytus* 13 (1959): 1–82; 15 (1964): 95–110; 17 (1966): 49–59; 23 (1974): 5–26; 26 (1978): 85–123.

Vermeule, C. C. "Jewish Relations with the Art of Ancient Greece and Rome: Judaea Capta Sed Non Devicta." *Art of Antiquity,* vol. 4.2. Boston, 1981.

Vermeule, C. C. "Numismatics in Antiquity." *Swiss Numismatic Review* 54 (1975): 5–32.

Vermeule, C. C., and A. Brauer. *Stone Sculptures: The Greek, Roman, and Etruscan Collections of the Harvard University Museums.* Cambridge, Mass., 1990.

Versnel, H. S. *Triumphus.* Leiden, 1970.

Vigeon, E. "Clogs or Wooden Soled Shoes." *Journal of Costume Society* (1977). Offprint.

Ville, G. *La gladiature en occident des origines à la mort de Domitien.* Bibliothèque des Écoles Françaises d'Athènes et de Rome 54. Rome, 1981.

Vin, J. P. A. van der. "The Return of Roman Ensigns from Parthia." *BABesch* 56 (1981): 117–39.

Volbach, W. *Elfenbeinarbeiten der Spätantike und des frühen Mittelalters.* Mainz, 1976.

Volbach, W., and M. Hirmer. *Early Christian Art.* New York, 1961.

Wagner, J. "Die Römer an Euphrat und Tigris." *Antike Welt* 16 (1985): 3–72.

Walde, A., and J. B. Hofmann. *Lateinisches Etymologisches Wörterbuch.* 2 vols. 3d ed. Heidelberg, 1938–54.

Walker, S. *A Portrait Head of a Life-sized Statue of a Vestal.* British Museum Occasional Paper 22. Department of Greek and Roman Antiquities, New Acquisitions 1, 1976–79. London, 1981.

Wallace, R., and L. La Follette. "Latin *seni crines* and the Hair Style of Roman Brides." *Syllecta Classica* 4 (1992): 1–6.

Warren, L. *See* Bonfante-Warren, L.

Waterer, J. *A Guide to the Conservation and Restoration of Objects Made Wholly or in Part of Leather.* London, 1974.

Waterer, J. "Leather." In *A History of Technology,* ed. C. Singer, E. J. Holmyard, A. R. Hall, and T. I. Williams, 147–86. Oxford, 1956.

Waterer, J. "Leatherwork." In *Roman Crafts,* ed. D. Strong and D. Brown, 179–93. London, 1976.

Watkins, C. *The American Heritage Dictionary of Indo-European Roots.* Boston, 1985.

Weber, W. *Constantinische Deckengemälde aus dem römischen Palast unter dem Trierer Dom.* Trier, 1984.

Weber, W. *Die Darstellungen einer Wagenfahrt auf römischen Sarkophagdeckeln und Loculusplatten des 3. und 4. Jahrhunderts n. Chr.* (Rome, 1978).

Weitzmann, K., ed. *Age of Spirituality: Late Antique and Early Christian Art, Third to Seventh Centuries.* New York, 1979.

Weitzmann, K., and H. L. Kessler. *The Frescoes of the Dura Synagogue and Christian Art.* Washington, D.C., 1990.

Welles, C. B. "The Gods of Dura-Europos." In *Beiträge zur alten Geschichte und deren Nachleben,* ed. R. Stiehl and H. E. Stier, 50–65. Berlin, 1970.

Welles, C. B., R. O. Fink, and J. F. Gilliam. *The Parchments and Papyri.* The Excavations of Dura-Europos. Final report 5.1. New Haven, 1959.

Wells, P. S. *Culture Contact and Culture Change: Early Iron Age Europe and the Mediterranean World.* Cambridge, Eng., 1980.

Wernicke, K. "Arimaspoi." *RE,* vol. 2 (1895), 826–27.

Wessner, P., ed. *Scholia in Iuvenalem vetustiora.* Leipzig, 1931.

Wheeler, M. *Roman Art and Architecture.* London, 1964.

Wiedemann, T. *Greek and Roman Slavery.* Baltimore, 1981.

Wiggers, H. B., and M. Wegner. *Caracalla, Geta, Plautilla, Macrinus bis Balbinus.* Berlin, 1975.

Wilcken, U. *Griechische Ostraka aus Ägypten und Nubien.* Leipzig, 1899.

Wild, J. P. "The Clothing of Britannia, Gallia Belgica and Germania Inferior." *ANRW* 2.12.3 (1985): 362–422.

Wild, J. P. *Textile Manufacture in the Northern Roman Provinces.* Cambridge, Eng., 1970.

Wild, J. P. "Textiles." In *Roman Crafts,* ed. D. Strong and D. Brown, 167–78. New York, 1976.

Will, E. "La Syrie romaine entre l'Occident gréco-romain et l'Orient parthe." In *Le rayonnement des civilisations grecque et romaine sur les cultures périphériques,* 511–26. Paris, 1965.

Will, E. "Nouveaux monuments sacrés de Syrie romaine." *Syria* 29 (1952): 60–73.

Williams, R. D. *The Aeneid of Virgil, Books 1–6.* London, 1972.

Wilpert, G. "Zum Sarkophag eines christlichen Konsuls." *RM* 65 (1958): 100–120.

Wilson, L. *The Clothing of the Ancient Romans.* Baltimore, 1938.

Wilson, L. *The Roman Toga.* Baltimore, 1924.

Winkes, R., ed. *The Age of Augustus.* Louvain, 1985.

Wissowa, G. "Supplicationes." *RE,* 2d ser., vol. 7 (1931), 942–51.

Witt, R. E. *Isis in the Graeco-Roman World.* Ithaca, N.Y., 1971.

Woelcke, K. "Beiträge zur Geschichte des Tropaions: Der Tropaion am Panzer der Augustusstatue von Primaporta." *BJ* 120 (1911): 180–91.

Wunderlich, E. "Die Bedeutung der roten Farbe im Kultus der Griechen und Römern." *RVV* 20.1 (1925): 1–116.

Yadin, Y. *Bar Kokhba: The Rediscovery of the Legendary Hero of the Last Jewish Revolt against Imperial Rome.* London, 1971.

Yadin, Y. *The Finds from the Bar Kokhba Period in the Cave of Letters.* Jerusalem, 1963.

Yadin, Y. *Masada: Herod's Fortress and the Zealot's Last Stand.* London, 1966.

Yonge, C. D., ed. *The Orations of Marcus Tullius Cicero.* 3 vols. London, 1856.

Zaloscer, H. *Porträts aus dem Wüstensand.* Vienna, 1961.

Zanker, P. *The Power of Images in the Age of Augustus.* Trans. A. Shapiro. Ann Arbor, Mich., 1988.

Zinserling, G. "Der Augustus von Primaporta als offiziöses Denkmal." *Acta Antiqua* 15 (1967): 327–39.

# INDEX

Flammarii, 67

Flammeum: color of, 48, 55, 56; Juvenal on, 55; and Flaminica Dialis, 55–56; fire symbolism of, 56; in Roman paintings, 56; reconstruction of, 228; mentioned, 60, 150, 213

Flammeus, 67

Flax. *See* Linen

Flowers: in bridal costume, 56

Footwear: *See* chapter 6 *passim*

—animal head decorations on, 123

—archaeological finds: 104, 114, 119, 127; in Britain, 109, 110 *fig. 6.13*, 111, 112 *fig. 6.14*, 114, 117 *fig. 6.20b*, 119, 121 *figs. 6.25, 6.26*, 122, 123, 126, 126 *fig. 6.31*; Celtic, 103 *fig. 6.3b*; Etruscan, 103 *fig. 6.2*, 107; in northern Europe, 101, 105, 109, 110 *figs. 6.12a, 6.12b, 6.13*, 111, 113 *fig. 6.17*, 114, 115 *fig. 6.19a*, 117 *fig. 6.20a*, 119, 121 *fig. 6.25*, 122, 123, 124 *fig. 6.27b*, 126; in Palestine, 103 *fig. 6.3a*, 190 *n. 53*; restoration of, 104

—in art, 101, 104; problems of artistic depiction, 107, 114, 119, 122, 127; unusual depictions of, 111, 112 *figs. 6.15, 6.16*

—bare feet, 105; sign of divinity of heroism, 105 *fig. 6.4*, 114

—boots, 101, 102 *fig. 6.1g*, 104, 105, 123, 125, 126; chukker, 164, 168 *fig. 10.1*; dress-parade, 102 *fig. 6.1w*, 124 *figs. 6.28, 6.29*, 125

—bridal socci, 56

—buskin, 102 *fig. 6.1g*, 103 *fig. 6.1y*

—calcei, 14 *fig. 1.1*, 102 *figs. 6.1h, 6.1n, 6.1q*, 105, 109, 116, 119, 120 *fig. 6.22*, 121 *figs. 6.25, 6.26*, 122, 125, 126 *fig. 6.30*, 128 *n. 31*, 129 *nn. 41, 46*, 136–37, 229

—calcei equestres, 116

—calcei patricii, 102 *fig. 6.1n*, 105, 109, 116, 119, 120 *figs. 6.22, 6.23a, 6.23b*, 125, 127 *n. 5*

—calcei repandi, 102 *figs. 6.1a, 6.1c, 6.1j*, 116, 118 *figs. 6.21a, 6.21b*, 126, 214 *fig. 13.2a*, 216; Cicero on, 116; reconstruction of, 215 *fig. 13.2b*

—calcei senatorii, 105, 109, 116, 119

—calicae, 127 *n. 5*

—caligae, 102 *figs. 6.1o, 6.1p*, 104, 105, 114, 122–23, 124 *fig. 6.27b*, 127 *n. 5*, 128 *n. 31*, 174, 188, 195; Isidore of Seville on, 122; reconstruction of, 124 *fig. 6.27a*

—campagus, 122, 127, 127 *n. 5*

—carbatinae, 105, 109, 114, 115 *figs. 6.19a, 6.19b*, 116, 117 *figs. 6.20a, 6.20b*, 128 *n. 31*; Catullus on, 114; reconstruction of, 115 *fig. 6.19b*

—Celtic, 101

—Cicero on improper, 109;

—classification of: MacConnoran's, 128 *n. 31*; Morrow's, 101, 104, 107, 123; van Driel-Murray's, 105, 109, 111, 114, 116, 119; terminology, 125, 126, 128 *n. 31*, 129 *n. 46*

—colors of, 104, 114, 116, 119, 125, 127 *n. 5*, 129 *n. 46*

—of common people, 127

—cothurni: Frontinus on, 125

—crepidae, 102 *figs. 6.1b, 6.1d, 6.1f, 6.1h, 6.1i, 6.1u, 6.1v*, 104, 114, 115 *fig. 6.18*, 135, 143 *n. 16*

—Dacian, 203

—effeminate, 77

—embades, 123

—emperor's: *see* Emperor's costume

—empress': *see* Empress' costume

—endromides, 123, 129 *n. 41*

—Etruscan footwear: *see also* Etruscans; footwear: calcei repandi

—gallicae, 102 *fig. 6.1r*, 109, 110 *fig. 6.11*, 127 *n. 5*, 136–37; Aulus Gellius on, 109

—German, 203

—gold used in, 85, 101, 107, 109, 111, 125, 127 *n. 5*

—Greek, 116, 125–26

—hobnails, 109, 110 *figs. 6.12a, 6.12b*, 111, 112 *fig. 6.15*, 114, 122, 123, 124 *fig. 6.27b*, 126, 188, 190 *n. 53*; Mishnah on, 122; Josephus on, 122; Jewish prohibition of, 188

—impilia, 125, 183

—indoors of Roman citizen, 116, 125; for banquets, 111

—jeweled, 83, 84 *fig. 5.8*, 102 *fig. 6.1q*, 103 *fig. 6.1z*, 119, 121 *fig. 6.24*; of Caligula, 83

—Jewish, 183, 188

—of Lares, 123

—latchet, 103 *fig. 6.1z*, 126–27

—literary sources for, 101

—luna (of calceus), 119

—magistrates', 105, 125, 126 *fig. 6.30*

—manufacture of, 104, 111, 126

—materials used in, 101, 103 *fig. 6.3b*, 104–105, 107, 109, 116, 122, 126

—military influence on, 111

—modern reproductions of ancient, 104–105, 115 *fig. 6.19b*, 116, 123, 124 *fig. 6.27a*, 129 *n. 52*

—outdoors of Roman citizen, 116

—Parthian-Palmyrene, 164, 165, 174

—pellytra, 123, 126

—pero, 102 *fig. 6.1n*, 105, 125, 129 *n. 46*

—piloi, 123, 125

—podeia, 125

—price of, 109, 116, 122, 125, 127 *n. 5*

—Roman influenced by other cultures, 101, 105, 107, 116

—sandals (sandalia), 101, 102 *figs. 6.1e, 6.1k, 6.11, 6.1m, 6.1t, 6.1u*, 103 *figs. 6.1x, 6.1y, 6.3a*, 104, 105, 106 *figs. 6.5a, 6.5b*, 107, 107 *fig. 6.6*, 108 *figs. 6.7, 6.8, 6.9, 6.10*, 109, 110, 110 *figs. 6.12a, 6.12b, 6.13*, 112 *figs. 6.15, 6.16*, 115 *fig. 6.18*, 116, 134, 167, 196, 229; strap styles, 105, 106 *figs. 6.5a, 6.5b*; worn at banquets, 111

—sculponeae, 111, 113 *fig. 6.17*, 114

—slippers, 105, 111, 112 *fig. 6.14*, 125

—socci: bridal, 56; Pliny the Younger on, 125; mentioned, 105, 111, 127 *n. 5*, 128 *n. 31*, 135

—social importance of, 101

—socks, 72, 122, 123, 125–26, 126 *fig. 6.31*

—soleae, 102 *fig. 6.11*, 103 *fig. 6.1x*, 105, 107, 109, 110, 127 *n. 5*, 128 *n. 31*, 134, 139–40, 143 *n. 12*

—styles of, 104, 109, 111; trends in, 101, 111, 116, 119, 122–23, 125, 127

—taurinae, 109, 127 *n. 5*

—theatrical, 125

—triumphal, 116

—trochades, 102 *figs. 6.1r, 6.1s*, 109, 110 *fig. 6.11*

—tyrrhenicae, 107

—udones: Martial on, 126

Formae, 102 *fig. 6.1o*, 122, 127 *n. 5*

Freedman: ring of, 78

Freedwoman: stola of, 49

Fringe, 190 *n. 57*, 193 *fig. 12.4*, 196, 221. See also Tzitzit

Frontinus: on cothurni, 125

Fullonica, 74

Fulvus, 67

Fur, 74 *n. 9*, 167

Fuscus: as cheap purple dye, 65; mentioned, 67

Gabinius, Aulus, 138, 142, 143

Galbinus, 70

Gallic costume, 101, 103 *fig. 6.3b*, 193 *fig. 12.5*, 196; influence of, on Roman clothing, 146, 231

Gallienus (emperor): costume of, 83

Nudus, 136–39, 140, 143, 197, 199, 203, 206. *See also* Improper dress/costume

Offectores, 74
Olbia Treasure, 80
Openwork jewelry. *See* Jewelry
Orange: crocotulus, 66; flammeus, 67
Ostrinus, 69
Osztropataka: archaeological finds of jewelry at, 86, 86 *fig. 5.12*
Ovid: on matron's costume, 49; on hasta caelibaris, 60; on colors of textiles, 65; on silk, 69

Paenula, 182, 217; reconstruction of, 229, 231 *fig. 13.20*
Palestine: costume of, chapters 9 and 11 *passim*, 197, 198 *fig. 12.7*, 199; archaeological finds, 103 *fig. 6.3a*, 183, 184, 186, 188, 190 *n. 53*; Christian sources on costume of, 182; proper male costume in, 183, 184; women's clothing in, 186, 187 *fig. 11.6*; children's clothing in, 188. *See also* Jewish costume
—textile production, 182–83; weaver's marks, 184, 185 *figs. 11.2, 11.3, 11.4*
Palla: in *Aeneid*, 149, 150–51; at Palmyra, 169 *figs. 10.3a, 10.3b*, 172 *fig. 10.11*; reconstruction of, 215 *fig. 13.2b*, 221 *fig. 13.9*, 228; mentioned, 48, 116, 179, 214 *fig. 13.2a*, 217, 225 *fig. 13.14*, 230 *fig. 13.17*
Pallium: Tertullian on, 6, 8; and toga, 17; mentioned, 134–36 *passim*, 143, 143 *n. 16*, 165, 179, 183, 184, 217, 228, 229
Palmyrene costume: influence of, on Roman jewelry, 78; jewelry with, 79, 80 *fig. 5.3*; of women, 165, 166, 170 *fig. 10.5*; of Gods, 166; Roman dress worn, 166–67, 172 *fig. 10.10*; thematic distinctions in, 173; influence of, on Dura-Europos costume, 174; mentioned, 164–67, 168 *fig. 10.1*, 173 *fig. 10.13*, 179
Paludamentum: of emperor, 34; related to chlamys, 34; dyed with coccinus, 69; of governor, 134, 135; reconstruction of, 232–33, 233 *fig. 13.24*; mentioned, 36 *figs. 1.19a, 1.19b*, 150, 155, 191, 192 *fig. 12.1*, 195, 217
Paphiae myrti, 68
Parthian(s): and Palmyrene costume, 164; costume, 164, 193 *fig. 12.3*, 195; at Dura, 167, 173; and Iranian costume, 168 *fig. 10.1*; influence on Hatran costume, 174, 179; mentioned, 163, 166, 194, 197, 206
Patagium, 67
Patchwork, 70
Patrician dress: Johannes Lydes on, 6
Paul: on veiling, 188
Pausanias: on Jewish textile production, 182
Pendilia: earliest appearance of, 89; mentioned, 83, 85, 93, 94, 94 *fig. 5.30*, 95, 95 *fig. 5.32*, 96 *fig. 5.33*, 98, 236
Peplos: reconstruction of, 223–24, 224 *figs. 13.13a, 13.13b*, 226 *figs. 13.15a, 13.15b*; mentioned, 174, 179, 217, 219 *fig. 13.7*, 220 *figs. 13.8a, 13.8b*, 224 *fig. 13.13a*, 236 *n. 5*
Perizoma: reconstruction of, 234 *fig. 13.25*; mentioned, 138, 233
Persian costume, 147
Persius: on toga praetexta, 47; on hyacinthinus, 71
Phoenicia, 163; costume of, 165
Phoenicius, 67
Phrygian cap. *See* Headgear
Piazza della Consolazione: jewelry, 87 *fig. 5.16*
Pilleus. *See* Headgear
Pissyrgos, 104
Plautus: on matron's costume, 49, 56; on bride's hairstyle, 56; on colors and textiles, 65; on dyers, 67; on cerinus, 68; on cumatilis, 68
Plinius Secundus (the Elder), Caius: on toga, 13; on tunica recta, 54; on flammeum, 55; on gausapa and amphimallia, 72; on cothurni, 125

—effeminate costume, 77
—hair style of Vestal Virgins, 57
—hasta caelibaris, 60
—jewelry, 77; bulla, 77; rings, 78; brooches, 80; necklaces, 82
—yellow, 55; indigo, 68–69; conchyliatus, 69; hysginum, 69; coccinus, 69, 71; dye colors, 71; mordants, 73–74
Plinius Secundus, (the Younger), Caius: on cothurni and socci, 125
Plumatilis, 67
Plumeus, 67
Plutarch: on hasta caelibaris, 60; on veiling, 188
Poenicius, 67; in footwear, 125
Polymita, 69
Praetexta. *See* Purple; Toga: praetexta
Prasinus, 70
Precious stones: in jewelry, chapter 5 *passim*; on Elagabalus' clothing, 83; of Jewish High Priest's ephod, 156, 157; mentioned, 165, 166, 217, 236. *See also* Footwear: jeweled; Jewelry
Priapus: footwear of, 123
Priestly costume: Julian on, 4; priestess' veils, 56; footwear with, 102 *fig. 6.1n*, 119, 120 *fig. 6.22*; in *Aeneid*, 147–49 *passim*; reconstruction of, 216 *fig. 13.4*. *See also* Flamen Dialis; Flaminica Dialis; Vestal Virgins
—of Jewish High Priest, 156, 183; in Josephus, 156–57; cosmic symbolism of, 157
—of priests of the Argei, 50; of Luperci, 137, 138, 143; of Rex Sacrorum, 216, 216 *fig. 13.4*; of Arvales, 235–36
—Rome origin of Christian, 231
—mentioned, 47, 57, 82
Probus (emperor): jewelry of, 91 *fig. 5.24*
Procopius: on gifts of jewelry, 79, 96; on imperial costume, 86
Proper costume of Roman citizen, 229
Propertius: on toga praetexta, 47; on silk, 69
Prostitute's costume, 53 *n. 50*, 140–41. *See also* Toga: muliebris
Provinces, personifications of. *See* Iconography of costume
Pteryges: 166, 174, 191, 194, 195, 199
Pullus, 65, 67, 68, 134, 135, 141. *See also* Atratus; Mourning; Toga: pulla; Widow's costume
Puniceus, 67
Purple, hues of: Cornelius Nepos and Vitruvius on, 69. *See also* Clavi; Flaminica Dialis; Toga: praetexta, purpurea; Violet
—conchyliatus, 69, 71
—dye trade, 66, substitutes/counterfeits, 65, 71; Palestine dyers, 183
—footwear, 104, 125; on Palmyrene tunics, 165
—heliotropium, 71
—hysginum, 69, 74
—ostrinus, 69
—purpura dibapha Tyria, 65, 68, 71; first use of, 65, 69
—purpurea amethystina, 68
—purpureus laconicus, 71
—ruber Tarentinus, 69
—symbolism of color, 47, 51 *n. 12*; border on priestess' veil, 56; on Vestal's suffibulum, 57
—thalassinus, 69
—use of, restricted to emperors, 70
—mentioned, 127 *n. 5*, 134, 135, 139, 140, 143, 149, 155, 191, 228, 229, 231, 233, 236
Purpura. *See* Purple
Purpureus. *See* Purple

Quintilian: on draping of toga, 6, 16, 21, 24; on toga praetexta, 47

Rabirius Postumus, Gaius: improper dress of, 135–36
Ralla, tunica: 66

Vergil: on costume, Chapter 8 *passim;* toga, 13, 149, 151; pero, 105; mitra, 147; vestis, 147; vittae, 147; infula, 147–48; tunic, 148–49; amictus, 149; chlamys, 149, 150; laena, 149–50, 229; palla, 150–51; sagulum, 231–32; tiara, 147

Verres, Caius: improper dress of, 133–35, 139, 143

Vespasian (emperor): and portrait rings, 78

Vestal Virgins: costume of, 54, 57–60; 58 *figs. 3.1, 3.2, 3.3, 3.4,* 59 *figs. 3.5, 3.6,* 228; symbolism of seni crines, 56–57

Vestem mutare, 142, 143

Vestes Coae, 69

Vestiarii, 67

Vestis. *See* Vergil

Violaceus, 69

Violarii, 67

Viola serotina, 71

Violet: dyers of, 67; violaceus, 69; amethystinus, 71; hyacinthinus, 71; ianthinus, 71; Tyrianthina, 71

Virgin Mary: and imperial costume, 94

Viridis, 69

Vitruvius on: indigo, 68–69; hues of purple, 69

Vitta, 46–48 *passim,* 50, 99 *n. 39;* of matron, 49; purpurae of Flaminica Dialis, 52 *n. 40;* of Vestals, 57; and seni crines, 60; emperor's, 82; in *Aeneid,* 147–48

Weaves: kinds of, 66. *See also* Gold

Weaving, 66, 70, 71, 73, 217, 221; industry in Palestine, 182–83; marks (gammadia), 184, 186, 189 *n. 37*

White, 68; symbolism, 48; and suffibulum, 57; albus, 65; footwear, 104

Widow's costume, 50; Festus' definition of, 50

Women's costume: Roman, Chapter 2 *passim;* in early and middle Republic, 66–67; jewelry with, 78, 80 *fig. 5.4;* and Palmyrene jewelry, 165. *See also* Bride's costume; Girl's costume; Matron's costume; Toga; Undergarments; Unmarried woman; Widow's costume

—Dura-Europos, 173–74

—Jewish, 186

—Palestine, 187 *fig. 11.6*

—Palmyrene, 165, 170 *figs. 10.4, 10.5*

Wool: symbolism of, 47, 48, 51 *n. 19,* 55, 63 *n. 37,* 183; natural colors of, 65, 67, 70; breeding sheep for, 67; Columella on, 70; in footwear, 123, 126; mentioned, 65–66, 67, 70, 72, 159 *n. 34,* 191, 195, 203, 217

Wreaths, 82, 166, 167, 222. *See also* Corolla; Crowns

Yellow, hues of: calthulus, 66; aureus, 68; cerinus, 66, 68; cereus, 68; croceus, 68; galbinus, 70. *See also* Bride's costume: reticulum; Luteus

—symbolism, 48, 55–56; Pliny the Elder on, 55; effeminate color in *Aeneid,* 150

Zealots, 156

Zenobia: diadem of, 83

# WISCONSIN STUDIES IN CLASSICS

*General Editors*
Barbara Hughes Fowler and Warren G. Moon *(1945–1992)*

---

BARBARA HUGHES FOWLER
*The Hellenistic Aesthetic*

F. M. CLOVER and R. S. HUMPHREYS, *editors*
*Tradition and Innovation in Late Antiquity*

BRUNILDE SISMONDO RIDGWAY
*Hellenistic Sculpture I: The Styles of ca. 331–200 B.C.*

BARBARA HUGHES FOWLER, *editor and translator*
*Hellenistic Poetry: An Anthology*

KATHRYN J. GUTZWILLER
*Theocritus' Pastoral Analogies: The Formation of a Genre*

VIMALA BEGLEY and RICHARD DANIEL DE PUMA, *editors*
*Rome and India: The Ancient Sea Trade*

DAVID CASTRIOTA
*Myth, Ethos, and Actuality: Official Art in Fifth-Century B.C. Athens*

BARBARA HUGHES FOWLER, *editor and translator*
*Archaic Greek Poetry: An Anthology*

RICHARD DANIEL DE PUMA and JOCELYN PENNY SMALL
*Murlo and the Etruscans: Art and Society in Ancient Etruria*

JOHN H. OAKLEY and REBECCA H. SINOS
*The Wedding in Ancient Athens*

JUDITH LYNN SEBESTA and LARISSA BONFANTE, *editors*
*The World of Roman Costume*